The Uses of Literature

LIFE IN THE SOCIALIST CHINESE LITERARY SYSTEM

PERRY LINK

PRINCETON UNIVERSITY PRESS

PRINCETON, NEW JERSEY

Library of Congress Cataloging-in-Publication Data

Link, E. Perry (Eugene Perry), 1944–
The uses of literature : life in the socialist Chinese literary system / Perry Link.
p.   cm.
Includes bibliographical references and index.
ISBN 0-691-00197-9 (alk. paper). — ISBN 0-691-00198-7 (pbk. : alk. paper)
1. Chinese literature—20th century—History and criticism.   2. Socialism
and literature—China.   3. Literature and society—China.   I. Title.
PL2303.L543   2000   895.1′09358—dc21   99-41856   CIP

This book has been composed in Janson

The paper used in this publication meets the minimum requirements
of ANSI/NISO Z39.48-1992 (R 1997) (Permanence of Paper)

http://pup.princeton.edu

Printed in the United States of America

1   2   3   4   5   6   7   8   9   10

1   2   3   4   5   6   7   8   9   10
(pbk.)

CONTENTS

ACKNOWLEDGMENTS

I WISH TO THANK the Committee on Scholarly Communication with the People's Republic of China for funding research for this book during 1979 and 1980. During that year I had two "host units" in China, each of which also deserves special thanks: Zhongshan University in Guangzhou provided my wife and me with an apartment on campus and access to university life that was unusually free and relaxed for foreign visitors at that time. In Beijing, where I spent four months, the atmosphere was less relaxed and research more difficult than in Guangzhou, but the Literature Research Institute of the Chinese Academy of Social Sciences took the trouble to arrange a large number of interviews for me, not only with writers and officials but with the headquarters of the Xinhua Bookstore, Central Television and Radio, and the major literary publishers.

Since 1980, my research and writing on this topic has benefited from support by the Center for Chinese Studies and the University of California at Berkeley, the Wang Institute of Graduate Studies, and the Chiang Ching-kuo Foundation for International Scholarly Exchange. Some parts of this book draw upon articles I have published elsewhere, and I am grateful to the following for permission to borow from them: Harvard University, Council on East Asian Studies; Indiana University Press; *Modern China*; University of California Press; and Westview Press.

I am grateful to Stanley Rosen for sharing his collection of opinion and attitude surveys, to Mary Jacob and Jennifer Hunt for research assistance, and to Margaret Case for her meticulous editing. Michael Duke and Jeffrey Kinkley read the entire manuscript and offered many useful criticisms. Errors they may have missed are mine, not theirs. Others who have kindly helped with materials or criticisms include Robert Epp, Lung-hua Hu, Huang Weizong, Steven Kotkin, Inge Nielsen, Paul Pickowicz, Su Wei, William Tay, Rudolph Wagner, Wang Jinmin, and Wu Xiaoling.

Perry Link
Princeton, N.J.

Most references in the notes are stated briefly, omitting publication data and Chinese characters. Readers should refer to the bibliography for complete citations and characters. When a complete citation does appear in a note, it is not repeated in the bibliography.

The Uses of Literature

INTRODUCTION

THE RISE AND FALL of communism is likely to be one of the major stories in future accounts of the twentieth century. During decades when much of human life changed immensely, under the largely unguided and even anarchic influences of the industrial and technological revolutions, a great experiment went forth on the assumption that new and better patterns of social life could be molded by conscious human design. In China, at the peak of Maoist fervor for the experiment, some even thought that social engineering could rework a person's innermost character, and that selfishness itself might be consigned to the dustbin of history. But by century's end it was clear the experiment had failed. Apologists could still claim that it had not really had a fair trial, since the major sites of its adoption, Russia and China, had inherited strong authoritarian traditions that had skewed the experiment. But most of the people who had actually lived under the system and understood how it worked in daily life concluded that fundamental elements in its blueprint were flawed. The system had failed to produce what it promised, and not just by accident. It brought neither wealth nor freedom but often the opposite and, far from eliminating selfishness, only changed the rules under which selfishness was pursued.

The failure of the great experiment does little to reduce its historical interest, however. Humanists especially should examine it, not from a dubious hope that tinkering might save it on a second try, but because of the evidence it reveals about the variety that is possible in human experience and feeling. The ways in which people responded under its pushes and pulls reveals facets of human nature and expression that otherwise are less obvious. Study of these not only illustrates a variety that is interesting in itself but can show that the familiar patterns that we often consider normal, or even inevitable, in fact are as conditional as any. Literature is an especially interesting case. In the West (the North Atlantic and its tributaries), we speak as if we know what "modern" literature is; in academe, even the term "postmodern" is used with confidence. Such usage seems to gain solidity when young people from elsewhere, including former socialist countries, adopt it. The culture of the North Atlantic can come to seem the "natural" one, into which others merge as circumstances allow.

But creative writing can have more functions than this pattern suggests. When people's situations differ, some of their spiritual, intellectual, and emotional needs differ as well; when they read and write to fill these distinctive needs, their literary results will also differ. Can we really say which results are the "natural" ones? We sometimes feel we can do this because, in cases such as Stalinist Russia or Maoist China, it is easy to observe the gross intrusion of nonliterary factors; a writer or artist forced to extol a smelting vat is not creating "naturally." But such judgments, although unobjectionable when applied to extreme cases, are not in principle so simple. First, all writers have nonliterary contexts, and contexts always impinge. (Were the many paintings of Madonna and Child that the West honors in art museums produced free of context?) Differences from one situation to another are matters of manner and degree, which are things we need to measure carefully if they are to be our criteria for "naturalness" or quality. Second, we must be able to distinguish between a nonliterary intrusion and a literary response. We can rightly say that a political leader's command is extraneous to literature, but it does not follow that the writer's response is also extraneous. Writers comply, resist or, more often, do a mixture of the two, and such responses might be carefully thought out, unconsciously reflexive, or somewhere in between. But all are "genuine" human responses, at least worth noting and often worth studying. Some, moreover, produce good literature. If works written in opposition to coercion seem wanting as "pure art," they can nevertheless be very good, as Irving Howe has noted, at filling the special and sometimes intense spiritual needs that tyranny can generate. In referring to Aleksandr Solzhenitsyn's *One Day in the Life of Ivan Deni-sovich*, which describes life in a Stalinist labor camp, Howe holds that "only a cretin could read such a book 'purely' in literary terms."[1]

This book is based in large part upon an in-depth look at how literature functioned in Chinese society as of the late 1970s and early 1980s. This was a choice of necessity, because these years were the first since the 1940s during which foreign scholars were allowed to work in China. It was a period that became known for "scar literature," which was primarily an outpouring of bitterness about what was then called the "ten years of catastrophe" from the onset of the Cultural Revolution in 1966 until the death of Mao in 1976. In remarkable ways, scar literature resembled the "thaw literature" that followed the death of Stalin in the Soviet Union. In both cases, readers in large numbers turned to literature to purge themselves of pent-up resentment and to try to restore a sense of normalcy; many themes were similar; after about three years, in both cases, what could be done had been done, and the "scar" and "thaw" phenomena subsided. Because of this similarity—as well as others that resulted from China's borrowing of the Soviet model in cultural matters—I try to offer comparative comments in this study when they seem useful.

I also seek to explain more than just the late 1970s and early 1980s by using those years as an entrée to what I will call "the socialist Chinese literary system" as it existed from about 1950 to about 1990. The late 1970s, when I had my best access, were years when Chinese officials were working busily to restore the literary establishment of the 1950s, and study of this restoration became my avenue to study of the 1950s themselves. Although the bureaucratic apparatus of the 1950s was modeled on Soviet

[1] *New Republic*, 11 May 1963, p. 19. For more on what "good" means in various literary contexts, see chapter 6.

precedents,[2] Chinese behavior within the system was also colored strongly by Mao Zedong's views on literature and by some powerful assumptions that survived from Confucian tradition. The system that China borrowed from the Soviet Union established central and provincial literary magazines, editorial boards of prescribed political composition, a National Publication Administration that reviewed publishing plans and rationed paper, a Writers' Association that set down rules about writers' pay and privileges, and much more. The whole edifice collapsed with the outbreak of the Cultural Revolution in 1966, and was slowly rebuilt beginning in the late 1970s. The revived system remained fairly vital through the 1980s, although it was not as dominant as it had been in the 1950s. By the early 1990s, extreme disillusionment with the socialist bureaucracy and a rapidly increasing role for commercialism in literary publication made the official literary establishment increasingly irrelevant. Literary work began to stratify into two levels that resembled the case in the non-Communist world: at an elite level avant-garde literature—primarily short fiction and poetry—had high prestige but scant readership, while at a popular level there thrived a commercially profitable fiction that featured romance, sex, crime, and combat, as well as television drama featuring primarily family issues and social satire.

We can, in short, identify a distinctive socialist literary system that operated during the second half of the twentieth century in China except for a ten-year hiatus during 1966 to 1976 and during a declining phase in the 1990s. Because the system is unlikely to see a revival in the twenty-first century, this book is primarily an historical study aimed at illustrating the ways in which the twentieth century's experiment with socialism affected the roles and functions of literature in China. The socialist literary system never developed much in the Chinese countryside (except in the negative sense of repressing popular cultural expression), hence most of this book is about Chinese urban life.

One of the most striking features in the situation of literature under Chinese communism was the widespread assumption of its importance to the rest of life. Today, when we look at the stereotyped and generally mediocre works that were produced, it may be hard to imagine how people could find them interesting or useful. But in life within the system, Chinese writers, readers, critics, and political authorities—although sometimes holding very different or even opposing views on various matters—agreed almost unanimously in the assumption that literature is relevant, or even essential, to morality, social life, and politics at every level from the policymaking of the highest leadership to the daily life of the average reader.

In order to understand the system on its own terms, we should try to appreciate the mood in which this centrality of literature seems natural.

---

[2] The Chinese Communist Party began to adopt literary-control methods from the Soviet Union as early as 1930, when the League of Left-Wing Writers was founded, but the national system was built in the early 1950s. See Anthony J. Kane, "The League of Left Wing Writers and Chinese Literary Policy," and Merle Goldman, *Literary Dissent*, pp. 9–17, 67–157.

Some of the assumptions of the system can strike the outsider at first as odd, or even quaint. Below I list a few examples. These are not random, but have been selected in order to highlight certain aspects of the socialist Chinese system. I challenge the reader to join me in imagining the kind of general situation and outlook that could give rise to them.

—When tens of thousands of Beijing people came to Tiananmen Square in April 1976 to honor Zhou Enlai, who had died four months earlier and who was admired because of his presumed opposition to the Gang of Four (Mao Zedong's wife Jiang Qing and three colleagues, on whom the Cultural Revolution was later blamed), these citizens carried with them not only wreaths but thousands of classical-style poems painted in their own calligraphy. At the twilight of modern China's most radical episode, classical poetry and calligraphy remained their preferred means of expressing their strongest political and moral views.

—Three years later, young modernist poets who were publishing the unofficial literary magazine *Today* (*Jintian*) held two public poetry-reading sessions behind the Military Museum near Muxidi in Beijing. On the first occasion, 8 April 1979, it rained, and the organizers later reported regretfully that "only five hundred people" attended. The second session, on October 21, enjoyed clear weather, and about a thousand people came.[3]

—High communist officials used poetry and calligraphy to claim political and moral legitimacy and to extend their power symbolically to others. Mao Zedong's idiosyncratic calligraphy adorned the masthead of the *People's Daily* (*Renmin ribao*), the Beijing Railway Station, and many other more modest sites—including, to name but one, mosquito nets at Fujian Normal University in Fuzhou.[4] In 1978, a collection of the poetry of Chen Yi, who had been mayor of Shanghai and later foreign minister, was published in two volumes, extending to 550 pages.[5]

—During the literary drought of the late Maoist years (roughly 1964 to 1978), when published works were limited to stereotyped and highly tendentious pieces of fiction and opera, young Chinese readers passed around their own "hand-copied volumes" (*shouchaoben*) of popular fiction that told of spies, detectives, horror, romance, sex, and other popular themes. In some cases, these hand-copied volumes spread widely, throughout the whole nation, as readers recopied stories and passed them to others.

—In early 1979, China's political leadership suddenly announced that the public would again be allowed to buy and read a certain list of nineteen classics of Chinese literature (*Dream of the Red Chamber, Three Hundred Tang Poems,* and others) and sixteen Chinese favorites of foreign literature (*1001 Nights, Anna Karenina,* and others). On the day the books went on sale, the main branch of the New China Bookstore on Beijing's Wangfujing Street attracted a line of

[3] Interview with staff on *Jintian* (Today), 4, August 1980, Beijing.
[4] See Richard C. Kraus, *Brushes with Power,* p. ix.
[5] *Chen Yi shici xuanzhu.*

people two miles long. The store sold its entire stock of 800,000 volumes within a week, and could have done so faster had not sales been temporarily halted a few times when the line of customers deteriorated amid shoving and fisticuffs. Afterward, the store reported the recovery of twenty shoes that customers had apparently lost or forgotten.[6] Such symptoms of enthusiasm were not the common case within the socialist literary system; they were only a brief episode, but one that tells much about the long period of literary privation that preceded them.

—When the officially published provincial literary magazines were revived after the Cultural Revolution, and began to carry exposures of the social problems of the late Maoist period, their circulations skyrocketed. By 1980 the circulations of a few magazines reached half a million or more, and print runs of some novels ran into the millions. The numbers of actual readers were even higher, because copies of popular books and magazines were passed around and read by several—sometimes several dozen—different people.

—In a 1982 survey of middle-school students in Guangzhou, "reading" was named as the favorite after-school activity; moreover 9.5 percent chose "writer" as their preferred career—compared, for example, to 7.5 percent who chose "doctor" and 2.5 percent for "official."[7] Similarly, a 1984 survey of university students in Beijing found "reading literature" to be the favorite "cultural activity" outside of schoolwork. Reading was preferred to its alternatives, which included watching film and television, by a ratio of 2:1 or more.[8] In yet another survey, farmers living in the outskirts of Beijing in 1982 said that their favorite radio programs were readings of contemporary short stories, which they rated somewhat higher than traditional opera and far higher than the news.[9]

—Some of the writers who emerged (or reemerged) in the late 1970s became celebrities among students and other young intellectuals. Details of their off-the-record statements, especially those having to do with politics, were passed around though an oral grapevine that could spread news and gossip through a city, and sometimes across the country, in just a few days. Following the appearance of Liu Binyan's "People or Monsters?" in 1979, Liu and his publishers received tens of thousands of letters from nearly everywhere in China.[10] Readers cheered him, thanked him, told him what he should do next. And it was not just the most famous writers who received letters. The Guangzhou

[6] Interview at Xinhua shudian (New China Bookstore), Wangfujing Branch, Beijing, 30 October 1979.

[7] Wang Zhisheng and Li Zibiao, "Guangzhoushi zhongxuesheng sixiang zhuangkuang," pp. 43–44. The term "cadre" is used widely in China in the singular, to refer to officials of many sorts; it will be used in this sense in this book as well. The claims of Guangzhou youth that reading is their favorite extracurricular activity must be understood in the context in which they are made. When answering the written questionnaires of investigators there are strong reasons for describing one's ideal, as opposed to actual, behavior. This does not destroy the significance of the finding, however.

[8] Shen Jiming, "Guanzhong shenmei xinli," p. 17.

[9] Brantly Womack, ed., *Media and the Chinese Public*, p. 81.

[10] Liu Binyan, "Ren yao zhijian."

essayist Qin Mu, who had a good reputation but largely a local one, received an average of three hundred letters per month in 1980. Many of these were from young people seeking advice on how to write. Some, according to Qin, were even "hooligans" who wrote to him "as a benevolent neutral party" about how they might get a fresh start in life.[11]

—In June 1980, the leadership of the People's Liberation Army announced a list of thirty works of fiction that it was recommending to all soldiers. The works featured modern Chinese military heroes, whom the leaders wished to set forth as models for emulation.[12] The assumption the generals were using—that people's behavior has much to do, for good or ill, with the fiction they read—has deep roots in Chinese culture and has been especially strong in the twentieth century.[13] It was also clearly evident in a 1982 study by the Communist Youth League in Xi'an of the "worldviews" of young urban workers. In their summary analysis, the investigators classified youth into four groups: selfless idealists (18 percent), practical profit-seekers (67 percent), cynics (12 percent), and decadents (3 percent). They went on to characterize each group in various ways, including, in considerable detail, what kind of fiction each read.[14] They seemed to take it for granted that the whole range of young people, idealist through decadent, could be properly associated with some kind of fiction, and clearly felt that preferences in fiction were good ways to uncover "worldviews."

—In February 1980, Hu Yaobang, at the time minister of propaganda and soon to be general secretary of the Communist Party of China, delivered a "Talk at the Conference on Playwriting." Later his talk was disseminated in printed form for study in Communist Party meetings at all levels. It began with strong statements about the necessity of distinguishing sharply, as Mao had decreed, between political "friends" and "enemies," and about the indispensability of the Communist Party to China's salvation. Hu then turned to his major topic of how to write plays, not in terms of craft—where he was unqualified, and allowed as much—but in terms of moral and political correctness, where his views were not only relevant but authoritative. He clearly assumed that playwriting had much to do with public morality as well as with the stability of Communist Party rule.[15]

—Even foreign affairs could be involved. In the spring of 1980 the Liaoning provincial literary magazine *Yalü River* published an article calling for more literary treatment of heroic scientists and intellectuals, and crediting a father

---

[11] Interview with Qin Mu, 29 April 1980.

[12] "Zongzheng wenhuabu xiang quanjun tuijian sanshibu youxiu wenxue zuopin" *Yangcheng wanbao*, 18 June 1980.

[13] Liang Qichao's essay "Lun xiaoshuo yu qunzhi zhi guanxi" is a classic statement of the view and had a role in strengthening it.

[14] Gongqingtuan Xi'an shiwei xuanchuanbu, "Yige gongchang qinggong renshengguan de diaocha," pp. 12–14.

[15] Hu Yaobang, "Zai juben chuangzuo zuotanhuishang de jianghua," pp. 7–10.

figure of Soviet literature, Maxim Gorky, for the inspiration.[16] After someone brought the article to the attention of the Soviet embassy in Beijing, officials there wondered whether a new diplomatic attitude toward "revisionism" had been signaled. Was China's official attitude toward the Soviet Union changing? Was this, perhaps, a subtle sign of a split in opinion among the top Chinese leadership? It turned out that no signal had been intended, but the incident did leave the Chinese Foreign Ministry needing to make an embarrassing explanation.

Some of the uses of literature just noted present obvious, not to say amusing, contrasts with the contemporary West. What would Americans think if the mayor of New York published a two-volume edition of his collected poems? If the president of the United States lent his calligraphy to a major newspaper? If the Pentagon recommended thirty novels to the Marines? Could dissident poets attract five hundred people to a reading in Central Park—in the rain? How many college students would list reading fiction as their favorite extracurricular activity? Or how many farmers would prefer short stories on the radio? Could the U.S. State Department feel diplomatic embarrassment over an article in a middling literary magazine? In the 1980s, Western writers sometimes expressed sympathy for their beleaguered colleagues in China, who were seldom free to write just what they thought, were paid little, and could be harshly punished if they stepped out of bounds. These concerns were appropriate, but on the other hand, how many American writers could see their work occupy the central locations in society that the work of their successful Chinese counterparts did?

One of my aims in this book is to offer a picture of the Chinese literary scene that is comprehensive enough to make the "startling" facts listed above seem natural in their context. Some features of the scene will contrast with the modern West and others will not; I do not intend that every observation be seen as an implicit contrast.

In Western scholarship thus far, there have been basically three approaches to Chinese Communist literature. The earliest was to read literary works as social documents. For the three decades of 1949 through 1979, during which very few Western scholars could go to China, there was an extreme dearth of information in the West on Chinese daily life. It was possible to interview refugees, but this method seemed to raise questions of sampling and bias. One could read official pronouncements, but one never knew how much they described actual patterns rather than ideal ones. Literature, especially fiction, seemed to be another useful source, if not on specific events, then at least on general life patterns.

The assumption that Chinese fiction "reflected" daily life was not just the invention of Western sociologists, but in some ways a consequence of the

---

[16] Ye Boquan, "'Tamen shi zhenzheng de xin renwu': you Gaoerji de yige guandian suo xiang dao de."

way socialist Chinese literature presented itself. "Socialist realism," which China borrowed from the Soviet Union, held that literary works should "reflect reality in its revolutionary development"; hence literature was intended, in part, to be a mirror for life.[17] But it was also supposed to be more than that, as the phrase *in its revolutionary development* suggests. The mirror was supposed to be an inspired mirror, able to "train the people in the spirit of socialism" by showcasing ideals. For the Western sociologist, the injection of ideals into "realism" raised problems of how to account for distortions, and yet, in a larger sense, the "reflective" value remained because the values themselves were genuine parts of mental life and of the political struggles involved in the Party's attempts to inculcate "correct" attitudes. How to interpret "socialist realism" became more complex, but the value of literature as an entrée to mental and physical worlds that were otherwise cut off from the Western researcher was not therefore diminished. The social-document approach to socialist Chinese literature is perhaps best represented by Joe C. Huang's *Heroes and Villains in Communist China: The Contemporary Chinese Novel as a Reflection of Life*, in which major novels are used to discuss both the actuality and the ideals of guerilla warfare, agricultural collectivization, the cleanup of "bourgeois" cities, and other topics that were especially salient in the 1950s.

A second approach, well illustrated by Merle Goldman's books *Literary Dissent in Communist China* and *China's Intellectuals: Advise and Dissent*, has been to study the adversarial relations between writers and the Party leadership. Beginning in the early 1930s, with the founding of the League of Left-Wing Writers in Shanghai, the Chinese Communist movement took political ideas as the starting points for literary creation and used "literary" criticism as a venue for political battle. Writers who grew up in the movement accepted these premises, but in the 1940s, at the revolutionary base in Yan'an, some of them found themselves wanting to criticize the movement itself. This brought them into conflict with the movement's leaders, especially Mao Zedong, and from then on there was always an underlying tension, to a greater or lesser degree, between writers and the top leadership. The balance of power between the two sides was lopsided, since the leadership could, and sometimes did, crack down on writers. But writers—whether motivated by idealism, by traditional Chinese notions of the duties of an educated person, by careerist calculations, or (most often) by a mix of these things—repeatedly returned to the perilous push and pull of literary politics. Their right to speak out became itself one of the issues that they contested. Yet despite the differences between them and the ruling authorities, both sides seemed to begin from the assumption that literature, morality, and politics are closely intertwined—indeed, little more than different aspects of essentially the same thing.

---

[17] A full definition of socialist realism, as worked out by Stalin and Gorky in 1934, is quoted and discussed in Harold Swayze, *Political Control of Literature in the USSR*, p. 113.

The two scholarly approaches just mentioned originated in the 1960s, when Western study of contemporary China was done almost exclusively as part of "area studies" that were dominated by the social sciences. A few years later, beginning in the 1970s, the field of modern Chinese literature began to emerge on its own in Western universities, and in so doing spread from area studies centers to East Asian literature departments, which in turn were beginning, around the same time, to shift emphasis from philology and classical Sinology toward modern literary analysis. Accordingly there arose a call to view contemporary Chinese literary works as art, not as documents for social science. This call was seconded by Chinese writers themselves, who, when they emerged onto the world scene after China's opening in the late 1970s, wanted to be viewed not as mere reporters on Chinese society but as serious artists. Few, at first, produced any works that the Western world took seriously as art, and to this day there has been little consensus in the West about what the "canon" for recent decades should be. As of the late 1990s, we still have no book that surveys post-Mao Chinese literature from an artistic point of view, although there do exist some anthologies that use artistic quality as their primary criterion for selection.[18] One problem in reaching critical consensus, in both China and the West, has been a lack of implicit agreement about what constitutes quality. Debate over which works are "good" has involved—more than debaters have sometimes recognized—different understandings of what goodness is and how to measure it. These questions, difficult under any circumstances, can be especially perplexing when reasoning across cultures and political systems.

The approach I take in this book shares certain concerns with all three of the approaches sketched above, but in basic conception differs from them. My starting point is to be as empirical as I can. I try to look at how people who lived and worked within the socialist Chinese literary system—including writers, readers, editors, officials, and others—wrote, read, thought about, and argued over literary works. In the end I find, more than I had expected at the outset, a wide variety in the "uses" of literature, by which I mean different purposes that people who wrote, read, edited, or criticized literature wanted literary works to fill. Depending somewhat on time and place, different players in the system wanted literary works to teach correct political attitudes, to teach resistance to such attitudes, to entertain a person at the end of a hard day, to lift the curtain on what was going on in the outside world, to signal shifts in state policy, to complain in public about something one does not dare to say oneself, to explore new ideas or life

---

[18] These include Michael S. Duke, ed., *Contemporary Chinese Literature* and *Worlds of Modern Chinese Fiction*; Jeanne Tai, ed., *Spring Bamboo*; Henry Y.H. Zhao, ed., *The Lost Boat*; David Der-wei Wang, ed., *Running Wild*; Today editorial board, ed., *Abandoned Wine: Chinese Writing Today*; Henry Y. H. Zhao and John Cayley, eds. *Abandoned Wine: Chinese Writing Today, II*; and Wang Jing, ed., *China's Avant-Garde*. Bonnie McDougall and Kam Louie make a first step toward surveying post-Mao writing from an artistic point of view in *The Literature of China in the Twentieth Century*.

styles in a vicarious context, to provide the security of joining a group identity, to set history right for the sake of posterity, to bring fame to an author, to bring money to a publisher, and much more. Some of the literary "uses" are familiar in Western societies—or indeed all societies—whereas some are more distinctive to socialist systems or to China's in particular. In my empirical approach I try to account for all of them, with no implied judgment about how specifically "Chinese" each is.

My larger point is that the variety of literary uses in socialist China was greater than we have yet recognized. Each of the "social-document," "literary-dissent," and "artistic-quality" approaches has been by itself too narrow a lens to capture the entire variety. By itself, each of these approaches can lead to the conclusion that literary life in socialist China was simplistic or thin; but this only deepens the mystery of how something simplistic or thin could occupy the very central place in life that literature in socialist China obviously did.

Chapter 1 describes the literary setting in China during the late 1970s and early 1980s; it also introduces the broader perspectives that are available through comparison to other times and places, including the post-Stalin thaw in the Soviet Union and aspects of literature in Japan after World War II. Chapter 2 analyzes China's system of literary control. Chapter 3 discusses writers—their types, generations, groups, livelihood, and ways in which they viewed their roles. Chapter 4 surveys the literary media and market—the ways in which literature reached people and how (if at all) their preferences affected availability. Chapters 5 and 6 look at different kinds of readers and, using evidence of their preferences in literature, discusses some of what might be inferred about their values and outlooks. Chapter 7 reviews the major "uses of literature" and explores the problem of literary evaluation, that is, what do we mean by a "good" work when a variety of uses are at play?

CHAPTER 1

Historical Setting

FOR UNDERSTANDABLE historical reasons, China has never easily viewed itself as one nation among others. The division between China and "the rest of the world" has always made intuitive sense to Chinese and, in the last two centuries, the concept of comparison between China and the nations that have led the world in wealth and power has also become a national preoccupation. But comparison with nations whose modern experiences have more closely paralleled China's have not come so easily. Chinese people have not shown much interest in the parallel experience of Japan in responding to the West, despite the fact that Japan, at least in the initial stages, responded much more successfully than China. Similarly, in the struggle to understand what went wrong in their tremendous experiment with socialism, Chinese in recent times have paid strangely little attention to the obvious relevance of Soviet and Eastern European experience, where certain parallels with China are strong, and have preferred to focus on comparisons with Western Europe and the United States, where they are not. To some extent China scholars have also respected this Sinocentrism, allowing China's case to seem sui generis and sufficiently distinctive to be treated singly.

In this chapter—and, in passing, later ones—I want to compare aspects of the Chinese and Soviet socialist literary systems. The similarities between the post-Mao and post-Stalin "thaw" periods in the two countries raises the question of whether there are even broader patterns in how writers and societies respond to human-caused disaster and to the closely associated problem of literary repression. Many other twentieth-century cases in Europe, Africa, and Asia are relevant here, and I will occasionally make comparisons with some of them, especially from Soviet-dominated Eastern Europe and from Japan after World War II. I begin by looking closely at the Chinese scene in the late 1970s and early 1980s, choosing these years not only because they are a good baseline for the comparisons just noted but because they were the first for which an outside researcher like myself could get a close look at the Chinese socialist literary system in daily practice.

The same years are, moreover, a good entrée into the study of all the other phases of the Chinese socialist literary system from the 1940s to the early 1990s. The literary-bureaucratic system that was revived in the late 1970s was, in important respects, the one that had been built in the 1950s by borrowing from a Soviet model and that had lasted in China until the mid-1960s. The Maoist "Cultural Revolution decade" (1966–1976) brought a collapse of the Soviet-style system, but the "catastrophe" of those years also became the preoccupation of writing in the late 1970s and early 1980s. Debate in the late 1970s and early 1980s over how far to depart from Maoism revived issues of the Yan'an era of the 1940s, when Mao Zedong had laid down rules that underlay all phases of the socialist Chinese literary experience. Then, through the 1980s, the growth of the Chinese economy and increased contact with the outside world gradually eroded the fundaments of the socialist literary system, leaving readers, writers, and editors ever-greater latitude to stray from its patterns and prescriptions, provided only that writers not directly attack the government. By the early 1990s, the revival of popular fiction, the rise of film, the emergence of elite avant-garde writing, and the gradual replacement of political controls with market forces essentially ended what I am calling the Chinese socialist literary system. Although some of the bureaucratic labels remained, the functions they referred to had largely changed. This study does not, except occasionally in passing, seek to address the situation of the 1990s.

. . .

The national literary "weather," to use a metaphor that was customary in socialist China, was a ubiquitous fact of the socialist literary system. It referred, in general, to the amount and type of pressure or other interference that the national political leadership applied to the literary scene. In good weather, freedom of expression was broader, themes more varied, criticism more common, and readers generally more enthusiastic. In bad weather, just as many words went down on paper, but less literary life was visible both on and off the page, as writers and editors took cover and readers bided their time. How much freedom any given writer enjoyed at any particular moment was determined by more than the general weather. As we shall see in the next chapter, it could vary with who one was, who one's supporters were, where one published, who the supporters of one's publishers were, one's reputation among readers, and many other factors. The same literary manuscript could easily meet with very different fates depending upon the circumstances of its submission. Nevertheless, this variability operated within limits, and everyone's limits tended to shift when the weather changed. Literary editors monitored the weather closely, as did writers, critics, and even some readers. Because political leaders sometimes used literary outlets to broach purely political moves, the literary weather could have significance not just for stories and poems but for all of society. Hence a "meteorological" history of our period is important background.

The period of the late 1970s and early 1980s began with the arrival of a major warm front and ended with some thunderstorms during a cooling trend. The chronicle that follows is a "big picture." Its two major phases—warming until late 1979 and cooling afterward—encompassed smaller countertrends at specific times and places, and I note only the more salient of these in passing.

WARMING, 1976–1979

In 1979, the warmest year in more than twenty, Chinese intellectuals often pointed to 5 April 1976 as having been the first sign of important change. That was the date on which thousands of supporters of the recently deceased Premier Zhou Enlai, who was popularly thought to have stood for political moderation, challenged police in the heart of Beijing in order to pay tribute to Zhou and, indirectly, to protest the excesses of Maoist rule. A more important milestone—although no one could say so publicly at the time—was 9 September 1976, the day Mao Zedong died and supreme power fell within the reach of people with more practical ideas. Following Mao's death, Chinese writers and artists were invited to ridicule Mao's wife Jiang Qing and three of her associates, dubbed the "Gang of Four," yet for the first year remained hesitant to do so publicly. Certainly most were willing, but they faced deeply conditioned inner barriers against risking anything so apparently dangerous. The first actually to respond were cartoonists and comedians, whose skewerings of the Gang of Four met with enthusiastic popular response.[1] Yet they ventured only caricatures, whose implications about responsibility for China's recent suffering barely reached beyond the four approved targets. Because of their humor, cartoons and comedians' dialogues were generally viewed as "light" entertainment that would be relatively easy to shrug off if something went wrong. The more weighty question of what one might dare to put in a literary magazine— where both the leadership and the public were accustomed to look for significant political messages—still paralyzed most writers and literary editors.

   The first editors to venture significantly out of paralysis worked in Guangzhou (Canton), where traditional affinities with the culture of Hong Kong and other overseas Chinese communities were important in making the bold step seem possible. In March 1977, the magazine *Guangdong Literature and Art* published an article by Qin Mu called "Exploring and Interpreting Questions of Literary Art Dialectically."[2] By standards that applied two years later, the essay was timid and turgid with Marxist jargon. But Qin Mu had been labeled a "rightist" in the great Anti-Rightist Campaign of 1957, and for him to publish anything was a bold step for both him and his editors to take. Moreover, the article was primarily a challenge to the position of Hao Ran, the "peasant writer" who for the preceding ten years had been the only contemporary novelist in China to receive official praise—or indeed, to be allowed any public reputation at all. Before publishing the essay, Qin Mu and his sympathetic editors organized support for their posi-

---

[1] By "comedians" I mean performers of *xiangsheng* comedians' dialogues, one of the first of which to appear was Ma Ji and Tang Jiezhong, "Baigujing xianxingji." For a sample of the best cartoons, see Liao Bingxiong, *Liao Bingxiong manhua*.

[2] Qin Mu, "Bianzhengde tantao he chuli wenxue yishu wenti."

tion not only in Guangdong province but elsewhere in China, even in Hao Ran's home base of Beijing. In the predictable backlash that followed, *Guangdong Literature and Art* was able to argue the issue to a standoff. But a standoff, during a thaw, is actually a victory. The editors pressed forward, including in their June 1977 issue a children's story that satirized the absurdities of adhering to ultraleftist policies in the classroom.[3] Just as Qin Mu could be partly protected by using Marxist terminology, and comedians by using "light" humor, so this story was partly covered by being "merely" a children's story.

During the first year after Mao's death, the clearest political sign that a literary thaw could be expected was the gradual reappearance of pre-Cultural Revolution literary figures. The "exoneration" of writers and literary officials like Zhou Yang, Xia Yan, Mao Dun, Liang Bin, Sun Li, Zhou Libo, Ma Feng, and others proceeded quietly but with a seeming inexorability whose portents were very loud.[4] As readers followed these events in the press, they began to anticipate an eventual return to a literary climate that might approximate that before 1966, when the Cultural Revolution began. The parade of exonerations was accompanied by the gradual return of the Soviet-style literary administration that had been in place from the early 1950s until 1966. In December 1977, the Guangdong branch of the Chinese Writers' Association announced its reopening. The Shanghai branch followed in the next month,[5] and the first post-Mao national meeting of the association followed four months after that.[6] Within two years, all other provincial branches of the association—each publishing its own family of literary magazines and many sponsoring seminars, retreats, and funds to support travel or writing leaves—were revived. In many cases the same editors and managers returned to their posts and, as before, a central-provincial structure held the net together. The center, where membership carried more prestige, set national guidelines for such things as manuscript fees and royalties.[7] The number of literary magazines distributed by the Chinese Post Office increased from only a handful in 1976 to 110 by April of 1979, and the number of copies per issue grew rapidly, as well.[8] Circulation of the monthly magazine in Guangdong province, *Literary Works*, grew from 70,000 in mid-1978 to 500,000 by early 1980.[9]

---

[3] Lu Zhenkang, "Yuanyuan qiyu ji."

[4] I translate the Chinese term *pingfan*, literally "invert [back to upright position]," as "exonerate" rather than "rehabilitate," which the Chinese government uses and Westerners have adopted uncritically. "Rehabilitate" in English suggests that a person has a flaw or disability that is being overcome. But *pingfan* clearly connotes that the original fault lay not in a person's condition but in a wrong judgment.

[5] On the revival of the Guangdong Writers' Association, see "Jiepi 'wenyi heixian zhuanzheng' lun," *Renmin ribao*; for Shanghai, see *Wenyibao* 1978.1.8.

[6] *Wenyibao* 1978.1.8.

[7] See chapter 3 for details.

[8] Interview with Beijing Municipal Post Office, 16 October 1979.

[9] Interview at *Zuopin* editorial offices, 4 March 1980.

The first literary work to attract national attention for venturing into territory that for years had been off limits was Liu Xinwu's "The Homeroom Teacher," published in November 1977 by China's premier national-level literary magazine, *People's Literature*.[10] On the surface, the story's audacious departure is its portrayal of a juvenile delinquent who cuts class, has a surly attitude, and reads bad books like Ethel Voynich's *The Gadfly*. (Voynich, a socialist born in New Jersey, moved to England where she wrote *The Gadfly*, which eventually became known in China through its mention in two Soviet novels.[11] During the Cultural Revolution, these Soviet associations were part of what made *The Gadfly* a licentious book.) Before Liu Xinwu's story appeared, Chinese were not supposed to admit in public that the Cultural Revolution had produced any footloose hooligans. An even bolder implication of the story, although more subtly put, was set forth in the character of a young woman whose "model leftist" characteristics—energy, unquestioning loyalty, puritanical attitudes, disdain for any view that does not originate in the official press—turn her into an ignorant and insensitive bigot who is as flawed in her way as the juvenile delinquent is in his. The story suggests that the flaws of both characters spring from a common origin: the madness of the Cultural Revolution, then mentionable only under the code name, "Gang of Four period." Although politically tepid by the standards of two years later, "The Homeroom Teacher" generated unusual excitement nationwide because nothing remotely like it had been seen for over twenty years.

The next work to bring a significant change in the literary weather was Lu Xinhua's "Scar," which was published in Shanghai in August 1978, after a lengthy behind-the-scenes debate over political costs and benefits.[12] To look at the story out of context, it can seem peculiar to imagine that such a mediocre work might draw a tremendous reader response—enough, in the end, to establish its name as a collective label for thousands of other works published in the next two years. Fundamentally, the response stemmed less from the story itself than from the traditional Chinese emphasis on family. Under Mao's command to put "class struggle" above all else, young people had denounced their parents during the Cultural Revolution, and countless families had been torn apart. "Scar" tells of a young woman whose relations with her parents (her family of birth) as well as her boyfriend (her potential family of marriage) are both destroyed for no good reason by the mindless zealotry in her environment. For readers, the story provided a vital link between their own daily lives and the widely trumpeted but far too abstract "evil" of the Gang of Four. Millions apparently read "Scar" and thought:

---

[10] Liu Xinwu, "Ban zhuren."

[11] The two novels were Nicholas Ostrovskii's *How Steel Is Tempered* and Lyubov Kosmodemyanskaya's *The Story of Zoya and Shura*, which in the 1950s were translated in China and published in 1.4 and 1.6 million copies, respectively. Interview at China Youth Publishing House, 8 October 1979.

[12] Lu Xinhua, "Shanghen."

This family was ruined. *My* family was ruined! Hooray for this story! Meanwhile those in the political leadership who opposed the story asked: Can we allow a story to dwell on the negative, to elicit tears? What kinds of thoughts go along with the tears? Where will such a trend stop?

Despite such questions from conservatives in the Party, the top leadership continued to call for a warming trend.[13] Other stories like "Scar" appeared in newspapers and magazines. In November 1978, the Tiananmen Incident of 5 April 1976 was officially declared to have been a good, correct, "revolutionary" action. Even more surprising, the national leadership announced a blanket recision of "rightist" labels that hundreds of thousands of intellectuals had borne since the Anti-Rightist Campaign of 1957. Some wondered why the leadership would do something so drastic. Were they really repudiating such a large and significant campaign? (Fourteen months later, in January 1980, Deng Xiaoping answered this question by explaining that he had meant not to repudiate the spirit of the Anti-Rightist Campaign, but only to say that it had gone too far.)[14] In any case, the policy was a dramatic gesture of conciliation toward intellectuals. It came during preparations for the Third Plenary Session of the Eleventh Party Congress in December 1978, and probably had something to do with that meeting. Deng was about to announce major plans for China's "Four Modernizations" (of industry, agriculture, the military, and science and technology), a cause in which he needed the cooperation of intellectuals.

Speeches at the Third Plenum called upon intellectuals to "liberate their thought." Writers were encouraged to break into previously "forbidden zones" and not to fear a return to repressive policies. The leadership's goal was modernization of China's science, economy, and military—not its art or politics. But the effects of a "warm wind," whether intended or not, are to heat everything at once. The leadership probably knew, in any case, that to set down separate policies for scientific and nonscientific intellectuals would not have been practical. The trauma of the Cultural Revolution, during which intellectuals of every kind suffered similarly, was still too fresh a memory for one group to feel secure while another was subject to attack.

The first quarter of 1979 was the warmest season for literature and art in thirty years. Then in April, May, and June the weather was chilly again. Wei Jingsheng, a former Red Guard who had become a leading figure at Beijing's "Democracy Wall," was arrested on 29 March. Wei had been an editor of the unofficial journal *Explorations* (*Tansuo*) and had published an essay holding that Deng's Four Modernizations would not work without a fifth, which Wei said was political modernization or democracy. Wei's arrest and trial were well publicized, clearly in an attempt to warn others away from his example. In Guangzhou, editors of unofficial publications were arrested

---

[13] Beginning in the late 1970s, reform-minded Chinese began using the term "conservative" (*baoshou*) to refer to orthodox leftists—not, as in the contemporary West, to the political right.

[14] Deng Xiaoping, *Muqian de xingshi he renwu.*

without publicity on the grave charge of "counterrevolution." The handful of unofficial publications that had sprung up in several Chinese cities in the late 1970s never recovered from this "chilly wind."

Although such shifts in the national "weather" undoubtedly originated among the highest leadership, no one at that level provided a clear statement of what the disapproved opinions were. (This kind of vagueness could be useful to the leadership. When boundaries of the permissible were left unclear, intimidation produced a wider scope of self-censorship; the absence of having issued a negative command left leaders with more "face," which was important in symbolizing legitimacy.) The rationale for the spring chill of 1979 was delivered through surrogates. Two of the most widely noticed statements were by a little-known provincial official named Huang Ansi and an entirely unknown youngster named Li Jian, who clearly was speaking on behalf of more powerful people.

Huang Ansi, deputy minister of propaganda in Guangdong province, published a newspaper article on 15 April 1979 entitled "Look Forward, Literature!"[15] Huang held that literary works about the Gang of Four catastrophe fall into three categories. First were works that praise the brave people who dared to fight back—for example, Zong Fuxian's prize-winning play "From the Silent Zones," which extols the young heroes of the 5 April 1976 Tiananmen Incident.[16] Such works were fine, according to Huang, because they aroused people's courage. Second were works that examined social problems caused by the Gang of Four—for example, Liu Xinwu's "The Homeroom Teacher." These works were all right, too, because they made people think.

But the third category of works, which bemoaned the suffering that people had endured, were not so fine. Huang did not name examples, but seemed to have been thinking of stories like "Scar" and Chen Guokai's almost equally popular "What Should I Do?!," which had recently been published in Guangdong.[17] Chen's story tells of a pregnant young woman who learns during the Cultural Revolution that her scientist husband has been hounded to death. She attempts suicide, is rescued by a brave young worker, gives birth, eventually falls in love with her rescuer, marries him, and has a second child. Then she discovers that her first husband has not, in fact, died. As she sees his battered, ghostlike apparition approach her door, she can only think "What Should I Do?!" Huang Ansi argued that "depressing" works should be curtailed because they only cause negative feelings among readers. They go against the directives of the Third Plenum, which included, in addition to "liberate thought," the behest to "unite as one and look to the future."

Li Jian's article, called "'Praise' and 'Shame,'" was published in June in

[15] Huang Ansi, "Xiang qian kan a, wenyi!"
[16] Zong Fuxian, "Yu wusheng chu."
[17] Chen Guokai, "Wo yinggai zenme ban?"

Hebei Literature and Art.[18] Speaking with the tacit encouragement of this journal's conservative leadership, which included the veteran poet Tian Jian, and probably having backers at the central level as well, Li Jian argued that any writer who fails to remember the great Chairman Mao, or to sing the praises of the socialist motherland, is shameful. His article, more than Huang Ansi's, came to be viewed as a standard-bearing statement of the "praise faction"—people who championed the Maoist legacy (attributing wrongdoing only to the "Gang of Four"), and who felt that "liberation of thought" could have dangerous implications.

But soon the weather changed once again. On 20 July, Wang Ruowang, a Party member and intrepid veteran of literary wars since the 1930s, attacked Li Jian's "'Praise' and 'Shame'" in an article called "A Cold Wind in Springtime."[19] Other intellectuals—and more importantly, reformers in the Party leadership—had been waiting for an opportunity to rally against the "praise faction" and now supported Wang. With open derision, they called the praise faction "whateverists"—people who support "whatever" Mao said, literally interpreted, regardless of changing circumstances. Within a few months, the unfortunate Li Jian had become a pariah; even his girl-friend left him, denouncing his whateverism, and he is said to have at-tempted suicide. He apparently found reprieve only when Deng Xiaoping summoned him, Wang Ruowang, and editors of *People's Daily (Renmin ribao)* to meet and recognize that, although Li had made some mistakes, it was also wrong for the "older people" to attack him.

The warm literary weather that arrived in autumn 1979 was even better than that of the early spring.[20] Liu Binyan's startling work of reportage, "People or Monsters,?" which exposed massive corruption in a county in Heilongjiang Province, was published in the September issue of *People's Lit-erature* after an exceptionally expeditious editorial decision.[21] This piece and the enthusiastic response of readers throughout China enlivened the literary scene for several weeks. The warming trend was reinforced when, from October 30 to November 15, the Fourth Congress of the All-China Federa-tion of Literature and Art Workers convened in Beijing. At this huge meet-ing, Liu Binyan, Bai Hua, and other writers who had been repressed since

[18] Li Jian, "'Gede' yu 'quede.'"

[19] Wang Ruowang, "Chuntianli de yigu leng feng."

[20] A spate of anthologies, including several in English translation, collected the surprising literary harvest of this season. See Lee Yee, ed., *The New Realism*; Helen F. Siu and Zelda Stern, eds., *Mao's Harvest*; Perry Link, ed., *Stubborn Weeds* and *Roses and Thorns*; Stephen C. Soong and John Minford, eds., *Trees on the Mountain*; and Michael S. Duke, ed., *Contemporary Chinese Literature*. For analytic comment in English, see Michael S. Duke, *Blooming and Contending*, and Jeffrey C. Kinkley, ed., *After Mao*.

[21] "Ren yao zhijian" was dated August 1979 and appeared in September 1979, having passed through editing and typesetting in only a few days. It is also noteworthy that the piece is located near the end of the issue and is printed in small type, whereas in the table of contents the title is listed first and printed in boldface type. For more see Duke, *Blooming and Contend-ing*, chap. 4, and Li Oufan, "Liu Binyan yu 'Ren yao zhijian.'"

the 1957 Anti-Rightist Campaign brought standing ovations with their speeches about political hypocrisy, falsity, and distortion of literature and art.[22]

At the same meeting, the Deng Xiaoping leadership began the very serious process, which took about eight months to complete, of changing the guiding slogan for Chinese literature and art. Ever since Mao Zedong's "Talks at the Yan'an Forum on Literature and Art" in 1942, the slogan "Literature in Service of Politics" could not be publicly opposed in China.[23] People could, and occasionally did, argue about what should be understood by the vague phrase "service of politics." But whatever its meaning, that meaning was indubitably "correct." This was the case with all slogans that had originated with Mao. Thus it was potentially momentous when Hu Qiaomu, a long-time political secretary of Mao, pressed the Congress of Literature and Art Workers to abandon "Literature in Service of Politics." Hu held that the record of the previous thirty years had shown the slogan to have done more harm than good. Orthodox Maoists in the "whatever" faction, such as Wang Zhen, Lin Mohan, and Liu Baiyu, opposed Hu's speech, and the meeting reached no clear result on this issue. But the slogan itself disappeared from the public media, and for eight months Chinese literature and art did without a supreme slogan, until "Literature in Service of the People and of Socialism" was unveiled.

In the interim, some less official policy watchwords were used. These clearly had the approval of Deng Xiaoping, but were tentative and colloquial in tone. One that emerged from the Congress of Literature and Art Workers was aimed at reassuring writers and artists that there would be no return to the abuses of the Cultural Revolution period. It promised "Three Noes": no "cudgeling" (Cultural Revolution slang for harsh ad hominem attacks), no "capping" (affixing unchangeable negative labels), and no "grabbing of pigtails" (seizing upon a small mistake to discredit everything about a person).[24] Writers well knew that the "Three Noes" would have effect only as long as the top leadership saw fit; even so, this slogan was a considerable advance. By December 1979, Chinese writers and artists had freedoms they would not have dared to suggest five years earlier. The state had permitted not only a wider scope for writers but considerably more volume of publication. Volume was controlled though allocation of paper. In 1977, literary publishers were assigned 596,000 reams of paper; by 1979, this figure had risen to 1,476,000 reams, an increase of 148 percent in two years.[25]

[22] A selection of their speeches is translated in Howard Goldblatt, ed., *Chinese Literature for the 1980s*. Liu Binyan's speech appears in Liu Binyan, *People or Monsters?*, pp. 1–10.

[23] The best translation of Mao's talks is Bonnie S. McDougall, *Mao Zedong's "Talks at the Yan'an Conference on Literature and Art"*.

[24] In Chinese, "san-bu" zhuyi: buda gunzi, bukou maozi, buzhua bianzi.

[25] Interview at the National Publication Administration, 4 August 1980.

COOLING, 1980–1983

The first sign of what turned out to be a long-term cooling trend was the closing of "Democracy Wall" in Beijing in December 1979.[26] Democracy Wall was never very large, and was not primarily concerned with literature. But its abrupt shutdown cast a shadow over literary publication throughout China. The general association of political protest and literary expression was too close for this to be otherwise. More specifically, the ferment at the wall was associated, in the minds of readers as well as the leadership, with the unofficial literary magazines that had arisen in the late 1970s. *Today (Jintian)*, published in Beijing, was the best known of these, but others had appeared on the campuses of leading universities in many parts of China. A month earlier, in the final communiqué of the Congress of Literature and Art Workers, these unofficial journals had received explicit endorsement as important contributors to China's flourishing literary scene. Now this important point was being repudiated on the highest authority. Not only did the reversal severely undermine the security of the unofficial literary journals; the prestige of the Congress had been tarnished, as well. The literary cost of closing the wall was far less in the few additional poems that might have appeared on it than in the setting down of guidelines that editors everywhere knew they would violate at their own peril.

Some of the official literary periodicals continued through January and February 1980 to publish path-breaking works. But these were largely works written in the fall of 1979, whose unseasonal appearance was due more to the publication time lag than to resistance to the "wind." On 16 January 1980, Deng Xiaoping drew the new line clearly in a speech that was later circulated in printed form to Party branches throughout China. Many youth, Deng said, had become infatuated with "bourgeois liberalism" and did not appreciate the important distinction between socialist democracy and bourgeois democracy. In China's socialist democracy, literature and art must observe the Four Basic Principles, popularly known as the "Four Upholds": of socialism, the dictatorship of the proletariat, the leadership of the Communist Party, and Marxism-Leninism-Mao Zedong Thought. Although we should reevaluate the slogan "Literature in Service of Politics," said Deng, it does not follow that "literature can be separate from politics."[27] In the days after Deng's speech, newspapers at every level echoed one another with articles supporting its "spirit."[28] In meetings, literary officials

[26] Technically, the wall was not closed but only "moved" to Moon Altar Park, where participants were required to register their names and the names of their work units. Since Party officials in work units controlled nearly all aspects of a person's livelihood, the "move" immediately killed free speech at the wall.

[27] Deng Xiaoping, *Muqian de xingshi he renwu*, p. 23, and paraphrased from pp. 16, 17, and 36.

[28] For example, "Manhuai xinxin, polang qianjin," a major policy statement in the Shanghai *Wenhuibao* attributed to "Commentator," 22 January 1980; and *"Wenhuibao* fabiao pinglunyuan wenzhang 'manhuai xinxin polang qianjin,'" *Guangzhou ribao*, 25 January 1980.

spread the new message that, although the Party would maintain its policy of the "Three Noes," writers could not, on the other hand, expect "a World of Three Withouts": without leadership, without criticism, without imperatives.[29] Simultaneously, officials began to criticize stories and plays that contained "errors."

These errors were basically of two kinds. The more serious of the two was writers' forthrightness in exposing corruption, bullying, and sycophancy in officialdom. Such writing was especially troubling to the leadership because of the enthusiastic and widespread response it drew from readers. The intensity of the response clearly implied the severity of the problems. To stimulate such a response thus amounted to a challenge to political stability. Liu Binyan's "People or Monsters?" was obviously an example of this offense, and some in the leadership wanted to use it as a negative example in press attacks. But the great popularity of the piece, and its solidity as well-researched nonfiction, made this difficult.[30] Instead, the press began to criticize a satirical play called "What If I Really Were?" by three young playwrights from Shanghai.[31] The play features a young man who pretends, for an evening, to be the son of a high official, only to have grasping bureaucrats take him at his word and shower him with gifts and favors, followed by personal requests, not only for that evening but for many days thereafter. Although never published in the public media in China, the story of "What If I Really Were?" spread widely by word of mouth.

The second kind of error that official critics began to find in literary works was the setting of bad moral examples for youth. A filmscript called "Girl Thief" was criticized for showing a young female hoodlum—clever and quick in the tradition of China's female *xia* (knights errant)—who could run circles around bumbling police.[32] Other bad examples exhibited "un-Chinese" frankness about sex. A novella called "Work Transfer" told of a young man who, in trying to arrange a job reassignment from the countryside back to a city, was ready to do any favor for anyone—including sleeping with the wife of a director of personnel so that she might put in a good word for him via the "crucial pillow connection."[33] Some works committed both kinds of errors, the political and the moral. The filmscript "In the

[29] Li Yingmin, talk at a conference on teaching materials and Hong Kong-Taiwan literature, Nanning, winter 1980. The "World of Three Withouts" is "'san-wu' shijie: wu yaoqiu, wu lingdao, wu piping."

[30] Local leaders in Heilongjiang, whose reputations were most hurt by "People or Monsters?," were the only ones who decided to sponsor published attacks on the piece despite the risks of opposing something so popular and irrefutably true. See Wu Yungang, "Ping 'ren yao zhi jian' de shishi."

[31] Sha Yexin, Yao Mingde, and Li Shoucheng, "Jiaru wo shi zhende." The play was published in classified (*neibu*) periodicals in China and later in Hong Kong. It was performed for politically restricted audiences in Shanghai and Beijing and publicly for three days in Guangzhou before being shut down.

[32] Li Kewei, "Nüzei."

[33] Xu Mingxu, "Diaodong." For a criticism, see Shi Cheng, "Ping zhongpian xiaoshuo 'Diaodong.'"

Archives of Society"[34] and the story "Feitian"[35] both told of high officials in the military raping young women who were in their charge.

The pairing of political and moral errors was not accidental. It had several advantages from the leadership's point of view. To oppose only political challenges would amount to a blunt "don't criticize us," and such bluntness would in itself entail a certain loss of face. On the other hand, to assume the almost parental role of caring about the proper instruction of young readers not only preserved face but suggested that those who dissented politically were in the same category with common hoodlums and devotees of sex. "What If I Really Were?" was attacked for encouraging youth to "sympathize with a charlatan," even though this charge fit very poorly with the theme of the play and had virtually nothing to do with the reasons for its popularity.[36]

The leadership's new direction was emphasized and refined in the middle of February 1980 at a Conference on Playwriting in Beijing. Hu Yaobang, then secretary general of the Central Committee of the Party, delivered the keynote address, a fact that signaled the importance of the meeting. While singling out "What If I Really Were?," "In the Archives of Society," and "Girl Thief" for special criticism, Hu also took pains to seem as reasonable as possible: "I am not saying that shady or backward things should not be reflected in literature. Provided they are representative things, or characteristic things, they indeed should be reflected. But if a work reflects backward or shady things exclusively or incessantly, then I feel it cannot be said to reflect fully or correctly the nature of our society."[37] Hu then went on, more ominously, to speak of "poisonous weeds"—a label that had spelled doom for stories and disaster for writers during the Anti-Rightist Campaign in 1957. "Since our literary comrades are especially sensitive," said Hu, "I will try to avoid the two words 'poisonous weeds'; but poisonous weeds do exist, you know."[38]

The basic principle that Chinese writers were supposed to take from the Conference on Playwriting was formulated in a new slogan, "Literature and Art Should Consider Social Effects," which was widely publicized in February and March.[39] In newspapers, literary journals, and official meetings, Party officials pointed out the ill effects of irresponsible literature and art—such as a case in which children murdered their siblings with a candlestick after seeing this happen in a foreign film. But among writers, the "social

[34] Wang Jing, "Zai shehui de dang'anli."

[35] Liu Ke, "Feitian."

[36] Chen Yong, "Cong liangge juben kan wenyi de zhenshixing he qingxiangxing." See chapter 2 for more on this tactic in the political criticism of literature.

[37] Hu Yaobang, "Zai juben chuangzuo zuotanhuishang de jianghua," p. 18.

[38] Ibid., p. 28.

[39] The first public statement of the "social effects" policy, which must have either originated with Deng Xiaoping or had his approval, appeared in a piece called "Tantan wenyijie de sixiang jiefang wenti," published in *Hongqi* on 1 February and attributed to "Commentator."

effects" slogan only led to an oblique counterattack in the form of a long list of rhetorical questions: How can a writer, working from that inner fire one calls "inspiration" (*linggan*), at the same time stand back, like a social scientist, and try to calculate the effect each line might have on countless readers? Even if a writer tries to do this, how can he or she be responsible for the immensely complex relationship between a work of art and the psychology of a reader? Or the equally mysterious relationship between readers' ideas and their behavior? If writers are blamed every time a reader commits a crime, quipped Wang Meng, a leading writer who in 1986 became China's minister of culture, then shouldn't a writer get credit every time a reader does not commit a crime?[40] When something goes wrong in society, asked Wang Ruowang, whose dissidence eventually led to his expulsion from the Communist Party in 1987, why assume that it all started with writers? What about parents, schools, and political leaders?[41] Isn't it clear from the disastrous rule of the Gang of Four, asked Liu Binyan, that the "social effects" of a politician's mistake can be much worse than any attributable to a writer?[42] And who, after all, should judge the effects of art—those "above," meaning officials, or those "below," meaning readers? If officials decide, then how, ultimately, can we guarantee no return to the abuses of the Cultural Revolution?[43]

The leadership had no interest in addressing such questions, and "consider social effects" was certainly not a call to do research on public attitudes. (When such research was done anyway in the 1980s, it showed that readers themselves felt that literature had, on average, a highly positive effect on their morale and sense of social responsibility.)[44] In spring 1980 writers and editors who opposed the "social effects" slogan rallied behind the argument that the only true way to know the social effects of a work is

[40] Interview, 3 August 1980, Beijing. In a later essay called "Manhua wenyi xiaoguo," Wang Meng points out that Cervantes' *Don Quixote* could be said, in the terminology of the Chinese left, to "viciously attack" Spanish society of its time, yet the book also became an item of pride in Spanish culture; that Hollywood films are regarded as low art even by Americans, yet do wonders for America's prestige around the world; and that humor is so complex that no one should have to try to figure out what its "social effects" might be.

[41] Interview at *Shanghai wenxue* editorial offices, 18 June 1980. A 1983 survey of nearly 12,000 young readers in eight cities confirmed the point of Wang Ruowang's rhetorical question from the viewpoint of young readers themselves. It found that only 11 percent felt that literature and art had a major influence on their attitudes toward life. The Communist Party and Youth League, the example of prominent people, and the influence of family, friends, and teachers were all rated as more important. The young readers also felt that the influences literature did have on them were overwhelmingly positive ones. See Huang Ruixu, "Young Laborers' Attitudes towards Literacy and Artistic Works" and "Daxuesheng yuedu wenxue zuopin xianzhuang qianxi."

[42] Liu first raised the question in his speech at the Conference of Literature and Art Workers in November 1979. See Liu Binyan, *People or Monsters?*, p. 2.

[43] These last two questions were discussed, among other places, at a Conference on the Writing of Comedians' Dialogues, 7 May 1980, Beijing (transcript, n.p.,n.d.), p. 4.

[44] See pp. 252–53, below.

to let it be published so that the people, and eventually history, can be its judges.[45] Thus, although everyone accepted the "social effects" slogan superficially, the real issue was argued to a standoff. The wind grew no warmer, but the freezing tendency abated for a time.

In their creative work, writers faced the problem of how they could be innovative now that hard-hitting social criticism—at least for most people, most of the time—had been ruled out of bounds. Some turned toward innovation in literary technique. For several months, Wang Meng had been using interior monologue in stories such as "Eye of the Night," and his experiments were partly responsible for an interest in Western "stream of consciousness."[46] Many writers, partly influenced by film, were experimenting with nonlinear presentation of time. There was also much talk in literary circles about Western "black humor"—partly because it seemed to preserve space for negativity—but few actual examples were attempted.

The official response to these technical initiatives was mixed. On the whole, the leadership held them to be basically harmless, and certainly preferable to work that could stir up political trouble. In at least some locations, Propaganda Department officials made it known to editorial boards that foreign influences, provided they were not political, could be given more scope for a while. Even such things as photographs of nude statues and paintings were acceptable so long as they served to dilute the preoccupation with social criticism that had been so strong in fall of 1979. But the Western influences drew significant criticism, as well. Conservatives like Liu Baiyu, an essayist and critic who worked in the People's Liberation Army, argued that "stream of consciousness" writing, because it is inherently unclear, cannot perform the proper functions of literature. "If I can't understand it," Liu reasoned, "then the masses can't, either; and if the masses can't, then it doesn't belong in socialist art."[47] Criticism of the technical experiments also came from a few, mostly senior writers, such as the poet Ai Qing, who agreed with Liu Baiyu that literary messages should be clear, but who still generally opposed the leadership's demand that writers leave social problems alone. On this Ai Qing agreed with Liu Binyan and many others that a writer's duty is to "speak for the people."

On 26 July 1980, the Party leadership unveiled its long-awaited replacement for the formal slogan "Literature in Service of Politics." It was a care-

---

[45] The argument that "social effects" take time to measure, and that only readers—not political authorities—can determine what the effects actually are, was repeated in very similar terms by Wang Ying (editor of the Anhui literary journal *Qingming*), interview 24 June 1980; Wang Ruowang, interview 18 June 1980; Wang Meng, interview 3 August 1980; Kong Jiesheng, interview 2 April 1980; Zhao Zhenkai (Bei Dao), 4 August 1980; and Zhang Jie, interview 2 August 1980. These and other writers and editors seem to have been basing themselves on a 1961 speech by Zhou Enlai that was widely republished in early 1979 (see *Beijing Review*, 30 March 1979).

[46] Wang Meng, "Ye de yan." Wang Meng himself does not use the term "stream of consciousness" to describe this story, and denies any conscious influence from Western writers.

[47] Interview, 11 August 1980, Beijing.

fully wrought compromise: "Literature in Service of the People and of Socialism." On the one hand, by omitting the word "politics," the new slogan signaled that writers would no longer need, as they did during the Maoist period, to write works that actively supported the most recent updating of the agenda of the Party's Propaganda Department. Now writers could be political or apolitical as they chose. But on the other hand, if they chose to be political, they still would have to be political only in the correct ways. Anything that ran counter to socialism (specifically the "Four Upholds") was out of bounds. Around the same time, two other inner-Party decisions, seemingly trivial yet of considerable importance in the sensitive context of China's literary politics, were quietly implemented. First, newspapers were now allowed, indeed required, to begin referring to the Cultural Revolution in quotation marks. This small point of punctuation, suggesting that it had been only a "so-called" Cultural Revolution, allowed widely held private opinion some vindication in the public realm. Second, one could now attack Mao's long-time deputy Kang Sheng, the much feared and hated "central adviser" during the Cultural Revolution, by name. Until then one had to use the euphemism "that authority on theory."

Accompanying these small measures was another guideline—attributed on the literary grapevine to Deng Xiaoping himself—that said the new slogan should not be allowed to stultify literature, because the literary scene in a socialist society should be rich and lively. There ensued in the fall of 1980 an orchestrated public debate over the questions "How can we enliven literature?" and, more specifically, "How can the Party's leadership of literature be improved?" Views on these questions from a wide range of literary figures appeared on the pages of the *Literary Gazette (Wenyibao)*, the Party's premier publication on the politics of literature. One contribution that was too frank for the leadership's taste was delivered by Zhao Dan, a famous film actor, as he lay dying of cancer. The best way to "improve" Party leadership, wrote Zhao, was simply to keep hands off: "If the Party controls literature and art too closely, then such work is hopeless—it is finished."[48]

Two works of fiction further enlivened the fall of 1980. Yu Luojin's "A Winter Fairy Tale," a startling account of the author's first divorce and a paean to her brother Yu Luoke, who had been executed in 1970 for openly questioning Maoism;[49] and Dai Houying's *People, Oh People!*, especially its afterword, were read as a plea to revive "humanism," thus implicitly rejecting Mao's theory that there is no human nature, only class nature.[50] In

---

[48] Zhao Dan, "Guan de tai juti, wenyi mei xiwang."

[49] Yu Luojin, "Yige dongtian de tonghua." The version published in China was rather severely edited before publication. For an unexpurgated English translation by Rachel May and Zhu Zhiyu, and an introduction by John Minford, see *A Chinese Winter's Tale*, published in Hong Kong.

[50] Dai Houying, *Ren a, ren!*, translated by Frances Wood as *Stones of the Wall*. For comment see Duke, *Blooming and Contending*, chap. 6. For a summary in English of contemporary commentary in Chinese see *China News Analysis*, no. 1,231 (23 April 1982).

Guangzhou, provincial officials in late December oversaw the founding of a "Literary Association of Guangzhou Youth," whose vice president was the student editor of *Red Bean*, an unofficial literary magazine at Zhongshan University. The move was significant because *Red Bean* was the sole survivor of the crackdown on unofficial publications at the beginning of the year. The Guangdong leadership was subtly signaling that it thought such publications were permissible.

But in early 1981, the wind temperature shifted again and blew mostly cold all year. On 14 January an article in *People's Daily* by "Commentator" (indicating high authority) warned that some people "want to tear down every one of the literary guidelines of Marxism-Leninism" and that such an attitude is "incorrect."[51] On 4 February the same "Commentator" voice said that "literature and art should contribute to the establishment of spiritual civilization"[52]—meaning, essentially, that there should be more praise of model heroes and less exposure of actual conditions. A number of top-level Party meetings, which are difficult to date with precision, led to the circulation of three classified documents whose potency was not suggested by their drab names, "No. 2," "No. 7," and "No. 9." No. 2 opposed "dissidents" and other "troublemakers"; No. 7 sought an end to the exposure of social problems in journalism and creative writing; No. 9 came down hard on unofficial publications, finally wiping out even *Red Bean*.[53]

In the spring, an orthodox line in literature and art emerged from the military. On 10 April *Liberation Army News* published a major article, which apparently had been in careful preparation for some time, on the proper evaluation of Mao Zedong.[54] Stiffly countering the drift away from Mao in recent years, the article listed Mao's "key" contributions to the Chinese revolution beginning in the 1920s, and sought to disperse responsibility for his disastrous policies during the Great Leap Forward (1958–1960) and the Cultural Revolution. His record as a whole, according to the article, still made him a hero of epic proportions. The grandiose style of the article recalled Cultural Revolution writing. Although not about literature per se, this article was the direct forerunner of the literary shock that came ten days later: the attack on Bai Hua, his filmscript "Unrequited Love," and Chinese "bourgeois liberalism" in general.

"Unrequited Love," an unremarkable piece in literary terms, and largely unnoticed until it was attacked by the government, suggested that Chinese intellectuals' love for their country (or "state," as the term *guojia* can also be

---

[51] "Jianchi Makesizhuyi de wenyi piping," *Renmin ribao*, 14 January 1981.

[52] "Wenyi yao wei jianshe shehuizhuyi jingshen wenming zuochu gongxian," *Renmin ribao*, 4 February 1981.

[53] On these documents, see *Zhengming* no. 43 (May 1981), pp. 90, 50; *Dongxiang* no. 30 (1981), translated in Foreign Broadcast Information Service 19 March 1981, pp. U1–U3; and *Dongxifang* no. 28, p. 65.

[54] Huang Kecheng, "Guanyu dui Mao zhuxi pingjia he dui Mao Zedong sixiang de taidu wenti."

understood) has not been reciprocated; intellectuals during the Maoist period were cruelly abused.[55] One scene also suggested that reverence for Mao was superstitious—akin to incense burning and idol worship. On 20 April *Liberation Army News* published an article by "Special Commentator" which said that "Unrequited Love" had violated the "Four Upholds."[56] This was a very serious charge, even after the thaw of recent years; it situated a person outside the revolutionary ranks, where, during the Mao period, one had been utterly defenseless. It was unclear what it might mean in the shifting winds of 1981. Three days after the "Special Commentator" article, on 23 April there appeared a tabloid "special supplement" to *Report of the Times*— a newly arisen magazine that had a Maoist flavor and enjoyed strong support within the army. The supplement carried revolutionary songs and poems, a tribute to Mao's talks on literature at Yan'an, a report of the glorious victories of the army's basketball team against South Korean and U.S. opponents—and, at most length, harsh attacks on Bai Hua's "Unrequited Love."[57]

For about three months it was unclear whether this cold wind from the army would have a lasting effect. Writers and readers hoped it would simply blow by. But after a number of high-level Party meetings in the summer, it became clear that it would not.[58] Party leadership of the arts was to be

---

[55] The selection of Bai Hua as the target in this campaign was a puzzle that aroused speculation both inside and outside China. "Unrequited Love" did not stand out as an especially provocative piece during 1979. Based on the life of the painter-poet Huang Yongyu, it was published in September 1979 in *October* (*Shiyue*), a major literary magazine in Beijing. Yet it received little notice, either pro or con, through the exciting fall of 1979, when works like "People or Monsters?" and "What If I Really Were?" were so controversial. Why was it suddenly singled out two years later? A rumor inside China had it that Deng Xiaoping himself had not noticed the work until he viewed a predistribution screening of its film version; he was shocked, according to the story, said "this won't do," and that was that. Another theory, printed in the Hong Kong magazine *Qishiniandai* (Mu Fu, "Yichang daijia gaoang de biaoyan"), claimed that Bai Hua's connections with the top leadership were good enough that he could tacitly accept his selection as a target for attack, and even provide a "self-criticism" to the Party's liking, in confidence that no truly serious trouble would be in store for him personally. The fact that Bai Hua was in the army may explain why he was a fitting example from the point of view of his leading attackers, who were also in the army. But the truth of this matter is not known outside the very small group who were involved in the decision. In broad perspective, moreover, the reasons for selecting Bai Hua as a target are largely beside the point of the overall campaign, whose purpose was not to punish Bai Hua personally but to use him as an example through which to oppose "bourgeois liberalism" generally. For more on the Bai Hua affair, see Merle Goldman, *Sowing the Seeds of Democracy*, chap. 4 and Duke, *Blooming and Contending*, chap. 5.

[56] "Si xiang jiben yuanze burong weifan," *Jiefangjun bao*, 20 April 1981.

[57] "'Kulian' de shifei, ging yu pingshuo," *Shidai de baogao zengkan*, 23 April 1981.

[58] These meetings included a national conference on "the thought front," convened by the Party's Propaganda Department on instruction of the Central Committee and held in Beijing from 3 to 8 August 1981. The results were handed down at a one-day meeting of key people from the Ministry of Culture and the All-China Federation of Literature and Art Workers— on, perhaps purposely, the fifth anniversary of Mao Zedong's death, 9 September 1981.

"strengthened"; the "lax and flabby" leadership of recent times must be stopped; and "Unrequited Love" should be exposed to another round of criticism. Around the same time, Yu Luojin and her story "A Winter Fairy Tale" were denounced. The story had told too frankly of divorce and remarriage; Yu Luojin herself was a "fallen woman."

In late September, the Party's general secretary, Hu Yaobang, delivered the formal public statement on the general retightening.[59] Hu was personally the most liberal of the top leaders, and his choice as the one to deliver the crackdown message seemed to have been intended as a signal that the leadership was unified on the issue. The occasion also carried some irony: it was an international conference to commemorate the great modern Chinese writer Lu Xun. In a speech that might have made Lu Xun squirm in his grave, Hu proclaimed the dangers of an ill-defined "bourgeois liberalism," issued a warning to those who were tainted by it, and called for a return to the Party's outstanding tradition of "criticism and self-criticism." In a revival of Maoist style, Hu's speech was full of military metaphors: writers were "warriors," wielding "weapons," engaged in "battle" on the "thought front." The slogans "liberate thought" and "let a hundred flowers bloom," which had been so prominent two years earlier, did not get even perfunctory mention. Articles in *Red Flag*, the Party's major journal for theoretical statements of contemporary relevance, reinforced the cooling trend that Hu's speech had signaled. An article in the 1 October issue sought to add the mantle of moral paternalism to the Party's political crackdown by identifying "bourgeois liberalism" with sexual excesses portrayed in film.[60] On 1 December the journal carried a hard-hitting speech that Hu Qiaomu had delivered at a high-level Party conference in August.[61] "Bourgeois liberalism," Hu said, was not just a problem in film or other art, but an "ideological" trend. It "departs from the socialist path" and "breaks from Party leadership." In short, Hu's article publicly vindicated the charge in the *Liberation Army News*, eight months earlier, that people like Bai Hua were violating the "Four Upholds."

The next year, 1982, although grayish throughout, showed how literary weather could vary from place to place. In February, Zhou Yang, a powerful figure in political criticism of literature since the 1940s, told writers in Guangzhou that literary policy cannot—try as it might—control what people do and do not find attractive; traditional Chinese opera, with its "feudal" emperors, generals, scholars, and beauties, persists because people like it, Zhou said.[62] In this guardedly liberal statement, Zhou appeared to be giving

---

[59] Hu Yaobang, "Zai Lu Xun dansheng yibai zhounian jinian dahuishang de jianghua."

[60] Chen Bo, "Dianying yao wei jianshe shehuizhuyi jingshen wenming zuochu gongxian," p. 30.

[61] "Dangqian sixiang zhanxian de ruogan wenti," *Hongqi* 1981.23.2–22.

[62] "Zhou Yang zai Guangdong zuojia luntanshang de jianghua," *Dagongbao*, 9 February 1982 p. 3; translated in Foreign Broadcast Information Service, China Report, 10 February 1982, p. W5.

tacit support to a more challenging position that Wang Ruowang, the Party gadfly from Shanghai, had recently been pushing: that literary policy should learn from the Daoists and "govern through nonaction," meaning live and let live. In May, editors at *Anhui Literature*, whose liberal tendency from the late 1970s still faintly survived, criticized the official view that "the sixteen years" from 1949 to 1966 had had "normal conditions in literature and art." The "abnormalities" would have to be counted from the Anti-Rightist Campaign of 1957, the editors held.[63]

But these and other cases of local warming were countered by a cold blast from Beijing in April, when three important literary works were criticized by name. Zhao Zhenkai's *Waves*, a long story that employed modernist techniques and was the most important work of fiction to appear in the unofficial journals, was criticized for "existentialist" tendencies;[64] Lu Yanzhou's filmscript "The Fable of Heavenly Cloud Mountain" was singled out for its unflattering portrayal of a Party secretary;[65] and Yu Luojin's "A Spring Fairy Tale," a sequel to her "Winter" tale, was charged with a host of "bourgeois liberal" errors.[66] Attacked in dozens of publications throughout China, Yu Luojin became second only to Bai Hua in the post-Mao period as a negative example used to warn other writers. From 6 to 12 May, a major conference in Beijing reaffirmed Mao Zedong's "literary thought" and called for its "continued development."[67]

The temperature of the wind from the center shifted again in the second half of 1982, when "leftist" voices at *Report of the Times (Shidai de baogao)* and *Liberation Daily (Jiefang ribao)* were chastised in the authoritative *Literary Gazette*.[68] The slow warming continued into spring 1983, when Zhou Yang published an essay suggesting that both "humanism" and "alienation" were possible, indeed actual, under China's socialist system.[69] Humanism remained important to intellectuals as a theoretical counter to Mao's insistence on class nature and "class struggle." Zhou's acknowledgment that socialism could give rise to "alienation"—a term Marx had used to describe the alienation of workers from the means of production under capitalism—was something that intellectuals had long wanted to say but until then could not. The gaps between pompous political language and actual conditions ("ideological alienation," in Zhou Yang's phrase) and between arrogant offi-

---

[63] *Anhui wenxue*, "Dui 'shiliunian' tifa de yiyi," p. 73.

[64] Ai Shan (pseud.), *Bodong*; (see bibliography under Zhao Zhenkai).

[65] Lu Yanzhou, "Tianyunshan chuanqi."

[66] Yu Luojin, "Chuntian de tonghua." The issue of *Huacheng* in which it was published was recalled as part of the attacks on Yu Luojin, and two issues later the editors published a self-criticism entitled "Our Mistakes" (Women de shiwu) on the very last page of the issue, where editors in socialist China sometimes placed pieces that they published only reluctantly.

[67] Zhongguo shehuikexueyuan wenxue yanjiusuo dangdai wenxue yanjiushi, *Xin shiqi wenxue liu nian*, p. 530.

[68] See Yu Dong, "Yige zhide zhuyi de yuanze wenti"; Xin Xu, "'Shiliunian' wu chabie ma?"; and Guan Lin, "Fenqing shifei, bianming zhenxiang."

[69] Zhou Yang, "Guanyu Makesizhuyi de jige lilun wenti de tantao."

cials and ordinary people (Zhou's "political" alienation) had been obvious
for years. Even "economic alienation" had long been visible in workers' lack
of care for equipment at their workplaces.

But Zhou Yang's initiative was not accepted in the highest counsels of the
Party. Zhou was obliged to write a self-criticism, and by fall his claim of
"socialist alienation" had become a primary target in a new campaign to
"Oppose Spiritual Pollution."[70] This movement, which began in September
1983, peaked in early November, and ended rather abruptly in January
1984, brought the chilliest weather since the mid-1970s. A few senior
writers, who had been irritated by "modernist trends" for essentially literary
reasons, were willing to speak in favor of the campaign; some others, because they held official positions, were obliged to offer perfunctory support;
but most writers pointedly eschewed comment—as if competing to see who
could maintain the most meaningful silence until the weather changed
again.

The continual fluctuation of literary policy in the early 1980s can be seen
as ripples and eddies resulting from the major shift from Mao Zedong's
political regime to Deng Xiaoping's. But for many, among both political
leaders and intellectuals, there was a deeper factor at work, as well. The
problem of how to find a proper balance between Western influences
(whether called "bourgeois liberalism" or something else) and a more basic
Chinese "essence" was a question that had been in the background of
China's predicament for more than a hundred years. This problem, chron-
ically resistant to solution, had created in many a deep and lasting ambivalence that led more easily to changes of mind than to firm answers. People
on several sides of the literary battles of the post-Mao years exhibit this
ambivalence, sometimes dramatically. For example, Deng Liqun, deputy director of the Chinese Academy of Social Sciences, supported "liberal" views
in 1979 but by 1983 was the leader of the Anti-Spiritual Pollution Campaign. The veteran poet Ai Qing, who in 1980 protested controls on literature with such hard-hitting lines as "Only an idiot / Argues with an idiot,"
in 1983 took the other side, saying that "exposure" writing could "pollute
readers' souls."[71] Switching in the opposite direction was Li Jian, who wrote
"'Praise' or 'Shame'" during the chill wind of spring 1979 but was himself
writing exceptionally lurid "exposure" stories in 1981.[72] There were, to be
sure, other factors involved in such changes of mind, but the abiding search
for a definition of China that would be at the same time modern and dis-
tinctively Chinese underlay most of the other factors. It is implausible to
suppose that someone like Ai Qing—famous for his stubborn independence

---

[70] See Xing Bensi, "Yihua wenti he jingshen wuran."

[71] Ai Qing, "Hua yu ci" and "Wenyi kanwu yinggai shi jianshe jingshen wenming de
zhendi."

[72] See Kam Louie, "Between Paradise and Hell: Literary Double-Think in Post-Mao
China."

through wars, prisons, and political campaigns of the past—would perform an about-face in obedience to anything but his deepest worries.

Yet the overall trend of literary policy in the early 1980s was to stop the political and social criticism that had gushed forth in the scar literature of the late 1970s. This cooling trend seems to have been guided by Deng Xiaoping himself. Originally scar literature had served Deng's political interests, because it discredited the policies of the late Maoist period and paved the way for the basic changes that Deng wished to institute. But by late 1979 the discrediting function had gone far enough for Deng's purposes. He apparently concluded that further critical probing of the Maoist period would undermine the authority of the Communist Party itself, and that was something he could not risk.

.   .   .

Changes in the literary weather continued through the 1980s, but, since our sample of fine fluctuations is already sufficient, I will pass over them here and point out only a few highlights. The most liberal days of the 1980s came in December 1984 at the Fourth Congress of the Writers' Association, where Hu Qili, who represented the top leadership, spoke in favor of "creative freedom" for writers.[73] At the same meeting, Chinese writers were allowed, for the first time, to elect the Board of Directors of their association by popular vote. Ba Jin, the famous author of *Family* and other fiction published in the late 1920s and the 1930s, who also had written essays after the Cultural Revolution that had broken ground in confronting those events honestly,[74] was elected president of the association, and Liu Binyan was elected vice president.[75] In the summer of 1986 there was hope that the viewpoint of writers might finally get an institutional base when Wang Meng was named minister of culture and brought in other active writers and artists as his assistants. But this tentative advance was outweighed by the intimidation that accompanied the fall of Hu Yaobang, the relatively liberal general secretary of the Party, in January 1987. Liu Binyan, who had long benefited from Hu's support, was expelled from the Party in a prelude to Hu's own fall. Wang Ruowang, whose persistent demands for more openness had earned him the enmity of conservatives, was also expelled from the Party. The slogan "oppose bourgeois liberalism" was revived.

As it became clear, in the early 1980s, that contemporary social and political criticism would be increasingly risky to write and difficult to publish, writers were obliged to turn in other directions. Some turned toward politi-

---

[73] Hu Qili, "Zai Zhongguo zuojia xiehui di si ci huiyuan daibiao dahuishang de zhuci." Hu's endorsement of "creative freedom" had more power in Chinese than in English translation. In Chinese, the word *ziyou* is the same in *chuangzuo ziyou* "creative freedom" and in *ziyouzhuyi* "liberalism," a term that had recently been under strong attack in the phrase "bourgeois liberalism."

[74] Ba Jin, *Suixianglu*.

[75] *Renmin ribao*, 6 January 1985, p. 3.

cally innocuous material, such as travelogues, sketches of unusual people, or stories of peculiar coincidences. Others turned toward experiments in modernist technique, where there seemed plenty of room to explore without having to venture onto politically dangerous ground. Some sought to leave contemporary issues behind by exploring China's cultural roots.

But departure from contemporary concerns was seldom if ever complete. Gao Xingjian's "absurdist" play *Bus Stop* (*Chezhan*, 1983), apparently inspired in part by Samuel Beckett's *Waiting for Godot*, shows several ordinary citizens waiting for a bus that never comes; but the errands that each wishes to accomplish by taking the bus—which they discuss at length as they wait together—lead directly into concerns about contemporary society, and the overall effect is much more socially engaged than *Waiting for Godot* is. Modernist technique also made an implicit political statement by its inherent "unclarity." Party critics were leery of "misty" (*menglong*) poetry precisely because they could not be sure what it said. Some lines invited political readings, but nothing could be proven, and the fact that poets had carved out a space that was beyond political adjudication did not sit well with them.[76] The young writers in the mid-1980s who became known as the "root-seeking group" (*xungen pai*) were even more bound to China's contemporary situation despite their appearance of plunging into the past. They were among the young intellectuals who had formed high hopes during 1978 and 1979, with the calls for "liberation of thought" and the outpouring of socially critical literature. By 1983 they began to ask, "Why is our country headed back to its old ruts? Is there something deep in our culture that keeps pulling us back to them?" Thus their turning to look at the past was not only an avoidance of contemporary problems, whose direct address had become forbidden, but a very important way of exploring those problems indirectly. The young writers sought "roots" of basically two kinds, and for two very different reasons: some wanted to discover lost cultural resources that could be tapped in order to fill the void left by the failed experiment in socialism,[77] while others sought to identify the roots of contemporary afflictions so that they could be dug out and thrown away.[78]

---

[76] For translations and an introduction to some of the controversies that attended both misty poetry and *Bus Stop*, see Stephen C. Soong and John Minford, eds., *Trees on the Mountain*. See pp. 98–99 below, for more discussion of this problem.

[77] The most frequently cited example is probably Zhong Acheng, "Qiwang" (The king of chess), in which a footloose and destitute young man during the late Mao years roams the countryside perfecting his skill at Chinese chess. The game provides him not only an escape from the mindless turmoil around him but a transcendence into another, vaguely Daoist kind of China that seems to have been existing all along on a higher plane. See translations by W.J.F. Jenner in *Chinese Literature*, and by Bonnie McDougall in *Three Kings*.

[78] The most famous example of this type is Su Xiaokang and Wang Luxiang's *Heshang* (River elegy), a television script that was produced and broadcast with tremendous effect in summer 1988. *Heshang* finds despotism, conservatism, closed-mindedness, and xenophobia in China's imperial past and suggests that contemporary China, including the Communist Party, has substantially inherited all of these in altered guises. See Richard W. Bodman and Pin Pin Wan, trans., *Deathsong of the River*.

A few writers continued, despite the obstacles, to write literary reportage in the tradition of Liu Binyan's "People or Monsters?"[79] Exposure of the Maoist period occasionally appeared in fiction, as well, notably in the labor-camp fiction of Zhang Xianliang.[80] But in the 1980s such writing was always constrained by limitation of the depth and breadth of exposure, by admixture of faith in "true Marxism," or by both.

The limitations on socially and politically critical writing led to a sharp decline in the enthusiasm of readers and, accordingly, in the circulations of the periodicals that had carried such writing in the late 1970s. *Shanghai Literature (Shanghai wenxue)*, which had sold about 500,000 copies per issue in 1980, fell to a circulation of only 30,000 in 1986. Nationwide, the circulations of provincial or municipal literary magazines parallel to *Shanghai Literature* fell an average of 27 percent between 1984 and 1985 alone. In April 1986, the Chinese Writers' Association convened an urgent meeting to study why subscriptions to nearly 700 of its literary periodicals had been steadily dropping.[81] The related medium of film, for similar reasons, fell in urban viewership an average of 6 percent a year after 1979, until 1985, when it fell 25 percent in a single year.[82]

A rise in television viewing partly explains the decline in the film audience. At the beginning of 1980 there were about 3.5 million television sets in China, and by the end of 1984 about 42.3 million.[83] But television aside, there clearly remained a reading public looking for things to read other than the innocuous pieces and avant-garde literary experiments that were filling the literary periodicals. In Shanghai a survey of college students—who had been among the most avid readers of the literary periodicals during 1979–1980—showed that reading actually increased between 1982 and 1984 for every category of material except literature.[84] For literary publishers there was a crisis, too, because the terms of the economic "responsibility system" of the 1980s obliged publishing houses, who previously had enjoyed large state subsidies, to find ways to balance their own budgets. This economic pressure, combined with reader demand, led to a revival of

[79] Liu Binyan himself was one of these; see, for example, *Liu Binyan baogao wenxue jingxuan*. Zhang Shengyou and Hu Ping, a generation younger than Liu, followed his tradition and wrote specifically about him. For interviews with Zhang and Hu, see Laifong Leung, *Morning Sun*, pp. 53–64 and 240–50.

[80] For translations of major examples, all by Martha Avery, see *Half of Man Is Woman*, a translation of *Nanren de yiban shi nüren; Getting Used to Dying*, a translation of *Xiguan siwang; Grass Soup*, an abridged translation of *Fannao jiushi zhihui;* and *My Bodhi Tree*, a translation of *Wo de puti shu*. For comment, see articles by Jeffrey C. Kinkley, Yenna Wu and Philip F. Williams in *Asia Major*.

[81] "Literary Editors Discuss Drop in Subscriptions," Joint Publications Research Service, CPS-86-049, p. 24.

[82] Zhongying gongsi, "Jing Jin Hu deng shiyige chengshi shangbannian dianying shichang qingkuang," p. 26.

[83] Brantly Womack, ed., *Media and the Chinese Public*, pp. 25, 27.

[84] Ye Jun et al., "Shanghai shifan daxue xuesheng sixiang guannian bianhua de qingkuang diaocha," p. 14.

the kind of modern popular fiction that had first boomed in Chinese cities in the early twentieth century.[85]

Again Guangdong led the way. In 1981, the Guangdong People's Publishing House began to reprint A. Conan Doyle's *The Adventures of Sherlock Holmes* in hundreds of thousands of copies. These sold out as soon as they became available. Beginning in 1984, when China's publishers were allowed to reprint popular fiction from Hong Kong and Taiwan, the "knight-errant" (*wuxia*) stories of Jin Yong became best sellers. In 1986, the love stories of the Taiwan writer Qiong Yao became a fad among young readers on the mainland. By the early 1990s, the bifurcation of China's literary scene into elite and popular levels was well established.

PERSPECTIVES

A season-by-season chronology of China's literary scene in the late 1970s and early 1980s begs larger questions about how to interpret the whole. Are we studying primarily what happens when repression of literature gives way to more freedom? How a society that had been preoccupied with internal matters begins to look outward? How a nation recovers from trauma and gropes to understand what has recently happened to it, and where it should now go?

Although all of these questions, and others, are important to the case of post-Mao China, they were largely absent from public discussion in China at the time. Perhaps still too close to painful events, and in any case limited in what they could publish, Chinese intellectuals did little more than affix some chronological labels: first were the tentative breakthroughs of "scar" (*shanghen*) literature, from late 1977 to late 1978, when "the ten years of catastrophe" (1966–1976) were blamed on "Lin Biao and the Gang of Four"; 1979 and about half of 1980 were the time of "contemplative" (*fansi*) literature that sought deeper explanations of what had happened; then came a "pluralist" (*duoyuan*) stage that included "roots" (*xungen*) literature, modernism, and some reportage, Taiwan literature, popular writing, and other trends side by side. When Chinese scholars did seek to go beyond these superficial labels, they encountered obstacles. In 1979, some young researchers at the Literature Research Institute of the Academy of Social Sciences began working on a history of contemporary Chinese literature, only to hear Hu Qiaomu, president of the academy, instruct them to stop, on the grounds that it would be too difficult to arrive at "correct" answers to all the controversies, and that the results of their labors would probably be unpublishable.

Some broader perspectives on the post-Mao thaw are available in comparisons to other times and places. In Mao's China itself, the phenomenon

---

[85] See Perry Link, *Mandarin Ducks and Butterflies*.

of literary thaw and refreeze has a precedent in the 1956–1957 Hundred Flowers period and the following Anti-Rightist Campaign. A similar but less pronounced example occurred in the early 1960s, when many of the tenets of the post-Mao thaw were enunciated in a 1961 speech by Zhou Enlai.[86] Elsewhere in the socialist world, the emergence of a Soviet-style literary system from the shadow of a repressive dictator has a richly instructive parallel in the post-Stalin thaw in the Soviet Union in the mid-1950s, and literary rebellions in Hungary in 1956, Czechoslovakia in 1968, and Poland in the early 1980s also offer useful perspective on the Chinese case. Comparisons outside the communist world—to Japan and Germany after World War II, for example—can be useful in interpreting how much of the post-Mao literary scene was a response to a communist system in particular, and how much was a more general case of response to extremity. Holocaust literature and Japanese "atomic-bomb literature" both offer the possibility of much deeper study of how human beings, over a considerable time span, seek to come to terms with unfathomable catastrophe.[87] This deeper question is largely beyond the scope of what I will address in this book, however. As of the late 1990s, China's writers still had not faced their country's Maoist episode squarely enough to provide examples commensurate with Holocaust literature or atomic-bomb literature.[88]

Comparing the Hundred Flowers

On 2 May 1956, and again on 27 February 1957, Mao Zedong delivered speeches in which he invited Chinese intellectuals to speak their minds on public matters, including criticisms of the Communist Party. "Let a hundred flowers bloom, and a hundred schools of thought contend," Mao declared, using a phrase that originally referred to contention among philosophical schools during China's Warring Sates period (475–221 B.C.). Four or five years into his revolution, Mao had already grown impatient with the tendencies of his Communist Party to ossify into a new ruling group. He wanted an end to "bureaucratism, dogmatism, and commandism," and felt that a good way to achieve it would be to reach outside the Party to encourage criticism from the "masses" and their willing spokespeople, the intellectuals, both of which groups were themselves dismayed by the growing bureaucratism.[89] Mao had already conducted several public purges of intel-

---

[86] Zhou Enlai, "Zai wenyi gongzuo zuotanhui he gushipian chuangzuo huiyi shang de jianghua."

[87] For a good bibliography of "atomic-bomb literature," see John Whittier Treat, *Writing Ground Zero*.

[88] Still, Vera Schwarcz is able to open the question of comparing Holocaust literature and some examples of post-Mao writing in *Bridge across Broken Time*.

[89] Li Zhisui, who was Mao Zedong's personal physician from 1955 to 1976, reports that another reason for Mao's wish to reach outside the Party was that Mao "was furious over the slights he had received at the Eighth Party Congress [September 1956]—the call for collective

lectuals for "bourgeois" tendencies, "counterrevolution," and other disloyalty, but did not appreciate how much fear he had already spawned. He
assumed that the great majority of intellectuals were loyal to the revolution
and would trust him to listen to their accounts of its flaws. But in fact, to
many intellectuals, the problems with the new ruling group were bigger
than mere flaws, and one of these problems was whether one could dare to
say so in public.[90]

Initially very few writers responded to Mao's call for criticism. In 1956,
Wang Meng, at age 22, and Liu Binyan, 31, published widely noticed stories
that criticized bureaucratism, waste, and inefficiency.[91] Not until May 1957,
after several more encouragements from Mao, did underlying discontent
really begin to surface. In increasingly critical articles, intellectuals questioned not only the Party's techniques of rule but whether its monopoly on
government was appropriate. Some of the articles appeared in the *People's
Daily*, the Party's own central newspaper. It began to seem that an anti-
Communist uprising of the kind that had happened in Hungary the previous year might be possible in China. Mao, apparently furious, and realiz-
ing he had miscalculated, began to plot revenge on those who had spoken
out. But he purposely delayed for a month, allowing the liberal atmosphere
to continue long enough to "lure snakes out of their holes."[92]

The broad crackdown, called the Anti-Rightist Campaign, began in June
1957. Mao abruptly announced that China was infested with "Rightists" in
need of reform. In the ensuing months, public humiliation, written confession, deprivation of Party membership, and assignment to the countryside
for reform through labor were among the techniques used to carry out
Mao's will. The Chairman's arbitrary estimate that about 5 percent of Chinese intellectuals were Rightists turned into a de facto quota that work units
such as schools and universities, editorial boards, libraries, museums, and
hospitals were obliged to fill. People who had spoken out during the immediately preceding months were the first to be fingered to fill the local

---

leadership, the assertions that China would never have a cult of personality, the removal of
Mao's thought as the guiding principle for the nation" (*The Private Life of Chairman Mao*, p.
192). But other well-placed people, such as Ruan Ming, maintain (interview, 21 November
1994) that Mao's inspiration for the Hundred Flowers policy was genuine populism; Mao dis-
liked Stalin and had hopes for Khrushchev, Ruan Ming says, until the Hungarian uprising in
1956 convinced him that a hard line was better.

[90] The interpretation of Mao's thinking presented in this and the next paragraph, although
substantially presented to Western scholarship in Merle Goldman, *Literary Dissent in Communist China*, chaps. 8–9, Richard Solomon, *Mao's Revolution and the Chinese Political Culture*, pp.
268–329, and elsewhere, are confirmed and given more precise detail in Li Zhisui's *The Private
Life of Chairman Mao*, pp. 197–202 and passim.

[91] Wang Meng, "Zuzhibu xinlai de nianqingren"; Liu Binyan, "Zai qiaoliang gongdishang"
and "Benbao neibu xiaoxi." For a broad selection of "hundred flowers" works, see Hualing
Nieh, ed., *Literature of the Hundred Flowers*.

[92] *Yin she chu dong*, long rumored in China to have been the Chairman's plan, is confirmed by
Li Zhisui to have come from Mao himself (*The Private Life of Chairman Mao*, p. 201).

quotas. When their numbers fell short of the required 5 percent, witch hunts followed. These naturally gave rise to intense dissension and backbiting among people who only a few months earlier had been "speaking out" together. Families were torn apart as people were pressured to denounce their Rightist members. Rightists themselves sometimes opted for divorce in order to protect their loved ones from their taint, which could spread. Some (no one knows how many) were driven to suicide. In the 1980s, the Chinese government acknowledged a figure of 500,000 victims in the Anti-Rightist Campaign.

There are obvious differences between the 1956–1957 experience and the post-Mao events. The methods used in the retrenchment of the early 1980s were considerably more gentle and subtle than those of the Anti-Rightist Campaign. Still, in literature, the overall patterns of thaw-and-refreeze were similar: in both cases an enlarged scope for expression for writers and a brief sense of euphoria among the reading public were followed by contractions and gloom. Many of the specific complaints that surfaced—about hidden poverty, official corruption, and dogmatic and ignorant leadership—were similar, as well. In both periods there were debates over "humanism," over "obscurity" in poetry, and over the duties of the writer, especially over whether a writer should give higher priority to telling the truth or to portraying model behavior for emulation.

Why was the retrenchment in the early 1980s less harsh than in 1957? The general pattern in the socialist world, to judge from such cases as Hungary in 1956 and Czechoslovakia in 1978, was that a greater episode of speaking out induces greater force of repression. But although the outpouring of 1979 went well beyond that of 1956, it induced a repression that was less in amount and more gradual in its application. The famous protest stories by Wang Meng and Liu Binyan in 1956 seem long-winded and dull by comparison to literally hundreds of works from 1979, including new works by Wang and Liu.

One important factor in the difference is that the top leadership was continuous in the 1950s under Mao but was shifting from Mao to Deng Xiaoping in the late 1970s. When writers exposed recent social and political abuses, Mao, under whose rule the abuses had occurred, could not tolerate as much protest as could Deng, who had recently been out of power. Like Khrushchev in following Stalin, Deng had little need to lure snakes from holes, and clearly welcomed the effect that literary dissent had in discrediting his predecessors, so long as it did not go so far as to call into question the basic legitimacy of the regime he was inheriting. Deng's cliché "ten years of catastrophe," which frequently appeared in literature, as elsewhere, to refer to the years 1966–1976, not only served to glorify Deng as the liberator from catastrophe but prepared public opinion for the far-reaching policy changes that were in Deng's plans.

The two retrenchments also differed in the depth of change they sought to bring about. Mao, flush with optimism over the success of his revolution, assumed that human nature could be fundamentally remolded, whereas Deng, picking up the pieces after the Maoist disaster, was content simply to control key aspects of outward behavior. In the Anti-Rightist Campaign, Mao expected fully 5 percent of Chinese intellectuals to remake themselves "from the bone marrow outward." In the early 1980s Deng—who in 1957 had prosecuted Mao's campaign against intellectuals—could not have pursued character remolding even if he had wanted to, given the greatly diminished prestige of the regime. In the early 1980s, his aim was simply to find a literary work he could use as a negative example in order to frighten writers into observing certain bounds. For this purpose, he wisely chose to sidestep the most warmly received works of 1979, such as Sha Yexin's "What If I Really Were?" and Liu Binyan's "People or Monsters?," and settled on Bai Hua's less-noticed work, "Unrequited Love." Then he focused on Bai's literary errors rather than reform of Bai's inner self. By the standards of 1957, Deng scarcely punished Bai Hua. Bai was denied foreign travel, but did not lose his job or his salary, and was not called before public criticism meetings; his family was not pressured to turn against him, and he was allowed to continue publishing.[93] Moreover, the government denunciation of Bai cut both ways. It made him instantly a heroic figure among Chinese intellectuals. It increased his international stature and seemed to reserve a spot for him in history books. These benefits drew admiration, and even envy, from his fellow writers. Under Mao in 1957, the designation of Bai Hua and others as Rightists had caused others to shun them.

But from Deng's point of view, the purpose of limiting public expression was served quite well. Deng's methods in the early 1980s, while much gentler than Mao's in 1957, owed their quick effectiveness to people's vivid memories of Maoist times. Here, too, is an important difference between the contexts of the two crackdowns. In the early 1980s, traumatic memories of the Cultural Revolution still haunted intellectuals—enough, as Anne Thurston has shown, to explain unusually high rates of physical illness.[94] The leadership's plea in the late 1970s and early 1980s that intellectuals "banish residual fear" was an insufficient guarantee against a return of what the regime itself was calling a "nightmare." In sharp contrast, most active writers in 1956–1957 were young communists who had invested their ideals in the revolution. They were largely free of nagging inner fears and thus, from Mao's point of view, needed strong external pressure in order to achieve remolding. They were—and many of them said so after 1979— naive about Mao in 1956. But now that they had seen the revolution at its worst, a powerful cynicism had grown where youthful optimism had been.

---

[93] People less famous than Bai Hua were actually punished more severely than he was during the campaign aimed at "Bai Hua and bourgeois liberalism." Local officials used the vague term "bourgeois liberalism" to punish enemies of many kinds and for various reasons. Still, the extent of such punishments fell far short of those of 1957.

[94] Anne F. Thurston, "Victims of China's Cultural Revolution: The Invisible Wounds, Part II"; also chap. 8 of Thurston's *Enemies of the People*.

To them, the national criticism of Bai Hua looked, despite the disclaimers of the leadership, like the onset of a Maoist campaign: criticisms were dogmatically repetitive, no dissenting views were published, and the offender was associated with a vaguely defined charge ("bourgeois liberalism") that could, variously interpreted, threaten almost anyone. These signs alone, without any actual punishments, were enough to bring a jolting chill. Although much less force was used in 1981 than in 1957, this is partly because much less was needed.

Comparing Soviet and Eastern European Examples

From the first signs of the relaxation of literary controls after Mao, Chinese intellectuals spoke of "thaw" (*jiedong*), which was an implicit reference to Ilya Ehrenburg's 1954 novel *The Thaw*. Ehrenburg portrayed life under Stalin, specifically the plight of artists, with unprecedented realism, and drew from Soviet readers the same kind of immediate recognition ("that's what *really* happened!") that Lu Xinhua's story "Scar" brought in China. Although "Scar" was much less substantial than *The Thaw*, the two works both came to be used loosely as labels for all the literary works that appeared around the same time and shared the function of exposing previously forbidden truths.

   Close examination of the two cases reveals that their similarities run much deeper than the question of labels. Some of the likenesses, such as the appearance of the word "thaw" in both contexts, are the result of China's borrowing from the Soviet precedent. Much more significant, however, are similarities that spring from the basic structures of the two historical situations and that have nothing to do with which case came first. In each case, a period of literary deep freeze, when almost all independence and originality were impossible (1946–1953 in the Soviet Union, 1966–1976 in China), ended with the death of a dictator (Stalin on 5 March 1953 and Mao on 9 September 1976) and led to a period during which the dictators' successors sought a return to a more "normal" socialist situation, while writers led readers in a chorus of protest over recent conditions. In both thaw periods, a tradition of the educated person as the conscience of society, bearing a responsibility to speak in behalf of its overall welfare, led writers to speak out against corrupt and incompetent authority. There were calls in both cases that literature be "sincere,"[95] meaning that writers be allowed not only to describe observable events truthfully but to invest their literary characters with believable individual thoughts and feelings.

---

[95] Ehrenburg issued a plea in October 1953 that literature describe the inner life and be based on a writer's own inspiration. Then Vladimir Pomerantsev's famous article "On Sincerity in Literature" (December 1953) suggested that literature be judged for its frankness and truth telling rather than, by implication, its "Party spirit." A year later (December 1954), Olga Bergolts gave a hard-hitting speech in support of the "inner voice" of the poet. See Dina Spechler, *Permitted Dissent*, p. 22, and Swayze, *Political Control*, pp. 86, 111.

In both cases, the fluctuating literary "weather" was an issue, and editors, writers, and certain readers all became their own weathermen. Although details naturally differed, the major trends in the two cases were remarkably similar: each included three major warm spells within the decade after the dictator's death (in the Soviet Union late 1953, fall 1956, and 1959–1962; in China winter 1979, fall 1979, and 1984–1986). In both cases, the second was the warmest time, and came just three years after the death of the dictator. The third in each case was the longest and most stable period of relatively good weather.

These similarities of pattern may be due mostly to chance; but the equally remarkable similarities in literary theme seem clearly accountable to the contexts from which they sprang. For example, Zhang Jie's story "Love Must Not Be Forgotten" (1979),[96] which describes a woman deeply in love with a married man, drew a powerful and basically favorable response in China simply for raising subjective questions such as this in print; a similar claim for space in which to discuss private feelings was more common, and pressed considerably further, in prominent works of fiction and drama in the Soviet thaw.[97] The special privileges of officials, so vividly lampooned in Sha Yexin's "What If I Really Were?," as well as the related problem of smug laziness among the children of high officials—as portrayed, for example, in Bai Hua's "A Bundle of Letters"—are themes in works of the Soviet thaw such as Yury Nagibin, "A Light in the Window" and Leonid Zorin, "The Guests."[98] Liu Binyan's anguished observation in 1979 that official ideology and ordinary life had diverged so much as to produce "two kinds of truth"[99] echoes nicely the "old joke" in Russia, repeated by Alexander Fadeyev during the Soviet thaw, that "one incorrect viewpoint is better than two correct ones."[100] These are but a few of the points on which the concerns of writers in the two countries can be compared; for more, see chapter 5 below.

Popular responses to thaw literature, insofar as they can be inferred, were also remarkably similar. Readers in both societies seem to have found reading and discussing truth-telling literature to be good ways of releasing pent-up feelings. Writers became instant heroes when they managed to get into print things that readers had long had in mind without daring to express

---

[96] Zhang Jie, "Ai shi buneng wangji de."

[97] These include Ilya Ehrenburg, *The Thaw*, and Vladimir Dudintsev, *Not by Bread Alone* (1956), as well as Nikolai Podogin, *Petrarch's Sonnet* and Samuil Alyoshin, *Alone*, two plays that reportedly drew packed houses in Moscow and elsewhere.

[98] As a critique of special privilege, Yury Nagibin's "A Light in the Window" (translated in Hugh McLean and Walter N. Vickery, eds., *The Year of Protest*, pp. 224–33) is less clever and less funny, but more quietly poignant, than "What if I Really Were?" Bai Hua, "Yishu xinzha" and Leonid Zorin, "The Guests" (see Swayze, *Political Control*, pp. 98–99) tell similarly of spoiled sons of revolutionary fathers.

[99] Liu Binyan, "Qingting renmin de shengyin," translation taken from Liu Binyan, *People or Monsters?*, p. 3.

[100] Quoted in Swayze, *Political Control*, p. 253.

publicly. This function of literature seems closely correlated with the rapid increase in the numbers and circulations of literary periodicals during the two thaws. It is also one factor in the rise of unofficial journals, called *samizdat* in the Soviet Union and *minjian* in China.[101] The similarities are clearest in cases where popular responses were strongest. Liu Binyan's "People or Monsters?" and Vladimir Dudintsev's *Not by Bread Alone*, for example, both set forth paradigm cases (Wang Shouxin and Drozdov, respectively) of corrupt, manipulative, and materialistic abusers of power, and both works drew nationwide responses whose intensity can be viewed as defining the high points of the two thaws.

Given the readiness of writers to speak out, and the eagerness of readers to applaud them for doing so, the leadership in both China after Mao and the Soviet Union after Stalin needed to make some difficult calculations. Deng and Khrushchev both knew that they could gain popular support by permitting more freedom of expression. Each surely knew, moreover, that popular denunciation of the Mao or Stalin regime would serve to justify his own reform program, thereby strengthening his hand against opponents of reform. But how much denunciation of the former regime could one permit without implicating the whole system, which still was the basis of present rule? For both Khrushchev and Deng, writers could be useful, but also dangerous.

In general, Deng's use of writers proceeded more easily than Khrushchev's. For this Deng owed much to the fortuitous fact that Hua Guofeng, who served briefly as Communist Party chairman after the death of Mao, had distinguished clearly and immediately between Mao and the "Gang of Four." Chinese writers were therefore free to denounce Maoism, under the euphemism of the Gang of Four, without directly assailing Mao, who was still the most important symbol of Party power. This is why, during the times of freest expression, such as fall 1979, there could be a happy three-way convergence in China among what writers wanted to say, what readers were waiting to hear, and what the leadership wished to see expressed. Literary "alienation" was at a low point.

Khrushchev enjoyed no similar distinction between Stalin and convenient scapegoats. He had to decide when and how much to discredit Stalin directly. It took him three years from Stalin's death to make his bold move in his famous "secret speech" at the Twentieth Congress of the Soviet Communist Party in 1956. Until then, Soviet writers who wished to venture criticisms of Stalinism could rely only on the cautious approval of editors, the tacit consent of censors, or the negotiated support of Party leaders such as Georgy Malenkov. There were several ways in which the absence of surrogates for the former dictator made Khrushchev's use of literature in his transition to power more awkward than Deng's. Deng gained much by rid-

---

[101] The functions of the Soviet unofficial journals differed in some ways from those of their Chinese counterparts. For more on this comparison, see chapter 4.

ing the anti-Gang-of-Four tide of the late 1970s, whereas Khrushchev needed, during the three years before criticizing Stalin, to restrain Soviet popular impulses to denounce the former regime.[102] Khrushchev also had to delay for three years the "rehabilitation" of writers who might have been useful to him,[103] whereas in China, as noted above, such rehabilitations were among the harbingers of Deng's return to power. When the time finally came to distance himself from Stalin, Khrushchev had to target Stalin directly, thereby implicitly raising the deeper questions about the political system that Stalin still symbolized and upon which he, Khrushchev, still depended. Khrushchev's situation obliged him to negotiate a transition from the role of Stalin's heir to that of liberator from the worst of Stalin's legacy. Deng, thanks to the device called the Gang of Four, could present himself as simultaneously heir and liberator.

As the two thaws proceeded, the Deng and Khrushchev regimes established and began to enforce some new rules about what writers could and could not do. Again there are remarkable similarities, and they seem to stem from the congruence of the two situations rather than from any imitation of Khrushchev by Deng. In both countries, writers took aim at corruption, cruelty, and incompetence in officialdom, and both regimes, which wanted such realities to be known euphemistically as "the dark side" of society, gradually made it clear that they would permit literary discussion of the dark side only on two conditions: first, that criticisms be offered in the spirit of improving the regime, not opposing it; and second, that writers state or imply that the overall condition of society is good and that dark-side phenomena are aberrations.[104] In both countries, writers and editors who wished to press the borderlines of these rules sought tacit support among officials— either by looking for areas in which officials had naturally overlapping interests, or by building personal relationships that implied mutual loyalty and protection.[105] But even as these post-thaw ground rules settled in and began to form a tentative stability, some of the more penetrating writers in both countries objected that the new accommodations were superficial and premature as bases for optimism. The dictators may be gone but their legacies are not, these writers warned. "We carried him out of the mausoleum," Yevgeny Yevtushenko wrote in a famous poem, "But how to root Stalin / Out of Stalin's heirs?"[106] And Liu Binyan, in ending "People or

---

[102] I do not mean that Chinese felt no restraints when they denounced the Gang of Four, but only that the Soviet people were restrained more and longer before they could criticize Stalin. In the late 1970s, intellectuals in China felt considerable discontent, which they expressed only in private, over the fact that Mao was not grouped with the Gang of Four, where he belonged. This is one point on which they and their archenemies the ultraleftists agreed.

[103] Harold Swayze judges that the Soviet rehabilitations were "unthinkable" before 1956; *Political Control*, p. 151.

[104] For the Soviet case, see discussions in George Gibian, *Interval of Freedom*, pp. 23–24 and Spechler, *Political Dissent*, pp. 3–16; for the Chinese case, see details in chapter 2.

[105] See Spechler, *Political Dissent*, pp. 4–5, and chapter 2 below.

[106] Priscilla Johnson, *Krushchev and the Arts*, p. 94.

Monsters?", says "People, be on guard! It is still too early to be celebrating victories. . . ."[107]

In sum, the parallels between the post-Stalin and post-Mao thaws warrant study on several points and will be further noted in chapters that follow. But there are also some important differences in the larger cultural and historical contexts. The humanist tradition of the great Russian nineteenth-century realist writers does not have a parallel in China. It was perhaps for this very reason that Chekhov, Tolstoy, and Dostoyevsky had a major impact during China's May Fourth years in the late 1910s and the 1920s.[108] During the Chinese thaw, "humanism," as represented by Dai Houying, for example, was sometimes conceived as a Russian answer to Mao's insistence on the primacy of Marxian social class. Later in the 1980s, Chinese writers and critics began again to notice the ideas of sin and repentance in nineteenth-century Russian fiction and to express the wish that Chinese culture had more of these things.[109]

To some extent, examples from Soviet-dominated Eastern Europe can further refine the question of how distinctive China's socialist literary system may have been. Literary revolts in Hungary and Poland in the mid-1950s, and in Czechoslovakia during the spring of 1968, can help to illustrate the range of what could happen when communist parties temporarily relaxed their literary controls. It is, first, striking that the range of these responses seems fairly narrow—a fact that suggests that basic human responses to repression count for more in determining behavior than do the cultural differences that often draw first attention. The Eastern European cases include the same hallmarks as those of China and the Soviet Union: "rehabilitation" of purged writers, freer contacts with the West, increased latitude for subtler and more artistic literary expression, increased criticism of the government (along with government demands that criticism stay "constructive"), and, most pronounced of all, a rush to tell the truth about social reality. Polish writers in the mid-1950s began to describe World War II truthfully,[110] and the Polish emigré Czeslaw Milosz wrote scathing attacks on the Party orthodoxy that opposed such honesty.[111] The truth telling of

---

[107] Liu Binyan, "Ren yao zhijian," p. 102.

[108] Mau-sang Ng, *The Russian Hero in Modern Chinese Fiction.*

[109] One of the best statements of such views was a 1986 essay by Liu Zaifu entitled, "Wenxue yu chanhui yishi" (Literature and the awareness of repentance). After agreeing to publish the piece, the Shanghai *Wenhuibao* backed off because of opposition from the conservative Politburo member Bo Yibo. With the backing of the prominent playwright and literary official Xia Yan, the piece was later published in abridged form in *People's Daily*, but was immediately followed, on instructions from above, by two articles criticizing Liu's piece. The full essay was published in 1988 in Harbin (*Liu Zaifu ji*, pp. 313–26). Liu continued to write on the idea of China's lack of a "repentance consciousness" after leaving China in 1989; in 1998, in Colorado, he was completing a book manuscript on the topic, coauthored with his junior colleague Lin Gang.

[110] Leopold Buczkowski, *Black Torrent* (1954); Roman Bratny, *Kolumbowie, rocz nil 20* (1957).

[111] Czeslaw Milosz, *The Captive Mind*, especially chapter 1, "The Pill of Murti-Bing."

the Hungarian writers' "Petofi Club" left a lasting impression on Chinese intellectuals. People in Hungary and Poland who took the government side began to earn the label "conservative" in spite of their ostensibly Marxist stance—an anomaly that arose during the "Prague spring" in 1968 and again in China after Mao. Writers in all five cases objected that Party officials and their families had become a new ruling class, and that socialist language was becoming a kind of fraud. In the acid words of Milosz, "let us not forget that the connection between the New Faith and Marx is rather superficial."[112]

One characteristic of the three Eastern European cases that is different from China's is the comparative lack of a need for soul searching about the recent past. Readers in these countries apparently needed less than did Chinese readers to believe, as the "scar" metaphor in China suggested, that the process of writing and reading the truth can lessen people's pain and purge society of some of its ills. True, the European countries had been invaded and their societies forcibly transformed; but their wounds still were not as deep as China's, and they did not bear China's burden of having to figure out why they had inflicted wounds upon themselves. Of the three cases, Hungary's may have been closest to China's because of the close proximity of its Stalinist rule (under Matyas Rakosi from 1946 to 1953, and again in 1955–1956) to a more relaxed regime (under Imre Nagy, 1953–1955). The Chinese and Hungarian cases raise the question of whether the intensity of literary protest is due more to the intensity of repression or to the suddenness of release from repression. The Czech case, in which Stalinist rule declined more gradually and over a longer period before the appearance of the intense 1968 protests, suggests that repression is the greater factor and that protesters' memories are long.[113]

Another major difference among the Eastern European cases, China's, and Russia's lay in the relations of communist rule and nationalism. The literary rebellions of the Hungarians, Poles, and Czechs were in significant part protests against Moscow's political invasion of their countries. The issues of foreign-imposed rule and communist rule were so intertwined in these countries as to make it practically impossible to weigh the two separately as causes of the revolts. In sharp contrast, in China and Russia the communist movements had grown from native soil, where nationalism worked very much for them. In the 1940s, the Chinese communist movement gained crucial popular support when it led national resistance to the Japanese invasion. After 1949, the Party leadership made it quite clear, in

---

[112] Milosz, *The Captive Mind*, p. 74.

[113] By "Stalinist rule," I mean that of Klement Gottwald, from 1946 to 1953. Although Gottwald's successors, Viliam Siroky and Antonin Novotny, remained staunchly Stalinist for a few years after the deaths of Stalin and Gottwald, both in 1953, by the 1960s they and Siroky's successor, Jozef Lenart, were gradually relaxing literary controls and restoring people who had been purged under Gottwald. Thus Alexander Dubcek's "Prague spring" of 1968 was the endpoint of a longer trend than one can trace in the Hungarian and Chinese cases.

media as diverse as theoretical journals and children's songs, that loyalty to the Party and to the nation were coterminous. This propaganda effort succeeded, and the identification of Party and nation in the popular mind did not begin to break down until the 1980s. In the 1990s, when socialist ideals became all but useless to the Party and only nationalism was left as a tool for stimulating popular support, the Party stressed its role as the champion of Chinese national pride—in economics, in international sports, and even in such things as mystical martial arts and Daoist healing techniques that it had once called "feudal."

The Soviet Party leadership, although it exploited patriotism in a similar way, also had the problem, which the Chinese leadership did not, of how to handle nationalist sentiment in the countries of its empire. In calibrating how much "thaw" to permit, Soviet rulers had to worry about consequences not only within the Soviet Union but in several other countries as well. De-Stalinization set the stage for mid-1950s literary protests in Hungary and Poland, and even indirectly in China. Because local populations were waiting to protest when given the chance, a policy move in Moscow could have volatile and unforeseen consequences; when Khrushchev sacked Matyas Rakosi in Hungary in 1953, apparently in a gesture to assuage Tito in Yugoslavia rather than with the intention of bringing relaxation to Hungary, he probably did not foresee that his decision would help pave the way to a Hungarian revolt.

In all of these "thaw" experiences, writers seemed anxious about time. They were eager to express themselves as soon as possible, not only because they had a backlog from years of enforced silence but because they were unsure how long their interlude of freedom might last. When their writing caused excitement, the reasons usually had less to do with new insights in their works than with the simple fact that they had given public expression to well-known but formerly unspeakable truths. Readers, far from bored at reading what they already knew, were often exhilarated to see their cherished truths appear in official media. Publication in these media was important not because of greater circulation (since the truths were well known anyway) but because of the implication that the government, with its moral claim to represent the society's center and its hegemonic reach to every part of it, now officially recognized the truth sufficiently to allow it to appear in print. Even people who loathed the government but had no choice about the matter of dealing with it felt this effect.

The parallel between the post-Mao and post-Stalin thaws, instructive though it is, obscures an ambiguity. The literary outpouring in each case can be viewed as the coincidence of two effects: the natural result of the lifting of literary controls by a Leninist party, and an indictment and examination of a catastrophe that a nation has just been through. These two issues can be separated, to some degree, by looking at cases that involved recovery from catastrophe, but where literary restrictions were weaker or different in nature. For this purpose the cases of Japan and West Germany after World War II can offer useful comparisons. The Japanese example is especially fruitful because of Japan's underlying similarities to China as a Confucian society that has had to answer challenges from the modern West.

Comparing Japan and Germany after World War II

The revival of the *bundan* or "literary world" in postwar Japan bears a number of general similarities to the return of the Chinese *wentan* (which is the same term) after the Cultural Revolution. In both cases, the relaxation of censorship, the appearance of new writers, and the return of silenced writers led to new enthusiasm about literature, a mushrooming of literary publications, a renewed emphasis by some writers on literary quality as opposed to politics, and the establishment or reestablishment of national literary prizes. Both countries saw a revival of popular entertainment fiction and of frankness in the description of romantic love and sex. Reader demand for books and periodicals surged so strongly as to produce temporary shortages of paper in both countries.[114]

Although writers in both cases enjoyed increased latitude in what they could express, the breadth of what was permitted was still considerably greater in postwar Japan—and West Germany—than it was in post-Mao China. Several factors in the political environments made this so. First, the change in national leadership was more drastic in the Japanese and German cases than in China's, where the new leadership had a vital interest in continuity of the government's prestige. In Japan, the transition from the wartime government to the United States Occupation, in both policies and personnel, was about as thorough as a governing change can be. But in China, despite the vitriolic denunciation of the "Gang of Four," the Communist Party was still in charge, and many of its policies, practices, and personnel remained. As we have seen, the top leadership in both China after Mao and the Soviet Union after Stalin for several years faced a problem of how much literary denunciation of the former regime could be tolerated without undermining present rule. In Japan, although writers did have their inner struggles over how to balance national guilt against national pride, they did not have to contend with a government that put limits on how much its predecessor could be criticized.

Postwar Japan and West Germany were, moreover, aiming to establish liberal democracies and thus were committed in principle to permitting broader freedom of expression than communist regimes allowed. This difference, although crucial, was not entirely clear-cut. In Japan, the Occupation government compiled lists of writers who had been "war criminals." Some were also "purged," although this meant the very mild punishment,

---

[114] See Donald Keene, *Dawn to the West*, pp. 963–65, and chap. 4 below.

by Chinese standards, of banishment from government office and deprivation of certain political privileges. Purged writers could still publish.[115]

The abrupt transition in national government in Japan and West Germany did not, however, bring equally radical shifts in their literary worlds.
In several respects, literary continuities in Japan and Germany were stronger than they were in China. Many of the same Japanese and German
writers remained active during and after the war. This was possible largely
because militarist Japan and Nazi Germany treated their writers less harshly
than did Maoist China, and the postwar governments in Japan and West
Germany were also less restrictive than was Deng Xiaoping's China.[116] On
both sides of the divides, therefore, Japanese and German writers had more
latitude than did Chinese writers for pursuing their own interests. Most of
Japan's notable writers published during their country's war years, some
supporting the militarists in varying degrees and some bending their unsup-
portive messages to avoid trouble. After the war, even those who had been
strongest in their support of the militarists could continue to publish. In
China, the names of published writers during ten years on either side of
1976 were almost entirely different. Post-Mao writers were almost exclusively either new figures, who had never published before 1976, or established writers who had not been allowed to publish for ten or twenty years.[117]

In Japan and Germany, there was also literary continuity in the sense that
some kinds of nonpolitical writing went forward regardless of the war or its
end. In Japan, Tanizaki Junichiro's masterpiece *The Makioka Sisters* was published in part during the war and in part afterward, and Kawabata Yasunari's

[115] Keene, *Dawn to the West*, pp. 926, 933.

[116] Under Japan's militarist regime, dissident writers were often forced to choose between
imprisonment and commission of *tenkō* (conversion), which required explicit declaration of a
reversal in viewpoint comparable to that of the "self-criticism" during China's Cultural Revolution. In both cases, the sincerity of these about-faces varied widely with individuals and is not
easy to fathom. But in China, writers who did self-criticisms were harshly punished in many
other ways as well, and certainly were not allowed to resume publishing, whereas in Japan,
those who had committed *tenkō* were generally left alone and allowed to continue publishing,
and sometimes even to continue issuing veiled signs of unrepentence. A 1941 poem by Tsuboi
Shigeji illustrates a degree of literary dissidence that would easily have cost the life of its writer
in late-Maoist China. It is called "Kumo" (Spider), where spiders mean government agents: A
butterfly quietly dances / into my deserted yard / Butterfly / what brings you stumbling / into
my flowerless garden? / Don't you know about the spider / who has spun a silken snare under
that tree / who holds his breath / waiting for fellows like you? / Day and night / I pit myself
against him / becoming ever more antagonistic / I want to tatter his web / with a stone / but
fear that if I do / a larger net would soon be spun across my sky / Another wasted day. (*Tsuboi
Shigeji zenshishū*,1970, pp. 267–68; unpublished translation by Robert Epp).

[117] A few of the prominent post-Mao writers, including Jiang Zilong, Chen Rong, and Chen
Guokai, had published a few inconsequential pieces before 1976; Wang Meng published translations from Uighur during his exile in Xinjiang. The only post-Mao writer to have published
substantially during 1966–1976 was Hao Ran, author of the long novels *Yanyangtian* (Bright
sunny days, 1966) and *Jinguang dadao* (The golden road, 1972–1974); but Hao Ran, on the
other hand, published very little after 1976.

Snow Country was begun in 1935 and finally completed in 1947. Similarly in Germany, the reputations of writers Franz Kafka and Robert Musil solidified after the war on the basis of works whose interest was not directly tied to problems of Nazism or the war. By contrast, in post-Mao China the social and political problems of recent Chinese history preoccupied writers and dominated discussions of literature. Works that completely skirted such questions were rarely published and little noticed.

In addition to a greater variety of literary works in postwar Japan than in post-Mao China, the creation and revival of a large number of literary groups in Japan led to spirited and sometimes arcane debate over what literature should be and do. Such debate far outstripped the range it had in the Chinese case.[118] Japanese Marxists alone raised a wider range of issues than did all of the obligatorily Marxist Chinese. From an orthodox faction of Japanese Marxism came arguments that would have fit the mood of China's Cultural Revolution.[119] But a liberal group included people like Noma Hiroshi, who could be "terrified" by Solzhenitsyn's revelation of the Soviet gulag, could advocate that Marxist writers depart from socialist realism if they wished, and could himself write grotesqueries that no Chinese or Soviet censor, even in the warmest weather, would have tolerated.[120] Shiina Rinzō, who also began as a Marxist, turned to Existentialism and finally to Christianity as he became obsessed with problems first of freedom and then of life and death.[121] Such intellectual journeys were rare among post-Mao Chinese writers, and private when they existed at all.

Despite the differences we have just sketched, the "scar" phenomenon, broadly conceived, was an important part of postwar Japanese and German literature. Like writers and readers in post-Mao China, those in postwar Japan and Germany faced problems of how to come to terms not only with

---

[118] A notable exception to this generalization was the Chinese debate over the relative merits of overseas (including Taiwan) writers and in-country writers. Who is better prepared to speak for China? Who produces better art? Who best inherits China's May Fourth tradition, or best brings China into the international world of letters? On these issues the Chinese case has a much better parallel in postwar Germany, where writers who chose to stay in Germany throughout the war sometimes charged those who went abroad, such as Bertolt Brecht, Thomas Mann, and Alfred Doblin, with living comfortably and not really enduring the experience of war with their fellow Germans. On the other hand, those who stayed in Germany sometimes had to answer accusations that they were partly complicit with the Nazis or that they did artistically inferior work. Essentially the same charges were traded, in the Chinese case, between mainland and overseas writers.

[119] For example, the argument that the *Man'yōshū*, an eighth-century compilation of Japanese verse, represents the progressive creativity of the peasant class (as did China's ancient *Book of Songs* for Cultural Revolution theorists); or that the seventeenth-century fiction of Ihara Saikaku was (like Cao Xueqin's eighteenth-century *Dream of the Red Chamber* for Chinese Marxists) launching a covert but bitter attack on the ruling order. See Keene, *Dawn to the West*, p. 1,003. The terms "orthodox" and "liberal" in the present characterization are my own, not Keene's.

[120] Keene, *Dawn to the West*, pp. 976, 982, 983.

[121] Ibid., pp. 986–98.

national devastation but with the militarism and political extremism that had precipitated it. Resemblances to Chinese scar works were sometimes uncannily close. An example is Akira Kurosawa 's film *No Regrets for Our Youth* (1946), which tells of a courageous opponent of militarism who, during the war, is falsely accused as a spy, then imprisoned, then killed. His lover, loyal to him and filial to his parents, who are peasants, goes to live with the parents and helps them to plant rice. Other villagers trample their fields and stridently accuse the three of being spies as well. After the war the dead man is posthumously exonerated. Hundreds of works of Chinese scar literature included similar elements: an oppressive ruling ideology; resistance, at great personal cost, by courageous individuals; groundless accusations of espionage; ostracism by fanatic crowds; the importance of romantic attachments and family loyalties; and exoneration at the end. In Germany, during the five to seven years after the war, a "ruins" literature included themes of personal and family devastation that were broadly comparable to Lu Xinhua's "Scar" in their sense of shock and of groping to rebuild personal lives and families.[122] Some critics, mostly in Hong Kong and Taiwan, borrowed the term "ruins literature" (*feixu wenxue*) for application to post-Mao China.

The sense of truth telling pervaded all themes in Chinese scar literature. Not only could forbidden statements now be published, but at least some official lies could be contradicted. Viewed from this angle, postwar Japanese novels such as Noma Hiroshi's *Zone of Emptiness* and Ōoka Shōhei's *Fires on the Plain*, both published in 1952, were also powerful revelations of the true nature of war and military life, and contradicted the rosy chauvinism of wartime writers like Hino Ashihei and Ozaki Shiro.[123] And in Germany, works like Heinrich Boll's *The Train Was on Time* (1949) dramatically revised the notion that Nazi soldiers were happy to fight and die. But on the whole, truth telling was more important in China, where government manipulation of language in the Maoist years had forced mendacity and hypocrisy deep into daily life, and where, even after Deng's ameliorations of the problem, resistance still bore a special spice. Disillusioned and cynical Chinese youth, sometimes referred to in post-Mao China as "the lost generation," were a large part of the scar readership. These readers would no doubt have championed a truly "alienated" writer like Japan's Dazai Osamu, who refers in *The Setting Sun* (1947) to "the lost tribe," meaning the younger generation emerging from Japan's war years.[124] But no one remotely as idiosyncratic as Dazai could be published in China in the 1980s.

With few exceptions, Chinese scar works are overt, unsubtle, and explicitly didactic.[125] The suffering of victims is often described with self-right-

---

[122] See Wolfgang Borchert, *The Man Outside*.

[123] Keene, *Dawn to the West*, pp. 916–33, 950–52, 980–82.

[124] Dazai Osamu, *Shayō*, translated by Donald Keene as *The Setting Sun*.

[125] One of the exceptions is an understated and subtle work, Yang Jiang's "Ganxiao liuji," which has two good English translations (see bibliography). Another example, quintessentially

eousness and effusive sentimentality. In contrast, postwar Japanese writers, even when looking at very ugly facts, frequently used understatement, humor, or simulated inadvertence. Tsuboi Sakae's *Twenty-Four Eyes*, published in 1952 and later made into a well-received film, tells about a teacher's love and concern for her twelve students (the "twenty-four eyes"), one of whom is her own son; as a side theme, it shows how militarism in the wartime atmosphere subtly warps this son's attitude toward his mother/ teacher.[126] Ibuse Masuji, who wrote several works about the war, always with indirection, sometimes employed humor. Donald Keene summarizes his *Lieutenant Lookeast* (1950) as "the story of Yuichi, a Japanese army lieutenant whose chosen manner of demonstrating absolute allegiance to the emperor is to order his unit to bow in the direction of the Imperial Palace every day, especially after news of a victory. His unit becomes famous for this conspicuous display of reverence, which extends to fresh rounds of bows toward the distant palace even when repeat announcements are made of the same victories."[127] The "loyalty dance" that Chinese people performed during the Cultural Revolution, typically each morning and evening, has at least as much potential for humor as the bowing lieutenant. But post-Mao Chinese writers, although certainly eager to denounce the loyalty dance, apparently could not bring the attitude of genial detachment to the topic.[128]

Commenting on the postwar situation, Ibuse's award-winning *No Consultations Today* (1949) uses the figure of a kindly old doctor to symbolize the quiet strength of the Japanese people, who will somehow pull through and see better days. The doctor's patients, ignoring his sign "No consultations today," come to see him anyway, and he sees them as usual.[129] This theme of "enduring" runs more explicitly through "Midnight Feast" (1947) and other stories by Shiina Rinzō about the lower depths of postwar Tokyo.[130] But for Chinese writers of scar literature, enduring was not a congenial theme. Enough enduring had already been done, and it was the writer's duty to try to end it and prevent its recurrence.

The tendency in Chinese scar works toward direct and confident didacticism contrasts not only with Japan after the war but also with Italy, where understatement and indirection do not have the same tradition they have in Japan. In the late 1970s Li Yi, editor of the Hong Kong magazine *The Seventies (Qishiniandai)*, began publishing Chinese scar literature and calling it "new realism," pointing out its similarity to Italian neorealism after

---

a scar work except for its remarkable avoidance of authorial comment, is Wang Ruowang's "Ji'e sanbuqu," translated by Kyna Rubin as *Hunger Trilogy*.

[126] Tsuboi Sakae, *Nijūshi no hitomi*, translated by Akira Miura as *Twenty-Four Eyes*.

[127] Keene, *Dawn to the West*, p. 947.

[128] Chinese *xiangsheng* comedians could do this. See Jiang Kun and Li Wenhua, "Ruci zhaoxiang." For an example of serious indignation toward the loyalty dance, see Kong Jiesheng, "Zai xiaohe neibian."

[129] Ibuse Masuji, "Honjitsu kyūshin," which won the first Yomiuri Literary Award in 1950.

[130] Keene, *Dawn to the West*, pp. 989–92.

World War II.[131] But "neorealism" in the Italian case was considerably more naturalistic, and less explicitly didactic, than its counterpart in China. Vittorio De Sica's Italian neorealist film, "The Bicycle Thief" (1948), for example, shows in plain, daily-life terms how a bicycle is stolen and its owner, an humble and unoffending man, is put through great trouble and distress. When the film was shown in Beijing in 1979, a group of young viewers, who were devotees of scar fiction, found it boring. "A stolen bicycle? So what? It happens all the time! Who goes to the movies to see this?"[132] They would have preferred that the thief be caught, his crime related to the policies of the fascists, and he and the fascists roundly denounced.

China's scar writers were often ready to locate the roots of evil in individual people, whether at the highest or local levels. When they hesitated to name names, it was usually from their perception of the risks involved rather than from uncertainty in their own minds or a preference for artistic indirection. By contrast, Japanese writers blamed more diffusely, if at all. They did sometimes express resentment of the militarists, or of Americans for dropping the bomb or for arrogant attitudes during the Occupation. But on the whole, they presented a more multifaceted response to the war catastrophe than Chinese writers did to the post-Mao catastrophe. They certainly showed more toleration for "enemies" within their own midst. Three years after the war, for example, Nakayama Gishu could publish, without incurring controversy, a fairly sympathetic account of a militarist staff officer who, just before committing suicide, recites the Imperial Rescript for Military Men ("A soldier must consider loyalty as his absolute duty, a soldier must be correct in his deportment"). The narrator, while not approving, can understand the officer: "It was clear that he must have something to cling to in order to achieve internal calm. This was the moment when, if he had been a samurai of the past, he would have recited 'Namu Amida Butsu.'"[133] This degree of sympathy with the "internal enemy" did not appear in post-Mao scar literature—or indeed, at any time since in mainland Chinese publications. Zheng Yi's story "Maple" (1979) does reveal a human side of the Red Guards,[134] and Jin He's "Reencounter" (1979) shows the reader the internal dilemmas of a municipal official who is complicit in the Cultural Revolution.[135] But both Chinese authors are careful to show that the objects of their understanding are victims of the Gang of Four as well as its agents; and both stories still drew criticism for allowing any sympathy whatsoever.

Neither Japanese nor Chinese writers, in their postdisaster situations, did much introspection about the question of possible guilt among the Japanese

[131] Li Yi, "Zhongguo xinxieshizhuyi wenyi de xingqi," p. 21.
[135] Personal observation, Friendship Hotel, Beijing, 28 October 1979.
[133] Nakayama Gishūu, "Teniyan no matsujitsu" (The last days of Tinian, 1948), quoted in Keene, *Dawn to the West*, p. 953.
[134] Zheng Yi, "Feng."
[135] Jin He, "Chongfeng."

or Chinese people generally. In Japan, the continuity in the group of active writers before and after 1945 might lead one to expect a considerable focus on the question of war guilt, but the question was not often raised. A few post-Mao Chinese writers did raise the question of whether the extensive cruelty of the Cultural Revolution might have arisen from more people than a Gang of Four. Some did this by honestly examining their own complicity, thereby indirectly challenging readers to do the same;[136] others, such as Gao Xiaosheng and Liu Zaifu, began to write about ways in which many or all parts of the Chinese population were partly guilty.[137]

For some writers in postwar Japan, the question of blame became diffuse enough to merge with the question of evil in human nature generally. The material that Ōoka Shōhei uses in *Fires on the Plain*, for example, is certainly graphic enough to make a Chinese-style scar work: an imperial soldier in the Philippines at the close of the war wanders through forests and villages constantly in search of food and in fear of being killed by the enemy Americans, the native Filipinos, or other Japanese soldiers in straits like his own.[138] He comes to realize that others are eating human flesh, and even, through an accident, finds himself eating some himself. Having killed an innocent Filipina woman, he wonders if the evil deed is attributable to the emperor's rifle or to his own evil nature. He ends up back in Tokyo in a mental hospital. But his sordid story, unlike scar works, conveys no sociopolitical lesson. Although his needs are excruciatingly material, his biggest questions are spiritual: What is flesh and blood? What is evil behavior? What is madness? He is, as noted by Arthur Kimball, "putting the whole concept of 'human' on trial."[139] Chinese writers of scar literature almost never used their material to raise questions at this level.

Their preoccupation with the fate of China does much to explain their failure to address more universal questions, but so does pressure of time. Uncertainty about how long the literary-political weather could hold created an urgency to produce responses quickly—and therefore not as reflectively as one might like. In longer historical perspective, this is, at least so far, one of the most significant points of comparison between post-Mao

---

[136] Shi Tiesheng, "Wenge jikui"; on Ba Jin, see chapter 3, note 135.

[137] Gao Xiaosheng was, I believe, the first Chinese writer to say publicly, at a conference in Nanjing on 29 April 1981, that it is absurd to suppose that only four people manipulated eight hundred million others. Gao made similar statements in print, although less directly. See his reports of "superstition, gambling . . . and even beatings" among peasants during the Cultural Revolution in "Xiwang nuli wei nongmin xiezuo," p. 13. Liu Zaifu, director of the Institute of Literature of the Chinese Academy of Social Sciences, delivered his influential paper called "Wenxue yu chanhui yishi" (Literature and the awareness of repentance) at a conference in Beijing in 1986 (see note 109 above). Liu argued that the novels of Tolstoy and Dostoyevsky could achieve an elevated moral vision because of the religious concepts of sin and repentance in Russian culture. Chinese culture lacks such concepts, Liu said, but would do well to cultivate them when trying to come to grips with a moral catastrophe like the Cultural Revolution.

[138] Ōoka Shōhei, *Nobi*.

[139] Arthur G. Kimball, *Crisis in Identity and Contemporary Japanese Novels*, p. 32.

China and postwar Japan or Germany. The more mature responses to extremity and disaster in Japan and Germany took some time to appear. In Germany, Gunter Grass's *The Tin Drum*, which established him as a major literary and moral spokesman for the generation that grew up under Nazism, appeared fourteen years after the end of the war. In Japan, although literary responses to the atomic bomb disasters appeared quickly, the more mature and penetrating responses of Ōta Yōko, Ibuse Masuji, Ōe Kenzaburō, and others appeared one to two decades later. The special power of these writers stemmed, in part, from the moral depth of their narrative voices—a quality whose appearance seems to have required some time. Perhaps it is not too late to hope that China's Maoist period will also eventually receive its mature artistic treatment.

The Mechanics of Literary Control

LITERARY CENSORSHIP under the Chinese socialist system was seldom done by blunt intervention of the kind that could leave blanks or obliterations on printed pages, as censorship under China's Nationalist Party did earlier in the twentieth century. It was at once more subtle and more totalistic than that. In some ways it resembled the Soviet system, whose Hungarian version Miklos Haraszti described in *The Velvet Prison* as creating a "new aesthetic culture in which censors and artists are entangled in a mutual embrace."[1] But in some ways it exceeded even the Soviet system in its reliance on psychological pressures rather than bureaucratic functions. The Soviet Union maintained a huge censorial bureaucracy that was responsible for cleansing manuscripts of illicit words and ideas that were specifically listed for bureaucrats in periodic handbooks. In China there was no such bureaucracy, but self-censorship, induced by fear of punishment, more than made up the difference. Every Chinese writer and editor had to be his or her own judge of the foggy and treacherous political-literary "weather."

A SPECTRUM OF VIEWPOINTS

Before examining how this system worked, we must look at some basic political labels, some of which had uses different from, indeed opposite to, those that are standard in the West. "Left" and "right" had several senses in China. In one technical sense, a "rightist" was someone who had been officially marked as such during the Anti-Rightist Campaign of 1957. But the evaluative connotations of the term, even in this precise sense, changed radically between the late 1950s, when rightists were shunned, and the post-Mao period, when the term "'57 rightist" implied a collegial solidarity. Among some, the term "heroes of '57" came into use for these rightists. Beyond this narrow technical sense, "right" referred generally to opinion that favored relaxation of social controls, a more democratic style in politics, a freer economy, toleration of variety in life-styles, openness to the outside world, and a deemphasis of the military. Rightism was, in sum, an orientation that the modern West might call liberalism or moderate leftism. "Left," in China, generally referred to preference for a planned economy, a prominent role for the military, and the fostering of "correct" behavior through use of social controls, strong leadership, and public ideology.

For most of the Mao years, "left" was a synonym for "revolutionary,"

---

[1] Haraszti, *The Velvet Prison*, p. 5.

and, during the high fever of the Cultural Revolution, both terms were essentially synonyms for "good."[2] In the post-Mao period, leftism lost its unquestioned correctness, but it did remain respectable. "Ultraleftism," which connoted Cultural Revolution fanaticism, did not.[3] Ultraleftism was called "fascist"—a term that identified it as sharing the basic nature of European ultrarightism during World War II. Chinese state-controlled media officially linked ultraleftism and fascism, but it was too much to allow a related usage—entirely normal in the daily-life talk on Chinese city streets—that identified "leftism" and "conservatism." "Conservative," in the post-Mao years, referred to opinion that favored preservation of Mao's legacy and maintenance of strong Party authority against the rising tide of "liberation of thought." The synonymity of "left" and "conservative" in Chinese popular usage, although paradoxical from a Western point of view, was actually common in other societies ruled by state socialism. When Chinese people began using "conservative" to mean "leftist" in the late 1970s, people in Russia, Hungary, Czechoslovakia, and elsewhere had already been doing so for several years.

In the early 1980s the term "liberalism," like the term "rightism" in the late 1950s, suffered the overlay of negative connotations produced by political campaigns. "Liberalism" (ziyouzhuyi) and/or "liberalization" (ziyouhua) became primary ideological targets in the 1981 campaign against Bai Hua, the 1983 Anti-Spiritual Pollution drive, and the 1987 crackdown on Liu Binyan, Fang Lizhi, Wang Ruowang, and others. Originally the term ziyou, which was invented in Japan in the late nineteenth century to accommodate the translation of Western terms like "free," "freedom," and "liberty," had basically positive connotations in modern China. In the 1980s campaigns, the Party used the terms ziyouzhuyi and ziyouhua with connotations of selfishness and irresponsibility, and to some extent these connotations stuck in popular usage. But the term ziyou itself remained basically positive. The terms "Party" and "non-Party" were not as useful in China as they were in the Soviet Union to label positions in literary politics. Party members were arrayed on all sides of controversies. Some of the boldest challengers of repression—Liu Binyan, Bai Hua, Wang Ruowang, and others—were themselves Party members. The controversial student-run and unofficial magazines often had key support from the offspring of top officials.

The clearest terms that were used to describe positions either favoring or

[2] A post-Mao comedian satirized the excessive use of "revolutionary" by imitating the clerk in a Cultural Revolution photography shop: "Whatever revolutionary comrade enters the revolutionary door of my revolutionary photography shop to ask revolutionary questions about taking a revolutionary photo must first shout a revolutionary slogan." Jiang Kun and Li Wenhua, "Ruci zhaoxiang."

[3] A rare case of public expression of ultraleftist opinion in the post-Mao period is reported in Tang Xiaolou, "Zhou Yang, Xia Yan, 'san bu'!," p. 26. In early 1980 a museum in Guizhou went further than was currently permissible in restoring the name of Liu Shaoqi in an exhibit. The event was published in a Shanghai newspaper, and the next day banners saying "Down with Liu Shaoqi, Down with Deng Xiaoping!" appeared briefly in Shanghai.

opposing more freedom for writers were *shou* (pull in, restrict) and *fang* (let go, set free). These were normally verbs, and hence were used differently from the nouns and adjectives listed above. But they do better than other terms in clarifying a paradox-free spectrum of opinion in Chinese literary politics.

At one end, advocating strongest *shou*, were those who held that Mao's talks at Yan'an must be upheld and interpreted strictly: Literature must serve revolutionary functions, Mao had said, and in the post-Mao period this meant the current government and all its policies. A less extreme position was the one commonly called "conservative," which allowed that some writing could be apolitical, provided that the writer's basic attitude clearly supports the government, and some could even be critical, provided it is clear that the criticism is constructive. Overall emphasis must be on "the bright side"—on optimism and Party-approved ideals that would draw readers in the right direction.[4] One step further toward *fang*, but still in the middle of the spectrum, was a position that many older intellectuals adopted. It said that ideally writers should not be limited at all, but for now stability, and especially avoidance of another upheaval like the Cultural Revolution, has to be a more important goal, and for this reason some limits are acceptable.

But although some argued that minor differences be suppressed for the sake of societal unity, others argued the exact opposite position, that the airing of differences is the best way to iron them out so that unity can be achieved. This position goes a bit further in the *fang* direction but not too far, because it still makes societal unity a basic goal. Hu Yaobang enunciated such a view at the Conference on Playwriting in 1980. "We must have full and free discussion," Hu said, "and must solve our disagreements using the test of practice. . . . We will do our best to unify thought, but this cannot be done overnight."[5] Many writers went further than this, to the position called "liberal," by holding that pluralism is valuable for its own sake, whether or not it eventually leads toward an ideal unity. Advocates of this position were criticized for abandoning socialism, but usually denied doing so, taking the much less dangerous position of saying that ideal socialism should include literary pluralism. A comparative few went all the way to the dangerous end of the spectrum, holding that no Party limits on expression are justifiable because Party rule itself should be debatable. This position could not be voiced publicly, even in the warmest political-literary weather.

---

[4] The following statement from the elder writer Ouyang Shan, a standard-bearer for the "conservative" position, can be taken as representative: "Before Liberation, back in Shanghai, we writers fundamentally opposed the social system. We criticized it with the aim of tearing it down. Today writers are free to criticize society, but are expected to do so from a fundamentally positive stance, criticizing in order to help the society be better. Are there problems in society? Yes, definitely. And they should be dealt with. But it is not permitted to take a negative stance toward the society as a whole. Some young writers have not considered this adequately." Interview, 22 April 1980, Guangzhou.

[5] Hu Yaobang, "Zai juben chuangzuo zuotanhuishang de jianghua," p. 5.

The positions of individuals were not always fixed at one point on this spectrum. In addition to changing their minds, people sometimes took different positions on different topics. Senior intellectuals, for example, sometimes favored *fang* on questions of literary control ("let young people write what they want") but *shou* on cultural behavior ("it's better if they don't wear dark glasses and bell-bottom trousers"). Moreover, in the complex shadowboxing that political-literary debate sometimes became, it could be a useful tactic to state a position of one's opposition—temporarily but publicly— in order to have more face for voicing contrary views in private or at a later time.

WHAT WAS CONTROLLED?

The literary control system was used to limit a variety of things: political disloyalty to the leadership or its ideology; exposure of social problems such as corruption and poverty; decadence and cultural "pollution" from abroad; and unclear writing such as "misty" poetry or stream-of-consciousness fiction. In the end, all of these issues were essentially political.

Explicit dissent could not be published. It was not even submitted for publication, because writers saw no point in doing something that would lead only to penalties. Normally, even the thought of direct dissent was absent. Political criticism, if dared at all, was always indirect—suggested through historical analogy, fable, allegory, or the like.[6] Indirection had the advantage of allowing writers to deny inferable meanings, but it also created the disadvantage that writers could be accused of meanings they had not meant to imply. In the late 1970s, many tales surfaced about political zealots of the Maoist era who had forced writers to confess to implications they had not intended.[7] As political and social criticism became more possible under Deng, officials became sufficiently sensitive to it that even a straightforward report about well-known social problems could be seen as political challenge to the leader within whose area the problems had been found. As in imperial China, an official's power depended on maintaining face before higher officials as well as before those who were ruled; exposure of a problem could diminish an official's face even in the absence of any charge that the official was connected to it. To insecure officials, exposing a problem could seem as great an offense as causing it.

Exposure was especially troublesome when the problems had no ready solutions. Dai Qing's 1979 story "Anticipation," for example, drew a tremendous response for showing the suffering of intellectuals' families when

---

[6] Famous examples of such writing from the pens of Wu Han, Deng Tuo, and Liao Mosha in the early 1960s, published in Beijing newspapers, indirectly led to the first salvoes of the Cultural Revolution. See Merle Goldman, *China's Intellectuals*, pp. 27–38.

[7] As shown, for example, in Feng Jicai's story "Dou han tu," in which a Party authority accuses a baffled painter of treason for seeming to suggest in his painting of nature that the wind is blowing from the West.

husband and wife were given job assignments in different cities.[8] But the story was criticized for raising a problem that the leadership could not handle, at least not quickly. Similarly, in May 1980, at an ideological conference on comedians' dialogues (*xiangsheng*), China's comic actors were warned against making too much fun of problems like unemployment and the housing shortage. Such problems "cannot be solved overnight," and to rile the populace over them will only lead to "suspicions about the superiority of our social system."[9] To keep the exposure of social problems acceptable, a writer normally had to state or clearly imply that the unhappy events were aberrations from a general case that was much different. At the 1980 Conference on Playwriting, Hu Yaobang allowed that there did exist corrupt officials and cynical youth in China, and then asked rhetorically: "But are most of our officials, and most of our youth, like that?"[10] Always under pressure to say "no" to such questions, writers could take refuge in scapegoating particular villains, be they "landlord elements" (1950s), "capitalist roaders" (1960s), or "Gang-of-Four" followers (late 1970s). The literary scapegoat was a compromise between writers and the leadership, and vitally useful to both: it allowed writers a way to register their criticisms, and allowed leaders to hold that the criticisms applied to only a few.

The device produced a dilemma, however. When literary works narrowed their indictments to a specific few, writers would hear from people who suspected they were the ones being written about. In 1980, editors in Guangzhou found this happening even when their authors had been trying to write pure fiction. In the case of one story, the editors received letters from twelve different people protesting that the alleged villainies were not so, or (more interesting, since it amounted to a kind of confession) not *exactly* so.[11] The pattern was common enough to acquire the nickname "self-assigned seating," a topic that inspired one nationally famous comedians' dialogue.[12]

For the highest leaders, who symbolized the whole of the regime and wanted that the regime be identified with China generally, foreign cultural influences, which could be seen as undermining "Chineseness," became a political as well as a cultural threat. From time to time throughout the socialist years, Party leaders complained about the intrusion of Western music, dance, dress styles, and other debilitating foreign influences, including literary works that described sex and romantic love too frankly. They held that such influences were the outward signs of a self-centered and so-

[8] Dai Qing, "Pan."

[9] Xiangsheng chuangzuo zuotanhui bangongshi, ed., "Xiangsheng chuangzuo zuotanhui jianbao," p. 3.

[10] Hu Yaobang, "Zai juben chuangzuo zuotanhuishang de jianghua," p. 42. Although the implied answer to Hu's rhetorical question is clearly "no," it is also apparent that many of the millions who enjoyed the play he was criticizing, Sha Yexin's "Jiaru wo shi zhen de" (What if I really were?), might well have answered "yes." It was precisely the widespread appeal of the play that so aroused the leadership's concern.

[11] Interview at *Zuopin* editorial board, 4 March 1980.

[12] Jiang Kun, "Duihao ru zuo."

cially irresponsible approach to life. Although there can be no doubt that such views were often sincere (and by no means limited to officials), they also clearly had a number of important functions within the political control system.

The most important of these was to associate the Party with nationalism, a sentiment that had broad and deep popular appeal. The campaign in the early 1950s to "Resist America and Aid Korea" was important in stimulating national pride and in associating Party with nation. In the 1950s, "nation" meant primarily the "new" China, forged of socialist ideals and opposed equally to the "feudal" past and the "bourgeois" West. By the late 1970s, however, Mao Zedong's disastrous experiments had left socialist ideals practically dead and, among some, even despised. By the time Deng Xiaoping took over, it was clear that only Chinese pride of a more traditional sort could serve as a foundation on which to build legitimacy for his reformist regime. Deng climbed onto this foundation and began to phase out the old Communist objections to "feudal" traditional culture. By the late 1980s, even claims about mystical Chinese essences, for example in the martial arts or in herbal medicine, began to appear in government tourist brochures and as advertised parts of the training of Chinese Olympic athletes—who themselves also became a tool for eliciting national pride and channeling it toward support of the regime.

Deng's embrace of a more traditional nationalism, no longer called "feudalism," allowed him to continue in resisting "bourgeois" foreign influences. But the problem of how to import science and technology while resisting the cultural baggage that seemed to come with it required a constant push and pull that marked Deng's rule to its end. It also continued a battle that Chinese leaders of many kinds had been waging off and on for more than a century. In the late nineteenth century, Zhang Zhidong's formula of "Chinese learning as a core, Western learning for practical use" had seemed to modernizers the right compromise. In the twentieth century, leaders as diverse as the liberal Hu Shi, who spoke of "taking what it makes sense to take," and communist Mao Zedong, who called for "Western things as they fit China's purposes," continued to look for a balance that would allow China to modernize and yet remain—"purely," in some sense—China. In 1985, Party Chairman Hu Yaobang invoked a well-established theme when he said, "As we bring in advanced technology and advanced management experience from foreign countries, it is inevitable that some decadent bourgeois thought will also come in. This decadent thought is 'bacteria'—it spreads like a disease."[13]

On the whole, the need to protect cultural integrity seems to have been somewhat stronger in socialist China than in the Soviet Union during comparable periods. The difference lay not so much in strength of national pride itself, where Russia rated high, as in cultural distance from the West-

[13] Hu Yaobang, "Guanyu dangqian wenyi gongzuo yixie wenti de jianghua."

ern adversary. Russia's traditional ties with the culture of Western Europe, especially France, made Western influences in the Soviet Union, however loudly denounced as "bourgeois," less profoundly upsetting to Soviet leaders than were Western challenges to China. From a Chinese viewpoint, Russia itself was part of "the West," broadly speaking; the big divide was between America and Europe (including Russia) on one side and China and adjacent parts of Asia on the other. For more than a century, the magnitude of the perceived gulf between China and the West had produced deeper and more painful dilemmas for China than it had for Russia.

The Party's defenses of Chinese culture and ethics gave it, in addition to legitimacy, some rhetorical high ground when it turned to the nasty business of suppressing political dissent. During campaigns against "spiritual pollution" in 1983 and "bourgeois liberalization" in 1987, for example, the Deng regime painted a wide spectrum of behavior with a single brush. To question Party leadership, to expose social problems, to write modernist poetry, to wear bell-bottom trousers, to watch pornographic videotapes, and to murder taxi drivers were all, in the rhetoric of these campaigns, presented basically as mutations of a single problem: improper behavior. Public executions of common criminals increased, as did press attacks on wayward thinking and foreign influences. An official survey of young people in the city of Chengdu, for example, found that 9.4 percent held the "degenerate" view that one's youth should be spent "pursuing pleasure whenever possible." This attitude could be understood, according to the report, by considering that 58 percent of those in the degenerate group named foreign radio broadcasts—from America, Australia, or Hong Kong—as their preferred ones. Only 8.6 percent of this group preferred Chinese stations.[14] This kind of lumping together of dissidence and "decadence" served the leadership's interests not only by sullying its opponents but also by elevating its own image to something resembling a parenting role. The rhetoric of Party pronouncements sought to appropriate the assumed benevolence of a father's voice as it spoke for the common good and—as if by the way—against the few who were misbehaving.

"Decadence," for the leadership, was not just another kind of misbehavior that could be useful in stigmatizing political dissidents. It was itself politically threatening because of its apparent connections with liberalism: the two seemed to be conducive to each other. The leadership's fear that liberalism could lead to decadence is illustrated in Hu Yaobang's statement, quoted above, that opening to the West can allow spiritual "disease" to spread. The fear that decadence, in turn, could lead to liberalism was not so obvious but very real. It can be seen, for example, in a 1981 criticism of love stories and other "bourgeois liberalism" in the authoritative theoretical journal *Red Flag*. "Romantic writing," according to the article, leads readers, especially

---

[14] Wu Benxue, "Qingnian wenhua shenghuo yu jiazhi quxiang," pp. 20, 22.

young ones, to think "only of personal life" and thus to neglect "the future of the motherland."[15] Worse than that, preoccupation with romance encourages youth to understand and respect their most intimate feelings—not only about the opposite sex but, potentially, about other things as well. They might look inward for guidance in how to behave, rather than outward toward the public rules set down by the Party leadership. Love stories therefore breed "skepticism," according to the *Red Flag* article, and "lead to moral *and political* degeneration" (my emphasis), that is, to both "decadence" and "liberalism."

What worried the leadership about private and subjective literary experience was not just that it might breed political dissent that could pop up unexpectedly in the public arena, but that it defined an area into which Party controls could not reach even if they wished. How could one control the reflections of a young person reading a love story in silence? Basically the same frustration underlay the leadership's opposition to literary modernism. What, after all, is a writer saying in a "misty" poem, or a stream-of-consciousness short story? In 1983 Hu Yaobang explained that the West sends China two kinds of "candy artillery shells": "material" shells include stylish women, fancy commodities, and lust for money; "spiritual" shells include such things as literary modernism and talk about "humanism" and "alienation."[16] While arguing that modernist writing was cultural pollution, the leadership's real fear was of the political unknown. Literary experiments that were conducted under one or another elusive Western "ism," such as existentialism or poststructuralism, were especially threatening. But it was, ironically, the leadership's refusal to allow explicit criticism that made these fears of hidden dissent somewhat realistic.

THE LITERARY CONTROL SYSTEM

In his "Talks at the Yan'an Conference on Literature and Art" in 1942, Mao Zedong laid down some basic rules about what literature should do—and must not do—in Communist China. From then until the 1980s, when their influence gradually waned, Mao's "Yan'an Talks" were the foundation of China's literary control system. Literature had to "serve" politics, both by teaching socialism to readers and, more concretely, by supporting the current political campaign of the leadership, be it "resist Japan" (in 1942), "ex-

---

[15] Sha Tong, "Renzhen kefu wenyi gongzuozhong de ziyouhua wenti," pp. 35–38.

[16] Hu Yaobang, "Guanyu sixiang zhengzhi gongzuo wenti," pp. 1, 4. The distinction was stated even more explicitly, if less colorfully, by Minister of Culture Zhu Muzhi during the "oppose spiritual pollution" campaign of 1983 (*Renmin ribao*, 2 November 1983, p. 3). It is worth noting in this regard that the "oppose spiritual pollution" campaign itself, which is best known for its curbing of intellectuals, began amid a crackdown on murder, rape, and burglary.

pose landlords" (1952), or "smelt iron at home" (1958).[17] Individual literary works were to be judged by political as well as artistic criteria, with political criteria taking precedence.

Mao's 1942 guidelines have been well analyzed in Western scholarship.[18] Here, rather than to summarize them in theory, I offer an analysis of the actual workings of the system as seen primarily in the immediate post-Mao period. In using the word "system" I mean to imply a certain stability—not in literary policy, which fluctuated under Deng and sometimes lurched wildly under Mao, but in the principles that tended to govern the relations among the five kinds of actors who were importantly involved: readers, writers, editors and publishers, critics and cultural officials, and the top leadership.

By "top leadership" I mean officials and their families at the highest levels of national, or sometimes provincial, government. During the post-Mao thaw, members of the ruling Politburo monitored contemporary literature and sometimes worried about its influence. Writers cultivated friendships with the children of national leaders in order to learn what the people on top were saying about them. The attention that top leaders paid to literary policy could be surprisingly minute. For example, at the Fourth Congress of Literature and Art Workers in November 1979, a document on the spirit of the meeting was distributed in the name of the Party's Central Committee. Zhou Yang, a leading political critic of literature, had drafted the document, which was then edited by Party Chairman Hua Guofeng and by Deng Xiaoping.[19] Deng used it as the basis for his keynote address that closed the Congress, but then, three days after delivering his address, began to have second thoughts about one of its carefully crafted phrases. He had said that the "cultural line" during 1949–1966 had been "correct." But was it entirely right to imply that the Anti-Rightist Campaign of 1957 had been "correct"? After thinking it over, Deng specifically notified Hu Yaobang, who was then director of the Propaganda Department, to add the word "basically" before the word "correct" in the printed version of the speech.[20]

By "critics" I do not mean literary critics in a Western sense, but political critics who were responsible to the government. The main job of these critics was to monitor literary publication and, if necessary, to criticize particular works according to the ideological criteria that the leadership was currently stressing. Cultural officials and some of the more conservative senior writers—such as Tian Jian, Ding Ling, and Ouyang Shan during the scar years—also sometimes played the role of political critic. There were, in

---

[17] As noted in chapter 1, the shift in summer 1980 to the slogan "literature in service of the people and in service of socialism" relaxed the demand that writers support specific campaigns. But this change did not bring radical change to the overall control system.

[18] Bonnie S. McDougall, *Mao Zedong's "Talks at the Yan'an Conference"*; Tsi-an Hsia, "Twenty Years after the Yenan Forum," in *The Gate of Darkness* pp. 234–62; and Goldman, *Literary Dissent in Communist China*, chap. 2.

[19] Hu Yaobang, "Zai juben chuangzuo zuotanhuishang de jianghua," p. 2.

[20] Ibid., p. 3.

Chinese universities and research institutes, literary scholars with interests in form, language, and literary history, but these academics had little access to the mass media and seldom played much of a role in the control system.[21] By "readers" I mean primarily urban readers. This is not to slight the peasant masses in China but simply to note the fact that, despite periodic literacy campaigns in Maoist China, rural people never did become a significant part of the literature-reading public. Urban readers were of many kinds, as we shall see in chapter 5.

To understand how socialist China's literary control system worked, the Western observer must first set aside deeply ingrained notions about the primacy of the writer. In the design of the system, the primary relationship, which all the other relationships were supposed to support, was that between top leadership and readers. The purpose of literature was to lead readers to think what the leadership determined it was best that they think. This conception assumed that top leaders could know what thoughts would most benefit readers, and therefore what writers should write, better than these groups themselves could know these things. Sometimes this assumption was explicitly spelled out. In 1980, for example, the conservative critic Chen Yong offered the following as justification for his denunciation of Sha Yexin's "What If I Really Were?":

> The main line of attack that Party Central chooses in any current struggle is determined by a multiplicity of factors. Writers and artists usually rely more on their own direct observations, and thus may have deeper impressions of, and a greater readiness to emote about, the life that they have experienced personally. But for the complete picture, for all the factors that must go into determining the direction of the current political struggle, Party Central's understanding will be the clearer one.[22]

The authoritarianism of such pronouncements had close analogies in the Soviet Union and elsewhere in the socialist world. But in China the paternalistic tone ("I know best what is good for you and have a responsibility to guide you") also owed something to the familism in Confucian political culture. In the 1950s and 1960s, before cynicism reached deep into their society, Chinese people of all ages tended to view their leaders as father figures. The leaders knew what was best, and it was their role to issue prohibitions and permissions as appropriate.

In the political jargon, the term "correct" (*zhengque*) was reserved for views that Party leaders agreed with. Every literary text theoretically had its "correct" interpretation.[23] The Party might or might not have had time to

---

[21] After the mid-1980s, elite modernist writing did find its way into large-circulation periodicals. Editors used such material for its prestige value, while relying on popular fiction to reach marketing goals.

[22] Chen Yong, "Cong liangge juben kan wenyi de zhenshixing he qingxiangxing."

[23] Confirmed in an interview (Beijing, 13 July 1980) with the prominent critic Zhu Zhai, Literature Research Institute, Chinese Academy of Social Sciences.

determine what this was, but only the Party could do so. When writers expressed correct thoughts for readers to absorb, the interests of the Party, and therefore, in theory, of society as a whole, were served. Borrowing a phrase from Stalin, Party theorists referred to the "engineering of readers' souls";[24] borrowing from Lenin, they spoke of writers as "screws in the socialist machine."[25]

But their favorite metaphors for the workings of the political-literary control system were drawn from medicine. A good literary work was "healthful" to its readers; a bad one could be "unhealthful" or even "poisonous." The assumption that the leadership knew better than readers themselves what was good for readers was reinforced in the analogy of the leader to a doctor, whose understanding of disease and whose ability to prescribe medicine ("healthful" works) was beyond question. Whether readers found the medicine palatable or not was a separate point.

In fact, in daily life from the 1960s on, the benevolent paternalism of the medicine metaphor was a poor description of the ways in which leaders and readers, especially young readers, viewed each other. A 1985 survey in Shanghai, while finding young workers indignant at "unfair, despotic, and unresponsive" leaders, also discovered that leaders viewed the following as the primary traits of young workers: slick-talking and deceptive, greedy and manipulative, materialistic, profligate, and uncultured.[26] But in its official rhetoric, the leadership could not afford to admit such gaps, and could be embarrassed if it became too obvious that readers did not enjoy the literature that was prescribed for them. Hence the fiction was maintained that readers did like it. A prescribed medicine became a prescribed preference of the palate as well. Because such preferences are something different from genuine palatability,[27] I will use the following technical terms below: "actual reader preferences" were for what readers enjoyed; "prescribed reader preferences" were for what the top leadership felt readers ought to enjoy.

One could, with care, draw a line graph of actual reader preferences and prescribed reader preferences over time, showing when and to what extent the two converged or diverged in the history of socialist China from Mao's "Talks" in 1942 until the mid-1980s, after which the control system was too weak for the exercise to be possible. Separate graphs would sometimes be necessary for different kinds of works, yet certain overall trends are also clear. In the Communist base areas of the 1940s, there was great conver-

---

[24] The phrase "engineers of the soul" was invented by Stalin, assisted by Gorky. See Herman Ermolaev, *Soviet Literary Theories, 1917–1934*, p. 167. The phrase was adopted in China and got considerable use even during the post-Mao period.

[25] See Rudolf G. Wagner, *Inside a Service Trade*, pp. 12, 117.

[26] Dong Xijian, "Qinggong yu lingdao ganqing de zhang'ai ji shutong," pp. 40–43.

[27] This fact, although perhaps too obvious to need documentation, is confirmed in a 1984 survey of 488 film viewers in Lanzhou, whose most frequent complaint about films made under the Chinese literary control system was that they seemed "untrue and unnatural," and who preferred foreign films because they were "natural and realistic." See Pang Junlin and Li Jie, "Dianying: xibu qingnian de kewang yu xuqiu," pp. 126–27.

gence of actual and prescribed preferences for resist-Japan war stories, especially when the anti-Japanese message was delivered through oral or performing arts that circumvented the problem of illiteracy. Peasants wanted to resist Japan, and that is what the Communist leadership wanted them to want. The Soviet Union experienced a similar convergence of preferences during World War II, when the leadership's call to defend the motherland coincided with strong popular sentiment; during those years, in Boris Pasternak's phrase, "the spell of the dead letter was broken."[28] On the other hand, during the same war years in China, Mao Zedong's pronouncements that the proletarian masses love the difficult language and subtle art in the works of Lu Xun is a good example of wide divergence between actual and prescribed preferences.

Convergence appears to have declined only slightly in China with the optimistic revolutionary novels of the 1950s. Readers genuinely liked stories of the revolutionary struggle and early socialist transformation, such as Yang Mo's *The Song of Youth* and Zhou Erfu's *Morning in Shanghai*. The horrific problems of the 1930s and 1940s were still vivid in readers' minds during the early 1950s, and the self-sacrificing idealism projected in these works was fresh and attractive. Several years passed before the 1957 Anti-Rightist Campaign and the famines of 1959–1961, which had resulted from Mao's Great Leap Forward, called the revolutionary idealism into question. Stories and poems praising the Great Leap led to a divergence of actual and prescribed reader preferences. For many readers, the gap continued to grow during the Cultural Revolution, when stereotyped stories of model behavior, sometimes written by committee, dominated China's published writing. Among Red Guards, the divergence of actual and prescribed preferences did narrow somewhat, but for a new reason. These young idealists, infatuated with the idea of model behavior and identifying with the leadership they served, asked themselves less whether they liked a story as readers than whether it was good medicine for others.

The outpouring of scar literature from 1978 to 1980 marked a reconvergence of prescribed and actual preferences. Both the leadership and a great majority of readers wanted to denounce the "catastrophe" of the late-Mao years, and writers were eager to write about it. Although purposes differed, the coincidence of interests on this large issue meant that little engineering was required to produce literary works that pleased all sides. Editors and publishers could relax in their censorial roles. Only the political critics, whose job was to monitor for "correctness," appear to have felt uneasy—not because of any problem in their work but because they feared their entire role could disappear if relaxation were to remain permanently the norm in Deng Xiaoping's China.

---

[28] Quoted in Max Hayward, Introduction to Hayward and Labedz, *Literature and Revolution in Soviet Russia*, p. xvi; see also Harold Swayze, *Political Control*, p. 27; George Gibian, *Interval of Freedom*, p. 5.

With the retightening of 1980 and the criticism of Bai Hua in 1981, it became clear that the relaxation of the late 1970s had been a temporary internal configuration of the control system, not a sign of its demise. Many of the old devices for transmitting "correct" thought from leaders to readers reemerged. We can look at the relaxation and retightening in these years to analyze what actually happens among writers, editors, critics, and others during such phases of the system.

THE MECHANICS OF RELAXATION

The question of political control of literature was both pervasive enough and sensitive enough that euphemisms became badly needed. As a result, an extraordinary range of physical and biological metaphors came into in popular use to describe functions of the control system. As noted in the last chapter, the broad, national picture was frequently characterized in terms of weather. Winds blew in one or another direction, the atmosphere could be warmer or colder, and writers could be under higher or lower pressure. There were freezes and thaws. Flower gardens could thrive or wilt. Weeds could invade. Some weeds were poisonous. To touch them was unhealthful. Many other things could be unhealthful, including whole societies. Sometimes medicine was needed; sometimes the surgeon's scalpel. As these and related metaphors recur in this and the next section, the reader should bear in mind that they are not my inventions but standard clichés of the socialist Chinese literary world.

The basic mechanism of relaxation was that a warm wind would blow from the highest political levels, signaling a certain "spirit" (*jingshen*) that could allow writers and editors to move forward. But the questions of how to read the spirit from the top and how to apply it within one's own particular situation could be extremely subtle.

Top leaders sometimes showed that they were aware that their casual observations could have inordinate power. Hu Yaobang opened his "Talk on Playwriting" in February 1980 with the words, "Comrades! I'm here just to offer a few opinions—they are not 'instructions.'"[29] He went on, however, to make comments that he clearly expected to be viewed as more than "opinions." Generally everyone, including the top leaders, took it for granted that the leadership could decide the fate of any literary work. In 1979, for example, leaders in the Office of National Defense Industry wanted to decide whether to allow public staging of the play *The Future Beckons*, which seemed to sully the image of senior officials.[30] Special arrangements were made for top authorities to view the play and render their decision. Afterward, according to an eyewitness, Hu Qiaomu went over to

[29] Hu Yaobang, "Zai juben chuangzuo zuotanhuishang de jianghua," p. 1.
[30] Zhao Zixiong, "Weilai zai zhaohuan."

the young playwright, who was sitting in the theater perspiring and tense, and said only, "take a shower and have a good sleep—your play's okay."[31]

Only in especially important cases, however, did the top leadership have time to render specific decisions. For the vast majority of writers, the questions of exactly where and how to move forward when "the wind blew warm" were immensely complex. They depended on all the specifics of one's own situation as well as the question of how to interpret a "go" signal from the top that was inspiring but also frustratingly imprecise. Even when the leadership meant to include some precision and specificity in its guidelines, the message tended to get simplified or twisted as it was passed rung by rung down the bureaucracy. Usually, by the time a wind blew all the way down from the mountaintop, having been repropelled by functionaries at many intermediate stations, only its temperature was sensible in the valleys. For example, beginning in late 1979 and throughout 1980, the leadership stipulated, successively, that the Democracy Wall should be regulated; that official literary journals should not reprint materials from the unofficial journals; and finally, that unofficial journals should not be sold at retail on the streets. But to most people involved, all these specifics were not as noteworthy as the basic fact that the leadership's "spirit" was now to oppose the unofficial journals.

As people at lower levels sought to interpret high-level "spirits," the ability to notice and evaluate subtle changes became a specialized science. How to study the text of a speech or report by a national leader was a basic skill, but the particular slant of one's own immediate superior also had to be read not only in verbal signs but also in such things as tone of voice and gesture. In a story published in 1980, a young writer satirizes the process this way:

> [The director's] right-hand man transcribed everything the director said with lightning speed, scrupulously including every tiny inflection and evocative grunt or sigh. It would be a great mistake to dismiss those little "ahhs," "hmms," "wells," "tsks," and so on. These little noises would be of inestimable value to all the subordinates in their efforts to puzzle out and comprehend the head man's thinking.[32]

The role of middle-level officials could be important. When the top level came out with a spirit of relaxation in the late 1970s, the first to respond were writers and editors at the bottom, while bureaucrats in the middle, who had less to gain from a warming trend, moved more slowly if at all. In literary circles this phenomenon generated the catchphrase, "two ends hot and the middle cold."[33]

[31] The source is Li Yingmin, at the Conference on Literary Teaching Materials, Nanning, Guangxi, winter 1980. The quoted phrase is, "xi ge zao, shui ge jiao, shi hao xi."

[32] Cao Guanlong, "San'ge jiaoshou"; excerpt translated by John Berninghausen in Link, ed., *Roses and Thorns*, p. 135. The author is denouncing life in the Cultural Revolution years, but clearly wrote, and was read, with more general problems in mind.

[33] Liang tou re, zhongjian leng.

As writers studied their environments for signs of how to move forward, spatial metaphors became useful in addition to those based on weather and health. There were "boundaries" of a permissible "scope." One could challenge the boundaries and perhaps "break into forbidden zones" (*dapo jinqu*), thereby opening them to others. A dramatic success could earn one the epithet of "ground-breaking hero" (*chuangjiang*). Liu Xinwu was known as such a hero after his story "The Homeroom Teacher" in 1977, as was Lu Xinhua after "Scar" in 1978. These two works stimulated thousands of youngsters to send their own would-be "ground-breaking" stories to literary magazines. Young writers exhibited a speculative mentality that, for all the obvious differences, bore some resemblance to speculation on a stock market: both involved bets on future trends; for both there circulated inside "tips"; both could ultimately bring success or ruin; and for both the logic of events was nearly always clearer in retrospect than in advance.

A variety of tactics were available to writers and editors who wished to break new ground. Many involved manipulation of political language: turning the categories, axioms, slogans, and metaphors of officialdom to one's own purposes. One advantage of such tactics was that they implied a basic loyalty to the Party worldview, and such an appearance provided insulation against the fearsome charge of being a public enemy. Another important advantage of language-based tactics was that the Party's terminology could not be assailed. Whatever the purposes of their use, the terms themselves were indubitably "correct." Harold Swayze describes the same basic tactics at work in the Soviet literary world under Khrushchev in noting that "recalcitrant elements . . . leave an undeniable trace on the unfolding of any particular policy, deflecting the policy in unforeseen directions, . . . exploiting its hidden loopholes, clothing it with unintended meanings."[34] In China, exposés of suffering among the downtrodden were clothed in the Party's "glorious tradition" of going to the masses or "listening carefully to the cries of the people."[35] Calls for more freedom of expression, including the right to be somewhat contrary, were cloaked in officially condoned metaphors, such as the "flowers and weeds" that senior writer Yang Mo used to make her point in the late 1970s: "if there is a bit more rain, and a little more fertilizer, and the earth is a little richer, your sprouts will grow somewhat better; but the weeds will do better, too. Now, if you decide that the weeds have taken over, and decide to alter the growing conditions, reducing the water and withholding fertilizer, then the weeds will wither, but so will your plants."[36] It could also be helpful to invoke the sovereignty of "the masses." Virtually no one believed that the masses were, in fact, "the masters of the People's Republic," but the fact that this phrase expressed an unassailable truth in the official ideology could be useful in argument.

---

[34] Swayze, *Political Control*, p. 27.

[35] Mai Junru, whose argument is typical although his terms are unusually eloquent; see "'Wei wei,' 'e e' yu 'jingzi.'"

[36] As paraphrased by Liu Binyan in "Tan xin shiqi de wenxue chuangzuo wenti," p. 6.

In the summer of 1979, for example, the editors of a magazine called *Cartoon Strips* came under fire for publishing a picture version of Zheng Yi's story "Maple," which went too far in implicating Mao Zedong in Cultural Revolution violence, and which showed the disgraced leader Lin Biao in too favorable a light. The editors moved quickly to defend themselves, using only three days to convene a conference on what "the masses" thought about their cartoon strip. They invited to the conference representatives of factories, communes, and neighborhoods, as well as people who worked at the editorial offices of major magazines and newspapers reading letters to the editor. Not surprisingly, the conference concluded that the masses, on the whole, viewed the "Maple" cartoon extremely favorably. Transcripts of the conference and "representative" letters from the masses were compiled and forwarded to major art magazines and institutes around the country, as well as to the Central Propaganda Department, from whom the final decision on "correctness" finally had to come.[37]

Besides the irrefutability of the masses' standpoint, another advantage in pretending to refer questions to them was that this required that works be published. How else could the masses judge them? In 1961, Zhou Enlai had said that "whether a work of art is good or bad must be decided by the people and not by the leadership."[38] Zhou's remark, which writers and editors revived and touted in the late 1970s, implied not only that a work had to be published in order to be fairly judged but that some time must pass before the judgment was reached. "After a work as been published it becomes a social thing," wrote the prestigious elder writer Ba Jin. "The good ones are passed on to the next generation and the bad ones wither away by themselves."[39] This plain-looking statement was actually a sharp challenge to Party intervention in literature; Ba Jin was rejecting the idea that propaganda officials could decide in advance of a work's publication what its "social effects" (reader response) might be. The advantage of arguing this way was that the desired goal—publication—was a necessary step in the process of running the very test that Party rhetoric called for; hence the outcome of the test in a sense did not matter. The vulnerability of the argument was that Party officials could claim—and did, when the literary weather changed in the early 1980s—that their axiomatic closeness to the masses did indeed enable them to know in advance what "the masses" would think, and that it was not only their right but their duty to intervene.

Liberal-minded editors could also use language, especially during relaxations, to put conservatives on the defensive. During 1979, when the wind from the top was warm, an obstructionist official could be tagged "ultra-

---

[37] *Lianhuan huabao* bianjibu, "Guanyu lianhuanhua 'Feng' de zuotanhui fayan jilu." The cartoon strip in question, painted by Chen Yiming, Liu Yulian, and Li Bin, was published in *Lianhuan huabao*.

[38] Zhou Enlai, "On Literature and Art," p. 13.

[39] Quoted from *Zhengming* (Hong Kong) January 1984 in *Inside China Mainland* February 1984, p. 15.

leftist" or a "remnant of the Gang of Four." These labels were not generally as dangerous as "bourgeois liberal" and "antisocialist" were for the liberals, but they were certainly negative enough to induce conservatives to do what liberals had to do more often—weigh the costs against the benefits of speaking their minds. At the Conference on Playwriting in February 1980, Hu Yaobang noted that "some comrades" were opposed to the play "What If I Really Were?" but were "afraid to say so; since we're stressing the Hundred Flowers these days, they were afraid that saying so would go against Party Central's policies."[40] Conservatives could feel sensitive about ultraleftist labels even when the winds were blowing their way.[41]

Literary intellectuals could also advance their interests by stressing their solidarity with scientists, whose political position was stronger than theirs in several respects. In official language, the word "science" itself bore positive connotations, as in "scientific Marxism." The importance of science in the "Four Modernizations" drive was beyond anyone's questioning. And scientists, even when they were criticized for their political ideas, could at least hope to separate such questions from their work in their special fields, which were apolitical, whereas a writer, whose work almost inevitably involved moral and political questions, risked his or her entire career when speaking out. One method that writers used in order to underscore their common identity with scientists was to make scientists the heroes of their stories. Among countless images of the persecuted intellectual in post-Mao writing, writers were strangely rare.[42] Scientists were much more common. The image of the doctor in a white coat (adding the good of "healer" to that of scientist) was almost a cliché. Choosing scientists as heroes not only strengthened the identification between scientists and writers but helped to shield from attack whatever observations the writer chose to have his fictional scientist make.

Chinese scientists, for their part, generally cooperated in building solidarity among intellectuals.[43] Memories of a common fate during the Cultural Revolution, when all kinds of intellectuals were stigmatized as "cow ghosts and snake spirits" and persecuted similarly, strengthened the solidarity of scientific and nonscientific intellectuals in the post-Mao years. Scientists wrote poetry and stayed abreast of literary events more, certainly,

[40] Hu Yaobang, "Zai juben chuangzuo zuotanhuishang de jianghua," p. 43.

[41] Conservatives who led the crackdown of 1987 apparently had such fears. See Shi Hua, "Zhuozhou huiyi mijian beijing," p. 26.

[42] Works about persecuted writers that did appear were among the most moving, however. Wang Ruowang's "Ji'e sanbuqu" is a powerful autobiographical account of a writer in prison. Yang Jiang, "Ganxiao liuji" is an elegantly restrained account, also autobiographical, of a writer's life in a labor camp. The 1979 film *Ku'naoren de xiao* (Shanghai zhipianchang, directed by Yang Yanjin and Deng Yimin) explores the excruciating pressures on a journalist who wants to write truthfully.

[43] For example, the slogan "Let a Hundred Flowers Bloom," which was so important to writers and other humanists, was strongly advocated by scientists, as well. See Xu Liangying and Fan Dainian, *Science and Socialist Construction in China*, chap. 5.

than their colleagues in the West normally did. In 1989 scientists, social scientists, and humanists alike wrote petitions to the government asking for the release of political prisoners; a personal friendship between the prominent physicist Fang Lizhi and the equally well- known poet Bei Dao was a key element in the cooperation on those petitions. Other one-party states have been able to use differential treatment to split scientists, whose services they have needed, away from other intellectuals, whom they have found expendable and often irritating.[44] But in China this split was never very wide.

Once a writer or editor had decided to make a move, and had selected appropriate rhetorical tactics, he or she often sought what was called "backstage" (*houtai*) support from a like-minded person who wielded some power. Alliances between writers and their backstage supporters were based on a number of things, including shared goals as well as any of a wide variety of personal connections. Ties based on family and close friendship were taken for granted and tended to be strong. The children of high-ranking officials often did quite well in their efforts to become "ground-breaking heroes," even if their powerful parents had negative or mixed feelings about what their offspring were doing.[45]

Other connections had to be built. This could be done through trading gifts, favors, public praise, deferential visits, and the other ways in which connections are cultivated in Chinese culture. A practical symbiosis often lay at the base of such a relationship. A backstage supporter could help a writer to get published, and also, to a degree, protect him or her from attack after a piece was in print. In return, because backstage supporters were often officials whose formal responsibilities made it "inconvenient" for them to say certain things publicly, writers could help them by getting their points of view out. Perhaps because literature was conceived to be closer to one's inner thoughts and morality than were other things, a good literary alliance usually involved a degree of "personal feeling" (*jiaoqing*) or "understanding" (*liaojie*).

Still, a backstage supporter also had to calculate privately the balance of gains and risks that were involved in supporting an independent-minded writer, and had to be ready to back off if necessary. A similarity in this regard between literary life in socialist China and the Soviet Union is apparent in a story called "One's Own Opinion" by Daniel Granin, which liberal-

[44] See Samuel P. Huntington, "Social and Institutional Dynamics of One-Party Systems," in Huntington and Moore, *Authoritarian Politics in Modern Society*, especially pp. 33 and 37 on the division between "intellectual" elites and "managerial" or "technical" elites.

[45] The offspring of several high officials were involved in the controversial unofficial publications of 1978–1980. See pp. 189–90. In addition, the audacity of the Shanghai magazine *Shouhuo* (Harvest) owes something to its being edited by Li Xiaolin, daughter of the famous senior writer Ba Jin; and few if any Chinese film directors could portray sexual attraction as frankly as did Ling Zi, daughter of Marshall Ye Jianying, in her directing of the film *Yuanye* (Wilderness).

minded Soviet writers and editors championed after it appeared in 1956. It tells the inner dilemmas of an official, Minayev, who would like to continue supporting a heretical report by a young engineer, Olkhovsky, but finds that "Olkhovsky had gone too far; to support him openly would mean to enter into conflict with too many influential people. But in the depths of his heart Minayev keenly envied Olkhovsky's reckless daring."[46] The necessary caution of the backstage supporter implied a corresponding necessary caution in the writer. For the writer, the possible unreliability of one's supporter meant that he or she had to be evaluated for both "firmness" and "weight," which were different things: weight was a measure of such things as the supporter's public office (the higher the better), personal contacts (the more concretely relevant the better), and general prestige. Firmness was a measure specifically of how loyal a supporter was to a writer.

Unless there were strong personal ties involved, the firmness of backstage support varied considerably with the nature of the cooperation. Support was relatively firm when a writer was simply speaking for his or her backstage supporter. This was the case when the little-known Li Jian, in spring 1979, wrote his "'Praise' and 'Shame'" on behalf of the conservative provincial leadership in Hebei.[47] When the connection between writer's expression and supporter's intent was vaguer, support inevitably was less firm. If a work were criticized, the supporter would defend its basic spirit while perhaps acknowledging, if necessary, that the writer had been unwise in selecting some of its phrases. An even more diffuse kind of support was that which provided general approval of a point of view but no endorsements of particular works. An example of this case was the general support that Wan Li, first secretary of the Party Committee in Anhui Province, gave to a whole group of editors and writers who spent much of the late 1970s exposing social problems in stories and reportage in the Anhui literary journals.

At its softest, backstage support could be symbolic and nearly impossible to pin down. But even then it was useful; when a supporter was powerful, greater weight could compensate for lack of firmness. In late 1978, for example, students at Zhongshan University in Guangzhou were having difficulty in launching their literary magazine *Red Bean* (*Hongdou*). Then Zhou Yang, a literary official with credentials dating from the 1930s, who was attacked during the Cultural Revolution but "exonerated" afterward, and who was in 1978 the new vice chair of the Chinese Writers' Association, came to Guangzhou for a meeting. A student sought him out with a question: "What do you think of our plan to start a magazine, respected comrade Zhou Yang?"

"Very good," Zhou reportedly answered.

"Will you do us the honor of donating your calligraphy?"

Zhou Yang did, and the students used the calligraphy for their front cover. Reversing themselves, the university authorities granted not only permis-

---

[46] Quoted in Hugh McLean and Walter N. Vickery, *The Year of Protest, 1956*, p. 261.
[47] See pp. 19–20, above.

sion to publish but a subsidy of 1,000 yuan (four to six months of a professor's salary). It is hard to say whether Zhou Yang's abstract and temporary patronage had anything to do with *Red Bean*'s daring to be one of the more outspoken student magazines in China, or its being the last of these magazines to fall in the chilly wind of 1980. In cases where backstage support was as symbolic as this, the involved parties themselves could not say with precision just what was being done or made possible.

Personal relationships could be useful even between people who were basically opponents. A young writer, for example, could pay a deferential visit to an elder conservative critic and perhaps thereby gain a greater scope for expression of his liberal views, while the conservative gained a symbolic acknowledgment of the Party's centrality and an opportunity to keep the young writer basically within its fold. Conservatives sometimes actually sought such ties. During the Anti-Spiritual Pollution Campaign in 1983, the senior conservative Hu Qiaomu invited Wang Ruowang, a radical advocate of free expression, and Zhang Xinxin, an outspoken young writer, to visit him "for a talk." During the cold literary weather of those days, Hu could certainly have pursued more direct means of throttling people like Wang and Zhang, but chose the subtler approach of trying to build personal ties.[48]

When controversies arose, two sides, or sometimes more, organized different camps of backstage support. The decision of whether to publish or not—or, if a piece was already published, whether to attack it or not—could hang in the balance of whose backstage support was the firmer and weightier. For example, when writers at the Guangzhou magazine *Literary Works* launched criticisms of Hao Ran in 1977, charging that he had been too close to the Gang of Four, Hao Ran found his own support in Beijing.[49] As both sides built their support, it gradually became clear that the question of whether Hao Ran could publish in the post-Mao period would depend on which side won. "Weight" in such matters varied inversely with the distance (meaning political distance, in which geographical distance played a role) between support and the location of a problem. Writers everywhere in China knew that if they wanted to criticize Hao Ran, they could do so more easily in Guangzhou than in Beijing. And Hao Ran's supporters knew that, if they wanted to use Beijing clout to quell opponents in Guangzhou, they would need much more of it than if the decision were to be made in Beijing. As it happened in the Hao Ran case, the result was a stalemate; for a time the two cities treated him oppositely.

Writers and editors who wanted to break new ground had to work within the hierarchical structure of state and Party bureaucracies. They could use personal connections to reach outside this structure, and from outside bring

---

[48] Hu's efforts were not very successful in this case. Zhang Xinxin appeared for the appointment but Hu kept her waiting for what she felt was an impolitely long time; she left a note and departed. Hu did meet with Wang Ruowang for about three hours, but the meeting seems not to have produced much of a connection.

[49] See pp. 15–16, above.

pressure to bear, but there was no escape from the structure itself. The Party leaders on editorial boards held key power. Without them an initiative would get nowhere. Even with them, questions that involved political risk were often referred to higher levels in the Party Propaganda Department. For a local official, asking higher approval was always the safer course; the record of having done so could be invaluable if a work were later determined to be "incorrect." The question of whether to publish or not could go all the way to the provincial or even national level if both sides had supporters. In 1979 Hu Yaobang, then head of the Propaganda Department, personally made the final decision to allow publication of the cartoon version of Zheng Yi's story "Maple." Basically the same phenomenon appeared in socialist systems elsewhere. In the Soviet Union in 1962, Nikita Khrushchev personally authorized publication of Alexander Solzhenitsyn's controversial *One Day in the Life of Ivan Denisovich.*[50]

Higher officials, who were busy people and usually not literary people, often lacked the time to look at literary questions carefully. During relaxations, when a large number of questions were referred upward, they could lie for months on the crowded desks of middle- or high-level officials before receiving attention. Decisions, when they did come, might be hasty and idiosyncratic, but were nonetheless crucial. Popular clichés about "one-sentence courts" (*yi yan tang*) where "one person's word goes" (*yige ren shuole suan*) applied to many questions in the society, but seemed especially useful in describing the fate of literary manuscripts. Lu Xinhua's story "Scar," for example, first appeared publicly when a longhand copy was pasted on a wall at Fudan University. Later the author submitted it to *Shanghai Literature* (*Shanghai wenxue*), where it stimulated great controversy but was eventually rejected. Next he tried the newspaper *Wenhuibao*, whose editors deliberated at length and could not reach a decision. They referred the question to the Shanghai Propaganda Department, where it was passed directly to Hong Ze, deputy chief of propaganda. According to the story that found its way back to the author, Hong Ze showed the story to his daughter during a family meal. The daughter reportedly was so moved that she ignored her food and spent the rest of the meal time arguing—successfully, in the end— that her father should approve publication.[51] Such stories were common. They were no doubt embroidered, but nonetheless are good indicators of the widespread belief that high officials made literary decisions quickly and arbitrarily, if they got around to them at all.

Some writers, especially among the young, complained that the system amounted to "rule by people" (*ren zhi*) instead of "rule by law" (*fa zhi*). Certainly it was true that personal authority within bureaucratic structures, influenced by informal connections of whatever kind actors could bring to

[50] Priscilla Johnson, "The Politics of Soviet Culture, 1962–1964" in *Khrushchev and the Arts*, pp. 5–6.

[51] Interview with Lu Xinhua, Los Angeles, 22 January 1987.

bear, was much more important than any written document in determining what authors could publish. Written documents played a role, but not that of law. The function of written rules, from official slogans to the constitution, was to provide language upon which people could draw as they needed. Usually it was officials who referred to written rules, but writers and editors could borrow them as well to bolster their arguments. To align one's opinion with a written law, policy, or slogan gave it moral authority, but no one assumed that an appeal to a written rule could overturn a personal decision that in other ways was dominant. How and when to invoke the authority of written rules was an art. The rules themselves were many, and sometimes contradictory. (The Chinese constitution in the post-Mao period guaranteed freedom of speech but outlawed opposition to the Communist Party, for example.) For individuals, the art lay in when and how to "mention" a relevant rule. In a published speech in 1961, Zhou Enlai made some unusually liberal statements on literature and art, and at the time these were very useful to writers and editors. During the Cultural Revolution, Zhou's speech, although not attacked, was simply not "mentioned." To cite it would have been dangerous. It remained unmentionable from the mid-1960s until February 1979, when the authoritative *Literary Gazette* (*Wenyibao*) republished it with fanfare. Similarly, political-literary slogans existed in a kind of limbo, emerging when policies called for them and receding when they were out of favor. In the Deng Xiaoping years, the countervailing slogans "let a hundred flowers bloom" and "oppose bourgeois liberalism" were both theoretically accessible at all times; which to use and how to use it depended on the political-literary weather. People who invoked slogans inappropriately could be told "that's not the way it's used" (*bushi neme tifa*).[52] The "mentioning" of a slogan could even turn its original sense on its head. "Freedom of Creation," which was championed at the Fourth Congress of the Chinese Writers' Association in December 1984, was used in the crackdown on writers in winter 1987 on grounds that the Party, too, should have its "freedom to create" criticism of writers.

The primacy of human beings over written documents helps to explain the unpredictability of the political-literary weather in socialist China. When differing views on literary questions vied for supremacy, the crucial factors were not public opinion or historical trends but the changeable minds of people who themselves might move up or down in power. Because such mind changes or fluctuations in power often had nothing to do with literature, literary trends usually were not predictable from literary phenomena.

The other side of invoking the right language was to exploit the misstatements of one's opponents. Although this was primarily a weapon that political authorities used against writers and editors, during relaxations editors could use it as well. Liberal editors sometimes published submissions from

---

[52] On *tifa* (way of mentioning), see Schoenhals, *Doing Things with Words*, pp. 6–29.

Figure 1. Back cover of *Masses Cinema*, May 1979.

the opposing side when they judged that the pieces would be self-defeating. In May 1979, for example, the highly popular magazine *Masses Cinema* printed on its back cover a photograph of a Chinese actor and actress kissing. The two were playing Cinderella and her prince—two foreigners—and this fact made the photo less shocking than it would otherwise have been. Nevertheless, it drew criticism. From among the critical responses, the editors of *Masses Cinema* chose to publish a letter from an agitated Youth League official in Xinjiang Province who wrote somewhat ridiculously that "A foreign poisonous weed is attacking the Party and Chairman Mao!"[53] That letter, in turn, stimulated many letters in support of the magazine's editors, some of which were published. The editors made sure that the positive letters showed much more "support from the masses" than did the negative letters. In the fall of 1979 the Cantonese artist Liao Bingxiong

[53] Letter from Wen Yingjie, of the Political Office of Youth League group 129 of the Kui Village Agricultural Reclamation Bureau, Xinjiang, *Dazhong dianying* 1979.8.4–5.

Figure 2. "Enough to Blow Your Hat Off," cartoon-painting by Liao Bingxiong, exhibited in Guangzhou, fall 1979.

painted a color cartoon (*manhua*) called "Enough to Blow Your Hat Off," satirizing the critics of the kiss.[54]

When people on the conservative side saw such tactics coming, they nat-

[54] The Chinese title of the cartoon, *nufa chongguan* (literally, "angry hair raises the hat") is a literary cliché most famously associated with the hero Yue Fei, who became furious about the Jin invasion of north China in the twelfth century. In depicting the flying hair as a queue, which was a symbol of Chinese humiliation at the hands of the ruling Manchus during the Qing dynasty (1644–1912), Liao Bingxiong archly suggests that the outrage over kissing in 1979 was narrow-minded and backward-looking. The cartoon was exhibited at the People's Park in Guangzhou in fall 1979.

urally sought to avoid them. For example, in its first issue of 1981, the Guangzhou literary magazine *City of Flowers* published, under the by-line "Our Commentator," an article containing the unusually bold argument that lower-level officials need not obey higher levels, and that, moreover, if they are quite certain that the higher levels are in error, it is actually their duty to disobey.[55] This was a very radical claim, and all of the newspapers in Guangzhou, as if by reflex, immediately prepared to publish criticisms of it. Before the criticisms went to press, however, the first secretary of the Provincial Party Committee, Ren Zhongyi, intervened to stop them. Ren could foresee that in the current climate in Guangzhou, official criticism of *City of Flowers* would only draw more attention to the troublesome article and bring more public sympathy to its authors. Instead of approving the criticism, Ren negotiated for the editors of *City of Flowers* to publish a partial retraction, "Asking Ourselves Once More," in the magazine's next issue.[56] The problem then went away quietly.

Ren's goals were not only to avoid turmoil locally in Guangzhou but to preserve the reputation of Guangdong province nationally. During the late 1970s, certain provinces and cities, especially Guangdong, Anhui, and Shanghai, gained national reputations for especially "liberated" literary publishing, while others, notably Hebei, were known as centers of conservatism. Writers began, more than they had before, to submit their work on a national market, passing over editors in their own city or province in favor of more sympathetic editors elsewhere. Liberals, more than conservatives, benefited from China's unmanageable size. It was easier for a groundbreaker to shift an attack from one area to another than it was for his or her opponent to maintain effective repression at all possible locations.

As they pressed forward, liberal editors around the country monitored one another's advances in order to gauge how large a step to take next. Priscilla Johnson has found that Soviet writers after Stalin would "weigh each new step forward, lest that particular step be the one to precipitate a reversion to the methods of the past."[57] In China the reason for caution seems to have been much the same. The writer Wang Meng argued that all writers should exercise self-restraint because

> In the Cultural Revolution years, high pressure kept a smooth facade on society. All the problems were pressed underneath. What's happened now [after Mao] is that the high pressure is off and all the problems come out. It looks as if the new policies have brought on the difficulties, but actually they've only let them emerge. If all of us writers now let loose and shoot freely, the high-pressure people will have an argument for coming back to put the smooth face back on.[58]

[55] Benkan pinglunyuan, "Buji zi wen," *Huacheng*.

[56] Benkan pinglunyuan, "Zai yi ci zi wen," *Huacheng*. My version of the incident is from and interview (February 1981, San Francisco) with Huang Qiuyun, senior writer, editor, and literary official in Guangzhou.

[57] Johnson, *Khrushchev and the Arts*, p. 7.

[58] Interview, 3 August 1980, Beijing.

In particular, if one ground-breaker were to get too far out in front of the others, it would become easier for the opposition to single that person out and use him or her as a negative example in a campaign of repression against everyone. This is why, in the early 1980s, the intrepid free-speaker Wang Ruowang worried his colleagues at the editorial offices of *Shanghai Literature* as much as he delighted them. They knew him affectionately as "the broadcasting tower," but the nickname cut two ways.[59] Their fear that he might become a negative example in a national campaign came true in 1987, when Deng Xiaoping declared Wang to be "crazily out of control" and used his case to bring the tightest controls on expression that China had seen in ten years.[60]

THE MECHANICS OF TIGHTENING

Socialist China did not have the kind of formal censorial organs that other autocratic regimes have maintained. Literary control was less mechanical, and more psychological, than it has been elsewhere. It depended primarily on the private calculation of risks and balances in the minds of writers, editors, and those who supported them.[61]

The Chinese bureaucracy most responsible for censorship was the Communist Party's Department of Propaganda, whose general functions were to announce and advance Party policies through the news media, the education system, and Party committees in work units and neighborhoods. But there was no fixed pattern in the relationship between a literary editorial board and its local Propaganda Department. In the late 1970s and early 1980s in Shanghai, for example, literary magazines routinely sent their galleys to the Propaganda Department, where officials examined them and cut problematic phrases or paragraphs. In most other places, the Propaganda Department did not edit but simply approved or disapproved entire works. In Anhui province, editors did not send their galleys to the Propaganda Department at all, but straight to printers; censorship amounted to the self-censorship that was induced by fear of what might be said after a work appeared in print.

Whatever its relationship with the local office of the Propaganda Department, each editorial board had its own Party committee that exercised in-house censorial control. The chair of this committee, who was usually a chief or deputy chief editor appointed on political criteria, had a crucial voice in publishing decisions. More professionally qualified editors, as well

[59] Personal interview with Sun Xiaolan, board member of *Shanghai Literature*, Los Angeles, 6 February 1987.

[60] Deng reportedly described Wang as *changkuang de hen* in "Document No. 1," early January 1987; quoted in Ji Wen, "Zhongyang hongtou wenjian yi lan," p. 33.

[61] Edith Frankel and Alan Schwartz both hold that internalized self-censorship was also important in the Soviet case. The contrast with China is a matter of degree.

as writers, often chafed under such "rule by the unqualified." But it was difficult to complain openly, since there was seldom any alternative to continuing to work under the very person about whom one would be complaining. In 1980 a well-known film actor named Zhao Dan decided to voice this issue two days before he died of cancer: "Why should we invite so many cadres who know little or nothing about art and literature to lead several million [of us]? . . . May I ask, which countries in the world are like ours, where so many nonprofessionals occupy such a high percentage of posts in literary and art circles?"[62] Yet the "nonprofessionals" did have one essential skill: they knew how to read, and could sometimes modulate, the political winds that blew from the top. Since local writers and editors needed this help, the nonprofessionals could also be useful insofar as they chose to side with local interests.

At the first sign of a cold wind, writers and editors wanted to know just what it meant. Who was behind it, how strong would it be, and what "spirit" (general policy) did it represent? There were several ways to look for answers: by studying nuances in the speeches and articles of top leaders and authoritative critics; by reading, if one had access to them, the classified "internal circulation" documents and directives that were sent down through the Party hierarchy or, if one did not have such access, by studying the speech and behavior of people who had it; and by making enquiries among one's supporters or other well-placed acquaintances. The literary rumor mill, although not always reliable, was another constant source of interpretations. Until the "spirit" and extent of a cold wind became clear, most writers and editors reflexively drew back a bit just to be on the safe side. Wang Cunli, a writer of comedians' dialogues, described the onset of the chilly wind of 1980 with a touch of whimsy: "Whenever the leadership starts talking about 'social effects,' a heavy cloud descends. If we write our usual satires, the local officials start mincing their words, editors get long-winded, and publications pull in their reins. The message is loud and clear that 'retrenchment' is the spirit of the day, and that it's better to stay on the safe side with 'praise only,' no satire."[63] Jiang Kun, another writer of comedians' dialogues as well as a leading performer, described his personal experience of the same chilly wind this way: "I wanted to try a piece about a bull-headed factory manager. But just as I was working on it, I sensed a new spirit of retrenchment in the air, so I rubbed off a lot of his rough edges and gave him a bright side. The piece was a total failure."[64] These examples illustrate the self-censorship that, by the late 1950s in socialist China, had become the primary mechanism of literary control.

The major incentive for self-censorship was a vague but omnipresent fear

---

[62] Zhao Dan, "Guan de tai juti," p. 5. For more on the Zhao Dan incident, see Michael S. Duke, *Blooming and Contending*, pp. 19–20.

[63] Xiangsheng chuangzuo zuotanhui bangongshi, ed., "Xiangsheng chuangzuo zuotanhui jianbao," p. 5.

[64] Ibid., section 8, p. 2.

of criticism and punishment. This fear was like a great anchor that exerted a constant, directed pull on all the big ships and little sailboats that criss-crossed in pursuit of various other interests. Major criticism of writers centered in "campaigns" of fairly predictable pattern: a writer was singled out for criticism and his or her "mistakes" listed; the press then expounded upon these mistakes for several weeks or even months; everyone in literary circles—and, in the case of major campaigns, in the larger society as well—was urged to join in the criticism. To refuse to join was to bring suspicion upon oneself. Writers under attack were pressured to produce self-criticisms, which in turn were used to justify and sometimes to continue the campaign. During the Maoist period, the failure to produce a good self-criticism could lead to a sentence of labor reform.

A campaign was totalistic in two senses. First, no one was allowed overtly to disagree, or even to strike a middling position. (Sometimes, especially during the Deng period, writers found ways to signal dissent indirectly.) Second, all aspects of a targeted person, for purposes of the campaign, were negative. Hence any association with the person, whether literary or non-literary, was a bridge over which taint could spread. People to whom it spread could become the campaign's secondary targets. But any person, connected or not, could be subject to attack if a local powerholder determined that the person's mistakes—concerning "the capitalist road," "bourgeois liberalism," or other campaign watchword—were generically the same as those of the targeted person.

Physical punishment was most severe during the Cultural Revolution, when campaign victims had their homes ransacked, were paraded through the streets in public scorn, and could be sent for hard labor or be shot. In the Deng period punishments of this severity were rare, but the vivid and widespread memory of such things, coupled with the perpetual uncertainty of Chinese politics, was enough to make even mild criticism an effective deterrent. Anne Thurston has noted that China's Cultural Revolution affected its survivors differently from wars and catastrophes in other nations because the Cultural Revolution had no distinct end.[65] The decline of extremism after 1969 was gradual and intermittent; temporary resurgences of "ultraleftism" continued through the mid-1970s. Two years after Mao's death in 1976, the Deng Xiaoping leadership was exhorting writers and other intellectuals to banish "residual fear" and wholeheartedly throw themselves into the work of the Four Modernizations. But this was easier said than done; people bitten by snakes, in the Chinese cliché, fear ropes ever after. Threats of criticism still loomed "like the weight of Mount Tai," as Wang Ruowang put it.[66]

Continuing fear was, moreover, not just paranoia. The Deng regime, in implicit contradiction of its behest that people banish their fears, continued

---

[65] Anne F. Thurston, "Victims of China's Cultural Revolution," part 2, p. 7.
[66] Wang Ruowang, " 'Yuyong . . .' zhi lei," p. 59.

to breathe life into those very fears by using them for purposes of control. Recurring "cold winds" during the Deng period brought with them slogans and viewpoints that were at least reminiscent, if not secretly supportive, of "ultraleftism." In early 1980, authorities in a county in Hubei sent the Public Security police to arrest a poet who had dared to protest corruption among senior revolutionaries, and then launched a countywide campaign of criticism against him.[67] Although the Deng leadership was at pains to point out that the criticism of Bai Hua in 1981 was not a "campaign" in the Maoist sense, nevertheless the resemblance to a campaign was strong in the way the press was orchestrated and limited to one point of view.

Although seldom acknowledged as such, the vilification of the Gang of Four was itself strong implicit confirmation that Mao-style attack remained acceptable in the post-Mao regime. Even though their numbers were now limited to a mere handful, targeted people could be totally discredited and denied the opportunity of rebuttal. It also remained true that the key factor in placing someone in this status was personal word from the highest leadership.

In the campaigns of both the Mao and Deng periods, only a few writers were actually named as targets at the national level. The control of the great majority of writers and editors happened on the local level and through local work units. For the relatively few writers with professional status, the work unit was a municipal or provincial branch of the Writers' Association; others usually had a factory, school, or something else as a work unit. But in either case, the leadership of the work unit held considerable power over many aspects of one's welfare—salary, housing, medical care, schooling, and permission to travel, to purchase rationed commodities, or even to have children. Within this "organized dependency," as Andrew Walder has aptly called it, housing in particular was a major problem for writers.[68] Normally, no amount of national fame or adoration by readers counted as much in a writer's housing assignment as did the single opinion of the Party secretary of one's work unit. Zhang Jie, one of the best-known writers in the post-Mao years, lived in the 1970s and early 1980s in a small room in the dormitory of a machinery institute that had been her work unit during the Cultural Revolution. A less famous writer, Su Wei, the young editor of the Guangzhou student magazine *Red Bean*, was assigned to work in Beijing but then denied any housing at all—not for any "mistake" of his but because of the general crackdown on writers in winter and spring of 1987. Opportunities for writers to publish, to take "writing leaves" from work, to participate in seminars, to accept invitations to go overseas, and much more, were similarly subject to approval by immediate superiors. All of these activities were much envied within the society as a whole, and writers who enjoyed

---

[67] Luo Rujia, "Jiujing shei 'chouhua' Zhonggong?," pp. 56–57. The problematic poem was Xiong Zhaozheng's "Qing juqi senlinban de shou, zhi zhi!"

[68] Andrew G. Walder, "Organized Dependency and Cultures of Authority in Chinese Industry." See also Walder's *Communist Neo-Traditionalism: Work and Authority in Chinese Society*.

any of them were a privileged group. But when fear of political criticism was used in the control of literature, it applied, depending on time and place, all the way from fear of loss of privilege to fear for life.

Its operation followed some basic techniques. One was to make criticized persons feel isolated. In the 1981 campaign against "bourgeois liberalism," for example, newspapers declared that "the masses" see things differently from the "tiny minority" of bourgeois liberals. Hu Yaobang, in his major speech at the Lu Xun Memorial Celebration in September 1981, used the "tiny minority" phrase repeatedly.[69] He extended the point with the simile of lice (the liberals) on the body of a great lion (the masses). At first glance this might seem odd: if the opposition were indeed as minor as lice are to a lion, why would the Party chairman need to deliver an austere and well-publicized speech about "the crucial need to maintain vigilance" against this "grave danger"? But to wonder this is to look in the wrong direction. The point of the lice simile and the "tiny minority" phrase was not to estimate the size of any group but to work on the psychology of everyone.

First, to tag the opposition as a "tiny minority" automatically undermined its political legitimacy in the official rhetoric, where correct opinion was associated with "the masses." On the same principle, if the opposition was a tiny minority, the Party leadership appeared to be representing the main-stream. In literary circles, use of the "tiny minority" phrase said to writers and editors, most of whom were complexly involved in compromises and balancing acts, that compliance would surely bring safety; after all, only a "minority" were causing the trouble. To writers who had been provocative toward the leadership, and who thus risked membership in the "tiny minor-ity," it held out the possibility of forgiveness if they changed their ways and joined the majority. Sha Yexin, the main author of "What If I Really Were?," resisted considerable pressure to make changes in his play after Hu Yaobang criticized it in winter 1980. In the spring, when Sha finished writing *Mayor Chen Yi*, a clever but politically docile play that praised a revolutionary leader, the political critics were quick to give his new work favorable publicity. To show that Sha had apparently rejoined the "mainstream" gave face to the Party leadership as well as shoring up Sha's own personal security.

Key phrases such as "tiny minority" and "bourgeois liberal" normally combined two components of meaning: a moral component that was unmistakably clear and a denotative component that was purposely and very effectively vague. The negativity of moral terms was often apparent in their root meanings. *Ziyou*, in the term *ziyouzhuyi*, "liberalism," could have positive connotations when used in translation of Western words like "freedom" and "liberty," but in its root sense suggested self-indulgence and social irresponsibility. *Wuran*, "pollution," which referred to Western influences in the phrase "spiritual pollution" (against which the Party launched a campaign in

---

[69] Hu Yaobang, "Zai Lu Xun dansheng yibai zhounian jinian dahuishang de jianghua," p. 2.

1983), is an even better example of built-in negativity. No one (not even a Westerner) would stand up to defend *wuran*; whatever it referred to, *wuran* was clearly a bad thing. After the Beijing massacre in 1989, the Party warned against *aizibing*, "love-capitalism-disease," socking the negativity home through a pun on *aizibing*, using the same sounds but different characters to mean "AIDS."

But the denotative components of such terms were highly elusive. What tiny minority was bourgeois liberal? What exactly was the definition of the flaw? Did the labels apply only to behavior that threatened the leadership— or could, for example, a writer be guilty of bourgeois liberalism for accepting royalties? Wanting better housing? Wearing long hair? (How long?) Since at least some traces of bourgeois liberalism, "correctly" interpreted, could be found in almost anyone, the very ambiguity of a phrase like "tiny minority" made its menace ironically very broad: almost everyone had at least some incentive to play things safer. In the end, whether or not one fell within the pall of negative terms depended far less on the meanings of the terms themselves than on whether one had enemies who possessed the desire and the power to apply them.

For guidance, writers and editors could look to positive catchwords as well as negative ones. But positive terms carried the same purposeful vagueness. Writers knew, for example, that they were supposed to reflect the *benzhi* "basic nature" of socialism; but what exactly was this "basic nature," when one set pen to paper? Just as the only reliable fact about "bourgeois liberalism" was that it was bad, the only clear fact about the "basic nature" of socialism was its goodness. In the late 1950s, and again in the early 1980s, Chinese comedians were told that they should downplay satire and do more "praising" (*gesong*) of socialist society's "bright side" (*guangming-mian*). This left them spewing words to no effect—as if, as one put it, pressing the accelerator of a car that was out of gear.

With every political-literary campaign, the leadership named at least one or two concrete examples of what it deemed offensive. But these did little to clear away ambiguity. Bai Hua's "Unrequited Love" was prominently cited as "bourgeois liberal" in 1981. But what—other than just to play safer— could other writers infer from such an example? Why was "Unrequited Love" found to be in error when so many other pieces published in fall 1979 were much harder hitting and yet went uncriticized? Why did it take nearly two years for the criticism to emerge? Plainly the politically crucial factors included much more than what Bai Hua set down on paper. Speculation about the other factors dominated attention on the literary grapevine.

Vagueness also enshrouded the seriousness of offenses. If a literary work were criticized for "casting a shadow over our socialist motherland" (as happened to Chen Rong's "At Middle Age" in 1980),[70] the author could not

---

[70] Xiao Chen, "Buyao gei shenghuo mengshang yiceng yinying," p. 3. Chen Rong is also commonly spelled Shen Rong in English. Chen, from Sichuan, prefers the Shen spelling be-

know if this was a reminder to be a little more optimistic next time or an innuendo that one was anti-socialist and perhaps anti-Party. Even if a charge seemed clear when it was made, its gravity could change abruptly later on, following changes in the political-literary weather. Its seriousness also depended greatly upon who was actually making it. Top leaders were reluctant to make criticisms in their own names, preferring to serve as backstage support for someone else or, if they wrote directly, to use a pseudonym or call themselves "Commentator." So when a work was first criticized, its author would not necessarily know how powerful his or her opposition was. This ambiguity, too, served a purpose in literary control. It allowed leaders to stand behind general principles while leaving the hatchet work on particular cases to surrogates. This allowed the leader to maintain a nonhostile face before those being criticized, who could, therefore, choose to return to the leader's fold without the humiliation of capitulating to the hatchet man.

The leadership sometimes handled dilemmas in literary policy by issuing contradictory guidelines. It would warn against two undesirable extremes, vaguely defined, and leave the burden of finding a proper middle way to writers and editors. Around 1980, for example, writers were being told to "liberate thought" but also to "oppose bourgeois liberalism." From month to month the winds might shift somewhat, but the basic dilemma stayed in place, and the risk of error fell to writers and editors. The more strongly the leadership stressed both sides of contradictory guidelines, the greater was the freezing effect on all initiatives they might take. In 1983 Liu Baiyu, the major literary authority in the People's Liberation Army, used the tactic of contradictory guidelines repeatedly when he explained that China must "oppose spiritual pollution" but adopt "good things" from the West. China should also accept "healthful" works of literature and art while rejecting "unhealthful" ones, and oppose "humanism" but do nothing to stifle "expression of the inner self." "Bourgeois liberalism" must be criticized, but without relaxing our guard against "left excesses." China should "insist upon" Marxism-Leninism-Mao Zedong Thought, but "not oppose emancipation of the mind." This can be achieved in cultural policy by opposing both "lax leadership" and "indiscriminate intervention."[71]

Contradictory guidelines were said to have been a favorite device of Mao's wife Jiang Qing during her reign over Chinese literature and art in the 1970s. The following is from a 1977 comedians' dialogue:

A: If you try to go up, you can't go up; go down, you can't go down; live, you can't live; die, you can't die.

---

cause it more closely reflects actual pronunciation in Sichuan dialect. I opt for the standard Mandarin spelling not out of any disrespect for Chen, whom I have met several times and consider a friend, but from a fairness principle. If we allowed spelling changes to reflect the local dialects of all Chinese authors, it would be pretty hard to keep things straight.

[71] Zhongguo xinwenshe (China News Service), broadcast 10 November 1983; Foreign Broadcase Information Service, 14 November 1983.

B: What if I'm defiant toward her [Jiang Qing]?

A: Defiant? She'll charge you as a dyed-in-the-wool Party-hater.

B: Then I'll keep my distance from her.

A: And she'll charge you with lack of feeling for the Party.

B: I'll be formally correct but stay noncommittal.

A: She'll charge you with an unsteady class standpoint.

B: Then I have to go over to her side!

A: And she'll charge you with pressuring her—making counterrevolution!

B: Gee! How'm I supposed to live?[72]

Even if a writer could find exactly the safest position at the center of various countervailing forces, there was no guarantee that this optimal position would remain the same over time. It shifted, by large or small margins, almost constantly. In a popular 1979 play called *The First Flower of Spring*, the Party secretary in a factory is trying to implement the new policy of judging workers on performance, not class background. But his deputy secretary advises caution: even if we feel the new policy is right, isn't it better not to be too active about it? What if another Gang of Four were to come along?[73] Complete safety was impossible even for those whose only goal was to fit Party policy.

The resulting self-censorship in the Chinese system was, in general, more effective than the explicit editorial censorship that was used in places like wartime Japan. (Soviet and East European cases fall between the Chinese and Japanese examples in this regard.) The Chinese system was, first, more extensive in its reach. When the blocking mechanism of censorship is based on personal fear, is shrouded in vagueness, and operates inside the minds of writers, it suffocates many things, even beyond what safety would require if guidelines were more external and clear. In 1986, Liu Binyan commented that Chinese writers normally used only about 30 percent of the freedom they actually had; their reluctance to use the other 70 percent was born of self-protective conservatism.[74] A second strength of the Chinese system was its invisibility. There were no blacked-out characters, no blank pages, no news stories about rifled files—in short, no external signs of any kind that the leadership was suppressing dissent. Everyone concerned knew that suppression was in fact going on, and in this sense no one was fooled. But the surface appearances were very important, anyway. They allowed the leadership to maintain face on the stage of Chinese politics, and propriety at this level remained important to political power. In China, the prestige of the leadership fell whenever it had to acknowledge explicitly that it was silencing its critics—or even that it had any critics, other than hostile foreigners.

Together with the mechanics of suppressing dissent, therefore, we should

---

[72] Ma Ji and Tang Jiezhong, *Baigujing xianxingji.*

[73] Cui Dezhi, "Baochunhua."

[74] Liu Binyan, oral statement at the International Conference on Contemporary Chinese Literature, Shanghai, 4–6 November 1986.

note the closely related mechanics of how the leadership preserved its face. Here a basic device was euphemism. The leadership's commands and prohibitions were too unseemly to be stated bluntly in public. Since writers and editors understood the leadership's codes quite well, the great advantage of a euphemism was that it could communicate a command even while supporting the fiction that it was not a command. In 1980, for example, writers throughout China were asked to "consider the social effects" of what they wrote. "Social effects" meant influences on readers. But writers and editors also knew that the slogan was not a call for serious inquiry into the opinions and behavior of readers. Its real point was to direct attention in exactly the opposite direction: toward the leadership, not the readership. The message was not "consider what readers think" but "pay more attention to what we want readers to think." The immediate target of the policy was not "social effects" so much as the motives of writers.[75] Similarly, the frequent admonition that writers emphasize "the bright side" of life meant—as they well knew—that they should show the Party to be doing well and should create more heroes to represent the Party and its policies. When writers portrayed heroes who struggled against Party leadership (as Liu Binyan sometimes did, albeit only against local, "misguided" Party leaders),[76] these heroes did not count as "the bright side," and portraying them could draw serious criticism. Writers and editors were not at liberty to expose official euphemisms. They were integral parts of the power system, and the costs of violating the rules for their use were similar to those for violating other policies.

We have seen how the leadership claimed to represent "the masses" in order to make dissenters feel isolated. The same device had the advantage of describing Party power euphemistically. By cloaking itself in the masses' mantle, the leadership could claim the selfless motive of serving the people rather than the actual one of protecting its own power. For example, in the winter of 1980, when the top leadership decided that scar literature had served its purpose of discrediting the Gang-of-Four leadership and was now beginning to undermine its own rule, the central Propaganda Department sent word down its hierarchy that the masses were getting tired of baleful tales and wanted more writing about heroes of the Four Modernizations. But to judge from all available direct evidence of popular preferences (see chapter 5), no such shift actually occurred.

When it wanted to, the leadership could summon "all the masses" to produce artistic criticism of laughable precision. For example, in early 1980 a large mural painting by Yuan Yunsheng called "Water-Sprinkling Festival:

[75] Liu Baiyu acknowledged this quite clearly in an interview, 11 August 1980, Beijing. See also Wang Ruowang, "'Yuyong . . .' zhi lei," p. 59.

[76] Liu Binyan's "People or Monsters?," widely regarded by supporters and opponents alike as purely a revelation of the "dark side" of society, in fact includes a section called "Little Guys Do Some Big Things" that praises two common people who courageously stand up for what is right. (See Liu Binyan, *People or Monsters?*, pp. 56–62.)

An Ode to Life" was unveiled in a dining room of the Beijing airport. A panoramic depiction of a festival of the Dai minority people, the painting showed, in one of its corners, two nude female figures bathing. A debate ensued over whether the nudes should remain, and the question apparently could not be resolved until it went to high levels in the leadership. Eventually an order came down directing that a small curtain be placed in front of the offending corner of the mural. But the publicly stated reason for this action was not that high officials had objected; it was that the "Dai masses" were upset. The announcement did not explain how any of the Dai masses could have gained access to this dining room, where only foreigners and very privileged Chinese were allowed to go.[77] It was not necessary to claim that one of them had, somehow, wandered in and suddenly been shocked. No competent reader of the Chinese press needed to be told that the invocation of "mass opinion" was a debating tactic, not a report of fact.

Another common use of euphemism was to charge a writer or artist with an offense other than the one that really mattered. The advantage of this tactic was that it could censor an offensive viewpoint without drawing increased public attention to it. The more truth a viewpoint contained, the more important it was to draw attention elsewhere. For example, the artists who did the 1979 cartoon strip "Maple" broke far into "forbidden territory" when they depicted Cultural Revolution violence in a series of unambiguous realist paintings. Even more provocatively, they implicated Mao Zedong by including posters of his beaming visage over scenes of shocking cruelty. But the official criticism of their work did not mention these affronts. It said they had portrayed Jiang Qing and Lin Biao too realistically. Lin Biao and the Gang of Four, in those years, were always supposed to be omitted from pictures or otherwise "uglified" (*chouhua*). Doesn't the realistic portrayal of ultraleftists, the criticism asked rhetorically, imply secret support for the ultraleftist line?[78] This criticism not only obscured the real issue; it turned it on its head. The cartoon strip was spectacular precisely for its bold attack on the ultraleft; and it was the Deng Xiaoping leadership who felt that anti-Mao sentiment had to be kept within limits. But rather than to acknowledge the actual situation, the leadership preferred to turn things around and accuse the cartoonists of supporting the ultraleft. The red herring did not confuse other Chinese artists and writers, however; they knew the codes. Seven months later, the play "What If I Really Were?" (see pp. 23, above) was criticized for encouraging youth to sympathize with a deceitful impersonator, a "swindler." But this work, far from glorifying deceit, was satirizing it. The play's whole point, which could hardly have been more colorfully portrayed, is to denounce the deceit, bribery, sycophancy, and string-pulling not of the impersonator but of the official circles he moves in. Yet viewed against its own goals, the official critics' emphasis on the

---

[77] See Chang Er, "Beijing jichang bihua de fengbo."
[78] *Lianhuan huabao* bianjibu, "Guanyu lianhuanhua'Feng' de zuotanhui fayan jilu," p. 17.

swindler was brilliant. It drew attention away from the sore point—the play's devastation of officialdom's face—and toward an issue where the leadership had not only face but the upper hand. Sympathize with a trickster? Socialist China may have its problems, but we need socialist solutions, not bourgeois-individualist ones.[79]

Recognizing the leadership's jealous regard for "face" and the dangers of challenging it, writers often attacked by indirection, buffering their criticisms with a layer of what American politicians sometimes call "deniability." This indirection had the added benefit of allowing people who shared a fairly widespread but forbidden view to signal—in public but in code—their tacit comradeship. An example is the use of code names in poems at the 1976 Tiananmen demonstrations to refer to unnameable villains. Jiang Qing was a "clear river" (*qing jiang*), "green duckweed" (*qing ping*, suggestive of her 1930s stage-name Lan Ping, "blue duckweed"), or a "demon" (*jing*) of various sorts; her associates Yao Wenyuan and Zhang Chunqiao could be a "shaking bridge" (*yaoqiao*) and other things.

Authors could also use indirection to make criticisms that they supposed were accurate but could not stand behind in formal terms; or ones that, although known to be defensible, might come too close to incurring counterattack. Chen Dengke's allegations about Lin Biao in the novel *Record of the Broken Wall* (1980),[80] and Duanmu Hongliang's attacks on Jiang Qing in a television drama called "Dawn Bugle on a Frosty Day,"[81] are examples. Both were attacks on people who were already officially public enemies, but the authors still found it advisable to present their detailed allegations as "creative work."

Such protection of the leadership's face depended upon separating the leader's public persona from his or her private motives. Maintaining appearances mattered even when private opinions varied widely. In extreme cases, in order to maintain the face-enhancing appearance of balance, leaders emphasized in public points to which they were opposed behind the scenes. Thus Deng Liqun, a major supporter of the "Oppose Spiritual Pollution Campaign" in fall 1983, made public statements in early 1984 announcing the campaign's end. Hu Qiaomu, another leading opponent of Western cultural "pollution," received a delegation of American writers in May 1984. Conversely, Hu Yaobang, known as champion of reform in the mid-1980s, and Chen Huangmei, a propaganda official widely appreciated for his be-

---

[79] Many critics voiced this line in the spring of 1980, after Hu Yaobang first broached it at a closed high-level conference in February. See "Zai juben chuangzuo zuotanhuishang de jianghua," p. 42. One of the most important statements was Chen Yong, "Cong liangge juben kan wenyi de zhenshixing he qingxiangxing." It is noteworthy that, despite the critics' charge, "What If I Really Were?" never suggests that its protagonist's deceit is a solution to the social problem of corruption. Even as a way out for an individual, it is presented as a forbiddingly hazardous strategm, because in the end—and Chinese audiences always look to the end for the lesson—the young trickster is crushed.

[80] Chen Dengke and Xiao Ma, *Pobiji*.

[81] *Shuangtian xiaojiao* (Dawn bugle on a frosty day), Guangzhou dianshi, 20 March 1980.

hind-the-scenes protection of writers, both delivered a number of conservative public speeches on literature and art through the mid-1980s. Feng Mu, a senior official widely known for his relatively liberal outlook, undertook to criticize Huang Weizong, a scholar at Zhongshan University in Guangzhou who tried to promote "socialist critical realism" as a way of defending free literary expression. Feng argued that regular socialist realism, without the word "critical," already allowed for reflection of both the positive and negative sides of society, and that therefore no bold new "ism" was necessary; but his real purpose, apparently, was to adopt a conservative-leaning public stance so that he would have more credibility to spend when he tried to protect liberal-minded writers and editors.[82]

The distinction between public presentations of policy and the actual positions of leaders was institutionalized in the system of "internal" (classified) reports. In the public media, policies were reported in ways that made the leadership look as good as possible, whereas in internal reports editors and publishers received more candid guidelines. For example, when Bai Hua was criticized in 1981, and Liu Binyan in 1987, officials were quick to make the point publicly that the two writers remained in their jobs and free to write. In reality, though, no Chinese publisher at those times would dare to print anything by Bai Hua or Liu Binyan short of a self-criticism or, perhaps, an innocuous piece whose publication would be tantamount to surrender. There were several levels in the internal-report system, and sometimes different shades of literary policy appeared at more than two levels. In late 1983, Party policy toward Ba Jin, the senior novelist who had gained wide respect for his probing essays in the late 1970s, was to treat him in the public media as a grand old man of Chinese letters; at the first internal level, accessible to most editors, the word was that his virtues should not be magnified; at a still more internal level, Party propaganda officials were told that he should be actively deemphasized, and references to him avoided.

The distance between public presentations and actual goings-on also made it possible to prettify the silencing of writers. In September 1981, Hu Yaobang praised the Party's "tradition of criticism" and stated that although writers have their freedom to write, they must also accept the critic's freedom to criticize.[83] Such a formulation, casting the two kinds of "rights" as equal and parallel, had the surface impression of even-handedness, and thus helped maintain face for the leadership when it announced unpopular crackdowns. In practice, as everyone knew, the two "rights" were not parallel at all.

---

[82] Feng Mu, "Jianchi geming de xianshizhuyi."

[83] Hu Yaobang, "Zai Lu Xun dansheng yibai zhounian jinian dahuishang de jianghua." In "Lun dang de xinwen gongzuo" Hu also says, referring to the control function of the Party committee on editorial boards that "writers can never use their own freedom to deprive the editorial board of freedom."

Psychological pressures based on the manipulation of language and fear were the primary means of literary control in socialist China, but they were not the only ones. There were blunter means that utilized legal, economic, and physical barriers. The tactic of bureaucratic stonewalling, for example, is well illustrated in the way the unofficial Guangzhou literary magazine *The Voice of the People* was suppressed in 1979. In March, the magazine's editors, seeking to comply with a long-ignored Publications Registry Law that had been passed in 1951, hand-delivered applications for registration to the municipal and provincial Party committees. Hearing no answer after several months, they decided to announce in December their intention to sell copies on the street. A provincial official promptly informed them that they could not do so, explaining that their application in March was void because it had been misaddressed; it should have gone to the Provincial Publications Bureau. On December 11, the editors went to this bureau and were told they had come to the wrong place. Ten days later, after more inquiries, they returned to the same bureau and were told that, yes, this actually was the correct place, but applications must be submitted in writing. The editors submitted a written application on December 22. By January 12, having no reply, they went to enquire and were told that the application was insufficiently detailed; moreover, since they were going to do their own printing, they would need to apply to the Control Bureau of the Industrial and Commercial Administration for a permit to enter the printing business. Two private shops would need to serve as guarantors for this purpose. When the editors pointed out that private shops did not exist as they had in 1951, the reply was that the 1951 law had not been superseded, and therefore was still in effect.[84]

In 1981, the Guangzhou student literary magazine *Red Bean* was closed down by a ruling that acknowledged its right to exist but denied it the right to be sold in public, either on the streets or by mail subscription. *This Generation*, another student magazine, saw only half of its first issue reach print after authorities intervened directly with the printing shop. "For reasons that everyone can guess and comprehend," wrote the editors in an open letter to readers, "our printers have suddenly had to stop, and this publication of student literary exercises can reach its readers only in this crippled and incomplete form."[85] Three months later Deng Xiaoping, in a major address, reinforced the correctness of cutting off access to printing as a means of curtailing unofficial publications: "It is absolutely forbidden for a

---

[84] *Renmin zhi sheng* bianjibu, "Guangzhou 'Renmin zhi sheng' bianjibu shengming." In 1980 the conservative critic Liu Baiyu was advocating a national "publications law" that would require registry of all publications and provide Party leaders with the power to withdraw licenses in order to terminate "harmful" publications; interview, 11 August 1980, Beijing.

[85] "Gao duzhe shu" (Notice to readers), inside front cover of *Zheiyidai*, issue 1.

Party member to peddle notions like freedom of speech, freedom of the press, or freedom of assembly if these are extended to counterrevolutionaries. . . . How, for example, did some of those secret publications get printed so prettily? Where did they get their paper? Who did the printing? Don't tell me those people have their own printing presses!"[86]

When paper was in short supply, as it often was, its rationing provided authorities with another tool for literary control. All official publications in China were subject to the scrutiny of the State Publications Administration (SPA), a bureaucracy with several planning and review functions, one of which was to allocate paper. Individual publishers could try to supplement their allocations through informal arrangements with paper mills or through barter with other publishers, but the size of the state allocation was still crucial. The leverage of the SPA was diffuse. It could not withhold paper specifically for one or two offensive works, because its annual allocations were done in response to overall yearly plans submitted by the publishers. But it could assign a paltry allocation of paper to a publisher whose plan contained too many objectionable items. From the perspective of a liberal-minded publisher, the same trade-off meant that provocative pieces could be included in a plan so long as they were properly balanced by more orthodox works.

The SPA's paper came in different grades at different prices, and this fact could introduce a financial component into the question of allocation. In 1980, the SPA was allocating two kinds of paper, one priced at 1,500 yuan per ton and the other at 1,350 yuan per ton. Since the difference in quality was very slight, publishers preferred the lower-priced paper. This gave the SPA financial leverage when it determined the mix of the two grades that each publisher would receive. Because the "responsibility system" that began around 1980 required publishers to be increasingly self-sufficient, finances were tight and even small price differences could, at the margins, have a surprising impact. For example the Guangdong People's Publishing House (Guangdong renmin chubanshe), beginning in 1980, adopted a policy of returning 15 percent of its profits to staff as bonuses. In the first year everyone received a bonus of 400 yuan; in the next year, after Guangdong had to buy paper from neighboring Hunan Province, the bonus fell to only 6 yuan per person.

Although the SPA did not have line-item censorial powers over the annual plans of publishers, it did have the power to prohibit the sale of a particular book or magazine after it had been produced. Financially, this was the H-bomb of pressures on publishers. It threatened a loss equivalent to the entire cost of producing the problematic issue. Again, the controversial cartoon strip "Maple" provides a good example. It appeared in the August 1979 issue of the magazine *Cartoon Strips*, which had already been printed and sent to the Post Office for distribution when the SPA suddenly

---

[86] Deng Xiaoping, *Muqian de xingshi he renwu*, p. 20.

announced on the morning of 8 August that it was forbidding sales, effective immediately.[87] Expressing "astonishment" that must have been based in panic, the editors immediately appealed to the Central Propaganda Department, where the decision went all the way to its chief, Hu Yaobang. Two days later Hu decided in *Cartoon Strips'* favor and disaster was averted. But decisions could go the other way, too. One year later, the entire August issue of *Hebei Literature and Art* (*Hebei wenyi*) had to be destroyed because of a story—whose content has never been revealed—called "The First Secretary of the Provincial Party Committee."[88] More than 100,000 copies of the issue had already been printed, representing a financial loss of about 20,000 yuan for paper alone.

The risk of "execution"—as the sudden ban of a finished product was popularly called—was especially serious in the case of film. When a literary work was executed the monetary losses, including the time of author and editor, ranged in the 10,000s of yuan at most. Producers of drama could also alter their shows, or entirely dismantle them, with losses in the same range.[89] But a finished film was more costly. When the 1980 film *In a Twinkling* (*Shun jian*) was banned, the losses to its producers reached about one million yuan. However tiny an amount in Hollywood, in socialist China this was an equivalent of about eight hundred person-years in salaries.[90] For filmmakers, the specter of such losses loomed from the outset as another powerful reason—besides the normal political punishments—for exercising self-censorship.[91]

In addition, the Propaganda Department watched film considerably more closely than it did printed literature. Provocative stories could, with local support, be slipped into provincial journals, where central authorities might not notice or care much. But the audience impact of film was different and clearly worried the leadership more. The film audience was, first, especially large; it included the literary readership plus large urban (and sometimes rural) groups who read little or no literature.[92] Moreover, the effect of film on audiences was more potentially volatile. People read fiction singly, separately, and usually in private places, but film viewers congregated in the hundreds or even thousands, exchanged views during and after showings, and thus could more easily generate trends in public attitudes. Film was, as an authoritative "commentator" in the Party's journal *Red Flag* put it, the cultural artifact "closest to the masses."[93] It had to be watched.

[87] *Lianhuanhuabao* bianjibu, "Guanyu lianhuanhua 'Feng' de zuotanhui fayan jilu," pp. 2, 32.

[88] Luo Rujia, "Jiujing shei 'chouhua' Zhonggong?," p. 57.

[89] Interview with Sha Yexin, Los Angeles, 24 November 1986.

[90] Luo Rujia, "Jiujing shei 'chouhua' Zhonggong?," p. 57.

[91] For leading filmmakers, whose reputations were international, this fear abated in the late 1980s, as overseas royalties became reliable. By the early 1990s, films such as Chen Kaige's *Farewell, My Concubine* and Tian Zhuangzhuang's *The Blue Kite* actually benefitted from Chinese government bans, which only increased overseas interest.

[92] See chapter 5 for a discussion of film audience versus literary readership.

[93] Chen Bo, "Dianying yao wei jianshe shehuizhuyi jingshen wenming zuochu gongxian."

Whereas decisions to publish literary works were made at local editorial boards and approved, if necessary, at municipal or provincial Propaganda Departments, films had to be referred to central authorities in Beijing. Like literary writers and editors, filmmakers would do what they could in advance to calculate their risks, find backstage support, and weigh their opposition. But it remained the case that only a finished film could elicit a final answer, and only large investments could produce a finished film. The high stakes of this gamble were compounded by the idiosyncratic nature of judgments that sometimes came down from the top. When a film was politically sensitive, the question of approval could be passed from level to level in the central bureaucracies until it reached a high-ranking leader who had only casual knowledge of the film world and no time to give more than a personal reaction to one viewing of the film. Informally, intellectuals exchanged anecdotes about the ways in which the leadership and its propaganda officials could misunderstand films. Liu Binyan observed that novelists should consider it their good luck that top leaders, while finding time for television and film, almost never read books.[94]

The casual opinions of top leaders could have great power. In 1986, the provocative film *The Black Cannon Incident* (*Heipao shijian*) was under a cloud of suspicion, and not widely shown, until word suddenly spread that Hu Yaobang had seen it and had nodded his approval; theaters across China began to show the film, but then word spread that Hu Qiaomu had seen it and had shaken his head no, whereupon many theater managers reversed themselves again. Top leaders themselves sometimes commented on their inadequacy as instant critics. In a major address to China's filmmakers in 1982, Hu Qiaomu opened with the self-effacing admission that "I am quite unacquainted with the film world, and have seen very few films. . . . Recently, when comrade Hu Yaobang invited me to come and meet with you, I felt both happy and honored, and so rushed out a few evenings to watch films. Of course, I still didn't get to see very many."[95] Hu's reticence was not, however, so great as to impede his delivery of the rest of his lengthy, authoritative discussion of basic principles. Two years later, in July 1984, Hu Yaobang issued his own tersely worded directive "to abolish the practice of letting a single person arbitrarily decide whether a film can be screened publicly or not."[96] But after two more years, during the imbroglio over *The Black Cannon Incident* in 1986, the two Hus again found themselves making personal and arbitrary decisions.

---

[94] A milder version of this observation appears in Liu Binyan, "Tan xin shiqi de wenxue chuangzuo wenti," p. 15.

[95] Hu Qiaomu, "Zai huijian quanguo gushipian dianying chuangzuo huiyi daibiao shi de jianghua," p. 6.

[96] Hu Yaobang, "Guanyu dianying de pishi."

SOVIET COMPARISONS

There were strong similarities in the methods of literary control between socialist China and the Soviet Union. Some of these arose from China's borrowing of the Soviet model in the early 1950s, but others seem, more basically, to have been parallel outgrowths of strongly similar situations: authoritarian regimes with activist agendas seeking to use writers as intermediaries in guiding the thought of reading publics. Some of the differences between the two systems, such as the greater Chinese emphasis on the connection between "face" and political power, seem to reflect cultural predispositions. Other differences had more to do with the differing personalities of the men who ruled.

There were similarities, first, in the kinds of writing that rulers sought to control. In both countries, leaders found that exposure of "the dark side" of society threatened their sense of security. Hence bearers of bad news themselves became bad news. Writers learned that, if they did reveal problems, they were expected to present them as anomalies that were either limited to unusual times and places or attributable to declining residual influences (of the bourgeoisie, the Gang of Four, or the like).[97] In both countries, this principle generated conflicts with writers, who often wanted precisely to reveal systemic problems. A 1956 Soviet poem called "The Three Portraits" by S. Mikhalov expresses frustration at having to reflect only "the bright side": three painters are charged with doing portraits of "The Great Khan" (Stalin), who had a deformed left arm and pockmarks. The first painter, a "varnisher of reality," covers the blemishes, but the Khan is angry: "That is not me!" The second, a "naturalist," shows the defects: "This is a base and cunning plot directed against me!" The third, a "socialist realist," paints a profile, thus showing the good side while hiding the bad. The Khan is pleased.[98] In both China and the Soviet Union, writers who failed to maintain "balance" between the bright and dark sides of life could be criticized. Just as Daniel Granin was faulted for not showing "a single ray of hope," or any positive character, in his story "One's Own Opinion,"[99] Liu Binyan's stories and reportage were criticized for omission of the upbeat endings, or "bright tails," that other writers used.[100]

[97] George Gibian, "Soviet Literature during the Thaw," pp. 135–36; Swayze, *Political Control*, pp. 162–163.

[98] Translated in McLean and Vickery, *The Year of Protest*, pp. 120–21.

[99] Swayze, *Political Control*, p. 164.

[100] "Bright tails" are not entirely attributable to state control of literature. They have roots in traditional Chinese storytelling, where endings were conventionally uplifting, through either happy outcomes or didactic moralizing. In a broader context, one can also argue that artificiality of ending is a somewhat inevitable feature of the fictional form. E. M. Forster, speaking of Western fiction only, observes that "nearly all novels are feeble at the end ... because the plot requires to be wound up" (*Aspects of the Novel*, p. 91). Chen Rong's "Ren dao zhong-

In both societies leaders also feared unclear messages. During the post-Mao relaxation, Chinese authorities were leery of the "misty" poetry and other literary modernism that cropped up. What was the poet Gu Cheng really saying in a poem like "Feeling"?

> The sky is gray
> The road is gray
> The building is gray
> The rain is gray
>
> In this blanket of dead gray
> Two children walk by,
> One bright red
> One pale green.[101]

Soviet leaders were equally bothered by oblique expression. It seemed to undermine socialist realism, Stalin's reliable formula for advancing society and protecting Soviet power. Harold Swayze has observed that "true creativeness implicitly threatens a doctrine [socialist realism] which, in spite of its dynamic appearance, is deeply conservative and inflexible in its hostility toward the undetermined, the uncertain, the inexplicable."[102] Put more bluntly by Victor Erlich, "It is difficult to control what you don't understand."[103] China's "misty" poems, even when they bore no encoded political messages (as they usually did not), still implied an important political statement: that there could be a domain in which private thought and morality operate beyond the reach of the state's system. Nikolai Pogodin gave explicit voice to this principle in his play *Petrarch's Sonnet*, which ends with a plea for "certain intimate sides to life" that a person need "not reveal to anyone."[104] In both the Soviet Union and China, to recognize private autonomy was to challenge the hegemonic claims of the control system, within which every public thought had to be either "correct" or refutable. Enigmatic literary expression introduced the neither-correct-nor-refutable, an inconvenient category that not only seemed to clear a space within which encoded dissidence might grow but also, simply by existing, undermined the control system's claim to definitiveness.

---

nian," which appeared during the high tide of scar literature, ends when the heroine, after nearly dying from a heart attack brought on by overwork and mistreatment, walks unsteadily, but in the sunshine, down hospital steps and into an automobile specially despatched for her by the leadership. This "bright ending" displeased many readers, who saw in it the heavy hand of literary control. But Chen Rong (interview, 7 August 1980, Beijing) said that her conception of the ending had nothing to do with external pressures and was exactly what she herself wanted to write.

[101] Gu Cheng, "Ganjue," in Link, *Stubborn Weeds*, p. 185.
[102] Swayze, *Political Control*, p. 23.
[103] Erlich, "Post-Stalin Trends in Russian Literature," p. 414.
[104] Quoted in Swayze, *Political Control*, pp. 176–77.

For this reason, ironically, the *silence* of writers could sometimes be annoying to political authorities. In 1957, in response to a tightening of pressure on them, Russian writers protested by organizing a boycott of speech. Party officials, wanting to strike back but lacking concrete statements of which to disapprove, were nonplussed. One wrote, "It is well known that in music a pause sometimes expresses greater feeling and thought than a melody or chord. Hence your silence is dangerous. It disorients readers. What does it mean? What does it indicate? A haughty disregard for the opinions of others? A disdainful conviction of one's own infallibility? An insulting 'however could you hope to understand me'? The drama of sacrifice? Just what *does* this silence signify?"[105] Writers in socialist China never organized the same kind of collective "vow of silence"; this would have been a more explicit form of dissidence than they were accustomed to, or than their system allowed. But, somewhat like writers during the Hungarian rising of 1956, who were accused of "the heroism of silence," Chinese writers sometimes acted individually, or in purely tacit concert, to use silence as a expressive tool. Using the metaphor of physical health for political mood, they sometimes withdrew for a hospital stay or "convalescence" at home. ("I'm not feeling well" could be a richly ambiguous phrase.) When several acted at the same time, they could establish an atmosphere of "nonverbal nonsupport" for unpleasant cultural policies. During the "spiritual pollution" campaign in fall 1983, for example, it was well noticed in literary circles who did or did not *biaotai*, or "take a stand," in favor of the government's position. Many did not. Among those who did, there were gradations in how significant the act was. If one were obliged to support the policy (perhaps because of one's job as a chief editor or cultural official), the act could seem partly pro forma. Feng Mu, as head of the Writers' Association, could not easily stay on the sidelines; but Ding Ling, who could, decided to "take her stand" anyway, and thus actually invested more of her prestige in the government's campaign than did Feng Mu, who was an official. It also mattered how one took a stand. Wang Meng and Cao Yu both chose to denounce "spiritual pollution" when they could have avoided it; but Wang Meng coupled his stand with a reaffirmation of the "hundred flowers" principle, whereas Cao Yu did not. Among those who refused to "take a stand," there were also gradations in how significant the silence was. The more one was in the spotlight because of position or reputation, the louder would be one's silence. Because silent dissent was admired, there was, among some, a subtle competition to see whose closed mouth could be most obvious.

The methods of control in the Chinese and Soviet systems were also similar in several ways. Both clothed the censoring power in the garb of beneficent paternalism. Like the Chinese, the Soviet leadership presented itself as knowing what was good for the reading masses better than they themselves could know it. It followed that any writer or editor who ques-

[105] Quoted ibid., p. 193.

tioned or opposed directives from above must have ill intentions. As in China, but to a lesser extent, medical metaphors like "healthful" and "poisonous" buttressed these assumptions. "Criticism from below?—that's poison. From above?—that's medicine!" noted the Soviet poet Vladimir Mayakovsky during the post-Stalin thaw.[106] For writers and editors seeking to find ways into print for their more challenging works, the building of "backstage" alliances with like-minded leaders was a feature of the Soviet system as well as the Chinese.[107] In both cases, a few prominent writers were able to survive through top-level connections.

But the most striking technical similarity in the two control systems is probably the political-literary campaign, certain features of which China learned from the Soviet Union. Chinese campaigns, from those against Hu Feng and Ding Ling in the mid-1950s to those against Bai Hua in the early 1980s, resembled Soviet prototypes—such as the attacks on Boris Pilnyak and Evgeni Zamyatin in 1929 and on Mikhail Zoshchenko and Anna Akhmatova in 1946—in a number of ways.[108] In both countries, literary campaigns were used to signal political shifts; in both, the errors of targeted persons were less important per se than as negative examples for others; and, in both, the victims were encouraged to assist in the propaganda efforts by contributing "self-criticisms." In both cases campaign rhetoric sought to isolate the targets of attack. Just as followers of Bai Hua were "a tiny minority," so "the whole Soviet public" was indignant at Zoshchenko and Akhmatova;[109] consequently, in both cases, all writers and editors felt pressure to side with the "majority" and perhaps even join in denouncing the victims. The risk of resisting such pressures, in both cases, included vulnerability to guilt by association. Political taints could last a long time, even reemerging after they had seemed to disappear: Zoshchenko was attacked in 1946 for his associations in the early 1920s; the Chinese playwright Xia Yan was attacked in 1967 under a group epithet that had been invented in the 1930s.[110] Political taint could be potent even in times of thaw, as Soviet writers found in 1956 when Khrushchev tied them to the "anti-Party" leaders Shepilov and Kaganovich.[111] In both countries, an important and widespread effect of the political-literary campaign was to frighten writers and editors into curbing themselves.[112]

On the whole, though, the role of self-censorship was smaller in the So-

---

[106] Quoted ibid., p. 82.

[107] Dina Spechler, *Permitted Dissent in the USSR*, pp. 4–5.

[108] Hayward, "Introduction" to Hayward and Labedz, *Literature and Revolution in Soviet Russia*, pp. xi–xii; Swayze, *Political Control*, p. 38; McLean and Vickery, *The Year of Protest*, pp. 12–13.

[109] McLean and Vickery, *The Year of Protest*, p. 13.

[110] "Si tiao hanzi" ("the four guys") also included Zhou Yang, Tian Han, and Yang Hansheng. See Goldman, *China's Intellectuals*, pp. 74–76, 126.

[111] Gibian, *Interval of Freedom*, p. 20.

[112] Spechler, *Permitted Dissent*, chap. 3; Alan J. Schwartz, "The State of Publishing, Censorship, and Copyright in the Soviet Union," p. 34.

viet Union than in China because of certain more bureaucratic and explicit features of the Soviet system. The official route that a manuscript had to travel in order to pick up approvals for publication was more standardized in the Soviet case.[113] The Soviet Writers' Union, according to some sources, played a role in censorship that went considerably beyond that of the Chinese Writers' Association, which at most offered prudential advice to writers and editors.[114] The role of the Soviet KGB as "the highest rung in the publication process" was far more overt than that of the Chinese secret police.[115] In a public denunciation of Ilya Ehrenburg, Khrushchev once threatened to cite KGB archives, thereby reminding all listeners how these records could be tapped at any time;[116] in China such an explicit reference by a top leader would have been shocking. But the clearest examples of the more bureaucratic and overt Soviet style in literary control can be seen in the functioning of the Chief Administration for the Preservation of State Secrets in the Press, or Glavlit for short.

This bureaucracy, which had about 70,000 employees working under an elite corps of supercensors, had at its disposal large handbooks that were periodically updated, and that made clear which topics and even which specific phrases were out of bounds. Officials in the system reviewed and controlled all literary publication in two basic stages.[117] First, most editorial boards included a Glavlit person who did in-house checking. Second, after an issue was prepared, but before printing, it was sent for review to a Glavlit office, where it stayed for a few weeks or even months. (In China, at some times and places, this second censorial function had a parallel in the sending of edited issues for approval to local offices of the Propaganda Department. But the practice was less systematic in China. It was more important when "sensitive" works were involved, it usually did not take weeks or months, and it frequently did not occur at all.)

In general, the Soviet review process was both more overt and more cumbersome than the Chinese. It made conflicts formal and explicit that in China were, comparatively speaking, more confined to the private calculations of individuals. Whereas Soviet writers could get relatively clear-cut (even if distasteful) answers from Glavlit, Chinese writers were routinely left to judge the "wind direction" for themselves, relying on resources in their own situations and personal networks. What the Chinese control system

[113] The steps have been analyzed into (excessively?) neat hierarchical order in Edith R. Frankel, *Novy Mir*, p. 188, note 57; see also chap. 6, pp. 122–41.

[114] George Gibian calls the Soviet Writers' Union "the Party's main means of controlling authors" (*Interval of Freedom*, pp. 11–12, note). Edith Frankel, on the other hand, attributes a considerably smaller control function to the Writers' Union, calling it "comradely criticism" (*Novy Mir*, p. 138).

[115] Frankel, *Novy Mir*, p. 140.

[116] Johnson, *Khrushchev and the Arts*, p. 25.

[117] On Glavlit, see Frankel, *Novy Mir*, pp. 127–41; Schwartz, "The State of Publishing," pp. 32–37, especially p. 33; and Maurice Friedberg, "Soviet Books, Censors, and Readers" p. 198.

lost in explicitness was more than compensated by the two big advantages of vagueness which, as we have seen, were to magnify the inducement for writers to censor themselves and to provide officials with the flexibility to apply rules arbitrarily. The difference was only of degree, however. Self-censorship based on fear of the unpredictable was an important feature of the Soviet system, as well.

The Chinese and Soviet systems also differed somewhat in the way they used financial threats to control literature and art. Because Glavlit guidelines were fairly accessible and moderately reliable, Soviet writers and artists could get a sense in advance of whether their initiatives might be approved. Hence the danger of investing time and money only to see a finished work suffer "execution" was not as great as in China. In the Soviet case, a more common financial threat was direct cut-off of funds. Khrushchev claimed several times that the state was "wasting" money on cultural activities. After viewing an exhibition of abstract art in Moscow in 1956, he forthrightly declared that "we aren't going to spend a kopeck on this dog shit" and that the artists can go "cut trees until you've paid back the money the state has spent on you."[118]

Such colorful bluntness could also be found among Chinese leaders, especially Mao, but only in private. To speak or write publicly in this way would be too costly to a leader's public face, and hence power. This difference in cultural styles also helps to explain why literary dissent, when tolerated at all, was allowed to be more overt in the Soviet Union than in China. Although Khrushchev might rail openly at artists, he was also ready, within limits, to let them register public complaints. Thus Vladimir Dudintsev, the author of *Not by Bread Alone*, in 1957 could stand up in a public meeting and openly rebut official charges against him;[119] a few years later Valentin Ovechkin, the writer of reportage who had inspired China's Liu Binyan, even criticized Khrushchev personally in public;[120] an editor of *Novy Mir* could threaten to bring his case to court;[121] artists could openly hoot an official off stage for his record under Stalin;[122] Ilya Ehrenburg could face down a vicious verbal attack and then, while still inside the Kremlin room where the attack had occurred, remark to some young people that "I shall never see the flourishing of Soviet arts, but you will—after twenty years."[123] The explicitness of literary dissent in the Soviet Union's Khrushchev era went well beyond what was possible in Deng's China.

Writers in the Khrushchev era were also more fearless and overt in their

---

[118] Nikita Khrushchev, "Remarks at the Manezh," pp. 101–5 in Johnson, *Khrushchev and the Arts*, p. 103.

[119] McLean and Vickery, *The Year of Protest*, p. 159.

[120] Johnson, *Khrushchev and the Arts*, p. 49. Ovechkin's act may have had severe costs, however, as his subsequent attempt at suicide suggests.

[121] Swayze, *Political Control*, p. 189.

[122] Johnson, *Khrushchev and the Arts*, p. 7.

[123] Ibid., p. 23.

choice of publishing outlets than were their counterparts in Deng's China. They concentrated their literary bombshells in a few places, namely, the journal *Novy Mir* and two large anthologies called *Literary Moscow*; their conservative opposition also centered in one main outlet, the journal *October*.[124] If this situation resembled trench warfare, Chinese dissenters looked more like guerrillas: mobile, deft, carrying small weapons. They used ambiguous language and published from time to time in several places, availing themselves of sympathetic editors who themselves were involved in precarious balancing acts.

In both China and the Soviet Union, literary dissent increased the consternation of the leadership when it caught the notice of foreigners. Khrushchev found it appropriate to threaten banishment to the West as a means of controlling writers. "Do you want to go abroad?" he asked some artists in 1956.[125] "Go on, then; we will take you as far as the border. Live out there in the 'free world.'" It was not until the early 1990s that the Chinese leadership began to see the advantages of sending its dissident writers into foreign exile, but even then was loath to say so publicly. Liu Binyan, Wang Ruowang, Su Xiaokang, Zheng Yi, and others were banished under a 1994 directive so secret that border officials were ordered to memorize and then destroy the copies that were sent to them.[126] Another connection to the world stage for Soviet leaders, unlike Chinese, was the burden of empire. Soviet literary policy could influence Eastern Europe. For example, when samizdat journals appeared in 1956, the Soviet Party's response, which was to provide them with Komsomol "guidance," was chosen in part in order to counter challenges to socialist realism that had emerged in Poland and Hungary.[127]

In sum, the socialist Chinese system of literary control, although less overt and heavy-handed than its Soviet counterpart, was not therefore less effective in stifling dissent. Chinese writers and editors had less foreign support and were somewhat more vulnerable to financial punishments. But most important, the psychological engineering of the Chinese system, operating subtly but powerfully on feelings of fear and calculations of risk in particular situations, created greater inducements to self-censorship in the Chinese case.

[124] Erlich, "Post-Stalin Trends," p. 409; McLean and Vickery, *The Year of Protest*, pp. 4–5; Spechler, *Novy Mir*, pp. xv–xvi.
[125] Khrushchev in Johnson, *Khrushchev and the Arts*, p. 103.
[126] Human Rights Watch/Asia, "China: Enforced Exile of Dissidents," pp. 6, 9, 11, 12, 16.
[127] Swayze, *Political Control*, p. 154.

Writers

As NOTED ABOVE, literary art in socialist China could have surprising power. A short story could stimulate broad national debate about a social problem; the highest political leaders might become temporary literary critics; poetry fans could gather by the hundreds. This power of literature was in part a result of its truth-telling function, which is observable in many other authoritarian states. Every regime that tells a public story of itself grants a measure of power to people who tell other versions of the story; if those other versions are repressed, they naturally emerge less often, but have even greater power when they do. Words that might otherwise seem innocuous can be made exciting and highly significant by such a process. Vaclav Havel writes, for example, that Soviet rulers had to muffle Solzhenitsyn not because he was, or could have become, a rival politician, but in order to protect "the integrity of the world of appearances" on which the regime vitally depended. "As long as it seals off hermetically the entire society," writes Havel, the regime's version of itself "appears to be made of stone. But the moment someone breaks through in one place . . . everything suddenly appears in another light."[1] The same basic mechanism operated in Havel's own case in Czechoslovakia, as well as in, to one degree or another, those of Alex La Guma in South Africa, Liu Binyan in China, Catherine Lim in Singapore, and many others.

TRADITION OF RESPONSIBILITY

In some countries more than others, specific cultural factors have added to the moral and political weight of the writer's voice. Chinese cultural assumptions of ties between writing and governance are centuries old. However "modern" Chinese writers have seemed in their language, manner, and conscious ideologies, some of their most basic assumptions about what their relationship to the state should be and about how they should play their social roles are embedded so deeply in their culture as to be beyond question, and often beyond notice. To speak with extreme parsimony, the basic assumptions can be summarized as three.

Written Chinese embodies moral and political power. The very earliest examples we have of Chinese writing—scratches on tortoise shells and the shoulder

---

[1] Havel, "The Power of the Powerless," in *Living in Truth*, p. 59.

bones of oxen—were done to allow emperors to consult with heaven about matters of rule. The Confucian classic *The Great Learning*, claiming to explain the methods of ancient kings, specified how learning leads to cultivation of character, which in turn leads to harmony in the family, regulation of the kingdom, and finally pacification of all under heaven. This theory— which implicitly held for all human beings, not just ancient rulers—found institutional expression in the civil service examination system for more than thirteen centuries of Chinese history. A moral power, rooted in texts, could be absorbed into a person's character through memorization and study, and then radiate outward to the benefit of ever-larger circles of society. Formal language, literary education, morality, politics, and public service were conceived as a seamless continuum. Good calligraphy showed moral character. The ability to write a good extemporaneous poem was admirable in an official.

A literary intellectual has a responsibility to help set the world in order. Learning brought not only the power but the duty to extend morality to the world. One did this by caring for the areas under one's influence and by offering advice to those, including the emperor, who ruled in larger spheres. Such duties properly took precedence over any risks involved. In the 1980s, Chinese intellectuals liked to cite maxims, both attributed to Fan Zhongyan (989–1052), that said "take responsibility for all under heaven" and "be the first in the world to assume its worries, the last to enjoy its pleasures."[2]

A literary intellectual can reasonably expect that the state will utilize his talents.[3] This assumption broadly underlay China's civil service examinations since Sui times. It also underlay the system of "recommendation" that was used in the Han and Six Dynasties, and the notion of "selection of worthies" that operated before that. In all cases, the best talent was to be identified and then used, via the ruling authority, for the benefit of the whole country. A corollary principle was that, if a scholar's abilities were not properly appreciated or used, he could withdraw to await a more auspicious time, but should not compromise principle, even to death. Cultural heroes like Qu Yuan (343–289 B.C.), the scholar-poet who suffered wrongful banishment from his king's court and became a martyr to his patriotic principles, were powerful symbols of this ideal even in the twentieth century.[4]

[2] The textual source of the first maxim is obscure. The second appears in Fan's "Yueyanglou ji" (Recorded at the Yueyang pavilion). See *Guwen guanzhi* (Essence of the classics), vol. 9 (Shanghai: Shanghai shudian, 1982), p. 411.

[3] I use the pronoun "his," rather than "his or her," not from stylistic preference but because women in China were not allowed to become scholar-officials. "His or her" would be misleading.

[4] On the many and shifting mythological conceptions about Qu Yuan over more than 2,000 years, see Laurence A. Schneider, *A Madman of Ch'u.*

The Modern Crisis and the Idea of a "Path"

The arrival of Western gunboats on China's coast in the mid-nineteenth century, and the whole challenge of technical modernization of which those gunboats were, to China, the leading edge, led to ever-increasing intensity in Chinese intellectuals' worry over the fate of their nation. China's loss of the war with Japan in 1895 was especially humiliating, and was followed by a few years in which Chinese feared their country might be carved up, like the "slicing of a melon," into areas controlled by Western powers and Japan. Social Darwinist notions that China might lose a "struggle for survival" among nations spawned a fear that verged on panic and that was especially painful because of the implication that China was, compared to others, "unfit."[5] How could China, land of Confucius, Mencius, Qu Yuan, the First Emperor of Qin, Tao Qian, Wang Wei, Li Bai, Du Fu, Zhu Xi, and countless other incomparable statesmen, philosophers, poets, painters, courtesans, rebels, and others, be "unfit"? The idea would be almost unthinkable if history had not made it so actual.

The sense of national crisis intensified until, in the early twentieth century, some of China's intellectual elite began to feel that only radical change of Chinese tradition could save the modern Chinese nation in any form.[6] During China's "May Fourth" period in the late 1910s and early 1920s, young intellectuals experimented with a wide variety of foreign ideas, almost invariably with the question "How might this help China?" either clearly in mind or as an implicit assumption.[7] Creative writers were at the center of this ferment. Although their factions and stances were various, and their debates sometimes acrimonious, very few departed from what C. T. Hsia has perceptively called an "Obsession with China: The Moral Burden of Modern Chinese Literature."[8] Nearly all the varying viewpoints of the May Fourth years can be seen as one or another way to handle the China obsession.

In the 1930s, the Japanese attacks on China, especially the occupation of the northeast provinces in 1931 and the invasion of north China in 1937, brought the question of national survival to white-hot intensity and, for many writers, channeled the free thinking of the May Fourth years onto the single track of how to resist Japan. Many writers concluded that Chinese unity was the key to resistance, and that it was therefore their duty to concentrate on resistance themes and to "popularize" their writing as much as possible.[9] This brought a marked downturn in the subtlety of much Chinese

[5] See James R. Pusey, *China and Charles Darwin.*

[6] See Yü-sheng Lin, *The Crisis of Chinese Consciousness.*

[7] On the May Fourth movement, see Tse-tsung Chow, *The May Fourth Movement*; and Vera Schwarcz, *The Chinese Enlightenment.*

[8] The title of an appendix (pp. 533–54) to Chih-tsing Hsia's *A History of Modern Chinese Fiction.*

[9] See Chang-tai Hung, *War and Popular Culture.*

writing between the beginning and end of the 1930s.[10] At the same time, the cacophony of May Fourth answers to the question of how to save China began to give ground to a quest for greater national strength through unity of thought and expression. The sense of crisis had grown into a sense of impending doom (*wangguo yishi*) that was strong enough that intellectuals willingly subordinated individual judgment to a collective voice. Writers who in the late 1910s or early 1920s had joined May Fourth groups based on natural affinities in viewpoint began in the 1930s to join groups from a sense of patriotic duty.

The largest such group, the League of Left-Wing Writers, was founded in Shanghai in 1930.[11] The league's faith in the Marxist idea of "objective historical truth," when added to its members' burning desire for an escape route from China's plight, produced the notion of a true "path" (*daolu*) for the nation to follow. This idea of a path remained prominent in Chinese literary politics until the 1980s, and survived in basic political thinking beyond that. There were still, in the 1930s, various groups with different notions of what the true path was. Factions in the League of Left-Wing Writers disagreed, for example, over whether resistance of Japan should or should not take precedence over social revolution within China. But in these disagreements, unlike the May Fourth debates, the disagreeing parties tended to acknowledge that there was, somewhere, an objectively "correct" (*zhengque*) answer. This assumption implied the important corollary, which had powerful consequences for the next half century, that writers could be "incorrect"—not just thought or said to be incorrect, but objectively incorrect.

A problem in the 1930s was that there was no final arbiter of correctness in China. According to Marx, history should determine which ideas are ultimately correct. In Leninist states like the Soviet Union, from which China had borrowed the idea of correctness, a "proletarian party" with advanced consciousness was supposed to foresee the inevitable course of history and determine correctness with no need to wait. China did have a Communist Party, but no leader strong enough to support a claim to ultimate correctness. This confusing problem was resolved beginning in 1942 in the Communist base area at Yan'an, Shaanxi province, and in the rest of mainland China after 1949, with the ascendence of Mao Zedong. In May 1942 at Yan'an, Mao delivered his famous "Talks at the Conference on Literature and Art," in which he distinguished "political" from "artistic" criteria in the evaluation of literary work and stressed that political criteria must take precedence.[12] In practice, this stipulation removed the determination of correctness from writers and handed it to political authorities. Given the

---

[10] Edward Gunn shows in his *Unwelcome Muse* that China did produce some good fiction and drama during the war, despite the national mood as well as Japanese censorship.

[11] Although a number of Ph.D. dissertations have been written on the Left-Wing League, the best secondary reading remains Tsi-an Hsia, *The Gate of Darkness*.

[12] McDougall, *Mao Zedong's "Talks at the Yan'an Conference on Literature and Art."*

strictly hierarchical structure of Mao's Party, it also meant that higher officials could and should overrule lower ones, even if the lower ones knew
more about literature and more about the specific cases they were judging.
Hence it happened, during more than four decades after Mao's "Talks," that
the crucial events in Chinese Communist literary history were all nonliterary. The "correct path" for writers shifted often, and sometimes abruptly,
with political changes at the top. The control system described in the previous chapter remained basically intact, adjusting to the sharp political turns
by altering its goals, not its structure.

ESTABLISHING NATIONAL GUIDELINES

Yan'an was Mao's laboratory for setting forth what literature and art should
do in his revolution, and after a few criticism campaigns the model became
clear there.[13] But Yan'an was only a small place. The extension of Mao's
model throughout the Chinese mainland after 1949 was another major task.
Mao decided to use both push and pull, laying down a number of prohibitions and warnings while setting up a new system that offered both material
and spiritual rewards to writers who cooperated.

The prohibitions were introduced gradually, lest rebellion by intellectuals
disrupt the transition to the new regime. Writers were admonished to learn
from the Soviet Union and to "remold incorrect ideological outlooks," but
there were no guidelines about what to write or to avoid writing until
spring of 1951, when a film called *The Story of Wu Xun* was criticized in the
official press. Wu Xun was a nineteenth-century educator who, according to
the film, had begun with nothing and worked hard for thirty years to
strengthen China by establishing new schools.[14] The film was criticized for
suggesting that education, rather than social revolution, was the right path
for China. The purpose of making this point in a nationwide press campaign was to warn all creative artists that the boundaries of acceptable expression would now begin to be enforced. Also in 1951, the first examples
of national criticism campaigns against individuals established the point that
each writer and artist should censor his or her own expression in order to
avoid a similar fate. Mao Dun, the famous novelist, and Ai Qing, the nearly
equally renown poet, both were targeted in 1951. But the main target that
year was a little-known writer named Xiao Yemu, who was accused of a
"petit bourgeois mentality" in a story called "Between Husband and Wife"
(*Fuqi zhi jian*). As soon as the criticism appeared in the press, Xiao Yemu's
mentality, not just his story, became officially offensive, and this fact gave

[13] See Merle Goldman, *Literary Dissent in Communist China*, chaps. 1 and 2. The extremes of
Mao's methods, such as the way in which Wang Shiwei was executed, took many years to come
to light. See Dai Qing, "Wang Shiwei yu 'ye baihehua.'"
[14] See Jay Leyda, *Dianying*, pp. 197–98.

Party officials everywhere the power to warn or threaten any writer or artist who thought—or who could be said to think—in similar ways.

After a brief relaxation in 1953, the pressure on writers with incorrect ideas was reapplied with greater force in late 1954 and in 1955. In fall of 1954, the writer Hu Feng published his objections to the "crude sociology" of political criticism of literature and his claim that creative inspiration must be based on the personal impressions of individual writers. The question was debated for several months in Chinese newspapers, but Party leaders increasingly steered the debate toward repudiation of Hu Feng and his ideas. The crucial difference between the campaign against Hu Feng and the earlier one against Xiao Yemu was that Hu's mistakes were identified as not just cultural but political. Indeed, they were not "mistakes" but purposeful and sly efforts to undermine Party power; Hu was charged, without evidence, as a "counterrevolutionary" who had conspired with Nationalist agents.[15] The turning of errors into evidence of serious political attacks came to be called *zhengzhi shanggang*, "raising to political principle," and the Hu Feng case, its first example, sharply escalated the stakes in disobedience of the Party. Simple fear became a clearer factor in literary control than it had been before. (Hu himself spent most of the next twenty-five years in prisons. He was released in 1979 and partially "exonerated" in 1980, but his case was still politically sensitive when he died in 1985.)[16]

The positive side of the Party's approach to writers included the establishment of an All-China Writers' Association that offered its members prestige and official sanction, as well as, for some, salaries, bonuses, travel opportunities, writing leaves, and other perquisites.[17] The Party's approach also appealed to writers' idealism. Party-sponsored "socialist realism," a term and idea imported from the Soviet Union, had its strongly idealistic side. In 1952 Zhou Yang, a prominent Chinese Communist literary authority, defined socialist realism as literature "good at combining the reality of today with the ideals of tomorrow."[18] In later years, especially in the unusually free ones of 1956 and 1979, there were lively debates over whether "the reality of today" could also include the dark side of life; but for the most part, the socialist realist writers of the first fifteen years of the People's Republic took "reality" to mean success stories of the revolution from the Japanese invasion of China in the 1930s through the state-planned industrialization and agricultural collectivization of the 1950s. The admixture of

---

[15] Goldman, *Literary Dissent*, pp. 151–54.

[16] Li Hui, *Wentan beige*, is a sympathetic and richly detailed account of the Hu Feng case. For accounts in English see Donald A. Gibbs, ed., *Dissonant Voices in Chinese Literature*, and Goldman, *Literary Dissent*, chap. 7.

[17] For more on the Writers' Association, see pp. 118–22, below.

[18] Zhou Yang, "Shehuizhuyi xianshizhuyi" in Beijing Shifan Daxue, ed., *Zhongguo xiandai wenxueshi cankao ziliao*, p. 203. As Philip Williams has noted, socialist realism "is not actually realism at all but rather a variety of heavy-handed didactic romanticism" (Review, p. 177).

"ideals" meant, in practice, exposition of the advantages of the "correct path" and of the role of heroes in pursuing it.

Leading examples of full-length socialist realist novels were Yang Mo's *The Song of Youth*, about the anti-Japanese and anti-Nationalist student movement between 1931 and 1935; Qu Bo's *Tracks in the Snowy Forest*, about Communist counterinsurgency against remnants of Nationalist armies in the late 1940s; Liu Qing's *The Builders*, about agricultural collectivization in the mid-1950s; and Luo Guangbin and Yang Yiyan's *Red Crag*, about Communist martyrs in Nationalist prisons in the late 1940s.[19] The idealism of those who wrote and read these books was overwhelmingly sincere. The authors were revolutionaries who were emerging from the turmoil and suffering of the 1930s and 1940s, and who had high hopes for the new regime. Readers were primarily the young, whose natural idealism had been reinforced by the new revolutionary rhetoric. Socialist realism's call to "combine the ideals of tomorrow with the reality of today" seemed exactly the right prescription. During the post-Mao thaw, many in this 1950s generation looked back at the early 1950s, wiser but still nostalgic, as "the golden age" of the revolution, when socialist ideals were still authentic. Several things now seemed clearer in hindsight: that revolutionary ideals are harder to achieve than they first appear; that restraints on literary expression in campaigns such as the one against Hu Feng could not, ultimately, be separated from curbs on every kind of expression; and that, in retrospect, literary life in the 1950s had been rather narrow. Not only did the socialist realist works of those years resemble one another in important ways but there were, in fact, not very many of them. Compared to the years before 1949, the print runs of new novels increased sharply, but the number of new titles fell even more sharply. Before 1949, print runs for new novels usually ran only a few thousand copies, whereas in the 1950s, printings of tens or hundreds of thousands of copies were standard. But the number of new titles published, which had averaged several hundred annually before 1949, declined to fewer than eight per year for the period 1949–1966.[20]

EFFECTS OF THE ANTI-RIGHTIST CAMPAIGN

By the time the People's Republic was six years old, there seemed to be good reasons why writers could expect some stability in literary policy. Autonomy for writers had been clearly ruled out of bounds by the Hu Feng

---

[19] Yang Mo, *Qingchun zhi ge*; Qu Bo, *Linhai xueyuan*; Liu Qing, *Chuangyeshi*; Luo Guangbin and Yang Yiyan, *Hongyan*.

[20] In my *Mandarin Ducks and Butterflies*, I argued that between 1912 and 1949 there must have been between 5,000 and 10,000 average-length novels published in China's popular fiction tradition alone (see pp. 15–16). That would average to 135–270 per year, and not include all of May Fourth fiction, War of Resistance fiction, and other works in the elite tradition. The figure of an average eight novels per year for 1949–1966 is based on Joe C. Huang's citation of 120 for the period as a whole (*Heroes and Villains*, p. xii).

case; socialist realism had been set forth as the correct way to write and was already producing examples; and a nationwide bureaucracy that governed provincial literary magazines and chapters of the Writers' Association was in place. As we have seen, Mao Zedong himself felt the situation was stable enough that he could encourage intellectuals to speak out and be confident that their criticisms would aim only at improving, not undermining, Party rule.[21] The virulence of the Anti-Rightist Campaign of 1957 reflects in part Mao's sting of disillusionment.[22]

The 1957 events wounded Chinese writers more deeply than many people inside and outside China realized for many years. After 1978, when writers were encouraged to denounce the Gang of Four and the "ten years of waste [1966–1976]," many insisted on beginning their stories with the Anti-Rightist Campaign of 1957. It was the first campaign to target intellectuals in large numbers—estimated at half a million or more—and to apply punishments broadly enough to establish patterns of suffering that became widely recognized: forced confession, stigmatization in the work unit, deprivation of rights, banishment to labor camps, breakup of families, and suicide from despair. For many writers, the campaign was also the beginning of enforced silence that lasted more than twenty years.

The 1957 campaign had subtler but no less powerful effects in introducing alienation into language use. Although the distinction between formal official language (*guanhua*) and ordinary speech (*baihua*) was centuries old in China, it took on added significance in the People's Republic, and especially after the Anti-Rightist Campaign. The biggest difference from earlier times was that ordinary people had formerly left the official language to the officials, ignoring it in their own daily lives. But in the People's Republic nearly everyone had to learn to handle official language for use in politically sensitive contexts such as political study sessions or negotiations with local officials over housing, rationing, and many other things. During times of high political pressure, a misstep in official language use (even as simple as confusing *mao* "cat" and *Mao* "Mao Zedong") could have disastrous consequences for a person's life.[23] On the other hand, adroit use of the official language could also bring benefits. As manipulation of the official language became a valued skill in its own right, "correctness" of language use was measured more and more in the internal relations among words and less and less in their connections with what they ostensibly referred to. (If, for example, one could correctly use the slogan "Serve the People" to show that one was in tune with Mao Zedong's behest to produce "backyard iron," then it did not matter that seizing and melting down the cooking utensils of one's neighbors was by no means a service to the people.) A similar bifurcation of official and ordinary language is observable in other

[21] See pp. 37–38, above.

[22] Li Zhisui, *The Private Life of Chairman Mao*, p. 200ff.

[23] See, for example, Cao Guanlong, "Mao" (Cats), part 2 of "San'ge jiaoshou"; translated by John Berninghausen in Link, eds., *Roses and Thorns*, pp. 123–30.

communist systems. In a story called "Levers" by the Soviet writer Alexander Yashin, farmers complain about the officiousness of the higher-ups, but then, when they hold their own Party meeting, find themselves using the same kind of formal, long-winded language in order to fit in and protect themselves.[24] Between the beginning and the end of the 1950s in China, it became standard to use public-spirited language in the service of private goals. Victor Erlich, expressing the same point more sharply for the same transition in the Soviet case, writes that "what had been a rhetoric of crude yet genuine ideological commitment becomes a threadbare rationale for crass personal materialism."[25]

The problem of the official language affected virtually everyone, but especially writers. Not only did the political sensitivity of literature draw writers, more than most others, into situations where the official language was unavoidable in discussion of their work, but language was also the medium for writers, and work itself presented choices among linguistic styles of greater or lesser official flavor. Official language was more standardized, and somewhat more Westernized, than ordinary language in both vocabulary and grammar; its air of "correctness" conveyed a tone that, when credible, seemed morally exalted and, when not, somewhat pompous.[26] Ordinary Chinese included a much greater range of variation through different locations and social strata, generally was not very Westernized, and was no more exalted than your socks. With increased political pressure from the Anti-Rightist Campaign—and even more from the Cultural Revolution—the style of Chinese literature shifted more and more in the official direction. By 1967, even the dialogue of Chinese soldiers in battle was portrayed in impeccably Westernized grammar and vocabulary. The scar literature that appeared after the Cultural Revolution, while inverting certain judgments about who China's heroes and villains were, in its literary texture was quite continuous with the strong official-language influences of the preceding period. When Zhong Acheng's story "The King of Chess" appeared in 1984, one reason it drew so much attention was that its language seemed radically new.[27] In fact, though, the story's style was more a reversion to an older, less formal and Westernized style, reminiscent of Ming-Qing vernacular fiction, than it was invention of a new style. Zhong Acheng's story originated, significantly, in his informal, oral storytelling with friends.

The abrupt reversal of literary policy between the "hundred flowers" of

---

[24] See Harold Swayze, *Political Control of Literature in the USSR*, p. 173.

[25] "Post-Stalin Trends in Russian Literature," p. 407.

[26] It is easy to find irony in the use of Westernization to standardize the official language of Communist China. When Mao Zedong gave speeches in the early 1950s opposing U.S. imperialism in Korea, he used colloquial Chinese grammar and colorful idiom. When Hu Qiaomu and others polished his speeches for official release, they translated the colloquialisms into the modern compounds that had been invented in Japan to translate Western terms, and wrote sentences that rigorously followed the grammar and punctuation rules of European languages.

[27] Zhong Acheng, "Qiwang"; see chapter 1 note 77 above.

1956 and the anti-Rightism of 1957 also drove home the lesson that a writer cannot trust literary weather to hold. The reason why many intellectuals continued to speak very cautiously in 1979, even at the height of the post-Mao thaw, had much to do with this lesson. There was a noticeable divide between those who were about fifty years of age or more—old enough to have absorbed the lesson of 1957—and younger ones. Part of the lesson of changeable literary weather was to be wary of lengthy projects. Who could say what the weather would be like after a multiyear project is finished? Wang Meng, for example, finished his first novel, *Long Live Youth*, in the mid-1950s.[28] It told of idealistic high-school graduates in the years right after "liberation" in 1949, and began serial publication in the Shanghai newspaper *Wenhuibao* beginning in 1957. Within a few months, though, Wang Meng was labeled a Rightist for his story "A Newcomer Arrives in the Organization Department,"[29] and so *Long Live Youth* had to be dropped, even though it was a very different kind of work. Wang Meng was sent to do twelve years of labor reform, first near Beijing and then in remote Xinjiang province. *Long Live Youth* was finally published as a book after Wang Meng had returned to Beijing in 1979. In a preface he apologizes for what now seemed a "naive and immature" work.[30] Meanwhile, in 1973, during his stay in Xinjiang, Wang had begun a novel about life in a Uighur village and had finished two or three hundred thousand characters by the time of his return to Beijing; of necessity, the story included references to Cultural Revolution policies, and to Lin Biao and the Gang of Four, which were "correct" at the time. After 1976, when the political landscape changed, the manuscript became increasingly unpublishable, obliging Wang Meng to consider whether reworking it would be worth his time. By the mid-1990s he had decided simply to put it behind him.[31]

MAOIST UTOPIANISM IN COMMAND

Mao Zedong's "Great Leap Forward," launched in 1958 with the aim of catapulting China's economy ahead of England's within fifteen years, and Mao's "Great Proletarian Cultural Revolution," begun in 1966 with the aim of remolding society and even human nature, were prosecuted with such authoritarian zeal as to put China's writers basically out of business for twenty years. To be sure, stories and poems were published, and in great numbers. But they were written under strict guidelines, sometimes even to set formulae, and during the Cultural Revolution often by committee.

---

[28] Wang Meng, *Qingchun wansui*.

[29] Wang Meng, "Zuzhibu xinlai de nianqingren"; translated in Hualing Nieh, *Literature of the Hundred Flowers*, vol. 2, pp. 473–522. For analysis see David Arkush, "One of the Hundred Flowers."

[30] "Postscript" to *Qingchun wansui*, p. 346.

[31] Interviews with Wang Meng, 3 August 1980 and 16 March 1995, Beijing.

The Great Leap slogan to produce things "in greater quantity, faster, better, and more economically" applied to literary works as well as to home-made iron. The total number of poems written during 1958–1959, some-times in response to "production quotas," is impossible to calculate; but when we think of many millions of people, sometimes competing to see who can bring the most new poems to work every day, it seems quite possi-ble that more poems in Chinese were written during those two years than in all of Chinese history before then. One needs to use a permissive definition of "poem," as the following anonymous example from 1958 shows: "Big character posters / Big character posters / They're like stars / As well as cannon."[32] The late 1950s were also the years when underground poets in Beijing, who began the tradition that grew into the *Today* (*Jintian*) group in the late 1970s, began to write modernist poems that were politically du-bious. These works could not be published, and were passed around within a group that extended hardly beyond the poets themselves. Poets who stood between the tiny elite writing for themselves and the masses of workers writing to formula for their leaders were practically invisible. They watched as Mao raised the stakes in what they must produce in order to be pub-lished. As he began his overt split with the Soviet leadership, Mao declared Soviet-style socialist realism to be inadequate and said literary works should "combine revolutionary realism and revolutionary romanticism." The new slogan was not only an advance over the Soviets but, as Zhou Yang wrote in the leading theoretical journal *Red Flag*, "a scientific summation of all liter-ary history."[33] In fact, Mao's idea was basically the same as socialist realism except that it put more emphasis on the "romantic" projection of ideals in ordinary life, meaning that heroes should approach perfection even more closely.

The economic failures of the Great Leap, in addition to triggering the largest famine in human history, led to a temporary respite from Mao's romantic fervor during the early 1960s. In June 1961, Zhou Enlai gave a speech calling for more literary democracy; the same year Deng Tuo, an official and journalist in Beijing, published a series of veiled criticisms of Mao's Utopianism, and a propaganda official, Shao Quanlin, called for liter-ary portrayal of "middle characters," meaning figures more complex than the heroes and villains Mao preferred.

But the interlude was brief. In 1962, Mao admonished a Party Congress "never to forget the class struggle." In 1964 Shao Quanlin and his "middle characters" were criticized as part of a nationwide "socialist education cam-paign" that has been seen as a precursor of the Cultural Revolution. In 1966, Deng Tuo was attacked, and eventually driven to suicide, in an open-

[32] Xiao Yuying, "Ping yijiuwuba nian xin min'ge yundong."

[33] Zhou Yang, "Xin min'ge kaituole shige de xin daolu"; quotation taken from reprinted text in Beijing Shifan Daxue Zhongwenxi Xiandai Wenxue Jiaoxue Gaige Xiaozu, *Zhongguo xiandai wenxueshi cankao ziliao*, vol. 3, p. 697.

ing salvo of the Cultural Revolution itself.[34] In 1966 and 1967, Mao homed in on the "capitalist roaders" whom he saw as his political rivals. Young Red Guards, in the name of "destroying the four olds [old ideas, culture, customs, habits]," ransacked homes and "struggled" (that is, subjected to group criticism, including verbal and sometimes physical abuse) officials and intellectuals whose mentality they saw as "feudal." They eventually formed opposing groups, taking sides in the factional politics of their elders but always claiming the purest of loyalty to Mao, and began to fight, first with words and then with guns. Mao and other leaders encouraged the violence with slogans such as "bomb the headquarters" and "all-out civil war" until, in 1967 and 1968, they had to use the army to restore some order. The violence declined during 1969, and many historians mark the end of the Cultural Revolution in that year. But official use of the terms "Cultural Revolution" in post-Mao China has included the ten years of 1966–1976.

All provincial literary magazines ceased publication during the Cultural Revolution and all branches of the Writers' Association were closed. Some of China's established writers were sent to do labor reform in rural areas; others spent time in "cow sheds" (makeshift detention areas in work units where "cow ghosts and snake spirits"—one of Mao's terms for intellectuals—were confined); some just stayed at home; but the great majority published nothing for ten years. Although called ten years of "waste" in the immediate post-Mao years, in longer perspective many writers have credited their Cultural Revolution experiences with teaching them the true nature of suffering in the Chinese countryside, and, accordingly, giving them an independence of mind they had not had before. Having headed for the countryside at Mao's behest, many became deeply disillusioned with Mao.[35]

For the few writers who did publish—and for the workers, peasants, and soldiers who were mobilized to write, sometimes as parts of committees—there were strict guidelines. Characters in literary works should exhibit the "three prominences": among the masses, positive characters should stand out; among positive characters, the heroes should be apparent; and among heroes, there should be no doubt who the superheroes are. Partly to exemplify these principles, Jiang Qing promoted "eight model operas," modern adaptations of Beijing opera, which were to be emulated and, in theory, "adapted" to suit local customs and interests across China. In fact, however, the tyranny of the Cultural Revolution period was strong enough that no one dared to alter the model operas in the slightest. Widths of doorsteps were copied to the centimeter.

Fiction had only slightly more leeway than drama. Observance of the "three prominences" left stories bland and uniform, although it is far from true (as many said in the post-Mao years) that Hao Ran's novels were the

---

[34] See Merle Goldman, *China's Intellectuals*, pp. 47–50 and 101–4 (on Shao Quanlin), and 25–38 and 118–24 (on Deng Tuo).

[35] See Laifong Leung, *Morning Sun*.

only ones published for ten years.[36] Hao Ran's 1,336–page work *The Golden Road*, which recounts thirty years of Party organizational work in a north China village, includes colorful descriptions that represent perhaps the only artistically noteworthy passages of published fiction in China during ten years, but its failure to distinguish political ideals from actual life still leaves it seriously flawed.

The Cultural Revolution continued to affect Chinese writers for many years after the events. Scar literature was a first step in venting anger and regaining perspective, but remained far too superficial in its answers to the troubling question of how the people of a grand civilization could get caught up in treating one another so cruelly. This deeper question was difficult to face. First, it was by no means easy to figure out just what had happened. So many things happened in so many places, and so much depended upon secret decisions, that construction of a panoramic view seemed to demand a lifetime of research. Second, the facts were ugly. People had had their eyes gouged out. Parents had been forced to "reimburse the people" for the bullet used to execute their children. No one likes to look at such facts. The post-Mao leadership's call to get beyond them, to "look forward," appealed to a psychological need much deeper than those normally generated by politics in the ordinary sense. But on the other hand, not to look back, not to reflect on what happened and really get to the bottom of it, left Chinese writers uneasy. The concern was spiritual, but also had a side that was almost practical: if we don't figure out what really happened, how can we be sure such things will not recur? It was fairly common in the post-Mao period to hear Chinese writers refer to *War and Peace*, suggesting that the Cultural Revolution deserves such a work. But as of the late 1990s there still had been no sign of a grandly conceived literary account of China's harrowing Maoist episode.

KINDS AND GROUPS OF WRITERS

Superficially, it can seem that the socialist literary system effectively homogenized China's writers. In the first half of the twentieth century, especially during the May Fourth years, a wide variety of literary groups had populated the literary scene and generated overt controversies. Although the war with Japan induced China's writers to set some differences aside for

---

[36] Yang Lan, in "The Depiction of the Hero in the Cultural Revolution Novel," counts 126 novels published during 1966–1976, which averages, per year, to more than were published during 1949–1965. Hao Ran became the most politically favored writer of the late-Mao years, when Mao Zedong announced in 1963 that China should "pay attention to class struggle" and, within a year, Hao Ran was able to write and publish his 672–page novel *Yanyangtian* illustrating class struggle in just the way Mao preferred. Two sequel volumes of *Yanyangtian* appeared in 1966 (511 pages) and 1972 (603 pages), respectively.

the greater cause of resistance, even this unity was not much compared to the uniformity that seemed to blanket the scene after 1949.

In fact, however, what changed was not so much the variety among China's writers as the possibilities of expressing the differences through formal social groups. As in other spheres of Communist organization of society after 1949, in literary circles all social groups above the family and below the state were abolished and replaced by state-run bureaucracies. Thus differing tendencies among writers could not take the form of overt associations. On the whole (and this is ironic, given socialism's stress on public morality), the counsels of writers became more private, retreating into personal ties and the privacy of individual minds. Words for "group" or "faction" began to refer not to organized bodies but simply to writers whose commonalities (the "Shanghai group," "'57 Rightists," or "educated youth writers," for example) led others to categorize them together. Writing of the Soviet literary system, Edith Frankel notes that "one might more accurately speak of individuals who sometimes allied on a particular issue than of cohesive groups."[37] In China, the gathering of "backstage support" on different sides of particular issues seems similar to, but on the whole even less public than, the Soviet alliances that Frankel refers to.

During the optimism of the early 1950s in China, and again under the extremely high pressure of the Cultural Revolution years, the differences among Chinese writers were not too apparent. But at other times, it was fairly easy to discern writers with differing predominant concerns: to report on "social reality"; to "speak for the people"; to express oneself artistically; or simply to entertain readers. During the Cultural Revolution, when published literature was both monotonous and scarce, young people passed around "hand-copied volumes" containing stories of detectives, spies, love triangles, martial-arts heroes, and the unofficial lives of China's top leaders.[38] At an opposite extreme, some writers, even when the political pressure was off, were concerned with pleasing the leaders and illustrating political programs in literary form. Doing so could leave them vulnerable to charges of currying favor, but that was not the only insincere motive that writers were sometimes said to have. The young avant-garde writers who emerged in the 1980s were sometimes accused of faddishly imitating the West, and writers of popular fiction were sometimes said to be trying only to make money. Each of these characterizations of the motives and approaches of writers was enough to have them labeled as this or that *pai* ("group, school, faction"). But the *pai* were almost never organized groups.

A rare example of an organized group, although the organization was still loose, was the Today (*Jintian*) group of poets, fiction writers, and artists in

---

[37] Frankel, *Novy Mir*, p. 141.
[38] See Perry Link, "Hand-copied Entertainment Fiction from the Cultural Revolution" in Link, Madsen, and Pickowicz, eds. *Unofficial China*, pp. 17–36.

Beijing.[39] Formally founded in 1969, the group actually began informally as early as the late 1950s. The government considered it an "underground literary circle," but, perhaps because the offspring of well-placed officials were among the group, never moved against it except to limit its journal's circulation by blocking access to printing facilities. During the post-Mao thaw, unofficial literary groups sprang up on about a half dozen of Chinese major university campuses. Like the Today group, they centered around the publication of monthly or quarterly literary magazines.

There were many other, less formal associations among writers, but these ties were less visible and always subject to change. Writers from the same home area, or the same college class, or who had shared experiences of being sent to the countryside, tended to feel a certain group identity. Among peers, however, such associations bred envy as often as trust. Often more durable associations were built in unequal relationships, such as a senior writer with young protégés, or a writer with a powerful official. For example, both Cong Weixi (b. 1933) and Liu Shaotang (b. 1936) began publishing mediocre short stories in the 1950s with the help of Sun Li (b. 1913), an established author of 699 pages of socialist realism called *Stormy Years* (three volumes, 1951, 1953, and 1961), who had considerable influence with publishing outlets in Tianjin, where he was based. Both Cong and Liu began publishing in Tianjin, although both lived in Beijing; in 1980 interviews, both spoke effusively not only about Sun Li's reliability in editing and placing their work but of his personal warmth and their strong sense of loyalty to him.[40] Liu Shaotang spoke with almost equal gratitude about Hu Yaobang, who in the early 1950s was first secretary of the Chinese Communist Youth League and, in that role, invited Liu "for a chat" when Liu was only fifteen years old. Hu was impressed and issued an order that Liu be "cultivated," after which, says Liu, he "developed fast," publishing his first collection of stories and gaining entrance to the Communist Party both within two years, and then going to work under Hu in the Youth League. Hu Yaobang and Sun Li felt a certain tie because of their mutual sponsorship of Liu Shaotang, and Liu Shaotang and Cong Weixi were conscious of sharing the same web because of their common connection to Sun Li. Most informal literary "groups" were small and of this type.

THE WRITERS' ASSOCIATION

The big, official body that dominated the public sphere for writers and made all but the very small and unofficial clusters irrelevant was the Chi-

---

[39] See Pan Yuan and Pan Jie, "The Non-Official Magazine *Today* and the Younger Generation's Ideals for a New Literature" in Jeffrey C. Kinkley, ed., *After Mao*, pp. 193–219.

[40] Interview with Liu Shaotang, 9 August 1980; interview with Cong Weixi, 11 August 1980.

nese Writers' Association (Zhongguo zuojia xiehui).[41] Modeled on the Writers' Union in the Soviet Union, this association was the centerpiece of a comprehensive cultural bureaucracy called the All-China Federation of Literary and Artistic Circles (Zhongguo quanguo wenxue yishu jie lianhe hui), which included parallel but smaller associations for dramatists, film-makers, musicians, calligraphers, photographers, acrobats, popular perform-ing artists, students of folk literature, and others. In broad terms, the Writers' Association served the complementary functions of providing the Party with a means of monitoring and controlling creative writing and of establishing a clear-cut ladder of success for writers within the socialist liter-ary system. Through the association, the Party leadership organized the editorial boards of China's literary magazines (whose numbers grew to about eighty by 1960), sponsored lectures and meetings on literary issues, ran seminars and training sessions for young writers, assigned subcommit-tees to write or edit certain kinds of collective works, and handled liaison with other work units and other places in China and abroad.

Every province—as well as the cities of Beijing, Tianjin, and Shanghai (whose municipal governments were parallel to provincial governments in the People's Republic)—had its own branch of the Writers' Association, and all these were affiliated with the more prestigious national chapter in Bei-jing. Membership at the national level automatically conferred membership in all the provincial and municipal branches. By 1960, the national chapter included about 800 writers,[42] and the largest local chapter, in Shanghai, had about 1,000. The total for all branches was a bit over 8,700.[43] These num-bers all fell to zero during the Cultural Revolution—specifically between August 1966 and December 1977—when every branch of the association was closed. By 1982, the national association had rebuilt its numbers to 1,550,[44] and Shanghai's branch had about 300, about half of whom belonged by virtue of national membership.[45]

To writers, the Writers' Association offered prestige and access to a vari-ety of perquisites, including the privilege of attending lectures, seminars, and the banquets that came with them, as well as, for lucky or well-connected members, the possibility of joining excursions to other cities, to scenic retreats, or even—the rarest and highest prize—to foreign countries. Part of the rationale for domestic travel was to "experience life" (*tiyan sheng-huo*). Although Chinese writers generally knew little of Marxist literary theory, the tenet which says that all literary creation springs from an au-thor's "experience of life" was widely accepted, and especially welcome when it became grounds for requests to travel. Comparatively few members

[41] Between 1949 and 1953 the group was called the Association of Literary Workers (Wenxue gongzuozhe xiehui).

[42] Interview with Huang Qiuyun, San Francisco, 13 September 1981.

[43] Interview at the Shanghai branch of the Writers' Association, 17 July 1980.

[44] Feng Mu, "Guqijinlai, zhengqu wenxue chuangzuo de geng da de fanrong," p. 12.

[45] Interview at the Shanghai branch of the Writers' Association, 17 July 1980.

of the association were under thirty-five years old, but young writers were sometimes given special opportunities "for development." During the late 1970s and early 1980s, the national association invited two outstanding young writers from each provincial and municipal branch to come to Beijing for a summer "institute" that actually lasted five months. This glamorous and highly coveted activity included meeting older writers, hearing lectures from famous professors, and conducting workshops on one another's works, as well as banquets, sightseeing, and "social activities." According to one participant, there actually was little time for writing or reflection.[46]

Some branches of the Chinese Writers' Association had "creative writing funds" (*chuangzuo jijin*) to which members could apply for loans to replace salary as they took temporary or partial leave from work in order to write. If a writer earned manuscript fees or royalties from work done on such leaves, he or she was supposed to hand over that money up to the amount of the original loan.[47] Otherwise the association bore the expense.[48] Writing leaves were especially important if a writer worked at a factory, construction team, or other unit that did manual labor, and less important if one worked at a film studio, library, or other "cultural unit," where it was easier to explain to the leadership one's need for time off to write. Only in cases of very well-known writers, such as Kong Jiesheng in the late 1970s, did manual labor units (Kong's was a lock factory) allow time off for writing.

Beyond partial leaves, a small minority of association members could become full-time professional writers, which meant that the association itself became their work unit and paid their salary. Both the national and local branches of the association could sponsor professional writers in this way. The incentive to become a professional writer with the Writers' Association was naturally greater for writers at "noncultural" units. The number of professional writers sponsored by each branch depended on the finances and priorities of each. In 1981, the Guangdong branch had thirty-two professional writers, which was the highest number in the country, and Guangxi had three, which was lowest. In taking on a professional writer, the association normally pegged the salary to what the person was getting at the former work unit. Hence the incentive to become a professional writer was not primarily money, but prestige and free time.[49]

Many of the forms and functions of the Chinese Writers' Association were borrowed from the Writers' Union in the Soviet Union. The division of each branch into six or seven subgroups (for fiction and essays, poetry,

---

[46] Interview with Jiang Zilong, 10 August 1980.

[47] For details on fees and royalties, see below, pp. 129–38.

[48] Interview at the Shanghai Branch of the Chinese Writers' Association, 17 June 1980. According to Swayze, *Political Control* (p. 240), Soviet writers sometimes took loans and did not repay them, viewing them as legitimate supplements to their income.

[49] Not primarily money, but still in part money, even if the salary was the same, because the added time for writing could lead to more manuscript fees.

film and drama, children's literature, criticism and theory, and research on traditional or foreign literature), and the governance of these bureaus by a board of directors and a higher "secretariat" drawn from the directors, reflects both patterns and nomenclature of the Soviet example. The "creative writing funds" in China were also adapted from the precedent of a Soviet "literary fund," upon which writers could draw for loans, child care, or "creative missions."[50] In both the Soviet Union and China, there were inner and outer groups of writers who, depending on their status, enjoyed more or fewer of the benefits of the union/association. But the inner and outer circles were defined differently. Membership in the Soviet Writers' Union was very hard to attain, and all members automatically had professional status.[51] But many union-sponsored activities, such as lectures and conferences, were open to nonmembers.[52] In China, membership was broader and did not carry professional status. One had to be a member in order to take part in the wider circle of association-sponsored activities. The inner circle was defined by the professional status that only a few members enjoyed.

The Writers' Association had no competition. It was the only public ladder of success for writers. Its perquisites, even the small ones, were therefore attractive. Moreover, the prestige of membership carried over into important related matters such as placing one's manuscripts for publication, commanding higher manuscript fees, and having more leverage for privileges within one's work unit. For all these reasons, membership in the association was highly coveted.

Each branch of the association fixed its own criteria for what made a person eligible to join, but the criteria did not vary widely. There was usually a set standard for numbers of published works, but prizes and critical commentary could count, as well. Although an eligible person could technically apply directly for membership, the commoner route (which resembled the one that led to Communist Party membership) was to be recommended by two or more current association members.[53] Thus the first step for someone who sought membership was to cultivate contacts among current members. Just a few strong supporters were enough, because after a recommendation was made, the membership at large had no say in the matter. The candidate filled out a form that was processed by association staff (not writers) and forwarded to the branch secretariat, where officials, who might or might not be writers, made the decisions. Political control on membership was thus tight. As the scene relaxed in the 1980s, many complaints about the system surfaced. In 1980 Zheng Yimei, who had begun writing in

---

[50] Swayze, *Political Control*, p. 240.

[51] Alan Schwartz, "The State of Publishing," p. 32

[52] Swayze, *Political Control*, p. 240.

[53] Although it was unusual, the association sometimes solicited membership applications. For example, in the late 1970s the Shanghai branch approached two young writers, Lu Xinhua and Zong Fuxian, by sending application forms to them. Interview at the Shanghai Writers' Association, 17 June 1980.

the 1910s and was one of China's oldest and most prolific writers, still could not get admission to the Shanghai branch of the Writers' Association. Zheng's son complained, at the same time, that "there are people in the association who have no literary works at all, only connections."[54] Both membership in the association and professional status, for those who had it, were for life, and many young writers complained that all the slots were taken, leaving no room for the young. They pointed to cases of senior writers who had professional status, and continued to draw salaries, but no longer published.

GENERATIONAL DIFFERENCES

Chinese writers often divided themselves by generation. It was commonly said that there were three groups, the *lao*, *zhong*, and *qing* (old, middle, and young). To some extent these three categories derived from the official language of the Party, where *qingnian*, youth, was an especially common term, for example in the Communist Youth League (Gongchanzhuyi qingniantuan) and *China Youth News* (*Zhongguo qingnianbao*). The official definition of *qingnian* was "up to 36 years old," but in practice the borderline was flexible. In 1980, the national Writers' Association in Beijing invited the Cantonese writer Chen Guokai, who was then forty-two, to its summer "youth" institute. In terms of age limits, the border between "middle" and "old" was even more flexible.

The most useful basis for comparing the generations of writers is by period in which they were educated. Four periods stand out for having provided considerably different educational experiences: the years before 1949; the "seventeen years" of Maoist socialism, 1949–1966; the Cultural Revolution years of 1966–1976; and the years of Deng Xiaoping's reforms that began in the late 1970s.

The older generation of writers, educated from the 1920s to 1940s, had been formed by the lessons of May Fourth, including its liberalism and exploration of the West, as well as by the War of Resistance against Japan and its lessons in high-minded patriotism. Writers of this generation turned increasingly leftward as China's situation deteriorated in the 1930s and 1940s. The Communists won their respect, and in some cases deep devotion, because the Japanese attacks seemed truly to threaten dismemberment of China, and only the Communists, not the increasingly corrupt and incompetent Nationalists, seemed bent on resistance. In some cases, the pro-Communist sympathies of writers in this generation were magnified by feelings of guilt about their privileged and "bourgeois" backgrounds. But at the same time, the literary tastes of the several among them who had lived

---

[54] Interview with Zheng Yimei and Zheng Rude, 17 June 1980, Shanghai.

abroad were more Westernized than those of any generation before or since.

In 1949, most of this generation, because of sympathy with the Communists and a very strong patriotism, stood ready to sacrifice some of their literary freedom to suit the goals of the revolution. Very few left for Taiwan or elsewhere. Some, such as Lao She, Ba Jin, and Cao Yu, attempted to write under the new terms of the revolutionary regime, but were far less successful than before. Others, like Shen Congwen and Wu Zuxiang, did not even try to write creatively, and turned to historical scholarship instead. The more politically involved ones, such as Ding Ling and Guo Moruo, essentially became literary officials. Ouyang Shan is unique in his generation for attempting substantial novels such as *Three-Family Lane* and *Bitter Struggle* after the revolution.[55] That these works were harshly criticized confirms why others in his generation were reluctant to write.

The older generation did not participate much in the post-Mao literary ferment.[56] Although pleased, like others, that controls had been relaxed, they remained somewhat aloof from the frenzy over contemporary "path-breaking" works. Their literary identity remained rooted in prerevolutionary times, and a certain pride attended this fact. Not only was their generation, with its Western influences, more cosmopolitan than later ones; even their commitment to the revolution and to leftist ideology was, they felt, more genuine. Having followed the revolution from its roots, they understood why it had been necessary, and hence could preserve a basic loyalty to it despite the catastrophic Maoist interlude. Whether politically or artistically, they could see themselves as the high point in modern Chinese letters.[57]

By the 1980s, when the failures of Soviet-style socialism had become obvious, young writers looked with envy at the pre-Communist education of the oldest generation. That education, they felt, had been genuine and broad, and had provided the older generation with an inner steadiness and moral gyroscope that had helped them to weather tumultuous Maoist storms. In 1988, a young writer, whose own formative years had been spent in a Central Asian desert, asked, "How can we ever compare with Ba Jin [b. 1905, studied in France] or Qian Zhongshu [b. 1911, trained in England and France]? Back in those days, even the ones who didn't go abroad could

---

[55] *Sanjiaxiang* and *Kudou*.

[56] Some of the exceptions were Ba Jin, some of whose activities in the 1980s have been noted in chapters 1 and 2; Cao Yu, whose politically correct play *Wang Zhaojun* was staged with fanfare in 1979; and Ai Qing, who occasionally published barbed poems that did not seem entirely in tune with his proregime theoretical statements.

[57] Zhu Guangqian, a senior Marxist aesthetician trained in the 1920s, commented in 1980 that "no one [in literary circles] knows the first thing about Marxism these days" (interview, 23 July 1980, Beijing). Zhu was objecting to the notion that "Marxism" had obliterated "art" in China. He was sure he understood Marxism much more deeply than the political hacks who had obliterated art.

get a good education in China." At the same time, younger writers, especially the bitterly disillusioned Red Guard generation, always had trouble understanding the older generation's underlying loyalty to the Communists. To them, stories of the evils "before Liberation" were self-serving political rhetoric, whose peculiar hold on the consciences of the older generation was puzzling.

The formative experiences of the middle generation, who were born in the late 1920s or the 1930s, were the revolutionary optimism of the early 1950s, the Soviet-style education that followed, and the sting of rejection when the Anti-Rightist Campaign and Cultural Revolution arrived. In 1949, the middle generation was as devoted to the revolution as most of the older generation was, but the grounds of their commitment were different in important ways. The older generation, reacting to severe national crisis, had supported the revolutionary movement in its nascent stages, when revolutionaries were an embattled minority; but the middle-aged generation was joining the revolution at the high tide of victory and glory. Their enthusiasm came from participation in a great, centrally directed "progressive" effort. Unlike the older generation, their "hatred of society" came largely secondhand—through instruction from elders and from peer enthusiasm that sprang from youthful idealism and was shaped to a considerable degree by the political slogans of the early 1950s. Though quite sincere, the revolutionary optimism of this generation was partly artificial and, therefore, especially vulnerable to the shocks that lay ahead. No generation was more shattered by the Anti-Rightist Campaign of 1957. The hard labor may have been more arduous for older writers, but the sting of rejection was strongest among this group.

In the 1980s, after nearly all writers had been "exonerated" of the charges brought during the Anti-Rightist Campaign and Cultural Revolution, the middle generation was still trying to recover its balance by protesting its innocence and reaffirming its original ideals. Wang Meng's quasi-autobiographical "Bolshevik Salute" tells of a young party enthusiast who is sent for hard labor during the Cultural Revolution, all the while wishing he could deliver a "Bolshevik salute" to protest his innocence and the "mistake" of his punishment.[58] In one way or another, much of the 1980s writing of Zhang Xianliang, Liu Binyan, Chen Rong, Zhang Jie, Bai Hua, Cong Weixi, and others of the middle generation reflect the same aggrievement syndrome that is apparent in Wang Meng's story. As a whole, the generation wanted to say to the regime: You badly mistook us; we wanted to help and you knocked us down; now we are ready to help again but we want you to admit you were wrong about us.

This psychological need of the middle generation coincided with a need of the regime in the post-Mao period. The top leaders, in their seventies and eighties, were separated by two full generations from the angry and

[58] Wang Meng, "Buli," translated as *Bolshevik Salute*.

bitterly cynical group that had been Red Guards during the Cultural Revolution and were now the largest readership of scar fiction. The young people were in no mood to take the political cant of the old leaders seriously again. But they would listen to, and sometimes even make heroes of, middle-generation writers like Liu Binyan, Zhang Jie, or Chen Rong. The hybrid consciousness of writers in the middle generation—rooted in the idealism of the early 1950s but also deeply wounded by the disasters that followed—put them in a position to bridge the gap between the top leaders and young readers.

By the end of the 1980s, the need for vindication in the terms of the 1950s gave way to more critical perspectives on that decade. Younger intellectuals began to criticize the Soviet-style education of the 1950s as narrow and merely technical, with a goal only of making people into the happy tools of the party. They sometimes charged the middle generation with stunted intellectual growth, and in particular the inability to shake the "1950s mindset." Li Tuo, a middle-generation editor of *Beijing Literature* (*Beijing wenxue*) and a leading literary critic, agreed with the younger critics enough to say (exaggerating for rhetorical effect) that "my generation has been good-for-nothing; we're hopeless if we can't start by admitting at least that much."[59] But to most others in a generation that was now fifty or sixty years old, a radical rebeginning was too much. To deny the ideals of the early 1950s would have been to deny much of the self. There was a strong psychological need to salvage a continuity in sense of values, one way or another.

For the younger generation, born in the late 1940s or the 1950s, the defining life experience was the Cultural Revolution. Because schools were closed during most or all of 1966–1976, many in this group missed part of their education and later came to resent the loss. At first, though, their general reaction to the Cultural Revolution was enthusiastic. The idealism of "serving the people" was genuine, and the attack on "the new ruling class" that the Communist Party had become made sense in terms of their own life experience. When the slogans escalated to "Bomb the Headquarters!" and "Defend Chairman Mao to the Death!" few had second thoughts, so sure were they of the moral rightness of the epic struggle they had joined. For many, the dawn of disillusionment came when they volunteered to go to the countryside and found there not the beginnings of Maoist Utopia but wretched poverty and oppression.[60] As the gap between high-sounding political language and the dismal realities of daily life grew bigger, writers in this generation began to feel they had been used. The sting of betrayal turned many of them from Maoism to an anti-Maoism almost as

[59] Interview with Li Tuo, February 1989, Beijing. At a conference in Shanghai in November 1986, Ru Zhijuan felt that the "set pattern" of the 1950s was an ineradicable difference between her and her daughter, Wang Anyi, both of whom were writers. Wang Anyi had a flexibility that her mother could not develop even though she tried.

[60] See Leung, *Morning Sun.*

fervent. In this conversion, though, some came to see a silver lining in the "catastrophe" of the Cultural Revolution. The shock of disillusionment at least taught them to think for themselves, which is something the generation above them found much more difficult to do. The impatience of the Cultural Revolution generation with the one immediately above it resembles the "fathers and sons" generational split in the Soviet Union. In both cases, the older generation found the younger undisciplined and irresponsible, while the younger generation, the first to emerge after the reign of a tyrant, found fault with the older for an inability to shake the crippling mentality that the tyranny had imposed.[61] A difference is that the younger Soviet generation could transcend Stalin by returning to the relative purity of Lenin, whereas post-Mao Chinese writers, with no earlier model to fall back upon, had to look more within themselves. But in both cases the post-tyrant generation seemed to find a way to inoculate itself against the abused but still deep-seated credulity that its elders found hard to shake off. Liu Binyan, no friend of Mao's, commented in 1990 that without the Cultural Revolution, China in that year might have resembled North Korea.

The generation that went to school in the Deng Xiaoping years from the late 1970s to the mid-1990s received better education than any other since 1949. Its schooling was broader than the "socialist training" of the 1950s and more substantial than the zealotry of the late-Maoist years. An even more important factor in the overall shaping of this generation, however, was the money-making ethic of the Deng Xiaoping years, which led much of Chinese society into cynicism and naked pursuit of self-interest. A "popular ditty" (*shunkouliu*) of the mid-1990s, sarcastically entitled "A Short History of Comradely Sentiment," says:

> In the '50s we helped people
> In the '60s we criticized people
> In the '70s we fooled people
> In the '80s everybody hired everybody else
> In the '90s we "slaughter" whomever we see[62]

Here "slaughter" (*zai*), which corresponds fairly well in both sense and tone to "rip off" in contemporary American slang, is ironic. The sense is to condemn "slaughter" even while pointing out that it is rampant.[63]

Within this cynical atmosphere, however, Chinese writers of the generation schooled in the 1980s have produced a literary efflorescence unmatched since the May Fourth era of the late 1910s and the 1920s. I do not

---

[61] Prominent literary examples for the Soviet "fathers and sons" issue were Ilya Ehrenburg's *The Thaw* and Vera Panova's *Seasons of the Year*, both novels, and Leonid Zorin's play "The Guests." See Swayze, *Political Control*, p. 98, and Priscilla Johnson, "The Politics of Soviet Culture, 1962–1964" in *Khrushchev and the Arts*, pp. 26, 42–43.

[62] http://www.xys.org/xys/ebooks/literature/poetry/modern—ballads.gb.

[63] For a detailed account of the effects of China's economic boom in the 1980s and 1990s on social morality, see He Qinglian, *Zhongguo de xianjing*.

include a detailed look at their work in this book because in my view it represents a turning point, both institutionally and intellectually, out of what I call "the socialist literary system" that prevailed from the 1950s to the 1980s. Writers in the 1990s were no longer beholden to provincial editorial boards and branches of the Writers' Association. They could publish, and indeed find major followings, in Taiwan and overseas, and could see their work made into internationally successful films. Intellectually their work represents a departure from, and in several ways a rebellion against, the Party hegemony of the past.

Many in this generation can be viewed as growing out of the "root-seeking" mood of the 1980s and going on to achieve critical reflection of several kinds on Chinese history and culture. Su Tong looks back with an impish eye on family and village history;[64] Mo Yan and Ge Fei revisit glorified aspects of China's pre-1949 history, sometimes turning Communist myth to parody;[65] Yu Hua retells stories of the revolution, of China, and of human nature with an ironic distance alternately poignant, funny, and disgusting.[66] For a time in the early 1990s, such writing went under the nickname "rewriting history," which in one important aspect was also rewriting literary history. Wang Anyi, for example, seemed to recreate the Shanghai world of Zhang Ailing (Eileen Chang) with her *Songs of Eternal Sorrow*.[67] Ye Zhaoyan evoked "Mandarin Duck and Butterfly" style with his *Evening Stop with the Ladies of the Night*.[68] Jia Pingwa's *Capital in Ruins* was said to revive the pornographic tradition of the great Ming novel *The Golden Lotus*, but also echoes the anticorruption "exposure" novels of the late Qing years.[69] Chen Zhongshi's *White Deer Plain* debunked the romantic version of peasant warfare as portrayed in 1950s classics like Liang Bin's *Keep the Red Flag Flying*.[70]

A major problem for this generation was that taking a fresh look at Chinese history and literature required one to escape the deeply ingrained habits of Maoist language. The influential critic Li Tuo was assiduous in encouraging the younger generation to free itself of "Maoist literary style." For some, language itself became the main focus in writing. Poets such as Bei Dao and Duoduo, in their mature work of the 1990s, experimented with the limits of language.[71] Can Xue, Bei Cun, and others broke conventions

---

[64] See "1934 taowang" and "Yingsu zhi jia," in *Su Tong xiaoshuo jingpin xuan*, pp. 1–129, translated as "Nineteen-Thirty-Four Escapes" and "Opium Family" in Su Tong, *Raise the Red Lantern*, pp. 101–268; also *Mi*, translated as *Rice*.

[65] See Mo Yan, *Fengru feitun* and Ge Fei, "Da nian."

[66] On rewriting the revolution, see *Huozhe* and its film version, *To Live*, directed by Zhang Yimou, Shanghai zhipianchang, 1994; on reassessing human nature, "Xianshi yi zhong."

[67] Wang Anyi, *Changhen'ge*.

[68] Ye Zhaoyan, *Ye bo qinhuai*.

[69] Jia Pingwa, *Feidu*. See David Roy's translation of *Jinpingmei* (often rendered *The Golden Lotus*) as *The Plum in the Golden Vase*.

[70] Chen Zhongshi, *Bailuyuan*; Liang Bin, *Hongqipu*.

[71] For Duoduo, see Maghiel van Crevel, *Language Shattered*, chap. 7, "The Later Poems."

not only of literary form but of logic and grammar.[72] Han Shaogong's *Horse-bridge Dictionary* borrows dictionary form to write about life and colloquial language in southern China.[73] Some critics have called the language experiments of the late 1980s and 1990s "postmodernist," suggesting that they grew from Western influences. But such influences were superficial; the deeper causes lay in trends within Chinese culture, and had to do with the still-unfolding recoil from the Maoist episode.

In the 1990s, the readership of avant-garde writing, and all "serious" writing, dwindled to very small numbers, while pulp fiction boomed. Magazines on street stalls in Beijing in summer 1994 carried titles such as "Who Stole Napoleon's Penis?," "Sex Monger Uses Dog on Wife," and "Bestial Foreigners Make Gruel from Young Girls' Breasts." (No one has studied the popular fiction that has appeared at this level.) The full range of popular fiction and nonfiction encompassed a wide variety, but all of it had in common the potential to earn money for its writers and publishers. Through the 1990s, a number of "elite" writers began to write at the popular level. The big prize was to write a story that would be made into a film.

The popular writer Wang Shuo, whose sardonic approach to virtually everything brought him success both commercially and with readers, drew fire from two sides.[74] Cultural and political conservatives called his writing "hooligan literature," while dissident-leaning intellectuals said he abandoned social responsibility. Writers who defended Wang allowed that his work can be seen as "irresponsible," but said it was one of a number of authentic examples of what Chinese people liked and therefore by its very existence helped to establish an advance over the Mao period.[75]

Some writers and critics observed that neither of the two major categories of writing in the 1990s—the avant-garde and the popular—continued China's broadly humanist tradition from May Fourth times and earlier. They felt that the "spiritual" life of Chinese literature had been lost—whether to crass commercialism, political repression, academic fads from

[72] For example, Can Xue, "Lütuzhong de xiao youxi"; Bei Cun, "Da yaofang" and "Yundong."

[73] Han Shaogong, *Maqiao cidian*.

[74] See Geremie Barmé, "Wang Shuo and *Liumang* ('Hooligan') Culture," pp. 23–66. For a translated example, see *Playing for Thrills*, a translation by Howard Goldblatt of "Wan de jiushi xin tiao."

[75] Wang Meng, arguing that twentieth-century Chinese literature has been too dominated by writers' senses of exalted callings, defended Wang Shuo's counterexample in a piece called "Duobi chonggao" (Avoid the exalted). This piece drew a quick and sharp rebuke, but without naming names, from fellow writer Zhang Chengzhi, who referred to "people who shout sickening cheers about a Golden Age" in a piece called "Yi bi wei qi" (With pen as banner). Wang Meng restated his support for Wang Shuo at a conference in Shanghai in November 1994. See Chen Lingwen, "Wang Meng qidai kuanrong duidai dangjin wentan xianxiang." Then Zhu Xueqin, an historian in Shanghai, replied with an article criticizing both Wangs for irresponsibility. See "Chengtou bianhuan er wang qi" (The banners of two Wangs flashing above the city walls). A considerable debate ensued.

the West, or some combination of the three.[76] Although these complaints had considerable merit, it was never quite true that morally engaged work of the kind they favored had ceased to appear.[77]

LIVELIHOOD

Before the twentieth century, creative writing in China was not used to support a living. It was a side activity of people who made a living from official service, landowning, or other business of the literate elite. Popular storytellers did live from their art, but this was primarily oral performance, not literary creation. The first examples of professional creative writers appeared between about 1895 and 1920, when modern printing methods and changing education patterns created the conditions for mass-produced fiction in Shanghai, followed by Tianjin, Beijing, and Guangzhou. The harbingers were mainly journalists who began writing fiction on the side and later discovered they could make a living from it. They would sell their work to newspapers or magazines by the piece, and later (beginning in the 1910s) by a fixed rate of 1 to 3 yuan for a thousand characters. The more successful ones were able to sign on as salaried professional writers, earning in the range of 30 to 300 yuan per month. But most writers drew regular incomes from other roles—such as schoolteacher, journalist, clerk, or copyist—and took manuscript fees as occasional bonuses.[78]

For all the changes brought by the Communist revolution and the importation of Soviet models, the ways in which writers were paid remained largely the same in the socialist literary system. There were a few professional writers, but most were amateurs who held other jobs and who sold their work for fixed amounts per thousand characters. The biggest changes were the institution of nonmonetary rewards such as housing assignments and the benefits of joining the Writers' Association, and the flattening of the overall reward structure. The differences between well-paid and less-well-paid writers grew less and less; concomitantly, the psychological importance of small differences became greater and greater.

The Communist government's first regulations about payment for writing

[76] Following the "two Wangs" controversy, a debate over "humanistic spirit" in literature unfolded in the pages of *Reading* (*Dushu*), mainland China's leading magazine for intellectuals. Wang Xiaoming, Zhu Xueqin, Zhang Rulun, and Chen Sihe, who began it (*Dushu* 1994.3.3–13), argued that humanistic spirit was valuable but in serious decline. The "Search for a Conception of Humanistic Spirit" continued in issues 4 through 7, 1994, of *Dushu*. In later issues (nos. 6 and 8, 1995), Wang Meng, Li Hui, and Chen Jiangong countered. A supporter of the "humanistic spirit" side who commented with special strength on the problem of academic fads from the West was Lei Yi; see *Qujingji*.

[77] Among other examples, see Liang Xiaosheng, *'93 duanxiang: shei shi choulou de Zhongguoren?*; Liu Xinglong, *Fenxiang jiannan* (Sharing the hardships); Chen Zhongshi, *Bailuyuan*; and Zheng Yi, *Hongse jinianbei*.

[78] See Link, *Mandarin Ducks and Butterflies*, pp. 152–55.

appeared in 1951, when it set royalty rates according to a "double thousand" formula: a manuscript was bought for a set amount per thousand characters, and the purchase allowed the publisher to print up to a thousand copies. For every additional thousand copies printed, another payment of the same size was due. This system did not flatten the payment to authors very much. For example, Du Pengcheng's novel *Defending Yan'an* (*Baowei Yan'an*), which was printed in 970,000 copies in the early 1950s, brought the author 107,400 yuan in royalties, the equivalent of more than two hundred years of salary for a factory worker.[79]

Beginning in 1954, a "fixed quantity" (*ding'e*) system was adapted from the Soviet Union. Under this system a certain amount was paid for a manuscript each time a specified additional number of copies was printed. For example, Qin Zhaoyang was paid 4,000 yuan every time 50,000 copies (or fraction thereof) of his novel *Advancing through the Fields* (*Zai tianyeshang qianjin*) were printed. Altogether 440,000 copies were printed, for which Zhao received nine payments totaling 36,000 yuan.[80] This system lasted until 1958, when a dual system of "basic manuscript payments" (*jiben gaochou*) and "print-run payments" (*yinshua gaochou*) was announced. The basic payments, of a certain amount per thousand characters, were made when a piece was accepted for publication. Print-run payments were calculated as a percentage of the basic payment, depending upon number of copies printed. In the early 1980s, a writer got an additional 3 percent of the basic payment for every 10,000 copies printed. After 50,000, the percentage fell to 2 percent per 10,000, and after 100,000 copies it fell even lower. Rates for translation were roughly half. (See Table 1.) Print-run payments resembled Western royalties in some ways but not all. One difference was that in China the author's share went down, not up, with continued printings—reflecting the difference between the socialist assumption that the rich need not get richer and the capitalist's need to cover costs before distributing profits. Another difference was that, in China, the author's share was calculated not on the basis of the number of copies sold but by the number printed. Decisions on size of print runs were essentially political. Market considerations weighed more or less heavily depending on the political climate, but were always subordinate to political factors.[81]

Shortly after the new system of "basic" and "print-run" payments arrived, the Maoist fervor of the Great Leap Forward led to a deemphasis on material incentives and the temporary halving of basic payments and abolition of print-run payments. But after a few months the Ministry of Culture reversed itself, and the system continued to operate fairly well until early 1966.[82] Then Maoist fervor returned, and for the next eleven and a half

---

[79] He Bai, "Dalu zuojia na duoshao gaochou?"

[80] Ibid. He Bai lists Zhao as receiving 36,985 yuan, with no explanation for the 15 yuan shortfall.

[81] See pp. 171 and 214–15, below, on how decisions on sizes of print runs were made.

[82] He Bai, "Dalu zuojia na duoshao gaochou?"

TABLE 1
Print-run Payments for Literary Publications in August 1980

| | Rates per copy* | |
Copies printed	For original work	For translations
1–50,000	0.0003%	0.0002%
50,001–100,000	0.0002	0.0001
100,001–200,000	0.0001	0.00005
200,001–500,000	0.00005	0.00003
500,001–1,000,000	0.00004	0.00002
1,000,001 or more	0.00002	0.00001

Source: Interview at Chinese Writers' Association, Beijing, 9 August 1980.
*As a percentage of the basic payment.

years, until 1978, there were no payments to writers at all. The status of "professional writer" was abolished as part of the closing of all branches of the Writers' Association. In the late 1960s, there was very little publishing of anything except the works of Mao, and in the early and middle 1970s, when some publishing of fiction reappeared, authors were rewarded by gifts of a few books, or perhaps a pen or box of tea. During these years, writers sometimes *lost* money when they published, because the cost of the copies that friends and relatives expected as gifts was more than the value of what the author received. To have asked for monetary payment during the Cultural Revolution years would have been foolhardy as well as futile; it would have been a sign of the wrong class standpoint.

Mao Zedong grew wealthy from print-run payments. By 1960, Mao was receiving more than 230,000 yuan annually from this source, compared to only 400 yuan per month as his official salary.[83] (In this context, the many stories about his helping friends by dipping into "his own" royalty accounts are not hard to understand.) During the Cultural Revolution his harvest soared even higher. In the ten years 1966–1976 alone, forty billion copies of Mao's works, in one form or another, were published in China.[84]

Mao's case was exceptional not only in size but in its trend over time. For all other writers, the trend in pay was downward during the first two decades of the People's Republic. Differences between the better-paid and the less-well-paid also narrowed. When a Red Guard newspaper in 1967 published an exposé of the amounts that China's largest literary publisher had paid to sixteen writers during the "revisionist" years of 1949–1966, the large figures primarily reflected earnings from the early and middle 1950s.[85] Topping the list, which was based on payments by the People's Literature Pub-

[83] Wang Binbin, "Mao Zedong zao yi shi baiwan fuweng."
[84] Barmé, *Shades of Mao*, p. 9. See also Zhou Yunfu, "Ye tan Mao de gaofei."
[85] "Kan, zuiede xiuzhengzhuyi gaochou zhidu!" unsigned article in *Fenglei*. The same figures appear in He Bai, "Dalu zuojia na duoshao gaochou?" The figures in these reports are from sales by the People's Literature Publishing House (Renmin wenxue chubanshe).

lishing House, were Ba Jin, 229,624 yuan and Mao Dun, 182,266 yuan, for works written in the late 1920s and 1930s and republished in the early 1950s. The figures for 1950s bestsellers were lower. One source reports that Yang Mo received 100,000 yuan for *The Song of Youth* (1958).[86] Zhou Libo, author of *The Hurricane* (1952) received only 40,086 yuan, according to the Red Guard exposé, for a novel whose print run of 800,000 copies was the largest of any in the 1950s.

Manuscript payments were restored in 1978, and were paid retroactively for work published beginning in October 1977. But the rates were low. Editors, at their discretion within their budgets, could offer from 2 to 7 yuan per thousand characters. The major publishers usually paid within the 5–7 range, but this was still far below the 16 yuan standard that had been common before the Cultural Revolution. Moreover, for two years there were no "print-run payments" or payments for republishing of previously published work.[87] The Cantonese essayist Qin Mu recalled that during the War of Resistance against Japan the catchword for paying writers had been *qianzi doumi* "a *dou* [ten liters] of rice for a thousand characters"; now, said Qin, a *dou* of rice—thanks to the artificially low price enforced by the state—still cost about 5 or 6 yuan, which was about what a writer could get for a thousand characters of manuscript.[88]

In summer 1980 the official range for manuscript payments was adjusted upward to 3–10 yuan (or 13 yuan for "special manuscripts") per thousand characters.[89] At the same time, "print-run payments" and payments for re-publication were restored. There were major problems in enforcing the re-publication rules, however. Each republication of a work was supposed to yield manuscript and print-run payments in the same manner as original publication. But some publishers gave only half payment when a work was republished in an anthology. Others gave no payment at all. Writers across the political spectrum called for a "publications law" to protect copyrights and ensure proper payment of writers.[90] But no such law was forthcoming.

Thus even well-known works during the publishing boom of the post-Mao thaw did not bring writers much income. Wang Meng's story "Eye of the Night," for example, is about 5,700 characters in length and therefore brought him a "basic payment" of about 40 yuan when it was first published in the newspaper *Guangming ribao* in 1979. When the People's Literature Publishing House, who observed the regulations, republished the story in a collection of Wang Meng's works in 1980,[91] Wang received another basic

---

[86] Zhou Yunfu, "Ye tan Mao de gaofei."

[87] Interview at Renmin wenxue chubanshe, Beijing, 28 September 1979; interview at Wenyi chubanshe, Shanghai, 16 June 1980; He Bai, "Dalu zuojia na duoshao gaochou?"

[88] Interview with Qin Mu, Guangzhou 29 April 1980.

[89] Interview at Wenyi chubanshe, 16 June 1980.

[90] Interview with Liu Baiyu, Beijing, 11 August 1980; interview at Wang Meng, Beijing, 3 August 1980; interview with Wenyi chubanshe, 16 June 1980.

[91] *Dongyu*.

payment of about 40 yuan plus an additional 3 to 4 yuan in print-run payments for the 29,000 copies that were printed. But that amount, about 85 *yuan* (less than $25 U.S. by official exchange rates), was probably all that the story brought to the author. Certain other reprintings, done in distant places and without the author's permission, brought no payments.[92] The literary work that earned by far the largest sum during the post-Mao thaw years was Zhang Yang's *The Second Handshake* (*Di'erci woshou*). Originally a "hand-copied volume" that circulated underground during the Cultural Revolution, the novel was published, in a revised version, by the China Youth Publishing House in 1979. Within a year, 3.3 million copies had been printed, which ought to have earned Zhang Yang about 2,000 yuan in basic payment and—assuming that the summer 1980 restoration of print-run payments applied to Zhang's book—up to 2,320 more in print-run payments. But the total of 4,320 yuan is still less than 2 percent of what Ba Jin was paid for his fiction in the 1950s.

Manuscripts of fiction, essays, and "reportage" (*baogaowenxue*), which together comprised most of literary publishing, were paid by the same standards. There were special standards for certain other genres. Payments for poetry generally were calculated by treating 20 lines as the equivalent of 1,000 characters of prose. Translations were paid less than other prose; after 1978, when standard rates for original work were 2–7 yuan per thousand characters, the top two rates, 6 and 7 yuan, could not be used for translations.[93] Scholarly and theoretical work, on the other hand, could receive higher rates—from 13 to 20 yuan per thousand characters in the late 1970s.[94] Drama, when published in printed form in a book or magazine, was paid as fiction was. Payments for stage performances were more complicated. During the 1950s, playwrights usually received "performance payments" amounting to 3 percent of a theater's box receipts, but they complained that there was no system for obliging theaters to submit their payments. One anecdote tells of playwrights who scanned newspaper advertisements as the only way of discovering who was using their work and might be talked into paying for it.[95] During the Cultural Revolution, and even in the late 1970s, performance payments disappeared.[96] They came back in the early 1980s, at least in some cities. In Shanghai, for example, playwrights in the mid-1980s were paid 800 yuan for ten performances of a play and 3 percent of receipts after that.[97]

[92] For example, "Eye of the Night" was reprinted without Wang Meng's knowledge in a volume called *Zai shehui de dang'anli* (In the archives of society) (Guilin: Guilinshi shifan "yuwen jiaoxue" bianjishi, 1980), pp. 110–119.

[93] Interview at Renmin wenxue chubanshe, 28 September 1979.

[94] Interview at the Literary Section of *People's Daily*, Beijing, 14 July 1980.

[95] He Bai, "Dalu zuojia na duoshao gaochou?"

[96] Shu-ying Tsau, "Recent Developments in Spoken Drama," p. 13; and interview with Sha Yexin (co-author of the popular 1979 play *What If I Really Were?*), Los Angeles, 17 December 1986.

[97] Interview with Sha Yexin, Los Angeles, 17 December 1986.

Filmscripts were paid in two different ways. First, they could be published as written scripts and paid at the normal rates for prose. In the post-Mao years, "film literature" became a stylish genre. Thousands of texts were published and read as literature, with little expectation on anyone's part that they would ever be made into films. The monthly *Film Creation (Dianying chuangzuo)* was filled entirely with such texts. In addition, whenever a piece of fiction or film literature was actually made into a film, the creators received "shooting payments." Before the Cultural Revolution, these ranged between 2,000 and 6,000 yuan for full-length films, and half those rates for short films.[98] After the Cultural Revolution, payments were initially much lower; in 1980, the approved standards for full-length films were 1,000, 1,200, and 1,500,[99] but these amounts rose through the 1980s. Film directors had an incentive to participate in revising filmscripts, because this could mean that a portion of the shooting payment would go to them. The original authors sometimes welcomed this practice because, although it meant they had to share the shooting fee, it greatly increased the likelihood that their scripts would be made into films.[100]

In the post-Mao years, Chinese writers could win prizes that carried considerable prestige but only small amounts of money. In 1978 and 1979, twenty-five winners of national prizes for the short story received 200 yuan each; a few years later, prizes for middle-length fiction (*zhongpian xiaoshuo*) were 500 yuan.[101] By 1986, the national prize for full-length novels reached 2,000 yuan.[102] But even this figure (roughly $500 U.S. officially, or about half as much at free-market rates) remained paltry not only by Western standards but in comparison to the Stalin and Lenin prizes in the Soviet Union, which ranged between 25,000 and 100,000 rubles (roughly $5,000 to $20,000 U.S.).[103]

In sum, it was usually impossible in the Chinese socialist literary system for a writer to support a family on the various payments from manuscripts. During the 1949–1966 period, perhaps twenty or thirty writers in the entire country could do this, often because of pre-1949 writings; but from 1966 until the 1990s, when commercial publishing of entertainment fiction fully returned, it was impossible to make a reliable living on manuscript fees. The problem was not just that rates were low, but that writers could not count on the publishability of finished products. Even translations were not

---

[98] He Bai, "Dalu zuojia na duoshao gaochou?"

[99] Interview with Tong Enzheng, author of "Shanhudaoshang de siguang," Los Angeles, 11 March 1981.

[100] He Bai, "Dalu zuojia na duoshao gaochou?"

[101] Interview with Kong Jiesheng, who won both these prizes, Princeton, N.J., 20 February 1995. There were other prizes during the same years, usually for special political cases. Zong Fuxian, for example, received a prize of 1,000 yuan in late 1978 for his play *Yu wushengchu*, probably because its message—that the anti-Maoist demonstrators at Tiananmen in April 1976 were patriots, not counterrevolutionaries—was so useful to the Deng Xiaoping leadership.

[102] *China Daily*, 17 April 1986, p. 3.

[103] Swayze, *Political Control*, p. 241.

sure bets, because political standards could change between the beginning of a project and its completion. For their basic livelihood, writers depended on salaries, housing assignments, and other benefits from the "work unit" to which they were assigned.

Amateur writers, who were the great majority, drew salaries the same size as other workers in their units. In the late 1970s, normal salaries were 40 to 80 yuan per month for ordinary factory workers and up to 200 or 300 yuan per month for senior professors in universities or research institutes. In return for these salaries and the housing assignments that went with them, writers were normally expected to do a regular work load. Writing was an extra activity for which manuscript payments, if they came, were extra pay. It was sometimes possible to negotiate a reduced work load, especially if one had outside support from the Writers' Association. On the other hand, a reduced work load and/or extra pay could generate jealousies in the work unit. In 1980, a primary school teacher who wrote children's literature on the side sent a letter to the Shanghai newspaper *Wenhuibao* in which he told how he was taunted whenever he received a few yuan for his manuscripts. "How's the moonlighting going?" officials at his school asked. "Money from the pen is more civilized, isn't it?"[104] In a system where so much depended on one's relations with work-unit leadership, not just pride but very practical benefits were at stake.

Professional writers, whose work unit was the Writers' Association, received salaries at or only slightly above what the amateurs got. Professional salaries were fixed on an eight-step ladder that was used for all "literary and art workers"—or sometimes, if a writer was also an official, on the ladder of twenty-four steps that was used for state officials. In the late 1970s, salaries for professional writers ranged from about 70 yuan per month to, in rare cases, 300 or more.[105] A major problem with the professional salaries was that they were in no way tied to productivity. Appointment was for life, and one could move only up a ladder, not down. (Political trouble could knock one entirely off a ladder, but that was another matter.) As a result, senior writers who had essentially retired sometimes remained in the higher-paying positions, understandably reluctant to resign. But this could mean that younger, more productive writers were paid less, and still younger ones could not even hope for professional status because quotas were full. The same problem arose among nonprofessionals who won grants from the "creative writing funds" of the Writers' Association. Senior people with reputations had an advantage in getting these grants, even if they had burned out as writers. In some areas, "writing leaves" were renamed "reading leaves" in order to save face for grantees who had nothing to show when

---

[104] Letter from Hu Pengnan, *Wenhuibao* (Shanghai), 25 June 1980.

[105] Interview at Shanghai Writers' Association, 17 June 1980. "Publishing in China Past and Present," a pamphlet of the National Publishing Administration, cites 333.50 yuan as the highest monthly pay for writers (p. 5).

their leaves were over.[106] In the mid-1980s, reformers sought to reduce the role of fixed salaries and introduce more piecework incentives into the system. The writer Wang Meng called for better manuscript payments and fewer fixed salaries; Party leader Hu Yaobang observed that the "iron rice bowl" problem (of permanent jobs regardless of productivity) was "severe" among writers and suggested that China move toward a system of paying them "according to work."[107] One problem with piecework pay, however, was that it encouraged quantity rather than quality of writing. An established writer, who had no difficulty placing manuscripts, had an incentive for verbosity, and the deleterious effects were increasingly evident during the 1980s in China.[108] Poets had the opposite incentive: since poetry was paid by the line, cryptic lines of only one or two characters could have a special attraction.

In addition to salaries, work units provided housing, education, medical care, security, and access to rationed goods. Of these, housing was by far the most contested. Controlled rents were extremely low (only a few yuan per month), and hence ability to pay was a negligible factor in determining who lived where. Demand for housing was always intense, primarily because of extremely crowded conditions in Chinese cities, but also because quality of housing was a badge of social status. Housing decisions were in the hands of each unit's political leadership, who therefore had great power and could become the targets of gift-giving and bribery. Although most units published the criteria that were considered in making housing assignments (rank, seniority, family size, and other things), there was always discretionary space in which favoritism and corruption were widely assumed to operate and, in many cases, clearly did. During 1983–1984, Chen Jiangong, a young Beijing writer of considerable reputation, spent most of a year doing what was popularly called "running after housing" (*pao fangzi*), meaning running around giving the gifts and paying the respects that were necessary to get housing.

In the end, the quality and size of a writer's housing often had little to do with quality or quantity of writing, or with national or international reputation, and much to do with how the writer was perceived by the local leadership. For example, during the late 1970s in Guangzhou, the senior writers Ouyang Shan and Xiao Yin were assigned to comfortable, even somewhat elegant housing in large colonial-style buildings that had been built before the revolution. Ouyang and Xiao no longer wrote much, but were politically conservative and got along well with local Party leaders. By contrast, Qin Mu, who was writing much more actively at the time, was politically

---

[106] Interview with Shen Hugen, an editor of *Donghai*, a provincial literary magazine of Zhejiang Province, Hangzhou, 12 June 1980.

[107] Wang Meng, "Guanyu gaige zhuanye zuojia tizhi de yixie tantao"; Hu Yaobang, "Guanyu dangqian wenyi gongzuo yixie wenti de jianghua," p. 6.

[108] See Zheng Wen, "Chuangzuo de shuliang he zhiliang." The same dangers appeared in the Soviet literary system, where writers were paid by the "printer's sheet." See Swayze, *Political Control*, p. 244.

outspoken, and had troubled relations with his local leaders, lived in a tiny and drab apartment inside a large rectangular building. The "unfairness" of Qin Mu's housing assignment became a topic on the literary grapevine in Guangzhou.

In Beijing during the same years, Chen Huangmei, a powerful political critic of literature who mainly attended Party meetings and wrote for leading newspapers, but whose work unit was officially the Institute of Literature of the Chinese Academy of Social Sciences, lived comfortably in the Peace Hotel. Room charges, which the Institute of Literature paid, were 50 yuan per day, about the same as a beginning worker's monthly wage. At the same time, Zhang Jie, who wrote three stories that won national prizes in the late 1970s, lived in the dormitory of the machinery institute where she had worked as an accountant beginning in the early 1970s. She shared her room with her mother and daughter. When she became a professional writer, and her work unit officially became the Writers' Association, she still lived for a few years in the machinery institute dormitory because the Writers' Association could not make a better housing allocation. (It was fairly common for people to remain living in a former work unit if the new unit had no available housing. Squatter's rights were strong.) During the same years in Shanghai, the young writer Cao Guanlong, together with six other people, lived in a garret that had four slanting roof slabs for walls. The entrance was a trap door accessed by a ladder. Inside there were only a few square feet of space where an adult could stand erect. People slept in the crannies where the slanting roof met the floor. Cao's "study," which he reached through a second trap door, was, weather permitting, outdoors on the top side of the same slanted roof.

Although both the socialist literary system and the work-unit system in China drew much from Soviet models, Soviet writers were paid, in both money and perquisites, much better than were Chinese writers. We have noted above that Soviet literary prizes were between ten and a hundred times larger than Chinese prizes. Ordinary manuscript payments were higher as well, by about the same range of factors, in the Soviet case. In the Khrushchev era, Soviet writers were paid between 1,500 and 4,000 rubles per "printer's sheet" of Russian text,[109] which would be roughly 6,000 to 8,000 Chinese characters, an amount that would earn Chinese writers about 30 to 50 yuan. Officially, the ruble in the late 1950s and the yuan in the late 1970s were both about four to the U.S. dollar. In fact, the yuan bought considerably more, but not the fifty or eighty times more by which payments to authors differed. The difference in pay for poetry was similar: between seven and twenty rubles per line in Khrushchev's Soviet Union compared to between 0.1 and 0.35 yuan per line in post-Mao China.[110] Moreover, Soviet writers generally had better privileges, including housing

---

[109] Swayze, *Political Control*, p. 243.

[110] *Ibid.* The per-line calculation in the Chinese case is based on the standard rates of 2 to 10 yuan per twenty lines.

assignments, summer retreats, and special access to foods and commodities.[111] Most branches of the Soviet Writers' Union had automobiles that writers could sign up to use, at least occasionally. In post-Mao China there were senior writers who coveted interviews with foreign scholars partly in the hope that they might ride in a car for the first time.

Whereas the Soviet leadership apparently tried to raise living standards for writers in order to make the occupation more attractive, in China the leadership tried to be sure that writers' living standards were on a par with others, which could mean freezing or even lowering standards. Moreover, with anti-intellectual campaigns such as the Anti-Rightist Campaign and the Cultural Revolution, the leadership added some heavy disincentives to becoming a writer. It is a tribute to the respect for writing that lies deep in Chinese tradition that people chose to be writers anyway. In surveys in Shanghai and Guangzhou in the 1980s, high-school students rated "writer" and "journalist" very highly among alternative future careers.[112] What they aspired to achieve as writers varied in several ways, and could be either self-serving or idealistic, or both at once. As we will see in the next two sections, reasons for writing were, one way or another, often conceived in relation to a moral duty to China or some portion of it.

DISSENT

In the late 1970s, the parallel between what was emerging on the Chinese literary scene and what had happened earlier in the Soviet Union led Westerners to assume that *Today* (*Jintian*) and the other unofficial Chinese publications were the same kind of thing as Soviet samizdat ("self-published") journals. But the parallel is useful only superficially. Despite the strong similarities in the nature of the state systems that confronted them, Soviet and Chinese writers pursued dissent in ways that were importantly different.

On the whole, explicit dissent always had a more established place on the Soviet scene. The samizdat press grew to be strong enough that it could not easily be stamped out; mimeographed works circulated underground at

---

[111] Better supplies in the Soviet Union may have done nothing to reduce jealousies among authors, and indeed may have increased them. This is certainly the impression one gets from Vladimir Voinovich's short novel *The Fur Hat* (1989), a delightful insider's look at the tragicomic life of a journeyman Soviet writer.

[112] In a survey of 150 high school seniors in Shanghai in 1981 (Lan Chengdong et al., "Yingjie gaozhong biyesheng de zhiyuan qingxiang"), students were asked to rate 38 occupations, ranging from doctor to barber to garbage collector, for desirability; "journalist" was fourth and "writer" sixth among the 38. A 1983 survey of 267 Shanghai high-school students (Zhang Yongzheng, "Zhongxuesheng lixiang wenti de diaocha") found 4.6 percent aspiring to be a creative writers or journalists—clearly many more than could actually achieve these roles. In Guangzhou, a 1981 survey of 769 junior and senior high school students (Wang Zhisheng and Li Zibiao, "Guangzhoushi zhongxuesheng sixiang zhuangkuang de diaocha") found 9.5 percent wishing to be a writer or journalist.

nearly all times. Works like Boris Pasternak's *Doctor Zhivago* and Alexandr Solzhenitsyn's *The First Circle*, which appeared first in samizdat form, were picked up for publication in the West and eventually built powerful reputations for their authors. Westerners followed the fates of Soviet "dissidents" and prodded their governments to make their treatment an international issue. Even Soviet writers who kept their criticisms largely domestic (such as Ilya Ehrenburg and Yevgeny Yevtushenko in the post-Stalin thaw period) consistently expressed themselves more bluntly and openly than any Chinese writer until the late 1980s, when the socialist Chinese literary system was already collapsing. It was not until after the 1989 massacre at Tiananmen that Chinese writers in exile, such as Liu Binyan, Wang Ruowang, and Zheng Yi, began to accept the word "dissident" and the clear break that it implied.[113]

There were several reasons for the greater reluctance of Chinese writers to make an open break with their government. One was the difference between the Soviet and Chinese literary control systems, as noted in the preceding chapter. China's system relied less on explicit rules and more on psychological pressures that arose from vague threats; it was natural, within such a system, that dissent also rely on vagueness and indirection. A related factor was the presence in the Soviet Union—and absence in China—of a pretotalitarian phase at the beginning of communist rule. For about the first thirteen years of Soviet rule, Russian writers became accustomed to a communist system that allowed them considerable autonomy. Lenin felt that his competence did not extend to artistic matters, and Trotsky explicitly held that creativity depended on independence. These attitudes helped to make the 1920s the best decade in Soviet literature.[114] It was not until Stalin and Zhdanov, beginning around 1932, that the pretotalitarian phase gave way to a systematic "engineering of souls." By contrast, Chinese writers had to live under the strictures of Mao's "Talks at Yan'an" right from the outset of the People's Republic in 1949. They did not have, even in the back of their minds, a concept of what a "liberal" communist literary system might be like.

But there are also some deeper cultural reasons for the differing styles of Soviet and Chinese dissent. Soviet writers inherited the notion, established by the towering works of Tolstoy, Dostoevsky, Chekhov, and others, that literary artists could be custodians of an alternative culture to Czarist orthodoxy. They could claim a moral authority that diverged from that of official power. Chinese writers, emerging from the tradition of Confucian scholar-officials, were bound more to assume that literary, moral, and political au-

---

[113] Liu Binyan's newsletters *China Focus* (1993–) and *Dalu* (1994–1996) were explicitly dissident, as were Zheng Yi's books about Maoism and the political cannibalism in Guangxi province, *Lishi de yibufen* and *Hongse jinianbei*.

[114] Irving Howe has judged that the appearance, all in the 1920s, of writers such as Zamyatin, Pilnyak, Babel, Mayakovsky, Pasternak, and Essenin made that decade the "most brilliant" in Soviet literature. See "Predicaments of Soviet Writing," p. 19.

thority converge, indeed in some ways were the same thing. To them, a
dissenter owed a certain kind of political loyalty even to a ruler or regime
that was clearly wrong-headed. There was only one China, a writer had an
unquestionable duty to it, and its ruler was the party one had to deal with,
for better or worse. Zhao Zhenkai's short novel *Waves*, which was originally
published in the unofficial journal *Today* in 1979, contains the following
exchange between two young characters who, for that period in China, were
about as close to dissidence as writers could be:

> "No, I don't mean some hackneyed political cliché, I mean our common suffering,
> our common way of life, our common cultural heritage, our common yearning . . .
> this indivisible fate that constitutes everything; we have a duty to our country. . . ."
>
> "Duty?" she cut me off coldly. "What duty are you talking about? The duty to
> be an offering after having been slaughtered, or what?"
>
> "Yes, if necessary, that kind of duty."[115]

During the early 1980s, the Chinese writer Bai Hua was twice the target of
government-sponsored criticism campaigns, but in 1984 he told a national
convention of the Writers' Association that "a true Chinese writer must be,
first and foremost, a true son of China."[116]

For their part, China's political leaders assumed that because literature
fed the moral lifeblood of the nation, it deserved their attention and even
their participation in roles such as poet, calligrapher, and literary critic. In
1979, the China Youth Publishing House published *Poems of Ten Seniors* (*Shi
lao shixuan*)—meaning the traditional-style poems of senior revolutionary
leaders including Zhu De, Dong Biwu, and eight others—in 300,000
copies.[117] From time to time, *People's Daily* and other national publications
carried articles that glorified the literary efforts of leaders.[118] Poetry and
calligraphy, the most exalted literary arts, were the favorites for demonstrating the literary-moral power of leaders.[119] As in Confucian times, these two
arts could show that the leader had the moral qualifications to rule; calligraphy could have the added function of signaling patronage.[120] In these ways,
as well as in issuing occasional criticism of literature, the degree to which

[115] Zhao Zhenkai, *Waves*, translated by McDougall and Cooke, p. 21.
[116] *Renmin ribao*, 31 December 1984, p. 7.
[117] Interview at China Youth Publishing House (Zhongguo qingnian chubanshe), 8 October
1979. In the same year, the People's Literature Publishing House issued *Long-range Vision*
(*Yuanwangji*), a collection of Marshall Ye Jianying's poems.
[118] See, for example, Zhang Aiping, "Daxue ya qingsong."
[119] Fiction, a less prestigious genre even in communist times, was used in this way only
rarely. An example is Zhou Enlai, "You shenme fenbie?"
[120] Only male leaders used literature to play these symbolic political roles. The corresponding roles for women, which were minor by comparison, were typically limited to patronage of
children's literature and normally delegated to the wives of male leaders. For example, at a
meeting (Beijing, 30 May 1980) to distribute national prizes for children's literature, Song
Qingling, widow of Sun Yat-sen, gave the opening welcome, and Kang Keqing, wife of Zhu
De, gave a keynote address and served as chair of the judges' panel. Zhongguo shehui kexueyuan wenxue yanjiusuo dangdai wenxue yanjiushi, *Xin shiqi wenxue liu nian*, pp. 488–89.

Chinese leaders were willing to play personal roles in literary matters clearly went beyond what most Soviet leaders saw fit to do. Among the Soviets, Stalin may have come closest to a personal role with his advocacy of "engineering souls." But even this he did not try to do personally, or to conceive with much subtlety.

In China, public perception of a connection between the top leadership and literature was reinforced by the practice of representing top leaders, "correctly" interpreted, in stories, plays, and poems. Most such presentations were positive, and of course were hyperbolically so for Mao Zedong during the last decade of his rule. But they could also be "correctly" negative, as Liu Shaoqi, Lin Biao, and Jiang Qing in turn came to know. The images of leaders were somewhat more realistic during the thaw of the late 1970s, although they still lacked moral complexity. Zhou Enlai appeared in countless works of fiction and several plays, and some lifelike imitations of Mao Zedong, Zhu De, and Chen Yi appeared, as well.[121]

The various connections between China's rulers and its literature helped to maintain the preoccupation of Chinese writers with China. Even for the relatively "dissident," the primary audiences were domestic: Chinese readers, whom one could try to educate or arouse in various ways, and the Chinese leadership, to whom one could try to appeal. Foreign audiences might be important in building international reputations, which might lead to highly coveted opportunities to travel or other honors, but foreign audiences were not considered the right targets for statements of dissent. The government reinforced this view by issuing periodic warnings that "the inside and the outside are different."[122] It was not until the 1990s, when China's socialist system was dissolving, that Chinese dissident writers began seriously to address the West, and those who did so were primarily ones who had already moved to the West.

In this regard, the general Chinese situation was very different from that of Soviet writers who took on the "dissident" label. For Soviet writers, the presence of the West and its ability to create instant fame by conferring the "dissident" label loomed much larger than it did for Chinese writers.[123] The ties between Soviet writers and Western audiences were many-layered. In Czarist times the Russian cultural elite had spoken French, and the underlying connections between the worlds of Russian and Western European

---

[121] In the post-Mao years the main prohibition in representing the top leaders was to avoid any who were still alive. Writers generally did not object to this taboo, however, because of the risk inherent in presenting moral judgments of leaders whose power was still active and whose official place in history was still not fixed.

[122] *Neiwai you bie.* In one such appeal, Xia Yan, a senior writer and Communist Party official, warned the All-China Convention of Literature and Art Workers in fall 1979 that because "some propaganda organizations in the Western world have insatiable appetites for publicizing the details of whatever they can learn about our internal problems and temporary difficulties," all writers, especially Communist Party members, will certainly "consider the grave responsibilities they have toward the motherland." Yu Congzhe "Zhonggong de wenyi luxiang," p. 19.

[123] This condition is vividly illustrated in Voinovich, *The Fur Hat.*

letters continued into the Soviet period in a way to which there was nothing remotely parallel in the Chinese case. Despite the 1929 campaign against Pilnyak and Zamyatin (who were charged, among other things, with unauthorized publication in the West), Soviet writers consistently felt they could address the West in ways that Chinese writers found both less palatable and more difficult to carry out. The hardest-hitting works in Soviet literature were often conceived with foreign audiences in mind; in China, with rare exceptions, the domestic readership was primary. For their part, Western audiences watched the Soviet literary scene much more attentively than they—or anyone outside China—ever watched for "dissident" writing in China. Not only did the cultural similarities between Russia and the West make Russian writing more accessible and congenial to Western readers; more important, Western interest in Soviet dissent was constantly stimulated by the place of the Soviet Union as the West's adversary in the Cold War. Western readers were attracted to Soviet dissidence as a source on the dark side of a harshly repressive society; not until the massacre at Tiananmen did many in the West view China in such a way, despite its having been for decades at least as repressive as the Soviet Union. Moreover, issues such as free emigration from the Soviet Union touched Westerners personally in ways that had no parallel in the Chinese case.[124] The relative cultural distance of China, and its smaller threat in Cold War terms, allowed a long survival in the West of China's image as an exotic place whose "interesting" ways need not be questioned.

PURPOSES

An alien observer of the Chinese socialist literary system might, at first look, want to ask, "Why do they write? What impels them to fill so many pages?" Practically nothing that one could call distinguished art emerged from China for decades. Explicit and powerful dissent of the kind found in Pasternak, Solzhenitsyn, and other Soviet writers was also rare. Writers were not especially well paid, and could be subjected to blistering political attack. Why pick up the pen? What did they think they were doing?

The conception of the writer as standing between political rulers and the general populace, able to address one on behalf of the other, has roots in both Chinese tradition and communist theory, and is sturdy enough to serve as a framework for analyzing the motivations of writers in socialist China generally. Most writers most of the time liked to think of themselves as doing something for someone else in China. Sometimes they directly addressed the people they were trying to help, be they leaders who needed good advice or readers who needed such things as comfort, support, or

---

[124] Rights of emigration of Chinese to join relatives living overseas could have presented a similar issue but did not. An analysis of the national loyalties and relative political docility of Chinese populations in the West is an important topic, but clearly beyond our scope here.

explanations. Other times the side addressed and the side to be helped were different, as when writers addressed the general populace in order to help rulers spread policies, or, conversely, when they addressed rulers in order to plead the case of people below. Moreover, address could have several purposes and directions simultaneously, and messages as received naturally could differ from messages as intended. Some writing did not fit the pattern of the writer as intermediary between rulers and populace; sometimes writers wrote, at least in part, for the outside world or for history, or for a circle of friends, or just for themselves. But the question of address can shed light on that of purpose, and below we will consider three major aspects of it: addressing "the people," addressing authorities, and (as in self-expression or writing for history) addressing no one in particular.

Addressing the People

Few writers in socialist China viewed themselves as their readers' peers. Whether because they felt they understood more deeply, or had a generally higher level of moral or political awareness, their implicit attitude toward readers was nearer to that of teacher than of conversation partner. Such an attitude was prescribed in the literary theory of state socialism, captured perhaps most notably in Stalin's phrase about "engineers of the soul." But it had deeper roots in Chinese cultural tradition, where the associations between written language and moral instruction were pervasive, ancient, and strong. Chinese modernizers early in the twentieth century, before the arrival of communist influences, were convinced that the writing of a good, new kind of fiction could help to build a strong and modern China.[125] Major works of the 1950s such as Du Pengcheng's *Defending Yan'an*, Zhou Erfu's *Morning in Shanghai*, Wu Qiang's *Red Sun*, and Yang Mo's *The Song of Youth* were intended to teach the second revolutionary generation a broad and morally engaged version of how the revolution had come about. Political teaching—why and how to reject revisionism and the "capitalist road"— also underlay the fiction and revolutionary operas of the last ten Mao years. Deng Xiaoping chose to use literature much less as a way of disseminating national policies. A general dismantling of the Gang of Four, which came easily to writers, was most of what Deng needed.

But the disappearance of the demand that literature teach the political thought of the top leader did not lead immediately to a decline in the general notion that literature should teach. Nearly all of scar literature had a strong didactic bent; writers set forth morally correct and incorrect behavior in unambiguous fashion, ranging from blanket rejection of the Gang-of-Four mindset to fairly concrete instruction about how to live daily life. In a short story by Zhang Jie called "Who Lives Better?," for example, a young

---

[125] Zhou Zhiping (C. P. Chou) has pointed out that, despite their differences, both Hu Shi and Lu Xun accepted Liang Qichao's premise that "fiction is a good tool for reforming society." "Hu Shi yu Lu Xun de jiaoyi," p. 14.

male student learns that showing off his knowledge of Spinoza or *Dream of the Red Chamber* is not the way to approach a fine-featured young woman who sells tickets on a bus, and throwing a tantrum is not the way to respond when she declines an advance. It can turn out that she is not only an impeccably responsible citizen but an accomplished poet who happens to work on a bus.[126] The lessons that one should regard the sexes equally, that a student should not look down on a worker, and that one should be generally civil are all clear.

As scar literature matured and led to deeper reflection on China's problems, the teaching of specific lessons gave way to more open-ended probing of large questions. Writers began to pose questions rather than deliver answers. There were calls for national "self-examination" (*fanxing*) about the Maoist period. What happened? How could we Chinese have treated one another so cruelly? During the Cultural Revolution in particular, the whole country had seemed to turn mad for a while. How was this possible? Who is responsible? Although these questions did not have ready answers, the writer's role in leading people to face them was still implicitly that of a teacher.

As long as Mao was alive, no one dared speak of the problem of blame for the Cultural Revolution, because Mao's personal share, though obvious, could not be mentioned. After Mao died, when it became possible to vent one's anger at the "all-evil" Gang of Four, popular euphoria was genuine. But at a deeper level, people knew that the question of blame had barely been opened. Were only four people, by themselves, responsible for "all evil"? Obviously there were others. In 1978, the "Gang of Four" was formally expanded to "Lin Biao and the Gang of Four"; in 1980, Kang Sheng became an officially acknowledged accomplice. But, counting Mao, that still added up to only seven people. Did only seven people victimize eight hundred million others? The idea, however convenient, was absurd. More digging was necessary. Scar literature offered the personal stories of victims, but in so doing only underscored the sense that much remained to be explained without going very far in explaining it. The villains in scar stories were usually stick figures; authors avoided sensitive questions about their character and the culture that brought it about.

With the "root seeking" of the 1980s, especially that aspect of it that sought the roots of "feudalism" that were seen as holding China back, the fate of contemporary China was seen as something that lay deep in Chinese culture.[127] But where, precisely? Where could one focus attention when something as vague as one's whole culture seemed possibly at fault? The need to concretize the problem became one of the causes of a surge of interest, beginning in the late 1980s and extending into the 1990s, in a literary trend to "reevaluate history." Consciously rejecting the false history

---

[126] Zhang Jie, "Shei shenghuo de geng meihao?"
[127] See chapter 1, note 78, on *Heshang* (River elegy).

in official accounts, some writers began trying to reconstruct what "really happened" during the May Fourth movement, the Yan'an period, the Great Leap Forward, and so on. Dai Qing spurred this trend in 1988 with her sharply revisionist articles about the fates of Wang Shiwei, Liang Shuming, and Chu Anping, all of whom had dared to dissent during the 1940s and 1950s.[128] In the same year, Su Xiaokang published *Memorial to "Utopia,"* about the truth of the Lushan Plenum in 1959, when Mao's intransigence set China irrevocably on the road toward the colossal famine of 1959–1961.[129]

Although the political, moral, and historical reflection went through stages, the violence of the Cultural Revolution remained the big, haunting problem that would not go away. In 1989, Zha Jianying, one of China's most perceptive young writers, said, "The Cultural Revolution is still treated like an embarrassing secret. In the publicly acknowledged version of what happened, *everybody* was a victim—intellectuals, workers, peasants, old revolutionaries, honest officials, everyone. But this is an impossible version of history. We might better say we all turned abnormal for a while. But then, how do we explain *that*? We won't be done with the history of the Cultural Revolution until we can answer this question."[130] Zha seemed to feel that if her fellow Chinese could not isolate the problem—could not, as it were, pull it out of themselves, lay it on the table, point at it, and call it a name—then they might never know whether it would lie dormant inside them and some day rise up to wreak havoc again.

Introspection of this sort was not easy. It could also be painful. China's literary record since the death of Mao shows a consistent pattern of ambivalence about facing the inhumanity of the Cultural Revolution. Although many writers look at the topic, as they draw closer to it most sooner or later turn aside, as if a huge reverse magnet lies at the heart of the puzzle. Addressing the topic has generally been easier in private conversation than in the formality of print, where descriptions often fell far short of what could have been said. In 1989, the literary critic Li Tuo pointed to such understatement in Zhang Xianliang's 1984 novella *Mimosa*, which tells of a "rightist" who was sent to the countryside for labor reform in the late 1950s.[131] The story includes striking detail on how the man suffered hunger, and Zhang Xianliang drew praise for daring to be so realistic in print. But Li Tuo flared up at this praise. "It only shows the double standard between what we know and what we write," Li said. "The man in that story suffered? Yes, he suffered. But he still *did eat*. And he could write. He even had a woman's love. You think that was the worst of labor reform? Nonsense! I

[128] Dai Qing, "Wang Shiwei yu 'ye baihehua,'" "Liang Shuming yu Mao Zedong" (with Zheng Zhishu), and "Chu Anping yu dang tianxia."
[129] Su Xiaokang et al., *"Wutuobang" ji.*
[130] Interview, 3 May 1989, Beijing.
[131] "Lühuashu," translated by Gladys Yang as "Mimosa."

know a man who went to a camp that held thousands. He and only six others came back. Seven out of thousands. But nobody writes about *that*."[132]

Censorship and political intimidation explains part of the difficulty of writing about the ugliest facts. *Mimosa* pressed the borderlines of what could be published in China at the time. But there were much deeper reasons, which began inhibiting Chinese writers even before censorship came into play. One was the natural human response of emotional recoil from horrible events. Regardless of what role one might have played in events, certain facts can be just too awful to look at. If one can face them at all, it helps if a few years have passed to allow the emotional recoil to subside. The dropping of the atomic bomb on Hiroshima stimulated some Japanese poems in the late 1940s, but more than a decade was required for the first detailed looks at the event to appear in Japanese literature.[133] The emergence of "Holocaust studies" in the West required a similarly long time to emerge. For Chinese writers, the question of national pride and the dignity of the written Chinese language were additionally inhibiting. "Chinese have a long tradition of exalting our written language," said a young writer at a literary salon in 1989. "We still think there should be a certain decorum about the printed word. It is undignified (*butimian*) to put such awful things in writing." Another thought it had to do with national "face." "All the world can read scar literature," she said. "Chinese feel embarrassed to admit to others that such uncivilized things happened in China. It doesn't matter that we intellectuals were the victims. We are still embarrassed for China to admit that it happened."[134]

Finally, there was a fear of sharing the blame—a sense that, if one dug too deeply into the origins of the mindset that led to violence, one might find some of them within oneself. The use of the Gang of Four as moral scapegoats served (somewhat as Lieutenant Calley did for Americans during the Vietnam War) as a way of deflecting responsibility by finding someone else to be the cause of the trouble. In neither case did people want to face the terrible question, "Was *I* partly at fault?" Only a few Chinese writers in the 1980s and 1990s dared to raise this question publicly; and these, ironically, have been people with relatively tiny amounts of guilt to confess. In a 1978 essay about the death of his wife, Ba Jin wonders whether his complicity in the Cultural Revolution mind-set contributed to her suffering.[135] In 1982, Liu Binyan publicly announced his "good fortune" to have been declared a Rightist in 1957, because, "had I not been, I too might have been drawn into attacking others; I was fully behind the Cultural Revolution

---

[132] Interview, 24 November 1988, Beijing.

[133] See John Whittier Treat, *Writing Ground Zero*.

[134] Personal observation, 17 October 1988, Beijing.

[135] "Huainian Xiao Shan," in *Suixianglu*, pp. 14–35; translated by Michael Duke as "Remembering Xiao Shan" in Mason Wang, *Perspectives in Contemporary Chinese Literature*, pp. 113–33, and by Geremie Barmé as "In Loving Memory of Xiao Shan," in Ba Jin, *Random Thoughts*, pp. 21–42. By 1986, Ba Jin's courage in addressing the question of personal guilt had received praise in China's official media.

when it began."[136] In 1989, Shi Tiesheng published an essay in which he admits having been tempted to sell out a friend in order to save himself.[137] There are a few other examples, but none from people whose involvement in persecution was very deep.

Acts of gruesome cruelty were raised, but not very directly, by writers in the late 1970s and the 1980s. For example, Chinese writers knew then (well before the outside world did) about the practice of "harvesting" organs from prisoners who were scheduled for execution.[138] Cao Guanlong, in his story "Fire" (1979) writes of a Party official who makes certain that a particular young prisoner gets good food and care, right until the day he is shot, because the official needs his corneas.[139] But the story is vague about place and time, and includes a surreal ending that pushes the account further into an imaginative realm and thus insulates the reader from the shock of confronting the very recent past. Only when an editor questioned the "believability" of the story did the author write a letter naming specific people and places.[140] Yu Hua's story "One Kind of Reality" presents a farcical scene in which a bevy of greedy physicians huddle around a still-living prisoner and jostle for access to the skin, kidneys, stomach, liver, kidneys, and several other parts.[141] Here the spirit of raillery does the insulating, even to the extent of making the object of satire ambiguous: are we belittling the harvesting of organs or the many stories in society about the practice?

In the early 1990s, the question of facing the gruesome reached its extreme with Zheng Yi's reportage on the politically inspired cannibalism that took place during the Cultural Revolution in Guangxi. The topic of ritual eating of bits of the liver, kidneys, and other body parts of slain "class enemies" formed so repulsive a set of stories that even China's most outspoken writers had turned aside, more from reflexive revulsion than from fear of criticism. Liu Binyan, for example, heard about the Guangxi cannibalism in the early 1980s and did some initial investigation but, as he became convinced that the stories were based in truth, concluded that he would not write about them. They were just "too ugly"; how could one handle them before readers? Yet when Zheng Yi asked Liu's advice, Liu encouraged the younger writer's determination to face facts no matter what. Eventually Zheng Yi produced detailed interviews and photographs of Party documents that made denial of the cannibalism reports no longer possible.[142] But Zheng's writing, far from resolving the problem of facing facts, only turned it into a question of whether the facts should be published. Even outside

---

[136] Liu Binyan, "Tan xinshiqi de wenxue chuangzuo wenti," p. 7.

[137] "Wenge jikui."

[138] The first detailed account outside China was "Organ Procurement and Judicial Execution in China," *Human Rights Watch/Asia*. Some brief press accounts had preceded this report.

[139] "Huo" (Fire), part 3 of "San'ge jiaoshou," translated in Link, *Roses and Thorns*, pp. 130–45.

[140] *Anhui wenxue* 1980.1.31.

[141] "Xianshi yi zhong."

[142] Zheng Yi, *Hongse jinianbei*, front matter and pp. 2–113, 683–84. For an overview in English, see Liu Binyan, "China's Hidden Cannibalism."

China, far from the reach of the censorial system, Chinese people worried over the consequences of publication: "That was twenty-five years ago; why raise it again now?"; "It makes a person sick; why does Zheng Yi want to go around making people sick?"; "That happened in a national minority area, not among Han Chinese"; and so on. At a conference in Princeton, New Jersey, in 1993, reporters from the overseas Chinese press spent an afternoon in a debate with Zheng Yi, Liu Binyan, and others over whether and how much to publish. Zheng Yi and Liu Binyan held that no good comes from avoiding the truth, but most of the reporters feared that publication of such gruesome facts would hurt the image of Chinese in the world.

Zheng's and Liu's position in this debate illustrates the role of the author as a teacher who is confident about what is to be taught, and in doubt only over how to teach it. The tradition of the morally and cognitively confident author and narrator has been strong in modern Chinese literature ever since the realism of the May Fourth movement in the 1920s. But in the 1980s, even socially engaged writers like Zheng and Liu began to back off somewhat from the confident pose of the possessor of correct answers to the role of the teacher who raises important questions, even when the answers are unknown and maybe even unknowable. Three years after publishing his hard-hitting "People or Monsters?," Liu announced that it had hardly got to the bottom of things. Exactly what the ties were between Liu's chief villain, Wang Shouxin, and more senior Party leaders in the county and province were questions that he could not get clear on at the time, and that would probably always remain murky.[143] In 1986 Feng Jicai, moving away from his positivistic scar stories, published *The Three-Inch Golden Lotus*,[144] a work that explored the premodern problem of bound feet but led readers to ponder questions that indirectly raised contemporary questions: Why were bound feet considered beautiful? How could we Chinese have thought something so peculiar? How could we have been indifferent to the crushing of children's bones? Such questions were asked metaphorically about the more recent past.

The asking of questions, even if answerless, could have a cathartic effect. In a short story, "Who Am I?," Feng Zongpu tells of a woman who is persecuted during the Cultural Revolution until she loses her grip on whether she is a human being or, as her tormenters charge, truly a "cow ghost" or "snake spirit."[145] Her groping among variant versions of herself, apart from its realism, could be read as a metaphor for the search for China's true identity during confusing times. The author provides a clear view of the "correct answer" in the woman's case, but offers none in China's. Her role is to lead readers to ponder the parallel, only as a first step in coming to terms with the national confusion.

---

[143] Liu Binyan, "Tan xinshiqi de wenxue chuangzuo wenti," p. 12.

[144] "Sancun jinlian."

[145] "Wo shi shei?" I am indebted to Anne Thurston for pointing out this story; see "Victims of China's Cultural Revolution," Part 1, pp. 614–15.

On the whole, however, works that led readers to face ugly facts or ponder difficult questions were unusual. Even during periods of speaking out, most writers stuck with conventional knowledge and moral certitude. The mainstream of post-Mao scar literature, far from illustrating a search for unknown answers, spelled out in case after case truths that both writers and readers already had well in mind: that the Cultural Revolution had been violent, that officials had behaved unfairly, that corruption and bureaucratism were out of control, and so on. To people who live outside the context of the times, it might seem puzzling that simple stories bearing well-known truths could elicit such excited reader response. In societies where free public expression is possible, the public discusses such issues as they arise, and their complaints, whether answered or not, become commonplace. But in situations where public expression is difficult or impossible, pent-up popular needs to hear forbidden truths can grow until, when public expression finally does become possible, even prosaic views can seem exhilarating, and even agreed-upon truths count as "breaking new ground." Of Soviet writing during the post-Stalin thaw, Victor Erlich has written that "when bureaucratic euphemisms displace the unbearable actuality and explain it away, the simple act of calling a spade a spade, of naming the unspeakable, becomes an epiphany."[146]

This phenomenon of socialist systems was, perhaps, even more pronounced in China, where the cultural importance of morally correct public language added to the public's need to see their moral points of view receive the dignity of formal written expression. In the immediate post-Mao years, readers, writers, and even some officials called the pattern *jiehen* (release of resentment).[147] A writer who could put into print problems or truths that had previously been restricted to the oral grapevine, thereby taking responsibility for any "mistakes" in what was said, could give like-minded readers the chance to cheer with relative impunity. This cheer, in turn, could earn for the author a place, at least temporarily, in the pantheon known as "the literary scene" (*wentan*). In 1979, a young Cantonese writer wondered if he dared to write down the Cultural Revolution story about how he and fellow Red Guards had been induced to form a human dyke against typhoon-driven storm waves on the south China coast. Clutching their "Quotations from Chairman Mao" and singing revolutionary songs, they were swept away and drowned by the dozen. The story became widely known unofficially, but not until Chen Haiying's "Black Tide" ("Hei haichao"), published in the student literary magazine *Red Bean*, could people feel a "release of outrage" publicly.[148] The salubrious effects of such release were widely appreciated, indeed sometimes vitally important, to many readers and

---

[146] Victor Erlich, "Post-Stalin Trends in Russian Literature," p. 418.

[147] For an official reference see Li Shusheng, "Zhongguo wenlian lilun yanjiushi zuotan 'shei shi qiangzhe?,'" where attacks on corruption and influence peddling are officially praised as "saying incisively what the great majority of people, in their hearts, want to say."

[148] The story was published in three versions; see bibliography.

writers. This fact helps to explain another condition that has puzzled out-siders who look at literature in socialist China: why did writers who were kept under tight political controls, when they were released from some of those controls, continue to write politically? After Deng Xiaoping an-nounced in summer 1980 that, for the first time since Mao's "Talks at Yan'an" in 1942, Chinese literature need not "serve politics," hardly any writers turned immediately to apolitical topics. Outsiders tend to assume that habit was the only reason: these were political writers, they conceived things only in political terms, and political writing was all that they could do. But although habit was certainly part of the story, the behavior of post-Mao writers cannot be understood without accounting for the strong natu-ral attractions—pursued by choice, not reflex—in sticking with political writing but shifting one's political standpoint. Two years after Deng's change of policy, Liu Binyan observed that "the slogan 'serve politics' con-stricted literature. But does it follow that the further literature departs from politics, the better off it is? . . . the question is not whether literature should serve politics, but *what kind* of politics it should serve. . . . I don't like the word 'serve,' so prefer to say literature should 'deal with' (*chuli*) politics."[149]

Writers who "released resentment" could earn quick popularity when the points they made corresponded to widespread concerns. But they also drew criticism, not only from representatives of the leadership but also from cer-tain other writers. In the 1980s, a number of young modernist writers, many of them under the spiritual stewardship of the senior literary critic Li Tuo, wished genuinely to escape the guidance of politics, be it the Commu-nist Party's or Liu Binyan's. To them "releasing resentment" was essentially political, and in any case an artistically shallow literary function. Among other, more established writers, there was criticism that appeals to popular sentiment could be used opportunisticly, and even cynically. Wang Meng, despite his strong record of opposing Maoist literary controls, nonetheless had his doubts about "ground-breaking heroes." "Pointing out a problem is easier than solving it," Wang observed in 1980, when "releasing resent-ment" was at a peak. "For example, on the question of unemployment among urban youth today—a serious problem whose existence the govern-ment denies—it would be easy to write a very popular story. But would that solve the problem, or only make it worse?"[150] By 1986, Wang's doubts had hardened into fierce satire. In a story about a man who happened across a dirty public kitchen, Wang wrote:

> Too bad he wasn't a writer, otherwise [this kitchen] would have been enough for high-flown literary creation. All he'd need would be a couple of characters, a twist

[149] Liu Binyan, "Tan xinshiqi de wenxue chuangzuo wenti," pp. 4, 15. Emphasis added.
[150] Interview, 3 August 1980, Beijing. See also Wang's criticism of young playwrights who use "mellifluous standard Chinese" to put on stage lines that "everybody has been eagerly awaiting for a long time" instead of doing the harder work of characters, plots, and new in-sights. "Zhongguo wenxue chuangzuo de huanjing yu qiantu."

of plot, a bit of sentimentalism and a sentence or two of hard-hitting criticism, and there he'd have it—a bold work of fiction exposing the dark side of society. He could have gotten famous overnight, been invited to join the Writers' Association, and turned into a swaggering, gesticulating, uniquely revered hero, more correct than anyone. It is, in any case, easier to curse a public kitchen than to run one—and more fun, too.[151]

Wang drew criticism for this hyperbole, especially after others speculated that he was writing with certain actual people in mind. But there can be no denying that the side of writers' motivations that he refers to was there. Writers in socialist China, as elsewhere, thought about matters of fame, money, and status, and calculated ways to improve their chances at these rewards. The urge to be—or at least appear—courageous and self-sacrificing existed simultaneously, and the distance between the two kinds of goals created a perennial problem of the appearance of hypocrisy. A morally correct set of goals, whether expressing socialist ideals or courageous dissent, defined a public image for the writer to live up to; at the same time, privately, every writer paid more or less attention to mundane calculations.[152] There was, though, a considerable range in how writers handled the dilemma in terms of the mix of motivations, methods used, and degrees of openness.

In 1985, the writer Feng Jicai analyzed the problem in terms of "the limited number of places," at any given time, on the "literary scene."[153] "It's like the number of seats on a bus," Feng said. "If you don't get one, then you either stand or don't get on." The basic reason for the limitation, Feng felt, was just that the human brain takes note only of fairly short lists. When some new writers arrive on the "literary scene," some others, in the public mind, disappear from it. Implicitly there develops a competition that includes both established writers seeking to hold their places and large numbers of little-known writers always seeking to break in.[154]

The ways of breaking in were various, and almost always susceptible to cynical interpretation. Feng Jicai felt that experimentation with modernist literary technique was primarily a way to attract attention; it made one appear stylishly Western, but had little to do with Chinese daily life, which was, for the most part, still far from modern. Another way to gain a reputa-

---

[151] Wang Meng, "Hudie," p. 30; translated by Gladys Yang in Wang Meng *The Butterfly and Other Stories*, p. 87, but not to the normal standards of Gladys Yang.

[152] In a poem called "Confession" (Kougong, 1926), Wen Yiduo captured the condition with brutal honesty. After explaining that, as a poet, he naturally does feel moved by such things as white rocks, green pines, and the vast sea, sunset colors on the backs of crows, heroes, and tall mountains: "But there's another me / Are you ready for it? / The mentality of a fly / Crawling up a garbage can" (*Wen Yiduo xuanji*, p. 71).

[153] Interview, 5 December 1985, Los Angeles.

[154] Although most literary publishers balanced the pressures to introduce new writers (including numerous personal appeals) with their own interests in maintaining contacts with established writers, one magazine, published in Cangzhou, Hebei Province, called itself *Anonymous Literature* (*Wuming wenxue*) and published only the work of unknown writers.

tion was to write some hard-hitting social criticism or political dissent. Although this kind of writing had much better roots in daily life than modernism had, it was at least as easy to use opportunisticly. During the post-Mao thaw, when one could become a "ground-breaking hero" by breaking into "forbidden zones," young writers talked among themselves about which taboos to challenge, which stories could be used for the purpose, and how to achieve the most impact for the least risk. But if political dissidence could help build a literary career, so could political sycophantism. Whenever the Party announced a preference for a certain literary theme (progress in rural life, success in a military adventure, or the like), it created special opportunities for writers who were willing to comply. This was true even during times of relaxation, when a variety of writing was publishable.

For writers who gained some initial fame, there was the additional possibility of using a literary reputation as an entrée to a political career. Wang Meng's appointment as minister of culture in 1986 stimulated considerable speculation of many kinds about his motives in joining officialdom. At one extreme, some said he had sold out his independent integrity as a writer. Others said no, he was only trying to get into a position to do some good for everyone. There were many other rumors, all unconfirmable, about well-known writers who were jealous that they had not been chosen to be minister. When, two years later, Feng Jicai agreed to serve as vice chair of the All-China Federation of Literary and Art Workers, there was similar debate on the literary grapevine about his motives and about the pros and cons of a writer becoming an official. Even a young writer like Lu Xinhua, after publishing only one widely noticed story ("Scar," 1978) considered briefly whether to make a trip to Beijing in an effort to parlay his brief literary fame into the beginning of a political career. His method, he thought, could be to pay his respects to some high cultural officials and then to sit back and wait until one of them, for whatever reason, might want "to make use of me."[155]

Among some writers in the 1980s, the search for avenues to fame became strong enough to induce a kind of speculator's mentality. How one positioned oneself today depended upon one's sense of where political guidelines, literary fads, and popular tastes might turn tomorrow. Credit for an innovation, whether political or literary, could come and go very quickly, so that only the first few examples in a new trend were useful in building a reputation. Literary editors complained that after a literary breakthrough, their offices would be flooded by imitative works of little or no value. In 1979, the senior playwright Xia Yan wrote that every day he found in his mailbox three to five, and sometimes seven, manuscripts of lengthy, five-act plays from young writers seeking his help; he would have more patience, he wrote, if the manuscripts did not seem so hastily produced—full of contra-

---

[155] Interview with Lu Xinhua, 22 January 1987, Los Angeles.

dictions, vagueness, and technical errors.[156] Chen Canyun, a senior Cantonese novelist, complained that even plagiarism had become a tool for breaking into literary publication.[157] Even established writers felt the pressure to continue breaking new ground, lest the trends of the times gallop ahead of them. The staying power of a writer like Liu Xinwu, from his ground-breaking story "The Homeroom Teacher" in late 1977 through a series of stories and novellas extending into the 1990s, never far behind the twists and turns of the times, is an achievement that most sojourners on China's post-Mao literary scene have not been able to match.

The material and careerist concerns of individual writers often pulled in considerably different directions from what was prescribed by the exalted image of the writer as moral guardian of the public interest. Different though they were, neither of these two levels of the writer's life could be ignored without serious consequences, and learning how to combine the two, without seeming shamelessly hypocritical, became one of the skills of living. A sufficiently pedestrian example of the problem would be the occasion, in the early 1990s, on which a small group of writers, very short on money and also known for their literary exposure of corruption, boarded a train and found that the ticket taker failed to collect their tickets. "I wonder where the collector is," one mused. "They'll probably come later," another said. But no collector did come, and the topic went away.[158]

The interface of grand ideals and the nitty-gritty of daily living caused problems in literary creation, as well. Most works, even of fiction, were based on actual occurrences, and then were made to fit morally charged general patterns. When Jiang Zilong wrote his prize-winning story "Manager Qiao Assumes Office,"[159] in which the right-minded Manager Qiao cuts through bureaucratism in order to get things done, the municipal government in Tianjin, where Jiang Zilong lived, initially repressed the story, saying that the "old cadres" whom Manager Qiao swept away were, in actual life, good cadres whom the Gang of Four had kicked out, and that Jiang Zilong was, therefore, indirectly supporting a pro-Gang-of-Four point of view, which in 1979 was anathema.[160] In fact, the argument against the story appears to have arisen from certain old cadres themselves, who feared that they might be understood to be the deadwood that the story's hero was

[156] Xia Yan, "Gei yige qingnian zuozhe de xin."

[157] Chen pointed to a story called "Gui jie" (Ghost sister), which was published in *Guangzhou wenyi* (no. 3, 1980) and later exposed as a plagiarism of a story by the Hong Kong writer Xu Yu. Interview, 7 May 1980, Guangzhou.

[158] Personal observation. Names of writers withheld.

[159] Jiang Zilong, "Qiao changzhang shangrenji."

[160] Interview with Jiang Zilong, 10 August 1980, Beijing; interview with Wang Jinmin, a professor of Chinese, Zhongshan University, 4 January 1980, based on Wang's reading of current classified materials. "Manager Qiao" was published after authorities in Beijing sided with Tianjin editors against the Tianjin city authorities.

opposing. The author denied this was so, but an author's intentions in such cases were basically irrelevant.[161] After Ye Wenfu published a poem called "General, You Can't Do This," about a military official who embezzles funds intended for a nursery school, both readers and officials asked him repeatedly to reveal who he was actually writing about.[162] Some generals took pains to clear their own names.[163]

Only rarely did writers use literary works as a way of launching personal attacks on people other than national targets like the Gang of Four. But they did, commonly, draw on actual life situations for the material of their creative writing, and it was this tenuous connection that potential targets feared. Lu Wenfu, after publishing his story "The Gourmet," a tour de force of subtle political satire about a ne'er-do-well glutton, quite politically incorrect but landing on his feet at every stage of the revolution, explained why he could not be too precise about the social background of his story: it would bring too many meetings down on the heads of his fellow citizens of Suzhou.[164] According to Jiang Zilong, the tendency of officials to see themselves in literary works, especially as the negative characters, created inhibitions in writers who had to worry that their own leaderships would do this "self-assigned seating" and seek retribution. During his stay in Xinjiang in the 1970s, Wang Meng discovered yet another kind of misunderstanding born of the disjunction between the ideal and actual levels of a writer's life. Because he was in political disgrace, Wang had to write under pseudonyms. As his readers became accustomed to this, they began congratulating him on pieces he hadn't written.[165]

The genre of literary reportage, closely related to fiction, avoided certain ambiguities because it named actual names. People who merely resembled literary villains could relax, and writers needed to face objections only from people who were connected to those they named. But the difficulties that reportage shed in these regards were more than compensated by others that the genre entailed. The need to investigate carefully, gather opposing stories, cross-check facts, and satisfy government review were all greater for reportage than for fiction, drama, or poetry. In 1982, Liu Binyan, perhaps China's definitive writer of reportage, complained that the versions of a story from opposing camps could be diametrically opposed, and even a single witness's story might change drastically after the application of political pressure or the inducement of bribes.[166]

---

[161] Jiang Zilong, "'Qiao changzhang shangrenji' de shenghuo zhang," p. 14. Interview, 10 August 1980.

[162] See Li Yi, "Zhongguo xinxieshizhuyi wenyi de xingqi," p. 23.

[163] Interview with Wang Jinmin, 4 January 1980.

[164] Lu Wenfu, "Meishijia," p. 5.

[165] Interview, 3 August 1980, Beijing.

[166] Liu Binyan, "Tan xin shiqi de wenxue chuangzuo wenti," p. 12.

Addressing the Leadership

When political controls were relaxed within the system, as during the Hundred Flowers of 1956 and the post-Mao thaw, some writers seized the opportunity to "plead for the people" (*wei min qing ming*), asking the leadership to pay proper attention to sufferings among ordinary folk. In premodern China, this role of the Chinese literati had been primarily a matter of personal address to the ruler. The people who were spoken for were not involved. But in socialist China, the writer's rhetorical turn toward the leadership was seldom unidirectional in this same way. A story or poem, although formally addressed to no one, implicitly could be read as saying to the leadership, "You should do something about this"; to the people spoken for, "Look what I'm doing for you"; and to the general readership, "Observe how I perform the role of the principled literatus."

A wide variety of works from the post-Mao years exhibit this kind of public address of the leadership in one way or another. Liu Qingbang's "Look Whose Family Is Blessed" (1980) shows how a mother, pinching every edible morsel she can find in order to feed her children during the Great Leap Forward famine, breaks her commune's rules and is eventually driven to suicide.[167] The case of intellectuals who want to help build socialism but are slapped down by an uncomprehending regime had many examples, especially from the middle generation of writers. The theme of unappreciated patriotism was dramatized in stories about loyal intellectuals who returned from overseas after 1949 to help the new regime, only to be abused by it;[168] or, conversely, about some who had the chance to emigrate and have a wealthier life abroad but chose to be guided by ideals and to stay behind, only to suffer.[169]

The address of leaders in such cases was usually respectful, even adulatory. In a 1980 story called "Lost Piano Notes," a pair of young lovers, both pianists, perform together and win the approval of Zhou Enlai: "Premier Zhou attended our evening performance, and even met with us in person to encourage us. . . . Later we made a trip abroad together, and before we left, Premier Zhou again personally inspected our programs and warmly greeted us."[170] Later the young woman pianist is attacked as a "white expert" (someone who puts technical expertise above Communist ideals) and a "traitor," and is driven to death, apparently by suicide. She is attacked, according to

---

[167] Liu Qingbang, "Kankan sheijia you fu."

[168] Bai Hua's "Kulian" (see chapter 1, note 55) is the best-known example. A less-well-known but purer example is the film *Haiwai chizi* (The overseas compatriot) (Guangzhou: Pearl River Studios, 1979).

[169] The most famous example is Zhang Xianliang's "Ling yu rou," made into a film called *Mumaren* (The herdsman's story) (Shanghai zhipianchang, 1982). A much more subtle example is Wang Zhecheng and Wen Xiaoyu's "Jixu."

[170] Liu Shijun, "Xiaoshile de qinsheng," p. 20.

the story, as a surrogate for Zhou Enlai, who is the real target. The story "speaks for" Zhou as well as for the heroine. Zhou is exalted, as are, implicitly, the post-Mao leaders who are assumed to be Zhou's true comrades and to whom the appeal is addressed. The story illustrates a more general type of works that "spoke for the people" in the limited sense of speaking for particular individuals—usually not ordinary people, but political leaders who had been treated "incorrectly" at some point during the revolution. When the reputations of Chen Duxiu (1879– 1942) and Qu Qiubai (1899–1935) were officially restored in the late 1970s, the first public signs of the revisions came in commentaries on the two men's contributions to literature.

Leaders who had helped to build the socialist system in the 1950s and later suffered in Maoist purges got some literary support, both as a group and individually, in the immediate post-Mao years. General Peng Dehuai, purged in 1959 for opposing Mao on the Great Leap Forward, was defended in works by Liu Zhen and a collection of reminiscences called *At the Side of General Peng*, (*Zai Pengzong shenbian*) which was published in a remarkably large print run of 500,000 in the first half of 1980.[171] Chen Yi, a military leader and Politburo member who was purged in 1969 and died in 1972, received an unusual amount of literary praise, most notably in Sha Yexin's clever play *Mayor Chen Yi* (1980). Even Soviet novels were used for this political purpose. Semyon Babayevsky's *The Wide World*, winner of a Stalin Prize in the Soviet Union, was selected for translation in the late 1970s apparently for its message, relevant by analogy to China, that the "retirement" of senior Stalinist officials in Russia had been premature.[172]

Addressing the leadership obliged writers to think about whether and to what extent they would "illustrate policy" (*tujie zhengce*). The theory of illustrating policy was often different from its practice. In theory, writers were supposed to absorb policy guidelines that the leadership handed down, and then incorporate these into literary works to pass on to readers. In practice, from the late 1950s onward writers often bore leaders, not readers, in mind when deciding how to do policy illustrations. During times of high political pressure, such as the late Mao years, writers had no choice but to conform closely to policy. During more relaxed times, when a variety of options were available, close conformity to policy left a writer vulnerable to charges of sycophancy and to a lack of independent creativity. Yet some writers continued with the project of illustrating policy, using interestingly different degrees of specificity.

In 1979, a play called *Wang Zhaojun* by Cao Yu, whose fame dated from the 1930s, opened in Beijing amid much official fanfare. It also drew considerable criticism among intellectuals for being "literature written to order"

---

[171] Liu Zhen, "Heiqi" and "Pengzong de gushi." On *Zai Pengzong shenbian*, see Wen Lu, "Zhongguo de changxiaoshu."
[172] See Miriam London and Mu Yang-jen, "What Are They Reading in China?," p. 42.

(*zunming wenxue*), a term attributed to Lu Xun. The play was about a court lady of the Western Han dynasty who, in 33 B.C., agreed to marry a chieftain of the "barbarian" Xiongnu tribe of Central Asian nomads in order to try to buy peace with them. Wang Zhaojun's self-sacrificing spirit later came to be celebrated in Chinese poetry, drama, and storytelling of many kinds. In the late 1970s, according to the program notes at the performance, Zhou Enlai suggested to Cao Yu that a play be written that properly appreciates the Xiongnu point of view. Wang Zhaojun should be presented not as a martyr who fell to a barbarian tribe but as the wife in a happy marriage between peoples of equal respectability. This was the only proper reflection of the Party's policies toward the national minorities. The resulting work was a fairly pure example of "illustrating policy."

In most other cases, writers responded not to this kind of specific suggestion but to general guidelines. Writers of detective and counterespionage stories, for example, could submit their work in the mode of illustrating why and how the state should apprehend criminals and spies; the Ministry of Public Security ran a press, the Masses Publishing House, in order to publish such fiction, although the earning of revenue by selling entertainment became another important purpose. Although the rationale for detective fiction remained fairly constant over time, most other political guidelines came and went with changes in social policy. During the late 1970s, there appeared a spate of stories and films intended to illustrate the Party's policy that young people who had "lost their footing" during the Cultural Revolution and become cynics or even "hooligans" should be treated with sympathy and understanding, and should be trained in proper behavior, which is their own underlying wish.[173]

Even skilled and independent-minded writers would sometimes write works that illustrated policy if they found they agreed with a particular policy. For example, in 1981, Gao Xiaosheng, author of finely wrought stories that wonderfully capture the mental world of Jiangsu peasants and, sometimes, undercut the whole Maoist enterprise,[174] chose in 1981 to publish a story that illustrated the correctness of the current policies of rural economic reform. Entitled "The River Flows East," it tells of a young peasant woman who is engaged to a distant cousin, an honest and hard-working young man, but who instead falls in love with a technician, the son of a

---

[173] Liu Xinwu's "Ban zhuren" (1977) and "Xinglai ba, didi" (1978) heralded this trend, which became much more detailed in television films such as *Shiwangren de xiwang* (The hope of the hopeless) (Hunan dianshi dianying, 1979) and *Jiujiu ta!* (Save her!) (Shenyang huajutuan, broadcast nationally 13 January 1980). As noted in chapter 1, the top leadership felt that two filmscripts, Wang Jing's "In Society's Archives" and Li Kewei's "Girl Thief" went too far with the theme, producing the effect of teaching hooliganism instead of curing it.

[174] See *Gao Xiaosheng yijiubalingnian xiaoshuoji*, especially "Qianbao" (The purse), pp. 45–58, and "Yudiao" (Fishing), pp. 87–99; see translations by Wang Mingjie and Howard Goldblatt in Gao Xiaosheng, *The Broken Betrothal*, pp. 120–33 and 189–205.

factory manager.[175] She and the technician go on to illustrate the advantages of rural industry and a commodity market. Her peasant suitor, for example, feels that every family should make its own shoes. Why not save in this way, if possible? But the young woman and her new industrial boyfriend know that factory-made shoes are better, and are actually cheaper if you add up the cost of materials and *time*, which they now know is worth something.

The illustration of policy in literary work sometimes involved a harbinger function. New policies were broached or promoted before they publicly took effect. For example, Zong Fuxian's 1978 play "From the Silent Zones," which heralded the official "reversal of verdict" on the Tiananmen incident of 5 April 1976, was first published and performed in Shanghai in October 1978. Although no "reversal of verdict" on the demonstrations had yet been announced, Zong seems to have had assurance that his play accorded with a new policy that would soon be revealed. In the next month, November, *People's Daily* published a selection of poems from Tiananmen; in December, People's Literature Publishing House released a volume called *Poems from Tiananmen*. Then, also in December, the Ministry of Culture and the National Labor Union in Beijing jointly convened a big meeting to award a prize to Zong Fuxian's play.[176] Clearly the young playwright had been a pawn in the project of announcing a policy reversal. Yet, because he and his friends at Fudan University supported the reversal, which lifted the odious label of "counterrevolution" from the Tiananmen movement, we cannot say simply that Zong was illustrating someone else's viewpoint.

The same ambiguous pattern is illustrated by Chen Rong's "At Middle Age," although the political issue in the case of this story was less sensitive. When "At Middle Age" was published in January 1980, it drew wide attention and quick praise for pointing out the plight of middle-aged intellectuals like Lu Wenting, the opthamologist-cum-homemaker who worked herself nearly to death. To most of the public, this problem seemed newly broached and boldly put.[177] In fact, though, at high levels within the Party the problem of the special burdens of middle-aged intellectuals had already been under discussion for about a year and a half.[178] Chen Rong, whose husband wrote political editorials for *People's Daily*, was in a position to know that her story would fit with policies that the Party was preparing to announce.

---

[175] Gao Xiaosheng, "Shui dong liu." See also "On My Story 'The River Flows East,'" where Gao makes it clear that his intention in the story was to illustrate a new policy of which he approves.

[176] See Zhongguo shehui kexueyuan wenxue yanjiusuo dangdai wenxue yanjiushi, *Xin shiqi wenxue liu nian*, pp. 464–67.

[177] In a number of surveys of the film audience of the early 1980s, Lu Wenting drew the largest number of votes as "the film character you like best and who has left you with the deepest impression." See Gao Qixiang, "Dianying zhonggui yao kao sixiang he yishu yingde guanzhong" in Zhongguo renmin daxue shubao ziliao she, *Fuyin baokan ziliao*, p. 32.

[178] Liu Binyan, "Tan xin shiqi de wenxue chuangzuo wenti," p. 2.

Still, it would be wrong to see Chen Rong only as standing on the outside edge of the Party and broadcasting its new policy to readers. An even more important part of her address was toward the Party leaders, on behalf of intellectuals. Effectively she was saying to the Party: Now that you have formulated a policy, you had better carry it out; my story shows why. During the year after the story's publication, there were many appeals from below to "carry out the policy on intellectuals."

Works like "At Middle Age" that faced two directions, addressing both leadership and populace, had to be carefully done, because the interests of the two audiences did not overlap well. To match popular complaints very closely inevitably led a writer into political and social criticism that the leadership could not tolerate. One issue that generally allowed enough room to accommodate both groups was corruption. To readers, any amount of exposure of any corruption was welcome. To the leadership, too much exposure of corruption was of course unacceptable, but a limited treatment of corruption, combined with the creation of a heroic character who successfully deals with it, was not only acceptable but welcome. It could give readers the sense that the Party understood their grievances and was on the side that wanted to seek remedies. Stories such as Jiang Zilong's "Manager Qiao Assumes Office" and Ke Yunlu's *New Star* (1986)[179] both achieved for the leadership the effect of "a soft blow doing a lot of good" (*xiaoda da bangmang*). Jiang's story was awarded the official prize for the best story of 1979, and Ke's novel was adapted for nationwide television broadcast.

To the extent that writers chose to "illustrate policy," they were vulnerable to criticism as hacks, short on creativity and lacking independence. Such charges may often have been true, but it does not follow that being a hack was easy. It was, first, not easy to find out what the crucial policy issues were. Everyone had access to the slogans, such as "Build the Four Modernizations," but these were rarely sufficient to support even a bad story. Writers like Chen Rong, who were fortunate to be well situated, could know more; but for most, the details of policy remained obscure and elusive. In 1982 Liu Binyan observed that

> In this country of ours, if [young writers] really want to grasp the trends at work in society, [they] have to listen here and there for bits of information passed down through Party channels, and scour the Party documents they can get hold of. Many of them are not Party members, or anyway not high-ranking enough to have good access. . . . Hence a contradiction arises: the leadership asks that literature serve the Four Modernizations and make the most effective possible contributions to social progress; yet virtually no young writers are allowed any understanding of what the crucial problems are that the central authorities want to see solved.[180]

[179] Ke Yunlu, *Xinxing*.
[180] Liu Binyan, "Tan xinshiqi de wenxue chuangzuo wenti," p. 2

Even when writers could identify cutting-edge issues, there was no guarantee that these would stay the same long enough for them to conceive, write, and publish their literary work. Chen Canyun, a senior Cantonese writer known for his portrayals of village life and for his willingness to support Party policy, eventually gave up writing about the question of private plots of land, about which policy flip-flops were too hard to account for or predict.[181]

There was, moreover, the complex set of problems about how actually to produce in readers the kinds of responses that a policy called for. The acts of reading and writing proved too complex for writers to be able to control with precision what readers would take away. In the 1950s, a writer of comedians' dialogues, aiming to promote a literacy campaign by poking fun at people who used lame excuses for not reading, invented the line, "*The Liberation Daily* always carries the same old stuff; it gives me a headache just to look at it."[182] Later, when audiences laughed rather too hard at the line, the writer realized they were laughing more at the newspaper than at its reluctant reader. In 1979 a little-known Cantonese writer named Huang Tianyuan found a very specific issue on which he could illustrate the harm of superstition. In "Skating Love Song" he tells of a pretty young woman who works in a morgue dressing corpses.[183] She meets a boyfriend on a roller-skating rink and is afraid he will reject her when he learns what she does. The problem is not that people fear contamination by germs, which she can prevent by wearing gloves and other measures; it is the unscientific fear of occult curse, which is presumed to arise from contact with the dead and which no amount of washing can cleanse. Her boyfriend decides to stick by her, and faces down opposition from parents and friends. He properly illustrates freedom from superstition. But the effect on readers seems to have been different.

Editors at *Guangzhou Literature and Art* (*Guangzhou wenyi*), where the story was published, received letters from workers and directors in the morgues of Guangzhou complaining that now it would be harder than ever for their young workers to find boyfriends and girlfriends. More than spreading the right answer about superstition, they said, the story had only made matters worse by stimulating fears that would better have been left alone.[184] The story's "illustration of policy" had, in short, been counterproductive.

The story's author and editors could see its unintended effects because

---

[181] Interview, 7 May 1980.

[182] Li Qun, "Zhuanzhi kongmeibing."

[183] Huang Tianyuan, "Liubing lianqu." It is possible that the frame of this story was borrowed by the Hong Kong writer Xi Xi, whose 1982 story "Xiang wo zheyang de yige nüzi" examines the feelings of a young woman who dresses corpses for a living and faces having to reveal this fact to a suitor. In artistic sensitivity and subtlety, Xi Xi's story is a large improvement upon Huang Tianyuan's.

[184] Interview at *Guangzhou wenyi*, 7 March 1980. One of the letters was published; see *Guangzhou wenyi* 1980.1.71–72.

they had at least some access to reader response. But another, very considerable, danger in "illustrating policy" was that the political leaders who set policy usually had no such access. Not only were they too busy to look into such things; the staffs that surrounded them had strong incentives to buffer them from news they would not want to hear. As a result, they could easily make the naive assumptions that the intended effects of a literary work came close to its actual effects. To well-insulated leaders, a literary articulation of policy could appear to be essentially the same as a report on actual popular thinking: people could give up superstitions about corpses because stories told them to, or really support China's war with Vietnam because fictional heroes did. In 1979, Liu Binyan observed that, in Mao years, "Literature and life went forward on two entirely separate tracks. In the books things were this way, and in actual life they were that way, forming two very different worlds."[185] Li Yi, editor of the Hong Kong magazine *The Seventies*, argued that the confusion of policy and actuality among leaders could lead to a vicious circle: the more leaders became deluded into thinking that social life was as rosy as their policies prescribed, the more they were likely to set forth even more ambitious policies, only to have those, too, confirmed by the self-reinforcing patterns in the system.[186]

In 1980, as high-level political leaders sought ways to soften Mao's slogan "Literature in Service of Politics," they sent messages that writers should move away from "illustrating policy." In Shanghai's *Wenhui Daily*, the authoritative voice of "Commentator" said, "Practice has already shown that the old methods of turning literary work into illustration of policy, stressing the need to serve politics and setting forth rigid requirements about what to write and how to write it, has done more harm than good to literary development."[187] To most writers, such messages were good news. Were it not for habits developed over many years, they might have abruptly abandoned the illustration of policy in 1980. But the practice, periodically resuscitated by attacks on "bourgeois liberalism," died slowly during the 1980s, and was discernible even in the 1990s.

Writing for Self-Expression

Most of the creative writing in the Chinese socialist literary system was what James J. Y. Liu, in his classic *Chinese Theories of Literature*, has called "pragmatic": its purpose was to change the world in one way or another.[188] But the functions that Liu calls "expressive" were also sometimes at work. In these, the point of writing was to express what a writer had in mind—to "get it out," as it were, rather than to "get something done" once it was out. This distinction was never pure. No writer, however self-absorbed, has ever

---

[185] Liu Binyan, "Guanyu 'xie yin'anmian' he 'ganyu shenghuo.'"
[186] Li Yi, "Zhongguo xinxieshizhuyi wenyi de xingqi," p. 22.
[187] *Wenhuibao*, "Benbao pinglunyuan," "Wenyi yao wei sihua ouge."
[188] Liu, *Chinese Theories of Literature*.

completely eradicated the notion of a reader; at a minimum, an implied or ideal audience—even if this audience is oneself at another time, as in the case of a diary, or something as abstract as "history" or the mind of God— is always necessary before a writer undertakes to create something. It would be hard, moreover, to imagine a literary work that served purely a "pragmatic" or "expressive" function, instead of some combination of the two. Nonetheless there were, among literary works in socialist China, clearly differences of emphasis in these two kinds of literary function.

Some works that resembled state-sponsored socialist realism, and which thus appeared to be fully pragmatic in their concerns, in fact included an important expressive component. Like socialist realism, such stories were laden with moral judgments and populated by fairly flat characters; but they differed in that primary loyalty was to the writer's own vision of the truth, or to a vision shared by a coterie, rather than to the state's. In the post-Mao years, for example, a number of stories were written by and about the victims of the 1957 Anti-Rightist Campaign and undermined the official view that the campaign had been "necessary."[189] (Since Deng Xiaoping had personally prosecuted the campaign, to repudiate it entirely was out of the question.) These stories obeyed the alternate vision that "Rightists" were loyal and idealistic people whom Mao had misunderstood and mistreated. Although the act of writing such stories certainly did have the pragmatic goal of changing public perceptions of Rightists, it was often also the expression of an inner need, the need to put on paper one's own vision of the truth.

Some works of the "scar" period were a kind of personal documentary. A story called "Nightmare: Notes from a Mother's Hand" records the experience of a parent watching a child be drawn into mortal combat, and die, during the Cultural Revolution; as such, it sketches an important episode in Chinese history and does so in a way that represents millions of others.[190] But its heart is personal pain, and its purpose is more to express that pain than to wreak any particular effect. Its implied audience is less concrete than officialdom, or other victims; it is larger, perhaps all of "history," whom the author hopes to be "a fair and impartial judge."[191] The same spirit of recording the truth for posterity is at work in "Look Whose Family Is Blessed," the story about starvation during the Great Leap Forward. We noted above that this story addressed the leadership, asking it to recognize what happened during the famine. But in part, too, it was speaking over the leadership's head, toward history. Sometimes writers wrote "for history" without knowing if their work could ever be published. In the early 1960s, for example, Cong Weixi penned a novel about the Great Leap Forward called *The*

---

[189] An unusually good one, psychologically far more subtle than others of its kind, is Liu Binyan's "Diwuge chuan dayi de ren." A book whose publication broadly challenged the official view of the Anti-Rightist Campaign was Zuo Ni, ed., *Chongfang de xianhua.*

[190] Xu Hui, "Emeng."

[191] Link, ed., *Stubborn Weeds*, p. 56.

Children, knowing that it could not be published immediately but hoping that eventually it might be; a few years later, during the Cultural Revolution, his frightened mother burned the manuscript.[192] It was usually oppositional writers who addressed history in this way, but not always. When Party writers in the 1950s sought to set down the glories of the revolutionary struggle, their aim was also, in part, to address history. Du Pengcheng, a journalist who lived through the Yan'an days of the Communist movement, wrote *Defending Yan'an* (1954) as a "record for posterity" of the heroic people and events he had witnessed. In larger perspective, his work seems a propaganda tract; but his own sense of writing at the time was different.[193]

Expression that focused on the great events of history, no matter how deeply and personally it was felt, always remained somewhat ambiguous between the pragmatic and expressive functions of literature. Works that sidestepped the great events and focused on individual people were fairly rare; but when they did appear, they could provide better examples of expression of the self. Zhang Jie's story "An Unfinished Record" (1980) tells of an historian of the Ming dynasty, at the end of his life and about to die in a hospital, recalling his youth. In those days he had invited a young woman who beamed like sunlight to meet him in a park, only to have her not come, but instead introduce him the next day to her handsome and sturdy fiancé. This left the young scholar, sad but not jealous, to pass the rest of his life unmarried, his primary companion a stray cat whom he adopted and named "The Grand Historian."[194] Zhang's aim in this story, she said, was "to dig out what's really inside people" and "try simply to appreciate them as people."[195]

In a larger sense, "simple appreciation" of daily human life was part of Zhang Jie's quest to find, or build, a confident and satisfying personal identity. In 1981 she wrote, "Only through my work have I found myself. I don't know about others, but I feel to really know one's self is very difficult, sometimes a lifelong task. At any rate, it has taken me forty years, and though it comes late, I relish this new, strong sense of self."[196] Zhang omits mentioning that, until Mao died, she could not use literature in her forty-year effort to come to know herself. The literary styles and requirements of the Mao period had made introspective uses of literature, which had thrived in the first part of the century, practically impossible. When they did become possible again, most notably in the early 1980s, they gave rise to the kind of excitement that is normally associated with new discoveries. Especially to young writers, it could seem splendidly fresh that one could set aside moral

---

[192] Interview with Cong Weixi, 11 August 1980, Beijing.

[193] Interview with Zhang Zhong and Zhao Zumo, Chinese Department, Beijing University, 6 October 1979. During the Cultural Revolution, Maoists accused Du of writing *Defending Yan'an* in order to promote the "Peng Dehuai clique"; *Renmin ribao*, 12 November 1967, p. 6.

[194] Zhang Jie, "Weiliao lu."

[195] Interview, Beijing, 2 August 1980.

[196] Zhang Jie, "Pursuit."

lessons about social groups and explore the world of personal feelings. A high point in this trend came in spring of 1982, after the publication of Yu Luojin's short novel *A Spring Fairy Tale*, which is a frank account of the love life, and unsuccessful marriages, of an educated young woman.[197] The author had already stirred controversy by exposing some of her marital problems in the press; hence few doubted that her new novel was autobiographical. She seemed determined to pull down every inner barrier and social taboo, revealing her involvement with an editor nearly twice her age, and telling even what she knew of her father's love life. To some extent her aim, and her achievement, was simple iconoclasm, as if she were saying, "Look what I can get away with writing." But beneath the shock value was a strong interest, which many readers shared with the author, in probing private consciousness and personal relationships. The notion that insights could pop up in the course of such probing—truths not bound to conventional morality or officially declared to be "correct"—seemed both challenging and exhilarating. Some argued that such probing was more socially useful than the explicit didacticism of the past. "A school-marmish approach to fiction," Feng Jicai commented in 1985, "is not conducive to the production of interesting or great work."[198]

Although self-examination and self-release continued in Chinese writing through the 1980s and into the 1990s, it remained, on the whole, fairly tame by comparison with modern literature in Europe and America. Even Soviet writing after Stalin, which included an outpouring of the personal and subjective basically parallel to that of post-Mao China, clearly exceeded the Chinese case in the degree to which it allowed the unguarded release of inner feelings. Susan Chen, who has compared post-Stalin and post-Mao works systematically in this regard, finds Chinese cultural conservatism stronger than Russian.[199] Political intolerance of expression of the inner self was also at least as strong in China as in the Soviet Union. As noted in the previous chapter, Party leaders feared the release of inner thoughts less for their specific content than for the dangerous fact that they could not be predicted or controlled. In 1981, an authoritative article in *Red Flag* ridiculed the claim that "self-expression is the reflex of an artist's subjective self."[200] Only the artist could say what a subjective reflex was, and it was intolerable to have a situation in which the artist was sole arbiter. Hence "the life of the people," which was publicly accessible and therefore definable by the leadership, had to be "the only source of literature and art."

The probing of the inner self was accompanied by changes in literary technique, as some writers departed from realism in order to experiment with imagistic expression, free association, nonchronological narration, and

---

[197] Yu Luojin, "Chuntian de tonghua."
[198] Quoted in "The Asiaweek Literary Review," *Asiaweek*, 4 October 1985, p. 47.
[199] Susan Wilf Chen, "Literature of the 'Thaw' in China and the Soviet Union."
[200] Sha Tong, "Renzhen kefu wenyi gongzuozhong de ziyouhua qingxiang"; quotation from translation in Foreign Broadcast Information Service, 3 December 1981, pp. K11–K12.

other, often ambiguous, reflections of the subjective life.[201] In some cases, censorship encouraged such change, ironically, by its requirement that certain kinds of thinking be expressed only obliquely. For a good number of journeyman writers, "aesthetics" turned into a superficial matter of shifting erratically from one time or narrative viewpoint to another, or inserting some absurdities or shocking images. Certain other writers, reacting against this faddishness, and originally disposed to realism in any case, were confirmed in their realism. For yet others, art remained an elusive thing, to be captured neither by realism nor by hackneyed devices of antirealism. A senior writer in Anhui, having devoted most of his life to Mao's injunction that art serve politics, near the end fell in love with "pure art," whose essence, he said, could never be taught because it could never really be grasped.[202] Making the same point more concretely, Wang Meng questioned what it means to "understand" a piece of art. After a 1980 meeting in Beijing of writers and officials who had hotly debated the question of "non-understandable art," Wang observed that

> The question, "Do we understand art?" is too simple. A good piece of literature, like *Dream of the Red Chamber*, means many things and sustains many readings. What could it mean to say someone "understands" it? If I read it once, and find later that I can gain from a second reading, does that mean I "didn't understand" the first time? That I "got it" only the second? Will I never need a third? To me, so long as a reader is *interested* by a literary work, and feels some sense of beauty or truth—at least enough to keep on reading—then there's "understanding" enough.[203]

Wang's viewpoint disturbed more conventional writers and critics because it seemed to allow literature to grow separately from "life," or, in the Marxist cliché, no longer to "reflect" life. Merely to play word games seemed a betrayal not just of socialist realism but of deeply rooted cultural attitudes about the social responsibility of a writer. Rebutting this criticism, Yue Daiyun, a professor of comparative literature at Beijing University, wrote that

> Great literary works always reflect certain aspects of the spirit of their times, but this reflection does not have to happen only through "writing the truth." It can also come from writing about spirits and gods, the imagination, an atmosphere, the world of dreams, or the subconscious. The technique can be ornate or spare, analytic or "misty." The point, for art, is not whether the portrayed events are true or not, but whether or not the writer's approach to them is food for thought, and whether their telling bears the power to move.[204]

---

[201] In the early 1980s, Wang Meng was best known for these literary traits; by the end of the decade Can Xue, who far exceeded Wang Meng in their use, was most famous for them. See "Shanshang de xiaowu" and "Wo zai neige shijieli de shiqing." For translations see Can Xue, *Dialogues in Paradise*, pp. 47–53 and 87–93.

[202] Interview with Chen Dengke, 25 June 80, Hefei.

[203] Interview, 3 August 1980.

[204] Yue Daiyun, "Wo guan Zhongguo dangdai wenxue."

Although the spirit of Wang's and Yue's remarks was to defend the "unclear" modernist expression that was emerging at the time, their conception of literary worth was tolerant enough to make room for the broad array of uses of literature that we have reviewed in this chapter. Teaching, exposing, pleading for the people, "releasing resentment," "illustrating policy," "reversing verdicts," recording for history, confessing, exploring the self, experimenting with language, and even simply entertaining were all admissible under the standard that readers find "interest" in some kind of "beauty or truth." Such a standard is appropriate for application to the Chinese socialist literary system, in which, despite its sometimes monolithic appearance from the outside, a wide variety of things was going on.

CHAPTER 4

Media and Market

IN THE LAST CHAPTER we saw how the purposes of writing in socialist China, despite outward appearances of uniformity, could vary widely. In this chapter we will see how the literary media also involved greater variety than was suggested by the routine arrangements of the state's literary bureaucracy: a branch of the Writers' Association for each province, each branch associated with literary periodicals that looked about the same, and so on. The variety entered in part because literary work could appear in several forms (books, magazines, newspapers, radio, television, film, stage performance, hand-copied booklets, word of mouth), and in part because of differing relations to state authority. Some publication was "internal"—meaning restricted by state authority to politically defined readerships—and there were several grades of internality. There was also a variety of semiofficial, unofficial, and underground media that appeared from time to time, depending on conditions.

Here we look at the various categories of media, beginning with the official and public (that is, noninternal) kinds, which at all times reached the largest number of people. We look particularly at the late 1970s and early 1980s, when the state literary system was revived after its curtailment during the Cultural Revolution, and before it had lost much to the market-economy changes that began to undermine it by the late 1980s.

DISTRIBUTION: OFFICIAL AND PUBLIC

In 1979, Chinese publishers produced about 11,000 book titles, of which about 2,300 concerned literature or art.[1] Periodicals numbered over 1,100, and reached a combined circulation around 165 million;[2] the highest-circulating literary magazines were the central-level *People's Literature* at 1.4 million and *Literary Works*, published in Guangzhou, at 0.5 million.[3] The ques-

---

[1] "Books" here includes reprints, inexpensive paperbacks, including small-format editions (*xiaokaiben*), and cartoon-illustrated books; interview at the State Publication Administration, 4 August 1980. The total value of the output, including periodicals, was about 800,000,000 yuan, or a bit less than one yuan per capita; see Wen Lu, "Zhongguo de changxiaoshu."

[2] Interview at the Sidaokou Post Office, Beijing, 16 October 1979; Andrew J. Nathan, *Chinese Democracy*, p. 158.

[3] Interviews at *Zuopin* editorial board, 4 March 1980, and at *Renmin wenxue* editorial board, 9 August 1980. The periodicals that had the largest circulations were not primarily literary: *China Youth News* (*Zhongguo qingnianbao*, which did have a fiction column) circulated at 11

tion of distribution—which depended primarily on a system of bookstores, libraries, and subscriptions to periodicals—was critical.

Bookstores

The national network of New China Bookstores (Xinhua shudian, a name chosen by Mao Zedong at Yan'an) handled nearly all book sales in socialist China. In 1980 there were about 5,000 retail branches in its system, or about one per 190,000 people.[4] The branches were organized hierarchically by province, county, and district, similarly to other state-run bureaucracies. In addition, there were book "service departments" (*fuwubu*) in schools, factories, and other work units. In rural areas, "supply stations" (*gongxiaoshe*) that distributed food and other necessities often served as agents for the book-supply network as well.[5]

An important function of the bookstore system was to provide data on reader "demand" to the major publishers. Local branches were supposed to solicit the preferences of readers and report them upward though the bookstore bureaucracy, from where they were reported to publishing houses, who then "considered" reader preferences in making their publishing proposals to the State Publications Administration (SPA).[6] As we have seen in chapter 2, the SPA had both political authority and control of the paper supply, and publishers knew that they could publish only to the extent that the SPA could be pleased. This condition produced a pressure on publishers, and therefore on the bookstore system, to report that readers everywhere wished to read what the leading authorities wanted them to wish to read.

Parallel to the New China Bookstore system but considerably smaller were two others, the Foreign Languages Bookstores (Waiwen shudian), which sold all books printed in non-Chinese languages, and the China Bookstore (Zhongguo shudian), which dealt in used books as well as all "ancient" books (which usually meant, in practice, all pre-1911 books, whether original or newly reprinted). But in many places, the divisions among the bookstore systems was not strictly observed.

All branches of the New China Bookstore drew from a national supply network that was governed by distribution quotas. The quotas favored major cities, but were designed to ensure that small and rural bookstores had at least some access to books. Despite this system, however, there was little uniformity in what was actually on bookstore shelves—save the classics of Marxism-Leninism-Maoism, of which there was an unsold surplus of 450

---

million, *Reference News* (*Cankao xiaoxi*) at 9 million, and *Masses Cinema* (*Dazhong dianying*) and *Red Flag* (*Hongqi*) at 8 million each. See Nathan, *Chinese Democracy*, p. 158; interview at Sidaokou Post Office, 16 October 1979, for *Red Flag* figure.

[4] National Publishing Administration, "Publishing in China Past and Present," pp. 8–9.

[5] Interview at the Xinhua shudian, Wangfujing Branch, 30 October 1979.

[6] Interviews at the State Publication Administration, Beijing, 4 August 1980, and the Wangfujing Branch of the New China Bookstore, Beijing, 30 October 1979.

million volumes as of June 1979. (Mao's works alone comprised 8 percent of all unsold books.)[7] Large urban stores, although well supplied with books that were in demand, often sold out of them quickly. At the height of the frenzy over scar literature in 1979, relatively remote stores sometimes contained books that had quickly disappeared from downtown stores. (The rush to buy high-demand books was made worse by the general prohibition against browsing. Customers were separated from bookshelves by counters and clerks, and almost never were allowed to look at a book before buying it.)[8] Because the books that were openly available on a bookstore's shelves were often leftovers, as was the case in the Soviet Union, they could be a better indication of what was not popular than of what was.[9] As a first approximation of what books people were actually reading, it was more important to discover what had been supplied to a bookstore than what was left remaining on its shelves.

Most of the literary titles with large print runs came from two publishing houses: the People's Literature Publishing House (*Renmin wenxue chubanshe*) and the China Youth Publishing House (*Zhongguo qingnian chubanshe*), both in Beijing. (A third, the Writers' Publishing House [*Zuojia chubanshe*], did some big-circulation novels in the late 1950s and early 1960s.) One indication of the primacy of the two leading presses is that, for the three years 1977–1979, they together used 33.7 percent of the paper officially allocated for all literary publication in China.[10] The list of their most-published books—which is also therefore a list of what literary books were most widely available (not necessarily most widely read)—is interesting both for what it contained and for what it omitted.[11] It included socialist realist classics from the 1949–1966 period (Luo Guangbin and Yang Yiyan's *Red Crag*, Zhou Libo's *The Hurricane*, and Yang Mo's *The Song of Youth*),[12] whose spirit the leadership clearly wished to revive, as well as "ancient" classics (Luo Guanzhong, *Romance of the Three Kingdoms*; Feng Menglong, *State of the Eastern Zhou*; Wu Jingzi, *The Scholars*; and Wu Cheng'en, *Journey to the West*) that were in popular demand. But it skipped over the "May Fourth era" of the late 1910s through early 1930s, much of which may have been too probing, socially and politically, for the leadership to feel comfortable about releasing.[13] *One Thousand and One Nights* and Ethel Voynich, *The Gadfly*, which came to China via the Soviet Union, signaled in part a retreat

---

[7] According to secret statistics compiled by the Xinhua Bookstore; quoted in Geremie R. Barmé, *Shades of Mao*, p. 9.

[8] A letter to the *People's Daily* (*Renmin ribao*, 28 September 1978) complains about this barrier between readers and books, and calls for "restoration of open-shelf browsing."

[9] See Maurice Friedberg, "Soviet Books, Censors, and Readers," p. 202.

[10] Interview at the State Publication Administration, Beijing, 4 August 1980.

[11] My data for the list are taken from an interview with the State Publication Administration, 4 August 1980. A complete list of the "top twenty" books for these years, together with their print runs, appears my "Fiction and the Reading Public," p. 230.

[12] For comment, see pp. 110, above, and pp. 250–51, 315, below.

[13] The only exception, and an interesting one, is that Ba Jin's *Torrent Trilogy* (*Jiliu sanbuqu*) was republished in fairly large print-runs.

from the anti-Soviet spirit of the Mao years.[14] The selection of classical Chinese novels for republication was most notable for the downplaying of *Dream of the Red Chamber* and *Water Margin*. *Dream*, which officially had been a record of the "decay of feudal society" ever since the early 1950s,[15] was never published in numbers to reflect its stature or popularity.[16] *Water Margin*, presumably because Mao Zedong liked it, was the most-published classical novel of the Mao years. Its neglect during 1977–1980 was another subtle sign of the general retreat from Mao. Finally, some items on the list were apparently made as concessions to popular demand. Zhang Yang's *The Second Handshake*, which at 3.3 million copies was by far the most-published book of China's post-Mao years, had originated during the Cultural Revolution as an illicit "hand-copied volume" (*shouchaoben*). Editors at the China Youth Publishing House gave the officially published version of *The Second Handshake* a political face-lift, but still the overwhelming interest of the book lay in timeless staples of modern Chinese entertainment fiction: a love triangle, martial-arts heroism, detectives, exploration of the West, and a science-to-save-the-nation theme.[17] Alexandre Dumas, *The Count of Monte Cristo*, seems another concession to popular taste. The book became well known and an intensely sought prize during the Cultural Revolution, when Jiang Qing listed it with seven other works as "highly recommended" reading.[18]

Nearly all of the much-published literature was fiction. A volume of Shakespeare's plays was published in 720,000 copies, even more than the numbers for *Journey to the West* and *The Song of Youth*. But this decision seems clearly to have made as a bow to a "standard" great Western writer. The outstanding example of mass publication of poetry had a heavy political connotation. At least five volumes of the classical-style poetry that had been written at the

[14] See Friedberg, "Soviet Books, Censors, and Readers," p. 205.

[15] See Merle Goldman, *Literary Dissent in Communist China*, pp. 115–19.

[16] During 1949–1966, *Dream of the Red Chamber* (*Hongloumeng*) was published in 660,000 copies, which put it twenty-third among all novels for those years. During 1977–1980, the number added was 400,000, a figure that tied it with Mark Twain's *Tom Sawyer* and Du Pengcheng's *Defending Yan'an* (*Baowei Yan'an*) as thirty-first for those years. On the great continuing popularity of *Dream*, see chapter 5, note 2.

[17] On the special editing that was needed to convert *The Second Handshake* from an illicit underground book to an officially approved book, see Li Shuoru and Kuang Xiayu, "*Di'er ci woshou* chuban qianhou," which reports two major changes: adding more laudatory references to Zhou Enlai, and changing the names of the scientists in the story, many of which had been names of real people. A reader of both versions reports additional differences: that the romance of the original lovers was downplayed in the published version, and an episode in which the second woman in the love triangle dies giving blood to the man was omitted (interview with Lin Chanying, 10 December 1979, Guangzhou).

[18] Other works on Jiang Qing's list were Charlotte Brontë, *Jane Eyre*; Charles Dickens, *A Tale of Two Cities*; Margaret Mitchell, *Gone with the Wind*; Nathaniel Hawthorne, *The Scarlet Letter*; and Maurice Stendahl, *The Red and the Black*. *Monte Cristo* seems to have become the most popular of these books because of its theme of revenge, which was much on the public mind in the immediate post-Mao years.

Tiananmen demonstrations of April 1976 were published between 1977 and 1979.[19] These demonstrations had commemorated Zhou Enlai while carrying veiled attacks on Maoist zealotry. They were unpublishable at the time they were written, but three years later, when their messages had become officially welcome, they were not only published but promoted.

Local bookstores were encouraged to advertise their holdings. Large branches sometimes advertised in newspapers, and many did so using blackboards outside storefronts. Advertising was often a formalistic exercise, however, because the supply system left little elasticity in the market: books that were in demand sold quickly, whereas others hardly sold at all, advertised or not. Individual bookstores had no flexibility (except illegally) to change fixed prices. Not only were the bookstores' own commissions set by national policy at fixed percentages of book prices (22 percent for retail stores and 8 percent at the wholesale level); the book prices themselves were set by complex, rigid formulas that, although slightly variable from province to province, could not be changed by individual publishers or bookstores.[20] The factors that went into the formulae were number of pages, quality of paper, size of characters (because smaller characters required more labor per page), number of illustrations, number of colors used in illustrations or on the cover, and quality of binding. A book's content also affected price. In Guangdong province in 1980, materials were ranked in six categories according to content, and the price per page was calibrated in steps from 0.055 to 0.080 yuan accordingly.[21] The ranking reflected the relative costs of large and small print runs as well as the government's political priorities. The lowest per-page prices, for example, were reserved for primary school textbooks and mass political propaganda. The most expensive categories were technical and specialized works, and many "internal-circulation" works.[22] Modern and contemporary Chinese literature was in the middle, at 0.065 yuan per page. "Traditional literature worth recommending" was set at 0.070 per page, whereas other "traditional literature" (apparently not worth recommending, but worth publishing) was 0.075 per page.

[19] The five volumes were Liaoning daxue Zhongwen xi, *Tiananmen shichao quanji*; Beijing di'er waiguoyu xueyuan, *Tiananmen shiwenji* and its sequel (2 volumes); "Geming shichao" bianjibu, *Geming shichao*; and "Shijie wenxue" bianjibu *Xin bei*.

[20] Variability from province to province can be illustrated in the simple "broadcast newspapers" published in most provinces and major cities. The *Beijing guangbo bao* in 1980 cost .03 yuan per copy. The central-level *Zhongyang guangbo bao*, identical in size and most other features, cost .02 yuan per copy. Although both were published in Beijing, the central-level newspaper apparently fell under the center bureaucratically, where it enjoyed a more favorable price formula.

[21] For a complete account of the Guangdong formula, see Link, "Fiction and the Reading Public."

[22] Price was not too important for internal-circulation works because they were usually purchased by work units with public funds. Literature published internally was usually seen as so desirable that a private citizen lucky enough to lay hands on something would not balk at price, in any case.

With price largely out of the question as a mechanism for relating supply to demand, competition for limited supplies of books took on other forms. The system of "internal" publications and bookstores, and the privileged access that it ensured, was an important example. In major cities, the larger branches of the New China Bookstore had two or even three "counters," which in practice were special rooms into which only people qualified by rank in the cadre system—or sometimes by occupation—could be admitted. There were also separate, unmarked bookstores that sold "internal" books exclusively.[23] For the larger number of books that were not "internal," bookstores had other mechanisms to assure privileged access. Work units, for example, generally had priority over individuals in the purchase of books, and their priority rose against other work units if they could show that the books they wanted were necessary for their work. In early 1980, for example, the demand for a newly published edition of the dictionary *Cihai* far exceeded the available supply; copies were rationed first to research institutes and universities, and then to other schools and libraries, generally according to the need they could demonstrate.[24] There were, however, many complaints about abuses of the system, especially charges that books went to people with power or privilege even if they had little need for them. An article called "No More Book-Embezzling," which appeared in the intellectual journal *Reading*, deplored the practice of "wasting" books by handing them out as perquisites of office, only to see them gather dust or be eaten by rats.[25]

Another mechanism for regulating access to scarce books was a system of "purchasing coupons." These coupons gave priority in buying many hard-to-purchase things, not just books, to people who had received remittances of foreign currency and changed them, as Chinese law required, into Chinese currency. In 1979, Twenty-one purchasing coupons were issued for every foreign remittance equivalent to 100 yuan. To buy a copy of *The Count of Monte Cristo* in Shanghai, one needed to spend twenty of these coupons in addition to the regular purchase price. (Four years earlier, in 1975, one needed sixty coupons plus the purchase price.) Besides these var-

---

[23] I had entirely underestimated the sensitivity of such stores until one day a Chinese friend in Beijing played a practical joke on me. Knowing my interest in bookstores, he told me of an unusually good one at 83 Chaoyangmennei Avenue. I arrived there one day around noon, when, apparently, the doorkeeper happened to be taking a break. There was no sign to indicate a bookstore—only a small desk and chair next to an open doorway freshly painted in bright red. When I walked in, a middle-aged woman who was sitting inside jumped out of her chair and literally about two feet into the air. She came running toward me, waving her arms and shouting, "We're closed!" I apologized and explained that I had been told this was a bookstore. "No!" she shouted back, "It's an empty room!" Actually, books were piled everywhere, but I was of course in no position to examine them.

[24] Interview at Xinhua shudian, Wangfujing, Beijing, 30 October 1979. Unfortunately *Cihai*, like other books so dearly coveted by intellectuals in China, could easily be bought by anyone using foreign currency in Hong Kong.

[25] Xin Shan, "Zhizhi 'qintun.'"

ious formal regulations of access, there were many varieties of "back door" arrangement by which powerful people, people who worked in the bookstore, or people with friends or relatives who worked in the bookstore could put in "orders" for a book before it arrived at a store.[26] During 1979–1980, desirable books were so much in demand that sometimes, at some bookstores, all copies were sold through the back door before any reached the shelves. When hard-to-get books did appear on shelves (or, more often, in piles waiting to be shelved), bookstores would be temporarily packed with eager customers. Sometimes there were lines, but frequently hands and elbows did the job. When the first issue of the literary magazine *City of Flowers* (*Huacheng*) appeared in Guangzhou bookstores in April 1979, it sold out in one morning.[27] The whole system of book sales put at a disadvantage anyone who lacked special status and lived far from a bookstore. In 1980, the per capita concentration of branches of the New China Bookstore was two or three times greater in the cities than in rural areas,[28] and the urban branches were normally many times larger and better supplied. The giant Wangfujing branch in Beijing, for example, had a staff of over three hundred, whereas a rural branch might have had one or two clerks who also sold cooking oil and garlic. Even among cities, some were favored more— sometimes much more—than others. When officials at the SPA decided in 1978 that China should reprint thirty-five classics of Chinese and world literature—books that were in extremely high demand after their nearly complete disappearance during the ten years of the Cultural Revolution— they decided that one-fourth of the entire country's allocation of these books should go to the city of Beijing. The reason, according to officials at the New China Bookstore, was "the concentration of high-level intellectuals and high officials" in the capital city.[29]

Several measures were adopted to lessen the disadvantage of readers outside the big cities. One was the rule, noted above, that books be priced exactly the same everywhere, notwithstanding the greater transportation costs in the countryside and the better economies of scale in the cities. Another was the publication of small, low-priced paperback versions (called *xiaokaiben* "small format editions" or *pujiben* "popular editions") of the major Chinese communist novels of the 1950s as well as some of the scar stories of the post-Mao years. These were normally sold at small book stalls, both rural and urban. Another was the establishment of "postal purchasing sections," through which readers in remote areas could order books by mail

[26] Interview, 13 November 1979, with Zheng Yimei, a senior writer in Shanghai whose friends in the bookstore would wrap his orders in newspaper and, when he visited the store, unobtrusively hand him a package in exchange for a previously prepared envelope that contained payment.

[27] Interview, *Zuopin* editorial board, 4 March 1980. In nearby Hong Kong, this same issue of *City of Flowers* rested in great piles in the pro-mainland bookstores.

[28] National Publication Administration, "Publishing in China Past and Present," p. 9.

[29] Interview at Xinhua shudian, Wangfujing, Beijing, 16 October 1979.

from the New China Bookstore or major publishers.[30] But readers who sought books that were in high demand found mail order ineffective.

In the 1990s, when the socialist literary system as I am defining it in this book withered away, the book distribution system changed in fundamental ways. Private entrepreneurs built a separate web for book distribution, popularly known as the "second channel," in which profit was king. The source of books in the second channel did not matter; books could be officially published, unofficially published, illegally published (pirated or produced underground), or brought in from overseas. Although there were rumors of fraud in the second channel (about private entrepreneurs absconding with book supplies, for example), the existence of the second channel forced everyone in the book market—including the state bookstores, which were now largely responsible for their own profits and losses—to pay more attention to actual reader preferences, not just politically correct estimates of what those preferences should be. The supply of books thus became much more varied than before. Books on traditional China, including a popularized comic-book version of Chinese classics produced in Taiwan, circulated in large numbers. Old Western favorites such as Charlotte Brontë's *Jane Eyre* came back in over a million copies, and new translations ranging from James Joyce's *Ulysses* to illustrated children's stories appeared. The martial arts novels of Hong Kong writer Jin Yong and the travel fiction of Taiwan writer San Mao circulated widely, as did the satiric fiction of China's own Wang Shuo. A lurid tabloid press flourished. Political censorship still applied, but became largely a matter of self-censorship; people in the second channel did not want political trouble to complicate their money making.[31]

Libraries and Reading Rooms

Municipal libraries were not major suppliers of literature to the public. Many cities did not have libraries, and when they did, the purposes of the libraries were generally limited to reference, research, and preservation of materials. Those libraries that did offer literature to the public normally offered only a few kinds. Pre-1949 publications were seldom available to the general public; traditional Chinese novels were available only in a few post-1949 reprints. The many provincial and municipal literary magazines from 1949 to 1966 were normally not available to the public, either.[32] Works from the Cultural Revolution years of 1966–1976 had little appeal once the

---

[30] Interviews at Xinhua shudian, Wangfujing, Beijing, 16 October 1979, and Wenyi chubanshe, Shanghai, 16 June 1980.

[31] I owe much in this paragraph to Jianying Zha, "China's Popular Culture in the 1990s," pp. 137–38, and to Steven Mufson, "Let a Thousand Books Bloom."

[32] In libraries where I was able to find such materials during 1979–1980, invariably the issues from the liberal Hundred Flowers period in 1956–1957 were the most tattered and dirty, indicating heaviest use.

Cultural Revolution was over, and in the 1980s were offered in libraries only selectively.[33] When post-Mao works that exposed and examined social problems created unusually high demand, libraries generally avoided the role of satisfying it. Some simply decided that the difficulties were too great and did not handle such materials at all. Others did try to meet some of the demand, and looked for ways to get multiple copies of the most popular books and magazines. In 1980, the city library of Jiangmen, Guangdong, managed to get a few dozen copies of each issue of the magazines *City of Flowers* and *October* (*Shiyue*), but still found itself far short of supplying what the 130,000 residents could have used.

The literary publications that were most often borrowed from libraries, at least until about the mid-1980s, were the full-length novels of socialist realism published between 1949 and 1966.[34] *Red Crag*, a saga of communist revolutionaries who withstood torture in a Nationalist prison, was the most available, and by a wide margin. The number of copies produced by its 126 printings reached 6.8 million—more than double any other literary work published in socialist China, and this does not count 3.3 million of a less fictionalized account of the same story, at least another million in cartoon-strip version, and adaptations to film, stage drama, radio drama, and Chinese opera.[35] The next most widely available of the socialist-realist classics during the post-Mao years were Jin Jingmai, *The Song of Ouyang Hai*, Qu Bo, *Tracks in the Snowy Forest*, and Yang Mo, *The Song of Youth*. *Romance of the Three Kingdoms* led among premodern works. May Fourth works, except for Lu Xun's short stories and Ba Jin's *Torrent Trilogy* (Jiliu sanbuqu), were hard to find.

Public libraries varied in function, depending on their size. The municipal libraries in major cities like Beijing, Shanghai, and Guangzhou concentrated on expanding their collections and serving specialized researchers. In the late 1970s, the Beijing Library, 80 percent of whose holdings of more

---

[33] The novels of Hao Ran, the major novelist of the Cultural Revolution years, were still read after 1976. *Bright Sunny Days* (*Yanyangtian*), which actually was first published by People's Literature Publishing House (Renmin wenxue chubanshe) in 1964, before the Cultural Revolution, was generally more popular in the post-Mao years than *The Golden Road* (*Jinguang dadao*, 1972), which remained tainted by association with Cultural Revolution policies, and whose reader demand had, in any case, already been well saturated in the mid-1970s.

[34] According to data provided by the State Publication Administration (interview, 4 August 1980), the eleven socialist realist novels most widely available in libraries as of 1980 were, in descending order, Luo Guangbin and Yang Yiyan, *Red Crag*; Jin Jingmai, *The Song of Ouyang Hai*; Luo Guangbin, Liu Debin, and Yang Yiyan, *Immortality in the Raging Flames*; Qu Bo, *Tracks in the Snowy Forest*; Yang Mo, *The Song of Youth*; Li Yingru, *Wildfire and Spring Wind in the Old City*; Liu Liu, *Diamond in the Flames*; Liang Bin, *Keep the Red Flag Flying*; Wu Qiang, *Red Sun*; Du Pengcheng, *Defending Yan'an*; and Zhou Libo, *The Hurricane*. For more details, see Link, "Fiction and the Reading Public," p. 236. For analysis, see Joe C. Huang, *Heroes and Villains*.

[35] Interview at Zhongguo qingnian chubanshe, Beijing, 8 October 1979. The alternate, less-fictionalized version of the story is Luo Guangbin, Liu Debin, and Yang Yiyan, *Zai liehuozhong yongsheng*.

than 10 million titles were in the natural sciences, did not lend to the general public at all, although people who could show a student or worker ID were allowed to read inside the library.[36] The municipal Zhongshan Library in Guangzhou theoretically lent literature to the public but, according to one staff member, commonly saved itself trouble by turning away would-be borrowers of highly sought materials. The Zhejiang Provincial Library in Hangzhou did not even allow people to read *inside* the library unless they could show that they were university students or graduates.[37] The Shanghai Library lent literature to the public, but was very short on its stocks of popular items. In 1980, it circulated only two copies per issue of the immensely popular Shanghai magazine *Harvest* (*Shouhuo*). For a city of over 10 million people, the Shanghai Library issued only about 11,500 borrowing cards, or one for each 9,500 or so citizens.[38] The Tianjin Municipal Library did better, but still had an average of fewer than 8,000 literature books and about 7,000 literary periodicals lent out to readers on any given day in 1983.[39] It was not always true that people in the biggest cities were best served by libraries. For example, the public library of the small city of Xinhui, Guangdong, whose population of around 80,000 benefited from money remitted from overseas Chinese, held 130,000 volumes in 1980. It offered 6,000 borrowing cards, or one for every 13.5 people in the city.

Statistics from the Tianjin and Xinhui libraries both show strong reader preference for literature over other kinds of books. In Tianjin, 81.5 percent of the periodical borrowing was for literature, with only 7.0 percent for science and technology and 4.5 percent for theory, politics, and sociology.[40] In Xinhui, for the three months of January through March 1980, 75.0 percent of the book borrowing was for literature, and 6.7 percent was for other fields of the humanities, 16.1 percent for natural sciences and technology, and 2.2 percent for social sciences.[41] In the early 1980s, the library at the Beijing College of Economics found that literature books were checked out to students about three times as often as books in economics, the work of the school.[42] None of these reports breaks down the large category called "literature," but the staff at Xinhui were certain that fiction predominated.

---

[36] Interview at Beijing Library, 28 October 1979.

[37] Interview at the Zhejiang Provincial Library, Hangzhou, 12 June 1980.

[38] Interview at Shanghai Municipal Library, 13 June 1980.

[39] These figures are based on Huang Ruixu, "Young Laborers' Attitudes towards Literary and Artistic Works," charts on pp. 49–50. I have divided the listed numbers of annual borrowings by twenty-six to get an average number of materials lent out at any one time on a two-week basis.

[40] Based on a total of 231,067 instances of borrowing. See ibid., p. 50.

[41] Based on an average of 5,313 books borrowed per month. A complete tabulation of Xinhui library statistics appears in Jeffrey C. Kinkley, *After Mao*, p. 261.

[42] Yang Yiyin, "Cong dushu jiegou kan daxuesheng de sixiang jiegou," p. 33, charts 1 and 2. The apparent discrepancy between the charts may be explainable by the fact that chart 1 refers to the average number of books checked out at a given time, whereas chart 2 refers to the total number of borrowings.

Librarians at the Shanghai Municipal Library, whose borrowings in May 1980 were 74.8 percent in literature, were similarly confident that fiction was most popular.[43] Within fiction, the most frequently borrowed items were full-length foreign novels and Chinese scar stories in leading magazines such as *People's Literature, Harvest, Literary Works,* and *Anhui Literature.* Poetry, by most accounts, was the least borrowed literary genre, although Tang and Song poetry still drew a faithful few. Although it was often hard to borrow fiction because all the books were out, books in other fields rested on shelves for years. At the Xinhui library, books in biology and in military affairs remained largely untouched; they accounted, respectively, for only 1.2 percent and 1.5 percent of the borrowings. Least borrowed of all were books on "Marxism-Leninism-Mao Zedong Thought," which accounted for only 0.013 percent, or two books every three months.[44]

University libraries were surprisingly hard to use, even for university students. One copy of *Gone with the Wind* in translation was locked inside a cage in the Beijing University library, like a worm protected from a pool of trout, limited to borrowing by faculty only. At the Foreign Languages Department Library at Zhongshan University in Guangzhou, students were barred not only from borrowing but even from using the library's seven English dictionaries and other English-language books. Students could borrow from the Chinese Department library, but there were many restrictions.

The difficulty of securing borrowing privileges at libraries caused readers to seek access through the "back door." But back-door traffic only increased the pressure on books and became a reason to tighten restrictions even further. Of the Shanghai Library's approximately 11,500 borrowing cards in June 1980, about 10,000 were for individuals and 1,500 for work units.[45] There was a rule that no new cards for individuals could be issued unless someone surrendered an old card. But since there was no charge for holding a card, nor even fines for overdue books,[46] cards were seldom relinquished. The back door thus became one's only practical hope for getting a card, even though few had the clout necessary to open such a door. The majority of would-be fiction borrowers in cities resorted to "culture stations" (*wenhuazhan* or *wenhuaguan*) at the district and street-committee levels. It was the purpose of these small libraries, in sharp contrast to the research libraries, to supply fiction and other popular materials to the reading public.

But still there were major problems in meeting demand. First, the number of culture stations and books they contained fell short of borrowing

[43] Interview at Shanghai Municipal Library, 13 June 1980.
[44] The low borrowing rates for "political" books mirrors the situation in Soviet libraries. See Friedberg, "Soviet Books, Censors, and Readers," p. 202.
[45] Interview at Shanghai Municipal Library, 13 June 1980.
[46] The Zhejiang Provincial Library, like other big libraries, levied no fines but did fashion a mild disincentive for late returns: a person who returned a book late was "fined" the number days late by a reduction of that number of days from on his or her next borrowing of a book.

needs. The culture stations of Beijing, although better off than those of most cities, had combined holdings in 1979 of only about 250,000 volumes.[47] The public could check these books out, but they amounted to only 2.5 percent of the number of books in the main Beijing Library, which the public could not check out. In Guangzhou, there were about ninety culture stations in the early 1960s, all of which were closed down during the Cultural Revolution and slightly over fifty of which had been partly or fully reactivated by 1980.[48] Second, there were no effective incentives for the people in charge of culture stations to acquire books that readers really wanted. Why fight, a station-worker in Guangzhou asked rhetorically, to acquire copies of *The Count of Monte Cristo* when it was so much easier to stock song books of national-minority tea-pickers praising Chairman Hua? A clerk got the same pay whether there were many borrowers or few, and more leisure time if there were few. Third, when high-demand books did come into a culture station, it was often hard to control their circulation. Borrowing periods of two to three weeks were commonly ignored as readers exchanged high-demand books through private arrangements with friends and acquaintances. Fourth, since most libraries and culture stations did not have open stacks or card catalogues, it could be difficult to determine what was available for borrowing. The need to depend on library attendants to go in search of books put an obvious premium on cultivation of personal relationships with staff, who could be very helpful in reporting what "hot" books were available, as well as in discreetly setting them aside. Some libraries tried to simplify matters by using "half-open stacks," whereby books were placed behind sheets of glass with only an inch-wide crack left open, allowing the borrower to push a desired book inward far enough to indicate it to an attendant on the other side. But half-open stacks were expensive to build. The general presence of unmet demand is further apparent in the fact that libraries that were well stocked and run were heavily used. At the Xinhui Library in Guangdong, the maximum number of books that could possibly have been checked out per month, to calculate from the number of borrowing cards and the number of borrowings allowed per card, was about 12,600. In early 1980, the actual number of borrowings averaged 5,313 per month, which indicates very intense use of library privileges.

In addition to public libraries at several levels, factories, schools, and other work units, as well as branches of the Communist Youth League and some agricultural communes, ran reading rooms from which members could check out books. At the Youth League reading room of a commune in Nanhai county, Guangdong, the borrowing period was one month with a 0.50-yuan fine for late return of books. All workers at the commune could borrow books, but priority went to Youth League members. A survey of commune reading rooms in Shanxi province showed that cartoon books

---

[47] Interview at Beijing Municipal Library, 28 October 1979.
[48] *Guangzhou ribao*, 26 December 1979.

were most heavily borrowed, followed by "classical romance and adventure novels."[49] In general, large industrial work units in the major cities were most favored in their reading-room facilities. In 1979, the No. 27 Locomotive Plant in Beijing, which had 10,300 workers, had a library of 90,000 volumes housed in thirty-five separate reading rooms. Two-thirds of the books were literature, primarily fiction.[50] To belong to such a work unit, in which the ratio of books to people was almost 9 to 1, was a big advantage; it compared to a ratio of about 1 to 40 books-to-people between the culture stations and the Beijing populace at large. Some of the best work-unit libraries were in units concerned with education or "propaganda" (including news and film), where the variety was greater and even "internal-circulation" books were sometimes available.

Subscriptions to Literary Periodicals

With few exceptions, all periodicals in socialist China were sold through the Post Office.[51] The selling and delivering of periodicals was not just an additional function of the Post Office, but its main activity. In the early 1980s, the Post Office delivered nearly six times as many copies of periodicals as it did other items of mail.[52] In designated branches, periodicals were sold at retail in much the manner of a bookstore. The burden of the Post Office in handling periodicals was especially severe in the late 1970s, when there was startlingly fast growth in both the number of periodicals and their circulations.[53] Periodicals created a special strain when they were bulky, and for this reason were sometimes temporarily handled by the New China Bookstore during "adjustment periods."[54]

The SPA imposed quotas on the literary periodicals that were in most demand. This was done primarily in the name of paper shortage, but editors sometimes felt that political curbs were also at work. The quotas were of two kinds: ceiling circulation quotas, which were enforced by limiting paper supplies; and distribution quotas, which specified the number of copies that

---

[49] "Report on 'Rural Intellectuals' in Shanxi," *Jinyang xuekan* 1984.3, translated in *Inside China Mainland*, November 1984, pp. 15–17; quote on p. 15.

[50] Interview with "representatives of Beijing readers," arranged by the Chinese Academy of Social Sciences, 18 October 1979.

[51] The exceptions were, first, unofficial publications and, second, a small number of official periodicals that were sometimes sold through the New China Bookstore.

[52] *Beijing Review* 1982.25.6.

[53] Of the approximately 1,100 periodicals that the Post Office was handling in October 1979, 50 were literary. Only six months later, these figures were 1,500 and 110, respectively. By early 1980, the major literary periodicals such as *Renmin wenxue* and *Xiaoshuo yuebao* were reaching a million in circulation, or about ten times what they had been only three years earlier. This growth imposed considerable, and sometimes unmanageable, burdens on the postal system, and required postal officials occasionally to warn publishers that they must slow their production. Interviews at Guangzhou Municipal Post Office, 30 April 1980, and at *Zuopin* editorial offices, 4 March 1980.

[54] Interview at Xinhua shudian, 30 October 1979.

should go to the various cities and provinces. Ceiling quotas for the most popular literary magazines rose quickly during the late 1970s. Guangzhou's *Literary Works*, which began with a circulation of 50,000 when it was revived in 1972, had a ceiling quota of 70,000 in mid-1978, 210,000 in early 1979, and 500,000 in early 1980.[55] Ceiling quotas for the Guangzhou magazines were unusually high, not only because of liberal editorial and control policies but also because paper was relatively plentiful in Guangdong. The ceiling of 500,000 for *Literary Works* in 1980 was highest in China for provincial-level literary magazines; at 300,000, the ceiling for *Guangzhou Literature and Art* was highest for the municipal level.[56] The typical case for provincial literary magazines elsewhere is better represented by, for example, *Donghai* in Zhejiang province, which had a circulation of 20,000 when it was revived in 1975, then went to 40,000 in 1977 and 120,000 in 1980.[57] During the early 1980s, as demand began to decline and paper supplies continued to grow, ceiling quotas were gradually abandoned.

The goal of distribution quotas, which the Post Office was charged with enforcing, was to provide all provinces with at least some copies of the major magazines while reserving special concentrations to the home province and to the capital in Beijing. For example, *Harvest*, published in Shanghai but much in demand everywhere, had a distribution quota in June 1980 that allowed 60,000 copies to be kept for the Shanghai municipality and another 68,000 for adjoining Jiangsu province. Sichuan, despite its large population, got only 4,000 copies, and only 1,000 copies went to Guangdong. Beijing received 9,000 copies.[58] Readers in the various cities could learn what periodicals were available by reading quarterly tabloids published by the Post Office. In Guangzhou, the first-quarter announcement for 1980 listed 83 literary periodicals, of which 11—including the most popular magazines like *October* (*Shiyue*, Beijing), *Harvest* (Shanghai), and *Literary Works* (Guangzhou)—were subject to fixed quotas.[59] Another four titles were listed as having "flexible quotas," meaning that adjustments could be approved "according to reader needs." In practice, flexibility went beyond official policy and into the realm of informal deal making. Cities and provinces sometimes engaged in barter of their distribution quotas. In 1979, Hunan province traded 15 tons of paper to Guangdong in exchange for 12,500 extra copies of *Literary Works*.[60] In addition to this kind of trade, there was an unwritten understanding that local favoritism would be tolerated. *Literary Works* and *Guangdong Literature*, for example, were supplied to Guangzhou

[55] Interview at *Zuopin* editorial offices, 4 March 1980.

[56] Interview at *Guangzhou wenyi* editorial offices, 7 March 1980. "Municipal" here does not include Beijing, Tianjin, and Shanghai, which were directly administered cities parallel to provinces.

[57] Interview with Shen Hugen, deputy editor of *Donghai*, Hangzhou, 12 June 1980.

[58] Interview at *Shouhuo* editorial offices, 16 June 1980. The Guangdong figure is from the Guangzhou Municipal Post Offices interview, 30 April 1980.

[59] Guangdong sheng youzhengbu, "1980 nian diyi jidu baozhi zazhi jianming mulu."

[60] Interview at *Zuopin* editorial offices, 4 March 1980.

residents well in excess of the quotas for Guangzhou, which were 60,000 and 30,000, respectively.[61] Quotas for out-of-province publications were hard to change; 1,000 copies of *Harvest* was far from sufficient for Guangdong, but little could be done. The scarcity of out-of-province magazines could lead to a "grass is greener elsewhere" mentality among readers. In spring of 1980, for example, the magazine *Literary Works* in Guangzhou published a story by Liu Binyan that raised a furor in Shanghai, where it was hard to get, but not in Guangzhou, where it was fairly easy to get. Around the same time, Guangzhou readers were busy discussing a work by Wang Ruowang that was published in Shanghai, and hard to get in Guangzhou.[62]

Within provinces and cities, further regulations governed distribution to readers.[63] Two key questions were: How many copies were to be sold at retail, and how many reserved for subscribers? And among subscribers, what proportion were to be work units and how many could be individuals? Periodicals on technical or scholarly topics, as well as all "internal" (classified) periodicals, went exclusively and directly to approved subscribers. Such periodicals amounted to the majority of the 1,500 handled by the Post Office as of April 1980. Subscriptions to other periodicals, including most literary magazines, were offered first to certain high officials and to work units, especially those whose work was related in some way to literature. In Guangzhou in 1980, these priority subscribers absorbed nearly all literary magazines except the local ones, leaving few subscriptions for independent subscribers or retail sales. Ordinary readers could hope to get subscriptions to the local magazines, but there were waiting lists for this privilege, too, and would-be subscribers complained that connections were a more reliable means of access than patience. In Guangzhou, individual subscriptions, even for those lucky enough to get them, were normally limited to three months—a regulation the Post Office imposed in an effort to maintain reader morale by spreading the privilege of subscription around. Unless one had connections, it was far more difficult to subscribe to *Literary Works* in Guangzhou than it was in the United States, where anyone could subscribe.

A portion of the supply of local literary magazines was sometimes reserved for retail sales at local branches of the Post Office. In 1980 in Tianjin, 30 percent of the copies of *New Harbor*, the local literary magazine, were reserved for sale in this way;[64] in Beijing all of the locally published literary magazines were sold by subscription only,[65] but 40 percent of the copies of *People's Literature* (a national magazine, but produced locally) were

[61] Interview at Guangzhou Municipal Post Office, 30 April 1980.

[62] The works are Liu Binyan, "Jinggao" and Wang Ruowang, "Ji'e sanbuqu."

[63] The following discussion of Post Office distribution policies is based, except where otherwise noted, on interviews at the Guangzhou Municipal Post Office, 30 April 1980, and the Sidaokou Post Office, Beijing, 16 October 1979.

[64] Interview at *Xin'gang* editorial offices, Tianjin, 30 June 1980.

[65] Occasionally some copies did appear for retail sale, because of "adjustments" in distribution quotas.

sold at retail; in Guangzhou, the Post Office tried to reserve 50 percent of its copies of local magazines for retail sale at three of its larger local offices on Beijing Road, on People's Road, and at Dongshan. When an issue of *Literary Works* or *Guangdong Literature* was about the arrive at these places, news spread quickly and the supply sold out in a matter of hours.

Renting

In the early decades of the twentieth century, with the rise of modern popular fiction and new printing techniques, the custom of renting fiction in books, magazines, and cartoon books grew up in China's cities. The practice extended into the People's Republic years, and occurred both inside and outside the state-run bookstore systems, but no offices, it seems, kept systematic records on it.[66] Some of the smaller branches of the New China bookstore rented books, and in some places the Bookstore supplied books to streetside stalls that were not formally part of its system but worked on a commission basis under the system's guidelines.

In a small village in Guangdong (Xian'gang, Kaiping county), there was no New China Bookstore in 1980, but the "Rising Sun Book and Cultural Supply Store," in addition to selling pencil sharpeners, thermos bottles, and other such items, sold and rented many books of fiction, mostly contemporary Chinese fiction. A book could be rented for about a week for only 0.02 yuan, and was secured by a deposit of approximately the price of the book. In cities, "Youth Culture Palaces" often rented books on similar terms, and sidewalk book stalls sometimes specialized in the renting of cartoon book fiction. In the early 1980s, many of these cartoon books were adaptations of the major socialist realist novels of the 1950s, like *Red Crag* and *Tracks in the Snowy Forest*, but some were based on post-1977 short stories by writers like Liu Xinwu and Jiang Zilong. These cartoon books, according to their back covers, were printed in the hundred thousands of copies, and thus must have been an important source of fiction for the marginally literate portions of the reading public. On the streets of Huhehot in summer 1980, it cost only 0.01 or 0.02 yuan to rent a cartoon book, and sidewalk stalls provided little benches where one could sit and read on the spot, thus avoiding a security deposit.

In general, however, rented materials did not usually contain the works that were in greatest demand. These went elsewhere, and, if they had gone to the rental market, could not have been secured by ordinary deposits. When the Beijing Post Office experimented in 1979 with renting the highly popular *Masses Cinema* and *Harvest*, deposits in excess of the purchase prices of the magazines proved insufficient.[67] In Guangzhou, where *Harvest* and

[66] At an otherwise fruitful interview at the headquarters of the New China Bookstore in Beijing,(30 October 1979, six senior staff appeared to have no knowledge of any statistical information on renting.

[67] Interview at the Sidaokou Post Office, Beijing, 16 October 1979.

other high-demand periodicals sold on the black market well above their cover prices, the Post Office suspended all its rental activities in the late 1970s.[68]

DISTRIBUTION: RESTRICTED, SEMIOFFICIAL, AND UNOFFICIAL

In addition to the mainstreams of literary distribution, which were official and public, there were, at politically "higher" levels, distribution channels that were theoretically restricted to certain readerships, and, from time to time at "lower" levels, different kinds of semiofficial and unofficial, including underground, publication and distribution.

Restricted or "Internal" Distribution

A large number of literary publications were designated for "internal" (*neibu*) circulation only. Such publication had several grades of "internality" that corresponded to the ranks of the people who were allowed to see them or, sometimes, to the nature of a person's work. During the Maoist years, internal materials were guarded closely; when they did leak beyond restricted circles, as when Red Guards captured them in raids, they were passed around only surreptitiously. But in the early Deng Xiaoping years, materials at the lowest levels of internality, such as the newspaper *Reference News* (*Cankao xiaoxi*), which had a circulation of about 9 million and was theoretically limited to state officials, were easy to find in work-unit reading rooms or even on public park benches. Some materials, including a number of provincial literary magazines, were unrestricted inside China but were still "internal" in that they could not be exported.

The volume of internal literary publication, although it may at no point have exceeded that of the open publications, was sometimes very large, especially during the late years of Mao. From 1975 to 1977, more than 1,500 internal titles were published by Beijing publishers alone; for some publishers, more than half the titles were internal.[69] Lists of the titles and their print runs were themselves internal materials and not available to foreign researchers. But to judge from unofficial sources, many of the best known, and probably most printed, internal books were about great political figures and global politics.[70] These included memoirs such as *Khrushchev Remembers*; Richard Nixon, *Six Crises*; Marshal Zhukov, *Reminiscences and Reflections*; and the memoirs of Stalin, Churchill, Truman, Eisenhower, and S. M. Shtemenko, once a chief of staff of the Warsaw Pact. The Masses Publishing

---

[68] Interview at the Guangzhou Municipal Post Office, 30 April 1980.

[69] Yu Chen, "Jiefang 'neibu shu,'" p. 8.

[70] In addition to interviews with readers, my sources are: Yu Chen, "Jiefang 'neibu shu'"; Miriam London and Mu Yang-jen, "What Are They Reading in China?"; and Ding Wangyi, "Zhongguo dalu de dixia wenxue."

House (Qunzhong chubanshe), run by the Ministry of Public Security, was the publisher for the memoirs of Stalin, Khrushchev, and Eisenhower; as part of its program to publish counterespionage fiction, this press went further than others in the direction of pornography. Titles such as *Sex Spies* "warned" readers about the role of voluptuous women in international intrigue; an unexpurgated version of *The Golden Lotus*, a classic erotic novel of the seventeenth century, was published and limited to officials at the municipal committee level and above.

There were also biographies of Napoleon, Gerald Ford, and Henry Kissinger, as well as William Shirer, *The Rise and Fall of the Third Reich*; Kissinger's *Nuclear Weapons and Foreign Policy*; John Barron's, *KGB*; and a British pamphlet by Z.A.B. Zeman called *Prague Spring*. Books that touched on Chinese politics were rarer, because of the difficulties of publishing, even internally, on issues that were still alive. But they did include Edgar Snow, *Red Star over China* and, according to one source, a novel called *Plum Blossom Party*, which orginally was an underground story about intrigue among China's leaders during the Cultural Revolution, and later was published officially but only internally.[71] Another major category of internal publication was foreign popular fiction, mostly American, including Margaret Mitchell, *Gone with the Wind*; William J. Lederer, *The Ugly American*; Alex Haley, *Roots*; James Michener, *Centennial*; Herman Wouk, *The Winds of War*; Richard Bach, *Jonathan Livingston Seagull*, and Erich Segal, *Love Story*.

The purposes and rationales of internal publication were several. The restriction of readership was implicitly based on the elitist principle that ordinary readers were insufficiently sophisticated to interpret "correctly" such things as Western politics, idealist philosophy, or sex. Limitation of access to officials of certain ranks was supposed to ensure that the readership would already be immune from a book's potentially noxious influences. The fact that many internal books were translations of foreign works added a nationalist element to the protection principle. Internality was a shield against foreign contamination. But it gave rise, as well, to one of the sharpest ironies in Chinese literary politics, namely, that much from the outside, or *wai*, had to be stamped "internal," or *nei*.[72]

The primary justification for producing internal publications at all was that such materials, although potentially dangerous, could supply important information to those who were equipped to interpret it. The state was better off if high officials, theoretically immune from the ideas of Khrushchev and Kissinger, knew what these men thought. Some internal books, explicitly offered as "negative examples," were published with the message "sup-

---

[71] According to Ding Wangyi, "Zhongguo dalu de dixia wenxue," part 1, p. 19.

[72] Another principle that underlay internal publication was protection of information about China from the eyes of foreigners. This principle had very little effect on literary publication, because very few Chinese literary works were ever classified as internal. The principle did, however, have an interesting consequence for foreign authors, who occasionally were denied access to internal translations of their own work.

plied for criticism" prominently imprinted on the front and back covers. In addition, though, it seems clear from the publication of works like *Jonathan Livingston Seagull* that another reason for internal literary publication was simply that foreign works were interesting and that the Chinese elite wanted to enjoy them. Although this reason was not officially acknowledged, informally many people assumed it to be the case.

Another function of internal publication, sometimes including literary publication, was to broach changes in political trends. In 1971, many rank-and-file officials got their first inklings that Lin Biao had a problem, before the dramatic Lin Biao "affair," when the internal *Reference News* suddenly reported Edgar Snow's quotation of Mao that the Cultural Revolution epithets "Great Leader, Great Teacher, Great Commander, Great Helmsman" were not to Mao's personal liking. In March 1980, in a prelude to deemphasis of Mao, *Reference News* published, without comment, a Yugoslavian news service report that foreign opinion held Mao partly responsible for the catastrophe of the Cultural Revolution. Around the same time, Svetlana Stalin's *Twenty Letters to a Friend*, with its criticisms of the Soviet system, was published internally. The translator's preface wryly states that "some comrades have said this book shows that one must be careful in raising children. But I feel the situation is much more complex." The "complexity," apparently, had to do with possibilities of reading Svetlana Stalin sympathetically rather than critically. China had yet to denounce Stalin; hence, for a Chinese readership, to question Stalin's legacy was to open the door to questioning Mao's.[73]

In addition to the leadership's reasons for internal publication, writers and editors had their own, sometimes different, reasons. These were basically of two kinds. First, editors could publish internally books that they knew to be sufficiently problematic as to be unpublishable in the open category. The internal label allowed them a certain distance from a claim that their materials were formally "correct," and hence was especially useful in publishing books of prerevolutionary or foreign origin. Second, in cases where the "correctness" of a work truly was in doubt, because authoritative judgments had not yet been made, internality was a useful hedge. A work could be published "for comments," and if comments were negative, the political costs were less than those that open publication would have brought. Such a step was routine, for example, in publishing textbooks, whose "correctness" was unusually sensitive. In some cases, this kind of internal publication served editors simply by allowing them to sidestep the immense workload of combing materials for possible problems. This fact alone can explain why the Chinese translation of Joseph Needham's *Science*

---

[73] It was not always clear that the subtle messages sent through internal publications were from a unified leadership unveiling a set policy. They were also, frequently, the devices of participants in high-level factional strife. See London and Mu, "What Are They Reading in China?," p. 42.

and Civilization in China (which is more than 4,000 pages long in English) was published internally.

Internal publication spawned resentment among readers who did not qualify for access. Although the families of high officials and high-level intellectuals could usually find ways to lay hands on what they wanted to read, ordinary readers often found themselves limited to hearing about internal works on the rumor mill. Writing in a small Beijing tabloid in 1979, one irritated reader described "the imposing, mysterious, fearful new world" of internal publication, and then resorted to sarcasm: "I, after all, am only an 'external' and thus have never quite fathomed 'internality.' I have always naturally assumed that, since there's a distinction between 'internal' and 'external,' it must have to do with the needs of the revolution. That's why I've never bothered to look into it. I've just been content to serve as one of those things that the revolution also needs, an 'external.' It's only a division of labor, after all!"[74] Such resentment arose not only because of the much greater variety of internal publications but because it seemed that the especially interesting materials—about politics, sex, and foreign countries, for example—were inevitably classified. The very fact that materials were sealed off enhanced their allure, whatever their content.

Unofficial and Semiofficial Publication

In 1979, a pamphlet version of Ye Jianying's speech on National Day was circulated in 2.45 million copies in Beijing alone,[75] yet the pamphlet often lay untouched on tables in work units. Around the same time, Sha Yexin's play *What If I Really Were?* was not published or performed publicly at all in Beijing, but stimulated widespread enthusiasm among those who heard about it orally or read debates about it in the press. Such incongruity between popular preferences and official supply in literature is what gave rise, throughout China's socialist period, to various forms of unofficial and semiofficial literary expression. Unofficial outlets ranged from oral storytelling and underground hand-copied volumes during the Cultural Revolution to above-ground but unofficial (*minjian*) publications in the early Deng period; semiofficial publications included student literary journals on university campuses and tabloids called "mini-newspapers" (*xiaobao*) that had varying degrees of low-level official status.[76]

A tabloid was typically a single sheet printed on two sides and folded down the middle to make four small "pages." It had roots in the early de-

---

[74] You Yicun, "'Neibu' jianwen."

[75] Interview at Xinhua shudian, Wangfujing branch, 30 October 1979.

[76] From the mid-1980s on, the influx of popular material from Hong Kong and Taiwan and the rise of commercial publishing of entertainment fiction inside China were crucial developments in supplying "actual preferences" to Chinese readers. I omit analysis of this phenomenon, however, because I view it not as an issue in the socialist literary system but as part of the major change that ended it.

cades of the twentieth century, when the major Western-style newspapers in China's treaty ports created supplements, which later became independent publications, carrying fiction, curiosity pieces, cartoons, games, puzzles, letters to the editor, and other items of light entertainment.[77] These early tabloids also carried gossip about famous people and protests against official abuses—both themes that reappeared, although in muted form, in the tabloids of the Deng period. Compared to its predecessors, the Deng-era tabloids carried somewhat more items on popular science, such as medical explanations for why people grind their teeth in sleep.[78] Their publishers were various—from official literary organs to freelancing unemployed youth. *People's Literature* (*Renmin wenxue*), an official and central publication, issued a tabloid called *Window on Literature* (*Wenxue shuchuang*) that contained news about books and authors, and brief reviews. City-level publications like *Wuhan Literature and Art* (*Wuhan wenyi*) and *Guiyang Evening News* (*Guiyang wanbao*), among others, published separate literary tabloids featuring fiction and poetry. Most tabloids, however, were published by district "culture stations" under names, to pick three from Beijing, like *Maple Leaves*, *Dandelions*, and *The Bell and Drum Tower*.[79] These contained a variety of light-interest material in addition to literature, and were hawked on the street for 0.03 yuan per copy. All the tabloids associated with official cultural units, from the central level down to the culture-station level, were subject to normal literary controls. Their lively, informal style suggests a more relaxed application of the controls, but they still belonged, in the Party's view, under the broad aegis of the Propaganda Department. Their main purpose was to make money.

Other, primarily commercial tabloids began to appear in the early 1980s from unofficial publishers. One that appeared in Shanghai, featuring stories and pictures of attractive women, was called *Storehouse of Oriental Beauties* (*Dongfang meiren ku*); in Guangzhou, one called *The South* (*Nanfang*) specialized in historical romance about the Lin Biao affair and other episodes of the Cultural Revolution years. The publishers of these early examples of the unofficial tabloid did not identify themselves on the copies of their publications. They were rumored to be self-employed entrepreneurs or people from noncultural work units who wanted to make extra money on the side. In 1980, Li Yingmin, a central propaganda official, denigrated the unofficial tabloids as "husband and wife papers."[80] A 1985 survey of Beijing high-school students found that 51 percent believed that the unofficial tabloids "are pure trickery, not worth anything."[81] The survey researchers explained

[77] See Perry Link, *Mandarin Ducks and Butterflies*, pp. 118–24.

[78] *Zhonggulou* 1979.10.4.

[79] *Feng ye*, *Pugongying*, and *Zhonggulou*, published by the culture stations of the Xicheng, Haidian, and Dongcheng districts, respectively.

[80] Conference on Literary Teaching Materials and Hong Kong-Taiwan literature, Nanning, winter 1980.

[81] "Shi ze haoqi, ji er yanfan," *Beijing qingnianbao*.

the word "trickery" by citing complaints that the tabloids make attractive promises in their headlines, arouse a reader's curiosity to buy the paper, and then do not tell anything really substantive or new. But mischievous or not, the tabloids maintained a market. In 1985, Party chairman Hu Yaobang warned that "a great number of indecent tabloids have emerged in many cities in the recent period. . . . If these things are allowed to run unchecked, they will poison the minds of young people and sap the morale of the working people!"[82] A 1986 order to ban unofficial tabloids slowed but did not stop their growth.

The unofficial magazines that appeared between 1978 and 1981 were of several kinds. They generally came to be known in the Chinese press in Taiwan and overseas as "underground" publications, but this term is misleading. Although later banned, they were not illegal during the years when they appeared; they could be openly exchanged and sold, both on the street and through subscriptions. The term "Chinese samizdat," which was also used to characterize them, is inappropriate for the same reason. Soviet samizdat was illegal and had to be done in secret.[83] Among the Chinese unofficial magazines, some were primarily political, such as *Explorations* (*Tansuo*) and *Beijing Spring* (*Beijing zhi chun*), which thrived briefly at "Democracy Wall" in Beijing, or *The People's Voice* (*Renmin zhi sheng*) in Guangzhou. Others were specifically literary, such as *Today* (*Jintian*) in Beijing and *The Future* (*Weilai*) in Guangzhou. All of these examples were entirely "unofficial," run either by small groups of urban workers or by young unemployed intellectuals. In addition, there were a number of "semiofficial" magazines, either literary or "comprehensive" (*zonghexing*) in nature, which were run by students at some of China's major universities and monitored by Party personnel on campus. Prominent examples include *Unnamed Lake* (*Weiminghu*) and *Morning* (*Zaochen*) at Beijing University, *University Students* (*Daxuesheng*) at Fudan University in Shanghai, *Red Bean* at Zhongshan University in Guangzhou, *Mount Luojia* (*Luojiashan*) at Wuhan University, and *This Generation*, which was a national-level cooperative venture involving editors from thirteen different student magazines.[84] These unofficial and student magazines were sometimes associated with literary "societies" that sponsored literary readings, debates, and other meetings. In Beijing, the group of about thirty-five young people who supported the *Today* magazine organized public poetry readings and, every two weeks, held a round-table meeting to discuss one another's works and to decide what to publish in the next issue. These meetings were "like a big democratic editorial board

[82] Hu Yaobang, "Lun dang de xinwen gongzuo," translated in Brantly Womack, ed., *Media and the Chinese Public*, p. 192.

[83] Alan U. Schwartz writes that "The essence of *Samizdat* is secret circulation, . . . [because open circulation] would indirectly subject the writers and disseminators of this material to stringent criminal penalties." "The State of Publishing, Censorship, and Copyright," p. 35.

[84] *University Students* and *Unnamed Lake* were "comprehensive" in nature. The others named here, and the majority of semiofficial student magazines, were literary only.

meeting," according to one of the group's leaders.[85] Large work units also sometimes organized semiofficial literary magazines, but these seldom attracted much notice outside the work unit. The No. 3 Universal Machine Works in Beijing sponsored a magazine called *Ruby* (*Hongbaoshi*), but most readers in Beijing had never heard of it.

The official literary magazines often lost money and relied on subsidies from the state. Unofficial magazines were entirely on their own financially, as were most of the semiofficial student magazines. Balancing the books was not easy, and publications often survived hand-to-mouth. In early 1980, for example, *Red Bean* was printing 10,000 copies per issue. Each issue required just over a ton of paper, for which the editors had to pay 1,400 yuan. Typesetting cost about 450 yuan, printing 500 yuan, and binding 350, for total costs of about 2,700 yuan per issue. Of the 10,000 copies, 1,000 were given away to friends, political patrons, libraries, and "fraternal" student magazines in other cities. The other 9,000 were sold, at .35 yuan apiece, partly through subscriptions but mostly on the streets of Guangzhou, where they sold quickly. *Red Bean*'s total income of about 3,150 yuan per issue covered costs and left about 450 yuan for incidentals like postage, manuscript paper, and activities of the Bell Tower Society. In general this magazine had an easier time than others like it, however, because of an extraordinary grant of 1,000 yuan from its home campus, Zhongshan University.[86] At Beijing University, *Unnamed Lake* had greater financial difficulties throughout its existence, despite a circulation that was double *Red Bean*'s.

Finances for the completely unofficial literary magazines, like *Today* in Beijing, were more difficult than for the student magazines. The unofficial magazines usually had to pay more for paper, had less access to letterpress (*qianyin*) facilities, and survived on smaller circulations than the student publications, to say nothing of official publications. *Today*, despite its national and even international reputation, in summer 1980 had a circulation of only 1,000 copies, of which just over half were through subscription and the rest through street sales.[87] It probably had more readers per copy than any other magazine of its time, or perhaps any time, in socialist China. Stories and poems in the unofficial and student magazines sometimes had considerable "circulation" from being pasted to walls on campuses or in city centers, where crowds stood to read them.

The unofficial and student magazines, although frequently called *minjian* "among the people," often had key ties with established officials or literary figures. Zhang Andong, who wrote for *This Generation*, was the son of Zhang Guangnian, a former chief editor of the *Literary Gazette*. Wu Xiaonan, the son of Wu Nansheng, Communist Party secretary of Guangdong province, was a supporter of *Red Bean* at Zhongshan University. The

---

[85] Interview with Zhao Zhenkai, 4 August 1980.

[86] The grant was due to public patronage by Zhou Yang; see pp. 74–75, above. Information on *Red Bean*'s finances is from interviews with the magazine's staff in spring 1980.

[87] Interview with Zhao Zhenkai, 4 August 1980.

son of the famous socialist-realist writer Qu Bo was active in the *Today* group. *Today* also benefited from the moral support of liberal-minded editors like Jiang Liu at *Anhui Literature*, who made a point to express his approval at precisely the times when *Today* was under heaviest political pressure. Provincial Party committees (and for student publications, university Party committees) could be crucial in supplying or withholding support. *Red Bean* had strong support in the Chinese Department at Zhongshan University and at least toleration from the Provincial Party Committee. Conditions were not as good in the late 1970s in Fujian province, where university students in Xiamen (Amoy) were allowed a modest literary magazine but students in neighboring Fuzhou were not.

The extent of official support determined, among other things, whether a student magazine could be printed in handsome letterpress. *Unnamed Lake*, *University Students*, and *Red Bean* all had this privilege, as did *Jin River* (*Jin he*) at Sichuan University and *Hope* (*Xiwang*) at Northwest University in Xi'an. But most others were mimeographed. In Beijing, the unofficial political journal *Beijing Spring* was mimeographed in all its issues except January 1979, when it suddenly—and for one month only—came out in printed form. A year later, during the crackdown on unofficial publications, Deng Xiaoping complained specifically about unofficial access to printing facilities.[88]

Deng then carried out a suppression of the post-Mao unofficial and student magazines by exploiting their financial and logistic vulnerabilities. *This Generation* collapsed in November 1979, when printing presses in Wuhan were ordered not to touch it. *Today* and *Red Bean* both eventually fell, in mid-1980 and late 1980, respectively, after orders prohibiting sales on the street made financial survival impossible. *Voice of the People* closed after bureaucratic stonewalling frustrated all the editors' efforts to obtain a "commercial license."[89] Deng accompanied the suppression with ideological attacks, calling the unofficial magazines "illegal" and classifying them together with a remarkable list of other ills: counterrevolution, rumor-mongering, the Gang of Four, murder, arson, thievery, rape, gang rape, white slavery, organized prostitution, and the manufacture of explosives.[90] (Such all-out denunciation contrasts with Khrushchev's methods in 1956, following a surge of unofficial student publication in the Soviet Union. The Soviet policy, aimed at cooptation rather than annihilation, was to stress Party or Komsomol "guidance.")[91] Editors at *Voice of the People* tried to protest their innocence of Deng's charges; they "believed in the basic principles of Marxism, supported the reformist group in the Chinese leadership, and recog-

[88] Deng Xiaoping, *Muqian de xingshi he renwu*, p. 20.

[89] See p. 93, above.

[90] Foreign Broadcast Information Service, *Daily Report*, 4 May 1981, p. W8; and *Issues and Studies*, July 1981, pp. 115–16.

[91] Harold Swayze, *Political Control of Literature in the USSR*, p. 154.

nized the inevitability of the victory of socialism."[92] But such strained protests brought no reprieve.

Oral Literature and Related Venues

Gossiping, or "chatting" (*liao tian*), which has parallels in many other preindustrial societies, was China's most common form of entertainment until easy access to television and other modern forms and media began to dominate spare-time hours. Before television, friends would drop in on one another—unannounced but not quite unexpected—for the sole purpose of "chatting" about famous people, national politics, and interesting scandals, more or less fictionalized depending on the talents of the teller and the interests of listeners. People who were good at telling stories—who could embroider and dramatize them, and supply moral commentary—become known as adept chatters and were even somewhat honored as such. Chatting was partly a recreation, partly a social grace, and partly a supplement to the controlled press.

Major stories on the chatting network spread the length and breadth of China, and also reached Hong Kong fairly easily, where they were sometimes published in magazines. Many were news stories, leaked from high sources but unpublishable in China's controlled press. In summer 1980, for example, the grapevine carried the news that Kang Sheng would soon be identified by name as an associate of the Gang of Four; a few months later, another story spread that Wang Dongxing and other "leftists" were about to be demoted. Both these stories came true. Other items included the informal comments of top leaders, colorful and germane but usually impossible to verify. In winter 1980, chatters in Guangzhou were making much of Hu Yaobang's alleged characterization of the "Four Dares" in China: Beijing people "dare to speak" (referring to Democracy Wall); Sichuan people "dare to eat" (referring to the success of Zhao Ziyang's material-incentive policies there); Shanghai people "dare to wear" (referring to higher skirtlines and lower necklines); and Guangdong people "dare to run" (referring to illegal emigration to Hong Kong).

In some ways the chatting network was functionally parallel to the tabloid press of the modern West. It carried scandalous but seldom verifiable stories about the misbehavior of political leaders and other famous people. Anecdotes about the love life of Mao Zedong, for example, spread widely during the Cultural Revolution, thanks especially to the mobility of Red Guards and urban youth "sent down" to the countryside. In the 1980s, Gu Hua, a former Red Guard and writer of prize-winning fiction, recorded many of these stories in a 558-page book called *Mao Zedong and His Women*,[93] which can be regarded as a classic collection of chatting material in printed form.

---

[92] "Guangzhou 'Renmin zhi sheng' bianjibu shengming" *Guanchajia* no. 31 (May 1980), p. 15.

[93] Jing Fuzi (Gu Hua), *Mao Zedong he ta de nürenmen*.

In fall 1979, the grapevine carried a story that Ye Jianying had treated himself to an extravagant eighieth birthday party. In this case, in addition to the rumor itself, there were rumors about who may have planted the story in order to attack Ye Jianying. The eminent writer Ba Jin had recently written, in an essay called "Marriage," about how inaccurate or malicious rumor can drive people even to suicide.[94]

The grapevine often carried news about literary works and their authors. *Jonathan Livingston Seagull* became famous, despite the difficulty of obtaining copies of the "internally circulated" translation, after a summary account of it appeared in *Reference News* and set off a wave of storytelling on the rumor mill. The details of a "true episode" in Zhang Jie's life, allegedly the basis for her controversial story "Love Must Not Be Forgotten," spread about as quickly as did enthusiasm for the story itself. Chen Guokai's popular story "What Should I Do?!" had actually been circulating orally in several versions—in what was called *koutou wenxue* or "word-of-mouth literature"—before it was formally published in February 1979. Chen himself allows that he did not so much write the story as piece it together.[95] The play "What If I Really Were?," written in the summer of 1979, was published in China only "internally" and in very small numbers. Yet millions knew the basic story, and debated several versions of it, throughout the autumn of 1979. In sum, literature, oral storytelling, news, commentary, and rumor combined on the oral grapevine in inextricable ways, feeding on one another and comprising a great store of "things to talk about" when people sought to amuse themselves, to "release resentment," or to hear the latest.

In addition to its appearances on the informal grapevine, oral literature of several kinds was performed formally. In 1978, Lu Xinhua's story "Scar" was read aloud at public meetings in Shanghai.[96] Later, this and many other contemporary stories were broadcast on radio. Comedians' dialogues (*xiangsheng*) and fast tales (*kuaiban shu* and *Shandong kuai shu*), although largely absent from their prerevolutionary environments in marketplaces and teashops, came to be performed in auditoriums and before microphones. Because they could be adapted easily to the satire of contemporary social and political problems, comedians' dialogues were especially numerous and well attended, especially during the ten years after Mao's death.[97] They were broadcast almost daily at major radio stations. Traditional-style storytelling (*shuoshu*), which was not as successful in adapting to new performance conditions, by the 1980s was much less popular than it had been before the revolution. It was occasionally broadcast on the radio, as well, but more from deference to elderly aficionados than from any mass demand.[98]

[94] Ba Jin, "Jiehun."
[95] The writing took three nights. Interview, 2 April 1980, Guangzhou.
[96] Interview with Lu Xinhua, 24 June 1980.
[97] See Perry Link, "The Genie and the Lamp."
[98] Interview at Central Radio and Television, Beijing, 11 October 1979. An attempt to revi-

In June 1980, an official of the Shanghai Culture Bureau expressed concern that storytellers and practitioners of other traditional performing arts were doing private bookings in the Shanghai suburbs, outside officially established channels.[99] The same official complained of the number of "spontaneous drama troupes" that were "running around in society performing plays," sometimes including "bad plays," without "the leadership of any specific unit." To compound the difficulties of officials in the control system, "word-of-mouth literature" began during the post-Mao years to benefit from the rapidly growing availability of cassette audiotapes. A 1983 survey of students in work-study high schools (for delinquents) in Shanghai revealed the "harm" that audiotapes could do: the pornographic story "A Maiden's Heart" was easily available on tape; moreover, 29 percent of male students and 19 percent of females had "listened to" pornographic fiction, either on tapes or in oral narration.[100]

Underground Entertainment Fiction

As noted above, the term "underground" has been used widely but somewhat misleadingly in the overseas Chinese press to refer to unofficial magazines like *Today* and *The Future*. The label is problematic not only because these magazines, during the time they survived, were formally legal and could be sold or exchanged openly but also because there was another, very different kind of literature that truly was underground.

This other kind consisted of "hand-copied volumes" (*shouchaoben*) that circulated surreptitiously, especially during the Cultural Revolution,[101] and contained primarily entertainment fiction about lovers, spies, detectives, traitors, corpses, and wizards of the martial arts, as well as of China's top leaders, informally described.[102] Many of the readers and writers were "educated youth" assigned to the countryside, where looser surveillance made hand copying more possible than it was in the cities. Most of the stories were original creations, although some were recopyings of works that had

---

talize traditional storytelling, investing it with contemporary social messages, was made in the publication in Shanghai of the bimonthly magazine *Gushi hui*, which was printed in 400,000 copies per issue in mid-1980 and intended for use in public readings in villages. But despite optimistic initial reports (see "'Gushihui' zai ge di nongcun da shou huanying," *Wenhuibao*), there is no evidence that such readings became a widespread practice.

[99] "Jiaqiang dui zifa jutuan de zhengdun he guanli," *Wenhuibao*.

[100] Fudan daxue zhexuexi qibaji diaocha xiaozu, "Zhongshi huangse shouchaoben dui zhong-xuesheng de duhai," pp. 52–53.

[101] Zhang Yang's hand-copied *The Second Handshake* was first written in 1964. See Wang Weiling, "Zai jiankuzhong molian, zai douzhengzhong chengzhang." I have seen no reference to a hand-copied volume before 1964.

[102] See Ding Wangyi, "Zhongguo dalu de dixia wenxue"; also Miriam London and Tai-ling Lee, "Two Poems from the Chinese Underground." The editors of *Guangzhou wenyi* claim that their special column on Song poetry became a hand-copied volume in northwest China; interview, 7 March 1980.

been published before 1949.[103] After about 1970, when Red Guard raids had opened many privileged libraries of "internal" books, hand-copied volumes also included translations of foreign works such as A. Conan Doyle's stories of Sherlock Holmes or Jules Verne's science fiction.[104] A small portion of hand-copied volumes had serious content, including political statements, personal philosophies, and poetry. Some Christians had hand-copied versions of the Bible. But the physical appearance of surviving examples of the volumes suggests that those containing entertainment fiction, which were by far the most soiled and tattered, had been most in demand.

Because writing paper was difficult to obtain during the Cultural Revolution, the creators of hand-copied volumes normally began by obtaining— pilfering, presumably—a supply of paper from a work unit.[105] They would then find a secret place to begin writing—for example using flashlights under blankets, if we can accept a standard cliché on this point. Most hand-copied volumes were only ten or twenty pages long. When they were longer, sometimes those doing the copying would divide the task among several people. A 142-page hand-copied version of Wumingshi's *Woman in the Tower*, for example, clearly shows, by different handwriting styles, that the copying was shared about equally among eight different people, the last of whom recorded "copying finished" at the end. Once a story had been written down, the pages were bound with string and then passed around among friends. If well received, the homemade volume might be passed from hand to hand until it became a "flying book" (*feishu*) that never found its way home. When this happened the original author, if he or she desired a personal copy, had to begin again. Usually, but not always, hand-copied volumes "flew" from hand to hand without exchange of money.

Zhang Yang, whose story *The Second Handshake* eventually flew the length and breadth of China, had to rewrite his work a total of seven times. The first version, written in 1964 and called "Lang Hua" (Sea spray, or The vagabond beauty) was only 5,000 characters in length. Zhang wrote subsequent versions in 1966, 1970, and 1973 at lengths steadily increasing from

---

[103] Five original examples that I have collected, and that are listed in the bibliography under "Anonymous," are "Dixia baolei de fumie," "Kongbu de jiaobusheng," "Manna huiyilu," "Qingtian changhen," and "Renxing lun." I also have a hand-copied version of Wumingshi's 1944 novel "Tali de nüren." Works that originated as hand-copied volumes and later were published in China include Zhang Yang, *Di'erci woshou*, and Jin Fan, "Gongkai de qingshu." Hand-copied volumes later published in Hong Kong include You Kecun, "Daqiao fengyun"; Sha Tian, "Liulanghan de qiyu"; and Anonymous, "Yige gaozhong nüsheng de xing tiyan." Hsia Chih-yen's *The Coldest Winter in Peking* was published in English translation in New York; although it is unclear how much it circulated inside China, it bears a strong generic resemblance to hand-copied volumes.

[104] See Ding Wangyi, "Zhongguo dalu de dixia wen xue," part 2, p. 29. A pre-1949 work was Wumingshi's "Tali de nüren." Jules Verne translations included *Mysterious Island* and *From the Earth to the Moon*.

[105] Two originals in my library are written on the letterheads of the "Zhanjiang District Revolutionary Committee" and the "Revolutionary Committee of the Second People's Hospital of Kaifeng City."

15,000 to 80,000 characters (approximately equivalent to 25 to 130 printed pages). The titles changed to "How Red the Fragrant Hills" (Xiangshan ye zheng hong), then to "Homecoming" (Guilai), and finally to *The Second Handshake*. This last title, under which the book was officially published in 1979, was chosen not by the author but by an unknown reader-copier along the way.[106]

In general, the literary qualities of hand-copied volumes reflected their casual production and popular origins. They were often full of incorrect or nonstandard characters, and their action could leap with jarring abruptness from one time and place to another in urgent pursuit of a narrowly conceived story line. The detective stories, despite claims of scientific tightness, were full of logical lapses and inconsistencies. Occasionally, though, they offered some fairly good writing. "Strange Encounters of a Wandering Brave," at least in the form in which it was republished in Hong Kong, incorporates storytellers' conventions[107] and lively modes of description[108] that are reminiscent of traditional-style vernacular fiction at its best. To judge from internal evidence, the author of this work may be older than other creators of hand-copied volumes. He refers to himself as a "sorry old man" (*zao laotou*).[109]

During the early and middle 1970s, authorities tried, in desultory fashion, to stop the spread of hand-copied volumes. But this was not easy to do, given the spontaneous manner in which the booklets were written and passed around. At one high school in Guangdong, school officials responded to a surge of student interest by convening a public meeting aimed at suppressing the activity and uncovering its "backstage" ringleaders. But no ringleaders could be found; the contagion had been produced by the spontaneous enthusiasm of students.[110] After the Cultural Revolution, the Communist Party initiated a nationwide effort to wipe out hand-copied volumes. Readers were warned about holding "illegal materials" and offered amnesty if they handed over what they had. At the same time, the leadership offered a symbolic pardon to the former world of hand-copied volumes by approving the mass publication of Zhang Yang's *The Second Handshake*— albeit in a politically revised version. (In Guangzhou a group of young entrepreneurs, saying they took the pardon of *The Second Handshake* as a sign that the prohibitions on all hand-copied volumes had been reversed, began

[106] Data on *The Second Handshake* are from Wang Weiling, "Zai jiankuzhong molian, zai douzhengzhong chengzhang," and from an interview at the China Youth Publishing House, 8 October 1979.

[107] Such as *hua shuo* "we were saying" to begin a new episode; *zhijian* "and then it was seen that" to introduce action; and *ge wei* "all of you" for direct address of the reader. Sha Tian, "Liulanghan de qiyu," part 2, pp. 82.

[108] The phrases, lively and terse at the same time, are often in parallel: *lian zou dai pao* "running head over heels" (ibid., part 2, p. 82); *bafang la guanxi, sichu zou houmen* "pulling strings in the eight places, going the back door in the four directions" (ibid., part 2, p. 83).

[109] Ibid., part 2, p. 83.

[110] Ding Wangyi, "Zhongguo dalu de dixia wenxue," part 2, p. 30.

to convert hand-copied volumes to printed form and to sell them. The authorities promptly corrected their misunderstanding.)[111]

The liveliness of the story of hand-copied volumes belies the truly dangerous aspects of the activity. The author of *The Second Handshake* was arrested in 1975, charged with "opposing Chairman Mao's revolutionary line," and sent to prison, where he almost died of tuberculosis and pleurisy.[112] Ding Wangyi recounts the story of a young writer who was thrown into jail for staying up late at night to write a long story, in letter form, about the wrongness of a previous instance of his being thrown into jail.[113] The danger of underground writing explains why authors and copiers of hand-copied volumes never put names on their work and clearly sought to avoid detection however possible.[114] Sometimes even their families did not know. One young author described himself as a "guerilla," writing on the move as opportunity permitted.[115] The pressures of self-censorship also affected writers of hand-copied volumes. As if to doubt that they really could maintain complete secrecy, authors occasionally included formulaic bows to official ideology. Chairman Mao is quoted from time to time, and "workers" are sometimes described—incongruously in the context of dazzling thrillers—as properly proletarian. Such details would, to be sure, provide only mild extenuation if an author were discovered; that they were included for purposes of protection seems clear, however, from the fact that they are otherwise so out of place. Given the dangers involved, it might seem strange that hand-copied volumes were produced at all. Their very existence, so viewed, is powerful testimony to readers' needs for nonpolitical entertainment.

Although the different kinds of literary supply—open and "internal," official and unofficial, aboveground and underground—had generally clear borderlines, there were, in unusual cases, several kinds of crossover among these categories. Internal books intended only for high officials circulated underground in the early 1970s, after capture by Red Guards, and in the post-Mao years because family members leaked them. Sometimes they were officially reclassified from "restricted" to "open" status, as happened, for example, to Herman Wouk's *Winds of War* and Edgar Snow's *Red Star over China* in the late 1970s.[116] Another kind of crossover between categories occurred when stories and poems from unofficial publications like *Today* and

---

[111] Guan Lixiang, "'Duanxiang' de duanxiang."

[112] Wang Weiling, "Zai jiankuzhong molian, zai douzhengzhong chengzhang"; interview at Zhongguo qingnian chubanshe, 8 October 1979.

[113] Ding Wangyi, "Zhongguo dalu de dixia wenxue," part 2, p. 29.

[114] As noted above, audiotapes changed the situation of illicit fiction in post-Mao China. Underground storytelling became not only easier to recopy but easier to hide, as well. A homemade and tattered hand-copied volume on a shelf next to Marx or Shakespeare is identifiable at a glance. But an audiotape looks the same whether it contains Beethoven, the Party secretary's latest speech, or a horror story. The would-be censor is obliged to put in many hours of listening time in order to find what he is looking for.

[115] Ding Wangyi, "Zhongguo dalu de dixia wenxue," part 2, p. 30.

[116] Yu Chen, "Jiefang 'neibu shu,'" pp. 8–9.

Red Bean were selected by liberal-minded editors for publication in official journals of both the "restricted" and "unrestricted" types.[117] The main area in which the various publishing distinctions broke down, however, was that of informal exchange.

Casual Borrowing and Marketing

When literary controls relaxed (as during 1956 or 1978–1980) or substantially broke down (at some places during the Cultural Revolution), casual borrowing became one of the most important means of literary distribution. In the early and middle 1970s, informal libraries containing various kinds of illicit material sprang up in many places.[118] If a work was in high demand, it mattered little whether it was official or unofficial, bought, rented, or stolen—it was passed around.

During the post-Mao thaw, editors of some of the popular literary magazines estimated their number of readers per copy at ten or so; some guessed as high as thirty. Library officials estimated about two or three readers per borrowing of fiction books. If these estimates are even roughly accurate, it is clear that friends, not libraries, were the main source from which literature was borrowed. Library books popular enough to be passed around without revisiting the library became "flying books," and, once the books were out, there was little that libraries could do to stop the flying. Levying fines was ineffective, because a borrower could charge "subborrower's fees" to his or her friends, covering the fines and perhaps making a profit. Even at the prestigious Chinese Academy of Social Sciences in Beijing, someone checked out the only copy of *The Count of Monte Cristo* from the academy library in the late 1970s and set up his own system of waiting lists. The four-volume edition was lent out under a limit of only one volume per person per day, lest the precious set "fly" away. In an exceptional case such as this one, the number of readers per instance of library borrowing might have reached into the hundreds.

A bit further underground, but not as far down as hand-copied volumes, internal publications circulated informally. Workers at printing presses sometimes found ways to take copies home, or to manufacture extra copies informally.[119] There were also leaks in the supply of officially printed books.

---

[117] For example, Wang Jing's filmscript "Zai shehui de dang'anli" was published first in the unofficial journal *Wotu* and later in the official press, both "unrestricted" (*Dianying chuangzuo*) and "restricted" (Guilin Shifan "Yuwen Jiaoxue" Bianjishi, eds., *Zai shehui de dang'anli* 1:204–26 and 1:212–30). The official journal *Anhui wenxue* published a section of "wild grass" from unofficial publications in early 1980 (1980.1.33–45). The official *Guangzhou wenyi* published "Hei Haichao" by Chen Haiying after it had been published in the unofficial student magazines *Hongdou* and *Zheiyidai*.

[118] Interview with Chen Huangmei, deputy director of the Literature Research Institute, Chinese Academy of Social Sciences, 15 July 1980, Beijing.

[119] This normally required cooperation, because a single worker would not be assigned to produce a whole book, but only certain pages, or the binding or cover. Some informal volumes

When a high-ranking official could get hold of a copy of *The Rise and Fall of the Third Reich*, so could his family members; and if they could, so could their friends, and so on, and the book could begin to circulate illicitly. (To ordinary readers, the underground, ironically, could be the only place to find books that had once seemed "over head.") Another kind of technically illicit informal exchange was in Chinese-language books and magazines that travelers brought into China. Guangzhou often had more of such material than other cities because of its proximity to Hong Kong. Foreign and internal publications both sometimes became the material for hand-copied volumes.

Money sometimes changed hands with the informal exchange of reading material, although the precise proportions of this technically illegal market are difficult to fathom. When materials were in great demand, their black-market prices soared far beyond their cover prices. In the mid-1970s, *The Count of Monte Cristo* commanded a rent as high as 8 yuan for only twenty-four hours on Beijing's black market; in Guangzhou, around the same time, a hand-copied *Monte Cristo* could be exchanged for a highly coveted Phoenix Brand bicycle from Shanghai. In Shanghai, the Public Security Bureau revealed in the early 1980s that a prerevolutionary pornographic book called *Stranger than Strange* (*Qizhong qi*) was selling on the black market for 40 yuan, equivalent to about a full month's pay for a young worker. One sheet from a smuggled pornographic magazine could cost 10 yuan or more; a ballpoint pen in the shape of a nude, 20 yuan and up; and a pack of obscene playing cards, 50 yuan or more.[120] Less secret, but still unofficial, were used-book stalls run by individual entrepreneurs. Normally, used books and magazines could be sold to the China Bookstore, which was the official outlet for used books. In Shanghai in the early 1980s, while the China Bookstore was paying 30 percent of the cover price for used materials in good condition, young entrepreneurs stood outside the Shanghai branch to offer people slightly more than 30 percent, and then, at their own streetside book stalls, resell the materials at 60 percent or 70 percent of cover price.

RELATED MEDIA: STAGE, FILM, RADIO, AND TELEVISION

Although books and magazines in socialist China carried a much greater range of work than other media, some of the others, especially film and

---

were hand-strung together between cardboard covers. Readers, too, sometimes assembled their own books by clipping serialized installments from daily newspapers and stitching the pages together between homemade covers. This happened in the Maoist period with Luo Guangbin, Liu Debin, and Yang Yiyan, *Zai liehuozhong yongsheng*, when it was serialized in the *Beijing Evening News*; Interview at New China Bookstore, Wangfujing Branch, Beijing, 30 October 1979.

[120] Fudan daxue zhexuexi qibaji diaocha xiaozu, "Zhongshi huangse shouchaoben dui zhongxuesheng de duhai," p. 51. In the 1990s, after most other aspects of China's socialist literary system had disappeared, proscription of highly sought books still produced high black-market prices. In early 1995, Li Zhisui's *Mao Zedong siren yisheng huiyilu* sold for thousands and even tens of thousands of yuan in Chinese cities.

radio, reached far larger audiences. A full study of these other media is beyond our scope here; what follows are only some notes on how they related to the dissemination of literature, primarily fiction. Also beyond our scope is the rapid growth of the electronic media that began in the late 1980s and accelerated in the 1990s. This major change was part of the process that ended the socialist literary system in its classic form.

Stage and Film

At the beginning of the socialist period, traditional-style opera was, aside from "chatting," easily the most widespread form of popular entertainment. During the socialist years, interest in opera fell off sharply among young people and film came to rival it, at least in the cities. For contemporary writers this was a crucial change, because the content of traditional opera was fixed, whereas film needed new content, and often took it from fictional works. Film thus had much more flexibility to make social and political comment, and its quick access to a mass audience gave it considerable power.

The first two decades of China's socialist period witnessed a major effort by the new government to remold the nature of the Chinese stage, both by reforming traditional opera and by spreading modern-style "spoken drama." The reform of opera, which began early in the 1950s, was done on the principle of retaining its forms and techniques while removing "feudal" and "superstitious" content having to do with ghosts, immortals, imperial officials, and the like, and substituting socially progressive themes like equality in marriage. The famous modern playwright Tian Han headed a Bureau of Drama Reform whose purpose it was to screen and revise the content of traditional operas.[121] The effort to spread spoken drama led other established writers, notably Cao Yu and Lao She, to attempt—not very successfully—to write plays that suited propaganda themes of the time. Elite drama schools, coming under Soviet influence in the 1950s, promoted the study and use of the performance techniques of Konstantin Stanislavsky. The new government also did what it could to spread the new theater—both the "spoken drama" and the opera with reformed content—to China's broad rural audience. It sponsored itinerant drama troupes and encouraged the formation of amateur companies; by 1960, there were as many as seven million amateur actors in China.[122]

In the cities, many theater managers from before 1949 stayed in place after the revolution, and some theaters remained in part privately owned, until the eve of the Cultural Revolution.[123] But the physical arrangements of urban theaters, both through refurbishment of old facilities and construction of new ones, came increasingly to resemble Western theaters. People paid a fixed admission charge at the door, instead of sitting first and paying

---

[121] See Colin Mackerras, *The Chinese Theater in Modern Times*, p. 166.
[122] Ibid., pp. 184, 189.
[123] Ibid., p. 163.

as they saw fit later; they sat in rows, all facing one way, instead of around tea tables; they could bring in snacks from the outside, but not expect hawkers to ply the seating area; they commented on the performance (or whatever topic pleased them), but not as volubly as before. As the "work-unit" system became established, large groups began to attend theater together. Tickets to theater performances, of both modern drama and traditional opera, were prized items.

With the Great Leap Forward in the late 1950s, the government stepped up its campaign to tailor new, politically correct content for traditional-style opera. But as the Leap waned, the latent preference for traditional themes returned. By 1962, virtually all opera performances were once again using traditional stories.[124] That, however, was only the prelude to the final and most effective push to establish "revolutionary opera." The effort began in 1963, under the sponsorship of Mao Zedong's wife Jiang Qing, and resulted in the late 1960s and early 1970s in the emergence of "eight model operas" that became, until after Mao's death in 1976, nearly the only dramatic performances available in all of China. Entire texts of some of the model operas were printed in newspapers and journals, including *Red Flag*, the Party's highest-level theoretical journal. The model operas consistently filled the theaters—partly because they had little competition, but also because they were in tune with the frenzied times and were well crafted works.[125] They came closer than any earlier or later experiments to a genuine synthesis of traditional form and "revolutionary" content. Although excoriated in the post-Mao years both for the artistic tyranny they embodied and the political tyranny they portrayed, at least some of the model operas, such as *The Red Lantern* and *Shajiabang*, left nostalgic memories even among some of the intellectuals who were most critical.

With the release of controls in the post-Mao years, all forms of drama sprang back to life in a greater number and variety than at any time since 1949. Traditional opera seemed to reappear naturally and ubiquitously, and was in some ways encouraged by the regime. In 1980, the press carried stories about how top leaders in Beijing were meeting with peasant-amateur opera groups to congratulate them on their work.[126] Modern "spoken drama" flourished as well, led by a spate of plays on social problems such as corruption, juvenile delinquency, and political discrimination, all in more depth than the regime would allow in the electronic media. More than 200

---

[124] All the plays staged in Beijing in 1962 were classical, according to *Far Eastern Economic Review* 44.13 (25 June 1964), p. 634.

[125] During the Cultural Revolution, wrote a commentator in Guangzhou in 1980, it was prohibited to arrive late, leave early, carry packages, or laugh inappropriately. "Some plays might fill the hall, time after time; but while there could be quite a few people in the audience, there could also be quite a few complaints in the people." See Shen Shuzhi, "Xi shi yan gei guanzhong kan de."

[126] See, for example, "Nongmin yeyu yishu biaoyan zai Beijing bimu" (Festival of peasant-amateur artistic performance ends in Beijing), *Wenhuibao*, 12 June 1980.

new plays appeared during 1977–1979;[127] in September 1979, the *Beijing Daily* (*Beijing ribao*) carried announcements of 105 public dramatic performances that were running concurrently on the Beijing stage in honor of the thirtieth anniversary of the founding of the People's Republic.[128] Only Shanghai could rival Beijing in the number of plays produced, because only Shanghai and Beijing had so many stage theaters. Guangzhou, for example, had only twenty theaters suitable for dramatic performance, yet during the high tide of drama's popularity in 1980 the city had twenty-six active drama troupes.[129] These had to take turns on stage, and hence there was almost no time for inviting troupes from outside Guangzhou to perform in the city. The shortage of facilities limited the overall size of the theater audience, as well. If we assume, liberally, that every stage theater in Guangzhou was filled every night with about 500 people, the annual total audience still reached only about 3.6 million, or perhaps one million individuals, as most viewers attended more than once a year. A 1980 survey of students at Zhongshan University in Guangzhou shows an average of 3.2 visits to the theater per student per year, compared to 4.2 times they attended film showings each *month*, or about 50 times a year.[130] Ticket prices, in addition to shortage of space, was a considerable factor in limiting the size of theater audiences. In 1980 a drama ticket in Guangzhou cost 0.30 to 0.80 yuan, whereas film admissions were 0.30 yuan at most, and were free when one's own work unit showed the film.

Although films were shown in Chinese cities beginning in the last years of the nineteenth century, it was not until the 1950s, when they were used to spread the messages of the new government, that they became widely available in urban areas and began to penetrate the countryside. Films from socialist countries, especially the Soviet Union, were imported in large numbers, and many of the first socialist Chinese films were made in partial imitation of them. Other films from the early 1950s dealt with the Korean War, the "peaceful liberation" of Tibet, and China's minority peoples. Practically the only Western films shown in the 1950s were Charlie Chaplin's, which were both politically acceptable and infectiously popular. In the late 1950s, filmmaking turned toward problems in China proper; some famous examples were based on well-known short stories from the May Fourth era, but most were new scripts that reflected post-1949 problems.[131]

From the mid-1960s until the late 1970s, film's fate closely followed that of contemporary drama, and was widely blamed on Mao's wife Jiang Qing. A few of the model operas were made into films and shown widely, but only

[127] Ling Yang, "The Last Three Years," p. 8. Daniel S. P. Yang, in "Theater Activities in Post-Cultural Revolution China," finds 176 new plays in 1980 alone, among other related statistics (pp. 165–66).

[128] *Beijing ribao*, 27 September 1979, p. 4.

[129] "Guangzhoushi juchang buzu," *Yangcheng wanbao*, 20 June 1980.

[130] Kinkley, *After Mao*, p. 262.

[131] See Jay Leyda, *Dianying*, pp. 227–69.

a very few other films were ever available in public. (Jiang Qing herself apparently had access to a wide variety of films, including contemporary Hollywood products, but these were shown only "internally" to extremely small and privileged audiences.) Urban people were "organized" into large groups to attend film showings. Leaders at schools, offices, factories, and other work units could obtain blocs of tickets—or simply blanket permission, with no tickets involved—to see one of the small number of politically approved films. After the Cultural Revolution, intellectuals complained about how tedious these films had been. But ordinary viewers, for whom "chatting" was practically the only alternative entertainment, were generally eager to watch them.

With the post-Mao thaw, the first films to diversify the narrow and rigid Cultural Revolution scene were ones that had been in use during the 1950s and early 1960s and now could be exhumed from the archives that had protected them from Cultural Revolution campaigns. These included not only Chinese films but also some Soviet, North Korean, and East European works—and Charlie Chaplin, too. At the same time, Chinese filmmakers, doubly hungry because of their lengthy inaction and because of the new stories they had to tell, returned to their studios and produced feature films at a mind-boggling rate, reaching about a hundred per year in the early 1980s.[132] An additional supply came from abroad, mostly the United States. Their selection was determined primarily by cost. Chinese authorities, reluctant to spend precious foreign currency on entertainment films, limited what they were willing to pay for rental of foreign films to about $10,000 U.S.[133] In Hollywood this was enough only for films whose rental prices had been slashed because they had not done well. It thus happened, in 1980, that China imported films called *Convoy*, *Future Worlds*, and *Nightmare in Badham County*, which quickly earned undeserved reputations in Chinese cities as exemplars of American film.[134] But almost any Western film attracted audiences. A 1983 survey of the popular film audience in the city of Chengdu found that 43 percent of viewers, when they could choose, preferred films from the United States, Europe, and Japan, while only 20 percent

---

[132] "Jinnian jiang you neixie xin yingpian?," *Guangzhou ribao*, 13 January 1980. See also the estimate in Nathan, *Chinese Democracy*, p. 164.

[133] According to one Chinese film official, "They [in Hollywood] want to charge us their normal rentals based on audience size, as they say they charge everyone else around the world. But our audiences are far too large and too poor to permit this. If we paid 20 U.S. cents a person and then showed a film to a normal audience of 100 million, that would be $20 million, a fantastic sum, and even 2 cents would amount to $2 million." Parks, "Gene Kelly Makes a Hit," p. 5.

[134] In 1981, an American film delegation brought five other films (*Singin' in the Rain*, *Snow White and the Seven Dwarfs*, *Shane*, *Guess Who's Coming to Dinner*, and *The Black Stallion*), which were shown in five major cities to an audience of about one million. Although newsworthy in a Chinese context, this audience size was still far below the norm of about 100 million for the most widely viewed Chinese films, Parks, "Gene Kelly Makes a Hit," pp. 3 and 5. A few commercially successful American films, such as *Star Wars*, were also shown in China in 1980, but to very limited "internal" audiences.

preferred Chinese films and 8 percent films from other socialist countries.[135] Results of a survey in Shanghai were similar.[136]

Early in the post-Mao years, there were calls to set aside the system of group attendance and allow individuals the freedom to buy their own tickets.[137] By 1979, the open selling of individual tickets was again the common practice, but it still did not extend to most foreign films, including the better and more alluring ones, which were shown only "internally." As in the 1950s, but now even more so, tickets to "internal films," which normally were available only to political leaders and to people connected to film production or criticism, became extremely desirable items, and even a kind of currency in the "back-door" barter of favors and gifts.

With the return of the open market in film, a modest amount of advertising also returned. In the cities, some theaters printed single-sheet handbills, in black ink or dazzling red, giving story summaries and the names of actors and directors. In Shanghai, unemployed youth went into business by printing their own handbills, independently of theaters, and selling them on the street for 0.02 or 0.03 yuan. An unofficial handbill for the American film *Nightmare in Badham County* attributed it to the "United States Broadcasting Company, Limited" and begins "Two women students from Columbia University in Los Angeles . . . ." But the flier did capture the essence of the film in lively summary form; for local filmgoers, it served its purpose well.

In the early 1980s, China had about 150,000 "film projection units."[138] The term included theaters, both enclosed and open-air, as well as mobile projection teams that visited rural areas. Official estimates of the film audience, measured in "instances of one person viewing one film," ranged from ten billion to nearly thirty billion annually for the same years.[139] Such figures, which would imply an average of ten to thirty film viewings per person per year, are almost certainly too high. Film showings were still special occasions in most of the countryside, and did not reach at all to remote villages. If accurate, the estimates would have to be based on extremely heavy viewership in the cities. But in Shanghai, one of the most film-rich cities, a 1982 survey of high school students found that 62 percent went to films less than twice a month, and a 1985 survey of worker households found that people watched films and/or stage drama an average of 56 minutes per week, equivalent roughly to 24 films or plays per year.[140]

But even if film viewership reached only half the official estimates, it was still much larger than the readership of printed literature. Film's larger au-

---

[135] The remaining preferences were for films from other, "third world," countries. See Wu Benxue, "Qingnian wenhua shenghuo yu jiazhi quxiang," p. 19.

[136] Lan Chengdong, "Dui zhongxuesheng kan dianying, dianshiju de diaocha."

[137] See "Rang renmin qunzhong dou neng kandao dianying he xi," *Renmin ribao.*

[138] "Qunian nongmin siren ban fangyingdui jin liuqiange," *Wenyi qingkuang,* states that there were 159,830 projection units at the end of 1983. Nathan, *Chinese Democracy,* cites 140,000 in 1982 (p. 164).

[139] Cited in Nathan, *Chinese Democracy,* p. 164.

[140] Lan Chengdong, "Dui zhongxuesheng kan dianying, dianshiju de diaocha," p. 79; Wei Haibo et al., "Dianshi wenhua," p. 14.

dience had to do both with its lower demands on literacy and with its lower cost. Although only a small percentage of the Chinese populace was entirely illiterate after the anti-illiteracy campaigns of the 1950s and 1960s, many could read only slowly, or only certain kinds of materials.[141] For most people, rural and urban alike, watching films was much faster, easier, and more enjoyable than reading books. It was usually cheaper, as well. A novel in book form could cost 2 or 3 yuan and a literary magazine 0.30 to 1.00 yuan. These were large amounts, if we consider that households in Shanghai, for example, spent an average of less than one yuan per month on books and periodicals in 1984.[142] Admission to a film was only about .10 to .30 yuan in public theaters, and black-market prices for extraordinarily popular films also did not get much higher than the price of a book.[143] Film showings in work units were even less expensive. In 1979, a large industrial unit in Beijing was charging .05 yuan to its own workers and .20 yuan to outsiders for film showings in its theater.[144] When units that did not have theaters showed films outdoors, people from outside the unit would, if they could get onto the grounds, come to watch as well, "borrowing" access to a film in much the same way as written materials were commonly borrowed. At Zhongshan University in Guangzhou, open-air Saturday night film showings drew so many unruly youth from the city that university authorities had to suspend showings in early 1980.

Radio and Television

The connections between literature and the electronic media in socialist China were generally closer than they have been elsewhere in the modern world, including China itself before and after the prominence of the socialist literary system. Although some entertainment programming in socialist China was done specifically for radio or television, most was not. It was adapted in various ways from written literature. Performance literature— primarily drama and comedians' dialogues, but also clappertales (*kuaiban shu*) and other forms of storytelling—was usually broadcast from tapes of live performances, which, in turn, almost always corresponded to written texts.[145] Films, sometimes broadcast on television, also were often based on works of fiction.

---

[141] Illiteracy in China has been hard to measure; see pp. 213–14, below. Basic literacy was useful even in watching films because of the widespread use of subtitles, which were not limited to foreign-made films. Because the spoken dialects of Chinese vary so widely, Chinese films in Mandarin often used subtitles as well.

[142] From a survey of 500 households reported in Tao Ye et al., "Shanghai chengshi jiating wenhua xiaofei xianzhuang ji fenxi," p. 15, where intellectuals' households in the mid-1980s are reported to have spent an average 1.18 yuan monthly on books and magazines, while workers and cadres spent about three-quarters that much.

[143] In Guangzhou in winter 1980, the black-market price for a ticket to the extraordinarily popular French-Italian film *Zorro* was 3 yuan.

[144] Interview at the No. 27 Locomotive Factory, Beijing, 21 October 1979.

[145] Clappertales are stories in rhyme and are performed in a quick, syncopated rhythm to the accompaniment of bamboo or metal clappers.

Fiction was sometimes adapted for radio broadcast. In 1979, according to representatives of the Central People's Broadcasting Station in Beijing, a staff of twenty-two worked to identify suitable stories and prepare them for oral presentation.[146] Material had to be especially safe politically, because of radio's vast audience, and had to be reasonably adaptable to oral form. The staff made cuts and changes, sometimes consulting authors but often not, and arranged casting and musical accompaniment. Passages written as narrative were sometimes recast as dialogue. When stories involved much description and little dialogue, old-style storytelling techniques, including rhythm and lilting intonation, were sometimes used to enliven the narration.

In the years before the Cultural Revolution, and again after it, about half of Central Radio's air time went to "literature and art." As of 1979, the monthly average was about 47 percent to 48 percent. The figure included music and Chinese opera, which together accounted for over half the total. The rest was for fiction, poetry, popular performing arts (*quyi*), literary reportage, "revolutionary memoirs," and a program of literary commentary called "reading and appreciation." About one-fifth of the "literature and art," or about 9.5 percent of total air time, went to the narration of fiction. Before the Cultural Revolution, there was a rule that air time for fiction be divided fairly strictly into thirds—for premodern fiction, modern (May Fourth-era) fiction, and contemporary (post-1949) works. After the Cultural Revolution the formula was abandoned; contemporary Chinese fiction dominated, and a few Western stories appeared. Famous short stories such as Liu Xinwu's "The Homeroom Teacher" and Lu Xinhua's "Scar" were presented nationwide in somewhat saccharine narrations of twenty to thirty minutes each. Local stations had increasingly more latitude to create their own programming independently of the central stations, under the direction of local propaganda offices. On local Shanghai radio, "Cinderella," "Snow White," and "The Little Match Girl" made debuts to warm receptions. For months Yao Xueyin's voluminous contemporary novel *Li Zicheng*, about the late-Ming rebel, was serialized in thirty-minute installments. These were broadcast at 12:30 P.M. daily to coincide with lunch and siesta breaks, thus assuring that no one need miss a chapter of the broadly popular program.[147]

Being entirely oral-aural, radio fiction was one way that written texts turned into what we have referred to above as "word-of-mouth literature." A story heard on the radio could spread widely among people who had not read the text, or who did not even know that a text existed. During the late

---

[146] Interview with Liu Rongfa, Zhongyang renmin dianshi tai (Central People's Television) and Dai Jienan, Zhongyang renmin guangbo diantai (Central People's Radio Broadcasting), 11 October 1979. This and the following paragraph are based on this interview.

[147] Officials at the Zhongyang renmin guangbo diantai received an unusual number of letters regarding the timing of these broadcasts. Young people generally insisted that the noon hour was best, whereas older people complained that noontime naps were ruined by blaring radios. Interview with Dai Jienan (see previous note).

1970s, when "hot" books and magazines were difficult to buy, would-be readers wrote to radio stations pleading that this or that story be broadcast, since there was no other way to get hold of it.[148] Radio broadcast schedules were often printed in daily newspapers. The most complete schedule appeared in something called *Broadcast Program News* (*Guangbo jiemu bao*), but during the post-Mao thaw this little newspaper was itself so in demand that individuals could not subscribe to it. The magazine *Radio* (*Wuxiandian*) was also hard to buy, despite a circulation in the hundreds of thousands. A 1982 survey of households in Beijing and the surrounding countryside showed that rural people, on average, considerably exceeded urban people in their interest in serialized fiction. It was their favorite radio programming, well ahead of news, sports, and even traditional opera.[149]

Very little adaptation of written literature appeared on television, unless indirectly by way of film. In 1979, Zhang Jie's story "A Youth Like This" was adapted for television and broadcast nationally; but this was an exception.[150] Because of its visual capacity, television could draw more easily on a wide variety of existing stage performance—drama, opera, storytelling, comedians' dialogues, dance, acrobatics—that could be accessed fairly simply by getting permission from the leadership of a performance unit and then setting up cameras (using film before the Cultural Revolution, videotape afterward). For art forms that could carry political or social comment, such as modern drama and comedians' dialogues, a stricter censorship was applied before presentation on television. A play in a theater, over its whole run, reached only thousands or tens of thousands; but millions might see it on television, and all at once. Sha Yexin's "What If I Really Were?," barely acceptable for the stage, could never have been put on television. Even a play like *Thunder over China*,[151] which presented a meticulously correct version of the official view of recent political events, could not be put on television because Mao Zedong, Zhou Enlai, and other top leaders appeared in the play, portrayed by mere actors.

Films were one of the most popular kinds of television programming, and presenting them did not require political screening because films themselves were closely watched before release. In the Deng Xiaoping era, however, a financial barrier arose to the use of films on television. Because film theaters, like other work units, were charged with paying their own way financially, they moved to protect their markets by agreeing with film studios to keep new films off television. In Shanghai in 1980 there were protests of this policy from citizens who had invested large sums in home television sets and who said it was unfair that they still should have to go to theaters.

[148] Interview with Dai Jienan, 11 October 1979.

[149] Womack, ed., *Media and the Chinese Public*, p. 78.

[150] This detail, and others in this paragraph, are from an interview with Liu Rongfa, 11 October 1979.

[151] Zhao Huan, Jin Jingmai, et al., *Shenzhou fenglei*, produced by the Guangzhou budui zhanshi huajutuan (Drama troupe of army soldiers in Guangzhou), 1979.

But Shanghai officials decided in favor of the theaters, requiring that initial runs in fifty to sixty local theaters be protected from television.

The reach of radio into rural China grew tremendously during the 1950s, and television spread rapidly beginning in the late 1970s. The first rural inroads of radio were through hard-wired loudspeakers in town squares and village centers. In 1949, only eleven counties had rediffusion stations to feed such loudspeakers; by 1980 more than 2,600 counties had them, leaving very few that did not.[152] Loudspeakers were supplemented during the late 1970s by a rapid growth in the sales of individual radio sets. In 1974, 4.9 million radios were sold nationwide, and by 1982 the annual sales figure grew to 36.3 million. This still left only 18 percent of Chinese households owning a radio, but in 1978, just four years earlier, only 8 percent had had radios. In 1982, the national audience for radio was officially estimated to have amounted to slightly under half the population.[153] A 1983 survey of young workers in Heilongjiang found that "listening to radio" was about twice as common as "watching television," the second commonest "cultural activity," and even further ahead of reading and watching films.[154]

Television broadcasting began in 1958 as an amusement for the top leaders, when there were only twenty receiving sets in the whole country. The number increased into the thousands in the late 1960s, but took until 1978 to reach a million. Sales then skyrocketed, adding another half a million in 1978 alone, and nearly two million more during 1979. By 1984, the total number of sets in China had reached well over 40 million.[155] Much of the upsurge in television sales was due to purchases by work units, as the cost of sets remained well beyond the means of most families. In 1980, black-and-white sets cost about 400 to 900 yuan, while urban families spent only 3–5 yuan monthly on all "cultural" activities, including books, periodicals, radio, television, and tickets to films and performances.[156] The cost of color sets was even more exorbitant.[157] People with connections in Hong Kong or overseas did what they could to have friends or relatives bring in sets from outside, and the government established a rationing system that

---

[152] Ibid., pp. 25–26.

[153] Womack, *Media and the Chinese Public*, pp. 25–27. Although radio reached virtually everywhere in China by the 1980s, there were still proportionally more listeners in cities, where individual radio sets were easier to get. In 1982, 97 percent of surveyed Beijing residents reported listening to radio; see ibid., p. 90.

[154] Wang Yalin et al., "Qingnian zhigong yeyu wenhua huodong kaocha," p. 38.

[155] Interview with Liu Rongfa, 11 October 1979; and Womack, ed., *Media and the Chinese Public*, p. 27 and table I–3, p. 25. The figures in table I–3 account for 42.1 million television sets sold by the end of 1984, but apparently do not account for the substantial number of sets brought in by visitors from outside China.

[156] Tao Ye et al., "Shanghai chengshi jiating wenhua xiaofei xianzhuang ji fenxi," p. 15. The figures are from a 1984 survey; the 1980 numbers would, presumably, be slightly lower.

[157] In 1979, a 21-inch color television set in a Beijing shop cost 29,000 yuan, equivalent to about three decades' wages of a factory worker (personal observation, October 1979). By 1982, the cost had dropped as low as 2,000 yuan; see Nathan, *Chinese Democracy*, p. 165.

allowed a modest influx of such sets duty-free for use in private homes. But most television viewing before the mid-1980s was done in work units, town halls, or other communal space.

In 1982, when the number of receiving sets in China was somewhat over 20 million, official estimates put the national television viewership at around 350 million.[158] If the estimate is accurate, the average number of viewers per set, to lump all parts of the viewership together, was about fifteen. But availability varied greatly, especially between city and countryside. In 1982, according to one source, there was one television set for every 6.8 families in Chinese cities and one for every 53 in rural areas.[159] In the well-supplied city of Shanghai, 84 percent of households had black-and-white television sets in 1982; 1 percent had color sets.[160] A 1984 survey in the city of Lanzhou found, among all occupations and ages, that although people retained a strong preference for watching films in theaters, they had begun watching television much more frequently because of easier access to it.[161]

Collective television viewing took several forms. Most common, probably, was the practice of simply dropping in at neighbors' homes, work-unit facilities, or public places while a set was turned on. At the No. 3 Universal Machine Works in Beijing in 1979, a work unit of somewhat over 2,000 workers, three television sets were set up in an auditorium where workers could go to watch after hours.[162] In the city of Jiangmen in Guangdong, the public library in 1980 charged 0.04 yuan per evening to watch color television.[163] Authorities in the small village of Xian'gang (Kaiping county, Guangdong), who had been able in 1980 to purchase two black-and-white television sets through Hong Kong connections, placed the sets side by side in the village auditorium and charged 0.02 yuan admission. Television's newness gave it great attraction, and the charges for these public showings were only about 10 percent of what it cost to see a film in a theater. The big disadvantage, compared to film, was the difficulty of hearing clearly, or at all. About two hundred people came each night to look at the showings in Xian'gang, and they seemed to come in the mood of traditional fans of village theater. Besides watching, they chewed sugar cane, cracked melon seeds, admonished their children, and commented loudly and independently on what they saw on the magical flickering screens. They expounded upon other stories that the television images recalled to them. No one seemed bothered that the audio portion of the broadcasts was inaudible; those sitting near the back remained unaware that it existed.[164] They seemed to re-

---

[158] Womack, ed., *Media and the Chinese Public*, p. 25 (table I–3) and p. 27.

[159] See James Kenneson, "China Stinks," p. 14.

[160] Tao Ye et al., "Shanghai chengshi jiating wenhua xiaofei xianzhuang ji fenxi," p. 13.

[161] Of the 488 respondents, 94 percent watched television dramas more often than films, but only 23 percent preferred television. See Pang Junlin and Li Jie, "Dianying," p. 124.

[162] Interview with workers, Beijing, 21 October 1979.

[163] Interview, Jiangmen Public Library, 4 February 1980.

[164] Personal observation, 2 February 1980.

gard television as better than village opera in the wide new world it introduced; if its audio was inferior to that of opera, this shortcoming could be overlooked.

As television emerged in the early 1980s, it in some ways eclipsed the role of radio. Access to television was glamorous. Surveys showed, not surprisingly, that people of many kinds preferred television to radio.[165] Among urban elites, for whom owning one's own set was at least thinkable, television ownership became an important status symbol. Meanwhile demand for radio, which had always been high, leveled off in the early 1980s. In 1981, for the first time in China, newly manufactured radio sets went unsold, and production cutbacks were ordered for 1982.[166]

In sum, the popular Western notion of monolithic media in Communist China is too simple. It is quite true that the government, in its turn toward tyranny, sought monolithic control of all media, sometimes even all expression, and, at its extremes, no less than the internal workings of people's minds. But this effort, while causing much harm, never brought complete success. The natural tendency of people to think, say, and hear what they like, and to pursue a variety of purposes, always found ways to ooze through or around the monolithic structures, preventing their final petrification and allowing complex and changing patterns of communication to continue. In the next two chapters we will look more closely at the variety of reader (or audience) interests.

[165] An additional attraction of television was the possibility of viewing videotapes, including pornographic tapes brought in primarily from Hong Kong. A 1986 survey of "video projection sites" in Guangdong province found that 55 percent were showing pornography illegally. Xu Yihui, "Huangse luxiang dui qingshaonian de duhai."

[166] Womack, *Media and the Chinese Public*, p. 26. To note that new radios went unsold is not the same as saying supply exceeded demand, because distribution and pricing were far from perfect. In China's remote areas, radios were still highly coveted; only in the cities did supplies go unsold.

CHAPTER 5

Readers: The Popular Level

QUESTIONS OF READERSHIP in socialist China—How many readers were there? What sorts of people were they? What did they read, and why?—are not easy to answer with much precision. Reliable answers have remained elusive in part because formulaic ones have been too readily available. In the 1950s, the new regime set out to publish literature for "the broad masses"; but there never was much evidence that peasants, by far the majority of those masses, read it very much. During the Cultural Revolution, leaders who prescribed the form and content of "worker-peasant-soldier literature" had clear and forceful ideas of what was good *for* the masses of readers; but much evidence suggests that their prescriptions diverged considerably from what workers, peasants, and soldiers actually preferred.

The habit of conceiving readership groups in clichéd categories persisted as different categories came and went. After the Maoist years, as government-sponsored clichés faded, others arose to replace them. Writers, editors, and scholars continued in the habit of referring to readers in categories that were unexamined and somewhat too simple. "Educated youth," it was said, were the core readership of scar literature; young women preferred love stories; old people read traditional novels; and so on.

In the early 1980s, survey research for reader preferences became possible, and indeed was fashionable in academic circles for a few years. This research provided a more direct access to the question of preferences than did the anecdotes, memories, and gross figures for print runs that were—and remain—the only bases we have for understanding the 1950s through 1970s. But the surveys had their own problems, the biggest of which may be how to gauge whether respondents gave frank answers or provided what they thought the "right" answers to be.[1] Such pressures were in part political, especially when questions were related to attitudes toward the leadership. But more broadly, the pressures were also a reflection of the emphasis in Chinese culture on proper behavior. "Which are your favorite books?" could be understood not as "Which do you like best?" but as "Which are standardly regarded as the ones that one ought to like?" The 1980s surveys consistently found, for example, that Cao Xueqin's *Dream of the Red Chamber* was the most admired work of Chinese fiction, or even of all literary work of all time.[2] The surveys generally did not ask readers if they had read

---

[1] On the problems, see Stanley Rosen, "Value Change among Post-Mao Youth: The Evidence from Survey Data," in Link et al., *Unofficial China*, pp. 193–216.

[2] Two that find *Dream* the favorite for all time are Huang Ruixu, "Daxuesheng yuedu

the works they admired, and it strains credulity to imagine that they always had. Workers at a locomotive plant in Beijing said in interview that, although they and most of their colleagues regarded *Dream* as a classic and knew about the main characters and famous episodes from storytelling, popular clichés, and elsewhere, practically none had ever tried to read the book.[3] Even writers who claimed literary influence from *Dream* were sometimes uncomfortable with questions about whether they had actually read it.[4]

But despite the problems of survey research, some of its results are beyond question. For example, surveys from widely different parts of China in the early 1980s showed that students and young workers named virtually identical lists of titles as their favorites in foreign literature. These lists show again how "preference" was limited by availability; recurrent titles were Nicholas Ostrovsky, *How Steel Is Tempered*; Ethyl Voynich, *The Gadfly*; Leo Tolstoy, *Anna Karenina*; Alexandre Dumas, *The Count of Monte Cristo*; Stendahl, *The Red and the Black*; Charlotte Brontë, *Jane Eyre*; and a few others.[5]

The surveys yielded answers in broad categories of people by age, sex, occupation, or place of residence, but they did not go far toward subtler questions of what attracted people to read or what they took from their reading. A fairly simplistic notion that "group X reads works Y" and "group W reads works Z" could obscure complexly overlapping readerships. For example, detective stories, pornography, and other kinds of entertainment fiction were tested for popularity among workers[6]—rightly, no doubt—yet such works were also read, at least on the side, by university elites of the kind who were doing the surveys.[7] Similarly, officials whose public duties included the repression of politically audacious works sometimes read those same works with interest and sympathy in private. Surveys seldom reached these phenomena; they could yield only a rough-hewn picture of the many and complex uses to which reading was put.

---

wenxue zuopin xianzhuang qianxi," chart 5, p. 11, reporting a survey of university students in Beijing; and Perry Link, "Fiction and the Reading Public," pp. 263–64, on university students in Guangzhou. Huang Ruixu, "Young Laborers' Attitudes towards Literary and Artistic Works," p. 53, shows *Dream* second for all time; Yang Yiyin, "Cong dushu jiegou kan daxuesheng de sixiang jiegou," p. 36, finds *Dream* easily at the top among "ancient works."

[3] Interview, 21 October 1979, Beijing. One survey that did ask whether people had actually read *Dream* found that only 15 percent of its respondents, factory workers under thirty years of age, acknowledged that they had not. (Huang Ruixu, "Young Laborers' Attitudes," p. 53.) But the implicit claim that the other 85 percent all had read the monumental work only illustrates again the need for caution in interpreting survey results.

[4] An exception is Zhang Jie, who said with refreshing candor that she regretted never having read *Dream*, but only parts of it; interview, Beijing, 30 July 1980.

[5] See Huang Ruixu, "Daxuesheng yuedu wenxue zuopin xianzhuang qianxi," chart 5, p. 11; "Bashi niandai" diaochazu, "Guanyu dangdai Zhongguo qingnian gongren zhuangkuang de diaocha yu chubu fenxi," p. 34; Link, "Fiction and the Reading Public," p. 270.

[6] For example, Fudan daxue zhexuexi qibaji diaocha xiaozu, "Zhongshi huangse shouchaoben dui zhongxuesheng de duhai," pp. 51–53.

[7] See Zha Jianying, *China Pop*, pp. 151–53.

There is, further, the problem that "reading" and "literature" were in two different ways not coextensive. Some people read newspapers and technical materials but little or no literature; on the other hand, there were large numbers of people who seldom or never read printed material of any kind but absorbed versions of contemporary literature through adaptation in film, television, and radio, or enjoyed related forms as presented on stage in drama, opera, or popular perfoming arts.[8] As noted in the last chapter, simple word-of-mouth could be an important medium. In short, "literary" reception in this broader sense calls for a concept of readership/viewership/listenership that included people who did not read much or even could not read. Within this broader conception, four groups, or levels, can be roughly distinguished. Although there are several kinds of overlap among them, in broad outline the distinctions are significant.

READERSHIP (AUDIENCE) GROUPS

The Mass Audience

The "masses" in socialist China generally did not read. Illiteracy (to which we shall turn in a moment) was only part of the problem. Other problems were that written materials were too expensive, too hard to find even if one could afford them or, simply, required more effort to absorb than did radio, television, and other media. Audience surveys in the 1980s found that broadcasts of narrated short stories were among the most popular radio programs, especially in rural areas. News broadcasts were much less in demand. Where television was available, broadcasts of film and drama were the most popular items.[9] These preferences for literature seemed to hold across all age groups, but were especially pronounced among teenagers.[10] Officials at the Central People's Radio Broadcasting Station reported in 1979 that mail from listeners was overwhelmingly about the station's fiction broadcasts. The letters explained what moral lessons listeners drew from the behavior of this or that character, and if a plot left loose ends, would ask what happened to certain fictional people. Listeners also offered criticisms on how a story could be better presented. Some requested that staff at the broadcasting station buy books for them, and some, having given up the search for books, asked the station to broadcast a certain story as their only hope for access to it.[11] According to surveys, popular attachment to radio fiction, and later to films broadcast on television, generally varied inversely

[8] Comedians' dialogues (*xiangsheng*), although traditional in form, were almost entirely contemporary in content in socialist China, especially during the high tide of their performance in the late 1970s and early 1980s. Texts of *xiangsheng* were published as written literature in magazines such as *Quyi* and *Tianjin yanchang*.

[9] See Brantly Womack, ed., *Media and the Chinese Public*, p. 78.

[10] See ibid., p. 84–85.

[11] Interview with Dai Jienan, Zhongyang renmin guangbo diantai, 11 October 1979.

with education, although even college-educated people used the electronic media for fiction and film to some extent. Interest in films on television was highest among the illiterate and lowest among the college-educated, according to a 1982 survey in and around Beijing, whereas interest in news broadcasts varied sharply in exactly the opposite way.[12]

The extent to which people read literature instead of using aural media obviously depended on literacy. In China, as elsewhere, literacy has been notoriously hard to measure, in part because it has been hard to define.[13] If "literacy" includes the ability to handle certain written words in daily life— such as roadway signs, debit notices, family genealogies, certain parallel couplets hung at doorways, or the characters for *doufu* at a beancurd stall— then most Chinese were literate not only during China's socialist phase but well before. In the 1950s, the government undertook a number of campaigns to promote a more general literacy, especially in rural areas. But in the 1960s and 1970s, primarily because of the paucity of interesting reading materials, skills atrophied and many of the gains were lost.[14] Surveys indicate that rural people read little, compared to city dwellers.[15] Official figures on adult literacy in the early 1980s for the nation as a whole ranged from 76.5 percent to 95 percent,[16] but numbers as high as these could be accurate only under a liberal (for the 95 percent figure, almost meaningless) definition of literacy.

A more reliable approach to the question of how many people could become minimally competent readers of literature is to estimate the numbers who received education at least through six years of primary school. These numbers rose during the 1950s, fell as all schools were closed for several years during the Cultural Revolution, then began to rise again in the late 1970s. By 1979, the government claimed that 83 percent of Chinese children were completing primary education,[17] and in 1983 said that 70 percent

---

[12] See Womack, ed., *Media and the Chinese Public*, p. 88.

[13] See Evelyn S. Rawski, *Education and Popular Literacy in Ch'ing China*.

[14] Vilma Seeberg, whose studies in and around Hefei in Anhui province in 1979–1980 led her to estimate literacy in socialist China at somewhere between 20 percent and 40 percent, accounts for "recurrent illiteracy," the loss of literacy through disuse; see *Literacy in China*. In an "internal" speech about his investigations in Heilongjiang province in 1979, Liu Binyan commented that "there are plenty of high school graduates who are illiterate." See Liu Binyan, "Zai Heilongjiang jianghua quanwen," p. 13.

[15] See Womack, ed., *Media and the Chinese Public*, p. 66, table 5.1. It may be indicative that, among the many surveys of readers done in the 1980s in China, very few even inquired about rural areas.

[16] The 76.5 percent figure is from China's 1982 census (quoted in *Los Angeles Times*, 28 October 1982, part 1, p. 14); the 95 percent figure is from the United Nations, quoted in *Worldview* (New York) 24.3.38 (March 1981).

[17] Chen Muhua, a deputy prime minister of the People's Republic, told James Sterba of *New York Times* (13 August 1979, p. A4) that 6 percent of Chinese children were not going to primary school in 1979, and, of the 94 percent who were attending, 12 percent dropped out before reaching junior high school.

of the population as a whole had primary education or higher.[18] Chinese scholars have doubted these figures, however, and Western researchers have estimated the portion of the populace with primary education at less than 50 percent in the late 1970s and early 1980s.[19]

There were barriers to reading other than illiteracy. One, as we have seen in the last chapter, was the difficulty of finding attractive literary materials. Another was cost. A beginning worker in a Chinese city in 1980, for example, could draw a salary of only about 40 yuan per month. Food for one person could cost half this amount, and rent, water, and electricity for a small apartment took nearly all of the other half. A pair of standard blue pants cost about 6 to 10 yuan. A young family with two salaries could produce a small monthly surplus, but the decision to spend this precious resource on books or magazines had to be weighed against spending it on film tickets or other entertainment and against saving it for major, glamorous items such as bicycles (about 150 yuan), sewing machines (about 130 yuan), or electric fans (60 yuan and up). Editors at the jumbo-sized literary periodical *City of Flowers* were proud in 1980 to point out that young workers were eager to buy their publication in spite of its price of one yuan per copy.

The Popular Readership

This group can be defined as those who possessed basic literacy, who had access to attractive materials and at least sometimes could afford them, and who chose to read literature, at least sometimes, in preference to alternative amusements. The size of this readership, although impossible to measure with precision, seems to have been small in rural areas, lagging far behind the audience for radio and traditional performing arts. The much larger urban readership can be estimated in several ways, all of which roughly converge on a result between 20 percent and 40 percent of the population.

For example, the New China Bookstore used a network of "book-opinion stations" (*pingshudian*), located in its retail outlets, to monitor reader preferences for the purpose of estimating how many books to request from publishers. Based on this information, in addition to their own sales experience, editors at the Guangdong People's Publishing House estimated in 1980 that the popular readership in the city of Guangzhou was between one and two million, within a total population of about five million.[20] In 1980, the China

---

[18] See *Zhongguo tongji nianjian, 1983*, pp. 106, 112, 117–18.

[19] Seeberg found in the Hefei area that about 30 percent of children were not attending primary school in the late 1970s. In rural areas, transportation to school was a difficult problem. Moreover, a majority of female children who began school left before the fourth grade to do housework or to care for younger children. Seeberg estimates that 20 percent to 40 percent of the population had a fifth-grade education or better (*Literacy in China*). Andrew Nathan cites figures, for the early 1980s, that 65 percent of Chinese children were finishing five years of primary school, but only about 33 percent were passing the exam to get into junior high school, and that 50 percent to 70 percent of the rural populace were "nonreaders." See *Chinese Democracy*, p. 161.

[20] Interview at the Guangdong renmin chubanshe, 4 March 1980.

Youth Publishing House, after doing a survey, estimated the number of "young readers" in cities nationwide at 40 million,[21] a figure that was equivalent to about 20 percent of the total urban population. Since "young" in the survey meant "under thirty-six years old," it in fact encompassed a majority of the urban population, and thus implies that the upper limit of the total urban readership would fall somewhere below 40 percent.

These estimates can be roughly confirmed by calculations based on the circulation of periodicals. In Guangzhou in 1980, the literary periodical that had by far the largest local circulation was the *Literary Works*. With each issue, 60,000 copies were allocated to Guangzhou city and easily sold out. The magazine's editors estimated that an average of about ten people read each copy,[22] and this estimate is in line with many others for similar cases, as well as with survey research.[23] The Guangzhou readership of *Literary Works*, therefore, may have been about 600,000 or about 12% of the city's population. Popular though the magazine was, it would be too much to assume that every active reader read it. In particular, readers who preferred detective, romantic, or martial arts fiction would generally have found *Literary Works* too difficult, and perhaps too political, for their tastes. How much should therefore be added to the 12 percent figure is a question for speculation; but it does seem likely that the result would fall between 20 percent and 40 percent.

Most of this popular readership seems to have been young workers in cities, or *qingnian* (youth) as editors and officials generally called them. The cliché usage was confirmed, however, by surveys[24] as well as by the impressions of staff at bookstores and libraries. Statistics at the Shanghai Library for May 1980 show that "workers" or their units were responsible for 62 percent of all book borrowing, most of which was borrowing of fiction.[25] The evidence on division of the readership by sex is complex, but shows that both sexes were importantly involved.[26]

[21] Interview at the editorial offices of *Shouhuo*, Shanghai, 17 June 1980.

[22] Interview at the *Zuopin* editorial offices, 4 March 1980.

[23] Around the same time, editors at *Guangzhou Literature and Art* (*Guangzhou wenyi*), which was less prestigious than *Literary Works*, estimated 5 to 10 readers per copy of its magazine (interview, 7 March 1980). Other editors made the following estimates: at *New Harbor* (*Xin'gang*, Tianjin), 10 to 15 readers per copy (interview, 30 June 1980); at *Anhui Literature* (*Anhui wenxue*), about 5 per copy (interview 25 June 1980); at Hundred Flowers Publishers (Bai hua chubanshe, Tianjin), 10 readers per copy of magazines (interview, 29 June 1980); at China Youth Publishers (Zhongguo qingnian chubanshe, Beijing), more than ten readers per copy of books (interview, 8 October 1979). The China Youth editors said that they sometimes intentionally divided a book into two volumes so as to double the speed with which readers could share it. Officials at the Shanghai Library estimated that at least two readers, and sometimes three or four, would read a book of literature during the two-week periods for which the book was lent (interview, 13 June 1980). Based on survey data and official demographic statistics, Brantly Womack has been able to calculate that the *Beijing Daily* (*Beijing ribao*) had about eight readers per copy in 1982 (Womack, ed., *Media and the Chinese Public*, pp. 33, 36, 39, 104).

[24] See Womack, ed., *Media and the Chinese Public*, tables 11.3 and 12.3, pp. 83, 86.

[25] Interview, 13 June 1980.

[26] Editors of literary magazines often said that young women were their most numerous

Reading at the popular level seems to have grown during the 1950s and early 1960s, and declined somewhat during the Cultural Revolution years of the late 1960s and early 1970s. It grew markedly in the post-Mao years. It became a preferred extracurricular activity of high school students, among whom it was rivaled only by listening to the radio and, to a lesser extent, by sports, homework, and such things as strolling in parks or window-shopping. All of this was illustrated in 1980s surveys,[27] and was colorfully described by Liu Binyan in a 1982 speech: "Literature seems to have become an essential part of daily life. At least in the provinces and cities that I have visited, whether a factory is large or small, advanced or backward, its workers, while they may not read newspapers, or *Red Flag*, seem all to be walking around holding literature magazines. On the buses of Beijing, except for some foreign language textbooks, everybody is reading fiction."[28]

Although film and television were at least as attractive to the urban readership, they were limited by cost and (at least until the mid-1980s) availability. A 1982 survey of ordinary households in Shanghai found people using radio or television an average of an hour and a half per day, and reading about fifty minutes a day; rare trips to theaters averaged only about an hour per week.[29] Most reading took place in the evenings, although the noontime siesta period was also important.[30]

Socially Engaged Readers

Broadly speaking, the educated urban readership can be conceived in three categories, although we must understand that the three were not mutually exclusive: the same person, in different moods and for different purposes,

---

readers, especially of love stories; interviews at *Zuopin* editorial offices (Guangzhou, 4 March 1980), Literature and Arts Publishing House (Wenyi chubanshe, Shanghai, 16 June 1980), and *Renmin wenxue* editorial offices (Beijing, 9 August 1980). Some surveys confirmed this perception; see Liu Fengzuo, "Muqian daxuesheng baokan yuedu qingkuang de diaocha." But other surveys found more men than women reading popular literature overall. See Womack, ed., *Media and the Chinese Public*, where the readership in and around Beijing in 1979 was found to be 59 percent male and 41 percent female (p. 66). In many parts of the countryside, schooling patterns explain sex differences in literacy and reading; boys were sent to school for more years than girls, who were brought home earlier to work.

[27] Huang Ruixu, "Young Laborers' Attitudes," pp. 44–45; Wang Yalin et al., "Qingnian zhigong yeyu wenhua shenghuo kaocha," p. 38; Ye Jun, "Shanghai shifan daxue xuesheng sixiang guannian bianhua de qingkuang diaocha," p. 19; Wang Zhisheng and Li Zibiao, "Guangzhoushi zhongxuesheng sixiang zhuangkuang de diaocha," p. 44; Shen Jiming, "Guanzhong shenmei xinli de bianhua yu dianying de duice," p. 17; Pang Junlin and Li Jie, "Dianying: xibu qingnian de kewang yu xuqiu," pp. 123–24.

[28] Liu Binyan, "Tan xin shiqi de wenxue chuangzuo wenti," p. 5.

[29] Tao Ye et al., "Shanghai chengshi jiating wenhua xiaofei xianzhuang ji fenxi," p. 14. By official estimates, the overwhelming majority of workers at the No. 3 Universal Machine Works in Beijing in the late 1970s preferred films to fiction when they had the choice (interview, 18 October 1979).

[30] Womack, ed., *Media and the Chinese Public*, table 20, p. 108.

might fall into more than one category. Other than the popular readership that we have just sketched, there were socially engaged readers, who were drawn to literature for its critiques of society and politics, and elite readers, whose purposes were less time-bound, more "literary," and often more academic.

The socially engaged readers were primarily young and middle-aged workers and, more loosely, a group called "educated youth" (*zhishi qingnian*), meaning secondary-school graduates who were working, going to college, or awaiting work assignment.[31] (The term "educated youth" first gained prominence during the Cultural Revolution, when large numbers of urban youth were sent to the countryside for work and "revolutionary education," and it remained a common term after many young people returned to urban areas in the late 1970s. Publishers in the post-Mao years who received letters from the countryside urgently requesting books and magazines attributed these letters to "educated youth" who were still in the countryside, not to natives of rural areas.)[32] Along with younger cohorts of graduates, the returnees to cities formed a base for the popularity of the socially critical works that appeared after Mao.

Although they overlapped with the popular readership, the "educated youth" had certain attitudes and habits that caused them to be known as a special group. Maoist idealism was their pivotal experience; it brought them first inspiration, then sharp disappointment, and finally, in many cases, outrage. But through its ups and downs, this group maintained a sense of social concern, a stout oppositional spirit, and a lasting generational camaraderie. Literature also had a special place for it. Surveys show that as late as 1984, students at elite universities preferred literature to radio, film, television, sports, and a variety of other "cultural activities."[33] More than other groups, educated youth talked with one another about literature and related social and political issues. They also tended to write letters to editors and authors with disproportionate frequency. Within a few days after Lu Xinhua's "Scar" was published in the Shanghai *Wenhui Daily*, the newspaper's editors received 960 letters, and the author himself about 200. Two years later the author was still receiving letters.[34] Editors of literary magazines reported that even unremarkable pieces could cause dozens of letters to be written. Such numbers may not seem high for a readership that could reach the

---

[31] The number "awaiting work" was sometimes substantial. In 1981, Guangdong province reported that 500,000 people (about 1 percent of the total population) were in this category. See *Yangcheng wanbao* 13 May 1981, p. 2; also *Xuanchuan xuexi shouce* 1981.6.31.

[32] Interview at *Shanghai wenxue*, 17 June 1980; *Xin'gang* 30 June 1980.

[33] Shen Jiming, "Guanzhong shenmei xinli de bianhua yu dianying de duice," p. 17.

[34] Interview with Lu Xinhua, Shanghai, 14 June 1980. Chen Guokai's "What Should I Do?!" Jiang Zilong's "Manager Qiao Assumes Office," and Liu Binyan's "People or Monsters?" elicited still greater numbers of letters. Interview at *Zuopin* editorial offices, 4 March 1980, Guangzhou; with Jiang Zilong, 10 August 1980, Beijing; and with Liu Binyan, 4 April 1982, Los Angeles.

millions, but they go well beyond what readers elsewhere, for example in the United States, send to authors and editors.[35]

Elite Readers

These were generally older readers of Chinese and foreign classics whose interest derived from family traditions of learning or from academic work in universities, and whose supply of books came from family and school libraries and the "internal" circulation network. They were much fewer in number than the two categories just reviewed. Literary editors in major cities commented that "only a few intellectuals," or "older" or "more traditional" readers, liked to read things like essays, classical poetry, or great works of fiction.[36] Even May Fourth-era fiction, which remained largely unknown to most readers, had become "classic" in this sense;[37] a film of Lao She's classic *Camel Xiangzi* was rated "boring" in a 1983 survey of factory workers.[38] There were several reasons for the drop-off in reading after middle age. When people took on work and family responsibilities, they had less spare time for activities of any kind, including reading; and insofar as they still did read, surveys show that they turned increasingly toward reading news, technical and political reports, and other non-literary materials.[39] Many had lost their idealism, and hence did not need literature as a means to release it. The political elite, often overloaded with official reading materials, seldom read literature except to monitor the moods of the young or "the masses," or to study political signals or attacks that literature might contain. Through most of China's socialist years, there was practically no such thing (as there was in the Soviet Union) as an elite artistic vanguard in literature and art.[40] When modernist and "postmodernist" writing did emerge in the late 1980s, it came as part of a general reappearance of a split

[35] Lee Dembart, a literary reporter for the *Los Angeles Times*, once noted his surprise at receiving 87 letters or telephone calls in response to a literary piece. "In two decades in the news game," Dembart noted, "my lifetime average is about one letter per article. I can't recall any article on which I received more than ten letters"; *Los Angeles Times Book Review*, 28 December 1986, p. 9.

[36] Interviews at the editorial offices of Bai hua chubanshe, Tianjin, 29 June 1980; Renmin wenxue chubanshe, 28 September 1979; *Shouhuo* (Shanghai), 17 June 1980; and *Zuopin* (Guangzhou), 4 March 1980. See also Huang Ruixu, "Young Laborers' Attitudes," pp. 60–61.

[37] Interviews at the editorial offices of *Guangzhou wenyi*, 7 March 1980, and at Zhejiang Provincial Library, 12 June 1980.

[38] Huang Ruixu, "Young Laborers' Attitudes," p. 61.

[39] The survey presented in Womack, ed., *Media and the Chinese Public*, shows a falling off of the interest of readers over thirty-five in the categories of literature, sports, and letters to the editor, and an increased interest in news of the leadership, governmental policy, and science and technology. The same general pattern holds if high school graduation, rather than age thirty-five, is used as a criterion to separate two groups (pp. 86, 89).

[40] The forerunners of the elite *Jintian* group in Beijing began their activities in the late 1950s, but their readership, numbering in the dozens at most, was hardly bigger than the group itself.

between elite and popular literary levels that was common elsewhere in the world and that had last been seen in mainland China in the 1940s. Yet, although the literary elite in the 1980s remained only a tiny fraction of the overall readership, it was prestigious enough to reestablish the concept of "critical" acclaim in addition—and sometimes opposition—to popular or political acclaim.[41]

Modern poetry was an important form among the elite, but never had a very large readership. Poetry journals had small circulations and had to rely on subsidies either from the state or from publishers who could make money on fiction or other profitable forms. General literary periodicals included poems more to enhance their prestige than to attract readers. In 1980, a literary editor in Hangzhou reported that more than half of the unsolicited manuscripts that arrived at the offices of the Zhejiang provincial literary magazine were poems, and said he found this fact interesting because poetry clearly appealed to only a tiny fraction of readers.[42]

Traditional poetic forms remained more widespread and deeply rooted during the socialist period, and clearly were more popular when people wanted to reveal their "heartfelt feelings."[43] The poems of protest that appeared "like spring bamboo shoots after rain" at the Tiananmen demonstrations of 1976 were written overwhelmingly in traditional forms of five or seven characters per line.[44] Graffiti in parks, popular ditties, and official admonitions to wait for a green light before crossing the street all tended strongly to observe traditional rules of poetic meter. Mao Zedong's own poems were in ancient, and sometimes arcane, form. In contrast, the practitioners and audiences of artistic modernism were always small elites.

The interests of the four categories of readership (or audience) that we have just sketched spanned a wide range in genre, theme, language, medium, and literary origin. In the rest of this chapter and the next, I present some of the thematic interests of the readership/audience as well as some theories of why the interests were important within the daily-life contexts of people who had them. For convenience, I separate the discussion into the two levels of "popular" (about heroes, villains, lovers, adventure, and so on, dealt

---

[41] Bao Chang, head of the secretariat of the Writers' Association, noted in 1986 the beginnings of a bifurcation between highbrow and popular tastes in literature and related entertainment. See "Literary Editors Discuss Drop in Subscriptions" Joint Publications Research Service, CPS-86–049. Later that year, Chen Kaige's film *Huangtudi* (Yellow Earth) illustrated the problem dramatically. Elite viewers, both Chinese and Western, praised it immediately, and gave it prizes, but popular Chinese audiences found it boring and wrote letters to magazines like *China Youth* voicing their complaints. See Ruan Yuanzhao, "Dianying de xin kunhuo."

[42] Interview with Shen Hugen, deputy chief editor of *Donghai* (Eastern sea) (Hangzhou), 12 June 1980.

[43] Interview with Beijing readers from the No. 3 Universal Machine Works, 21 October 1979, as well as interviews with Zhongguo qingnian chubanshe, Beijing, 8 October 1979, and several literary editorial boards.

[44] See chapter 4, note 19.

with in the rest of this chapter) and "social engagement" (about corruption, violence, oppression, and other topics related to public affairs and the national fate, which I take up in chapter 6). Although the second of these levels is somewhat more "elite" than the first, I do not mean to tie the two kinds of themes to specific readership groups; many readers (or audiences) were engaged at both levels. The resulting two-level analysis inevitably omits some important things—notably, at one end, the traditional themes in opera and other indigenous and primarily rural performing arts and, at the other, the varied literary interests of the urban and primarily academic elite. But the analysis does include the broad mainstream of themes that people who read literature or who listened to its variant versions on radio, television, film, or the oral grapevine found, for various reasons, to be appealing.

POPULAR ENTERTAINMENT

The major themes of popular entertainment fiction in modern China have had strong staying power throughout the twentieth century. When Communist Party leadership took over Chinese publishing houses in the early 1950s, one of the first things they did, as part of a general "cleanup," was to end the mass production of entertainment fiction—primarily stories about romantic love, martial arts, and detectives—that had boomed in the first half of the century. But the abrupt end in production of such material did not end its allure to readers, and only partly curtailed its actual supply in society.[45] Some popular books and magazines continued to trickle into China in the baggage of travelers, especially between Hong Kong and nearby Guangdong. The strong influences from the Soviet Union in the 1950s, on which the Chinese socialist literary system was modeled, included a genre of Soviet "anti-spy fiction" whose resonances with pre-1949 Chinese detective and adventure stories were strong enough to satisfy the accustomed appetites of readers. In Shanghai and elsewhere, used-book vendors continued to sell and rent popular fiction, including pre-1949 works as well as Soviet stories, until 1966, when the Cultural Revolution finally ended this practice. But then, the complete banishment of printed materials only brought on the rise of "hand-copied volumes" peopled by the same kinds of lovers, heroes, and detectives that readers seemed so much to need.

In the post-Mao years, Chinese publishers returned to entertainment fiction, using it primarily to balance their financial books under Deng Xiaoping's new pay-as-you-go "responsibility system." Alexandre Dumas's *The Count of Monte Cristo* was republished in the late 1970s by the nation's premier literary publisher, the People's Literature Publishing House in Beijing. Shortly thereafter, the Zhejiang People's Publishing House republished

---

[45] See Perry Link, *Mandarin Ducks and Butterflies*, "Afterword," pp. 236–48.

Margaret Mitchell's *Gone with the Wind*, the Guangdong People's Publishing House began to reissue *The Adventures of Sherlock Holmes*, and several presses published Agatha Christie's *Death on the Nile*. By mid-1980, all these works, according to publishers in Shanghai, were circulating in about a million copies.[46] The numbers again shot up dramatically in the mid-1980s. In 1986, officials at the Federation of Literary and Art Workers said that Chinese publishers had, in the preceding two years, produced about 40 million copies of books filled with "kungfu masters, detective adventures, and love stories."[47] Around the same time, magazines featuring popular fiction sprang up in Wuhan, Taiyuan, Beijing, and elsewhere, and by the early 1990s had flooded urban bookstalls across China.

Although the revival in popular fiction publication was based on translations of foreign works, gradually the stories of contemporary Chinese writers also appeared. The trend began in 1979 in Shanghai, where the Literature and Arts Publishing House printed anti-spy stories by Mou Guozhang in 150,000 copies.[48] When the Party leadership in Beijing ordered that literary initiatives be directed toward Taiwan in an effort to pull Taiwanese popular sympathy toward the mainland, mainland publishers took the opportunity to introduce Taiwanese popular fiction as a way of making money. In 1986, the Guangxi People's Publishing House printed 160,000 copies of the love stories of the Taiwan writer Qiong Yao, and soon San Mao, another popular Taiwan writer, was also widely available.[49]

The thread that connects pre-1949 popular Chinese fiction to 1950s Soviet spy stories, Cultural Revolution hand-copied volumes, and post-Mao revivals of the entertainment press suggests an ineradicability of reader interest in certain popular forms and themes. Scar literature, although too politicized and serious to be viewed as pure entertainment, also drew heavily upon popular notions of heroism, romance, and twisting fate. So did traditional-style opera and storytelling, whether or not, in contemporary versions, it brought in modern characters such as detectives and spies.[50] In an address to Guangdong writers in 1982, the powerful literary official Zhou Yang acknowledged that Mao Zedong had been wrong in his assumption that the Chinese people's interests in storytelling could be radically overhauled. Although "Chairman Mao's views have stood the test of time," Zhou said, "he also made some mistakes. Operas depicting emperors, kings, generals, ministers, talented scholars and beauties have a history of several thousand years. How can we drive them off the stage in one swoop?"[51]

---

[46] Interview with editors at Wenyi chubanshe, Shanghai, 16 June 1980.

[47] Lu Chao, "Popular Novels Leave Serious Stuff Standing."

[48] Interview with editors at Wenyi chubanshe, Shanghai, 16 June 1980.

[49] Interview with Wang Jinmin (a scholar of Chinese fiction who was working with the Guangxi Press), 25 October 1986.

[50] On themes in contemporary rural storytelling, see "'Gushihui' zai ge di nongcun da shou huanying" *Wenhuibao*, 13 July 1980.

[51] "Zhou Yang Addresses Guangdong Writers Forum," *Dagongbao*, 9 February 1982, trans-

What follows is a discussion of some of those enduring popular interests that, throughout China's socialist period, could not be driven off stage, off paper, or outside the repertoires of oral raconteurs. The examples are from various materials, but I have relied especially on film, because of its broad audience and the fact that audience comments are audible to the researcher, and on Cultural Revolution hand-copied volumes, because these stories, which were free from any shaping by political authorities or the intellectual elite, tend to represent popular interests in a pure form.

Twisting Plots and Other Surprises

All sources point to strong popular interest in the unusual, the marvelous, and the unexpected. Apparently opposite features are combined in one character, as in a beggar with a grotesque face but a heart of gold, or an alluring young woman who is also a martial artist who can fling you twenty feet. Story lines frequently mislead the reader (or listener), as when, led into a strange all-glass room in a back alley in London, we see ninety-eight corpses on ninety-eight beds in a row, whereupon one "corpse" springs to its feet, embraces a visitor, and turns out to be a clever detective who has been waiting his chance to catch villains in action. The reader's assumptions can be undermined and carted away one by one until hardly anything remains predictable except that nothing can be predicted for sure. An evil temptress named Black Peony is in fact a blonde, and actually is not evil; she merely seeks revenge upon an Indian raja who had once sold her into slavery; she goes to India, tracks down the raja, lies in ambush, and showers him with bricks, only to discover that she has located the wrong raja and has pelted an innocent man, who by rights should be furious but, amazingly, turns out to be patient, kind-hearted, and so moved at hearing Black Peony's life story that he gives her fifty "toughs," fifty "braves," and 20,000 English pounds with which to continue her quest.[52]

Some stories seem to include abrupt twists simply in order to keep the action moving briskly. In the Black Peony story, when the need arises for a big mansion that can serve as Black Peony's haunted house, the narrator simply explains that the wealthy merchant who had owned the house fell off a cliff one day—unfortunately for him but very conveniently for the plot. Great leaps across time and place, and around piles of tedious details, are permissible in the hot pursuit of story lines. A young man riding a bus in search of his girlfriend suddenly spots her at a bus stop; later the woman, searching for him, enters a large city and easily finds him loitering at the railroad station.[53] In hand-copied volumes, some extremely sharp turns in

---

lated in Foreign Broadcast Information Service, *China Report* W3–6 (10 February 1982), p. W6.

[52] Anonymous, "Kongbu de jiaobusheng."

[53] Sha Tian, "Liulanghan de qiyu."

story lines seem caused by missing pages, perhaps accidentally torn out from earlier copyings of the text. But fundamentally, the twists and turns seem to be durable and consciously contrived features of the genre, born of an abhorrence of the possibility of reader boredom. It seems reasonable to speculate that the tedium and routine of daily life created some strong needs at least to imagine, through storytelling, some of the surprise and variety that otherwise was so rare. One imagines a young urban worker, riding the same bus back and forth between the same factory and the same small flat at the same time each day, or the "educated youth" assigned to work in the countryside and suddenly finding nothing to look at but rice fields and the same mountain for several years.

The use of surprising chance or coincidence (*qiao*), which has strong roots in traditional Chinese storytelling, became so common from the late 1960s through the mid-1980s that it practically ceased to be surprising. It was liberally employed in hand-copied volumes, in fiction and film of the scar period, and in late-1980s popular fiction, alike. In 1980, editors at *Shanghai Literature* reported receiving between 800 and 1,200 unsolicited fiction manuscripts per month, most of which were filled with twisting plots woven from highly imaginative coincidental events.[54] Frequently the coincidence was gratuitous—simply added to make an amazing tale even more amazing. In one story, a young woman is a clever thief and can always slip away from the police officer who pursues her; then she falls in love, and her boyfriend turns out to be the son of the judge who works with the same policemen.[55] A pair of Hong Kong lovers is separated when the young woman's parents send her to Europe for schooling; there she dies in an air crash, and the forlorn young man eventually marries the daughter of the principal of the high school at which he teaches; but, it turns out, the first young woman had miraculously survived the air crash and now returns to Hong Kong, where, by chance, she finds work at the same high school where her old boyfriend was working, and sets the stage for a series of tearful showdowns.[56]

In some cases the web of interlocking coincidence became so complex as to take on the interest of a puzzle. In a 1979 film called *Troubled Heart*, set in the late-Maoist period, an overseas Chinese surgeon returns to China to serve the people and operates on a young woman singer who dies during the operation.[57] The doctor is blamed for the death and charged by Gang-of-Four extremists with a wrong class standpoint. But actually the singer died because a nurse, acting for the Gang-of-Four people, had slipped poison into her arteries in order to provide a pretext for making the doctor into an illustration of incorrect class standpoint. Only the doctor's daughter stands by him during the crisis. By chance, one of this daughter's coworkers is the older brother of the deceased singer, and the two workers fall in love.

[54] Interview at the editorial offices of *Shanghai wenxue*, 17 June 1980.
[55] Li Kewei, "Nüzei."
[56] Anonymous, "Qingtian changhen."
[57] *Ku'nan de xin*, directed by Chang Zhenhua, Changchun dianying zhipianchang, 1979.

But when the boy learns that his girlfriend's father (apparently) caused his sister's death, he becomes severely distraught, swoons on the job, injures himself in a fall, and needs emergency surgery that—of course—only the same surgeon can provide. This operation succeeds, and the story ends happily when the doctor is also cleared of charges in the singer's death. This happens because the nurse who injected the poison becomes angry at her boyfriend for refusing to take proper responsibility for her pregnancy. She exposes her boyfriend and the Gang-of-Four people who had manipulated him in carrying out the murder plot. This end is ironically bitter for the boyfriend, who originally had been a promising student of, naturally, the same surgeon, as well as a budding suitor of the surgeon's daughter, who now was about to marry the brother of the woman that his new girlfriend, at his behest, had killed.

The appeal of coincidence seems to have lain partly in the marvelous compactness of the highly imaginary plots that could result. But it had other aspects, as well. It could dramatize issues by bringing two symbolic sides face to face. The anguish of losing one's sister on an operating table is made more vivid and concrete when the surgeon is one's girlfriend's father. The basic goodness of the doctor is underscored when he, of all people, has to do the operation on the bereaved, and the corresponding basic evil in the Gang of Four is put in sharper relief when the surgeon's own student turns out to be their tool. When two parties in a love triangle need to work through an emotional predicament, the drama is more intense if they find work at the same high school.

The use of chance occurrence to reunite kin or close friends was especially common. Drawing on devices of plot that had been well established since Ming times, storytellers of the socialist period found ways for people to locate one another, after years of intervening turmoil and longing, through improbable coincidence aided, at most, only by the recognition of a distinctive token or mark.[58] In a play called *Cherry Blossoms in Tears and Blood*, a Chinese student in Japan marries a Japanese woman, who conceives a son.[59] The year is 1941, and the Sino-Japanese War soon drives the couple apart. Thirty-two years later, after China and Japan have normalized relations, the Japanese wife sends her son on a mission to China to find his father. The son, frustrated by an evil uncle, attempts suicide and needs emergency surgery in China from a man who turns out to be his father. The father suspects the connection after noticing that the patient wears a token that looks just like the one he had left with his Japanese wife decades earlier. But he dares not draw the conclusion until his wife, who travels to China to thank the doctor who has saved her son, notices in the doctor's apartment the corresponding token that she had long ago left with her husband.

[58] For example, Baoweng laoren, "Maiyoulang duzhan huakui," in which the long-lost parents of both parties to a fanciful romantic match are reunited with the couple through coincidence and chance signs.

[59] *Leixue yinghua*, Guangdong huajutuan, Guangzhou, 9 January 1980.

Coincidence of this kind happened only to good people, and drew attention to the deep moral importance of family and other close ties, such as those between teacher and student or between sworn friends. In a play called *Love and Tears across the Straits*, a family long separated by the political split between Taiwan and the mainland is reunited when a strong and handsome young man in the mainland coast guard rescues a shipwrecked captain from Taiwan who turns out to be his father.[60] He also protects a beautiful young woman, who turns out to be his sister, from the lascivious intentions of guards from the Taiwan side. The fact that he starts to fall in love with the young woman turns out to be okay because she is, after all, an adopted sister unrelated by blood. Family and teacher-student ties are interwoven in a story called "Heroes Don't Weep," in which a blacksmith takes as his apprentice a boy whose parents have disappeared during the Cultural Revolution.[61] Eventually the blacksmith himself falls victim to Red Guards, who taunt him and smash his bellows. Wishing to help, the boy apprentice runs home and returns with an old bellows that his father had once used. When he looks at the bellows, the blacksmith is shocked to notice, engraved in its handle, the image of a fish that he himself had carved years before. This boy's father had been his first teacher! To the reader, the coincidence not only connects certain characters, but clearly establishes that all of the connected people are morally good.

During the post-Mao years, the use of coincidence to dramatize family separations produced a sentimentality that was much stronger and more explicit than the more wistful effects that were traditional in Chinese storytelling. In the film *Little Flower*, a mother and three children are all separated in the turmoil of civil war.[62] Eventually they all meet by chance near the front lines, rescue each other, and shout "Mother!" and "My child!" back and forth through tears. The chance meeting of kin reaches extremes of pain in Chen Guokai's story "What Should I Do?!"[63]

There is evidence that at least some of the appeal of coincidence, and of unexpected things generally, came from the enjoyment of taking the strange to be true. Editors reported receiving many letters that asked what "finally happened" to characters in fictional accounts,[64] and there were continued reports, as there had been for decades in China, of popular audiences who blamed actors on stage—and even off stage—as if they were themselves the people they portrayed. As a foreign researcher, I could sometimes get a direct sense of these assumptions by sitting among film or drama audiences and hearing occasional outbursts such as "Damn you, get out of here!" aimed at one character, or advice such as "*He* did it! The one in the big hat

---

[60] *Haixia qinglei*, Guangzhou huajutuan, Guangzhou, 10 January 1980.
[61] Cen Sang, "Haohan budiao lei."
[62] *Xiao Hua*, directed by Zhang Zheng, Beijing dianying zhipianchang, 1979.
[63] See p. 19, above.
[64] This habit is not entirely naive for the case of Chinese fiction, which is often a recounting, more or less embroidered, of actual events.

did it!" offered to another. In 1980, a high-ranking cultural official reported an incident in which an opera audience began spontaneously to take up a collection to help out one especially deserving character.[65] Even among more sophisticated readers and viewers, there were signs of the universal principle that stories are more fun when one can believe they are true. For years American readers of "Ripley's Believe It or Not" relied on this principle. "Chatters" on socialist China's oral grapevine, like readers of tabloid journalism in the West, have long been willing to stretch plausibility in order to gain the extra excitement that comes from believing that something actually happened.

The concept of *qi* (strange, marvelous), important in Chinese storytelling for centuries, depends for its allure on the natural tension between presentations that are too strange to seem true and the implicit claim that, nevertheless, they *are* true. A hand-copied story called "Strange Encounter with a Wandering Brave" presents *qi* in several ways.[66]

Set in 1969, the story introduces an accountant at a defense plant, a beautiful young woman named Fang Fang who has dozens of suitors but remains aloof. One day she goes into town to draw the factory's monthly wages. After stuffing the cash into a travel bag, she stops at a restaurant and orders two bowls of noodles. A large, scruffy-looking beggar walks over, rudely grabs one of the bowls, and guzzles the soup. Fang Fang flees in panic, forgetting her travel bag. The "food-grabber" (as such people were called) gobbles her other bowl of noodles, then turns his attention to her travel bag. Amazed at its contents, he then amazes the reader by reasoning that so much money can only be public funds, that this young girl will suffer a sentence of hard labor or worse if she loses it, and that, therefore, he must at all costs return it. By good luck he is able to find her at a bus stop, and insists on waiting while she counts every note to verify that he has taken nothing. He refuses even a token reward, but does accept her name and address and says he will look for her if he should ever really need help.

Some time later, roving the countryside and utterly destitute, he finds no alternative but to turn to her. In order to get past the gateman at her defense plant, he has to lie by saying he is her relative. She is delighted to see him and immediately lends him 50 yuan, but cannot prevent him from turning abruptly to leave and wander again. Shortly thereafter, the leadership at the plant announces that it will be hiring two hundred new workers and that priority will go to relatives of current workers. Inspired, Fang Fang sets out in search of her "cousin" the food-grabber, miraculously has little trouble finding him, and secures the back-door assistance of a deputy party secretary in getting him a job. The food-grabber takes a bath, gets a haircut, dons new clothes, and turns out, wonderfully, to be a strong and handsome

---

[65] Interview with Chen Huangmei, deputy director of the Institute of Literature, Chinese Academy of Social Sciences, Beijing, 15 July 1980. The collection was taken to aid Qin Xianglian (11th century A.D.), wife of the scholar Chen Shimei, who plotted to kill her and their children so that he could marry the emperor's daughter.

[66] Sha Tian, "Liulanghan de qiyu."

young man named Li Chunsheng. But then it emerges that the party official who had helped Fang Fang lusts for her and expects repayment of his favor. Frantic to avoid him, Fang Fang runs to Li Chunsheng and abruptly proposes that they marry. They do, and a year later have a baby. How strange, reflects the narrator, that this gorgeous prize of a young woman should end up bearing the child of a grimy food-grabber!

The story merits the word *qi* in its title not only because of this irony of fate, but because of the interplay between poverty and a huge sum of money, the intervention of chance in bringing people together and, perhaps most important of all, the enchanting incongruity between the crude exterior and the golden inner virtue of the food-grabber. His stout honor, shabby appearance, and wanderlust all recall standard elements of the righteous heroes known as *xiake*, or knights-errant, in Chinese storytelling tradition.

Heroes and Villains

Although tales of *xiake* (or *xia*, for short) have ancient roots,[67] they rose to unusual prominence in the latter part of the Qing period with novels such as *Seven Knights and the Five Righteous* (*Qixia wuyi*) and *Tale of Heroic Young Lovers* (*Ernü yingxiong zhuan*), and in the early twentieth century with Xiang Kairan's *Tales of Strange Roving Knights* (*Jianghu qixia zhuan*), Gu Mingdao's *Female Knight of the Wild Rivers* (*Huangjiang nüxia*), and other works.[68] Such stories were also the primary forebears of what became known in the late twentieth century as "*gongfu* films," although *xia* were generally not as flamboyant as the film heroes in their display of supernatural physical skills. Traditionally, *xia* concealed their unusual abilities, drawing on them only when and to the extent needed. Physical skill melded with—indeed, was ultimately the same thing as—superior intellectual and moral qualities. In the hand-copied *The Second Handshake*, the young male hero, appearing as a somewhat bookish student of science, gives no sign of his martial arts skills as he sits near a band of armed thugs on a railroad train. When the hooligans start to threaten his girlfriend, he judges that resistance has become necessary and coolly thrashes the lot of them. In another hand-copied story, the villains deliver to the police a mysterious shiny silver ball that appears to have some secret function. Aiming to open it, the police convene fourteen *xia*-like heroes, each shabby looking but famous for his prodigious skills. They gather to compete at opening the strange ball; when one finally succeeds, the others gallantly withdraw in deference to his superior skill.[69]

The female knight errant, or *nüxia*, was especially *qi* because of her sex. Since the *xia*'s martial skills—jumping, kicking, fighting, and so on—were normally associated with men, to suggest that a woman could be good at

[67] See James J. Y. Liu, *The Chinese Knight-Errant.*
[68] See Link, *Mandarin Ducks and Butterflies*, pp. 14, 22, 117, 162, 171, 237, 259, and elsewhere.
[69] Anonymous, "Dixia baolei de fumie."

them was *qi* already, and to show her doing things that would be strange for either sex was doubly *qi*. (The fact that she is presented as *especially* strange because of her sex indirectly supported male dominance by reinforcing the message that normally, and properly, women are less likely than men to have such skills.) A "girl thief" in a post-Mao film script appears as an unkempt street urchin, but she can outrun male police, elude them by leaping over walls or on and off moving trains, and later (in a revelation of her underlying morality) show up at a police station to return a wallet she has pickpocketed from one of them during the chase.[70] A related standard type is the temptress, a modern version of the fox fairy of traditional storytelling, who lures men to their deaths in a number of Cultural Revolution hand-copied volumes.[71] The temptress's composition—seductive on the outside and evil within—inverts that of the *nüxia*, whose ragged exterior covers a good heart. But the two are the same in presenting a strange combination of opposing qualities, thus producing the sense of *qi*.

The strong and enduring appeal of *xia* stories in Chinese culture is shown by the difficulty the Communist Party had in trying to stamp them out. Although they were successfully banned in the 1950s, the continuing interest of readers in *xia*-like heroes was evident in the appearance of various surrogates. Some of these were the detectives in Soviet spy fiction that became highly popular in the 1950s; others were the war heroes of certain Party-sponsored novels, such as Qu Bo's *Tracks in the Snowy Forest*. The reappearance of *xia* in the 1960s, in hand-copied stories that had contemporary backgrounds, suggests that these heroes had been alive continuously on the oral grapevine. In 1979, while the formal ban on *xia* fiction was still in place, authorities nevertheless allowed the importation of the French-Italian film *Zorro*. The righteous and mysteriously skilled Mexican swordsman-detective was not a Chinese *xia*, but was close enough to recall the *xia* tradition.[72] The film, which had added allure because it was from the West, played to packed houses and drove ticket prices to ten or more times their face value in some cities.[73] By the mid-1980s, when *xia* fiction and film (much of it from Hong Kong and Taiwan) had become almost as easily available as it had been in the 1940s, surveys of young workers in Wuhan, Lanzhou, and elsewhere found "martial arts" fiction and film the most preferred of several kinds.[74]

[70] Li Kewei, "Nüzei."

[71] For example, Huang Meifang in Anonymous, "Dixia baolei de fumie," and Hei Mudan (Black Peony) in Anonymous, "Kongbu de jiaobusheng."

[72] I am grateful to Jeffrey Kinkley for pointing out Zorro's background. For more see Ilan Stavans, *Antiheroes*, p. 66.

[73] In Guangzhou, where black-market prices reached three yuan per ticket, students at Zhongshan University struck classes in order to take advantage of a group admission that one of them, the daughter of the third-ranking member of the provincial Party committee, had been able to arrange through her connections.

[74] Mao Hanbin et al., "Bianhuazhong de qinggong sixiang guannian," p. 29; Pang Junlin and Li Jie, "Dianying," p. 124.

If we take the notions of "hero" and "villain" in a larger sense, to include realist and socialist realist works, we see strong continuity throughout China's socialist period in both the characteristics of heroes and villains and their popularity with readerships and audiences. The heroes and villains of Party-approved stories in the 1950s about the civil war, the war against America in Korea, and the "struggle" to form collectives and communes had many of the same characteristics as their counterparts in hand-copied fiction of the Cultural Revolution period and anti-Gang-of-Four stories of the late 1970s.

Heroes and heroines, first of all, looked good. They normally had straight noses, shining eyes, and light skin with a rosy glow. If young, they had jet-black hair and eyebrows, which, on men, were always thick; if old, the men had graying temples and the women salt-and-pepper hair combed straight back. They all looked—and were—sincere. They could be clothed in rags, but still appeared clean and neat. Villains, by contrast, had shifty eyes, signaling their insincerity, and drawn, gray, or greenish faces—although some had puffy faces to go with obese bodies. Males sometimes wore narrow moustaches reminiscent of the Japanese military, and females wore excessive makeup and ostentatious clothing that showed their self-indulgence. The color black was a metaphor for villainy. During the Cultural Revolution, Mao Zedong invented "five black categories" of social enemies (landlords, rich peasants, counterrevolutionaries, rightists, and common criminals); during the same years a villain in an underground story was called the Big Black Rogue, wore all-black clothes, and leered through an unshaven, "black" face. Even his laugh was "*hei!*," a homonym for "black."[75]

In the anti-spy fiction imported from the Soviet Union in the 1950s, the heroes were KGB operatives and the villains CIA agents. Chinese imitations of the genre used the same conventions, substituting Public Security Bureau (PSB) agents for the KGB. To judge from the content of the uncontrolled hand-copied volumes of fifteen years later, the PSB and CIA labels seem to have sunk in with the popular readership. By then, however, they seem to have become merely routine. They were often applied simply to identify the good guys and the bad guys, about as unreflectively as the labels "cowboys" and "Indians" were used around the same time in America. In fact, the villains were usually much more interesting—one might even say attractive—than the blander police. The villains had hidden two-way radios, underground munitions factories, soundproof chambers, and other evil equipment that made them seem very stylish technically as well as mysteriously unfathomable.

What villains do not have, and heroes do, is moral power and rightness (reminiscent of Confucian *de* and *yi)* that gives them authority among other moral people. A hero always keeps in mind what is right—meaning what is

---

[75] Anonymous, "Dixia baolei de fumie."

good for the largest number of people—and acts accordingly. He or she considers all angles of a problem (with furrowed brow, typically), reaches a principled and often overly simple conclusion, sticks to it with an iron will, at the cost of any personal sacrifice, and through such demonstration of virtue attracts the admiration and support of all other basically good people. The hero is always concerned about ultimate ends, which, so long as they are good, can justify just about any means. In the "Wandering Brave" story recounted above, the food-grabber can grab the food of others (which might seem wrong) because he really does need it to live (and thus do good). It is all right for him to lie in order to get past a gatekeeper, because in the long run his intentions are only good.

In a modern morality play called "Save Her!,"[76] widely shown on both stage and television in 1980, a young woman named Li Xiaoxia falls into a gang of thieving, drinking, fighting "hooligans" but eventually is saved in reform school by Teacher Fang, a broadly moral person who can see the big picture. As Li Xiaoxia is recovering, her original boyfriend (not a hooligan) writes her love letters, but Teacher Fang judges that these should be intercepted in order "to prevent her from being distracted from her studies." After she is fully rehabilitated and her boyfriend comes to visit her, Teacher Fang brings out all the love letters and gives them to Li Xiaoxia at once. The popular audience among whom I watched the play in Guangzhou seemed to identify entirely with Teacher Fang. They showed no sign of distaste at her decision to intercept the letters, and chuckled warmly when she brought them out at the end. The chuckle did acknowledge the teacher's minor transgression, but affirmed its appropriateness in context. She was doing what was best for the girl in the long run.

A hero's vision was not only long-range, but broad in accounting for all present realities. Just as Mao Zedong listened to the whole of the Yan'an Conference on Literature and Art in 1942 and then delivered his "definitive" summary of its significance, literary heroes in socialist China were good at taking in all aspects of a confusing issue and delivering a final judgment that was both analytically clear and morally proper. At the end of Sha Yexin's play "What If I Really Were?," no wrapping up of its lesson seems possible. Its indictment of corruption seems too strong for the Party possibly to accept, and yet to blame the young man who reveals the corruption seems morally unacceptable. Finally, a wise and elderly official, "Zhang Senior," comes forth to make a summary judgment that apportions blame even-handedly in several directions. A similar figure in the play "First Flower of Spring" comes up with the surprising decision that a worker's good job performance is more important than her bad class background.[77] Although a simple point (and exactly in tune with the propaganda initiatives

---

[76] Zhao Guoqing, "Jiujiu ta!" Shenyang huajutuan, broadcast nationally 13 January 1980; Guangdong huajutuan, live performance 23 February 1980; published in Jiangxi daxue Zhongwenxi, *Dangdai wenxue juben xuan*.

[77] Cui Dezhi, "Baochunhua."

of the day), in the play the judgment is presented as springing from a uniquely broad and deep view of current circumstances. Popular audiences seemed ready to assume that the highest-ranking heroes, such as Zhou Enlai, had an almost supernatural grasp of detail nationwide. In the play "Cherry Blossoms in Tears and Blood," noted above, Zhou, in Beijing, is aware of the accident in Guangzhou that has befallen a young visitor from Japan, and personally directs which physician should take charge. In a film called *The Young Swallow Flies*, Zhou has time to give his personal help to the training of gymnasts; he remembers to bring them a film of an international gymnastic competition that "foreign friends" had given to him.[78]

There was a strong sense of popular reliance on heroes to solve problems—not just a hero's own problems, but everyone's. The immense popularity of Jiang Zilong's "Manager Qiao Assumes Office" (1979) had a lot to do with the hero's ability to cut through bureaucratism and corruption of kinds that readers everywhere could recognize in their own environments. Ke Yunlu's novel *New Star*, published in 1985 and later tremendously popular in serial form on national television, depended on the same kind of imaginary hero that everyone wished for.[79] An important model for these modern fictional heroes was Bao Zheng (999–1063 A.D.), popularly known as Lord Bao (Bao Gong), a Song official whose reputation for upholding law and opposing corruption had long passed into legend, and who provided content for rural opera and storytelling throughout China's socialist period, except for the years when public expression of such things was forbidden. Sometimes more than a model, Lord Bao could have contemporary relevance. The high-ranking literary official Chen Huangmei reported in 1979 hearing peasants at an opera about Lord Bao shout "the Communist Party should learn from Lord Bao!"; Chen also noted that a poster asking "Where is Lord Bao today?" had been recently pasted onto the door of the offices of *People's Daily*.[80] When Deng Xiaoping returned to power in 1978, he was briefly compared to Bao Zheng because of the popular hope that he would magically "clear up" all of the "false, wrong, and unfair verdicts" of the Mao period.

The Lord Bao legend supported the interests of little people but was not at all the same as democracy. Law by itself, in this tradition, was useless unless one had a forceful hero to carry it out. Little people got justice by subordinating themselves to the hero. In popular film and fiction, the heroes often had a charisma that helped this subordination to take place instantly and absolutely. In the film *It Wasn't for Love*, a scuffle breaks out between protesters and provocateurs at the 1976 Tiananmen demonstrations in memory of Zhou Enlai.[81] The situation is confusing and deterio-

---

[78] *Ruyan fei*, Xi'an dianying zhipianchang, 1979; directed by Sun Min and Yao Shougang.
[79] *Xinxing*.
[80] Talk at the conference in Nanning, Guangxi, as reported by Wang Jinmin, 24 March 1980, at Zhongshan University, Guangzhou.
[81] *Bushi weile aiqing*, directed by Yin Xianglin, Emei dianying zhipianchang, 1980.

rates rapidly until the handsome young hero, bushy black eyebrows knotted in a frown, is somehow able to stand half-a-body taller than everyone else and call for order. All the scufflers freeze and give him their attention. The hero is powerful because he is good, and can do good because he is powerful.

But the popular assumption that goodness and power should go together could also have troublesome consequences for leaders. The failure to measure up, especially by the goodness standard, left officials vulnerable to satire of a kind that has been common in Chinese popular fiction since the eighteenth century. It led as well to a modern continuation of the traditional genre known as "unofficial history" (*waishi* or *yeshi*).

Unofficial History of the Powerful

Until the mid-1980s, there was an effective ban in socialist China on portraying living leaders in film, on stage, or in published fiction. Nevertheless, rich and varied accounts of life at the top thrived continuously on the oral grapevine. After the mid-1980s, tabloids (*xiaobao*) began to print some of this oral material from earlier years, for example about the Lin Biao affair in 1971, but under the unspoken principle never to contradict official accounts, only to flesh them out with juicy (and questionable) details. Some of the unofficial histories found their way into hand-copied volumes during the Cultural Revolution period, and this accident gives us some of the best evidence of what they were like.[82] One very widely circulated example was *Plum Blossom Party* (*Meihuadang*), author unknown, a fanciful but tightly knit account of elite political intrigue from the 1940s through the 1960s, ending dramatically when Wang Guangmei, wife of Liu Shaoqi (who was president of the People's Republic until he was purged during the Cultural Revolution), is found to be the head of a Guomindang spy ring taking orders from Taiwan.[83]

Another work, "The Great Bridge Affair," is set in 1969 and tells of an assassination plot by Lin Biao against Mao Zedong.[84] Mao is traveling from Beijing to Shanghai on a train that is scheduled to cross the Yangzi River over the great Nanjing bridge one day at 5:03 P.M. Using a complicated ruse, Lin Biao's people persuade an unwitting old lady to carry a "baby" (actually a time bomb) onto the bridge at precisely that time. The plot is discovered, and the bomb dismantled. Zhou Enlai is informed and dispatches an airplane from Beijing to pick up Mao. Zhou then reasons that the plotters, because they knew the top-secret details of Mao's itinerary, must have been highly placed and well connected. Hence the regular Public Security channels cannot be trusted to handle this case. The army, lacking

---

[82] Some stories leaked out of China and were published overseas. Hsia Chih-yen, *The Coldest Winter in Peking*, and Jing Fuzi (Gu Hua), *Mao Zedong he ta de nürenmen* are examples.

[83] Ding Wangyi, "Zhongguo dalu de dixia wenxue," part 1, p. 19.

[84] You Kecun, "Daqiao fengyun."

detective experience, also will not do. Zhou draws upon his virtual omniscience of individual good people throughout China and decides to call upon Sun Dasheng ("Great Victory" Sun), a detective genius who has been doing labor reform in the northeast wilderness because of his former association with the fallen general Luo Ruiqing.

Freed by Zhou, Sun heads for Nanjing, where he is formally met by Public Security people who are actually in the Lin Biao clique and among the plotters. They take Sun to a state guesthouse, where they try to get him drunk so that they can kill him. (It is not clear why he needs to be drunk before being killed, except that such an obvious shortcut would lop off a lot of good storytelling.) The clever Sun perceives the villains' scheme in advance, feigns inebriation, kills the intended assassin, and escapes to the roof of the guesthouse, where he uses a nifty radio to call in help from General Xu Shiyou, the Nanjing commandant who is loyal to Mao and Zhou. Xu responds with a battalion of troops, who rescue Sun. But the Lin Biao people escape through an elaborate maze of tunnels that lie beneath the guesthouse. The details of the whole matter became clear, we are told, after the Lin Biao affair of 1971.

Characters like Sun Dasheng are fictional, but their stories are intertwined with those of top leaders whose real names are used and whose political positions, on the whole, correspond to official definitions. (Wang Guangmei was certainly not the head of a Taiwan spy ring, as alleged in *Plum Blossom Party*, but the characterization is fully consistent with Maoist accusations against her husband in the late 1960s.) Points of orthodox ideology ("workers," for example, tend to be bland but reliably good people) and quotations from Mao ("Defeated enemies are never happy with their defeat," etc.) appear in the storytelling from time to time. But these aspects of general conformity with official ideology are not at all vital to the storytelling. Some, such as the Mao quotes, may have been included to provide at least some political cover in case a hand-copied volume were discovered. Usually, though, they appear simply as part of the landscape, worthy of neither praise nor blame. At one point in "The Great Bridge Affair," Mao is referred to as "the old man" (*lao touzi*), but in context the comment is only jocular sarcasm, not serious dissidence.

The real fun of the "unofficial history" genre seems to have been a kind of voyeurism. Ordinary people, denied accurate news reporting on the political superelite who held such fateful sway over their daily lives, naturally developed a great thirst for any account they could get about the ins and outs of happenings high in the clouds. The narrator of an unofficial history was immediately attractive to them, not only because of all the "facts" he or she could fill in but because of the sense of elevation a person could get by enjoying a panoramic view from a vantage point that seemed nearly at the same level as the mighty historical figures themselves.

There was a sense in these historical romances that the dramas played out on China's political stage were, naturally, the biggest ones in the world.

Nationalism in this broad sense was taken for granted, and patriotism was closely associated with other aspects of good character. As we have seen, even uncensored hand-copied volumes have a heroine working at a national defense plant, cast foreign spies as the standard bad guys, and generally accept that moral rot seeps into China from outside. The intersection of Sinocentrism and male-centrism is evident in the stories where a Chinese man marries a foreign woman, who, after suffering separation for a while, comes to China to find him.[85] (Although fictional marriages of Chinese women to foreign men did occur, they were rare, and were not used to illustrate Chinese nationalism. A Chinese woman who married a foreign man "married out.")[86] An apparent exception to the general acceptance of nationalism were the occasional fictional references to escaping China to Hong Kong. Such stories were set (and perhaps most popular) in Guangdong and other southern provinces, from which major waves of refugee emigration to Hong Kong occurred in the early 1960s, after the great famine, and again in the late 1970s when border controls weakened.[87] But the topic of "sneak passage" (*toudu*) was always highly sensitive. In published fiction the topic appeared only obliquely,[88] and in underground hand-copied volumes was somewhat more explicit.[89] But I call such references only an "apparent" exception to nationalism because they never entailed leaving China in a cultural or ethnic sense. Hong Kong and overseas Chinese communities were still part of China in terms of nationalist sentiment. There were strong popular interests in foreign lands, but these were of different kinds.

Foreign Things and New Things

Modern Chinese popular fiction, right from its beginnings in late-Qing Shanghai, was useful to its readers in coming to grips with the brave new world of modernization and Western cultural influences.[90] Readers could use fiction not only to learn about foreign things and practices, but to test them out. Attractive and *qi* as some modern things were—watches, telephones, automobiles, cinema, racetracks, street lights, traveling dentists,

---

[85] *Leixue yinghua* and *Haixia qinglei*; see notes 59 and 60, above.

[86] A character in the film *It Wasn't for Love* (*Bushi weile aiqing*, note 82 above) is the daughter of an Italian man and a Chinese woman. Since this daughter is a positive character, she does imply at least tacit approval of the marriage that produced her. But her mother was not extending Chinese nationalism by marrying a foreigner.

[87] Around Shantou (Swatow), people set off firecrackers in the late 1970s when they received telegraphic news that their loved ones had made it to Hong Kong.

[88] In Wang Jing, "Zai shehui de dang'anli," for example.

[89] An example is *Zhujiang shui chang* (Long runs the Pearl River), in which the bloody feuding of two Cantonese families ends when a young member of one of the families helps both families to sneak out to Hong Kong. See Ding Wangyi, "Zhongguo dalu de dixia wenxue," part 1, p. 20.

[90] See Link, *Mandarin Ducks and Butterflies*, chap. 6.

women pilots, boats with wings, and the whole accompanying sense of adventure about the unexpected—there was also the dark side of opium, gangsterism, venereal disease, humiliation of China, and other evil things that seemed tightly intertwined with the exciting things. What was an ordinary person—attracted and intimidated simultaneously—to do? By reading fiction one could experiment with—or "feel," as it were—various new kinds of behavior, without taking risks in real life. One could also look at decay, dirt, and deviance as much as one liked, without having to get involved with them.

These uses of modern popular fiction grew during the first half of the twentieth century, and then declined in the 1950s and early 1960s because the socialist realist novels of that era did not easily lend themselves to such uses. But explorations of the outside world reappeared in the hand-copied volumes of the late 1960s and 1970s. Some of these stories were translations of foreign works, and many of the indigenous Chinese stories seem in several ways to reflect a fascination with foreign lands and people. The tale of Black Peony, noted above, is set in England and India, and includes a Charlie (Chali), a Herman (Ouman), a blonde, a raja, and a couple of British detectives. In *The Second Handshake*, a young woman travels to America in pursuit of medical education, and lives in a southern mansion complete with white pillars, green lawns, black servants, telephones, and automobiles. Stories often take place either in foreign countries or in Westernized Chinese cities such as Hong Kong, Shanghai, or wartime Chongqing. Detective and spy stories introduce gadgets of warfare ranging from minuscule timers to underground munitions plants, which are both unusually effective and unusually mysterious because they are foreign-made. There were foreign touches even in pure pornography, as when a young beauty dons "brand new pure-white underpants" before setting out for an evening of sex.[91]

It may seem strange that interest in foreign things should have been so strong during years when China was often described as sealed off and inward-looking. But the very sealing off helps to explain why any scrap of material about the outside, with no need to be accurate, could become so fascinating to the ordinary person, and explains as well why such material was concentrated in an illicit medium like hand-copied volumes. There is ample evidence in the post-Mao years, when China "reopened," of a rush to peer outside and see where the world had gone in the last decade or two. The quick discovery of such things as pocket calculators and four-speaker portable stereos only increased the popular appetite for modern things and strengthened the reputation of "the West" as an unfathomed store of enigmatic things. A 1983 survey in Tianjin found "novels that reveal the inside story on Western societies" second only to detective and spy fiction in general interest,[92] and in 1984 a survey of young filmgoers in China's northwest

---

[91] Anonymous, "Yige gaozhong nüsheng de xing tiyan," p. 109.
[92] Huang Ruixu, "Young Laborers' Attitudes," p. 50.

found a main attraction of foreign films to be "the chance to learn about how other people do things."[93] The popular appetite to try some of those things out for oneself is suggested in a 1985 survey of young factory workers in Chengdu. Although few of them had ever seen a Western coat and tie except in film and on television, 74 percent rated the outfit "very spiffy" (*hen jingshen*), while 18 percent called it "fairly nice" and only 1.5 percent "not very pretty."[94]

The appetite of popular audiences to use film and fiction as a way of learning about life in other places could be measured, directly if imprecisely, by sitting in film theaters and listening for the Chinese exclamation *waaaahh!* that normally expresses surprise and wonder. An individual outcry was often useless for research purposes, but there were times when an entire audience would exclaim together, their uncoordinated *waah!*'s melding into a soughing, pure-vowel *u-u-h-h-h!* that rose and fell over about three seconds. A view of skyscrapers or a superhighway could elicit this response. At a showing of *The Second Handshake*, it came at the first glimpse of the American mansion with white pillars. It also came, notably, at the spectacle of the Beijing airport—a fact which shows that the distant places that the popular audience liked to explore through film and fiction were not just foreign countries but also other places and subcultures inside China. At a showing of the film *The Young Swallow Flies*, the audience produced its collective *waah* when the camera led them inside the home of the privileged protagonist. It had a fan, a couch, a refrigerator, and three rooms![95] Watching *The Heart Returns Like an Arrow*, a Guangzhou audience gasped when a peasant in remote Heilongjiang added some sticks to a fire.[96] Wood was precious in Guangzhou. And that woman just *burned* it?

Although a lively curiosity underlay much of the attention that audiences in socialist China showed for new things and distant places, there was also quite clearly a continuation of the deeper worries about how to handle the challenge of "the West." In *The Second Handshake*, as well as in the hand-copied volume called *Eternal Regrets in Love*, a love triangle involves a male protagonist who must choose between two young women: one who is more active, well educated, strong-willed, and ready to journey abroad, and another who is more traditionally Chinese, preferring to stay at home and be plain, deferential, and even a bit boring, but always familiar and reliable. This kind of love triangle, which has strong roots in the fiction of the first half of the twentieth century,[97] was a metaphor for the deep and intractable cultural question of how much China should westernize and how much it should preserve Chineseness. Which "girlfriend" should be China's future?

[93] Pang Junlin and Li Jie, "Dianying," p. 127.

[94] Weng Dawei, "Chengshi qingnian shenghuo fangshi de quxiangxing," p. 12.

[95] *Ruyan fei*; see note 78 above.

[96] *Guixin sijian*, directed by Li Jun, Bayi dianying zhipianchang, 1979.

[97] Notably in the fiction of Xu Zhenya and Zhang Henshui; see Link, *Mandarin Ducks and Butterflies*, pp. 23–30, 41–42.

In the 1960s and 1970s, just as in the 1910s and 1920s, the reader could use a triangular love story to test out the exciting but potentially dangerous aspects of the Western alternative, even while retaining the option of falling back on the tried and true Chinese alternative. The two-sidedness of Western influence, bringing allure and danger inseparably, was reflected in spy and detective fiction, as well. A Rolex watch that doubles as a secret radio transmitter is fascinating and desirable, while the foreign spy who created it and who alone can employ it represents iniquity incarnate.[98]

Science, Technology, Spies, and Detectives

Science fiction and detective fiction arrived in China together from Western Europe, appearing first in the reformist press of late-Qing Shanghai. Translations from A. Conan Doyle's *Memoirs of Sherlock Holmes* and *Adventures of Sherlock Holmes* began appearing in Liang Qichao's reform journal *Chinese Progress* in 1896,[99] and Lu Xun's translation (via Japanese) of Jules Verne's *From the Earth to the Moon* appeared in 1903.[100] The related genre of "novels of ideals" (*lixiang xiaoshuo*) sometimes projected social ideals, such as equality for women, and sometimes technical fantasies, such as a world in which all menial work is done by electric robots.[101] Science and detectives were linked not only chronologically but in spirit: Holmes's methods of observation and deduction seemed to illustrate the application of the scientific method to crime solution. His abilities seemed to be a concentrate of the more general self-help skills portrayed in the popular science writing in the Shanghai press. Holmes arrived in China as an overlay upon Lord Bao and other traditional heroes of crime solution, whose legendary skills and morality had for centuries been the stuff of immensely popular story cycles.[102] Lord Bao relied on logical deduction, as Holmes did, but went beyond Holmes in finding useful evidence also in dreams, natural signs, moral judgments of character, and forced confession. In the 1910s, when Cheng Xiaoqing began publishing his series of novels called *The Cases of Huo Sang, the Oriental Holmes*, his hero drew elements from both Holmes and Bao, and remained broadly popular through the 1940s.[103]

Banned in 1949, detective fiction was able to reenter China, at least in spirit, in the form of the 1950s anti-spy stories imported from the Soviet Union. *The Adventures of Sherlock Holmes* was republished in 1.5 million copies during the post-Stalin thaw, and imitative Soviet whodunits also be-

---

[98] Anonymous, "Dixia baolei de fumie."

[99] *Shiwubao* 6–7 (27 September and 7 October 1896); 10–12 (5, 16, and 25 November 1896); and 24–26 (22 April and 2 and 12 May 1897).

[100] *Lu Xun yiwenji*, vol. 1, pp. 3–145.

[101] For example, "Dian shijie" (The electric world), *Xiaoshuo shibao*, no. 1, September 1909.

[102] See Y. W. Ma, "The Pao-kung Tradition in Chinese Popular Literature." Here "Judge Bao" is the same as "Lord Bao" (Bao gong) referred to above.

[103] See King-fai Tam, "The Detective Fiction of Ch'eng Hsiao-ch'ing."

came broadly popular.[104] The Soviet detective fiction that reached China was apparently screened to permit only stories of international espionage— cracking spy rings, foiling plots to bomb factories or sink ships—in which the enemies were the Americans and their lackeys.[105] This subgenre gained enough popularity that during the Cultural Revolution, when uncontrolled hand-copied volumes appeared, its basic features remained unchanged. "The Annihilation of the Underground Stronghold," set during the 1953 "Resist America, Aid Korea" campaign, tells how Public Security operatives discover and destroy a chemical laboratory run by the CIA to develop poisons for use in warfare.[106] The plant is located beneath a graveyard in Chongqing, the wartime capital of the Guomindang, whose minions have lingered to assist the Americans. These include Huang Meifang, a sexy, westernized young woman who tempts police agents into deathtraps; Dr. Jiang, who tests American poisons on Chinese subjects; Clerk Wang, bribed to infiltrate Public Security for the United States; the Big Black Rogue (*hei dahan*), who does muggings and other errands; and an innocent-looking old lady whose wristwatch is a secret radio transmitter.

After Mao, popular interest in detective fiction resurfaced in dramatic ways.[107] By 1979, in major cities throughout China, *The Adventures of Sherlock Holmes* was by broad consensus one of the most sought-after books in China.[108] Ellery Queen and Agatha Christie soon became "hot," as well. In 1980, a film of Christie's *Death on the Nile* caused great excitement, and the Jiangsu People's Publishing House issued her *Murder on the Orient Express* in hundreds of thousands of copies, while officials in Shanghai complained that "some publishers pay no attention to quality."[109] By late 1980, *Holmes* and the book version of *Death on the Nile* both circulated in over a million copies.[110] In Beijing *Holmes* became a "flying book," lent hand-to-hand with no sense of ownership. When reader opinion surveys were taken beginning in late 1982, detective fiction was rivaled only by martial arts stories in the preferences of urban workers.[111] Surveys also seem to indicate that detective,

---

[104] Maurice Friedberg, "Soviet Books, Censors, and Readers," pp. 204–5.

[105] Of nine examples I have been able to find, *Meizhou bao di shisan hao* and *Youchuan "Tuapusi"* are typical. I have not been able to discover the original names of the authors in Russian, but have listed the books in the bibliography under *hanyu pinyin* romanizations of L. Shamoyiluofu and B. Sikeerbin for the first novel, and W. Kalining and T. Kusiniezuofu for the second.

[106] Anonymous, "Dixia baolei de fumie."

[107] See Jeffrey C. Kinkley, "Chinese Crime Fiction and Its Formulas at the Turn of the 1980s" in Kinkley, ed., *After Mao*, 89–129.

[108] According to interviews in Beijing at the Beijing Library (28 October 1979), Central Broadcasting (Zhongyang guangbo diantai) (11 October 1979), and the No. 27 Locomotive Factory and No. 3 Universal Machine Works (21 October 1979); in Shanghai at the Shanghai Municipal Library (13 June 1980) and the Wenyi chubanshe (16 June 1980); and in Guangzhou at the editorial board of *Zuopin* and the Guangdong renmin chubanshe (4 March 1980).

[109] "Chuban tushu yao kaolü shehui xiaoguo" *Wenhuibao*, 22 April 1980.

[110] Interview at the Wenyi chubanshe, Shanghai, 16 June 1980.

[111] Surveys in 1982 and 1983 showed strong preferences for detective stories in Wuhan,

anti-spy, and science fiction themes, more than other modern popular topics, have been responsible for shrinking the audience of traditional opera. Although themes of family, romance, historical drama, and moral heroism all have affinities with opera themes, modern detectives and scientific gadgetry do not. Surveys show that the decline in opera attendance was especially marked among young urban people, who were also the ones with the strongest preferences for detectives and science fiction.[112]

Science fiction, although never as popular as its cousin detective fiction, was continuously on the scene in socialist China.[113] It combined several of the popular audience's interests: it had strangeness (*qi*), it showed the wide world outside China, it had gadgetry, and it often brought in heroism. In the 1950s, while the import of Soviet anti-spy stories gave Chinese detective fiction an indirect boost, Soviet "science stories" also helped to keep science fiction alive, even though the Soviet stories were a somewhat different genre from China's fantasy-based science fiction. The state-sponsored idea of much Soviet science fiction was to showcase model scientists. Works with titles such as *The Wonderful Atom* and *How Steel is Born* told of scientists struggling to make major breakthroughs in their fields while maintaining correct political and social attitudes.[114] Although some Chinese works of this kind appeared, as well, the fantasy-based variety remained clearly more popular. In 1962, Tong Enzheng, an archeologist at Sichuan University, published *The Visitor from 50,000 Years Ago* about a boy who happens across a fragment of an alien spaceship and gets help from the Chinese Academy of Sciences in interpreting it.[115] After the Cultural Revolution, Tong and other writers turned again to science fantasy. Tong's story "Death Rays from Coral Island," about two patriotic overseas Chinese professors who invent a "nuclear battery" that emits deadly rays, and who keep it away from Soviet hegemonists by sending it back to China, was published in the prestigious *People's Literature* in 1978.[116] When readers were invited, in a poll sponsored by the Writers' Association, to name the stories they thought should be given national prizes, "Death Rays" received a tremendous (but unpublished) number of votes, leaving the panel of judges with the dilemma of

---

Xi'an, Heilongjiang, and Tianjin. See Mao Hanbin et al., "Bianhuazhong de qinggong sixiang guannian," p. 29; Gongqingtuan Xi'an shiwei, "Yige gongchang qinggong renshengguan de diaocha," p. 11; Wang Yalin et al., "Qingnian zhigong yeyu wenhua shenghuo kaocha," chart 3, p. 38; and Huang Ruixu, "Young Laborers Attitudes," p. 50.

[112] A survey of high school students in Wuhan, in addition to finding general distaste for traditional opera, found the following reasons for it: slow-paced, sluggish, long-winded; ancient stories with no contemporary relevance; stereotypical, boring plots; unattractive, dull music; unrealistic. See Fan Buyan, "Cong xia yidai guanzhong kan xiqu de mingtian," p. 130.

[113] See Rudolph Wagner, "Lobby Literature: The Archeology and Present Functions of Science Fiction in China," in Kinkley, *After Mao*, pp. 17–62.

[114] George Gibian, *Interval of Freedom*, p. 33.

[115] Tong Enzheng *et al.*, *Wuwan nian yiqian de keren*.

[116] Tong Enzheng, "Shanhudaoshang de siguang."

whether or not to bestow honor on a piece of flamboyant science fiction.[117] (In the end "Death Rays" did receive a prize, but was listed last among twenty-five prize-winning stories.) Shortly thereafter, in 1979, Zheng Wenguang's *Flying toward Sagittarius*, in which three young Chinese scientists are trapped in a spaceship commandeered by a Russian robot, sold out about as quickly as it could be printed.[118]

The goodness of the good people in spy, detective, and science fiction was established by tagging them in simple ways: as friends of China, or of people like Zhou Enlai, or as enemies of the CIA, Soviet hegemonists, or some kind of nefarious domestic gangster. But the "good guy" tags only told the reader which characters to trust; it did not make them interesting. Their interest lay in their technique. Great Victory Sun, the detective in "The Great Bridge Affair," likes to smoke a pipe because it "clears his head," but also because he can use its highly polished bowl as a convex mirror in which to observe people behind him. He also evades pursuers by jumping off the front of a moving train, waiting for them to jump off after him, and then leaping aboard the last car as the train rumbles on. In addition to such cleverness of stratagem, reminiscent in different ways of both Zhuge Liang and James Bond, the heroes of Chinese detective stories sometimes display a shrewdness in observation and rational deduction like that of Sherlock Holmes. When an old lady asks a soldier at the Nanjing Bridge to hold a well-wrapped baby for a few minutes, explaining that it belongs to their senior officer (*shouzhang*) and was entrusted to her by soldiers in the company, the soldier quickly reasons that first, he and his fellow soldiers never use the term *shouzhang* for their two company commanders (*lianzhang*), and second, neither of their two commanders is married, therefore third, there is something suspicious about this "baby." He unwraps it to find a ticking bomb.[119]

Other techniques involve secrecy and deception. These include personal disguises, such as that of the "old lady" just mentioned, or an agent who dresses stiffly in a coat and tie and acts the foppish overseas Chinese in order to put his adversaries off guard.[120] But deception could also be massive and multilayered, generating an interest simply in plumbing its depths. At the end of "The Great Bridge Affair," the villains escape into a labyrinth of secret tunnels, which Great Victory Sun discovers only when a guesthouse cook tells him that a button on the wall behind a portrait of Mao opens a trapdoor at the base of the wall. After determining, by Holmesian ratiocination, that the cook must be telling the truth, Sun finds the button, pushes it, and descends through the trapdoor, where he discovers a maze so vast that he abandons hope of chasing the villains and settles for dismantling a time bomb that he finds tied to a corpse. The same kind of delight in weblike

[117] Interview with editors at *Renmin wenxue* and *Wenyibao*, 9 August 1980.

[118] *Fei xiang Renmazuo*; see also Rudolph Wagner, "Lobby Literature," p. 21.

[119] You Kecun, "Daqiao fengyun," part 1, p. 82.

[120] Anonymous, "Dixia baolei de fumie," section 4.

intricacy can be generated by personal interactions whose interest depends on what different characters do or do not know. In a film called *Stormy Weather*, an elderly poet is harboring a heroic refugee of the 1976 Tiananmen demonstrations in her home. A Public Security detective is charged with catching the refugee, but he secretly sympathizes. When he knocks at the poet's door, the refugee hides behind a screen. The detective figures this out, but doesn't say so. The poet can perceive that he has figured it out, but also pretends innocence. The ensuing dialogue is fraught with double meanings. The detective says, "If you see her [the demonstrator], tell her this will never work." The poet answers, "It's cold outside, you should wear a hat." The film audience, commenting with zest, seemed happy with the assumption that the world of Public Security has many layers.[121]

It is doubtful that the daily lives of the audience included secrecy and deception on a scale anywhere near the kind that arose from the fecund imaginations of popular storytellers. But if the patterns were far-fetched, the enjoyment of thinking about them was utterly ordinary. In part, the popular preoccupation with secrecy seems to have fed on an interest in the mysterious and fearful Public Security bureaucracy. But at least as important, it seems simply to have been a consequence of a social context whose plainness and lack of privacy made huge secrets seem fun precisely because they were so impossible.

Love and Death, Fair and Foul

Surveys in the mid-1980s showed romantic love to be close behind detective and martial arts themes in the preferences of popular readers.[122] The surveys do not offer breakdowns of the love-story readership, but many literary editors held that it was young women who preferred the love themes, while young men went for detectives and fighting.[123] Although probably defensible on average, this judgment no doubt had many exceptions. For example, in the kind of triangular love story we have noted above, in which a boy chooses between two girlfriends, one who is more Westernized and the other who is more traditionally Chinese, a male protagonist remains at the center. The metaphorical dilemma arises from a male point of view. Women could still read the story with empathy, and unquestionably did. But it is likely that many men did, too.

At the popular level, the drama of Chinese lovers during the socialist

---

[121] *Fengyu xiaoxiao*, Zhujiang dianying zhipianchang, 1979.

[122] See Wang Yalin et al., "Qingnian zhigong yeyu wenhua shenghuo kaocha," and Mao Hanbin et al., "Bianhuazhong de qingnian sixiang guannian." Shen Jiming, "Guanzhong shenmei xinli de bianhua yu dianying de duice," p. 24, finds the love theme in first place among readers twenty-five years of age or younger. But Shen's survey does not specifically offer "detective" or "martial arts" as choices.

[123] Interviews at the editorial offices of *Renmin wenxue*, 9 August 1980; *Zuopin*, 4 March 1980, and Wenyi chubanshe (Shanghai), 16 June 1980.

period was continuous in many ways with the popular fiction of the early twentieth century and even with the conventions of "talent and beauty" (*caizi jiaren*) stories in Ming and Qing times. The least-censored love stories—in hand-copied volumes and the tabloids of the late 1980s—presented lovers who were unusually talented intellectually (especially the man, but the woman, too) yet poverty-stricken or otherwise underappreciated by the world. They inevitably faced some social problem that drove them apart (wrong class backgrounds, disapproval of parents, engagement to a third party, or the like) and met the challenge with vows of iron constancy that set the stage for the heart of the drama, which was a lugubrious downward spiral into suffering and toward death. Some writers flinched, allowing a happy ending. But the purity of death-for-principle had powerful allure, if not to the dying lover then at least to the reader, who could watch as the beautiful event fell upon someone else.

Death-observation of a related kind appeared in detective and spy fiction, which offered less understanding of the victim and generated a sense more of horror than of beauty. Scenes of bloodletting stemmed from the tradition of *Water Margin* and martial arts fiction as well as from Western horror fiction. A young woman falls in with bandits and, in an act of righteous defiance toward another member of the band, slashes herself across the upper chest to create a bright stripe of blood.[124] In another story, more Western in its conventions, another stripe of blood seeps silently under the door of a room in a dilapidated mansion; when the occupant opens the door, his skull is crushed by blows from the clubs of two giant thugs.[125] Hand-copied stories had plenty of corpses—lying in rows inside morgues, as one would expect, or suddenly appearing as one turned a corner in a secret tunnel. As "nude corpses," they could offer an appeal that was somewhat ambiguous between horror and eroticism.

Descriptions of sexual expression were almost entirely shut out of officially published literature beginning in the 1950s. They crept back in the late 1970s, beginning with such things as the embraces of morally correct lovers, illustrative sketches that included an extra curve or two in the human body, and metaphors about spring, rain, and plowing.[126] Despite the 1983 campaign against "spiritual pollution," by the mid-1980s one could buy fairly blunt pornography on city streets. An official of the Chinese Writers' Association complained in 1985 that bookstalls right outside the association's headquarters in Beijing were selling magazines that featured nudes on their covers and included stories called "Three Women and a Man," and "I'll Leave the Door Unlocked for You."[127] But the post-Mao growth of

---

[124] Wang Jing, "Zai shehui de dang'anli."

[125] Anonymous, "Kongbu de jiaobusheng."

[126] See, for example, the closing lines of Gu Hua's "Futuling," p. 379 in *Paman qingteng de muwu*; translated in *Pagoda Ridge and Other Stories*, p. 146.

[127] Interview with Bao Chang, managing secretary of the Secretariat of the Chinese Writers' Association, Shanghai, 16 November 1986.

pornography had not begun from scratch. From the evidence of hand-copied volumes, it seems clear that the pornography revival began in the late 1960s, when schools closed and Red Guards began to roam.[128] Mao's repression of pornography was effective for about fifteen years, from the early 1950s through the mid-1960s.

Two pornographic hand-copied stories, "Sister Xia" and "A Maiden's Heart," seem to have circulated nationwide in the 1970s. Each recounts the sexual adventures of a young woman, who narrates in the first person, and both existed in a variety of versions as a result of multiple recopyings. In "Sister Xia," which seems to have originated in Shanghai, the title character is a factory worker who is overwhelmed by her first experience of sex with her boyfriend.[129] When the boy is then unfaithful, she is so bitter that she turns to prostitution, both as an outlet for her insuperable sexual appetite and in order to teach her boyfriend the lesson that he is not essential to her getting what she wants. "I don't need you!" she repeats to herself in triumph at each orgasm with a customer whose five yuan are really beside the point. The protagonist of "A Maiden's Heart" is more docile. In a version of the story called "Manna's Memoirs," Manna is a comely sixteen-year-old preparing to enter the Shanghai Physical Education Institute. When she meets her cousin Xu Xiaohua, a strong and handsome student at Fuzhou University, she records her inner feelings—wonder, misgiving, longing, passion, and finally abandon—tying each to explicit descriptions of Xu's physical performances upon her voluptuous body.[130] Unfortunately, after two weeks Xu gets a notice that he is being sent to the Soviet Union for study. The two young sex addicts vow to write letters, and do, but it is soon obvious that neither letters nor self-stimulation can satiate Manna. She meets classmate Lin Feng, another splendid male specimen, and they marry. On the wedding night, Lin becomes so aroused that he fails to notice that Manna is not a virgin. This sets the stage for her to address her readers, at the end, with a little homily on the bliss and harmlessness of premarital sex.

A 1982 survey at a work-study school for high school delinquents found young men and women busy reading as well as recopying pornography.[131] The same survey indirectly confirms that characters like Manna and Sister Xia probably existed in reality as well as fiction: it found a higher percentage of men than women to be sexually promiscuous, and (naturally, therefore) a higher frequency of promiscuity among the few women who did fall into that category. "Female hooligans" also appear in several officially pub-

[128] A study of pornographic hand-copied volumes among high school delinquents could find no evidence of circulation before the Cultural Revolution. Fudan daxue zhexuexi qibaji diaocha xiaozu, "Zhongshi huangse shouchaoben dui zhongxuesheng de duhai," p. 54.

[129] See Ding Wangyi, "Zhongguo dalu de dixia wenxue," part 1, p. 19.

[130] Anonymous, "Manna huiyilu," a hand-copied volume recovered in Shanghai in 1984, containing basically the same story as "Yige gaozhong nüsheng de xing tiyan."

[131] Fudan daxue zhexuexi qibaji diaocha xiaozu, "Zhongshi huangse shouchaoben dui zhongxuesheng de duhai," p. 53.

lished works of the late 1970s and early 1980s, where they are presented as a social problem in need of cure. In official media the pornography is absent, of course; instead there is a moral overlay about how to rescue young people who have "learned bad habits" or "lost their footing."[132] Only in the strictly underground works do narrators try to articulate and defend the "hooligan" point of view. Manna revels in her sexuality, narrates its pleasures from the woman's point of view, and encourages others to follow her path.

Sister Xia takes the contrarian spirit much further, into protest themes carried in the official press and even toward something that superficially resembles feminism. Her quest for revenge on her boyfriend fits with the general popularity of the revenge theme during and after the Cultural Revolution, but she phrases her point in a way the official press could not have tolerated. "If men can wantonly take their pleasure with women, why can't women similarly take their pleasure with men?" When one of her customers for sex turns out to be the decorous Party secretary at her factory, and when he threatens to fire her if she denies him sex, her narrative briefly resembles a plethora of other, officially published stories about corruption and hypocrisy. But again it exceeds the official works when Sister Xia, standing alone and naked after the secretary has left, fantasizes that if only *she* could be a secretary some day, couldn't she take advantage of all the men in the same way?

The problem with calling Sister Xia feminist is that, as Yenna Wu has shown, feisty women in Chinese literature can be subtly confined even as they are celebrated.[133] Sister Xia is interesting because she is surprising (*qi*). But this interest is something different from empathy; it is enjoyment from a distance. Sister Xia is fun to read about but perhaps not to deal with. The fact that she appears as startling indirectly reinforces the idea that behavior not so startling, perhaps more docile and continent, is the proper norm. In the end, her rebelliousness is given only a fenced-in playground, not basic endorsement. This pattern in the treatment of underdogs—granting attention while avoiding any real challenge to the social order—appeared in other ways.

Underdogs and the Acceptance of Hierarchy

The humble, the dispossessed, and the unappreciated were frequently elevated to respectability in hand-copied fiction. Charlie in "Terrifying Footsteps" is penniless, and his mother a washerwoman, yet he can become a university student of physics. The world fails to appreciate the extraordinary literary talents of Cai Minghui, the lover in "Eternal Regrets," but no reader of the story can miss the point. The food-grabber in "Wandering

[132] Examples are Zhao Guoqing, "Jiujiu ta!"; Li Kewei, "Nüzei"; and Wang Jing, "Zai shehui de dang'anli."
[133] Yenna Wu, *The Chinese Virago.*

Brave" appears a slovenly thief but is actually a moral paragon who has had some bad breaks. Junior detectives are orphans, cast off by the world but saved by senior detectives who adopt them as apprentices.[134]

It seems possible that the popularity of these pro-underdog themes arose in part from needs among young readers to identify with people who are underappreciated and unfairly treated. Such needs were already at work in the reading of popular fiction in the first half of the twentieth century,[135] and the disruption of education during the Cultural Revolution, followed by the crashing collapse of Maoist idealism then and afterward, only exacerbated feelings among youth that their talents had been wasted, their efforts unappreciated, and their lots in life simply not fair. If public protest was impossible, one at least could find some comfort in reading stories about the talents of the penniless, the hidden potential of orphans, the immaculate morality of people who sometimes dress in rags, and the secret iniquity of some of the people, such as the Party secretary in "Sister Xia," who enjoy society's respect. Such stories could have an immediate effect of relieving a reader's sense of isolation; other people, including some wonderful people, also had the underappreciation problem. When the woes of fictional protagonists multiplied (as they did, especially, in the love stories), a reader could even begin to stand above them and gain some additional comfort from the sense that, however bad things are with me, I am still doing all right compared to these poor people in the story.[136]

This sympathy with the downtrodden, however, was not radical egalitarianism. It did not question the hierarchical structure of Chinese society or authoritarian values that underlay it, but protested only that people who deserved a higher place in the world were not getting it. The food-grabber was "really" a young urban intellectual who had been sent to the countryside; had he been a poorly schooled farmer, the sense of unfairness about his lot would have been much less. In another story, a general is banished to a small town, falsely charged as a "renegade" by the Gang of Four. But despite his demotion and humble new surroundings, his standing socially and morally is unchanged. The townsfolk view him as a person of higher class, and he plays the role by rectifying unfair situations among them.[137] Lowly characters themselves supported the correctness of hierarchical relations by offering deference to authority figures. The poor orphans adopted as apprentice detectives were permanently unequal to their senior partners,

---

[134] Examples are Little Zhang in Anonymous, "Dixia baolei de fumie," and Sai Ying in Anonymous, "Kongbu de jiaobusheng."

[135] See Link, *Mandarin Ducks and Butterflies*, chap. 6, especially pp. 232–34.

[136] I have no survey or interview evidence for this kind of fairly subtle psychological interpretation. My theory is based on the rhetoric of the stories themselves, including the many ways, whose description is beyond my present scope, in which the stories seem designed to stimulate and channel a reader's sentiments.

[137] Chen Shixu, "Xiaozhenshang de jiangjun." The story was among the top five vote-getters in the national poll of readers conducted by *People's Literature* in 1979 (interview at editorial offices of *Renmin wenxue*, 9 August 1980).

whom they called "older brother," obeyed unquestioningly, and regarded as saviors.

The punctilious observance of bureaucratic authority appeared in sharpest relief during tense situations in thriller stories. In "The Great Bridge Affair," the soldier who discovers the ticking time bomb judges that, first of all, he had better call headquarters to report; only afterward does he turn to the task of dismantling the bomb. Later, a detective is crawling along the top of a speeding train, leaping from car to car and heading for the engine, while the villains constantly shoot at him from behind. He reaches the locomotive, climbs into the cab, and—first things first—presents the panicky engineers with his documents, which include a personal letter from Zhou Enlai. In "Underground Stronghold," a Public Security team is in hot pursuit of a CIA agent. The team chief is suddenly wounded and disappears. His two assistants, instead of continuing the chase on their own, look at each other in bewilderment and decide that "since there's nothing we can do (*meiyou banfa*), we'd better return to the precinct and report to the leadership on all that has happened."[138]

The strongest evidence of the limits on sympathy with underdogs appeared in the attitude toward losers with whom the reader or viewer had no reason to identify. A food-grabber was sympathetic only for the part of a story in which the reader saw him as "one of us." Cut loose from the crucial tie of identification, a loser, however innocent, could become an object of scorn or ridicule, thus giving the reader (or audience) the privilege and comfort of feeling superior. Live audiences laughed at a wife whose husband slaps her hard in the face during an argument,[139] at a child whose mother scolds him for a theft we know he did not commit,[140] and at an athlete at a track meet who trips on a hurdle and falls.[141] Throughout the twentieth century, Chinese writers have noticed, and deplored, the popular habit of deriving pleasure from the observation of others' misfortune. Lu Xun, Lao She, and many others, from the 1910s through the 1970s, wrote bitterly about crowds of voyeurs at public executions.[142] In an essay called "The Chinese Sense of Humor," C. T. Hsia noted an abundance of jokes about cripples and deaf-mutes and wrote that "the Chinese still retain a childish

---

[138] Anonymous, "Dixia baolei de fumie," p. 11. Although this episode is not intended to be funny, socialist Chinese popular humor had plenty of comment on bureaucratism. An underground joke of Cultural Revolution vintage said: A large house has three storeys, one occupied by Vietnamese, one by Americans, one by Chinese. The house catches fire. The Vietnamese (cowards, of course) flee. The Americans run for buckets and ropes, splashing and shouting in a frenzy. The Chinese hold a meeting to summarize the current situation.

[139] *Ku'naoren de xiao* (Troubled laughter), directed by Yan Yanjin and Deng Yimin Shanghai dianying zhipianchang, 1979.

[140] *Lan fengzheng* (The blue kite), directed by Tian Zhuangzhuang, Beijing dianying zhipian chang, 1994.

[141] Personal observation at a live track meet, Capital Gymnasium, Beijing, October 1979.

[142] Lu Xun, "Nahan zixu" and "Shi zhong"; Lao She, final chapter of *Luotuo Xiangxi*; Wu Zuxiang, "Guanguan de bupin"; Cao Guanlong, "Huo" ("fire"; part 3 of "San'ge jiaoshou").

delight in taking notice of any physical and moral deviation from the norm; their fellow creatures, so unfortunate as to be physically deformed and disabled, are usually objects of ridicule."[143] In the 1950s, jokes about cripples, pockmarked people, and country bumpkins disappeared from public expression because of a government ban. But the underlying pattern of laughing at losers persisted, and appears even to have been magnified by the public cruelty of the late Mao years.

In sum, despite the import of socialist realism and an ambitious series of campaigns and programs aimed at remolding popular Chinese culture from the top down, the tastes of the popular audience and readership in socialist China showed strong continuities with earlier times. Centuries-old preferences for twisting plots, bizarre coincidence, and heroes with astounding skills persisted, both in traditional-style storytelling (as it appeared in opera, oral performance, and hand-copied fiction) and in modern adaptations to film, stage, and the printed page. Traditional devices for generating surprise were sometimes grafted onto socialist realism to produce hybrid works that both leaders and readers could find worthwhile. Socialist realism and traditional popular tastes coincided more fully in their common requirement that heroes be moral paragons, bearers of both power and virtue upon whom weaker people could depend. The two kinds of heroes differed, chiefly, in that socialist heroes had to look clean, strong, and handsome, whereas traditional heroes often hid their virtues behind modest exteriors. Other themes of perennial interest—"talent and beauty" love stories, pornography, and unofficial history of the powerful—were largely shut out of the socialist press, but survived in unofficial media, both written and oral.

Many of the newer interests of the popular audience and readership had to do with understanding foreign influences. The allure of modern science and technology, already strong before the socialist period, was magnified by Party endorsements of science in the 1950s, and then intensified even more by Mao Zedong's decision to cut the country off from the modernizing world for about fifteen years. By the mid-1970s, the idea of modern gadgets had become almost magical in Chinese popular culture. Interest in Western detectives and modern international spies, who employed the magical technology, also spread widely; detective and spy fiction eventually became by far the largest area of Western influence on socialist Chinese popular literature. On some questions, such as modern courtship patterns, popular thought was more skeptical about outside influences, and here love triangles and other modes of "testing" the new ways continued to have appeal. In the early Deng period, when the doors to the outside reopened, popular literature and film became important as a kind of explorer's skiff into the wide world outside. But, in greater or lesser degree, all of these uses of popular fiction and film had begun in the early twentieth century, well before the

---

[143] *Renditions* 9 (Spring 1978), p. 31.

revolution. Both the technical features of modern Chinese popular storytelling and several of the apparent uses of stories to their audiences—to enjoy the strange as a relief of boredom, to peer into high places and foreign lands, to test new ways, to comfort oneself in failure, to fantasize about a rescuer or a sexual partner, and others—show clear continuities throughout the twentieth century.

CHAPTER 6

Readers: Socially Engaged Level

MOST PUBLISHED LITERATURE in socialist China was both written and read on the assumption that literature could improve society. The readership was mainly young and urban, and in years when censorial pressure lessened—such as 1956–1957, 1961–1963, and after 1978—the popularity of socially critical works always increased. (This fact can be observed in the physical appearance of bound volumes of literary periodicals on library shelves in China. The pages of issues from late 1956 and early 1957, for example, are often much more tattered and soiled, obviously from heavy use, than are the pages of issues in adjacent years.) But some Party-sponsored works of long fiction were also infectiously popular and, because they were well supported by publishers, these constituted the literary mainstream during the 1950s and early 1960s.

It is not easy to find objective measures of the popularity of mainstream works in the 1950s, because we have no survey data and circulation figures are ambiguous because print runs, as we have seen in chapter 4, were based more on Party goals than on reader demand. But to judge from reminiscences and many anecdotal accounts, Zhou Libo's two-volume, 763-page *The Hurricane* (1949), about land reform and civil war in northeast China after 1946, was an early favorite.[1] Here the peasants are good, the landlords and Nationalists are evil, and the reader is led to identify with people who are struggling gloriously to make things better for everyone. Between 1957 and 1963, more than a dozen other very lengthy novels appeared, featuring communist heroes and high moral causes.[2] Each was aimed at presenting a romantic version of some chapter in recent Chinese history: landlord-peasant conflicts in the 1920s, radical students in the 1930s, the War of Resistance against Japan, the civil war with the Guomindang, and others. Most of the stories included armed struggle, and part of their appeal to readers was the timeless allure of heroes and martial arts that we have described in the previous chapter. Nearly all were set before 1949, when the

---

[1] Zhou Libo, *Baofengzhouyu*.

[2] Prominent examples are Liang Bin's *Hongqipu*, which describes struggles with landlords and the Nationalists in Hebei villages in the twenties; Wu Qiang's *Hongri*, which tells about civil war with the Nationalists in 1946–1947; Yang Mo's *Qingchun zhi ge*, about patriotic students between 1931 and 1935; Liu Liu's *Liehuo jin'gang*, which tells in storyteller's mode about anti-Japanese guerilla warfare in 1942; Ma Yixiang's *Chaoyanghua*, about a nurse who runs away from an arranged marriage to join the Long March in 1934; Luo Guangbin and Yang Yiyan's famous *Hongyan*, set in a Nationalist prison in 1949; and Qu Bo's *Linhai xueyuan*, about guerilla warfare against the Nationalists in the Northeast in 1946. For brief summaries in English of these and many other works see Meishi Tsai, *Contemporary Chinese Novels and Short Stories*.

villains—Japanese, Nationalists, U.S. imperialists—were easy to define and battles could be morally unambiguous.

Themes from after 1949 were harder to construe as good versus evil in a clear-cut way. Although literary characters were still fairly one-dimensional, the daily life to which they were supposed to be guides was not as black and white as the routing of Japanese invaders and other pre-1949 themes. Moreover, many readers, in approaching the post-1949 novels, had reason to feel at least some identification with the side being attacked, a fact that complicated the question of sympathy. Zhou Erfu's *Morning in Shanghai*, in explaining the need to eradicate Shanghai's capitalist class in the early 1950s, makes a pharmacy manager into a major villain.[3] Liu Qing's *The Builders* divides peasants in the 1950s into two groups, those who, by embracing collectivization, "wanted to build a society that would benefit all," and those who were "looking out only for [their] personal interests."[4] Persuading people not to look out for their personal interests was not easy, and *The Builders* never generated the same popularity that its similarly promoted predecessors achieved. Of the dozen or so prominent novels of the 1950s and early 1960s, only *Morning in Shanghai* and *The Builders* addressed post-1949 problems.

From a variety of evidence, it seems clear that the two most popular novels of 1949–1965 were Luo Guangbin and Yang Yiyan's *Red Crag* and Yang Mo's *Song of Youth*. *Red Crag* had few readers in the early 1980s, but the anecdotal evidence of its extreme popularity during the mid-1960s is widespread and persuasive. In the 1950s, Sister Jiang, the martyred heroine of *Red Crag*, was sufficiently well known to become a standard term in ordinary speech in Chinese cities. In 1962, queues to buy the book in Beijing were said to be 200 meters long.[5] A punning epithet applied to those who failed to get a copy, *hongyan*, meaning "red crag," could also mean, with a slight tonal change, "red eyes," a cliché for jealousy.

Song of Youth, an account of the personal and political struggles of patriotic students in Beijing after the Japanese occupation of Manchuria in 1931, held great attraction for students and other urban young people, who identified with its student heroine named Lin Daojing (Path-is-tranquil Lin). The novel was set during years when an intellectual who was devoted to resisting Japan and promoting ideals could be portrayed unambiguously as a good character. (Stories about intellectuals that were set in the 1950s or later had to account, one way or another, for major anti-intellectual campaigns.) *Song of Youth* had the fourth-largest circulation among the novels of its era (behind *Red Crag*, *The Hurricane*, and Yao Xueyin's *Li Zicheng*), but seems clearly to have been number one in staying power.[6] During the

---

[3] Zhou Erfu, *Shanghai de zaochen*.

[4] Liu Ching, *The Builders* (English translation of *Chuangyeshi*), dust-jacket flap.

[5] Interview with He Huoren, Institute of Literature, Chinese Academy of Social Sciences, 8 October 1979.

[6] Yao Xueyin's *Li Zicheng* is a five-volume and highly romanticized saga about the late-Ming rebellion led by Li Zicheng.

Cultural Revolution, even while its author was being severely denounced, *Song of Youth* held readers. Copies were passed around illicitly, just as "hand-copied volumes" were.[7] In 1980, a survey of university students in Guangzhou found it still first among "favorite [Chinese] works of the 1949–1966 period"; a 1982 survey of university students in Beijing found it ninth most favored of all works, foreign and domestic, of all times;[8] and in 1983 it got the third-best rating among fifty-five world-famous works in a national survey.[9]

The Cultural Revolution years of 1966–1976 were a watershed for readers of politically and socially engaged literature. Before 1966, readers warmed to accounts of Communist victories and were generally content with stories about prerevolutionary experience; after 1976, they preferred works that addressed present-day issues and included criticisms of their rulers' mistakes.[10] Since young people were the bulk of the readership on both sides of the divide, the change is also generational. By 1980, literary editors found that young people emerging from the Cultural Revolution had little use for stories about the guerrillas and martyrs of the 1940s, which now seemed a long time ago.[11] A writer who recalls watching the film *In the Misty Mountains* before the Cultural Revolution remembers how the audience had sat in silent awe during a scene in which one after another guerrilla hero rises in battle to shout "I am a Communist Party member!" and "I am a Communist Youth League member!" In 1981, viewing the same film among another audience of young people, the writer heard sarcastic laughter during the same scene.[12]

One of the clearest results of the 1980s reader preference surveys was the strong and pervasive preference for works about problems in contemporary Chinese society. Topics such as "attacking the Gang of Four," "learning about society," and "unveiling social problems" consistently ranked at or near the top in such surveys,[13] even when compared with such well-

[7] Wang Dawen claims that "a copy of *Song of Youth* could be read until it fell apart"; "Shouchaoben," p. 28.

[8] For the Guangzhou survey, see Jeffrey C. Kinkley, *After Mao*, pp. 267–68; for the Beijing survey see Huang Ruixu, "Daxuesheng yuedu wenxue zuopin xianzhuang qianxi," table 5, p. 11.

[9] Huang Ruixu, "Young Laborers' Attitudes towards Literary and Artistic Works," chart 11, p. 53.

[10] Although this general pattern is beyond question, there are interesting exceptions to it, for example: critical interest in contemporary problems appeared during the Hundred Flowers of 1956–1957, and would have gone further if allowed to; and there was considerable interest after the Cultural Revolution in Party history of the 1930s and 1940s, although it was interest not in heroic victories but in ferreting out the roots of disaster. See Perry Link, *Evening Chats in Beijing*, chap. 3.

[11] Editors at *Guangzhou Literature and Art* noted a swift decline in the popularity of *Hong Yan* and Qu Bo's *Linhai xueyuan* by 1980 (interview 7 March 1980). Editors at *Wenyibao* held that revolutionary war themes in general were much more popular before the Cultural Revolution than after (interview, 9 August 1980).

[12] Luo Rujia, "Jiujing shei 'chouhua' Zhonggong?," p. 57.

[13] A 1979 survey of its own readers by *Shanghai Literature* found the top three interests to be "crimes of the Gang of Four," "lives of educated youth," and "contemporary social problems"

established popular themes as detectives and romance.[14] In fiction, film, and even poetry, works that showed "the dark side" of society, such as Jiang Zilong's "Manager Qiao Assumes Office," Chen Rong's "At Middle Age," and Ye Wenfu's poem "You Can't Do This, General," led the way.[15] Informally these were called works of "exposure" (*baolu* or *jielu*), but there was a problem in using such terms officially, because Mao Zedong, in his authoritative "Yan'an Talks" in 1942, had denounced exposure as the kind of thing counterrevolutionaries do.[16] In official surveys, "reveal" (*jieshi*) was the most that literary works were said to be doing, and weaker formulations, such as "reflecting current society" and "showing the lives of today's youth," were also used.[17] There is some evidence, especially for more elite readers, that the interest in reading about society lay in learning new things and in understanding conditions one had not yet adequately understood.[18] On the whole, however, the cathartic function of such expression was clearly the more important. Readers were drawn less by the opportunity to learn than by the chance to express indignation at what they already knew.

We have seen in earlier chapters how Party officials viewed the expression of indignation as "negative" and blamed writers for creating such feelings. But the dynamics among reader, text, and society were more complex than that, and the responsibility for "negative feelings" much more ambiguous. A 1982 survey of university students in Beijing found 26 percent reporting "positive" influences after reading literature, only 2 percent sensing "nega-

---

(interview, 17 June 1980). A 1982 survey in Beijing of the readers of *Gongren ribao* (Workers' daily) showed the leading interests as "speaking for the common people," "exposure of problems," and "criticism of corruption" (Brantly Womack, ed., *Media and the Chinese Public*, p. 126). In 1983, surveys of elite students of economics in Beijing as well as of young workers in six cities around the country showed "revelation of social problems" at the top (Yang Yiyin, "Cong dushu jiegou kan daxuesheng de sixiang jiegou," p. 36 and Huang Ruixu, "Young Laborers' Attitudes," p. 59). A 1985 survey of young workers in eight major cities found "exposure of contemporary social problems" most popular ("Bashi niandai" diaochazu, "Guanyu dangdai Zhongguo qingnian gongren zhuangkuang de diaocha yu chubu fenxi," p. 34). Surveys of preferences in film found similar results; see Xu Miaoting, "Shanghai shiqu qingnian dianying quwei qianxi," p. 41.

[14] Huang Ruixu, "Daxuesheng yuedu wenxue zuopin xianzhuang qianxi," p. 13; Wang Yalin et al., "Qingnian zhigong yeyu wenhua shenghuo kaocha," p. 38; Shen Jiming, "Guanzhong shenmei xinli de bianhua yu dianying de duice," p. 24; Xu Miaoting, "Shanghai shiqu qingnian dianying quwei qianxi," p. 41.

[15] The "Manager Qiao" result for fiction was clear from a national survey by *Renmin wenxue* (interview, 9 August 1980); on the film *At Middle Age*, see Weng Mu, "Shanghai daxuesheng dianying suzhi yipie," p. 83; on poetry, see Yang Qingyun, "Dalu xinshi minyi ceyan de jieguo," reporting a survey by the literary magazine *Yalü River* in Shenyang.

[16] Mao Zedong, *Selected Works* (Beijing, 1965), vol. 3, pp. 91–92.

[17] "Bashi niandai" Zhongguo qingnian gongren zhuangkuang diaochazu (1985), p. 34; Huang Ruixu, "Young Laborers' Attitudes," p. 59.

[18] For example, Huang Ruixu, "Daxuesheng yuedu wenxue zuopin xianzhuang qianxi," finds among students at elite universities in Beijing that "extending knowledge" and "learning about life and society" are more commonly cited as the reason for reading literature than is "solving social problems" (p. 13).

tive" influences, and 49 percent feeling "both positive and negative" influences. In a related survey, 46 percent felt "more optimistic" about life after reading literature, whereas 14 percent felt "more pessimistic," and 25 percent reported "no effect." Toward people, 31 percent felt "more comradely" and 40 percent "more humanitarian" after reading, whereas only 2 percent felt stronger "self interest" and 1 percent "more cynicism."[19] These results can seem to present a puzzle of how reading bad news can generate good feelings. But the puzzle disappears when the picture is broadened to encompass more than just reader and text.

In a 1981 speech, Liu Binyan revealed that after publishing his "People or Monsters?,"

> more than 99 percent of readers' letters were positive. Some said, first of all, that the Party was great just for letting such a work be published. This meant the Party had a self-critical attitude, could face issues squarely, and could change its ways. People's optimism was strengthened. Were there any letters that said, "Forget it, this is hopeless!"? Certainly, but not very many. Most were stirred to action. Some asked me to forward their letters to Deng Xiaoping and other central authorities; the letters bore labels like "A Plan to Save the Country" and "A Plan for Rejuvenation." They all wanted to revive China. Wouldn't you call this "positive"? . . . And what is it, after all, that makes people feel pessimistic? Is it literary works that report on corrupt things and people, or is it those things themselves?[20]

Another positive effect of literary muckraking on readers who were beset with anger or depression could be to make such readers feel less lonely. By presenting a problem in print, a literary work could allow a reader to feel that a writer and official publisher—and many other readers—were on his or her side. According to Liu Binyan, "Some people have been doing battle with corrupt people and practices for many years, soldiering along in isolation and getting themselves into predicaments that make them feel like giving up. But when they read works like these, they regain their courage and forge ahead."[21]

At an extreme, as in the post-Mao years, the cathartic function of reading could produce the paradox of readers actually looking forward to more "bad news" because it could provide a vehicle for the venting of a general frustration. Such a use of literature partially explains why literary realism was popular at the time, because only through realism could the cathartic function work well. If a "negative" story seemed unrealistic, readers would reject it for missing the mark; only if it rang true would they sigh and nod.[22] Moreover, celebration of "bad news" in such contexts was not an abandonment of ideals but the opposite; it was a statement that things *should not* be as they

[19] Ibid., pp. 15, 18.

[20] Liu Binyan, "Tan xin shiqi de wenxue chuangzuo wenti," pp. 13–14.

[21] Ibid., p. 13.

[22] I owe this formulation of the point to Lu Xinhua (interview, Los Angeles, 22 January 1987).

are and should, therefore, reach toward a higher standard. In the middle of
the literary "negativity" of the post-Mao years, a survey of college freshmen
in Taiyuan, Shanxi, found that 64 percent were convinced that genuine al-
truism exists.[23] It was primarily idealism that drew readers and writers of
Chinese literature to the Communist Party in the 1930s and 1940s, and it
was idealism that later led them into criticism of the Communist movement. The criticisms were most evident during the five to seven years after
Mao's death, and can be summarized as a number of interrelated topics.

INTRUSIVE POLITICS

Problems of recognizing and resisting the intrusion of central ideology into
daily life—an intrusion that happened more during the Maoist period than
at any other time in Chinese history—were at the center of readers' concerns during the post-Mao years. But because they required difficult self-
examination, and needed to be expressed in the face of censorship, progress
was slow. A number of post-Mao works show in retrospect how the problem
took shape: how officials in the 1950s gradually became more dogmatic and
rigid; how they began to judge people by generic political labels rather than
as individuals; how families were distorted by separation through work assignment or torn apart when one spouse or another was accused of a political crime.[24] But even through the Anti-Rightist Movement of 1957, most
writers, and with them the reading public, were reluctant to attribute these
problems to ideas that were handed down from the top. It seemed more
natural to assume that difficulties arose from below—from unruly society or
from inside themselves. Mao Zedong and his Communist Party could not
be wrong.

It was the catastrophic famine of 1959–1961, which cost perhaps 30 million lives, that first brought a general recognition that the intrusion of Maoist politics into daily life was actually the cause, not a cure, for many contemporary problems. Like Stalin, Mao sought to cover his role in the
creation of famine by blaming bad weather, and as a result serious literary
analysis of the famine had to await the post-Mao thaw.[25] In 1980, Zhang
Yigong's "The Story of Criminal Li Tongzhong" explained how local officials got raises and promotions if their districts "overproduced" grain by

[23] Li Xinsheng, "Dui jixieyixi yinianji xuesheng youguan renshengguan wenti de diaocha
jieguo," p. 53.

[24] See Dai Qing's "Pan" on the problem of spousal separation; the story elicited more than
nine hundred letters to the *Guangming ribao*, the most the newspaper had ever received on any
piece (interview at *Guangming ribao*, Beijing, 26 July 1980). On the problem of the tainted
spouse, among many others, see Lu Xinhua "Shanghen," and Liu Binyan, "Diwuge chuan dayi
de ren."

[25] A Soviet story by Vladimir Tendrjakov called "Bad Weather" tells of an agronomist who
knows it is disastrous to sow in the rain but does so on political orders anyway. See Dina
Spechler, *Permitted Dissent in the USSR*, p. 10.

using romantic Maoist methods of "close planting" of seedlings, deep ploughing, use of homemade fertilizer, and other methods that actually destroyed crops rather than increasing them; the officials reported unprecedentedly large harvests while actual output plummeted.[26] When the state, on the basis of false harvest reports, took far too much grain in taxes, farmers starved. Other stories of the famine, although less historically analytical, were more hard-hitting emotionally. In Henan, one of the provinces where the famine was most severe, a play called *Wildfire* was banned for presenting coffins on stage in its final scene.[27] A popular story in Guangdong told of a young man driven to beg in order to feed his younger sister after their parents had died.[28]

The Cultural Revolution brought further examples of the havoc that Maoist theory wrought in daily life, and had especially disillusioning effects on the generation of Red Guards and other young people who had embraced Mao's stated ideals with the greatest enthusiasm. Having volunteered to work in the countryside, young idealists found that People's Communes were not actually governed by fairness and mutual concern, as Mao's theory had it, but by authoritarian bureaucrats who bullied, taxed, beat, and raped. "Serve the people" and other nice-sounding slogans now appeared at best to be tools for manipulating people, and at worst simply a kind of fraud.[29] Having set out to join the greatest movement in human history, the youngsters often found their own lives had been wasted—they had missed school, their families had been broken, and they bore the taint of having supported a wrong-headed political campaign.[30]

The relaxation of censorship in the post-Mao years allowed these aspects of the disillusionment with ideology to appear in print, although in muted form. Post-Mao literary works also showed how political labels—rigid, often arbitrary, and indelible—had been fixed on people: a "class enemy" was always a class enemy, and evidence to the contrary did not matter;[31] "class background" was sufficiently powerful that one's social label did not even depend on behavior so much as on accident of birth;[32] like a religion, the

---

[26] Zhang Yigong, "Fanren Li Tongzhong de gushi."

[27] Play entitled *Huanghuo*, playwright unknown. Information from interview with Wang Jinmin, reporting on a presentation by Chen Huangmei at a conference on "Literary Teaching Materials and Hong Kong-Taiwan Literature," Nanning, Guangxi, March 1980.

[28] Qian Yuxiang, "Lishi a, shenpan wo ba!"

[29] These themes are illustrated many times over in Laifong Leung, *Morning Sun*.

[30] Wang Zhecheng and Wen Xiaoyu, "Cuowei de kouzi," one of many works on this theme, tells of a young Shanghai woman who is sent to the countryside during the Cultural Revolution, rises to be a Party secretary, but ends as an impoverished streetside seamstress.

[31] See, for example, Lu Yanzhou, "Huhuan," in which an appeal to spare an honest official from punishment is rejected, not because there is evidence of guilt but because of the inviolability of the contemporary policy guideline to "support the left."

[32] See, for example, Cui Dezhi, "Baochunhua," in which a textile worker with a "bad" class background does work that is superior to workers with good class backgrounds, but sabotages her own work in order to avoid jealousies. Parents in "pure family lines" interfere in their

ideological system laid claim to a "correctness" that was not open to question or discussion.[33]

The sense of a confining rigidity in the Maoist political system invited parallels to "feudal" aspects of traditional culture, and several works wove these two together. In Zhang Xian's story "The Unbreakable Red Thread,"[34] a young woman is engaged against her will to a high official; she and her boyfriend flee, but the boyfriend dies, and she ends up back with the high official, who comments ironically that she and he were "fated." The subtly understated story creates the sense that life is stifling, drab, and inevitable. There is a need for rebellion, but it cannot happen. Because such a theme was hard to get published in the official press, some of its more explicit examples appeared in unofficial literary magazines. A poem called "If Tomorrow . . .", published in the unofficial Guangzhou magazine *The Future*, contained these lines:

> If tomorrow nothing happens
> If tomorrow is no different from today
> If tomorrow at breakfast, six o'clock sharp
>   It's that same old penny of rice gruel
>   And those same two pennies of dough
> If tomorrow at seven I set off to work
>   With that old beat-up lunchbox
>   On the same crowded bus
> I will roundly curse each frustration I've had
> And with each curse
> Become more freely insane.[35]

Because the Party's rules structured so much of daily life, the dull daily routine could seem part of the problem of ideological control. Step one of rebellion, accordingly, was often to take a stance deliberately opposite to official positions. During the controversy over "What If I Really Were?," students at Fudan University in Shanghai held a mock trial of Li Xiaozhang, the young man in the play who was convicted of fraud and impersonation, and inverted the play's result, finding him innocent; students at Zhongshan University in Guangzhou repudiated Zhang senior, the high official who delivers a political homily in the final scene, as a pompous oaf.[36] Stories like

children's romances in order to keep the blood lines pure. A right-thinking Party secretary denounces these attitudes as "feudal." On the same theme, see Yang Ganhua, "Jing zhe lei."

[33] See, for example, Lu Xinhua, *Mo*, in which a poor peasant throws his entire faith to the Party, believes all its doctrines religiously, and rises to become a production brigade leader, only to fall into one after another pitfall that he cannot understand, until he is driven to suicide.

[34] "Zhengbuduan de hong si xian."

[35] Xiao Feng, "Jiaru mingtian."

[36] Interviews with Lu Xinhua, 14 June 1980, and with editors of *Hongdou*, 6 May 1980. See chapter 1 above for the controversy.

Xu Mingxu's "Work Transfer" glorified the success of a young maverick who viewed the whole political system as a cynical game to be manipulated to one's advantage.[37]

An essayist in Guangdong in 1980 concluded that Goebbels' famous line "a lie repeated a thousand times becomes a truth" actually had another side, because lies repeated a thousand times could also engender disgust, and cause people to assume the opposite of what the liar says.[38] In 1986, a survey of film audiences in five cities indeed found that official praise for a film actually reduced the likelihood that people would go to see it. Only 6 percent of viewers said that official praise attracted them; 12.5 percent said they did the opposite of what the press recommended, and 78 percent said they preferred films that stirred controversies, "the bigger the better."[39] In 1979, a Canadian teacher in Guangzhou offered her students some books she had brought from home and found that the one about Norman Bethune, whom Mao Zedong had exalted during the Cultural Revolution, aroused no interest at all.

Rebellion against official guidance of thought raised the deeper issue of where to turn once official views had been repudiated. During a similar period in Soviet history, the poet Yevgeny Yevtushenko wrote that:

> I know others would give willing answers
> To all my questions: "How?" "What?" and "Why?"
> But suddenly it turned out that I
> Must find these answers for myself.[40]

The efforts of young Chinese to follow the rejection of official views with a probing of what might lie beyond can be seen in a story by Li Hong called "Wake Up, Big Brother," which began as a poster on the Zhongshan University campus in Guangzhou, and later passed through several hands before publication in the unofficial journal *The Future*.[41] The story is a satire of Liu Xinwu's officially published "Wake Up, Little Brother," about a teenager whose father is persecuted to death during the Cultural Revolution and who turns to alcohol, sloth, and cynicism as a refuge from the painful world.[42] Now that the Gang of Four has been smashed, Liu's story implies, this youngster should "wake up" and find an optimistic direction in life.

"Wake Up, Big Brother" turns things around to see them from the younger brother's point of view, and finds his cynicism still appropriate. It introduces an elder brother and sister in the family. The elder sister is courted by "Teacher Liu," a not-so-subtle reference to Liu Xinwu, whom the younger

---

[37] "Diaodong."

[38] Sima Yuchang, "Manhua 'guanggao.'"

[39] Wu Zhengxin, "Shishi qiu shi, qu xin yu min."

[40] "Zima Station," quoted in Harold Swayze, *Political Control of Literature in the USSR*, p. 180.

[41] Li Hong, "Xinglai ba, gege."

[42] Liu Xinwu, "Xinglai ba, didi."

brother finds disgusting because he made his fame by writing a story about how the younger generation has gone astray, lost its "revolutionary will," and so on. When Teacher Liu comes to visit the sister, the younger brother keeps his distance, fearing that anything he might say could end up in another brilliant story. The elder brother is a pleasant person but, after ten years of political tempering in the countryside, severely inhibited. At an evening class he meets a young woman called Sister Mei and feels attracted to her, but does not dare to say a word beyond strictly curricular matters. The younger brother, wanting to help, asks Sister Mei out to music and poker salons and tells her what a nice person his older brother is. But it doesn't work; Sister Mei only giggles and begins to feel attracted to him, the younger brother. As a desperate measure, he asks Sister Mei to meet him at a lonely spot in a park, and asks his big brother to meet him there, too. At the appointed time he and three friends disguise themselves using masks and dark glasses, then wait in ambush for the unsuspecting couple. When the pair arrive, the "bandits" jump out, surround them, and threaten their lives if they do not obey. They are ordered to embrace. Then they must kiss. They reject as insufficient the older brother's perfunctory effort at a kiss. The next, more powerful kiss begins to stir some passion, and soon the elder brother and Sister Mei become so involved that they forget the "terror" that surrounds them. The bandits begin to titter. The younger brother exults to himself that "Life is beautiful! Wake up, big brother!," and thinks again of how much he despises those "teachers" who always "turn life upside down."

SPECIAL PRIVILEGE AND ABUSE OF POWER

Hidden popular resentment of special privilege was strong in China, and it gushed to the surface during the post-Mao thaw just as it had in the Soviet Union after Stalin's death. Many works in both countries illustrated how state officials, who were charged with serving the laboring masses, had instead pursued their own comfort and developed bureaucratic attitudes as a way of protecting their privilege and power; the downtrodden, whom the revolutions were supposed to have saved, were shown still to be the downtrodden. Although it remained forbidden to use the term "class" in reference to the new society, in fact both Soviet and Chinese writers were describing a new ruling class.

In the Soviet Union, a widely discussed and richly detailed paradigm was the character Drozdov in Vladimir Dudintsev's 1956 novel *Not by Bread Alone*. As summarized by Victor Erlich, Drozdov "epitomizes the 'new class,' grasping, status-minded, and power-loving, glorying unabashedly in its material advantages and ever ready to invoke the 'tough' Marxist-Leninist lingo as an alibi for its moral callousness."[43] Drozdovian images are

[43] Victor Erlich, "Post-Stalin Trends in Russian Literature," p. 407.

plentiful in works from post-Mao China—allowing, however, the interesting difference that some of the most outstanding examples are female. The wives and children of revolutionary heroes grow selfish and materialistic in stories like Chen Rong's "At Middle Age" and Bai Hua's "A Bundle of Letters,"[44] while husbands and fathers appear as untainted, even somewhat naive, paragons of high-mindedness. These Chinese stories recall the case of Peter in Leonid Zorin's play "The Guests." Peter's father scolds him for turning out badly: "[After the revolution] I became, as they say, an important figure. And did my life change? Not at all. . . . All the blessings fell to you. [But then] insignificant toadies fawned on you because of your father, and you liked it, . . . you tasted power when you were a child, and it poisoned you."[45]

In both Soviet and Chinese works, the tendency of toadies to fawn is only the beginning of the problem. More serious is the well-entrenched and systematically articulated structure of privilege. Yuri Nagibin's story "A Light in the Window" tells of a vacation resort where one house is maintained in luxury—a fine TV and billiard table, fresh firewood, and so on—yet remains empty year round because it is kept in reserve in case one or another august personage should suddenly appear.[46] Meanwhile ordinary vacationers must do with faulty TVs, cracked billiard tables, and sex-specific dormitories, even for honeymooners. At a still lower social level, we meet Nastya, the maid who attends to the luxury suite, and whose humility is so genuine that she seems simply unable to question her own or anyone else's role in society. Finally, though, there appears a "light in the window," both literally and figuratively: one evening Nastya appropriates the privileged room for her own use. She and two children of the porter sit in plush chairs and watch TV, quietly having, thereby, reclaimed the revolution for the common people.

In post-Mao China, the issue of the haves and have-nots was famously depicted in Sha Yexin's play "What If I Really Were?" about the plucky young man who taps into a privileged world by impersonating the son of a high official.[47] More moving, however, and more closely parallel to Nagibin's story, are stories like Xiao Yi's "The Little Egg Girl," in which the material comforts of the ruling class are not only sharply distinct from those of the common people but are protected by some cruel bullying.[48] Ruling-class rapacity becomes true literally as well as figuratively in works like "In Society's Archives" and "Cries from Death Row," in which senior officials rape attractive young women and then use their power to avoid responsibility.[49] Chen Huangmei, a deputy director of the Propaganda De-

---

[44] Bai Hua, "Yishu xinzha."

[45] Quoted in Swayze, *Political Control*, pp. 98–99.

[46] Translated in Hugh McLean and Walter N. Vickery, *The Year of Protest*, pp. 224–33.

[47] See pp. 23, 65, and 90–91, above.

[48] Xiao Yi, pseud., "Mai jidan de xiao guniang."

[49] Wang Jing, pseud., "Zai shehui de dang'anli"; Jin Yanhua and Wang Jingquan, "Silaoli de nahan."

partment, blamed the editors who had accepted "Cries from Death Row" for "stooping to popular tastes," a denunciation that only confirmed, indirectly, that such works had considerable popular appeal.[50] A 1982 survey that asked factory workers in Xi'an what they "believed in" found that "socialism," "money," and "fate" all rated fairly well, but the phrase that got by far the most votes was "if you have power you have everything."[51]

PERVASIVE CORRUPTION

Literary satire of corruption, among officials, scholars, merchants, monks, and many others, has strong roots in Chinese vernacular fiction. The tradition of *The Scholars* (*Rulin waishi*, ca. 1750) gave rise in the early twentieth century to Li Boyuan's *Panorama of Officialdom* (1901) and Wu Woyao's *Strange Events Witnessed over Twenty Years* (1902), which attributed China's political, social, and military weakness to pervasive corruption.[52] During the war with Japan in the 1930s and early 1940s, satire of corruption in the Nationalist government was strong, despite repression.

When the socialist system arrived in the early 1950s, the reach of the government into society extended greatly, and by the end of the decade popular complaints about official corruption had extended equally far. The socialist system introduced large new official structures that were—just as in the Soviet Union and Eastern Europe—especially vulnerable to corruption. The essence of these new dangers was that nearly all money, goods, and services belonged to the state, yet decisions about how to allocate the resources were made by individual people. Theoretically every representative of the state made decisions by considering what was best for the largest possible group. In practice, however, the decision of whether to allocate something to this person or the next became a matter of which party was the more favored. The generation and exchange of favor thus became a vital part of the economy, and in many cases a functional equivalent of money. As Liu Binyan points out in "People or Monsters?," the steady supply of state-owned resources into the system continued to feed corruption because officials lost a sense of identity with the resources they controlled. They could "lend" state funds and not press for repayment, or even prefer that loans not be repaid, because the value of being someone's creditor, within the informal economy of personal favors, was more important than balancing the books of the state.[53]

After the death of Mao, corruption became one of the most widespread

[50] Conference on "Literary Teaching Materials and Hong Kong-Taiwan Literature," Nanning, Guangxi, March 1980; reported by Wang Jinmin.

[51] Gongqingtuan Xi'an shiwei xuanchuanbu, "Yige gongchang qingnian renshengguan de diaocha," p. 10.

[52] Li Boyuan, *Guanchang xianxingji*, and Wu Woyao, *Ershinian mudu zhi guai xianzhuang*.

[53] Liu Binyan, *People or Monsters?*, p. 25.

and persistent of popular complaints. During the scar years virtually all genres of literature and art, from poetry to cartoons, addressed the topic at many levels: from carrying a pack of cigarettes to offer here and there as general social lubricant, to the calculated barter of such things as grain for electricity, trucking services for cash, and so on, to the carefully cultivated, long-term investment in a powerful protector, or "mountain to lean on" (*kao-shan*). A great number of works in China's Deng era satirized "back door" connections. But most exposure of corruption was still fairly superficial in that it presented "back-doorism" as optional—as a temptation that could be resisted, and that only the morally weak succumbed to. Only a small number of works, beginning with Liu Binyan's "People or Monsters?," dug deeper by showing how corruption had become an integral part of the economy of state socialism. In a 1979 speech, Liu said:

> Originally I viewed back-doorism as merely a problem of operating style and personal integrity. I thought people used it only in order to leverage a bit of personal advantage. But in 1974 when I visited Luoshan County [in Henan province], I came to realize that the back door was not a problem of custom or ethics, but an indispensable feature of our economic system. Luoshan county has to get coal—you can't cook without it. The county doesn't produce coal, so you have to buy it from nearby mines; this you can do, but only if you pass out some goodies. Once you've bought the coal, you need the railroad—and the Railway Bureau extends its hand. When you get your coal to Xinyang station, the truckers want something. So what, if you are Party secretary of the county, do you do? Refuse the back door and prohibit others from using it? That would mean the ordinary people in your county couldn't cook food.[54]

In Ke Yunlu's 1980 story "Thirty Million," about a capital construction company caught in endless cost overruns because of corruption, officials shrug that "the whole country is this way" and "it can't be helped."[55]

Literary censors discouraged the publication of anecdotes about the bald routinization of corruption, but these circulated widely on the oral grapevine: a radiologist at a hospital could produce X-ray results in either four hours or twenty minutes—depending on how much pork he received as a gift; inspectors from the electric bureau would approve a store's meat slicer or not, depending on how much liquor and cigarettes were received.[56] A hand-copied volume from the late 1960s shows corruption so routinized that factory managers issue rules not to suppress it but to distribute its fruits equitably: a plant gets authorization to hire two hundred more people, and management stipulates that each official can open the back door only once.[57]

In a number of works, such as Chen Rong's "At Middle Age" and Bai Hua's "A Bundle of Letters," the wives of officials were portrayed as the

---

[54] Liu Binyan, "Zai Heilongjiang jianghua quanwen," p. 15.
[55] Ke Yunlu, "Sanqianwan."
[56] These particular examples are taken from James Kenneson, "China Stinks," p. 16.
[57] Sha Tian, "Liulanghan de qiyu," part 2, p. 83.

chief manipulators of the back door. It was the wife's job, as household administrator, to press a family's interests while the husband, whose power the wife capitalized upon, maintained a cleaner official image. During the Soviet thaw, a comparable trope of the materialistic wife of an official appears in Vera Panova's *Seasons of the Year*, although there the wife forces the husband into corruption rather than acting as his proxy. During the post-Mao years the image of the aggressive wife of a powerful man was also in some ways a symbolic attack on Jiang Qing. Qin Bo in "At Middle Age" was shrill, selfish, and narrow-minded in many of the ways Jiang Qing was said to be. Her image gave rise to the phrase "Marxist-Leninist Old Lady," which was used not only popularly but also in the official press.[58] As in earlier times in Chinese history, denunciation of corruption kept up with the spread of corruption itself. No matter how pervasive or routinized corruption became, the reading public seems never to have begun to condone it. Indeed, there is much evidence that readers enjoyed reading and talking about a topic on which it was so easy and refreshing to feel righteous indignation. In a play called *Who Is the Stronger?*, the manager of a textile mill learns that systematic bribery, which the playwright calls "contactology" (*guanxixue*), is a necessary part of running a mill, and some of his colleagues find him old-fashioned for not simply going along.[59] But the manager, the hero of the play, won't go along, just because it isn't right. A 1982 survey of high school student attitudes in Heilongjiang found "the back door" to be the most despised social practice on a list that also included "official privilege," "unfairness," "nasty plots," "total selfishness," and several other strongly worded choices.[60] The perceived harm of the back door was only in part that it made the front door less efficient—that a person visiting a hospital, for example, could not get an X-ray expeditiously in the proper way. More importantly, corruption was seen—and, as a literary topic, enjoyed—as moral misbehavior. When officials indulged in it, they lost their moral authority to rule in society. People who saw or heard about corruption took moral offense—and sometimes enjoyed doing so—whether or not material loss was involved.

Because of the strong moral disapproval of corruption, those who practiced it were careful to disguise it or to describe it with euphemisms. Television sets were supplied to official households "for testing"; public automobiles could be used for personal excursions called "official business"; junkets were designed as inspection tours. A supplicant might deliver a bribe by visiting an official, placing a gift on his or her desk without comment, and asking the official's "personal opinion" on the problem at hand. Officials' benefits, including both the proper and the improper, often outweighed official salaries. In Guangzhou in the early 1980s, officials could

[58] See Tian Zhongquan, "'Maliezhuyi lao taitai.'"

[59] Liang Bingkun, "Shei shi qiangzhe?"

[60] Liu Qingren et al., "Guanyu zhongxuesheng sixiang zhuangkuang de diaocha," p. 8.

not be induced to retire on 100 percent or even 110 percent of salary, because of the consequent loss of informal advantages.

The importance to officials of maintaining a morally presentable face meant that when the topic of corruption arose in literature, they always sought the implication that the author was describing an unusual case: this character was corrupt, but does not represent the society as a whole. (There is a chilling parallel in the counting of deaths from starvation in the labor camps during the great famine of 1959–1961: each inmate death was officially viewed as a separate occurrence because no one was allowed to say that a general famine was under way.)[61] Readers, however, tended to make the opposite inference: that any story about corruption probably represented a pattern.

Writers who specialized in exposing corruption knew this and wrote accordingly. The Soviet writer Vladimir Dudintsev, in creating the grasping bureaucrat Drozdov in his 1956 novel *Not by Bread Alone*, offered to readers what Liu Binyan did in describing the back-door artist Wang Shouxin in "People or Monsters?" Readers in both countries saw Drozdovs and Wang Shouxins everywhere in their own situations, while officials in both countries sought to deny the same generalizability. At a meeting of the Moscow Writers' Club in October 1956, Konstantin Paustovsky delivered a speech called "The Drozdovs" in which he concluded that "there are thousands of them . . . [they are] a new petty-bourgeois caste."[62] Paustovsky was promptly denounced in the authoritative *Literaturnaya gazeta* for drawing "a series of incorrect conclusions and generalizations to the effect that Drozdovs are a mass phenomenon."[63] Similarly Liu Binyan, in a speech at the Chinese Writers' Association convention in November 1979, read from one of the thousands of letters he had received about "People or Monsters?": "Your pen wove a net over Bin county, but why stop there? . . . To put it bluntly, Bin county is a microcosm of the whole country."[64]

The works of writers like Dudintsev and Liu not only gave readers the feeling that corruption extended to many places, including their own, but that it extended right to the present time, belying officialdom's perennial claim that corruption is a thing of the past. And yet corruption and its official denial were only a part of what readers wanted to see in print about bureaucratic behavior.

STYLES OF BUREAUCRATISM

A 1985 survey of young workers in Shanghai found that only 16 percent said they had "good, harmonious" relations with their factory leaders; 31

---

[61] Zhang Xianliang, quoted in Jasper Becker, *Hungry Ghosts*, p. 195.
[62] Swayze, *Political Control*, p. 168.
[63] Ibid., p. 167
[64] Quoted in Leo Ou-fan Lee, "Introduction" to Liu Binyan, *People or Monsters?*, p. x.

percent said relations were "ordinary," and 45 percent said there was no harmony because leaders were despotic, arbitrary, or unresponsive.[65] Surveys in other cities produced similar results, but the broadest indication of such concerns is probably the nationwide popularity of literary works such as, among many others, Jiang Zilong's "Manager Qiao Assumes Office" (1979), Zhang Jie's *Heavy Wings* (1981), Ke Yunlu's *New Star* (1985), and others that describe the frustrations of dealing with bureaucratism. "Manager Qiao" features an imaginary hero who can cut through bureaucratic problems with unrealistic ease, a fact that seems only to have increased its popularity. It placed first in a national poll for the best story of 1979, receiving more than 10 percent of all votes cast.[66]

For ordinary people, the most common experience with bureaucratism was the inordinate expenditure of time, effort, and patience necessary to get something done. In literary satire, bureaucrats appeared as masters of slippery language. They could speak in grand terms about policies, ideals, or reforms, but in practice resisted all change except what was specifically ordered from above. Pursued from below, even a simple task might require weeks or months. A 1979 comedians' dialogue, Ma Ji's "The Multi-level Hotel," exaggerated bureaucratic problems for humorous effect and drew an enthusiastic popular response because the essential complaints, while overdrawn, rang true.[67] A man visits another city and stays in a hotel that has two hundred levels—not storeys, but layers of bureaucracy. To get a room he has to register with the reception desk, the Party, the government, the army, the health bureau, the cashier, and several other offices, each of which has lengthy and repetitive forms to fill out and is staffed by people who prefer to read novels, play chess, or drink tea while treating customers as bothersome distractions. The charge for his room is small, but he has to add a management fee, a sanitation fee, a water and electricity fee, a furniture depreciation fee, a laundering fee, and several others. After registering, he wants a bowl of noodles, but the order requires so much negotiation that he finally gives up.

Along with complaints about too many formalities came complaints that processes were too slow. The registration clerk at the multi-level hotel, named Xiaoman (Little Slow), stays on lunch break until 2:30 and then needs about an hour to check a customer in. A small official in Liu Binyan's "People or Monsters?" earns the nickname "Liu Ha-ha!" because his standard response to anything is to chuckle and do nothing.[68] In 1985 Hu Yaobang, then secretary general of the Communist Party, acknowledged in a major speech that "the pace of our social life in many fields is still slow. This can be seen in our meetings, our work, and even our way of walking."[69]

---

[65] Dong Xijian, "Qinggong yu lingdao ganqing de zhang'ai ji shutong."
[66] Interview at *Renmin wenxue* editorial offices, 9 August 1980.
[67] Ma Ji, "Duoceng fandian."
[68] Liu Binyan, "*People or Monsters?*," p. 44.
[69] Hu Yaobang, "Lun dang de xinwen gongzuo."

Figure 3. "Inspiration upon Viewing a Toilet," cartoon-painting by Liao Bingxiong, November 1979. The inscription (upper left) says: A toilet scene that seems not to be there but in fact is everywhere."

Westerners who observed the deliberate pace of life in socialist China often attributed it to a lack of incentives: people were paid the same whether they worked efficiently or not. But Chinese literature and art, while including this explanation, more commonly offered another: bureaucrats felt strong incentives to please their superiors, which above all meant avoidance of "mistakes." Since the definition of a mistake could be highly flexible, the safest course for a bureaucrat was to be identified with nothing at all: no action meant no mistakes. A collection of stories by Zhang Jie on this general theme in 1988 was published in English translation under the apt title, *As Long as Nothing Happens, Nothing Will.* An outpouring of satiric cartoons in the post-Mao years made the same point: bureaucrats sat on toilets without defecating,[70] or appeared as dolls with rounded bottoms and no legs, so that, after any push this way or that, they would return to the upright position without having moved.[71] Bureaucracy was indigenous to China, and problems of bureaucratic rigidity were by no means new in the twentieth century. But socialist China's widespread problem of an immobility induced by fear of "mistakes" clearly has to do with its borrowing

[70] "Cesuo jijing" (Inspiration upon viewing a toilet), cartoon-painting by Liao Bingxiong, exhibited in the People's Park, Guangzhou, November 1979.

[71] "Tian hua luan zhui" (Flowers cascading from the sky), cartoon-painting by Fang Cheng, exhibited at the Central Art Gallery, Beijing, July 1980.

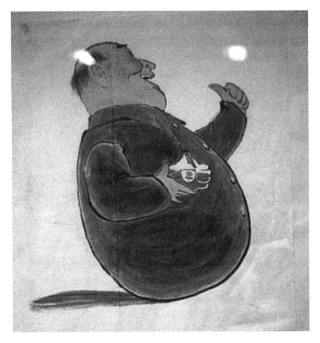

Figure 4. "Flowers Cascading from the Sky," cartoon-painting by Fang Cheng, exhibited in Beijing, summer 1980.

from the Soviet system. "The chief operating norm in the Soviet administrative system," writes Dina Spechler, "was to avoid taking initiative and wait for orders." Quoting reformist Soviet writers, Spechler says the Soviet bureaucrat awaited "a letter of instruction like a light in the darkness."[72]

Like their Soviet counterparts, Chinese intellectuals complained that their leaders could not grasp the fields they were charged with leading: Party secretaries in physics departments knew nothing about physics, and so on. Yet, as countless works of fiction showed, it certainly was not true that bureaucrats were intellectually vacuous. To attune oneself minutely to the "weather" from above, to be able to speak and act without a misstep, to change political directions instantly while pretending perfectly that no change had happened, to handle local situations without either disturbing the higher-ups or inviting rebellion from below, and to do all this without going on record as having done anything at all, required sensitivity, skill, and vigilance of a high order. Those who rose within the system were seasoned specialists in their roles.

If one made mistakes, and the mistakes were investigated and shown to be politically innocuous, one's file said "history is clear" (*lishi qingchu*). But it was better still if one's record showed nothing at all—no questions, no find-

---

[72] Spechler, *Permitted Dissent*, p. 10.

ings of innocence, no investigations to begin with. Such files were labeled "history is pure" (*lishi qingbai*), and it was the highest goal of a bureaucrat who had one to keep it that way. It was a lifetime investment, and indeed more: one passed it on to one's children. An official with a pure political record could seek to end the engagement of her son to a young woman of unpure background—on the grounds that the latter would almost certainly ruin his life, at least politically.[73]

The emphasis on political purity in socialist Chinese bureaucracy had a variety of consequences for bureaucratic behavior. Avoiding responsibility for decisions could mean just sitting on questions and hoping they would go away. Such behavior gave rise to countless popular jokes about the phrase *yanjiu yanjiu* ("we'll study it") as the way bureaucrats answered petitioners, while simply shelving their requests. (One such joke said that the only solution to *yanjiu* was *yan jiu*, meaning, in different tones, "cigarettes and liquor.") When decisions could not be avoided, the skilled bureaucrat knew how to transfer responsibility for the decision onto someone else.

One could pass the decision to superiors, so long as not to do this so often as to seem to be pestering. The hotel guest at the multi-level hotel needs his bowl of noodles in late afternoon, before the dining hall opens. The kitchen staff is willing, but wonders if this exception to the rules is permissible. "Would you mind filling out this form?" one of them asks, and then, when he finishes, asks him to bring the form to the kitchen supervisor, who approves, but only "pending approval of the section chief," who sends it to the department head, who wants the views of the Bureau of Culture. In frustration, the man goes straight to the hotel manager, who seems cordial and "very straightforward" but upon hearing the request says, "Check the documents for any possible guidance on the question of noodles," and a few moments later, "Better go back to your room, comrade. I can't approve this on my own." When the guest objects, the manager grows testy: "Comrade! We leaders must not be autocratic! Can we let a single pushy person decide things? Let's just wait for the assistant manager to come back. He and I will discuss it as quickly as possible." Where was the assistant manager, the guest wants to know. "On business in Guangzhou." Three days later, when the guest is on a railway platform preparing to leave the city, the hotel manager comes running up to him: "Comrade! Your bowl of noodles has been approved!"[74]

Buck-passing in daily life was, of course, not as far-fetched as this, or as funny. But the popularity of satire like "The Multi-Level Hotel," which appeared in countless works and a variety of genres, makes clear that both the phenomenon and popular resentment of it were very widespread. In 1979, a character on stage drew strong applause from a Beijing audience for

[73] Deputy Party secretary Wu Yiping treats her son's engagement in this manner in Cui Dezhi et al., *Baochunhua*.

[74] Ma Ji, "The Multi-Level Hotel," in Link, ed., *Stubborn Weeds*, pp. 265–66.

Figure 5. "Six Monks Carrying Water to Drink," cartoon-painting by Fang Cheng, exhibited in Beijing, summer 1980.

the line, "If we always have to wait for instructions from Party Central before doing anything, then what are our own brains for?"[75] Responsibility for decisions could be transferred downward as well as upward. A bureaucrat's request that petitioners fill out forms was in effect a way of sending responsibility for substantive matters downward.

The passing of responsibility up and down a bureaucracy not only created blockage and hence inefficiency. It also created pressures to expand bureaucracies, especially at the higher levels. Cartoonists and comedians made much of bureaucratic bloat during the post-Mao years. One cartoon showed a small bucket hung from a carrying pole shouldered by six monks.[76] Another showed an architect with a sketch of a new administrative building shaped, absurdly, like an inverted pyramid, each floor wider than the one below. "Officials can only go up, not down!" the architect cries.[77] A 1980 comedians' dialogue found at one (imaginary) organization so many chiefs

[75] Li Jian in Cui Dezhi et al., *Baochunhua*, viewed in Beijing 1 October 1979.

[76] "Liuge heshang da shui chi" (Six monks carrying water to drink), cartoon-painting by Fang Cheng, exhibited at the Central Art Gallery, Beijing, summer 1980. Without words, the cartoon plays off the popular saying "One monk carries water to drink, two monks share in the carrying by using a pole, three monks die of thirst (because they cannot decide who will do the work)."

[77] "Wei lou" (Precarious building), cartoon-painting by Liao Bingxiong, exhibited at People's Park, Guangzhou, November 1979.

Figure 6. "Precarious Building," cartoon-painting by Liao Bingxiong, exhibited in Guangzhou, fall 1979. The label at the top reads "Design drawing for the organization building." The official says: "If we build it like this it'll fall down!" The architect replies: "Lots of officials can only go up, and not down. So what can I do?"

of so many bureaus that it needed another bureau to coordinate them. Bureau Chief Bureau naturally needed a chief, who was the Bureau Chief Bureau Chief.[78] The excessive layering of bureaucracies led to a further problem of the top and bottom losing touch with each other. One cartoonist had a leader proclaiming that "everyone should get an annual inoculation," only to have bureaucrats at the next levels down simplify the message to "everyone should get a yearly shot" and then one level lower, roughly, "everyone should get shot."[79]

In the post-Mao years, when leaders at the top ordered a "reversal of verdicts" on people accused of rightism and other errors, bureaucrats at the bottom were faced with "welcoming" people whom they themselves had

[78] Wei Qiping, "Juzhangju."

[79] "Hao shi bian huai shi" (A good thing turns into a bad thing), cartoon-painting by Fang Cheng, created in 1953 and exhibited in summer 1980 at the Central Art Gallery, Beijing. In Chinese the pun is on *da zhen* "get inoculated" and *da* "beat." My translation "get a shot" and "get shot" captures the spirit but not the letter of the joke.

only recently persecuted.[80] To obey such orders created awkward personal relations and difficult work environments, and some local officials accordingly did not obey, but saved everyone's face by "obeying superficially and undermining in fact" (*yang feng yin wei*). This practice, in turn, led to a spate of petitions from people at the bottom who knew they were owed pardons but felt they had to go to higher rungs in the bureaucracy in order to get them.

During the Deng years there was considerable debate, which was amply reflected in literature, about the "problem" of the purely political bureaucrats left over from the Mao years. As making money was becoming the spirit of the times, and meticulous attention to political standpoint and Maoist campaigns seemed ever less relevant, Chinese society had to find some way of handling the literally millions of astute politicos who no longer had important functions but still occupied key positions. Popular stories and plays made fun of bureaucrats who could do nothing but politics, and live audiences applauded when characters on stage said these people should step aside, or that their claims to an inheritable "purity" were "nothing but feudalism."[81] More tolerant voices argued that, since the narrowness of Maoist bureaucrats was not their own fault, society should train them in other, more useful skills.[82] But in any case, the political bureaucrats should no longer be able to bar the paths of people who had practical expertise that could help China. An engineer who could put up a rocket should be trusted to put up a rocket—even if he had grown up and gone to school in the capitalist West.[83]

THE NEED FOR RULE OF LAW

In the late 1970s and early 1980s, a number of plays on the theme of criticizing special privilege appeared in urban theaters and on national television.[84] Because these plays were peppered with punch lines on social morality, a researcher who sat among live audiences or who listened to applause on television could get a direct, albeit unquantifiable, measure of the popularity of certain ideas. On a national television broadcast of Zhao Guoqing's "Save Her!" in 1980,[85] the audience cheered at length for the line, "We ought to have a legal system to guard against such power abuses." The longest applause in a broadcast of Xing Yixun's "Power and Law" was for the line, "All people are the same before the law."[86] Appeal to the law was

---

[80] Aspects of this problem are well treated in Liu Binyan, "Di wuge chuan dayi de ren," and Wang Meng, "Hudie."

[81] Cui Dezhi, *Baochunhua*, viewed in Beijing, 1 October 1979.

[82] Liu Binyan, "Zai Heilongjiang jianghua," p. 19.

[83] Zhao Zixiong, "Weilai zai zhaohuan."

[84] Cui Dezhi, *Baochunhua*; Zhao Guoqing, *Jiujiu ta!*; Xing Yixun, *Quan yu fa*; Sha Yexin et al., *Jiaru wo shi zhende*; and others.

[85] Shenyang Drama Troupe, viewed in Guangzhou 13 January 1980.

[86] China Youth Artistic Theater (Beijing), viewed in Guangzhou 29 December 1979.

widespread among educated readers and viewers, and no one questioned that law was a good thing; what the term meant, however, was not so clear.

"Power and Law" addressed the issue as squarely as any literary work of the time did. It tells of an honest woman named Ding Mu who wants to blow the whistle on her former boss, Party Secretary Cao, who embezzled money and lived extravagantly during the famine years of 1959–61, when millions of Chinese were starving. But Secretary Cao gets wind of Ding's intentions, frames her for the murder of her husband (who actually had been a victim of Cultural Revolution violence), and succeeds in frightening her into silence. Eventually another Party secretary, named Luo, appears, whom we know immediately to be a good man because of his jovial manner, bushy black eyebrows, and insistence on eating his simple bag dinner—a cold wheat bun—instead of Ding's home-cooked meal. When Luo discovers the truth about Cao he is furious (but in control, naturally) and urges Ding to make her complaint, saying to all parties that he, Luo, will take personal responsibility for all consequences. In the end we do not know whether Cao is brought to justice, but it seems that "law" will win because of the powerful backing of Luo.

The plot does not, in short, succeed in illustrating the ideal of "law above man," which appears to have been the playwright's aim. In the end, the Chinese cultural assumption that morality depends essentially on human character pulls hard enough that law, too, has to have a personal champion in order to work. The principle that everyone should be *treated* equally by the law does get clear support, but the notion that everyone should have equal *access* to law certainly does not. There is no actual law quoted in the play, and no court, no judge, no lawyer, and no mention of process. In place of all that is a good Party secretary, personally determined to see that justice is pursued without fear or favor.

If there were a sequel to the play, presumably showing Secretary Luo winning against Secretary Cao, Luo would eventually have to show up in court and adduce written law. But this could happen only after his defeat of Cao was assured. Socialist China did maintain legal organs and codes (except during the Cultural Revolution), but their functions were relevant only at the ends of criminal processes, to ratify decisions that had already been made. The ratification was a ritual that was something more than a mere rubber stamp. Courts were austere places, indeed gateways to prison, and legal language had to carry enough moral prestige to provide legitimacy for what the state was doing. In writing of the role of law in Communist Czechoslovakia, Vaclav Havel refers to "the purely ritualistic nature of the law" but warns that the rituals are crucial to state power: "The integrity of the world of appearances" depends on them, and a challenge to them "threatens the whole mendacious structure at its point of maximum mendacity."[87] The state's moral prestige, and hence power, depended on main-

---

[87] Vaclav Havel, "The Power of the Powerless," in Havel, *Living in Truth*, p. 98.

taining the public appearance that everything had happened in accordance with written law.

This is why, as noted in chapter 2, from the state's point of view, written law needed to include contradictory opposites. The 1980s version of China's constitution lists the freedoms of speech and the press, but also requires "upholding" the Communist Party and the socialist system. A similar document for China's writers (the constitution of the All-China Federation of Literary and Art Workers) "protects the . . . right to write, to study, and to carry out exchanges" for "writers and artists who support socialism, love the motherland, and safeguard the unity of the country."[88] Contradictory language gave powerholders the latitude they needed to cite the law differently in different situations. Written law normally had no role until an official needed the mantle of legitimacy for a specific act, whereupon invocation of the law amounted to finding the legal language to justify that act.

The conception of law as something to be used by rulers in order to regulate society and not by those who are ruled in order to protect their "rights" was broadly assumed among rulers and ruled alike. In 1980, the conservative writer Liu Baiyu seemed to be acknowledging the rights of the ruled when he commented, on the topic of the unofficial literary journals that were sprouting in China at the time, that China needed to strengthen its "publication law." Asked to elaborate, Liu made it clear that by "publication law" he meant law "to control unauthorized publication."[89] Around the same time, popular fiction and film were filled with images of police and the courts as fearful things, always to be avoided if possible.[90] The phrase "handle according to law" (*yifa chuli*) was, in practice, a synonym for "deliver official punishment."

THE PROBLEM OF TRUTH

A 1985 survey of science and engineering students in Guangzhou asked respondents to prioritize six virtues: communist ideals, patriotism, scientific and cultural knowledge, morality and discipline, professionalism, and insistence on truth. Among these, insistence on truth received most votes (30 percent), while communist ideals placed next to last (5 percent). (Morality and discipline were last, at 1.5%.)[91] Student comments suggested that the

---

[88] "An Organization of Chinese Writers and Artists," *Beijing Review* no. 52, 28 December 1979, p. 15.

[89] Interview, Beijing, 11 August 1980.

[90] Occasionally there were implications that things should not be this way, that police should be the friends of ordinary people. In the film *The Hope of the Downcast* (*Shiwangren de xiwang,* Hunan dianshi dianying zhipianchang, 1979), a young man captures a purse snatcher and delivers him to a local police station, only to learn that the station is run by Red Guards in the same band as the purse snatcher. From then on "downcast," the young man himself turns to pickpocketing.

[91] Xu Haohua, "Jin ji nian biye de ligongke daxuesheng zai xiang shenme?"

notions of truth and of communist ideals were divergent, as if following one meant abandoning the other.

We have noted in chapter 3 how, beginning in the 1950s, the use of official language in socialist China departed significantly from daily-life language in tone, vocabulary, and even grammar. Literary works from the Soviet Union show that a similar phenomenon existed there. In a story by Alexander Yashin called "Levers," for example, Russian farmers complain in ordinary language about officiousness among the higher-ups; but in a Party cell meeting, the farmers adopt the same long-winded political jargon that the officials use.[92] In broad outline, the reasons why official and unofficial language diverged were remarkably similar in the Soviet Union and China: each country fell under the control of a visionary who thought that agricultural collectivization was the first step toward communist utopia; in each country this effort led to a disastrous famine and rural violence; yet, in each case, the theory that the country was approaching utopia had still to be honored as "true." Eventually, two ways of speaking gave rise to two kinds of truth, a theoretical truth and a practical truth, which operated as if in different realms.

After the deaths of Stalin and Mao, when it became possible to hold up one kind of truth as a challenge to the other, the juxtapositions could be dramatic. A story called "Let History Be My Judge," which was immensely popular around Guangzhou in 1979, tells of a young man who is driven to beggary during the great famine in 1960 because all the grain in his commune has been shipped out to support false claims about bumper harvests.[93] Inside an urban restaurant, he happens across an official from his own commune, who is enjoying a banquet and is outraged at a beggar who dares to claim that the commune is short of food. The official reads from a newspaper report on the commune's splendid "overnight" success and its delivery of grain far "over quota."

"All of that is false," says the young farmer. "The quotas were filled by taking away our own grain."

"You dare to lie like that?" thunders the official. "Lazy bastard! Shirk off back at the farm and come to town to blacken the name of socialism?!"

The young man is strangely unafraid. "What I said is entirely true," he answers. "If you don't believe me, just come and live with us for a few days." In the end, however, the young man is handcuffed and led to prison. His version of truth cannot be allowed to stand.

Reflecting the Soviet case, Boris Pasternak uses a character in *Doctor Zhivago* to say that in order "to conceal the failure [of collectivization], people had to be cured, by every means of terrorism, of the habit of thinking and judging for themselves, and forced to see what didn't exist, to assert the

---

[92] In McLean and Vickery, *The Year of Protest*, pp. 193–210.
[93] Qian Yuxiang, "Lishi a, ni shenpan wo ba!"

very opposite of what their eyes told them."[94] From there, Pasternak held, it was but a short step to acceptance of paper constitutions and phony elections. Liu Binyan traces his own discovery of the "two truths" problem to his experience in the Chinese countryside during the great famine:

> The authorities told us that our impoverished gully of a village ought to build a zoo and a fountain. Now, what were peasants who hardly ate meat all year supposed to feed to lions and tigers in a zoo? With no water source—with man and beast still drinking rainwater—how were they to build a fountain? A struggle began to rage deep inside me: how could two diametrically opposed "truths" coexist in the world? The longings of the peasants were one truth, and the policies of the higher-ups and propaganda in the newspapers were quite another.[95]

With the arrival of the Cultural Revolution and its exaggerated praise of Mao and everything Maoist, the divergence of the two kinds of truth became a matter of "inverting black and white," to use the cliché of the post-Mao years. Wang Shouxin, the archvillain of Liu Binyan's "People or Monsters?," was "a heroine of her times."[96] When young people drowned as they sought to form a human dyke during a typhoon, armed only with "Quotations from Chairman Mao," contemporary press reports spoke of Mao's works having "forged intrepid warriors," who have "nothing to fear from wild winds and wicked waves, as their whole hearts are devoted to the people."[97]

Such wide divergence of fact and political myth naturally led to a kind of institutionalized hypocrisy. Several popular stories and films in the post-Mao years exposed how high-ranking leaders in Maoist times "participated in labor." In one such scene, a provincial Party secretary is poised to begin labor by removing large canisters from a truck. Facing a bevy of photographers, he admonishes them not to take his picture, but to focus their cameras on "the basic levels," meaning the ordinary workers. He then turns to lift a canister off the truck, while the lenses snap furiously. The moment he is done, an assistant runs over to tell him that he is needed at a meeting. He smiles to the cameras, waves his hand, and leaves.[98] The scheming Secretary Cao in "Power and Law," after living high during famine and blackmailing an honest reporter who knows about it, can produce immaculate political language nonetheless: "Every word we say and everything we do must be weighed against the interest of the Party and must be done on the basis of protecting our Party's sacred prestige and credibility with the people."[99]

---

[94] Quoted in George Gibian, *Interval of Freedom*, p. 148.

[95] "Listen Carefully to the Voice of the People," in *People or Monsters?*, p. 3.

[96] Liu Binyan, *People or Monsters?*, p. 30.

[97] "Kuangfeng elang he suo ju? Yipian danxin wei renmin," and "'Lao san pian' zhuzao de wuwei zhanshi," *Nanfang ribao*, 23 and 24 September 1969.

[98] *Ku'naoren de xiao*, (Troubled laughter), directed by Yang Yanjin and Deng Yimin, Shanghai dianying zhipianchang, 1979.

[99] Xing Yixun, "Quan yu fa," p. 7.

Middle-level bureaucrats, almost by necessity, became adept at the same kind of hypocritical role playing. A play that created a stir in Shanghai in 1979 presents an "old section chief" who wants his daughter to leave her boyfriend, the son of one of his servants, for someone of higher status. He cannot say this, of course, because "workers are the masters in the People's Republic." One of the boy's friends devises a scheme that persuades the old man that the boy is, in fact, the son of an artillery commander. Instantly the old man changes his mind, and turns remarkably eloquent on how the boyfriend's social standing has nothing to do with his approval of the match, because all workers play a valuable role in socialist society, and so on.[100] In a very short story called "The Truth Comes Out with Drink," by Sun Yuchun, the Party secretary of a commune is ordered by a superior to apologize to a young farmer whom he had imprisoned for putting up a critical poster. Arriving at the young man's house with his apologetic veneer intact, the official accepts an invitation to sit down for wine and fried peanuts. As he drinks more and more, the facade gradually comes loose, until his true feelings are fully exposed: "Don't think I can't squash you. . . . Just you wait, you little twerp!"[101]

Beginning in the 1950s, and especially after the Anti-Rightist Campaign of 1957, the two ways of speaking and two kinds of "truth" were generally confined quite separately to the public and private realms of daily life. People spoke one way at home, or in the confidence of friends, and another way in all public contexts. A film called *Troubled Laughter*, which was warmly received when it appeared in 1979, dramatizes the issue by showing the dilemmas of a young journalist who wants to tell the unofficial truth—the "real" truth—in his public reporting, but is faced with a variety of threats to him and his family if he goes ahead.[102] He consults with a senior professor of journalism, who sighs and passes along a story from Lu Xun: when a family has a son, they proudly show it to the neighbors and expect some compliments. Neighbors who say the boy will be rich or become an official will be thanked and flattered in return, but what they say may well be not true. If someone dares to say what is certainly true, that "this child will die," that neighbor will receive a beating. Faced with the choice of lying or being beaten, all an honest person can say is, "This child . . . heh, heh!"[103] Nowadays, the professor advised the young journalist, such feeble avoidance is pandemic.

According to Hugh McLean and Walter Vickery, the great popularity in Russia of Ilya Ehrenburg's *The Thaw* came because "it had been a long time since Russians had been allowed to entertain *in print* the idea that there

[100] Zhou Weibo, Dong Yangsheng, and Ye Xiaonan, "Paobing siling de erzi."

[101] Sun Yuchun, "Jiu hou tu zhen yan"; the translated quotation is from *Chinese Literature* 1979.12.117.

[102] *Ku'naoren de xiao.*

[103] Lu Xun, "Li lun."

might be such a thing as a cynical time-server."[104] Similarly during the Chinese thaw, the dramatic impact of sentences like Liu Binyan's famous line, "The Communist Party regulates everything, but does not regulate the Communist Party" was hardly to inform readers of anything, but to put well-known truths into official print.[105] Literary editors everywhere in China became aware of the opportunities of "saying what readers want said."[106] They were also aware of the risks. "People or Monsters?" stimulated so strong a reaction in Heilongjiang, where the corruption that Liu Binyan wrote about took place, that he could not safely travel there for many months. In Guangdong, even a little-known work like "Black Tide" aroused furious opposition from the army leaders who had been responsible for the senseless drownings.[107]

But readers overwhelmingly welcomed the official sanction of formerly forbidden truths. During a ten-day book sale in 1979, the New China Bookstore in Beijing sold out three editions, totaling more than 628,000 copies, of collections of poetry from the Tiananmen protests that had been crushed in April, 1976.[108] These were not great poems, but in 1976 represented the first public literary protests against Maoism that had been possible since 1956. Their publication in 1979 at the three largest literary publishing houses in Beijing was a clear if indirect signal that the government now approved the truths that they bore. Two films released the same year, in Sichuan and Guangdong, dramatized the crushing of the Tiananmen protests from the point of view of the protesters; although the scenes of actual violence were handled gently, the emotional impact on audiences was powerful.[109]

Important though it was, the issue of truth and falsity was subordinate to the principle of right and wrong. Readers and writers enjoyed the exposure of truth—about corruption, bureaucratism, waste, and so on—because they felt right in doing so, not just because the truth was there to be told. This point was especially clear in instances where falsity was condoned for the sake of doing good. In the film *Troubled Laughter* about the conscience-

---

[104] McLean and Vickery, *The Year of Protest*, p. 18, emphasis added.

[105] Liu Binyan, *People or Monsters?*, p. 43.

[106] The quotation is from an interview with Wenyi chubanshe in Shanghai (16 June 1980), but similar statements came from the editorial boards of *Zuopin* (Guangzhou, 4 March 1980) and *Renmin wenxue* (Beijing, 9 August 1980).

[107] Interview at the editorial offices of *Guangzhou Wenyi*, 7 March 1980; interview with Chen Haiying, Guangzhou, 31 May 1980.

[108] Interview at the Xinhua shudian, 30 October 1979, Beijing. The books were Liaoning daxue Zhongwen xi, *Tiananmen shichao*, of which 315,000 copies were sold in the ten days; "Geming shichao" bianji bu, *Geming shichao*, 113,500 copies sold; and Beijing di'er waiguoyu xueyuan, *Tiananmen shiwenji*, 200,000 copies sold.

[109] *Bushi weile aiqing* (It wasn't for love), Emei dianying zhipianchang, 1980, and *Fengyu xiaoxiao* (Stormy weather), Zhujiang dianying zhipianchang, 1979. *Fengyu xiaoxiao* took a softer position against the police who crushed the demonstrations by suggesting that they did not want to, but were forced by the Gang of Four.

ridden journalist, for example, the journalist feigns illness at one point in order to avoid filing a falsified report. A doctor discovers his deception but, as one pressured intellectual to another, looks him in the eye and says "I understand," then writes out a slip authorizing sick leave. In the moral rhetoric of the film, the false acts of both men are not only right, but courageous.[110]

Statements that can seem banal from an outsider's point of view sometimes brought strong reactions from readers and audiences who were waiting to release their feelings. In a 1979 stage play in Beijing, a character who dares to comment that "Communist Party members are not omnicompetent" received extended applause.[111] If a vapid truth like this could be exciting, one reason was that vapid falsities were much more common, and moreover could not be challenged. Around the same time, for example, Party propaganda chief Hu Yaobang delivered a major speech in which he claimed that the "superiority of socialism" is evident in "our complete removal of an exploitative system and our total eradication of oppression."[112] Hu also proclaimed that corruption, although it still existed under socialism, was only a vestige of the old society, not a function of socialism itself.[113] It was impossible to contradict Hu in public on these issues, but millions of readers knew that such claims were nearly the opposite of the truth. The dissemination of speeches like Hu's built a thirst among the reading public for truth telling, whether vapid or not.

In a 1985 speech Hu Yaobang said, "The issue of veracity is one over which we have argued for a long time with some writers. They always say that their works reflect the truth, but they fail to realize whether their works have faithfully reflected the overall situation in our society."[114] Hu offered writers the rule of thumb that it is best to "report good things" 80 percent of the time and "expose shortcomings" 20 percent of the time. It is not clear whether Hu's formula was meant to be descriptive or prescriptive— whether, that is, he felt Chinese society was in fact "80 percent positive and 20 percent negative" or only that this attitude was the best one to take if one wanted to do good for China. But the evidence from surveys and interviews is overwhelming that readers did not share Hu's preference for a "80 percent positive, 20 percent negative" formula. One writer from Gansu, publishing in Guangdong, noted that post-Mao scar stories focused primarily on the direct victims of the Cultural Revolution, whom Mao had once said were the "bad" 10 percent of the Chinese population. The other 90 percent were supposed to have been "good" and thus to have been spared

---

[110] The audience of university students among whom I viewed the film (at Zhongshan University, 5 January 1980) also showed no sign of disapproval of this kind of falsity.

[111] "Gongchandangyuan bushi shenme dou hui," pronounced by the character Li Jian in *Baochunhua*, and observed in Beijing, 1 October 1979.

[112] Hu Yaobang, "Zai juben chuangzuo zuotanhuishang de jianghua," p. 11.

[113] Ibid., pp. 23–24.

[114] Hu Yaobang, "Lun dang di xinwen gongzuo."

persecution and suffering. This writer submitted a story called "In the Ninety Percent," in which he showed how the suffering under Mao extended deep into the group whom Mao had called "good." After the story appeared, the publisher received hundreds of letters from readers who placed themselves among the good but still abused "ninety percent."[115] They praised the story for showing how the turmoil had affected ordinary people, not just political leaders or famous intellectuals.

Stories about particular cases that actually stood for large groups were welcomed for the same reason. Zheng Yi's "Maple," about armed combat among Red Guards, became celebrated because it put into a simple, plain story the forbidden truth about what had happened in many places during the Cultural Revolution.[116] Zuo Jianming's story "Shadow" tells about an old soldier who lost a leg before the revolution; during the famine of 1959–1961, his commune gives him a travel permit officially allowing him to visit other areas as a beggar.[117] Readers praised the story not just for showing how far the famine had pushed people, but because the author dared to reveal a phenomenon that was officially secret even though it had been common enough to acquire the nationally known nickname of "socialist beggary"; the story was based, moreover, on Deng Xiaoping's hometown area in Sichuan Province.[118] Such stories were a direct challenge to the leadership's claim that problem cases were always tied to particular places.

The leadership's guideline that literary works should attribute problems specifically to the past, so as to imply that the present and future are rosy, similarly created in the readership a thirst for statements that, even if bland, said the opposite. When "ten years of catastrophe" were being blamed on a Gang of Four who had already been arrested, Liu Binyan published a story called "Warning" that imagined the conversations of the ghosts of certain deceased ultraleftists, from their ashes inside funerary urns, as they reminisced about past glories and schemed to return.[119] It drew a strong response from readers.

THE PLACE OF ROMANCE

The literary theme of romantic love, repressed under Mao, resurged under Deng in ways that resembled its return after Stalin in the Soviet Union. We have noted in the last chapter how themes of love and sex survived repression at the popular level in China. At the level of the socially critical reader-

---

[115] Interview at the editorial offices of *Guangzhou wenyi*, 7 March 1980.

[116] Zheng Yi, "Feng"; for discussion see Michael S. Duke, *Blooming and Contending*, pp. 79–80.

[117] Zuo Jianming, "Yinying."

[118] Interview with student editors of *Hongdou*, Zhongshan University, Guangzhou, 6 May 1980.

[119] Liu Binyan, "Jinggao."

ship, the revival of romance brought a sense of individual liberation and, in consequence, generated some cultural and political controversies.

During the late Maoist years, romantic love in literature and art was reduced to the smallest of signs. Characters in the model operas of the Cultural Revolution period showed signs of heterosexual interest only through meaningful glances and symbolic pairings on stage. The fact that only heroes and heroines displayed even this much romantic interest suggested that love between the sexes was appropriate only for people whose highest priority was politics and whose political records were pure. The actual daily life of Maoist China was by no means free from sexual activity, as many post-Mao memoirs and works of fiction—as well as birth rates—make clear. But public expression of love and sex was banned, and activity was pressed into the private and even secret corners of life.

Early in the post-Mao thaw, some short stories broke the taboo with the bland assertion that love is not irrelevant. Liu Xinwu's "The Place of Love" (1978) tells of a boy and girl who meet on a bus and later meet again at a bookstore where they are properly buying the works of Mao.[120] Everything seems to be going well until she learns that his father is a mere vendor of sesame cakes. Others advise her to leave the boy, but she will not. Love has its place. Zhang Jie's "Love Must Not Be Forgotten" (1979) went further, suggesting that love had a place even if one lover was married to someone else. The strong reader responses to these stories, evident in thousands of letters to the publishers and authors as well as in debates in the press around the country, suggest that the stories played a cathartic role: they allowed long-repressed feelings to emerge, with at least some respectability, into the public sphere.[121] Data from surveys confirms this conjecture; in a survey of university students in Beijing, respondents said that reading literature produced more openness and independence in romantic life.[122]

Some stories addressed the problem of repression and inhibition directly. Zhang Xian's "The Corner Forgotten by Love" (1980) tells of a young couple who secretly make love during the Cultural Revolution.[123] One day they are discovered and hooted across town, after which the girl drowns herself from remorse while the boy is led away in handcuffs. These events leave such a deep impression on the girl's younger sister that when the sister's own body changes, and she feels attracted to a young man, she considers the feelings shameful. She will speak to her boyfriend only about official business and only at a distance of about four feet. When her parents begin to arrange a marriage for her, she rebels against the process and from there comes to realize that sexual feelings are not wrong and that her older sister

---

[120] "Aiqing de weizhi."

[121] The Beijing Publishing House, who published "The Place of Love," had received more 2,500 reader letters about it by mid-October 1979; the author had received 1,000 or more directly. (Interview at Beijing chubanshe, 20 October 1979).

[122] Huang Ruixu, "Daxuesheng yuedu wenxue zuopin xianzhuang qianxi," p. 18.

[123] Zhang Xian, "Bei aiqing yiwang de jiaoluo."

was not, after all, as depraved as society judged her. A story by Gao Xiaosheng called "Picking out a Pearl" tells about a peasant boy who is so inhibited that he cannot understand what is happening even when an adventuresome young woman, a Party member who appreciates his salt-of-the-earth honesty and hard work, literally jumps into his arms.[124] She begins by arranging for them to carry sacks of rice along the same route, but he, missing the point, offers to carry her sacks so that she will not have to. When she declines his offer and they set out together, he walks briskly ahead. After a while she sits down, claiming to need a rest, and asks him to carry her. He agrees, and suggests that she sit in a basket at one end of his carrying pole, with a load on the other end to balance. She says no, that's not comfortable enough, "You can just carry me on your back." He concludes that she is ill and says he will go for a doctor. At her wit's end, she leaps to her feet and shouts, "I don't want that!" They both reach for the carrying pole. When he yanks it toward himself, she falls into his arms. As he is saying, "Oops, oops!" she just nestles closer, and finally he catches on.

In the years immediately after Mao, the love theme became so standard as to seem almost a requirement. Works whose main themes lay elsewhere—in exposure of corruption, violence, and other somber matters—added romantic subplots as ornaments. An official critic writing in the *People's Daily* made fun of this practice. "A literary creation," said the critic, "is equal to X (any topic) + scars + love."[125] In some cases the addition of a romantic subtheme allowed an author to insert daring sexual descriptions, using the principal theme as a cover. In a story called "If the Rain Falls Endlessly" by Cen Sang, a husband and wife are separated for political reasons during the Cultural Revolution but, by passing secret notes, are able to agree that the next time it pours rain, they will steal away to meet inside a tunnel.[126] The reason for needing to meet, the reader is told, is that the wife possesses a pack of "materials," including a letter from a top leader in Beijing, that can clear the name of an elderly professor who is being wrongly punished by the Gang of Four. "You mustn't lose this no matter what," she says to her spouse when they meet. But, as if incidentally, the reader is also treated to a description of their meeting: she has lost her raincoat to the fierce wind, and her rain-soaked clothing clings to her body. From "concern," her husband helps her to peel it off, proceeding limb by limb, as the thunder and lightning continue to rage outside the dark tunnel in which the lovers huddle. Chen Dengke uses the Gang of Four as cover for titillation in a different way when he devotes chapter 10 of his novel *Record of a Broken Wall* to an exposé of the national beauty contest that Lin Biao arranged in order to find a match for his son; Chen also finds a way to insert background on Jiang Qing's reported claim that every woman deserves a gigolo.[127]

---

[124] Gao Xiaosheng, "Jian zhenzhu," section five.
[125] *Renmin ribao* 11 November 1981.
[126] Cen Sang, "Ruguo yu xia ge buting."
[127] Chen Dengke and Xiao Ma, *Pobiji.*

The question of romantic love raised some other cultural and political questions, which in turn stimulated several kinds of controversy. Stories like "If the Rain Falls Endlessly" and "Anticipation" (see chapter 3) raised the sensitive and widespread problem of the separation of spouses; "Anticipation" drew a record number of letters to its author and editors.[128] Stories like Zhang Jie's "Love Must Not Be Forgotten" (1979) raised deeper cultural questions and drew both strong support and determined opposition.[129] Zhang's story paints a sympathetic portrait of a widow who is attracted to a married man—a senior official who has spent his life in a loveless marriage that had been undertaken, originally, out of revolutionary duty rather than romance. The issue of obedience to the state and its laws is still present in the story, but the greater challenge is to Chinese cultural convention: should not genuine romantic feeling take precedence over preservation of social form? Why should people live in loveless marriages when love is a real alternative? This question smacked of what Party critics called "bourgeois individualism," but it also involved the traditional Chinese virtue of sincerity: is it not better to admit the true situation than to pretend? Some critics, such as Dai Qing, who defended Zhang Jie's story, pointed out that gender equality was also at issue. Traditionally in China, loveless arranged marriages had hurt women more than men.[130] More women than men wrote to the story's publisher, and many wanted advice on their own problems with unloving husbands.[131]

In Zhang Jie's story, the widow and the married official communicate their affections only through the subtlest of signs, such as glances at a distance. They never so much as hold hands. Their cerebral romance is revealed primarily through the inner monologue of the woman. But the challenge to conventional marital fidelity is nevertheless clear. It invites comparison to a similar challenge that emerged during the post-Stalin thaw in the Soviet Union, although Soviet writers and audiences were generally much more explicit and detailed on the issues. Ilya Ehrenburg's *The Thaw* (1954) and Vladimir Dudintsev's *Not by Bread Alone* (1956) both introduced extramarital romance more explicitly than did Zhang Jie or any post-Mao Chinese writer until Yu Luojin.[132] Samuil Alyoshin's play "Alone" (1956), which is said to have played to packed houses in Moscow, addresses Zhang Jie's questions in ways that Zhang Jie would have found unseemly for their directness.[133] Platonov, a married man, finding himself in love with Nefedova, who is also married—but not to Platonov—brings the fact of this adulterous love squarely before Nefedova's father, saying that the fact is there, so why should we be hypocritical? Later Nefedova also addresses her

---

[128] Interview with *Guangming ribao* editorial board, 26 July 1980.
[129] Zhang Jie, "Ai shi buneng wangji de."
[130] Dai Qing, "Buneng yong yi zhong secai miaohui shenghuo."
[131] Interview with *Guangming ribao* editorial board, 26 July 1980.
[132] On Yu Luojin's *A Spring Fairy Tale*, see chapter 3 above.
[133] McLean and Vickery, *The Year of Protest*, p. 37; play translated pp. 38–111.

father: "I think about him [Platonov] all the time. So why shouldn't I be with him? He is my life. Do you understand?"[134] The play also shows Platonov's wife as a strong and somewhat sympathetic character, whereas the wronged wife in Zhang Jie's ethereal tale is barely mentioned. Zhang's story also could not accommodate a character like Alyoshin's Lida, who, having abandoned herself to vodka and promiscuity, observes that she at least is better off than the lonely and hypocritical wives who hide behind the respectability of being "a married woman."[135] Susan Chen, who has compared the two works closely, argues that the greater detail and psychological complexity of Alyoshin's play makes it in the end a stronger statement of the case that both Zhang and Alyoshin wish to make.[136]

We have noted above (chapter 2) that Party leaders in China found the frank admission of romantic feelings to be not only culturally controversial but also politically unsettling. Obedience to innermost thoughts and feelings ran counter to the Party's preferred program of giving instructions from the outside. A close look at the available evidence on reader response to love stories shows that the Party's fear did have some basis. Editors at *Beijing Literature*, who published Zhang Jie's "Love Must Not Be Forgotten," reported that reader letters were overwhelmingly supportive of the story;[137] at *Guangming Daily*, where some criticisms of the story had been published, editors reported that mail still favored the story two to one.[138] From this and much anecdotal evidence it seems clear that many young readers (but not necessarily older ones) reveled in the story. Yet there is also evidence that the traditional taboo against adulterous love still had considerable force, among young readers as well as old. In a 1982 survey of 504 young workers in Beijing, for example, 85 percent said that romance with a married person is impermissible; only 4 percent said that it is all right, and the rest were unsure.[139] Part of the discrepancy between support for a story about adultery and opposition to the practice can be explained by the difference between the worlds of thought and of daily life: one should not look for a married lover, but it is all right to imagine such a thing while reading. Similarly, it is all right for political and social authority to forbid such a practice, but not all right to forbid the practice of thinking, writing, or talking about it. Yet, as we have seen in chapter 2, the practice of independent thought and expression is precisely what Party authorities did fear.

Conservative voices in the Party advocated suppression of writing about romantic love almost as soon as it began to resurge. At the height of the controversy over Zhang Jie's story, Xia Yan, vice minister of culture during

---

[134] Ibid., 77.

[135] See Swayze, *Political Control*, pp. 177–78.

[136] Susan Wilf Chen, "Literature of the 'Thaw' in China and the Soviet Union."

[137] Interview at the editorial offices of *Beijing Literature*, 7 August 1980.

[138] Interview at *Guangming ribao*, 26 July 1980.

[139] Zhongguo renmin daxue yi fenxiao "hunyin wenti diaocha zu," "Guowai 'xing ziyou' lilun dui bufen qingnian gongren de yingxiang," p. 22.

the 1950s and now newly returned to prominence, objected that the "embrace barrier" and "kissing barrier" had both fallen. Now the film cameras were aiming at the "third barrier," which meant "starting from the foot and heading for the thigh." Apparently without irony, Xia asked, "Is it right to keep going in this direction?"[140] In the fall of 1981, a coordinated official effort to repress writing about romantic love was launched in the Party's theoretical journal *Red Flag*. As was customary in such efforts, Party critics disguised its political interest in repression as something else, in this case as preservation of decency and cultural purity. *Red Flag* decried "vulgar trends in Western films," including stripping, kissing, slow-motion love scenes, "rolling around on the ground" (a misconstrual of "rock and roll") and "boys and girls playing together under water."[141] The *People's Daily* pronounced that love stories must "avoid unrealistic or unhealthy tendencies,"[142] and a conference of literary editors "decided" that love stories "must contribute to the construction of socialist civilization."[143]

But although *Red Flag* claimed that the "vulgarity" it had found in Western films "has made the audiences feel disgusted," it is clear that young urban audiences in fact were strongly attracted—if not to the practice of what they saw and read about, at least to watching, reading, and thinking about it. Some of the opinion surveys of the mid-1980s seem to have been aimed at rebutting the Party's disapproval of romantic expression. A survey of university students in Beijing showed in several ways that "sexual liberation" from abroad had not in fact done much harm.[144] Of students in a Tianjin high school, 78 percent approved of new-style "group dancing," and only 5 percent were opposed.[145] The theme of the rebuttal in such surveys was to say that romance and sex were natural processes, not necessarily either pernicious or foreign. A survey of university students in Taiyuan asked specifically whether the main cause of "love among college students" was "music, films, and videotapes from the West," and only 2 percent said it was; 55 percent chose "natural biological factors" as the main cause, and 40 percent said it was "the influence of general trends in society."[146]

---

[140] Tang Xiaolou, "Zhou Yang, Xia Yan, 'San bu'!"

[141] Chen Bo, "Dianying yao wei jianshe shehuizhuyi jingshen wenming zuochu gongxian," and Sha Tong, "Renzhen kefu wenyi gongzuozhong de ziyouhua qingxiang."

[142] Pinglunyuan (commentator), "Renzhen taolun yixia wenyi chuangzuozhong biaoxian aiqing de wenti," *Renmin ribao*, 4 November 1981.

[143] Conference of editors of *Zuopin yu zhengming* (Works and controversies), reported in Zhongguo shehui kexueyuan wenxue yanjiusuo dangdai wenxue yanjiushi, *Xin shiqi wenxue liu nian*, p. 519.

[144] Zhongguo renmin daxue yi fenxiao "hunyin wenti diaocha zu," "Guowai 'xing ziyou' lilun dui bufen qingnian gongren de yingxiang."

[145] Zhang Xu et al., "Zhongxuesheng dui jitiwu de kanfa."

[146] Guo Lihuai, "Wo yuan daxuesheng lian'ai wenti de diaocha," p. 57.

CHAPTER 7

The Uses of Literature

IN 1985, as the socialist literary system in China entered its waning years, Communist Party Chairman Hu Yaobang delivered a major speech on literary policy. Hu was the most liberal chairman the Party had had to that point, and he was speaking during an unusual warm spell in Party policy toward literature. But even under these conditions, the speech was grounded in Maoist assumptions about literature's "functions": "Our Party has always stressed the importance of the functions of literature and art within the overall revolutionary enterprise. On this point we have not changed for decades. During the Yan'an years, Comrade Mao Zedong said that our literature and art were weapons with which to unite and to educate the people."[1]

Confucian tradition before Mao had also held that literary texts—provided they were the right texts, and were learned properly—led the learner toward good behavior and thus brought harmony to society. But Mao's literary "functions," which had grown partly from European Marxism, were much more specifically targeted and enforced. At Yan'an, Mao had said, "Proletarian literature and art are ... in the words of Lenin, 'cogs and screws in the whole machine.' Therefore, the Party's literary and artistic activity occupies a definite and assigned position in the Party's total revolutionary work and is subordinated to the prescribed revolutionary task of the Party in a given revolutionary period."[2] The "cogs and screws" of Lenin continued to receive occasional mention throughout the life of the socialist literary system in China, but the metaphor never spread as widely as did medical metaphors and the military metaphors preferred by Mao. In literary journals from the 1940s to the 1980s—more often or less, depending upon the degree of ideological fervor of the time—writers were said to be in the "ranks" (*duiwu*) of the revolutionary "camp" (*zhenying*), where they used "(military) strategy" (*zhanlue*) to produce works that were "weapons" (*wuqi*) on the literary "front" (*zhanxian*). More specific formulations came and went in accordance with the "propaganda objectives" of particular times. For example in spring 1979, when the post-Mao short story was surging, official critics repeated the cumbersome phrase "the short story's combat function of the military scout."[3] Military metaphors eventually seeped even

---

[1] Hu Yaobang, "Guanyu dangqian wenyi gongzuo yixie wenti de jianghua," p. 4.

[2] Mao Zedong, "Talks at the Yan'an Forum on Literature and Art," *Selected Works*, vol. 4, *1941–1945*, note 9.

[3] See, for example, *Guangming ribao*, 28 March 1979, "Quanguo youxiu duanpian xiaoshuo pingxuan fajiang dahui zai jing juxing" and "Zhuhe he xiwang"; also Liu Xicheng, "Tan dangqian duanpian xiaoshuo chuangzuo zhong de jige wenti."

into the language of daily life, where, for example, it became normal in socialist China to propose that friends at a dinner table "annihilate" (*xiaomie*) the food remaining in a common dish. This phrase was used in a friendly manner, and sometimes bore a modest irony, but could seem strange and jarring to the ears of Chinese who had grown up outside the People's Republic.

In this chapter, I want to look not only at the Chinese Communist Party's use of literature for instrumental purposes but at all of the various "uses" that literature had inside the socialist Chinese literary system. As I argued in the introduction, Western scholarly approaches have tended to focus on one of three questions—dissent, sociological "reflection," or the search for pure art—and thus have yet to account for the full range of uses to which people who lived within the socialist system actually put the literature that they wrote, edited, read, criticized, praised, and argued about.

The word "use" in this chapter is meant in an especially broad sense. I certainly do not mean that all conceptions of literature were merely instrumental—that is, that reading or writing a literary work was done only with the aim of bringing someone's notion of a good effect to the world. Such a conception was, to be sure, very common in socialist China, and moreover had a variety of versions because not only Party authorities but writers and editors bearing many varying agendas pursued it. But by "uses" of literature, I also mean to include all the other functions that literary works actually had. These included such things as experimentation with new ideas, identification with an admirable person, vicarious travel to distant places, observation of someone doing or saying what one does not dare to do or say oneself, and simple diversion from daily drudgery. At an extreme of instrumentality, I include pursuit of fame and fortune as a "use" of literature; at the opposite, noninstrumental extreme, I also count the pleasurable experience of imagining rosy clouds at dusk a "use" of reading whatever text might stimulate this imaginative experience. It should be clear that this conception of "use" far exceeds the merely instrumental.[4]

I begin with the official uses of literature because they were central to the socialist literary system. These uses were indeed highly instrumental, and can perhaps be best summarized in the view that writers should be "engineers of the soul." This phrase—championed by Stalin but apparently invented by Maxim Gorky—was more adequate than Lenin's "cogs and screws" or Mao's "camps and ranks" in suggesting the comprehensive responsibility for society that writers in a communist system were supposed to

---

[4] This concept of "use" I owe primarily to the American pragmatists Charles Peirce and William James, who held that the meaning of anything, from the hardness of a table to the existence of God, is determined "exclusively in its conceivable bearing on the conduct of life" (C. S. Peirce, "What Pragmatism Is," in Philip P. Wiener, ed., *Values in a Universe of Chance*, p. 183). See also William James, "What Pragmatism Means" and "The Will to Believe," in *Essays in Pragmatism*. I am also influenced by Richard Hoggart's approach to working-class culture in Britain in *The Uses of Literacy* (1970).

have. Although Mao consistently preferred his military language, Zhou En-lai as well as some of the more pro-Soviet leaders referred to "engineers of the soul" from the 1940s to the 1960s, and again, after the death of Mao, in the 1980s.[5] The perennial demand that writers answer for the thinking and behavior of their readers shows how thoroughly the notion "engineering" pervaded the literary politics of socialist China. Even writers and editors whose conscious intentions were to criticize the Party generally assumed that their own proper role was to shape the attitudes of readers.

THE PARTY AND ITS "ENGINEERING"

The "engineering" idea gained remarkable power in China because it had both native and foreign roots. The strong Soviet influence of the 1950s represented not just Stalin but the whole Soviet model for doing things; Nikita Khrushchev, even while trying to depart from Stalin, continued to endorse literary engineering with statements like "art should ennoble the individual and arouse him to action."[6] Chinese leaders both pro- and anti-Soviet concurred in speaking of "healthful" literature that led to "correct" behavior. In some ways, they echoed Liang Qichao, who in the early twentieth century had argued that "new fiction" had the power to reinvigorate all aspects of Chinese life.[7] And Liang, in turn, had drawn heavily upon Confucian notions that good reading leads to proper thinking, good behavior, a healthy society, and a strong country.

Evidence of the engineering idea appeared in many contexts in socialist China: films about the motherland were to inculcate the "unconditioned duty" of patriotism;[8] literary depictions of fearless fighters were supposed to "steel" soldiers for new encounters;[9] leaders at the Ministry of Public Security invested in detective stories because of the benefits they thought it could bring to police work; science fiction was defended on the grounds that it produced dedicated scientists (in the West, according to one view, Jules Verne had inspired a great many scientists, including the inventer of the submarine).[10] Countless works were intended to teach specific lessons about correct political and social attitudes.

During the Mao years, literature was also supposed to serve timely goals, such as "aid Korea," "warmly celebrate China's nuclear bomb," "criticize Lin Biao," "oppose the rightist tendency to reverse correct verdicts" (that is, in 1975, oppose Deng Xiaoping's attempt at a second return to power), and

---

[5] For example, Zhou Enlai, "Zai wenyi gongzuo zuotanhui he gushipian chuangzuo huiyi shang de jianghua"; Hu Yaobang, "Lun dang de xinwen gongzuo" and "Zai juben chuangzuo zuotanhuishang de jianghua," p. 35; and Liu Xicheng, "Wenyi yu dangdai shenghuo," p. 36.

[6] Priscilla Johnson, *Khrushchev and the Arts*, p. 103.

[7] Liang Qichao, "Lun xiaoshuo yu qunzhi zhi guanxi."

[8] "'Kulian' de shifei, qing yu pingshuo," *Shidai de baogao zengkan*, 23 April 1981, p. 1.

[9] Interview with Liu Baiyu, 11 August 1980, Beijing.

[10] Su Manhua, "Qing guanhuai yixia kexue wenyi."

many, many others. In the 1950s and early 1960s, the Propaganda Department of the Communist Party issued periodic notices to literary editorial boards explicitly updating current propaganda goals. This practice was suspended during the Cultural Revolution and was not restored afterward, but media reports on the leadership's thinking never left editors in much doubt about what results they were supposed to be achieving.

The theory that well-engineered literature produced good social results had a corollary that poorly engineered literature created social problems. At a closed conference in winter 1980, for example, Chen Huangmei, deputy director of the Institute of Literature of the Chinese Academy of Social Sciences, criticized the film script "Girl Thief" by Li Kewei for depicting "hooligans." Arguing that such works taught young readers how to commit crimes, Chen recounted the case of a twelve-year-old boy in Beijing who, in a quarrel with his sister over five yuan, allegedly killed her, cut off her head, and placed it on the family incense burner; investigators later found that the boy had recently seen *"Death on the Nile* and many other foreign films," according to Chen.[11] Supporting Chen's view, a prominent Cantonese writer claimed that sexual crimes in Hong Kong had increased with the increasing availability of pornography, and cited a survey by the Chinese Department at Hong Kong University that purportedly showed this result.[12]

For important policy initiatives, the Party leadership organized writers, editors, professors, and others to play coordinated roles in a national plan. In 1979, for example, the leadership opened a propaganda offensive aimed at generating popular support in Taiwan and among overseas Chinese for reunification of Taiwan with the mainland. The leaders determined that literary exchange could serve a function of building bridges to Taiwan, with which there had been virtually no cultural intercourse for many years. On 10 September 1979, the *People's Daily* suddenly published six poems by Xu Zhimo, a leading poet in the 1930s who had always been banned in Communist China because of his identification with the Nationalists, who were still in power in Taiwan. In December, the People's Literature Publishing House in Beijing published a volume called *Selected Fiction from Taiwan* and another called *Selected Essays from Taiwan.*

During 1980, major literary magazines in Beijing, Shanghai, and Guangzhou began to introduce short stories by Bai Xianyong, Nie Hualing, and other overseas Chinese writers who had Taiwan ties. These writers were invited to visit China, and some (such as Nie) did, while others (notably Bai) did not. Meetings with returning Taiwan writers were organized with far more fanfare than their announced purposes seemed to warrant. In April, for example, a large public meeting was held in Shanghai to award prizes for the best literary works among "writers from Taiwan currently resident in

---

[11] At a conference on literary teaching materials and on Taiwan and Hong Kong literature, Nanning, winter 1980, reported by Wang Jinmin, March 1980.

[12] Interview with Chen Canyun, 7 May 1980, Guangzhou. Staff at the Chinese Department at Hong Kong University denied ever doing this nonliterary survey.

Shanghai."[13] In Beijing in August, the Chinese Writers' Association, Central Peoples' Broadcasting, and a new "Headquarters for the Alliance for Democracy and Self-Rule in Taiwan" held a major conference, at which Xu Juemin, Feng Mu, and other high literary officials gave addresses to commemorate the twentieth anniversary of the death of Zhong Lihe, a Taiwan novelist who was almost unknown inside The People's Republic and only moderately well known outside.

The initiative toward Taiwan included "organizing" literary scholars to write articles about Taiwan authors and to edit mainland editions of their works. Wang Jinmin, a professor of Chinese at Zhongshan University in Guangzhou, received a primary assignment, and within two years produced a book about Taiwan writers, six edited volumes of their works, a reference book of biographical sketches, and numerous articles.[14] In March 1981, an officially sponsored "Research Association on Taiwan Literature" was established with Wang as secretary general.

Wang's analysis of Taiwan writing was superficial. He grouped writers into "schools" and sketched their lives and works in bland ways. The political mission of his work was always evident in the way he couched it. For example, an article contrasting the "modern school" (*xiandai pai*) and "regional school" (*xiangtu pai*) of Taiwan writers ends this way: "We hope these two fraternal schools, in the months and years to come, will join hands more tightly, learn from each other, and move forward to promote realist Taiwan literature, national literature, and the splendor of the literature of all of China!"[15] This is just about what Party leaders wanted; deeper analyses would have raised thorny political questions and compromised the diplomatic purpose of the overall effort.

Still, within the context of 1979, Wang Jinmin's scholarly adventure seemed extremely bold. Mao had been dead only three years. To people who did not know that the new leadership had made a policy of reaching out to Taiwan through literature, Wang's attention to Taiwan-affiliated writers—especially to Bai Xianyong, who was the son of a Nationalist general—seemed almost reckless. Because local security officers in Guangzhou were among those who remained unaware that the central government was sponsoring Wang's research, Wang had the unusual problem of how to acquire prohibited research materials even though the government assigned him to work on them. Coincidentally, I arrived for an eight-month stay at Zhongshan University in November 1979, and soon became a pony for Wang. Every time I traveled to Hong Kong, Wang gave me a list of books by Taiwan writers to buy and bring back to Guangzhou. At the time I, too, thought Wang was very bold.

[13] Zhongguo shehui kexueyuan wenxue yanjiusuo dangdai wenxue yanjiushi, *Xin shiqi wenxue liu nian*, p. 485; the meeting was 11 April 1980.

[14] Wang's book is *Taiwan dangdai wenxue*. The edited volumes contain the works of Bai Xianyong, Wang Tuo, Chen Yingzhen, Zhang Xiguo, and others. The volume of short biographies is *Taiwan yu haiwai huaren zuojia xiaozhuan*.

[15] Wang Jinmin, "Jin sanshi nian Taiwan wenxue shuping," p. 28.

A year or two later, the political purpose of the whole effort had become unmistakable. In October 1981, there were reports of a meeting in Beijing between officials in the Ministry of Culture and "Taiwan compatriots in the cultural field," all of whom "spoke glowingly of the great enterprise of reuniting the motherland" and "warmly supported" Hu Yaobang and Ye Jianying in calling for talks with Taiwan authorities.[16]

PROBLEMS WITH ENGINEERING

In China, as elsewhere in the twentieth-century socialist world, the faith that human behavior could be understood and controlled through science eventually ran afoul the unfathomable complexity of the human mind. "Engineering" worked only crudely, and sometimes produced effects that were both unforeseen and unwanted. Writers and political authorities in socialist China found at least these three perennial problems in trying to engineer souls: Can literary inspiration be planned? Does engineering produce the intended effects, or others? Can literary ambiguities be eliminated?

Can Literary Inspiration Be Planned?

The question can seem peculiar, and yet many years of experience of the Propaganda Department of the Communist Party of China shows that, at least at one level, it is not. In 1958, there did appear millions of poems praising the Great Leap Forward; in 1973, millions of school children did draw pictures of Lin Biao's aircraft crashing in the Mongolian desert. But just as plainly, more complex kinds of literary creation could not be produced from instructions that originated outside of the creating mind. During the years when Chinese writers were supposed to "consider the social effects" of their work, writers Chen Rong and Zhang Jie objected that creative inspiration was such a private and unpredictable event that there was no way they could elicit it at will; indeed, the pressure of external guidelines not only was no help to inspiration but tended to inhibit it. When inspiration did come, it was the kind of thing that took them in unforeseen directions, so that often, as they sat down to write, they did not exactly know what would happen to the characters they were working with.[17] The actor Zhao Dan put it this way: "Did Lu Xun and Mao Dun become writers because they were requested to by the Party, and write what the Party asked them to? And who asked Marx to write? . . . The vigor of an artist or writer, and his philosophical outlook, cannot be determined by a Party, a faction,

---

[16] Zhongguo shehui kexueyuan wenxue yanjiusuo dangdai wenxue yanjiushi, *Xin shiqi wenxue liu nian*, p. 518.

[17] Interviews with Zhang Jie, 30 July 1980, and with Chen Rong, 7 August 1980, Beijing.

an organization, or a Party branch. If you insist on having too rigid a control, [you] only do harm to literature and art."[18]

Nevertheless, there was room for several intermediate positions on the
question of engineering versus inspiration. Some writers said they felt that
external guidelines do not kill inspiration so long as they are only general.
Some felt it was all right to begin a writing process with a fixed concept, so
long as the concept is one's own, not something imposed from without.
Wang Meng, for example, said that for him there is no necessary conflict
between "concept" and "inspiration," and indeed that the two are sometimes the same thing. In his story "Eyes," a librarian responds to a young
borrower differently after learning that, despite the gleam in her eyes, she is
not a "model worker"; according to Wang, this story grew from his fascination with the concept that the look in a person's eyes could have something
to do with moral character and with being a model worker. Wang's story
"Butterfly"—in which the protagonist seems somewhat confused as history
buffets him into and out of the roles of revolutionary, bureaucrat, laborer,
prisoner, husband, and father—was inspired by the concept in Zhuangzi's
famous conundrum about whether he is a man dreaming he is a butterfly or
a butterfly dreaming he is man.[19]

There was, in short, at least some agreement among some writers that
inspiration could be planned. But even if engineered messages could be
produced, no serious writer agreed that he or she could grasp the receiving
mind—that of reader or viewer—sufficiently to ensure that the interpretation of messages was reliable.

Does Engineering Produce Intended Effects?

In the immediate post-Mao years, the literary grapevine in China was filled
with anecdotes about how attempts to use literature to manipulate reader
response during the Mao period had sometimes brought effects quite different from those intended. For example, William Shirer's *Rise and Fall of the
Third Reich* had been published "internally" in order to illustrate the evils of
Hitler; but at least some readers took away lessons such as "our Workers'
Patrols are like the Gestapo" and "Red Guards were like the Hitler Youth."[20]
William Lederer and Eugene Burdick's *The Ugly American* was published
along with a preface explaining that the book shows how foolish Americans
are; yet some readers concluded from the book that Americans are "kinder
than the Soviets."[21]

To writers, the problem of counterproductive effects was especially sensitive because, as we have seen, writers could be held responsible for what

[18] Zhao Dan, "Rigid Control Ruins Art and Literature," p. 109.
[19] Interview, Beijing, 3 August 1980. For publication data on "Hudie" (Butterfly), see
bibliography.
[20] Miriam London and Mu Yang-jen "What Are They Reading in China?"
[21] Ibid., p. 43.

their readers thought and did. Yet reader opinion remained, in fact, noto-riously beyond any writer's effective control. Even the reputations of writers themselves could be read upside-down by readers. For example, the Party's use of quotations from Lu Xun to attack intellectuals during the Cultural Revolution produced the unforseen effect of tarnishing the memory of Lu Xun.[22] And if reputations could be tarnished by mistake, so could they be enhanced inadvertently. Nothing contributed more to the stature of Bai Hua during the 1980s than the two Party campaigns against him. Without these campaigns, Bai's "Unrequited Love" would never have been viewed as a major statement of Chinese humanism.[23]

Still, although it may have been impossible to use literature to get readers to adopt specific views on certain topics, there was a "soft" version of the "engineering of souls" theory, which claimed only that politically and morally correct literature would lead, in general, to better attitudes among readers. Party theorists retreat to this softer claim when confronted with examples of counterproductivity and writers and scholars also took it more seriously than its "hard" counterpart.[24]

There seemed to be evidence on both sides of the soft theory. Social surveys showed that, on the whole, positive role models were influential among high school and college students. In 1984, 80 percent of university students in a national survey said they "held in mind" someone whom they "revered."[25] A similar survey of high school students showed that, at least sometimes, "correct" attitudes were indeed inferred from literary examples.[26] In 1980, a high school teacher wrote to the Shanghai *Wenhuibao* favoring the continued importation of foreign films, which were explosively popular at the time, but warning, with examples, that his students do indeed some-times naively imitate whatever they see.[27]

But there remained, for other people, substantial doubt that even the soft version of the engineering of souls had very much to it. Not all viewers of murder mysteries commit murder, they held, and when murders do happen there are probably much stronger forces at work than the literary. In a 1981

[22] The Maoist slogan, "Learn from Lu Xun's spirit of beating dogs that have already fallen into the water," for example, had this effect.

[23] This kind of "favorable backlash" is also notable in the quasi freedom of the Soviet Union after Stalin; when Khrushchev unleashed vulgarities at young artists in Moscow in 1962, his words catapulted them from relative obscurity to a celebrity that brought crowds to their exhibit for days. Johnson, *Khrushchev and the Arts*, pp. 21, 101–5.

[24] The army writer Liu Baiyu argued that good effects would follow naturally, provided an author's basic "moral character" is good (interview, Beijing, 11 August 1980). Hu Yaobang, "Guanyu dangqian wenyi gongzuo yixie wenti de jianghua."

[25] Xu Qing, "Daxuesheng bangyang wenti diaocha," p. 48.

[26] More than 90 percent of high school students in one survey took away the "correct" lesson about patriotism from the example of Xu Lingjun in Zhang Xianliang's "Ling yu rou" (Spirit and flesh), later made into a film called *Mumaren* (The herdsman). See Liu Qingren et al., "Guanyu zhongxuesheng sixiang zhuangkuang de diaocha," p. 11.

[27] Hang Zhizhong, "Guanyu zenyang zhidao zhongxuesheng guankan waiguo dianying de tongxin."

speech, Liu Binyan recalled that "I, too, read some bad books when I was young. They were poor editions; you'd have to call them very 'unhealthful' books. I began [reading them] when I was twelve, but that didn't keep me from becoming a revolutionary."[28] Li Yi, editor of *The Seventies* magazine in Hong Kong, noted in 1980 that Tokyo bookstores and cinemas were awash in crime fiction, and yet Tokyo also had perhaps the lowest crime rate of any of the great modern cities of the world.[29]

In short, the minds of readers could be as complex and beyond "engineering" as those of writers. But even setting these two problems aside, there was the problem of what lay between writer and reader: the literary medium itself. By its nature, literary expression thrives on ambiguity and, in the context of socialist China, ambiguity had more than purely literary uses.

Can Ambiguities Be Controlled?

Chinese expression of political dissent through the use of ambiguity or indirection ("pointing at the mulberry tree to criticize the locust tree") was used extensively by seventeenth-century Ming loyalists, including painters as well as writers, and had been an established tradition even before then. When Deng Tuo and Wu Han used this method to criticize Mao Zedong in the 1960s (see chapter 3), the gentleness of their protests combined with the severity of their punishments made it seem that their thinking was fairly simple and straightforward. The many stories from the Mao era about people who were punished for inadvertently tearing or marking a photo of Mao, or a piece of paper that bore his name, can also make it seem that deviousness lay only in the imagination of a paranoid regime. The regime was indeed paranoid and did accuse many innocent people; but veiled expression of dissent was also at play in nearly every season, and was sometimes remarkably subtle.

An example of the subtlety can be seen in the experience of Li Jian, the young man whose article "'Praise' and 'Shame'" was used by the Party in June 1979 to quell a rising tide of scar fiction (see chapter 1). Li's article created deep resentment in intellectual circles, and in late summer of 1980, when the winds of cultural policy shifted in favor of openness, writers and critics were quick to attack him. Chastened, Li himself turned in 1980 and 1981 to writing lurid "exposure" stories about oppression, corruption, and sexual excess. These stories became targets in the Party's campaigns against "bourgeois liberalism" in 1981 and 1983, which meant that Li Jian was now vulnerable to attack from the conservative side, which in 1979 had supported him. But—and here we can see how subtle matters could get— some of the sharpest criticisms in this second round against Li Jian came not from true conservatives but from liberals. While ostensibly attacking

---

[28] Liu Binyan, "Tan xin shiqi de wenxue chuangzuo wenti," p. 10.
[29] Li Yi, "Zhongguo xin xieshizhuyi wenyi de xingqi," p. 26.

Li's excessive "exposure" stories, liberals could enjoy the satisfaction of denouncing someone who, in their own community, was still a symbol of
repression. Conservatives could not object to the attacks because, superficially, they defended the conservative position. For liberals the opportunity was especially valuable because it allowed an outlet for protest precisely during a season of increasing repression.

The use of double meanings was by no means restricted to arcane intellectual debate. It permeated literary culture and appeared even in popular
and ephemeral publications. In 1979, the Beijing tabloid *Dandelions* carried
a story about a young man with a "bad class background." The label ostensibly implied that he should be viewed negatively, but other characterizations of him used ambiguity to approve some of the values of a countercul-
ture that was rising among Beijing youth at the time. The young man's
"personal traits were not all that bad," the narrator confided. "In addition to
his gentle and honest nature, he had good looks, especially when his jet-
black hair grew somewhat longer and two ebony sideburns hung down past
his ears on both sides of his pure white face."[30]

Writers often played both sides of an ambiguity, using a single theme
both to advance an idea that the regime favored and to open a door to
popular messages or to advocacies of their own. Zong Fuxian's 1978 play
From the Silent Zones (see chapter 3) announced the top leadership's decision
to "reverse the verdict" on the 1976 demonstrations at Tiananmen, but also
served, from a popular viewpoint, as a protest against political repression
generally. When Chen Rong published her story "At Middle Age," she
knew that she was helping to introduce a new Party policy of giving better
treatment to middle-aged intellectuals who had been loyal to the regime,
but the story she wrote was a complex work that raised questions about the
whole meaning and fate of the revolution. The leadership's decision, noted
above, to use literature in an approach to "recovering" Taiwan also led to
much more than what the leadership originally had in mind. In the late
1970s, the allure of Taiwan to young Chinese had nothing to do with winning the island over to the "superiority of socialism" and everything to do
with the island's wealth, its freedoms, and the alternate mode of Chinese
modernity that it exemplified. In the 1980s, several "Taiwan writers," including Eileen Chang (although she lived in Los Angeles at the time) and
the popular writers Qiong Yao and San Mao, won large and devoted followings in mainland cities.

Sometimes literary ambiguity exceeded even what writers themselves had
in mind. Readers and audiences found their own messages independently of
any that were intended. Cao Yu's play *Wang Zhaojun*, as we have seen in
chapter 3, was meant to show that China's minority nationalities are just as
respectable as the Han people, so that marriage of a Han to a non-Han is
actually quite normal and fine; but some young people in Beijing took the

[30] Liang Deming, "Zhongsheng dashi."

play to mean that the Party could no longer object to marriages between Chinese and Westerners.[31] In 1980, the year the play was produced, such marriages were rare and required special permission.

The creativity of readers and audiences in adapting literature to their own uses was always present, even during the high tide of Maoism when literary texts seemed like shining steel that one could not possibly misinterpret. Stories about the fearless and selfless soldier Lei Feng seemed to describe a model so perfect as to be impervious to manipulation. In daily life, however, readers discovered a new use for Lei Feng. In more than one location in China, there were reports of "Lei Feng diaries" in which young people recorded their own "secret" sacrifices and noble thoughts, only to "lose" the diaries in public places in the hope that someone might discover their virtue and reward it.

In the post-Mao years, reformers began to reconsider whether, and how reliably, literature could be used to mold "correct" thinking and behavior after all.

RETREAT FROM ENGINEERING

The new debates were grounded in an appreciation of the complexity of the reading process. Revisionist voices pointed out that the best literary works before the communist period had no simple or reliable relation with speci-fiable reader response. In 1980, a critic in Guangzhou named Zhang Aolie recalled Lu Xun's comment that when they read *Dream of the Red Chamber*, "classicists see *The Book of Changes*, Daoists see pornography, romantics see pathos, revolutionaries see anti-Manchu spirit, and rumor-mongers see a trove of secrets." It is obvious, Zhang argued, that a single work can have many different "social effects."[32] Others argued that the "depressing endings of stories such as Lu Xun's "The New Year's Sacrifice" (1923) and Ba Jin's *Family* (1931) clearly had not depressed young readers of the time, but had had the opposite effect of spurring them toward social action.[33] Meng Wei-zai, a commentator for *Guangming Daily*, the central newspaper for intellec-tuals, made the flat claim that human behavior has so many causes that to expect writers to "engineer the soul" or to write "textbooks on how to live" is simply unrealistic.[34]

In 1992, Zhou Yang, whose career over five decades had been devoted to the project of using literature to mold reader attitudes, concluded that one assumption that had underlain his life's work—the assumption that popular preferences in literature and art themselves are malleable—could not be supported. As we have noted in chapter 5, Zhou was surprised to see how

[31] Interview with Wu Xiaoling, 11 July 1980.
[32] Zhang Aolie, "'Shehui xiaoguo' xiaoyi."
[33] See Li Yi, "Zhongguo xin xieshizhuyi wenyi de xingqi," p. 26.
[34] Meng Weizai, "Guanyu 'linghun de gongchengshi' he 'shenghuo de jiaokeshu' de lijie."

quickly village opera and other popular cultural forms sprang back to life after the lifting of Maoist bans in the late 1970s. "We can change governments," Zhou said, "but can we change literature and art overnight? . . . The answer is no."[35] Reform of cultural *policy* is quite possible, Zhou concluded, but reform of culture itself is another matter. Wang Ruowang and others took the radical position that a writer's duty is to tell the truth and nothing more, that no writer should have to think about reader response at all, and that no political authority should hold a writer accountable for adopting such an approach.[36]

These conclusions are broadly parallel to those that Soviet and Eastern European writers reached in their own experience with communist literary policy, although Chinese writers did not denounce cultural engineering in as fundamental a way as their European counterparts have. In *Doctor Zhivago* (1957), Boris Pasternak voiced a scathing view of Soviet "engineering":

> Reshaping life! People who can say that may have lived through a lot, but have never understood a thing about life—they have never felt its breath, its soul . . . they look on it as a lump of coarse raw material that needs to be processed by them, to be ennobled by their touch. But life is never a material, a substance . . . it is constantly renewing and remaking and changing and transfiguring itself. It is infinitely beyond your or my obtuse theories.[37]

Vaclav Havel, looking back in 1995 at the communist period in Czechoslovakia, concluded that "life, with its unfathomable diversity and unpredictability, would not be squeezed into the crude Marxist cage." While continuing to endorse the idea that writers should seek to improve society, Havel recommended a careful, almost reverent, approach to the immensely intricate world: "I believe . . . that neither politicians, nor scientists, nor entrepreneurs, nor anyone else should fall for the vain belief that they can grasp the world as a whole and change it as a whole by a single action. Seeking to improve it, people should proceed with the utmost caution and sensitivity, step by step, always paying attention to what each change actually brings about."[38] The 1980s in China were years when most of the writers, editors, and literary officials who had grown up with "engineering" moved in the direction of Havel's view, although only a few reached the same kind of

[35] "Zhou Yang Addresses Guangdong Writers Forum," *Dagongbao* (Hong Kong), 9 February 1982, translated in Foreign Broadcast Information Service, China Report, W3–6 (10 February 1982), p. W6.

[36] Interview, 17 June 1980, Shanghai. Wang used the example of Liu Xinwu's "Wake Up, Little Brother!" to say that no one can determine whether the story's young hooligan inspired more imitation or revulsion; the fact that hooligans do exist in society is enough to justify the writer's depiction. At a deeper level, however, Wang was clearly not so neutral about the social responsibility of writers. He felt that to be truly socially responsible, writers had to be able to criticize and oppose the Party; his argument that writers should be able to ignore the Party's demands about "social effects" was at bottom a tactical position.

[37] Quoted in George Gibian, *Interval of Freedom*, p. 149.

[38] Vaclav Havel, "The Responsibility of Intellectuals," p. 36.

reverence for complexity. A younger generation—Can Xue, Han Shaogong, Yu Hua, Su Tong, and others—broke radically with the whole idea of wreaking "social effects" and other aspects of the socialist literary system.

As the engineering system declined during the 1980s, the top leadership sought to adapt itself to more flexibility but still maintain control over key political matters. The result was a contradictory stance that could look considerably different at the public and internal (classified) levels. In 1985, Party Chairman Hu Yaobang gave a public speech that seemed to limit "engineering" to a minimal role:

> Party writers will display Party spirit in their writings . . . [and] will express the voice of the Party in their works, but the Party should at no time stipulate what this or that writer should write about. . . . Writers must to a great extent bring into play their individual creativity, perception, and imagination [and] must have complete freedom in expressing their own thoughts. . . . In this way they can write works that are influential and truly play an educational role.[39]

But less than two months later, in a classified speech to Party officials, Hu put more emphasis on "engineering":

> Regardless of whether we are speaking of ideology, morality, personal tastes and interests, or anything else, we have to bring analysis and guidance to the matter; we can't just let things go, to develop naturally as they will, but must add the element of the Party's leadership and make sure that this element functions powerfully, spreads, and exerts subtle and steady influence.[40]

The two countervailing emphases were to some extent known to writers, who were expected to find their own ways between them. This was (as we have seen in chapter 2) one way in which the Party induced self-censorship in writers and editors.[41]

SECONDARY USES OF ENGINEERING

The "engineering of souls" was intended to happen in a certain direction: Party leaders conveyed values to writers, who then took responsibility to get them into the minds of readers. The conception of literature that this view implied, however, became so dominant that it carried over to application in several variant ways. Party leaders sometimes tried to engineer one another; they also frequently viewed writers more as targets than as partners in the engineering process. Writers, for their part, sometimes vicariously adopted

---

[39] Hu Yaobang, "Lun dang di xinwen gongzuo"; translation is from Womack, *Media and the Chinese Public*, p. 176.

[40] Hu Yaobang, "Guanyu dangqian wenyi gongzuo yixie wenti de jianghua," p. 5.

[41] In 1985, writers were to write "their own thoughts" but also serve "the Party's leadership." In his public speech, Hu Yaobang provided a rough guideline: writers should "give 80 percent of their space" to the brighter side of things. See "On the Party's Journalism Work" in Brantly Womack, ed., *Media and the Chinese Public*, p. 188.

the role of leader and directed their own engineering toward readers, toward other writers, and toward officials. In all these efforts, literature and literary criticism served as tools.

Use in Factional Struggle

The point of using literature in intra-Party struggle was, as in other political combat, the expansion of someone's personal power, but this fact could not be stated bluntly. For reasons of face, much of the struggle proceeded in code. Just as in conflicts between writers and the leadership, the issue was often cast as "correctness"—except that now, because the two sides were both leaders, it could seem more a contest of rival correctnesses. Here again the example of Deng Xiaoping's brief sponsorship of Democracy Wall and scar literature is relevant. With these moves, Deng was able to undercut the Maoist holdovers who were his rivals for the top leadership in the late 1970s. But the first examples of using literature in factional combat in socialist China came much earlier.

In the 1950s, literary codes used in initiating such combat were intelligible only to a small elite. Other readers noticed the strife only later, when the attacked side published a counterattack or when the counterattack was rebuffed. For example, Du Pengcheng's *Defending Yan'an*, published in 1954, was attacked thirteen years later, in 1967, for upholding Peng Dehuai, who had been purged for opposing Mao in 1959; Li Jiantong's *Liu Zhidan* was said to speak for the leadership faction of Gao Gang and Rao Shushi, who were purged as a "renegade clique" in 1955. The novel was suppressed in the early 1960s, "rehabilitated" in 1979, and finally published in 1984.[42] In 1973, Mao Zedong, fearful that Zhou Enlai's prestige rivaled his own, but unable to confront the politically punctilious Zhou, used a national press campaign to criticize "Confucius"; two years later, Zhou and Deng Xiaoping were targeted in code as modern versions of "traitorous" Song Jiang, the rebel hero in the classic tale *Water Margin* who eventually joined with the emperor to suppress other rebellions.[43]

Use in Broaching New Policy

Factional jockeying could produce new policies, and these, too, were sometimes first broached indirectly and gently as literature or as literary criticism. The advantages of this method were that it avoided the shock of a

[42] *Renmin ribao*, 12 November 1967, p. 6; *Wenyibao* 1979.1.6. To what extent these novels really did advocate factional positions and to what extent they were merely accused of doing so by the side that perceived itself to be under attack is a question that would require further research.

[43] For discussion, see Merle Goldman, *China's Intellectuals*, pp. 166–76 and 201–13. "Shuihuzhuan," commonly translated as *Water Margin*, arose from popular oral tales of a twelfth-century rebellion. It is translated by Pearl S. Buck as *All Men Are Brothers* (New York: John Day, 1933).

sudden switch, which in turn had costs to the Party's prestige, and that it allowed the Party rank-and-file time to discern the shift and change direction "voluntarily." Examples we have seen above include the publication in China of Svetlana Stalin's memoirs, which signaled a coming deemphasis of Stalin, and by implication of Mao; the touting of a play about the 1976 Tiananmen demonstration, which heralded a political "reevaluation" of that event; and a story about overworked intellectuals, which paved the way for a change in policy toward the housing and salaries of intellectuals.[44]

During the major transition between the Mao and the Deng eras, the Party used pronouncements on literature to open and to recast large areas of intellectual turf not only in literature but in history, politics, and several other areas. When Deng Xiaoping announced his approval of "emancipation of thought" at the crucial Third Plenum in December 1978, many people were excited but few had any firm idea of exactly which doors were now open and which still closed. Ten months later, at a national convention of literature and art workers, many of the answers came in the form of a rambling speech by Zhou Yang, one of the Party's most senior and seasoned literary officials. Zhou reviewed twentieth-century Chinese literary history in what would seem to an outsider a plodding and unoriginal manner. But to readers of signals, including the bulk of the Chinese intellectual community, Zhou's report rewarded minute study. His comments on which were the "good works" of modern Chinese literature, as well as his "opinions" on long-standing literary controversies, held the keys to understanding what people, topics, and ideas were now open for public discussion.

Reading Zhou's speech for shifts in literary-political "wind direction" is a small part of the large topic, which we have examined in chapter 2 and will not repeat here, of how the Party used literary comment to control intellectuals. But we can note, in addition, that the leadership's pervasive use of literature for engineering purposes defined an attitude toward literature that eventually affected writers themselves, some of whom began to see themselves vicariously as stewards in charge of major societal trends.

Writers and Critics as "Engineers"

During the Deng years, from 1977 until the mid-1980s, successive phases of literary development were known as "thaw literature," "scar literature," "introspective literature," and "root-seeking literature." Writers and readers readily identified with these labels and assumed that the course of Chinese literature as a whole tended to veer one way or another from time to time. In Party jargon, popular thinking was said to have particular "tendencies" at any given moment. These tendencies, which also could be encapsulated in catchwords, were not entirely autonomous but could be "guided" by the intervention of literary theorists and critics. A writer, editor, or scholar

---

[44] See pp. 158 and 185, above.

could advance an idea, give it an appropriate label, point to some literary examples, and then watch for a "tendency" to develop. For example, in 1980 Li Yi defended his use of the label "new realism" by explaining that "On the China mainland we haven't yet seen anything that calls itself 'new realism.' But beginning last year . . . we have seen the return of 'intervening in life' and 'exposure of the dark side,' which can perhaps be viewed as examples of path-breaking literary theory."[45] Around the same time, Huang Weizong, a professor of Chinese at Zhongshan University in Guangzhou, wrote a series of articles advocating the carefully fashioned label "socialist critical realist literature," which he defined as literature that "exposes the dark side" of society and hence is "critical," but does not challenge the political order, and hence is "socialist."[46] In advancing his catchword, Huang was not just describing a trend but advocating it as well, hoping to clear a theoretical path for it. In the nonsocialist world a professor who sought to affect the entire course of a nation's popular thought by writing a prescriptive article on literature might seem amusing. But in China, Huang's initiative, although it did not get far, was treated seriously. Some writers supported it, high officials in Beijing worried over it, and Feng Mu, a deputy director of the Writers' Association and editor at the *Literary Gazette*, published a lengthy rebuttal to quash it.[47]

Readers as "Engineers"

The idea of social engineering was sufficiently pervasive that even readers could see themselves as the engineers. Socialist-realist works that reflected contemporary social movements in the 1950s and 1960s, such as Liu Qing's *The Builders*[48] and Hao Ran's *Bright Sunny Days*[49] used idealism and model behavior to show how agricultural collectivization and other social change was supposed to happen. When readers identified with the heroes in these stories, a vicarious shift in standpoint led them to see things from a leader's perspective. They temporarily were no longer the little people behaving dutifully toward the leadership, but themselves agents of the leadership whose duty it was to spread correct attitudes and behavior to the "masses" below. Fictional heroes, with their model characteristics, were one guide to how to behave in this enterprise. The trend reached an extreme in the late 1960s, when groups of Red Guards saw themselves as surrogates of Mao in the exalted project of annihilating classes and class consciousness among everyone else. In these extreme applications, the distinction between social life and literary creation could blur or even disappear. Sister Jiang was an

---

[45] Li Yi, "Zhongguo xinxieshizhuyi wenyi de xingqi," p. 22.

[46] Huang Weizong, "Shehuizhuyi pipan xianshizhuyi" (conference paper); published in revised form as "Tichang shehuizhuyi wenyi chuangzuo fangfa de duoyanghua."

[47] Feng Mu, "Jianchi geming de xianshizhuyi."

[48] Liu Qing, *Chuangyeshi*.

[49] Hao Ran, *Yanyangtian*.

historical character in the 1940s, a famous fictional character in the early 1960s, and virtually a resurrected living participant in the struggles of the late 1960s. The same progression marked the case of Lei Feng, whose apotheosis eventually grew so powerful that it dwarfed both the original facts and the original fiction about him.

But these large, politically colored "tendencies" were not the only currents in the literature of socialist China, and "engineering," although dominant, was by no means literature's only use.

THE VARIETY OF OTHER USES

Here I sketch some of the other, primarily unofficial, uses to which literature in socialist China was put. The categories are analytical, not taxonomic; any given literary work could be used in a variety of the following ways.

Entertainment

Routines and limited horizons were common features of daily life for most people in most parts of socialist China, less because of socialist cultural policies than because China remained, for the most part, a preindustrial society. During a century when people in the most modernized societies began to suffer from a surfeit of stimulation, people in most parts of China continued to have the opposite, age-old problem of an undersupply of diversion. Zoos and museums were limited to the major cities, and cost money to visit. Parks were free, but not especially diverting unless one brought along one's own chessboard, bird, lover, conversation partner, or other amusement. The playing of sports was limited by the availability of equipment; a row of bricks across a cement slab could build a makeshift Ping-Pong table; badminton was more accessible than other sports because, cut to the bare essentials, it needs no court. For many people in towns and cities, a common recreational activity was simply to stroll the streets watching for something unusual—a new item in a store window, a street argument following a bicycle collision, or the like.

Traditional storytelling, village opera, comedians' dialogues, clappertales, juggling, and other popular arts remained available, but not as widely as before 1949, and not at all during times when the Party was busy attacking "feudalism." As we noted in chapter 4, "chatting" was a common diversion and sometimes an admired skill, and an oral grapevine extended nationwide. Higher literacy rates and the spread of new media such as radio, television, and film in the socialist years sharply increased the possibilities for entertainment, but also presented the Communist Party with the question of how much entertainment to allow. Thresholds for entertainment were low: like a new item in a store window, a new film, television program, stage show, or novel might be diverting simply because it existed and because there was little else to compete with it for attention.

In the 1950s, there were internal debates in the Party over the proper relation between entertainment and didacticism: How much entertainment should be allowed? Do entertaining elements have to "enhance" a political or social message, or can they be separate from and "harmless to" the main point? Eventually, in a definitive speech in 1961, Zhou Enlai declared that the "educational role" and the "recreational role" of literature and art are "compatible."[50] Extremist thinking continued to differ, however, and a few years later, during the Cultural Revolution, the recreational role of published literature dwindled to practically nothing. Yet there may be a lesson about the ineradicability of the human thirst for diversion in the fact that, as we saw in chapter 5, it was also during the Cultural Revolution that "hand-copied volumes" containing the purest examples of entertainment fiction ever to emerge from socialist China were written and circulated underground. After the death of Mao, reformers uncovered and reprinted Zhou Enlai's 1961 speech, and the Party returned to qualified acceptance of literature's "recreational role." In 1983, a research group of the Beijing Journalism Association wrote that its radio series on fiction "enables the audience, while enjoying themselves, to receive moral and ideological lessons and to refine their character and taste."[51] By the early 1990s, when the socialist literary system had all but disappeared, entertainment, now on television as much as in the printed media, filled the void left by "engineering" and became the dominant function of published literature.

We have seen, in chapter 5, how film audiences in socialist China watched for every scrap of interesting material even if it might be only incidental to a film's story or theme: a southern audience gasps to learn that a farmer in the northeast can throw precious wood onto a fire; another audience oohs and aahs at the chance to see the inside of an official's fancy apartment; and so on. These responses illustrate the use of film and fiction not only as entertainment but as windows on parts of the world that one normally cannot see.

Learning about Other Parts of China

For all but a very few, travel in socialist China was not easy. It was expensive and required permission. Most people lived all or most of their lives within a few miles of where they were born. It is true that during the Cultural Revolution young Red Guards could ride the railroads free as they "established revolutionary ties" all across China; but the zest with which they seized this opportunity only underscores how unusual it was. To try to glimpse other parts of China through reading newspapers was unsatisfy-

[50] Zhou Enlai, "On Literature and Art," p. 13.
[51] Research Group, Beijing Journalism Association, "An Analysis of the Beijing Radio Audience," in Womack, ed., *Media and the Chinese Public*, p. 98.

ing; reports were superficial, gave only good news, and lacked human-interest detail.

But people remained curious, not only about other locations in China but about aspects of society that were administrative secrets. They passed around oral accounts of major events and famous people—how Lin Biao really died, what really happened during the Tangshan earthquake, how Deng Xiaoping got rid of Hua Guofeng, and so on. These stories, as we saw in chapter 4, sometimes found their way into written form, whether in hand-copied volumes, in materials published in Hong Kong or overseas and carried back into China, or, when political conditions permitted, in works of historical fiction or literary reportage that were published inside China. In addition to information, such stories offered readers a sense of release from captivity—from the humiliating status of "receiver of education"—that writing in the official press always implied. The teller or listener (writer or reader) of such stories enjoyed a position close to parity with the famous figures of whom the stories told.

Although many of the stories included exaggeration and embroidery, their appeal depended crucially on the implicit claim that they were basically true. True information was a precious commodity, and people sought it wherever they could; so long as a story was even possibly true, they preferred not to think that someone else had simply made it up. The extent to which readers would go in mining literary materials for nuggets of truth about their own society can be seen in the way Beijing intellectuals read Alexandre Dumas's *The Count of Monte Cristo* in the late 1970s. They knew the book was fiction, and that it was set in a time and place distant from China; and yet they thought it could shed important light on recent Chinese history, because they knew Jiang Qing had liked the book and had specially promoted its publication. Why had she done so? Clearly the novel held clues to the values and outlook of Jiang Qing.[52]

Informal versions of events were important (even if not wholly reliable) because of the narrowness of official versions of events, especially unfortunate events. News reports on strikes, demonstrations, risings, and repressions were classified, and reports on apolitical problems such as floods, earthquakes, or air crashes, although carried in the public media, only tantalized readers by omitting all but the most optimistic and sanitized of details. Oral "alleyway news" could fill some of the void immediately, but officially published accounts in the form of fiction or reportage were subject to long delays, often because writers and editors felt that time had to pass before they could dare to break official silence or contradict official accounts. The problem was especially severe during the Mao years.

For example, following the great earthquake at Tangshan in July 1976, news reports that appeared within days were vastly different from literary accounts that appeared after ten years. The quake measured 7.8 on the

[52] Interview with Wu Xiaoling, 28 October 1979.

Richter scale and struck in the middle of the night, destroying bridges, roads, and railroads. Rescue operations were difficult, and the government, citing self-sufficiency, declined offers of foreign help. Eventually about 242,000 people, or roughly a quarter of the city's population, perished, but the official media carried only brief stories stressing correct political attitudes toward rescue work. Three days after the quake, the *People's Daily* offered this description:

> The masses in the stricken areas . . . under the guidance of Chairman Mao's revolutionary line, and under the excellent conditions of having won great victories in the struggle to criticize Deng [Xiaoping] and to counterattack against the rightist move to reverse verdicts, are determined to press forward in the great revolutionary fearless spirit that humanity will certainly overcome nature, to unite as one, to go all out to make the country strong, and to seize victory in the antidisaster struggle.[53]

As anecdotes about what had really happened spread by word of mouth, some officials and journalists began collecting statistics and stories without publishing them. Mao Zedong died, Deng Xiaoping arose, and nearly ten years passed before anything of substance was put into print. Then, in March 1986, the monthly *Liberation Army Literature and Art* carried a work of reportage called "July 28: The Great Tangshan Earthquake" by Qian Gang.[54] Qian's piece reports not only on the earthquake's havoc but on the social decay—mainly looting, fraud, and prostitution—that followed in its wake. Qian cites official figures on the looting—how many wristwatches, items of clothing, kilograms of food, and so on, were stolen—and records episodes such as this one:

> The whole city was in a hysterical atmosphere. . . . An old woman was seen standing over the corpse of a young man, wailing, "My son, my son!" And then she took the watch from the dead man's wrist. Shortly afterward, she was found kneeling in front of another man's body, crying and saying the same thing as she took his watch. She did this in a dozen places before she was caught.[55]

The tremendous difference between Qian's account of the quake and the one that appeared in the *People's Daily* illustrates not only how much could be omitted from official reports. It also shows why those reports, instead of assuaging the public's curiosity, could actually stimulate and therefore increase it: a minimal sketch in rosified outline raised more questions than it answered. By stimulating popular demand for further information, one kind of writer could inadvertently create a literary opportunity for another. In

[53] "Zai qu renmin zai Mao zhuxi geming luxian zhidao xia fayang rendingshengtian de geming jingshen kangzhen jiuzai," *Renmin ribao*, 29 July 1976.
[54] Qian Gang, "Tangshan da dizhen."
[55] Translated by James Mann in "A New City Rises around Quake Ruins," *Los Angeles Times*, 24 May 1986, pp. 1, 26. I am grateful to Mann for pointing out Qian Gang's article.

other ways, though, the use of literature to achieve practical effects could be quite deliberate.

Achieving Practical Goals

For aspiring young writers, one use of literature was as a source of ideas. There are several kinds of evidence that such borrowing occurred. In interviews, young writers themselves acknowledged looking to published works not only as literary models but for information on what kinds of themes, characters, and writing techniques were currently contributing to the fame of other writers.[56] Librarians said that young borrowers visited libraries in search of ideas.[57] Literary editors noted—and sometimes complained—that the appearance of a successful work could elicit a tide of submissions of imitative works.[58]

If we extend the notion of the "uses" of literature to include pursuit of fame and fortune generally, then these uses, too, were abundant in socialist China, theoretical claims about "serving the people" notwithstanding. Yet such pursuits did have some distinctive forms in socialist China, as we have seen in chapter 3. The route to fame by performing as a "ground-breaking hero," for example, had parallels in other repressive societies but was an unusually subtle matter in the Chinese case because the Chinese censorial system relied so heavily on psychological pressure and self-censorship. Chinese writers' practices of satirizing one another through literary innuendo and in stories à clef also set them somewhat apart from norms elsewhere.

Readers as well as writers found practical uses for literature. The account by Qian Gang, just noted, of a woman's method of stealing wristwatches after an earthquake raises the question of how often readers turned to literature not just to learn about the world but to figure out specifically how to get by in it. As we saw in chapter 1, Party leaders occasionally criticized literary works as "textbooks for crime," arguing that young people imitate examples of bad behavior. In this view, Qian Gang's passage might teach readers how to steal during disasters—or, more broadly, that it is all right to think selfishly at such times rather than acting more responsibly.

Other, less sinister practical uses of reading were holdovers of the newspaper tradition that had arisen in Shanghai and other cities beginning in the late nineteenth century, when newspapers began regularly to offer readers advice about modern life and know-how, ranging from how a modern bank works to the proper use of an electric water heater or a new toothpowder.

---

[56] Interviews with Lu Xinhua, Los Angeles, 22 January 1987; with Wang Yaping, Los Angeles, 13 May 1981; and with Sun Xiaolan (a former editor at *Shanghai Literature*), Los Angeles, 6 February 1987.

[57] Interview at Shanghai Municipal Library, 13 June 80.

[58] Interview at the editorial boards of Zhongguo qingnian chubanshe, Beijing, 8 October 1979, where the example of *The Second Handshake* was cited; and of *Zuopin* (Guangzhou, 4 March 1980), where "What Should I Do?!" was the example.

This use of the press continued through mid-century and disappeared only during the Cultural Revolution, but returned in the Deng era. For example in the late 1970s, in the area around Chongqing in Sichuan, tales arose on the oral grapevine about a master teacher who had wonderful methods of annihilating rats. After the stories were gathered and published in the magazine *Story Collections*, interest in his methods spread nationwide. He began to receive invitations to lecture.[59]

Beyond the learning of such very concrete techniques lay the more amorphous but also more significant area of learning appropriate social behavior. Here, of course, the Party's engineering played a role, but certainly not the only one. Especially during the 1950s and early 1960s, large numbers of young readers did indeed take the heroes and heroines of socialist realist fiction as paragons of selflessness and courage, but to admire these people was one thing and to imitate them was quite another. They remained distant, somewhat ethereal ideals, but not very useful in getting a person through daily life, where mastery of certain mundane kinds of self-defense and social conformity were the more immediate problems.

The political campaigns of the Mao period forced people to attend with special care to how they appeared before others. Personal behavior is molded partly by social context in any society, but in Mao's China both the degree of required conformity and the punishments for aberration increased to a point where people had no choice but to work on new ways to present themselves. Characters in literature and film became important reference materials. One did not need to match the inner saintliness of heroes in order to simulate their speech and other outward appearances. People built their skills, in the metaphor of Zhang Xianliang, into a layer of armor that they put on before venturing into public: "When people get up in the morning, they put on their underwear, then their clothes, then a padded coat, and finally they wrap themselves up in an invisible suit of armor before going out. Everybody's huddled inside their own suit of armor, so even though there might be a lot of people working in a company, they never really get to know one another."[60] What appeared on a person's outside was his or her *biaoxian* or "showing." In *biaoxian* there is a suggestion of "acting," of taking life as political theater, and literature became one of the places from which one could learn role-playing. Although the notion of playing roles properly is ancient in Confucian culture, the rigidity and acute defensiveness of the Mao period has much stronger affinities with modern communist societies. Czelaw Milosz writes similarly of "acting" in communist Poland:

> one does not perform on a theater stage but in the street, office, factory, meeting hall, or even the room one lives in. Such acting is a highly developed craft that puts a premium on mental alertness. Before it leaves the lips, every word must be

---

[59] "'Gushihui' zai ge di nongcun da shou huanying," *Wenhuibao*, 13 July 1980, p. 1.

[60] Zhang Xianliang, "Xiaoerbulake," pp. 345–46; translation by Rui An in Zhang Xianliang, *Mimosa and Other Stories*, p. 199.

evaluated as to its consequences. A smile that appears at the wrong moment, a glance that is not all it should be can occasion dangerous suspicions and accusations ... everyone plays to everyone else, and everyone is fully aware that this is so.[61]

Milosz goes on to describe how role-playing, over a long period of time, can erode the identity of the person who plays the role, until only the role seems to be left:

> After long acquaintance with his role, a man grows into it so closely that he can no longer differentiate his true self from the self he simulates, so that even the most intimate of individuals speak to each other in Party slogans. To identify oneself with the role one is obliged to play brings relief and permits a relaxation of one's vigilance. Proper reflexes at the proper moment become truly automatic.[62]

Although the same kind of "automatic" behavior was evident in China, Chinese writers on the whole did not probe its anatomy as Milosz does, nor did they often write sympathetically about those who had collapsed into that state. In China, it was more common to portray dissimulation and hypocrisy—conditions, in other words, of people who have not lost their inner selves entirely but who are split between inner and outer layers and who develop patterns that straddle the two. In describing country folk in Hunan during the Cultural Revolution, for example, the novelist Gu Hua writes:

> For years they had trained themselves to be two-faced, trained themselves in double-talk. . . . In the daytime they wept, hung their heads, confessed their crimes; at night in the adobe cadre school, they cursed Wu Zetian and the Empress Dowager [surrogates for Mao's wife Jiang Qing] and the swine in the Cultural Revolution Group. By day, they attended classes to "struggle against the self and combat revisionism," then they smuggled home plexiglass and imported stainless steel to make a table-lamp or four-poster double bed. During meetings they contrasted past bitterness with present joys; but once home they griped because the commune's co-op had no kerosene, or even candles. They passed the day drinking tea, smoking, reading the newspaper and stressing the long-term importance of suppressing revisionism; the evenings, however, were spent jockeying for promotion or finding jobs for their relatives or places in the army or in college for their children.[63]

The phrase "reading the newspaper" in this passage does not refer, as might first appear, to a leisure activity parallel to "drinking tea" and "smoking"; Cultural Revolution newspapers did not carry recreational items. The phrase fits better with the one that follows, referring to the suppression of revisionism. Reading the press was a serious matter; it was a guide to the highest-level political winds, which were, ultimately, the reasons why all of language and

[61] Czeslaw Milosz, *The Captive Mind*, pp. 54–55.
[62] Ibid., p. 55.
[63] Gu Hua, "Futuling"; translation by Gladys Yang in *Pagoda Ridge*, pp. 131–32.

life were bifurcated. With the opening of the Deng era, reading became useful for a wider variety of purposes.

Learning about the Outside World

Socialist China was cut off from most of the outside world for the three decades from the 1950s through the 1970s. Hence it is not surprising that readers had a special interest in using literature to glean what they could about foreign lands. To some extent, their interest was just the natural curiosity that one feels about any unknown place, but, more important, the urge to look outside China sprang from the need for a standard against which to measure what was happening (or not happening) inside. Was the Great Leap Forward really bringing China past England? Was the rest of the world doing better or worse than China? In answering these questions, Chinese people naturally wished to compare themselves with the countries they took to be at the forefront, and therefore looked primarily, and perhaps inordinately, at the United States and Western Europe. Despite government rhetoric about "third-world solidarity," there was very little interest in Africa, Latin America, or the poorer parts of Asia.[64]

During most of the 1950s, interest in the outside world did not grow especially strong; China had not been cut off for very long, and many people were preoccupied with the country's own revolutionary experiments. By the late 1960s, however, a new curiosity about developments in the West was evident in literary activity both underground (that is, in hand-copied volumes, a surprising number of which were set in foreign lands) and "overhead" (in the classified "internal" publication of books on famous Westerners such as Winston Churchill, Richard Nixon, Henry Kissinger, and others). While Mao was alive it remained impossible to explore the West in the regular, above-ground press. In 1978 and 1979, however, sixteen Western classics were reprinted for public sale, a few recent American and European films were imported and shown openly, and publishing houses competed to identify themselves as "windows to the West."[65]

Depictions of life in the West could be highly fanciful, from the dreamlike mansion in the American south in *The Second Handshake*, to the abuse of young women on a forced-labor farm in the film *Nightmare in Badham County*, to the derring-do of Zorro. But accuracy was not a primary concern for a readership and audience whose consuming interest was to imagine and to "feel" ways of life that could offer diversion from their own environments. Although the prospect of actually traveling to the West was usually far beyond hope (as a number of stories about jockeying for precious spots

---

[64] Elite intellectuals did notice and admire Gabriel Garcia Marquez, but perhaps less for his Mexican context or Colombian roots than because of his European accolade, the Nobel Prize.

[65] On the sixteen Western classics, see the Introduction; on American films, chapter 4. The competition to be "windows to the West" is from interviews with editors of *Zuopin* and *Huacheng*, Guangzhou 4 March 1980, and *Guangdong wenyi*, 7 March 1980.

on overseas delegations made clear), a vicarious journey through fiction or film could hold great attraction.[66]

Although the novelty of the imaginary excursion seemed to wear off during the 1980s, a larger role for the imagined West continued through the end of the decade. The West was an idealized "other," a place that seemed to offer not only contrasts with China but remedies to be borrowed for whatever was wrong.[67] (Here we should note the quite reciprocal manner in which an idealized China has filled the needs of Westerners, from Sinophiles Montesqieu and Voltaire in the eighteenth century through radical Maoists in the twentieth.) Su Xiaokang and Wang Luxiang's television series *River Elegy* (1988), which contrasted Chinese "Yellow River civilization" (land-based, inward-looking, hidebound, authoritarian) with Western "Azure Ocean civilization" (seafaring, open, free, democratic), drew its distinctions too simply, but for that very reason fit well into the patterns in which millions of viewers wanted to interpret their world.[68] In the same way that reading about China was useful not only for information or diversion but as a way to learn how to behave, learning about the West also had practical relevance that could reach fairly deeply into daily life.

Negotiating the West

In deciding to face toward the West in the 1980s, socialist China revisited a problem that had been around for about a century: the absorption of Western ways seemed inevitably to diminish Chineseness. The problem of an eroding cultural identity was painful not only as a matter of national pride but because it raised practical problems in the conduct of daily life. Western values seemed to—and in fact often did—upset accustomed ways of doing things, and left people insecure about how to behave.

The problem began in the nineteenth century, when the Industrial Revolution arrived in China in the rude form of British gunboats defending an opium trade. China had little choice but to embark upon the long journey of having to learn from the same Western societies that seemed to be, and sometimes were, bullying it. The mix of excitement and humiliation that this process engendered is richly evident in literary materials, both popular and elite, at nearly every phase of Chinese history since. As we noted in chapter 5, the popular fiction of the early twentieth century offered readers ways of testing the "new style" (for example by imagining an exciting relationship with a Westernized girlfriend) while still extending the assurance

---

[66] A fairly realistic account of backstage jockeying appears in Jiang Zilong's "Jinnian diqi hao taifeng." A more romantic portrayal is in the film *Ruyan fei* (Young swallow flies), Xi'an zhipianchang, 1979.

[67] On the West as idealized "other," and for a needed corrective to global interpretations of Edward Said's *Orientalism*, see Chen Xiaomei, *Occidentalism*.

[68] Su Xiaokang and Wang Luxiang, *Heshang*. See also Xiaomei Chen, *Occidentalism*, pp. 27–48.

that the old style was there to be relied upon (by, for example, positing a classically "Chinese" girlfriend whom one could marry in the end).

China's inward turn during the 1950s brought a temporary halt to literary exploration of Western ways. But later, as the topic of the West reappeared, the use of literature for experimentation also returned. The hand-copied volumes of the Cultural Revolution years revived the formula of a romantic triangle that offered Westernized and un-Westernized love partners as metaphors for two possible modes of Chinese life.[69] During the post-Mao years, when the problem of the West returned to above-ground Chinese writing, the problems of cultural Westernization returned in a rich variety of ways.[70]

Stories like Zhang Xianliang's "Spirit and Flesh" (later made into the film called *The Herdsman*) drew a stark contrast between materially backward but spiritually advanced life in rural China and materially advanced but spiritually adrift life in urban, Westernized China. The story is not very subtle, but its very lack of complexity made it useful in the symbolic statement of a deep cultural dilemma. The question of which way a person should go is posed sharply when the hero must decide whether to remain a simple herdsman with his small family or to move to Los Angeles or Hong Kong to inherit the glittering financial empire of his long-lost millionaire father. His decision to stay in China seems a satisfying vote for honesty, purity, and rooted Chineseness, and against superficiality, moral squalor, and rootlessness.

But in other works, the balance tips the other way; and in yet others, compromise is sought. The *River Elegy* series, as we have noted, promotes the Western cultural alternative about as one-sidedly as "Spirit and Flesh" recommends the Chinese side. Moreover, in nearly all works at all times, the allure of one feature associated with the West—technological modernization—remains fairly constant. Paeans to Deng's "Four Modernizations" as well as to Mao's "Great Leap Forward" find nothing but good in technology and no incompatibility between technology and Chineseness. And the benign view of technology is the same underground: the detectives in hand-copied stories always can rely on wonderful electronic gadgets.

In some works, the moral purity of the "Chinese" side of the cultural dilemma is called into question. Bai Hua's "Unrequited Love," for example, shows an overseas Chinese who returns to help the motherland and instead is persecuted. Gu Hua's "The Log Cabin Overgrown with Creepers" symbolically portrays China as a tradition-bound place (metaphorically choked by creeping vines), both isolated and arrogantly disdainful of interference from the outside.[71]

Ambivalence and compromise are evident in stories by Wang Meng such as "Bolshevik Salute," "Eye of the Night," and "Butterfly," in which pro-

---

[69] *The Second Handshake* and "Eternal Regrets in Love," discussed in chapters 4 and 5, are examples.

[70] I have written about the dilemma between Western and Chinese values in post-Mao stories in "'Tu' yu 'yang': shi xi si pian dangdai Zhongguo xiaoshuoli de yige changjian de zhuti."

[71] "Paman qingteng de muwu."

tagonists negotiate a middle ground between a rural, un-Westernized China and an urban, partly Westernized one. Wang's characters are not just caught between the two but inextricably tied to both; they feel not only pulled in different directions but confused about where they stand. The sense of dilemma is simpler but clearer in Chen Rong's "At Middle Age," where one of the major characters decides, after long and careful consideration, to move to Canada, where material life is obviously better but the connection to China will be greatly weakened. Although she lacks the moral heroism of her classmate who decides to stay in China, her decision to emigrate also seems understandable.

A 1980 story called "Nest Egg," by Wang Zhecheng and Wen Xiaoyu, a husband-and-wife team, explores the issues of dilemma and compromise especially vividly.[72] Inverting the love triangle often found in popular fiction, the authors describe a young woman in the 1950s choosing between two young men, both university students of Chinese literature. One is handsome, suave, popular, and has relatives in Indonesia who can help him emigrate from China. The other, his friend and classmate, is a shy, awkward bookworm, but solid in his knowledge of classical Chinese poetry and the "true spirit" of Chinese culture. The girl is outgoing and popular like the suave boy, but has unexpected depth of character. She turns down his offer of marriage and emigration and rather abruptly declares her love for the bookworm, quite to his surprise. Eventually they marry and have two boys. He becomes a professor.

Meanwhile the suave student goes from Indonesia to America, where he, too, becomes a professor but remains single. Two decades later he returns to China wearing fancy ties and cufflinks and sincerely wishing to look up his old friends. They, in turn, want to be good hosts but are mortified at the thought of entertaining a foreign visitor in their plain and tiny apartment. Their one resource is a nest egg that they were saving in order to buy a television set for their little boys. After some soul-searching, the parents resolve to spend all the money on a banquet at an expensive restaurant.

At the banquet the overseas professor, who remains unaware of the couple's pain and sacrifice, is puzzled by the strange reserve and stilted conversation of his old friend and former classmate. Telling of his plans for a research trip to the caves of Dunhuang, the overseas professor warmly invites his friend to join him. The proposal is entirely out of the question for the Chinese professor, who has just spent all his money on a banquet. Indeed, never in his life has he had either money or permission for a trip to Dunhuang, the important cultural site that he knew so well through books, and where, ironically, foreigners could now visit much more easily than he. Shocked into silence by his classmate's proposal, the Chinese professor can only gaze helplessly at his wife, who, superbly disguising her inner turmoil,

[72] Wang Zhecheng and Wen Xiaoyu, "Jixu."

carries the conversation. "I just wish he had time," she comments, covering for her husband and maintaining the veneer of the unruffled hostess.

After the banquet, when the couple has gone home, their sons accidentally knock a thermos bottle onto the cement floor of their small flat. As the bottle shatters, so does the composure of the heroic wife, who no longer has to maintain public appearances. She rages at her husband, who then, pressed to the very limit himself, knifes back with the cruelest line of all: "Well, for God's sake, why didn't you marry him back then?" She walks out, deeply hurt that her husband has so misunderstood her. The reader is left to ponder several questions: At what price does one save face, whether personal or national? What actual rewards come to people who choose to devote themselves to China and to socialism? What really is at stake, materially and spiritually, in the decision to emigrate? And broadly underlying these questions are the old, persistent, big ones: What is the proper course for modern China? Through what combination of Chineseness and Westernization can Chinese people best improve their lives and preserve their self-respect? Literary works could be useful not only in wrestling with these problems, but also in vicariously testing possible solutions to them.

Testing New Ways

In real life, a person might be too frightened to confront a Party secretary or too inhibited to ask a friend of the opposite sex for a new-style date, but to watch a literary character do these things, and at least get a "feel" for the experience, was another matter. During the Cultural Revolution, Western-style social dancing was condemned as bourgeois and decadent. By 1985, a survey of 1,654 "ordinary Shanghainese" found that only 7 percent still opposed social dancing, while 21 percent had already tried it. But, interestingly, an even larger group (27 percent) said they "only like to watch other people dance."[73] Literature, drama, and film had a role in allowing people to "watch" new behavior and get used to it. Stories about new-style things could bring one well beyond the confines of one's own daily life.

The gap between the worlds of the imagination and of daily life could be vast. One day in spring 1980, for example, a group of students in contemporary Chinese literature at Zhongshan University in Guangzhou was engrossed in discussion of works of the post-Mao thaw when their class period ended. Still chattering about "liberation of thought," "the Western world," and how different everything in China should be, they arrived at the doorway of their classroom building, where they found pouring rain. A young man opened his umbrella and set out across campus. The young woman he had been talking with had no umbrella and stayed behind to ask friends about sharing one. Later I asked the young man why he had not shared his

---

[73] Wei Haibo et al. "Wuhui, daigou, disanzhe," p. 27. The remainder in the survey chose the response "don't dance myself, but don't mind if others do."

umbrella with the young woman. "You don't understand," he said. "If we shared an umbrella, everyone would see. They would think we were a couple. If we didn't get engaged, they would find something wrong; it would be very embarrassing, especially for her." The fiction the students had been discussing went far beyond the mere sharing of umbrellas. Why had these two been so inhibited? It is too simple to say they behaved hypocritically, saying one thing while doing another. They were living life in one sphere, and testing new possibilities in another. The activity in both spheres was sincere. In the long term, moreover, the two spheres are related.

Fiction seems to have been marginally more useful than film, television, or stage performance in the vicarious testing of new ways, and indeed in many other uses of literature. This was because of the privacy of the reading experience. People watched film, television, or plays in groups that included family, neighbors, friends, and strangers. To some extent, therefore, members of the audience were themselves "on stage"; any visible or audible response to what happened on screen or stage might be judged by others. In varying degrees, therefore, a person's responses were conditioned by what he or she was willing to have others believe was present in his or her mind. Reading a work of fiction, on the other hand, was a freer experience. Alone with his or her book or magazine, a reader could choose what to read, how fast to read it, and what parts to reread; also which characters to identify with, and how far to follow them down their paths, always keeping one's sympathies and experiments locked within the sanctity of one's own mind. If this or that gambit went wrong, no one else knew. It was not as if someone had seen you sharing an umbrella with a boyfriend.

Escaping to Imagined Space

Beyond serving as a testing ground, fictional worlds could become places into which people escaped and stayed for a while. The writer Zhang Jie recalls that "When I first began to read, books were to me like a mirage, something outside of life that opened new vistas. Like many other people, I often became so immersed in a book that I regretted having to leave this imaginary world and come back to daily life."[74] In part, the appeal of other worlds lay simply in the contrast they offered to daily humdrum. But seldom, if ever, was the imaginary world into which a reader escaped entirely different from the one he or she actually inhabited. The appeal of imaginary worlds depended both on distancing from daily life and the preservation of at least some similarities to it.

Clichés in socialist China, borrowed largely from Marxist literary theory, described the relation of literature to life as "magnifying" or "concentrating." Zhang Jie, in the essay just noted, refers to the "heightening" of life in

---

[74] Zhang Jie, "Pursuit."

literature's imaginary worlds.[75] In a 1984 survey of Shanghai university students, the most preferred answer to a question about what "a good film" does to a person was "it passes its feeling and power to you, so that you leave the theater feeling fulfilled."[76] This sense of "fulfillment" seems to have depended on an underlying general resemblance between the actual and fictional worlds that viewers experienced; the "power" that a work provided came from the concentration of its presentation.

A story like Wang Anyi's "Life in a Small Courtyard" (1980), about the daily lives of four young couples living as close neighbors, might seem so plain in its naturalism as possibly to bore readers—who, after all, lived daily lives that were virtually the same as those described in the story.[77] But Wang's subtle psychological depiction of ordinary life—including petty squabbles and jealousies as well as touches of tenderness and whimsy—apparently served many readers as a sort of sounding board for their own ups and downs. The effects of such a story were diffuse; there was no special problem to be illustrated or lesson to be taught. But the story was hardly therefore "removed from life." On the contrary, its close tracking of daily life was key to the appeal it held for a wide variety of readers.

Certain "daily life" stories seem to have been intended for, and appreciated by, groups of readers who shared an overall life pattern with the stories' protagonists. Some of Wang Anyi's stories of the early 1980s, for example, were said to have been especially welcome among young women who, like the author herself, had returned to China's cities after several years of life in the countryside during the Cultural Revolution. These women shared a special pattern of problems: although legally urban residents, they often had no work assignments when they returned to the cities, and had to use connections to look for jobs. They also sought husbands, but were at a disadvantage in the romantic game because, in their age group, there were fewer men than women living in the cities (because urban families tended to recall daughters before sons when return to the cities first became possible); moreover, after a sojourn in the countryside, they were already "old" compared to their competition. Wang's stories such as "The Rasping Sound of Rain" and "This Train's Final Stop" could not solve these problems for readers, but offered the solace that came from airing the problems and from dispelling the notion that there was anything shameful about them.[78] Reading fiction became a way to escape a sense of isolation and to find a group, actual or imagined, of kindred spirits.

[75] Ibid.
[76] Of the respondents, 45 percent chose this answer; 20 percent chose "says what you yourself cannot say, letting you feel less alone"; 18 percent chose "opens your eyes and shows you new things"; 17 percent chose "regulates your feelings and cultivates your character." Weng Mu, "Shanghai daxuesheng dianying suzhi yipie," p. 81.
[77] Wang Anyi, "Xiaoyuan suoji."
[78] "Yu, sha sha sha" and "Benci lieche zhongdianzhan."

Identifying with Groups

Private reading experience, as noted above, was important because it allowed one to escape from the expectations and judgments of others. But on the other hand, the predominantly social nature of cultural experience in socialist China also had its uses. From the 1950s though the 1970s, tickets to films and stage performances were allocated to schools, factories, or other large groups, whose members were often organized to attend together. Officially organized discussions sometimes followed. These practices declined during the 1980s, but public audiences still tended to whoop or groan in unison, generally sharing their judgments, especially moral judgments, of what they were seeing.

Students and other young urban readers of what we have called the "socially concerned" kind formed groups for literary discussion and other activities. In 1980 at Zhongshan University in Guangzhou, for example, students in the Bell Tower Society, in addition to publishing their literary magazine *Red Bean*, convened a campuswide meeting to discuss Chen Guokai's "What Should I Do?!" and other controversial short stories. They also wrote and produced a play called "Our Generation" (*Women zheiyidai*) about their collective recollections of life on Hainan Island during the Cultural Revolution, and organized a group outing to sweep the grave of Xiao Hong (1911–1942), a writer whom they idolized, on the anniversary of her death.[79] Camaraderie and conscious attention to the group's role were essential elements in these events: the play was conceived as an account of the group's own part in Chinese history, and the notion that the same group—as a group—was paying homage to Xiao Hong made the grave-sweeping more significant.

The writing and reading of poetry as a social event—at banquets or parties, or at poignant junctures in life, such as the parting of friends—continued a tradition of premodern times. Poetry in these uses almost always adhered to traditional forms of five or seven syllables per line. Practitioners of modern free verse also had social uses of poetry, notably in public readings in cities, where they could attract large audiences (in the hundreds or even thousands) and impart to them a vivid if temporary sense of group identity. Calligraphy also persisted not only as a graphic art but as a mode of cultured social exchange, and sometimes even as a demonstration art performed before small groups.

Some readers, especially among the young, affiliated themselves loosely as devotees of one or another particular author. In Shanghai in the late 1970s, a reader who tried to read everything a certain writer had published was known as that writer's "dedicated reader." The term was different at other times and places, but the phenomenon occurred with writers as various as

[79] Personal experiences during a research stay at Zhongshan University, November 1979 to June 1980.

Yang Mo (author of *Song of Youth* and other socialist realism in the early 1960s), Liu Binyan (following the publication of "People or Monsters?" in the early 1980s), and San Mao (writer of popular fiction from Taiwan, widely read on the mainland in the mid-1980s). Other than to answer some of their fan mail, writers could not attend to their followings, and these "groups" were never formally organized. But for an individual reader the bond could still seem strong, and at least some group awareness could develop through contact with other dedicated readers.

Expressing the Self

On the whole, however, reader identification with an author or a group of readers was not as strong as with favorite literary characters. Identifying with a character was useful not only for exploring or testing new ideas, as we have seen, but sometimes just to express feelings. This was a simpler function than the "practical" ones noted above in that it did not aim at changing the outside world in any way, or even at learning to adjust to it, but only at transportation of inner feelings outward. Yet, although this function was simpler in this theoretical sense, the feelings themselves could be various, subtle, and complex, and the satisfaction that came from expressing them also was of various kinds. Sometimes the satisfaction came from the sense of release from external repression or one's own inhibitions. It could also come from seeing a feeling or concern that one had sensed only vaguely be put into especially vivid or eloquent terms.

The socialist realist novels of the 1950s and early 1960s provide one kind of example. As we have seen in chapter 3, the heroes and heroines in these works were sometimes less important as depictions of life than as models for the altruistic tendencies of young people. The heroes both stimulated idealism and gave shape to how it was expressed: Sister Jiang in *Red Crag* was loyal to communist ideals at tremendous personal cost, and young readers enjoyed the feeling of imagining themselves just as altruistic. Although the explicit purpose of *Red Crag*, from the viewpoint of the Party, the book's publishers, and likely the authors as well, was to "engineer" good effects in the world, it was also true that for many readers the main use of the story was to stimulate and enjoy heroic feelings. The imagination of oneself as a hero was satisfying to readers quite apart from whether they had occasion or inclination to do anything about it.

In works of scar literature a few years later, literary characters helped readers to release feelings of a somewhat different kind. These were the feelings not of heroes but of victims, who, as we noted in chapter 3, turned to literature to "release [pent-up] resentment." In this use of literature, the literary work did not need to stimulate the reader's feelings—because the feelings were already there, indeed, could have been there for a very long time. If a work were published in the official media, there was an additional validating effect by which people could feel that their secret feelings were all right after all, and nothing to be ashamed of. Reading literature could help to dispel their sense of isolation. Not only did literary characters share some of their formerly "secret" worries and travails but countless other readers, who applauded with them, were obviously their fellow sufferers and thus, in a sense, their allies. The result could be a sense of group identity, locally or even nationally, among those who now could see that they felt the same way about something.

For example, one day on the campus of Zhongshan University in Guangzhou in 1979, the appearance of an issue of the student literary magazine *Red Bean* led to some elbowing and tussling among students who were eager to buy one of the few copies that were being offered at retail. The students' eagerness came not from curiosity; they knew quite well what the magazine contained. Among other pieces, there was Chen Haiying's story "Black Tide," about the young people who died under the belief that Mao's little red book would protect them from a tidal wave. The students wanted to celebrate the exposure of this debacle and—in the mode of collector as much as reader, to own a copy of it. Similarly, when *Shanghai Literature* published Zuo Jianming's "Shadow," which describes beggars in Deng Xiaoping's home county in Sichuan (see chapter 6), only two copies of the magazine were allocated for sale in that county. Those two copies reportedly were passed around so rapidly that they were reduced to tatters within days.[80] This happened not because the message they bore was news but, in a sense, precisely because it was not.

In early 1980, during a season when "release of resentment" was running high, researchers doing a survey in Liaoning province asked an open-ended question about what poets currently should be doing. Most of the responses, they reported, used phrases such as "sing out the feelings of the people," "above all tell the truth," and "say what is on people's minds."[81] From one point of view, these phrases all represent what we have been calling release of feelings—of both poet and the poetry readership. Yet to some extent the phrases also exemplify one kind of "engineering," because the point of such phrases was also practical: to join battle with the Party, and to oppose its comprehensive hegemony. The reason these two functions often went together in the Deng era is simply that the content of popular "feelings" often had to do with wishing social and political conditions were different. When audience members at village operas rose to shout "The Communist Party should learn from [the incorruptible eleventh-century official] Lord Bao!" they were releasing feelings and asking for social change at the same time.[82]

There were two different modes of the release of feelings about the vic-

---

[80] Interview at the editorial offices of *Shanghai wenxue*, 17 June 1980.

[81] Yang Qingyun, "Dalu xin shi minyi ceyan de jieguo."

[82] Invocations of Lord Bao were common in the early Deng years. This particular example was related by Chen Huangmei, deputy director of the Institute of Literature, Chinese Academy of Social Sciences, at a conference on teaching materials, Nanning, Guangxi, February 1980.

tims in literary portrayals. In one, which we might call the "identifying" mode, the reader (or viewer) sees in the tragedy of the literary victim elements of his or her own suffering, or that of close friends or relatives, and in several ways can derive comfort from this newly established solidarity. We noted in chapter 1 how a simple story like Lu Xinhua's "Scar" could have a powerful nationwide impact because so many political victims could see their plight within its sparse outlines. Similarly, the editors who decided to publish Chen Guokai's "What Should I Do?!" attributed that story's popular response to the broad resonance it had among people whose own families had been broken apart, and who for years did not even know what happened to loved ones.[83] After Chen Rong spotlighted the intolerable pressures one woman faced in trying to combine family and career, one critic asked, "Isn't this family a perfect picture of the daily life of many middle-aged comrades all around us? This may be the reason why the story moved so many people so deeply after it was published."[84]

In the other mode of viewing victims, which we might call a "pitying" mode, the reader (viewer) stands back from the victim and, while sympathizing to some extent, also gains comfort from the implicit assertion that I the reader, however unfortunate, still am better off than the literary victim. This response, which fits the unflattering cliché of "rejoicing in the calamity of others," is not something that readers were quick to admit to or necessarily aware of in themselves. But it is a well-established principle, identifiable in Chinese fiction of earlier times and many other times and places, including the horror fiction (and film) of the modern West, and it clearly underlies the appeal of some of the baleful underground stories of the late-Mao years as well as many above-ground post-Mao scar stories.

The starkest examples are stories that spread orally on the uncensored rumor mill—for example, about a family in Anhui province driven to such desperate extremes of hunger during the Great Leap famine that they despatch a family member to a roadside at night to kill a passerby to eat. Only after the deed is done do they discover that the victim was a young son of the family, who had been returning home after a long absence and had not been recognized in the murky night. Hand-copied volumes such as "Terrifying Footsteps" or "Eternal Regrets in Love" (see chapter 5, especially on "Eternal Regrets") also encourage a "pitying" response. Stories such as Jin Yanhua and Wang Jingquan's "Cries from Death Row" (chapter 6) exemplify the possibilities of finding officially published stories to read in this way.

Although some texts seem to "invite" readings in one or another of these modes, there is, of course, no way to determine how any one reader will respond. How far a reader or viewer wished to identify with a fictional character and how much he or she wished to stand back and view the char-

---

[83] Interview at the editorial offices of *Zuopin*, Guangzhou, 4 March 1980.
[84] Zhu Xiao, "Yidai jiankuan zhong buhui."

acter from the outside was—like the "testing" of new ways we have noted above—a private decision. A single reader could also shift from one of these modes toward the other, even while engaging the same literary work. Yet the psychological structure of the reading (or viewing) experience remains distinct in the two cases.

Indeed, a similar ambiguity applies to all of the uses of literature that we have noted in this chapter. None of them is so powerful that it does not easily combine with others in the same act of reading or writing. A writer can engineer and entertain at the same time, or at least try to; a reader can learn about the world, negotiate the West, express feelings, and identify with a group in a single reading; and so on. Moreover, the uses of writer and reader need not match: a mother who writes a memoir of her child's death in Red Guard strife might only be expressing her personal grief and impressions, and yet seem, to readers, to be making a political criticism or putting the story to other practical uses.[85] Ultimately we can only note, not measure, the various ways in which the needs and personal decisions of readers and viewers affected their uses of literature and art.

But in general we can say that literature and art in socialist China opened possibilities for mental activity that otherwise would have been largely unavailable. Literary controls imposed obvious limitations, but because controls and routines applied to the rest of life as well, literature was still an unusual opportunity. The mental space that literature can open within relatively closed societies has special importance that people accustomed to open societies do not easily appreciate. Writing of Czarist Russia in the mid-nineteenth century, the Russian literary patron Pavel V. Annenkov observed that literature and art provided "the only path . . . to public affairs of some sort: art was virtually the salvation of people, for it permitted people to think of themselves as freely thinking human beings."[86] Annenkov's statement may be extreme, but the evidence from socialist China shows that he has a point. During the Cultural Revolution, when China was under the tightest of social controls, performances of the "eight model operas" were always well attended. People came not just to see the most perfect of heroes illustrate political points in the most correct of ways. They came, first, because the color, music, choreography, and general excitement of the performance situation was hard to find anywhere else; and they came also because the content of the operas, however narrow and sterile, still provided at least some space in which a viewer's mind could exercise itself with some of the uses of literature that we have noted in this chapter. After Mao, literature became even more important in expanding the space in which people could, as Annenkov says, be "freely thinking human beings."

Despite the importance of popular uses of literature, and in defiance, too, of the state's dominating use of literature, some voices occasionally called for writing that would bring "uses" to a higher plane.

---

[85] See Xu Hui, "Emeng."
[86] Quoted in Harold Swayze, *Political Control of Literature in the USSR*, p. 169.

TRANSCENDING "USES"

In 1986 Lu Shuyuan, a well-known critic, noted an "ingrown" tendency in socialist Chinese literature that he attributed to utilitarianism that had gone too far. Original Marxist theory had predicted a maturation of socialist literature that, Lu observed, had not come about.

> After the founding of the New China, the role of literature in "seeking food and shelter" and "providing livelihood" for people was supposed to have gradually matured into "enriching" and "elevating" them. Ultimately literature was to have remolded people's inner spirits. Unfortunately, though, the "set view" of literature, which had developed over many years, caused people to continue viewing it only as a "tool" or "weapon," and prevented it from moving to a higher level.[87]

Lu wrote that the efforts of certain "courageous people" (apparently referring to Shao Quanlin, Kang Zhuo, and others) in the late 1950s and early 1960s to promote "a broad road for realism," "literature as the study of people," and "writing about middle characters" were actually attempts to bring socialist Chinese literature to that elusive "higher level." But, Lu concluded, the inexorable march of Maoism in the 1960s had doomed these efforts.[88]

In the post-Mao years, a small number of writers, primarily poets, renewed the quest for literary transcendence and drew plaudits from elite critics and scholars. The attraction of transcending to a higher level lay mainly in the prospect of escaping the situation that literature was currently in. The certainty of what had to be avoided drew more attention than the problem of what should be done instead. Accordingly, the notion of "pure literature"—the pay dirt of the quest to transcend—was conceived mainly by negative definition: "pure" meant non-Maoist, nonpolitical, nondidactic, and noninstrumental. Some critics went further, wanting "pure" art to be free of any conscious purpose whatsoever—of writer, reader, or anyone else.[89] The extremity of this conception is an indication of how oppressive the political forces that caused it must have been.

When purity becomes as pure as this, a problem can arise of how it is possible for a reader or writer to be motivated to read or write at all. There is a tautological sense in which any reader or writer must have a motive, or else would not be led to read or write. (An exception could be a person's unintended noticing of a public sign, but "reading" in this sense does not happen with literary works; no one reads a story or poem inadvertently.) Part of the problem can be solved using a distinction between the interior (psychological) and exterior (in the world) effects of reading. A purist view,

---

[87] Lu Shuyuan, "Lun xin shiqi wenxue de 'xiang nei zhuan.'"

[88] For an example of Shao Quanlin's proposals and the attacks they incurred, see Kai-yu Hsu, ed., *Literature of the People's Republic of China*, pp. 642–52.

[89] Li Tuo, editor of *Beijing Literature* and a key figure in the nurturing of young avant-garde writers, argued this position in the late 1980s.

in these terms, holds that one's motives should not include any designs to change the world, but only wishes to experience ideas and feelings. Yet "purity" as conceived in post-Mao China seemed to ask for more than this; it asked that the feelings and thoughts themselves also be free from "politics"—meaning, given the excessively broad reach of politics at the time, free from any thought about why and how the world should be different from the way it is. This demand exalted the notion of pure literature but narrowed its realm severely. It was a good thing, but what was it?

Advocates looked to predecessors in China's May Fourth years, where they found calls for purity that were similar to their own, in addition to literary examples such as the "symbolist" poems of Dai Wangshu and the fiction of Shanghai "new perceptionists" Shi Zhecun, Mu Shiying, and Liu Na'ou.[90] They also looked outside China, but found the noncommunist world not so filled with "pure art" as they first imagined it should be. The works of Nobel Prize winners, which they took as representing the highest art, still often involved "politics." The best match for their quest to find and protect pure art came, not surprisingly, in examples from the Soviet Union and other communist societies. In the opening lines of his 1970 Nobel Prize lecture, Aleksandr Solzhenitsyn made the kind of statement that Chinese advocates of purity in art could celebrate:

> A primitive savage chances upon some strange object. He holds it, turns it this way and that. What can it be? Something cast up by the ocean? Something buried in the sand? Or could it have fallen from the sky? An object of intricate curves, he twists it round and about, watches the way it reflects the light first dimly, then with flashes of brightness. In his bewilderment he tries to adapt it to some use, to find some lowly purpose for it. Of its higher purpose he has not the vaguest notion.
>
> In exactly the same way we human beings, holding Art in our hands, arrogantly imagine that we are its masters. We boldly direct it, renew it, reform it, display it, sell it for money, indulge the powerful with it, use it for light entertainment, for popular songs or night club attractions. From time to time we arm ourselves with it to fill some passing political purpose or some limited social need. But Art cannot be sullied, in spite of our efforts. It loses none of its original genius. Every time and in whatever way it is used, it grants us some small part of its own inner, secret light.[91]

Although statements such as Solzhenitsyn's posed the issue well, they were not very helpful in showing Chinese writers how, in fact, one could create art that transcended worldly uses. Those uses seemed, one way or another, to seep into anything one wrote. And even if a writer could produce a "pure" text, there was no way to prevent readers from examining it for mundane

---

[90] These writers drew much attention in academic circles in both China and the West after they were rediscovered in 1983 by Yan Jiayan, a professor of Chinese at Beijing University. See Yan's "Lun sanshi niandai de xin ganjuepai xiaoshuo."

[91] Alexander Solzhenitsyn, *Lecture*, p. 7.

meanings and uses. In a highly politicized atmosphere, the purposeful demonstration of an apolitical alternative for art could itself be read as a political statement.

Still, writers tried. Poems, because they are short, seemed the best forms in which to attempt purity from beginning to end. (Fiction, with its inevitable loose-endedness, and film and drama, which involved interpretation by directors and actors, made expression of "pure art" practically impossible.) The "misty" group of poets who emerged in the late 1970s were among those who sometimes aimed at pure art. Gu Cheng's poem "Curves" is an example:[92]

> A bird in the gusty wind
> Deftly changes direction
> A boy tries to pick up
> A penny
>
> The grapevine in fantasy
> Stretches its tentacle
>
> The wave in retreat
> Arches its back

It seems hard to find any "use" of this poem other than that it lets the poet express some perceptions of curves and lets readers appreciate them. But if we allow the sense of "use" to become as tautological as this, we also make the quest to "transcend use" futile by definition. Moreover, we have the paradoxical consequence that an ideally pure work of art, if it could exist, would have to be both created and read only by accident.

Although Chinese advocates of pure art used terms like "utilitarian" and "pragmatic" in reference to the approaches that they opposed, the problem of exactly how to define a "use" of literature did not occupy them. On the whole, they assumed that their terms would be understood, and concentrated their worries on the tendency of political uses to pervade all literary activity. To be good, literature had to permit ambiguity, but ambiguity was precisely what allowed impurities to seep in. For example, Gu Cheng has another poem called "A Brief Stop":[93]

> The train was tired
> The delegates climbed out
> Still wearing their best clothes
>
> Under the eaves of the signal box
> A girl
> Mechanically crushed stones
> She never looked up

---

[92] Gu Cheng, "Huxian."
[93] Gu Cheng, "Zhan ting."

The poem presents well-dressed delegates and a laboring girl, and the poet's decision to divide his lines into two stanzas suggests a willingness to accentuate the distinction between them. Is he commenting on the social problems—which were much in the air at the time he wrote his poem—of official privilege and the poverty of ordinary people? Readers undoubtedly made such connections. The theoretically inclined among them might even have recalled Mao Zedong's piece of political jargon about "a new ruling class." In another poem called "A Whole Generation," Gu Cheng's cryptic language invites even stronger sentiments of political protest:[94]

> The black night has given me black eyes,
> Yet I use them to search for light.

Although the undertones of these lines seem to have escaped official censure, some other lines of Gu Cheng's did not:[95]

> The junk in mourning
> Slowly passes by
> And unrolls its dark-yellow embalmer's cloth

Here the "embalmer's cloth" seems to refer to the brown strip across the earth formed by a river when viewed from a distance. Officials wanted to know why it is an "embalmer's" cloth, and why the junk is "in mourning." Is the poet saying something about the motherland? The Party? The controversy that ensued had little to do with pure art.

The ambiguity of art made it virtually impossible to seal out all sociopolitical readings. Yet ultimately, the consequences of this fact were not uniformly destructive of literary quality. References to the social context could, depending on how they were made, either add to or detract from the literary value of a work. In "A Brief Stop," to associate the images of well-dressed delegates and a downcast girl with contemporary social inequalities made the poem considerably more moving, and at least in this sense better as art, than it would otherwise have been. But when politics invaded as far as the crass demand to know whether the words "junk in mourning" were a comment on the Communist Party, the effect was to destroy art. The theoretical question of how to measure quality in the use-dominated literary works of socialist China is thus more complex than it first appears.

USE AND QUALITY

The idea of literary quality in both Chinese and European tradition has tended to inspire a certain reverence, and rightly so. A good work of art nourishes and elevates the spirit, while the specific nature of the aesthetic response remains mysterious. The person who has such an experience has

[94] Gu Cheng, "Yidairen."
[95] See Gao Hongbo and Guo Xiaolin, "Zai jing bufen shiren tan dangqian shige chuangzuo."

little trouble recognizing it, but cannot explain it. Normally we do not even feel the need for explanation—any more than, in riding a bicycle, we insist on knowing how it is possible to balance on two thin wheels. Those who have done dissections of the aesthetic response—Plato, Confucius, Liu Xie, Immanuel Kant, and many others—have had some success, but the analytical interest of their results is something quite different from (and never as elevating as) the aesthetic experience itself. To artists, a philosopher's interest in the anatomy of beauty can seem irrelevant and even mildly irritating, because vivisection of art, as of animals, kills the living thing. Louis Armstrong, when asked why jazz is so great, is said to have answered, "if you have to ask, you'll never know."

In looking at literature in socialist China, the attempt to analyze literary value runs immediately against the problem that there are very few examples of high art. The mainstream of literary works, as Joseph Lau and others have argued, does not contain much art, or even seem to strive for it.[96] Readers, writers, and critics seem preoccupied with more practical uses of literature, and art becomes incidental. Mao Zedong's notion that art could, as it were, be tacked onto any message of any kind in order to "magnify" it misconceived the nature of art.[97]

And yet there is a great puzzle about the question of value in China's use-dominated art. Despite the general mediocrity, in the daily life of readers and other "users" of literature, some works were often called "good" while others were not. People who used evaluative terms were not making claims about high art, but neither were they applying the terms randomly or meaninglessly. One could say "X is a good story" while another nodded agreement—or expressed dissent—and both would assume that something measurable was at issue. What was it? What makes a literary work "good" when art is not very much involved?

If we look at actual uses, it is immediately apparent that the word "good" referred to a considerable variety of attributes.[98] In 1980, Gu Cheng's poetry was being called "good," at least by some people, but so was Liu Binyan's muckraking reportage "People or Monsters?," Zhang Yang's hand-copied entertainment novel *The Second Handshake* and Tong Enzheng's science fiction story "Death Rays from Coral Island," among many others. A few years earlier, the socialist realist classic *Red Crag* was often called "good," as was Mao Zedong's "Talks at the Yan'an Forum on Literature and Art." Clearly, if we are going to identify a single sense for the word "good" in reference to literary works, it will have to account for all these uses and more. (Analyzing

[96] Joseph S. M. Lau, "Text and Context: Toward a Commonwealth of Modern Chinese Literature," in Howard Goldblatt, ed., *Worlds Apart*, pp. 11–28.

[97] This concept underlay Mao's "Talks at the Yan'an Forum on Literature and Art," in which he held, for example, that "works of art which lack artistic quality have no force, however progressive they are politically." *Selected Works of Mao Zedong* (Beijing), vol. 3, p. 90.

[98] For present purposes I see no need to distinguish between English "good" and Chinese *hao*, although these two words do not always correspond in sense.

the senses in which the word is used does not mean we need to agree with any of the judgments, of course.)

I believe it is a mistake to turn primarily to theories of art to explain this puzzle. We need a theory of value that applies to things that are more instrumental and mundane than those which classical aesthetic theory addresses. We need a theory of more general applicability, one that can tell us not just what a good (including "instrumentally" good) poem is but also what a good hammer—or shoe, or weathervane—is. I will devote the remainder of this chapter to the experiment of choosing an example of this broader kind of theory and seeing what it can yield.

The distinguished philosopher John Rawls incorporates a broad theory of value within his classic work *A Theory of Justice*. Rawls does not specifically address the issue of literary value, and literary aestheticians seldom quote Rawls.[99] His book is a good starting point for our purposes precisely because of its general applicability and because he grounds his concept of value in the notion of "use." He writes that "criteria of evaluation differ from one kind of thing to another. Since we want things for different purposes, it is obviously rational to assess them by different features. It is helpful to think of the sense of 'good' as being analogous to that of a function sign."[100] Thus a good knife is sharp, but a good hammer, exactly to the contrary, is blunt, because the instruments have different uses and we need them to have very different qualities. Both sharpness and bluntness are "good" when found in the appropriate tool.

In this essential insight, the modern Rawls does not exceed Zhuangzi, who quotes Ruo of the Northern Sea as saying: "A beam or pillar can be used to batter down a city wall, but is no good for stopping up a little hole. . . . Thoroughbred horses like Qiji and Hualiu can gallop three hundred miles in a day, but in catching rats are no match for a wildcat or weasel."[101] But Zhuangzi leaves, and Rawls addresses, the question of how to characterize whatever it is that remains constant across all uses of the word "good." (Something, apparently, must remain constant, or the word could not be intelligibly spoken and understood in its wide variety of contexts.) For the word's instrumental sense, Rawls uses the following definition of "good":

---

[99] The bibliography of Wayne Booth's *The Company We Keep: An Ethics of Fiction* includes more than 900 titles drawn from virtually every time and place in the Western world, but does not list Rawls.

[100] Rawls, *A Theory of Justice*, p. 405–6. In the Chinese translation of Rawls's book by He Huaihong, He Baogang, and Liao Shenbai, "good" in this passage is rendered as *shan* rather than *hao* (*Zhengyilun*, p. 385). The translators may have wished to grace the discussion with a more morally exalted term, but *hao* is a much better term for the daily-life instrumental sense of "good" that Rawls is analyzing in this part of his book.

[101] *Zhuangzi*, "Qiu shui" (waipian no. 17); translation adapted from Burton Watson, trans., *The Complete Works of Chuang Tzu*, p. 180. I am grateful to Inge Nielsen for pointing out the Zhuangzi parallel.

A is a good X if and only if A has the properties (to a higher degree than the average or standard X) which it is rational to want in an X, given what X's are used for, or expected to do.[102]

The word "rational" here raises questions, especially for cross-cultural studies. Rawls's use of the word, which predates the prevalence of "rational choice" theory in American political science departments by about two decades, is not an outgrowth of that approach. But there are legitimate questions about whether the word is culture-bound and/or implicitly evaluative.

In recent decades, researchers in cross-cultural fields have grown increasingly sensitive to the danger of assuming that the patterns of the researcher's own culture are the natural (or "rational") ones, while the nonempirical beliefs of other cultures appear to be "irrational." But this danger, although quite real, does not impinge upon the essential claims of Rawls's theory, which are not culture-bound in this sense. Rawls could have stated the essence of his theory without using the troublesome word "rational," so long as the notion of "making sense for a certain purpose" remained, in one way or another.[103] And "making sense" or "rational" does not have to imply a modern (or Western, or scientific, etc.) worldview; it can refer just as well to the sense-making of other human belief systems. A good shaman, on Rawls's theory, would be one who has the attributes that it makes sense to want in shamans, for example the abilities to exorcise ghosts and to communicate with the spirits of ancestors. Whether or not one believes in the efficacy of shamans is beside the point of what characteristics make (for believers) or would make (for nonbelievers) a superior example of the kind.

A more nettlesome question is whether the word "rational" is implicitly evaluative. I cannot here address the long-standing debate in Western philosophy over ethical naturalism—the question of whether we can measure the applicability of terms like "good" by empirical standards, in the way we can measure "heavy" by force of attraction toward the center of the earth or "green" by a certain wavelength of light. If we can, then whether something is "good" or not should likewise be demonstrable. Rawls is a naturalist. But critics of naturalism, who have argued (among other things) for "emotive" theories of value, have held that differences in judgments of value are rooted not in different opinion about fact but in different feelings.[104] For them, "A is good" reduces to something like "I like A." The statement "Gu Cheng's poems are better than Ye Wenfu's" is, at bottom, the same kind of statement as "I prefer vanilla to chocolate ice cream." If the emotive theorists are correct, then evaluative judgments can only be recommended (not demonstrated)

---

[102] Rawls, *A Theory of Justice*, p. 399.

[103] Rawls uses the word "rational" partly because it is traditional; he observes that "many philosophers have been willing to accept some variant of goodness as rationality"; ibid., p. 434.

[104] Logical positivists Moritz Schlick and Rudolph Carnap, who saw aesthetic statements as unverifiable and therefore cognitively meaningless, laid the groundwork for the more detailed theories of A. J. Ayer (*Language, Truth, and Logic*, 1936) and Charles Stevenson (*Ethics and Language*, 1945).

to others. All differing judgments are equally "true," provided only that they are reported sincerely.

For the purposes of analyzing the socialist Chinese literary system, I feel comfortable in accepting the naturalist position in this debate because, in my view, uses of evaluative terms "on the ground" in Chinese society of the time were largely consistent with this view. When Chinese people called a work "good" they might have been referring to any of a wide range of qualities that made it so, but they usually meant to claim more, I feel sure, than just "I like it." When they disagreed in their judgments, they often behaved as if they were really contradicting one another, not just expressing different tastes.

In my view, the greatest strength of Rawls's theory for our present purposes is its ability to account for what seems to be a puzzling variety of different senses in which words like "good" were actually used in the socialist Chinese literary system. The key to this ability is Rawls's phrase "given what X's are used for, or expected to do." With this flexibility, we can explain that Gu Cheng's poems were called "good" because of terse expression, clear imagery, sharp contrasts, and certain other specifiable properties that varied greatly from the properties that led people to call Tong Enzheng's science fiction "good" (suspense, a sympathetic protagonist, a window on the outside world, an imaginative extrapolation of technology, and so on). Similarly, Liu Binyan's "People or Monsters?" was "good" reportage because it told the truth, spoke for the people, and allowed "release of resentment." The several kinds of works were indeed "used for, or expected to do" very different kinds of things. An example that counted as "good" in one use might not be good at all in another.

Rawls shows how his approach can account for subcategories of uses and measurements of value. As an example, he speaks of the features it is rational to want in a watch (it keeps time, is not very heavy, and so on), and then notes that additional criteria apply when one specifically evaluates wrist watches, stop watches, or watches to match a certain evening dress.[105] The same kind of flexibility can be useful in trying to account for how the word "good" was applied to literary works in socialist China. For example, we have noted above that Gu Cheng's poems were sometimes called good for their terseness and imagery. A puzzle arises from the fact that a poem like Ye Wenfu's "General, You Must Not Do This!," was also called "good." The poem is too long to quote in full here, but ends this way:

> On the road of this New Long March
> Listen to the progressive young
> And progressing laws
> Cry:
> "General,
> You can't do this!"[106]

---

[105] Rawls, *A Theory of Justice*, pp. 401–2.
[106] A full translation, from which these lines are taken, appears in Helen Siu and Zelda Stern, eds., *Mao's Harvest*, pp. 158–65.

The poem is hardly terse, and uses stale images; but in the context of its time, even professors of aesthetics called it a "good poem."[107] It does share with Gu Cheng's poetry some superficial similarities of form, and in their separate ways, both kinds of poetry also bore a power to move readers. Ye's poem capitalized on "release of resentment," putting on paper what many people wished to say but did not dare to. This may not be what we generally regard as an "aesthetic" response, but because the poem did well what things of its kind "were used for, or expected to do," it could be, and often was, said to be a good poem.[108] Rawls observes that judgments of "good" often beg the question "for what?" The statement "Wildcat is a good mountain," he says, can be puzzling until we learn that the speaker means "a good mountain for skiing."[109] Similarly, "Ye Wenfu's poem is good" may seem strange unless we understand "good for ventilating."

One consequence of being this flexible in assessing value is that "good" can apply to things that are so widely different as to seem opposite. Luo Guangbin and Yang Yiyan's *Red Crag* exalts communist martyrdom, and for large numbers of readers in the early 1960s was certainly "good" for this reason. But several years later Zheng Yi's "Maple" and Xu Hui's "Nightmare" were "good" for decrying essentially the same spirit, which was now cast as fanaticism.

It is easy to observe that the readers and writers in these two cases had different viewpoints and goals. But this observation does not solve the problem so much as deepen it. Do we want to say that literature can be "good" in the service of any goal, without judging the goal itself? Is a work that promotes fanaticism good if it "does the job well"? The underground stories "Sister Xia" and "A Maiden's Heart" (see chapter 5) are good pornography in Rawls's sense of "having the properties it is rational to want in an X, given what X's are . . . expected to do." It would be snobbish to deny that, in one sense, the word "good" does apply here. But it is equally obvious that in another sense it does not.

We need to distinguish means and ends, and to allow "good" somehow to apply to both. Rawls, in treating this issue, discusses the "good assassin," a term that can be used to recognize certain skills without having to approve of them.[110] Even a person who holds that assassination is absolutely wrong can make distinctions between high-quality and low-quality practitioners. Similarly, the writer Zheng Yi, who by age forty had grown contemptuous of Maoist romanticism, could recognize that *Red Crag* is good at what it

[107] Professor Chi Ke, a senior professor of aesthetics at the Guangzhou Academy of Fine Arts, introduced the poem to me with great enthusiasm in early 1980.

[108] Among favorable responses to literary works, the question of how to separate what we want to call "aesthetic" responses from other kinds of psychological responses that still warrant use of the word "good" is a complex issue that I will not try to address here. The essential dilemma, in my own view, is how to account for the important distinction between artistic value and other kinds of value while avoiding, on the other hand, the snobbish view that the pleasures of the elite are intrinsically better than those of the nonelite.

[109] Rawls, *A Theory of Justice*, p. 402.

[110] Ibid., p. 403.

aims to do, even while, in a deeper sense, despising the book. A theory of literary value must address that deeper sense.

Again, to begin empirically, one kind of actual use of this deeper sense of "good" is not in principle very different from the instrumental sense that we have just been considering. In some uses of "good," a thing can be good in the deeper sense provided only that we stipulate that the group "for whom" the thing is good is a large group—all of a community, a society, or humankind (or, in the broadest sense, the whole universe)—and that the time span taken into consideration also be fairly large. "A good person," writes Rawls, in addressing this sense of good, "is one who has to a higher degree than average the properties which it is rational for citizens to want in one another."[111] Using a similar approach, we can account for Zheng Yi's negative overall judgment of *Red Crag* in terms of his view that the book's naive idealism does not serve the interests of China and the world over the long term. Thus, too, "A Maiden's Heart" can be called good pornography (better than average at titillation, as young inmates of a detention school testified), but bad literature in a larger sense (because of socially deleterious long-term effects, as conservative critic Liu Baiyu claimed.)[112] Assassins, because they usually are seen as serving a limited group of conspirators, usually do not qualify as "good" in the deeper sense, however nifty with pistols. In instances where a speaker is convinced of the righteousness of an assassin's cause, for example in stopping a tyrant's genocide, the speaker might call the assassin "good" in the deeper sense; but this would still be a case of wanting the best for the world at large, and hence not an exception to our principle.

However, the theory of "good" as serving the wants of the world as a whole is still inadequate to cover all of what we mean by the word, especially as it applies to literature and art. The more ineffable aspects of art—as noted by Louis Armstrong, Aleksandr Solzhenitsyn, and countless others—cannot be entirely captured either by a technical definition of quality (parallel to sharpness in a knife) or by a concept of conducement to the collective good of a large group, or even by a combination of the two. The limits of the technical definition are evident if we ask whether Du Fu's poems, or Shakespeare's, are good only because they have certain rationally desirable properties to a higher degree than other poems. Aside, perhaps, from recoiling intuitively at the suggestion of such a mechanical measure of value, the proposition leads to absurd consequences: for example, that the best poem in the world would become valueless if, for some reason, it were to become the only poem in

[111] Ibid., p. 435. The question of moral value, as distinct from technical or practical value, of course opens a large and extremely complex problem that lies beyond the scope of this book. Rawls's own discussion is itself lengthy and complex (pp. 433–587), but the essentials of my characterization of his position in this paragraph are fairly clear. He holds explicitly that his theory does account for questions of "moral worth" (pp. 434, 437, and elsewhere).

[112] Fudan daxue zhexuexi qibaji diaocha xiaozu, "Zhongshi huangse shouchaoben dui zhongxuesheng de duhai"; interview with Liu Baiyu, 11 August 1980.

the world. Using the measure of "conducement to the collective good" is less obviously counterintuitive, but still highly problematic. Are Du Fu's poems good only because they bring about (presumably through effects on readers) conditions that are rational for humankind as a whole to want? We sense not; if we imagine a hermit, about to die in the wilderness and reading the last extant copy of a Du Fu poem, we still can quite easily imagine the hermit finding the poem to be good. Moreover, some of the much more mundane uses of literature, reviewed above as "escaping to imagined space," "expressing feelings," and so on, also involve values of essentially this kind. Hence we still need an account of the enjoyment of literature for its own sake, or, as this is sometimes called, the "intrinsic" value of literature.

Such a question does not bring us entirely beyond a distinguished theorist like Rawls, but it does bring us to an area where his theory is most vague. He writes at length about the kind of good that can come about when a personal activity is satisfying, but does not draw specific examples from the appreciation of art. He refers in passing to "the enjoyment of beauty" as one kind of experience that his theory can account for, but his examples are drawn from related areas, such as appreciation of algebra or chess.[113]

Rawls theorizes that a person's intrinsic satisfaction in mastering an activity (or comprehending an experience) has to do with its complexity or subtlety. He takes it as a psychological fact that "someone who can do both generally prefers playing chess to playing checkers, and . . . would rather study algebra than arithmetic."[114] Such facts illustrate, he says, the "Aristotelian Principle": "A person takes pleasure in doing something as he becomes more proficient at it, and of two activities which he performs equally well, he prefers the one that calls upon the greater number of more subtle and intricate discriminations."[115] The phrase "subtle and intricate discriminations" clearly gets us closer to what we want to mean by "intrinsically" good literature. Between Zhong Acheng's "The King of Chess" and Lu Xinhua's "Scar," for example, both of which are about young people cut loose from their families during the Cultural Revolution, we have no trouble identifying "The King of Chess" as the better work, and our reasons inevitably concern its greater subtlety.

It is important not to overlook Rawls's proviso about competence. In order for greater complexity to produce greater satisfaction, a person needs to perform the more complex activity at least "equally well" as the simpler one. The natural tendency to seek added complexity (the Aristotelian Principle) is offset by the difficulty that mastery of complexity entails. (It is more fun, but also more difficult, to master chess than checkers.) Without the required competence, a more complex activity can bring frustration, noncomprehension, and hence less enjoyment than a simpler one. (Being good at

[113] Rawls, *A Theory of Justice*, p. 434.
[114] Ibid., p. 426.
[115] Ibid., p. 414. Rawls's attribution of the principle to Aristotle is based on the *Nicomachean Ethics*, VII.11–14, and X.1–5, and explained in *A Theory of Justice*, p. 426 note 20.

checkers is more fun than being bad at chess.) In daily-life Chinese, the word *fuza* (complex) often has negative connotations; others things being equal, one avoids the *fuza*. But this kind of *fuza* clearly implies "unmastered complexity"; it is not a counterexample to Rawls's theory that competence in complex or subtle matters brings satisfaction. The point is important in application specifically to literary value because it can shed light on the perennial problem of "elite" and "popular" literature; it helps to explain why we regard subtler works (Acheng's "King of Chess," say) as better than less subtle ones (Zhang Yang's *The Second Handshake*, for example) even though Zhang's more popular work reaches many more people and thus brings, on a utilitarian calculation, greater aggregate enjoyment to the world.

It is possible to question whether we always do value (mastered) complexity more highly than simplicity. In mathematics and science, a principle of parsimony asks that theories be stated in their simplest possible forms; physicists pursue what they hope will be a few basic rules to comprise a Theory of Everything, and mathematicians refer to terse proofs as "elegant," thus explicitly associating aesthetic value with procedures that are less, not more, intricate. However, to value parsimony of expression is hardly the same as to value simplicity or unsubtlety in what is expressed. Terseness is considered elegant in the expression of something like $E = mc^2$; it is not regarded as especially valuable in $2 + 2 = 4$.

The tougher problem, if we accept that mastery of complex activities is intrinsically more satisfying than mastery of simple ones, is to specify why this is so. Here Rawls can only speculate. He does so in general terms, but his musings seem to suit the matter of literary appreciation rather well.

> Presumably complex activities are more enjoyable because they satisfy the desire for variety and novelty of experience, and leave room for feats of ingenuity and invention. They also evoke the pleasures of anticipation and surprise, and often the overall form of the activity, its structural development, is fascinating and beautiful. Moreover, simpler activities exclude the possibility of individual style and personal expression which complex activities permit or even require.[116]

The virtue of these lines, for our purposes, is that they touch upon several of the elements that we feel intuitively to be involved in the more ineffable aspects of literary value: novelty, ingenuity, fascination, beauty, individual style, and so on. The weakness of the same lines is that each key term seems to open its own little realm of mystery, leaving us hardly closer to final analytic clarity.

But Rawls stops here; he ventures no further toward explication of the elusive aspects of value, and I, too, shall desist. A final account of aesthetic value is not (I am relieved to note) the purpose of this book, and in any case the point we have now reached seems to me adequate for handling nearly all

[116] Rawls, *A Theory of Justice*, p. 427.

the cases that we encounter within the socialist Chinese literary system. In my view, Rawls's theory of the more instrumental senses of "good" fits the realities of the socialist Chinese literary system remarkably well. His accounts of the deeper senses of "good"—as serving needs of whole societies, or, alternatively, the needs of individuals in accordance with the Aristotelian Principle—are less fully satisfying but still, in my view, useful as far as they go. They can help, for example, to explain the artistic differences between "At Middle Age" by Chen Rong and "Nest Egg" by Wang Zhecheng and Wen Xiaoyu—two stories we have discussed in earlier chapters that have a common theme and raise similar questions. "Nest Egg," the shorter of the two, was probably more direct in its service of the practical needs of readers in probing the West, testing life options, and the like. But "At Middle Age" seems the better work of art. We can call it more "sophisticated," but simply to apply this overused word, without explication, does not move us closer to understanding. Application of Rawls's theory does seem to move us closer: "At Middle Age" is the more complex of the two works; it depicts life in more entangled detail, demands more effort of the reader who seeks mastery, and offers greater satisfaction when mastery is achieved.

In larger perspective, though, the artistic differences between stories like "At Middle Age" and "Nest Egg" are small matters within the broad panorama of life in the socialist Chinese literary system. That system, directly or indirectly, gave rise to a considerable variety of uses of literature. Those uses in turn produced a range of senses for what people who lived within the system meant by "good" when they referred to literary works. Some of those senses—especially the more "instrumental" ones—are not obvious to an outsider; only people who have lived in a closed society or under authoritarian rule grasp them easily.

It is tempting to try to place the uses of literature themselves into a value-ordered hierarchy. In addition to saying that each sort of use admits value of its own kind, do we not want to say that the thrall produced by a good poem is itself more valuable than the "release of resentment" produced by a piece of truth-telling reportage or the escape from humdrum that a hand-copied thriller provides? This kind of ordering could be done, I believe, on something akin to Rawls's Aristotelian Principle. A mind that could appreciate the full range of "kinds" of literary value simultaneously (although I doubt there ever has been such a mind) would, one might argue, extrapolating from less ideal experience, no doubt feel that the subtler kinds are intrinsically the more valuable; and that fact would, in my view, be enough to justify claims of a hierarchy in the intrinsic value of the uses of literature. I believe this kind of argument is valid. But it still does not imply, in my view, that one person's experience in one use of literature is necessarily more valuable than another person's in a different use. For ordinary minds situated in varying particular circumstances, it remains ultimately moot whether a person who loves a thriller but cannot grasp a subtle poem has an experience less valuable than a person who loves the poem and scorns the thriller. Even within the same particular mind, it seems to me hard to argue that joy derived from "releasing resentment" is necessarily less good than joy derived from reading a subtle poem. The release of resentment is a simpler and perhaps more transient response, but, if the context is right, can also be more powerfully euphoric.

In sum, although I find in the socialist Chinese literary system a variety of ways in which works were called "good," this result does not imply an absence of standards but only that different standards applied to different types of writing and contexts. Intrinsic aspects of art never did very well in socialist China. But it is a mistake to move from the observation that intrinsic value was rare to the conclusion that value of all kinds was thin. Other things were going on, and some profound human values were sometimes at stake in how well they went. It is an especially unfortunate mistake to look at the crass intrusions of the state—its "engineering" and its literary control system—and conclude that the people who suffered those intrusions must have been equally unsubtle. An antihumanist assault does not imply a lack of humanism in those who are assaulted. Indeed, there is a sense in which repression ironically can enhance humanism. When truth-telling and subtlety are restricted and become dangerous, they become rarer even as the public need for them grows stronger, and their value can soar beyond what it would be without the system that restricts them. The very meaning of truth and human dignity are sometimes more deeply understood when denied. Ba Jin, near the end of his long life, notes that "only after I had been deprived of my human rights and had lived in a 'cow shed' for a decade did I truly realize that I was a 'person.'"[117] Considerations such as these help to explain the "strange phenomena" with which we began in the Introduction: literary magazines circulating in the hundreds of thousands, high school students who list reading as a favorite after-school activity, and poets who can attract crowds of several hundred to a park, even in the rain.

[117] Ba Jin, "Suixianglu hedingben xinji" (New note on the single-volume edition of *Random Thoughts*), quoted in Wang Zisong, "Zhengzhixuejia de tianzhen," p. 15.

GLOSSARY

THIS GLOSSARY omits the following kinds of item:

1. names of writers, works, and periodicals that can be easily located in the bibliography;
2. the Chinese and Japanese names of authors of works published in English;
3. names of the Chinese provinces and of very well-known cities (such as Beijing) and people (such as Mao Zedong);
4. names of Chinese publishers and film production studios (although, for films, titles and names of directors are provided);
5. extremely obvious examples when meanings are given, such as *lao* "old."

Ai Qing — 艾青
aizibing — 艾滋病, 愛資病
bafang la guanxi, sichu zou houmen — 八方拉關係, 四處走後門
Bai Xianyong — 白先勇
baihua — 白話
Bao Chang — 鮑昌
Bao Zheng — 包拯
baogaowenxue — 報告文學
baolu — 暴露
baoshou — 保守
Bei Dao — 北島
Beijing guangbo bao — 北京廣播報
Beijing zhi chun — 北京之春
benzhi — 本質
biaotai — 表態
biaoxian — 表現
Bin (county) — 賓
Bo Yibo — 薄一波
bundan — 文壇
bushi neme tifa — 不是那麼提法
Bushi weile aiqing — 不是爲了愛情
butimian — 不體面
Cai Minghui — 蔡明輝
caizi jiaren — 才子佳人
Cangzhou — 滄州
Cankao xiaoxi — 參考消息
Cao Xueqin — 曹雪芹
Cao Yu — 曹禺
"Cesuo jijing" — 廁所即景
Chali — 查理
Chang Zhenhua — 常甄華
changkuang de hen — 猖狂得很

Chaoyangmennei — 朝陽門內
Chen Canyun — 陳殘雲
Chen Duxiu — 陳獨秀
Chen Huangmei — 陳荒煤
Chen Jiangong — 陳建功
Chen Kaige — 陳凱歌
Chen Muhua — 陳慕華
Chen Shimei — 陳世美
Chen Sihe — 陳思和
Chen Yingzhen — 陳映眞
Cheng Xiaoqing — 程小青
Chi Ke — 遲軻
chouhua — 醜化
chuangjiang — 闖將
chuangzuo jijin — 創作基金
chuli — 處理
Cihai — 辭海
Cong Weixi — 從維熙
da zhen — 打針
Dai — 傣
Dai Jienan — 戴介南
Dai Wangshu — 戴望舒
daolu — 道路
dapo jinqu — 打破禁區
Daxuesheng — 大學生
Dazai Osamu — 太宰治
de — 德
Deng Liqun — 鄧立群
Deng Tuo — 鄧拓
Deng Yimin — 鄧一民
"Dian shijie" — 電世界
Dianying chuangzuo — 電影創作
Ding Ling — 丁玲

Ding Mu — 丁牧
ding'e — 定額
Dong Biwu — 董必武
Dongfang meiren ku — 東方美人庫
Donghai — 東海
Dongshan — 東山
dou — 斗
doufu — 豆腐
Du Fu — 杜甫
Duanmu Hongliang — 端木蕻良
duiwu — 隊伍
Dunhuang — 敦煌
Duoduo — 多多
duoyuan — 多元
Ernü yingxiong zhuan — 兒女英雄傳
fa zhi — 法治
Fan Zhongyan — 范仲淹
fang — 放
Fang Cheng — 方成
Fang Fang — 方芳
Fang Lizhi — 方勵之
fansi — 反思
fanxing — 反省
feishu — 飛書
feixu wenxue — 廢墟文學
Feng Menglong — 馮夢龍
Fengyu xiaoxiao — 風雨瀟瀟
Fenxiang jianian — 分享艱難
Fudan — 復旦
"fuqi zhi jian" — 夫妻之間
fuwubu — 服務部
fuza — 複雜
Fuzhou — 福州
Gao duzhe shu — 告讀者書
Gao Gang — 高崗
ge wei — 各位
gesong — 歌頌
gongchandangyuan bushi shenme dou hui —
    共產黨員不是甚麼都會
Gongchanzhuyi qingniantuan — 共產主
    義青年團
gongfu — 功夫
Gongren ribao — 工人日報
gongxiaoshe — 供銷社
Gu Mingdao — 顧明道
Guangbo jiemu bao — 廣播節目報
Guangdong huajutuan — 廣東話劇團
guangmingmian — 光明面

Guangzhou budui huajutuan — 廣州部
    隊話劇團
Guangzhou huajutuan — 廣州話劇團
guanhua — 官話
guanxixue — 關係學
"Gui jie" — 鬼姐
"Guilai" — 歸來
Guixin sijian — 歸心似箭
Guiyang wanbao — 貴陽晚報
Guo Moruo — 郭沫若
guojia — 國家
Guomindang — 國民黨
Guwen guanzhi — 古文觀止
Haiwai chizi — 海外赤子
Haixia qinglei — 海峽情淚
hansen bungaku — 反戰文學
hanyu pinyin — 漢語拼音
"Hao shi bian huai shi" — 好事變壞事
He Huoren — 何火任
Hebei wenyi — 河北文藝
hei — 嘿
hei dahan — 黑大漢
Hei Mudan — 黑牡丹
Heipao shijian — 黑砲事件
hen jingshen — 很精神
Hino Ashihei — 火野葦平
Hong Ze — 洪澤
Hongbaoshi — 紅寶石
Hongloumeng — 紅樓夢
hongyan — 紅眼
houtai — 後台
Hu Feng — 胡風
Hu Pengnan — 胡鵬南
Hu Ping — 胡平
hua shuo — 話說
"Huainian Xiao Shan" — 懷念蕭珊
Hualiu — 驊騮
Huang Meifang — 黃梅芳
Huang Qiuyun — 黃秋耘
Huang Yongyu — 黃永玉
Huangjiang nüxia — 荒江女俠
Huangtudi — 黃土地
Huo Sang — 霍桑
Ihara Saikaku — 井原西鶴
Jiang Liu — 江流
Jiang Qing — 江青
Jianghu qixia zhuan — 江湖奇俠傳
Jiangmen — 江門

jiaoqing — 交情

jiben gaochou — 基本稿酬

jiedong — 解凍

jieben — 解恨

jielu — 揭露

jieshi — 揭示

Jiliu sanbuqu — 激流三部曲

Jin — 金

Jin he — 金河

Jin Yong — 金庸

jing — 精

jingshen — 精神

Jintian — 今天

Jiujiu ta — 救救她

Kaiping — 開平

Kang Keqing — 康克清

Kang Sheng — 康生

Kang Zhuo — 康濯

kao shan — 靠山

"*Kougong*" — 口供

koutou wenxue — 口頭文學

kuaiban shu — 快板書

Ku'nan de xin — 苦難的心

Ku'naoren de xiao — 苦惱人的笑

Kurosawa Akira — 黑澤明

Lan fengzheng — 藍風箏

Lan Ping — 藍平

Lang Hua — 浪花

Lanzhou — 蘭州

lao touzi — 老頭子

Lei Feng — 雷鋒

Leixue yinghua — 淚血櫻花

Li Bai — 李白

Li Chunsheng — 李春生

Li Jian — 李鍵

Li Jun — 李俊

Li Tuo — 李陀

Li Xiaolin — 李小林

Li Xiaoxia — 李曉霞

Li Xiaozhang — 李小璋

Li Yingmin — 李英敏

lian zou dai pao — 連走帶跑

liang tou re, zhongjian leng — 兩頭熱，中間冷

lianzhang — 連長

Liao Mosha — 廖沫沙

liao tian — 聊天

liaojie — 瞭解

Lin Biao — 林彪

Lin Chanying — 林嬋英

Lin Daojing — 林道靜

Lin Feng — 林峰

Lin Gang — 林崗

Lin Mohan — 林默涵

Ling Zi — 凌子

linggan — 靈感

lishi qingbai — 歷史清白

lishi qingchu — 歷史清楚

Liu Baiyu — 劉白羽

Liu Na'ou — 劉吶鷗

Liu Rongfa — 劉榮發

Liu Shaoqi — 劉少奇

Liu Shaotang — 劉紹棠

Liu Xie — 劉勰

Liu Xinglong — 劉醒龍

"*Liuge heshang da shui chi*" — 六個和尚搭水吃

lixiang xiaoshuo — 理想小說

Lu Wenting — 陸文婷

Luo Guanzhong — 羅貫中

Luo Ruiqing — 羅瑞卿

Luojiashan — 珞珈山

Luoshan — 羅山

Lushan — 盧山

Ma Feng — 馬鋒

manhua — 漫畫

Mao Dun — 茅盾

Mei — 梅 (Sister Mei)

Meihuadang — 梅花黨

meiyou banfa — 沒有辦法

menglong — 朦朧

Ming — 明

minjian — 民間

Mou Guozhang — 牟國璋

Mu Shiying — 穆時英

Mumaren — 牧馬人

Muxidi — 木樨地

Nakayama Gishū — 中山義秀

Nanhai — 南海

Nanning — 南寧

neibu — 內部

neiwai you bie — 內外有別

Nie Hualing — 聶華苓

Noma Hiroshi — 野間宏

Nufa chongguan — 怒髮沖冠

nüxia — 女俠

Ōe Kenzaburō — 大江健三郎

Ōta Yōko — 大田洋子

Ouman — 歐曼

Ozaki Shirō — 尾崎士郎

pai — 派

pao fangzi — 跑房子

Peng Dehuai — 彭德懷

pingfan — 平反

pingshudian — 評書點

pujiben — 普及本

qi — 奇

Qian Zhongshu — 錢鍾書

qianyin — 鉛印

qianzi doumi — 千字斗米

qiao — 巧

Qiji — 騏驥

Qin Bo — 秦波

Qin Xianglian — 秦香蓮

Qin Zhaoyang — 秦兆陽

Qing — 清

qing jiang — 清江

qing ping — 清萍

qingnian — 青年

Qiong Yao — 瓊瑤

Qiu shui — 秋水

Qixia wuyi — 七俠五義

Qizhong qi — 奇中奇

Qu Qiubai — 瞿秋白

Qu Yuan — 屈原

quyi — 曲藝

Rao Shushi — 饒漱石

ren zhi — 人治

Ren Zhongyi — 任仲夷

Renmin zhi sheng — 人民之聲

Ru Zhijuan — 茹志鵑

Ruan Ming — 阮銘

Rulin waishi — 儒林外史

Ruo — 若

Ruyan fei — 乳燕飛

Sai Ying — 賽英

"san bu" zhuyi: buda gunzi, bukou maozi, buzhua bianzi — '三不' 主義: 不打棍子、不扣帽子、不抓辮子

San Mao — 三毛

"san wu" shijie: wu yaoqiu, wu lingdao, wu piping — '三無' 世界: 無要求、無領導、無批評

Sha Yexin — 沙葉新

Shajiabang — 沙家浜

Shandong kuai shu — 山東快書

shanghen — 傷痕

Shantou — 汕頭

Shao Quanlin — 邵荃麟

Shen Congwen — 沈從文

Shen Hugen — 沈虎根

Shenzhou fenglei — 神州風雷

Shi lao shixuan — 十佬詩選

Shi Zhecun — 施蟄存

Shiina Rinzo — 椎名麟三

Shiwangren de xiwang — 失望人的希望

shou — 收

shouchaoben — 手抄本

shouzhang — 首長

Shuangtian xiaojiao — 霜天曉角

Shun jian — 瞬間

shunkouliu — 順口溜

shuoshu — 說書

si tiao hanzi — 四條漢子

Sidaokou — 四道口

Song — 宋

Song Jiang — 宋江

Song Qingling — 宋慶齡

Su Wei — 蘇煒

Sun Dasheng — 孫大勝

Sun Min — 孫敏

Sun Xiaolan — 孫小蘭

Tang — 唐

Tangshan — 唐山

Tansuo — 探索

Tao Qian — 陶潛

tenkō — 転向

Tian Han — 田漢

"Tian hua luan zhui" — 天花亂墜

Tian Jian — 田間

Tian Zhuangzhuang — 田壯壯

Tiananmen — 天安門

tifa — 提法

tiyan shenghuo — 體驗生活

toudu — 偷渡

tujie zhengce — 圖解政策

waishi — 外史

Waiwen shudian — 外文書店

Wan Li — 萬里

Wang Cunli — 王存立

Wang Dongxing — 汪東興

Wang Guangmei — 王光美

Wang Shouxin — 王守信

Wang Tuo — 王拓

Wang Wei — 王維
Wang Xiaoming — 王曉明
Wang Yaping — 王亞平
Wang Ying — 王影
Wang Zhaojun — 王昭君
Wang Zhen — 王震
Wangfujing — 王府井
wangguo yishi — 亡國意識
Wei Jingsheng —魏京生
"Wei lou" — 危樓
wei min qing ming — 爲民請命
Wen Yingjie — 聞英傑
wenhuazhan (guan) — 文化站 (館)
wentan — 文壇
Wenxue gongzuozhe xiehui — 文學工作
　者協會
Wenxue shuchuang — 文學書窗
Women zheiyidai — 我們這一代
Wu Cheng'en — 吳承恩
Wu Han — 吳晗
Wu Jingzi — 吳敬梓
Wu Nansheng — 吳南生
Wu Qiang — 吳強
Wu Xiaoling — 吳曉鈴
Wu Xiaonan — 吳小南
Wu Xun — 武訓
Wu Yiping — 吳一萍
Wu Zetian — 武則天
Wu Zuxiang — 吳組緗
Wuhan wenyi — 武漢文藝
Wuming wenxue — 無名文學
wuqi — 武器
wuran — 污染
wuxia — 武俠
Wuxiandian — 無綫電
xi ge zao, shui ge jiao, shi hao xi — 洗個
　澡, 睡個覺, 是好戲
Xia —霞 (Sister Xia)
xia (ke) — 俠 (客)
xiandai pai — 現代派
Xiang Kairan — 向愷然
Xian'gang — 蜆崗
Xiangshan ye zheng hong — 香山葉正紅
xiangsheng — 相聲
xiangtu pai — 鄉土派
Xiao hua — 小花
Xiao Hong — 蕭紅
Xiao Yemu — 蕭也牧
Xiao Yin — 蕭殷

xiaobao — 小報
xiaoda da bangmang — 小打大幫忙
xiaokaiben — 小開本
Xiaoman — 小曼 (慢)
xiaomie — 消滅
Xin'gang — 新港
Xinhua shudian — 新華書店
Xinhui — 新會
Xinyang — 信陽
Xiongnu — 匈奴
Xiwang — 希望
Xu Juemin — 許覺民
Xu Lingjun — 許靈均
Xu Shiyou — 許世友
Xu Xiaohua — 徐小華
Xu Yu — 徐訏
Xu Zhenya — 徐枕亞
Xu Zhimo — 徐志摩
xungen (pai) — 尋根 (派)
yan jiu — 煙酒
Yan'an — 延安
yang feng yin wei — 陽奉陰違
Yang Hansheng — 陽翰笙
Yang Yanjin — 楊延晉
Yangzi — 揚子
yanjiu — 研究
Yao Shougang — 姚守崗
Yao Wenyuan — 姚文元
yaoqiao — 搖橋
Ye Jianying — 葉劍英
Ye Wenfu — 葉文福
yeshi — 野史
yi — 義
yiyantang — 一言堂
yifa chuli — 依法處理
yige ren shuo le suan — 一個人說了算
yin she chu dong — 引蛇出洞
Yin Xianglin — 殷向林
yinshua gaochou — 印刷稿酬
Yu Luoke — 遇羅克
yuan — 元
Yuan Yunsheng — 袁運生
Yuanwangji — 遠望集
Yuanye — 原野
"Yueyanglou ji" — 岳陽樓記
Yue Fei — 岳飛
zai — 宰
Zai tianyeshang qianjin — 在田野上前進
zao laotou —糟老頭

Zaochen — 早晨
Zha Jianying — 查建英
Zhang Ailing — 張愛玲
Zhang Andong — 張安東
Zhang Chunqiao — 張春橋
Zhang Guangnian — 張光年
Zhang Henshui — 張恨水
Zhang Rulun — 張汝倫
Zhang Shengyou — 張勝友
Zhang Xiguo — 張系國
Zhang Xinxin — 張辛欣
Zhang Zheng — 張錚
Zhang Zhidong — 張之洞
Zhang Zhong — 張鍾
zhanlue — 戰略
zhanxian — 戰綫
Zhao Huan — 趙寰
Zhao Ziyang — 趙紫陽
Zhao Zumo — 趙祖謨
Zheng Rude — 鄭汝德
Zheng Yimei — 鄭逸梅
zhengque — 正確
zhengzhi shanggang — 政治上綱
zhenying — 陣營
zhijian — 只見
zhishi qingnian — 知識青年
Zhong Lihe —鍾理和
Zhongguo guangbo bao — 中國廣播報

Zhongguo qingnian bao — 中國青年報
*Zhongguo quanguo wenxue yishu jie lianhe
   hui* — 中國全國文學藝術界聯合
   會
Zhongguo shudian — 中國書店
Zhongguo zuojia xiehui — 中國作家協
   會
zhongpian xiaoshuo — 中篇小說
Zhongshan — 中山
Zhongyang guangbo bao — 中央廣播報
Zhongyang renmin dianshi tai — 中央人
   民電視台
Zhongyang renmin guangbo diantai —
   中央人民廣播電台
Zhu De — 朱德
Zhu Guangqian — 朱光潛
Zhu Muzhi — 朱穆之
Zhu Xi — 朱熹
Zhu Zhai — 朱寨
Zhuangzi — 莊子
Zhuge Liang — 諸葛亮
Zhujiang shui chang — 珠江水長
ziyou (hua) — 自由 (化)
ziyouzhuyi — 自由主義
zonghexing — 綜合性
zunming wenxue — 尊命文學
Zuopin yu zhengming — 作品與爭鳴

BIBLIOGRAPHY

Works Cited in the Notes

Acheng 阿城. *See* Zhong Acheng.

Ai Qing 艾青. "Hua yu ci" 花與刺 (Flowers and thorns). *Renmin ribao*, 10 July 1980.

———. "Wenyi kanwu yinggai shi jianshe jingshen wenming de zhendi" 文藝刊物 應該是建設精神文明的陣地 (Literary periodicals should be the battlefront for establishing spiritual civilization). *Renmin ribao*, 2 November 1983, p. 3.

Ai Shan 艾姍. *See* Zhao Zhenkai.

Anhui wenxue 安徽文學 (Anhui literature). Hefei.

———. [Unsigned]. "Dui 'shiliunian' tifa de yiyi" 對 '十六年' 提法的異議 (A objection to the way "the sixteen years" are referred to) 1982.6. 71–76, 79.

Anonymous. "Dixia baolei de fumie" 地下堡壘的覆滅 (Annihilation of the underground stronghold). Hand-copied volume.

———. "Kongbu de jiaobusheng" 恐怖的腳步聲 (Terrifying footsteps). Hand-copied volume.

———. "Manna huiyilu" 曼娜回憶錄 (Manna's memoirs). Hand-copied volume. Also widely known as "Shaonü de xin" 少女的心 (A maiden's heart).

———. "Qingtian changhen" 情天長恨 (Eternal regrets in love). Hand-copied volume.

———. "Renxing lun" 人性論 (On human nature). Hand-copied volume.

———. "Yige gaozhong nüsheng de xing tiyan" 一個高中女生的性體驗 (The sexual experiences of a girl high school student). *Xie zhen: haiwaiban* (Hong Kong) 1987.2.106–11.

Aositeluofusiji 奧斯特洛夫斯基. *See* Ostrovskii, Nicholas.

Arkush, David. "One of the Hundred Flowers: Wang Meng's 'Young Newcomer,'" Harvard University *Papers on China* 18. Cambridge, Mass, 1964.

Ba Jin 巴金. "Jiehun" 結婚 (Marriage). In Ba Jin, *Suixianglu*, pp. 11–13.

———. *Suixianglu* 隨想錄 (Miscellaneous thoughts). Hong Kong: Sanlian shudian, 1979. Translated by Geremie Barmé as *Random Thoughts*. Hong Kong: Joint Publishing, 1984.

Bach, Richard. *Jonathan Livingston Seagull*. New York: Macmillan, 1970.

Bai Hua 白樺. "Yishu xinzha" 一束信札 (A bundle of letters). *Renmin wenxue* 1980.1.24–40. Translated by Ellen Yeung in Link, ed., *Stubborn Weeds*, pp. 115–42.

Bai Hua and Peng Ning 彭寧. "Kulian" (Unrequited love). *Shiyue* 1979.3.140–71, 248.

Baoweng laoren 抱甕老人. "Maiyoulang duzhan huakui" 賣油郎獨占花魁 (The oil-selling lad takes sole possession of the ace of courtesans). In Feng Shang 馮裳, ed. *Jingu qiguan* (Strange sights old and new) 今古奇觀. Shanghai: Guji chubanshe, 1992, pp. 61–86.

Barmé, Geremie R. *Shades of Mao: The Posthumous Cult of the Great Leader*. Armonk, N.Y.: M. E. Sharpe, 1996.

———. "Wang Shuo and *Liumang* ('Hooligan') Culture." *Australian Journal of Chinese Affairs* 28 (July 1992), pp. 23–66.

"Bashi niandai" Zhongguo qingnian gongren zhuangkuang diaochazu 八十年代中國 青年工人狀況調查組. "Guanyu dangdai Zhongguo qingnian gongren zhuangkuang de diaocha yu chubu fenxi" 關於當代中國青年工人狀況的調查與初步分析 (An investigation and preliminary analysis of the conditions of young workers in contemporary China). *Shehui diaocha yu yanjiu* (Social investigation and research) 1985.4.32–42.

Becker, Jasper. *Hungry Ghosts: China's Secret Famine*. London: John Murray, 1996.

Bei Cun 北村. "Da yaofang" 大藥房 (Big medicine shop). *Jintian* 1992.4.1–14.

———. "Yundong" 運動 (Movement). *Shanghai wenxue* 1994.5.26–33.

Beijing di'er waiguoyu xueyuan tong huai Zhou 北京第二外國語學院童懷周. *Tiananmen shiwenji* 天安門詩文集 (Collection of poems and writings from Tiananmen). Beijing: Beijing chubanshe, 1979.

———. *Tiananmen shiwenji xubian* 天安門詩文集續編 (Continued collection of poems and writings from Tiananmen). Beijing: Beijing chubanshe, 1979.

Beijing qingnianbao 北京青年報 (Beijing youth news). Beijing.

———. [Unsigned]. "Shi ze haoqi, ji er yanfan—zhongxuesheng dui jietou xiaobao de taidu" 始則好奇, 繼而厭煩——中學生對街頭小報的態度 (First curious, then fed up: high school students' attitudes toward street-side tabloids), 26 April, 1985, p. 1.

Beijing Review. Beijing.

Beijing ribao 北京日報 (Beijing daily). Beijing.

Beijing Shifan Daxue Zhongwenxi Xiandai Wenxue Jiaoxue Gaige Xiaozu 北京師範大學中文系現代文學教學改革小組, ed. *Zhongguo xiandai wenxueshi cankao ziliao* 中國現代文學史參考資料 (Reference materials on modern Chinese literary history). Beijing: Gaodeng jiaoyu chubanshe, 1959. 3 volumes.

Beijing wenyi 北京文藝 (Beijing literature and art). Beijing.

Bodman, Richard W., and Pin Pin Wan, trans. and ed. *Deathsong of the River: A Reader's Guide to the Chinese TV Series Heshang*. Cornell University East Asia Series, no. 54. Ithaca, N.Y., 1991.

Booth, Wayne C. *The Company We Keep: An Ethics of Fiction*. Berkeley and Los Angeles: University of California Press, 1988.

Borchert, Wolfgang. *The Man Outside*. Translated by David Porter. New York: New Directions Books, 1971.

Bratny, Roman. *Kolumbowie, rocnik 20* (The Columbuses-Generation of 1920). Warsaw: Panstwowy Instytut Wydawniczy, 1958.

Buczkowski, Leopold. *Black Torrent*. Translated by David Welsh. Cambridge: MIT Press, 1969.

Can Xue 殘雪. *Dialogues in Paradise*. Translated by Ronald R. Janssen and Jian Zhang. Evanston, Ill.: Northwestern University Press, 1989.

———. "Lütuzhong de xiao youxi" 旅途中的小遊戲 (A little game at mid-journey). *Xiaoshuojie* 小說界 (World of fiction) (Shanghai). February 1992, pp. 23–25.

———. "Shanshang de xiaowu" 山上的小屋 (Hut on the mountain). *Renmin wenxue* 1985.8.67–69.

———. "Wo zai neige shijieli de shiqing" 我在那個世界裏的事情 (The things that happened to me in that world). *Renmin wenxue* 1986.11.92–94.

Cao Guanlong 曹冠龍. "San'ge jiaoshou" 三個教授. *Anhui wenxue* 1980.1.17–31. Translated by John Berninghausen as "Three Professors" in Link, ed., *Roses and Thorns*, pp. 112–45.

Cen Sang 岑桑. "Haohan budiaolei" 好漢不掉淚 (Heroes do not weep). *Zuopin* 1980.45.30–36.

———. "Ruguo yu xia ge buting" 如果雨下個不停 (If the rain falls endlessly). *Dangdai* 1980.1.181–87.

Chang Er 長耳. "Beijing jichang bihua de fengbo" 北京機場壁畫的風波 (The controversy over the Beijing airport mural). *Guanchajia* 31 (1980), p. 30.

Chau, W. C., ed. *Prize-winning Stories from China 1980-81*. Beijing: Foreign Languages Press, 1985.

Chen Bo 陳播. "Dianying yao wei jianshe shehuizhuyi jingshen wenming zuochu gongxian" 電影要爲建設社會主義精神文明作出貢獻 (Films must contribute to building socialist spiritual civilization). *Hongqi* 1981.19.29–33.

Chen Dengke 陳登科 and Xiao Ma 蕭馬. *Pobiji* 破壁記 (Record of a broken wall). Beijing: Renmin wenxue chubanshe, 1980.

Chen Guokai 陳國凱. "Wo yinggai zenme ban?!" 我應該怎麼辦?! (What should I do?!). *Zuopin* 1979.2.37–50.

Chen Haiying 陳海鷹. "Hei haichao" 黑海潮 (Black tide). *Hongdou* 1979.2.1–9. Reprinted in *Zheyidai* 1979.1.19–27. Republished with two politically pointed passages omitted in *Guangzhou wenyi* 1979.11.3–10.

Chen Lingwen 陳陵文. "Wang Meng qidai kuanrong duidai dangjin wentan xianxiang" 王蒙期待寬容對待當今文壇現象 (Wang Meng hopes for tolerant treatment of phenomena on the literary scene today). *Chengdu wanbao* 成都晚報 (Chengdu evening news), 22 November 1994.

Chen Rong 諶容. "Ren dao zhongnian" 人到中年 (At middle age). *Shouhuo* 1980.1.52–92. Translated by Yu Fanqin and Wang Mingjie in Shen Rong, *At Middle Age*. Beijing: Panda Books, 1987, pp. 9–85.

Chen Shixu 陳世旭. "Xiaozhenshang de jiangjun" 小鎮上的將軍 (A general in a little town). *Shiyue* 1979.3.106–15.

Chen, Susan Wilf. "Literature of the 'Thaw' in China and the Soviet Union." Typescript, 1991.

Chen, Xiaomei. *Occidentalism*. New York and Oxford: Oxford University Press, 1995.

Chen Yi 陳毅. *Chen Yi shici xuanzhu* 陳毅詩詞選注 (A selection of Chen Yi's poems). Beijing: Beijing chubanshe, 1978.

Chen Yiming 陳宜明, Liu Yulian 劉宇廉, and Li Bin 李斌. "Feng" 楓 (Maple). *Lian \huan huabao* 連環畫報 (Cartoon strips) (Beijing) 1978.8.1–2, 35–36, front and back inside cover, and back outside cover.

Chen Yong 陳涌. "Cong liangge juben kan wenyi de zhenshixing he qingxiangxing" 從兩個劇本看文藝的眞實性和傾向性 (The realism and trends of literature and art as seen in two plays). *Renmin ribao*, 19 March 1980, p. 5.

Chen Zhongshi 陳忠實. *Bailuyuan* 白鹿原 (White deer plain). Beijing: Renmin wenxue chubanshe, 1993.

China Daily. Beijing.

China Focus. Plainsboro, New Jersey, 1993–1999.

China News Analysis. Hong Kong.

Chinese Literature. Foreign Languages Press, Beijing.

Chow, Tse-tsung. *The May Fourth Movement: Intellectual Revolution in Modern China*. Stanford: Stanford University Press, 1967.

Cui Dezhi 崔德志. "Baochunhua" 報春花 (First flower of spring). *Juben* 1979.4.2–40.

Dagongbao 大公報 (Dagong daily). Hong Kong.

———. [Unsigned]. "Zhou Yang zai Guangdong zuojia luntanshang de jianghua" 周揚在廣東作家論壇上的講話 (Zhou Yang addresses Guangdong writers' forum) 9 February 1982, p. 3.

Dai Houying 戴厚英. *Ren a, ren!* 人啊, 人! (People, oh people!). Guangzhou: Guangdong renminchubanshe, 1980. Translated by Frances Wood as *Stones of the Wall*. London: Joseph, 1985.

Dai Qing 戴晴. "Buneng yong yi zhong secai miaohui shenghuo: yu Xiao Lin tongzhi shangque" 不能用一種色彩描繪生活——與蕭林同志商榷 (We must not use one color in describing life: discussing matters with comrade Xiao Lin). *Guangming ribao* 1980.5.28.

———. "Chu Anping" 儲安平 *Dongfang jishi* 東方紀事 (Eastern chronicle) (Nanjing and Beijing) 1989.1.94–135. Reprinted in uncensored form as "Chu Anping yu dang tianxia" 儲安平與黨天下 (Chu Anping and the world of the party) in *Mingbao yuekan* 1989.1.136–47, 1989.2.44–54, and 1989.3.54–64.

———. "Pan" 盼 (Anticipation). *Guangming ribao*, 25 November 1979, p. 4 and 2 December 1979, p. 4. Translated by Billy Bikales in Link, ed. *Roses and Thorns*, pp. 147–67.

———. *Wang Shiwei and "Wild Lilies": Rectification and Purges in the Chinese Communist Party, 1942–44.* Edited by David Apter and Timothy Cheek. Armonk, N.Y.: M. E. Sharpe, 1994.

———. "Wang Shiwei yu 'ye baihehua'" 王實味與 "野百合花" (Wang Shiwei and "Wild Lilies"). *Wenhui yuekan* 文匯月刊 (Wenhui monthly) (Shanghai), May 1988, pp. 22–41. Also in *Mingbao yuekan* May 1988, pp. 3–16; and June 1988, pp. 24–33. Translated by Timothy Cheek in Dai Qing, *Wang Shiwei and "Wild Lilies,"* pp. 3–72.

Dai Qing and Zheng Zhishu 鄭直淑. "Liang Shuming yu Mao Zedong" 梁漱溟與毛澤東. *Wenhui yuekan* 文匯月刊 (Wenhui monthly) (Shanghai) 1988.1.24–32.

Dalu 大路 (The great road). Plainsboro, N.J., 1994–1996.

Dangdai 當代 (Contemporary times). Beijing.

Dangdai wenyi sichao 當代文藝思潮 (Trends in thought on contemporary literature and art). Lanzhou.

Daxuesheng 大學生 (University students). Fudan University student magazine, Shanghai.

Dazai Osamu. *The Setting Sun.* Translated by Donald Keene. New York: New Directions, 1956.

Dazhong dianying 大眾電影 (Masses' cinema). Beijing.

Deng Xiaoping 鄧小平. *Muqian de xingshi he renwu* 目前的形勢和任務 (On our present situation and responsibilities). Pamphlet. Beijing: Renmin chubanshe, February 1980.

Denton, Kirk A., ed. *Modern Chinese Literary Thought: Writings on Literature, 1893–1945.* Stanford: Stanford University Press, 1996.

Ding Wangyi 丁望乙. "Zhongguo dalu de dixia wenxue" 中國大陸的地下文學 (Underground literature in mainland China). *Haineiwai* 海內外 (New York), 1979: part 1 (January), pp. 18–20; part 2 (February), pp. 29–31; part 3, on poetry (March), pp. 18–24.

Dong Xijian 董錫健. "Qinggong yu lingdao ganqing de zhang'ai ji shutong" 青工與領導感情的障礙及疏通 (Barriers and mediation in the feeling between young workers and the leadership). *Qingnian yanjiu* 1986.1.39–46.

Dongxiang 動向 (Tendencies). Hong Kong.

Dongxifang 東西方 (The east and the west). Hong Kong.

Du Pengcheng 杜鵬程. *Baowei Yan'an* 保衛延安 (Defending Yan'an). Beijing: Renmin wenxue chubanshe, 1954.

Dudintsev, Vladimir. *Not by Bread Alone.* Translated by Edith Bone. New York: E. P. Dutton, 1957.

Duke, Michael S. *Blooming and Contending: Chinese Literature in the Post-Mao Era.* Bloomington: Indiana University Press, 1985.

———, ed. *Contemporary Chinese Literature: An Anthology of Post-Mao Fiction and Poetry.* Armonk, N.Y.: M. E. Sharpe, 1985.

————, ed. *Worlds of Modern Chinese Fiction: Short Stories and Novellas from the People's Republic, Taiwan, and Hong Kong*. Armonk, N.Y.: M. E. Sharpe, 1991.

Dushu 讀書 (Reading). Beijing.

Ehrenburg, Ilya. *The Thaw*. London: Harvill Press, 1955.

Erlich, Victor. "Post-Stalin Trends in Russian Literature." *Slavic Review* 23.3 (September 1964), pp. 405–19.

Ermolaev, Herman. *Soviet Literary Theories, 1917–1934: The Genesis of Socialist Realism*. Publications in Modern Philology, vol. 69. Berkeley and Los Angeles: University of California Press, 1963.

Fan Buyan 范步淹. "Cong xia yidai guanzhong kan xiqu de mingtian" 從下一代觀眾看戲曲的明天 (The future of opera as seen from the next generation of the audience). *Dangdai wenyi sichao* 1985.2.129–32.

Far Eastern Economic Review. Hong Kong.

Feng Jicai 馮驥才. *Chrysanthemums and Other Stories*. Translated by Susan Wilf Chen. San Diego: Harcourt Brace, Jovanovich, 1985.

————. "Dou han tu" 鬥寒圖 (A sketch in resisting the cold). *Xin'gang* 新港 (New Harbor) (Tianjin) 1980.4.4–25. Translated by Susan Wilf Chen as "Plum Blssoms in the Snow" in Feng Jicai, *Chrysanthemums and Other Stories*, pp. 172–228.

————. "Sancun jinlian" 三寸金蓮. Chengdu: Sichuan wenyi chubanshe, 1986. Translated by David Wakefield as *The Three-Inch Golden Lotus*. Honolulu: University of Hawaii Press, 1994.

Feng Mu 馮牧. "Guqijinlai, zhengqu wenxue chuangzuo de geng da de fanrong" 鼓起勁來, 爭取文學創作的更大的繁榮 (Get things moving and make literary creation flourish even more). *Wenyibao* 1982.2.12.

————. "Jianchi geming de xianshizhuyi" 堅持革命的現實主義 (Persist with revolutionary realism). Conference paper. Changsha, Hunan Province, 17 May 1980.

Feng ye 楓葉 (Maple leaves). Haidian qu wenhuazhan, Beijing.

Feng Zongpu 馮宗璞. "Wo shi shei?" 我是誰? (Who am I?) in *Zong Pu xiaoshuo sanwen xuan* 宗璞小說散文選 (A selection of Zong Pu's fiction and essays). Beijing: Beijing chubanshe, 1981, pp. 130–40.

Fenglei 風雷 (Tempest). A Red Guard newspaper. N.p.

————. [Unsigned]. "Kan, zuide xiuzhengzhuyi gaochou zhidu!" 看, 罪惡的修正主義稿酬制度 (Look at the evil revisionist manuscript payment system!), no. 9 (9 June 1967), p. 4.

Foreign Broadcast Information Service. Washington, D.C.

Forster, E. M. *Aspects of the Novel*. London: Edward Arnold, 1949.

Frankel, Edith R. *Novy Mir: A Case Study in the Politics of Literature*. Cambridge and New York: Cambridge University Press, 1981.

Friedberg, Maurice. "Soviet Books, Censors, and Readers." In Hayward and Labedz, *Literature and Revolution in Soviet Russia, 1917–1962*, pp. 198–210.

Fudan daxue zhexuexi qibaji diaocha xiaozu 復旦大學哲學系七八級調查小組. "Zhongshi huangse shouchaoben dui zhongxuesheng de duhai" 重視黃色手抄本對中學生的毒害 (Take seriously the pernicious influence on high school students of obscene hand-copied volumes) *Qingnian yanjiu* 1983.5.51–65.

Gao Hongbo 高洪波 and Guo Xiaolin 郭小林, eds. "Zai jing bufen shiren tan dangqian shige chuangzuo" 在京部分詩人談當前詩歌創作 (Certain poets in Beijing discuss the composition of contemporary poetry). *Wenyibao* 1981.16.19–20.

Gao Qixiang 高起祥. "Dianying zhonggui yao kao sixiang he yishu yingde guanzhong" 電影終歸要靠思想和藝術贏得觀眾 (In the end film must rely on thought and art to win its audience). *Xuexi yu yanjiu* 學習與研究 (Study and research) (Beijing)

1984.12.41–43; reprinted in Zhongguo renmin daxue shubao ziliao she 中國人民大學書報資料社, *Fuyin baokan ziliao* 複印報刊資料 (Reprints of periodical material) (Beijing) 1984.12.31–33.

Gao Xiaosheng 高曉聲. *The Broken Betrothal and Other Stories*. Beijing: Panda Books, 1987.

———. *Gao Xiaosheng yijiubalingnian xiaoshuoji* 高曉聲 1980 年小說集 (Collection of Gao Xiaosheng's fiction from 1980). Beijing: People's Literature Publishing House, 1981.

———. "Jian zhenzhu" 揀珍珠 (Picking out a pearl). *Beijing wenyi* 1979.9. Translated by Yu Fanqin as "A Bride for Guoming" in Gao Xiaosheng, *The Broken Betrothal*, pp. 134–44.

———. "On My Story 'The River Flows East.'" Translated by Rui An in *Chinese Literature* 1981.10.69–73.

———. "Shui dong liu" 水東流 (The river flows east). *Renmin ribao* 21 February 1981. Translated by Hu Shiguang in *Chinese Literature*, 1981.10.49–68.

———. "Xiwang nuli wei nongmin xiezuo" 希望努力爲農民寫作 (Hoping we will work hard at writing for the peasants). *Wenyibao*, 1980.4.41–44.

Gao Xingjian 高行健. "Chezhan" 車站 (Bus stop). *Shiyue* 1983.3.119–38.

Gaodeng jiaoyu yanjiu 高等教育研究 (Research on higher education). Liaoning.

Ge Fei 格非. "Da nian" 大年 (New year). In Ge Fei, *Shu yu shi* 樹與石 (Trees and stones). Yangzhou: Jiangsu wenyi chubanshe, 1996, pp. 86–125.

"Geming shichao" bianjibu "革命詩抄" 編輯部. *Geming shichao* 革命詩抄 (Revolutionary poetry). N.p., 1977.

Gibbs, Donald A., ed. *Dissonant Voices in Chinese Literature*. 1.1 (Winter 1979–1980) of *Chinese Studies in Literature*. White Plains, N.Y.: M. E. Sharpe.

Gibian, George. *Interval of Freedom: Soviet Literature during the Thaw, 1954–1957* (Minneapolis: University of Minnesota Press, 1960.

———. "Soviet Literature during the Thaw." In Hayward and Labedz, eds., *Literature and Revolution in Soviet Russia, 1917–1962*, pp. 125–49.

Goldblatt, Howard, ed. *Chinese Literature for the 1980s*. Armonk, N.Y.: M. E. Sharpe, 1983.

———, ed. *Worlds Apart: Recent Chinese Writing and Its Audiences*. Armonk, N.Y.: M. E. Sharpe, 1990.

Goldman, Merle. *China's Intellectuals: Advise and Dissent*. Cambridge: Harvard University Press, 1981.

———. *Literary Dissent in Communist China*. Cambridge: Harvard University Press, 1967.

———. *Sowing the Seeds of Democracy: Political Reform in the Deng Xiaoping Era*. Cambridge: Harvard University Press, 1994.

Gongqingtuan Xi'an shiwei xuanchuanbu, Xi'an baoshi zhouchengchang tuanwei 共青團西安市委宣傳部, 西安寶石軸承廠團委 (Propaganda Department of the Municipal Committee of the Communist Youth League of Xi'an City, Youth League Committee of the Xi'an Jewel Bearing Factory). "Yige gongchang qinggong renshengguan de diaocha" 一個工廠青工人生觀的調查 (An investigation of worldviews among young workers in one factory). *Qingnian yanjiu* 1982.17.9–17.

Grass, Gunter. *The Tin Drum*. New York: Pantheon Books, 1962.

Gu Cheng 顧城. "Ganjue" 感覺 (Feeling) *Shikan* 1980.10.28. Translated by William Tay as "Feeling" in Link, ed., *Stubborn Weeds*, p. 185.

———. "Huxian" 弧線 (Curve) *Shikan* 1980.10.29. Translated by William Tay as "Curves" in Link, ed., *Stubborn Weeds*, p. 185.

————. "Yidairen" 一代人 (A whole generation). In Gu Cheng, *Gu Cheng shi quanbian* 顧成詩全編 (Comprehensive collection of Gu Cheng's poetry), p. 121. Shanghai: Sanlian shudian, 1995), p. 121. Translated by William Tay as "One Generation" in Link, ed., *Stubborn Weeds*, p. 185.

————. "Zhan ting" 暫停 (A brief stop). *Jintian* 8 (1980), pp. 29–30. Translated by W. J. F. Jenner in Link, ed., *Stubborn Weeds*, p. 184.

Gu Hua 古華. "Futuling" 浮屠嶺 (Pagoda ridge). In Gu Hua, *Paman qingteng de muwu*, pp. 234–379. Translated by Gladys Yang in Gu Hua, *Pagoda Ridge and Other Stories*, pp. 9–146.

————. *Mao Zedong he ta de nürenmen* 毛澤東和他的女人們 (Mao Zedong and his women). Taibei: Lianjing chubanshiye gongsi, 1990.

————. *Pagoda Ridge and Other Stories*. Translated by Gladys Yang. Beijing: Panda Books, 1985.

————. "Paman qingteng de muwu" 爬滿青藤的木屋 (The log cabin overgrown with creepers). *Shiyue* 1981.2.56–68, 212. Translated by W. J. F. Jenner in Gu Hua, *Pagoda Ridge and Other Stories*, pp. 147–85.

————. *Paman qingteng de muwu* 爬滿青藤的木屋 (The log cabin overgrown by creepers). Beijing: Renmin wenxue chubanshe, 1983.

Guan Lin 關林. "Fenqing shifei, bianming zhenxiang" 分清是非, 辨明眞相 (Distinguish right and wrong, discern actual facts). *Wenyibao* 1982.8.74–79.

Guan Lixiang 關荔降. "'Duanxiang' de duanxiang" "斷想" 的斷想 (Some random thoughts about "Random thoughts"). *Yangcheng wanbao*, 25 June 1980.

Guanchajia 觀察家 (Observer). Hong Kong.

————. [Unsigned]. See *Renmin zhi sheng* bianjibu.

Guangdong sheng youzhengbu 廣東省郵政部 (Guangdong provincial postal department). "1980 nian diyi jidu baozhi zazhi jianming mulu" 1980 年第一季度 報紙雜誌簡明目錄 (Concise listing of newspapers and magazines for the first quarter of 1980). N.p., n.d.

Guangdong wenyi 廣東文藝 (Guangdong literature and art). Guangzhou. Called *Zuopin* after June 1978.

Guangming ribao 光明日報 (Guangming daily). Beijing.

————. [Unsigned]. "Quanguo youxiu duanpian xiaoshuo pingxuan fajiang dahui zai jing juxing" 全國優秀短篇小說評選發獎大會在京舉行 (National meeting to present prizes for the best short stories held in Beijing), 28 March 1979.

————. [Unsigned]. "Zhuhe he xiwang" 祝賀和希望 (Congratulations and hope), 28 March 1979.

Guangzhou ribao 廣州日報 (Guangzhou daily). Guangzhou.

————. [Unsigned]. "Jinnian jiang you neixie xin yingpian?" 今年將有哪些新影片? (What new films will there be this year?" 13 January 1980.

————. [Unsigned]. "*Wenhuibao* fabiao pinglunyuan wenzhang 'manhuai xinxin polang qianjin'" "文匯報" 發表評論員文章 "滿懷信心破浪前進" (*Wenhuibao* published a commentator article called "Forge ahead full of confidence"), 25 January 1980, p. 4.

Guangzhou wenyi 廣州文藝 (Guangzhou literature and art). Guangzhou.

Guilin Shifan "Yuwen Jiaoxue" Bianjishi 桂林師範 "語文教學" 編輯室, ed. *Zai shehui de dang'anli: Zhongguo dangdai wenxue cankao ziliao* 在社會的檔案——中國 當代文學參考資料 (In the archives of society: reference materials on contemporary Chinese literature). 2 vols. Guilin: n.p., 1980.

Gunn, Edward. *Unwelcome Muse: Chinese Literature in Shanghai and Peking, 1937–1945*. New York: Columbia University Press, 1980.

Guo Lihuai 郭立槐. "Wo yuan daxuesheng lian'ai wenti de diaocha" 我院大學生戀愛問題的調查 (A survey on the question of romance among students in our institute). *Gaodeng jiaoyu yanjiu* 1986.1.57–60.

Gushi hui 故事會 (Story collections). Shanghai.

Han Shaogong 韓少功. *Maqiao cidian* 馬橋詞典 (Horse bridge dictionary). Beijing: Zuojia chubanshe, 1997.

Hang Zhizhong 杭志忠. "Guanyu zenyang zhidao zhongxuesheng guankan waiguo dianying de tongxin" 關於怎樣指導中學生觀看外國電影的通信 (Letter on how to guide high school students in viewing foreign films). *Wenhuibao* 1980.2.27.

Hao Ran 浩然 *Jinguang dadao* 金光大道 (The golden road). 2 vols. Beijing: Renmin wenxue chubanshe, 1972, 1974.

———. *Yanyangtian* 艷陽天 (Bright sunny days). Vol. 1, Beijing: Zuojia chubanshe, 1964. Vols. 2 and 3, Beijing: Renmin wenxue chubanshe, 1966, 1972.

Haraszti, Miklos. *The Velvet Prison: Artists under State Socialism.* Translated by Katalin and Stephen Landesman. New York: Basic Books, 1987.

Havel, Vaclav. *Living in Truth.* London and Boston: Faber and Faber, 1989.

———. "The Responsibility of Intellectuals." *New York Review of Books* 42.11.36–37 (22 June 1995).

Hayward, Max, and Leopold Labedz. *Literature and Revolution in Soviet Russia, 1917–1962.* London: Oxford University Press, 1963.

He Bai 何柏. "Dalu zuojia na duoshao gaochou?" 大陸作家拿多少稿酬? (How much do mainland authors get paid?). *Zhengming* 1980.4.62–63.

He Qinglian 何清漣. *Zhongguo de xianjing* 中國的陷阱 (China's pitfall). Hong Kong: Mingjing chubanshe, 1997. Politically abridged and republished as *Xiandaihua de xianjing* 現代化的陷阱 (A pitfall of modernization). Beijing: Jinri chubanshe, 1998.

Hoggart, Richard. *The Uses of Literacy.* New York: Oxford University Press, 1970.

Hongdou 紅豆 (Red bean). Zhongshan University student literary magazine. Guangzhou, 1978–1981.

Hongqi 紅旗 (Red flag). Beijing.

———. [Unsigned]. Pinglunyuan 評論員 (Commentator). "Tantan wenyijie de sixiang jiefang wenti" 談談文藝界的思想解放問題 (On the question of liberation of thought in literary and art circles) 1980.3 (1 February 1980).

Howe, Irving. "Predicaments of Soviet Writing" *New Republic*, 11 May, 1963, pp. 19–21; 18 May, 1963, pp. 19–22.

Hsia, Chih-tsing. *A History of Modern Chinese Fiction.* (New Haven: Yale University Press, 1961; revised 1971.

Hsia, Chih-yen. *The Coldest Winter in Peking: A Novel from Inside China.* Garden City, N.Y.: Doubleday, 1978.

Hsia, Tsi-an. *The Gate of Darkness: Studies on the Leftist Literary Movement.* Seattle: The University of Washington Press, 1968.

Hsu, Kai-yu, ed. *Literature of the People's Republic of China.* Bloomington: Indiana University Press, 1980.

Hu Qiaomu 胡喬木. "Dangqian sixiang zhanxian de ruogan wenti" 當前思想戰線的若干問題 (Some problems on the current thought front). *Hongqi* 1981.23.2–22.

———. "Zai huijian quanguo gushipian dianying chuangzuo huiyi daibiao shi de jianghua" 在會見全國故事片電影創作會議代表時的講話 (Speech to the delegates to the national conference on creation of feature films). *Shehui kexue cankao* 社會科學參考 (Reference on social science). (Xining: Qinghai Academy of Social Sciences) 1982.11.6–9.

Hu Qili 胡啓立. "Zai Zhongguo zuojia xiehui di si ci huiyuan daibiao dahuishang de zhuci" 在中國作家協會第四次會員代表大會上的祝詞 (Salute to the fourth congress of the Chinese Writers' Association). *Renmin ribao*, 30 December 1984, p. 1.

Hu Yaobang 胡耀邦. "Guanyu dangqian wenyi gongzuo yixie wenti de jianghua (zhai yao)," 關於當前文藝工作一些問題的講話 (摘要) (Speech on some current problems in literature and art work [abstract]). *Wenyi qingkuang* 1985.6.2–6.

———. "Guanyu dianying de pishi" 關於電影的批示 (Directive on film). *Dangdai wenxue yanjiu yu xinxi* 當代文學研究與信息 (Research and information on contemporary literature) 1985.1.1.

———. "Guanyu sixiang zhengzhi gongzuo wenti" 關於思想政治工作問題 (On questions in ideological and political work), *Renmin ribao*, 2 January 1983, pp. 1, 4.

———. "Lun dang de xinwen gongzuo" 論黨的新聞工作 (On the party's journalism work). *Renmin ribao*, 14 April 1985, p. 1. Translated in Womack, ed., *Media and the Chinese Public*, pp. 174–98.

———. "Zai juben chuangzuo zuotanhuishang de jianghua" 在劇本創作座談會上的講話 (Talk at the conference on playwriting). Pamphlet. N.p., n.d. The talk was given 12–13 February 1980.

———. "Zai Lu Xun dansheng yibai zhounian jinian dahuishang de jianghua" 在魯迅誕生一百週年紀念大會上的講話 (Speech at the meeting to commemorate the hundredth anniversary of the birth of Lu Xun). *Guangming ribao*, 26 September 1981, pp. 1–2.

Huacheng 花城 (City of Flowers). Guangzhou.

———. [Unsigned]. Benkan pinglunyuan 本刊評論員 (Our commentator). "Bu ji zi wen" 不繼自問 (On no longer asking ourselves), 1981.1.261–63.

———. [Unsigned]. Benkan pinglunyuan. "Zai yi ci zi wen" 再一次自問 (Asking ourselves one more time), 1981.2.88–90.

———. [Unsigned]. "Women de shiwu" 我們的失誤 (Our mistakes), 1982.3.228.

Huang Ansi 黃安思. "Xiang qian kan a, wenyi!" 向前看啊, 文藝! (Look forward, literature!). *Guangzhou ribao*, 15 April 1979, p. 3.

Huang, Joe C. *Heroes and Villains in Communist China: The Contemporary Chinese Novel as a Reflection of Life*. New York: Pica Press, 1973.

Huang Kecheng 黃克誠. "Guanyu dui Mao zhuxi pingjia he dui Mao Zedong sixiang de taidu wenti" 關於對毛主席評價和對毛澤東思想的態度問題 (On questions concerning the evaluation of Chairman Mao and our attitude toward Mao-Zedong-thought). *Jiefangjun bao*, 10 April 1981. Reprinted in *Guangming ribao*, 11 April 1981, pp. 1, 4.

Huang Ruixu 黃瑞旭. "Daxuesheng yuedu wenxue zuopin xianzhuang qianxi" 大學生閱讀文學作品現狀淺析 (A preliminary analysis of university students' readership of literary works). *Dangdai wenyi sichao* 1983.3.8–20.

———. "Young Laborers' Attitudes towards Literary and Artistic Works." In Joint Publications Research Service. *China Report*, 20 November 1984 (JPRS–CPS–84–077), pp. 41–61.

Huang Tianyuan 黃天源. "Liubing lianqu" 溜冰戀曲 (Skating love song). *Guangzhou wenyi* 1979.7.8–14, 41.

Huang Weizong 黃偉宗. "Shehuizhuyi pipan xianshizhuyi de xingcheng ji fazhan" 社會主義批判現實主義的形成及發展 (The formation and development of socialist critical realism). Conference paper, 30 May 1980, Guangzhou.

———. "Tichang shehuizhuyi wenyi chuangzuo fangfa de duoyanghua" 提倡社會

主義文藝創作方法的多樣化 (Support diversification of method in socialist literary creation). *Guangzhou wenyi* 廣州文藝 (Guangzhou literature and art) 1980.4.48–53.

Human Rights Watch/Asia. New York.

———. [Report]. "China: Enforced Exile of Dissidents," 7.1 (January 1995). Copublished with Human Rights in China.

———. [Report]. "Organ Procurement and Judicial Execution in China," 6.9 (August 1994.

Hung, Chang-tai. *War and Popular Culture: Resistance in Modern China, 1937–1945*. Berkeley and Los Angeles: University of California Press, 1994.

Huntington, Samuel P., and Clement H. Moore, eds. *Authoritarian Politics in Modern Society: The Dynamics of Established One-Party Systems*. New York: Basic Books, 1970.

Ibuse Masuji 井伏鱒二. "Honjitsu kyūshin" 本日休診. Translated by Edward Seidensticker and Glen Shaw as *No Consultations Today*. Tokyo: Hara Shobo, 1966.

Inside China Mainland. Taipei, Institute of Current China Studies.

Issues and Studies. Taipei.

James, William. *Essays in Pragmatism*. New York: Hafner, 1948.

Ji Wen 集文. "Zhongyang hongtou wenjian yi lan" 中央紅頭文件一覽 (A look at some crucial documents of Party Central). *Jiushiniandai* 九十年代 (The nineties) (Hong Kong) 1987.6.33–35.

Jia Pingwa 賈平凹. *Feidu* 廢都 (Capital in ruins). Beijing: Beijing chubanshe, 1993.

Jiang Kun 姜昆 et al. "Duihao ru zuo" 對號入座 (Sitting in assigned seats). *Tianjin yanchang* 1980.7.4.

Jiang Kun and Li Wenhua 李文華. "Ruci zhaoxiang" 如此照相 (Here's how you take a photo). *Tianjin yanchang* 1978. 5–6. 17–20.

Jiang Zilong 蔣子龍. "Jinnian diqi hao taifeng" 今年第七號颱風 (The number seven typhoon this year). *Wenhui zengkan* 文匯增刊 (Wenhui supplement) (Shanghai) 1980.4.19–23.

———. "Qiao changzhang shangrenji" 喬廠長上任記 (Manager Qiao assumes office) *Renmin wenxue* 1979.7.3–26. Translated in Lee Yee, *The New Realism*, pp. 56–85.

———. "'Qiao changzhang shangrenji' de shenghuo zhang" 喬廠長上任記" 的生活帳 (Record of the life of "Manager Qiao assumes office"). *Shiyue* 1979.4.13–17.

Jiangxi daxue Zhongwenxi 江西大學中文系, ed. *Dangdai wenxue juben xuan* 當代文學劇本選 (A Collection of contemporary drama). N.p., 1980.

Jiefangjun bao 解放軍報 (Liberation army news). Beijing.

———. [Unsigned]. Teyue pinglunyuan 特約評論員 (Special commentator), "Si xiang jiben yuanze burong weifan—ping dianying wenxue juben 'kulian'" 四項基本原則不容違反——評電影文學劇本 "苦戀" (The four basic principles cannot be violated: a critique of the literary filmscript "Unrequited love"), 20 April 1981, pp. 1–2.

Jin Fan 靳凡. "Gongkai de qingshu" 公開的情書 (Open love letters). *Shiyue* 1980.1.4–67.

Jin He 金河. "Chongfeng" 重逢 (Reencounter). *Shanghai wenxue* 1979.4.14–25. Translated by Michael S. Duke in Link, ed. *Roses and Thorns*, pp. 221–43.

Jin Jingmai 金敬邁. *Ouyang Hai zhi ge* 歐陽海之歌 (The song of Ouyang Hai). Beijing: Jiefangjun wenyi chubanshe, 1966.

Jin Yanhua 金彥華 and Wang Jingquan 王景全. "Silaoli de nahan" 死牢裏的吶喊 (Cries from death row). *Guangxi wenyi* 廣西文藝 (Guangxi literature and art) (Nanning) 1980.1.3–13.

Jing Fuzi 京夫子. *See* Gu Hua.

Jintian 今天 (Today). Beijing 1978–1980; Oslo 1990–.

Johnson, Priscilla. *Khrushchev and the Arts: The Politics of Soviet Culture, 1962–1964.* Cambridge: MIT Press.

Joint Publications Research Service. Washington, D.C.

Juben 劇本 (Drama). Beijing.

Kalining, W., and T. Kusiniezuofu [hanyu pinyin transliterations] 維 · 卡里寧 and 特 · 庫茲涅佐夫 *Youchuan.* "*Tu'apusi*" 油船 "圖阿普斯" (The tanker *Tuapusi*). Beijing: Qunzhong chubanshe, 1954.

Kane, Anthony J. "The League of Left Wing Writers and Chinese Literary Policy." Ph.D. dissertation, Department of History, University of Michigan, 1982.

Ke Yunlu 柯云路. "Sanqianwan" 三千萬 (Thirty million). *Renmin wenxue* 1980.11.3–20.

———. *Xinxing* 新星 (New star). Beijing: Renmin wenxue chubanshe, 1985.

Keene, Donald. *Dawn to the West: Japanese Literature of the Modern Era.* New York: Holt, Reinhart, and Winston, 1980.

Kenneson, James. "China Stinks." *Harper's Magazine*, April 1982, pp. 13–17.

Kimball, Arthur G. *Crisis in Identity and Contemporary Japanese Novels.* Rutland, Vt.: Tuttle, 1973.

Kinkley, Jeffrey C., ed. *After Mao: Chinese Literature and Society, 1978–1981.* Cambridge: Harvard University, Council on East Asian Studies, 1985.

———. "A Bettelheimian Interpretation of Zhang Xianliang's Concentration-Camp Novels." *Asia Major* 3d ser. 4.2 (1993), pp. 83–113.

Kong Jiesheng 孔捷生. "Zai xiaohe neibian" 在小河那邊. Translated by Charles W. Hayford as "On the Other Side of the Stream" in Link, ed., *Roses and Thorns*, pp. 172–73.

Kraus, Richard C. *Brushes with Power: Modern Politics and the Chinese Art of Calligraphy.* Berkeley and Los Angeles: University of California Press, 1991.

Lan Chengdong 藍成東. "Dui zhongxuesheng kan dianying, dianshiju de diaocha" 對 中學生看電影、電視劇的調查 (A survey of high school students on watching film and television drama). *Shehui.* 1982.1.79.

——— et al. "Yingjie gaozhong biyesheng de zhiyuan qingxiang: dui Shanghai shi san suo zhongxue de diaocha" 應屆高中畢業生的志願傾向: 對上海市三所中學 的調查 (The career preferences of high school seniors: an investigation of three high schools in Shanghai). *Shehui* 1982.2.22–25.

Lan, Yang. "The Depiction of the Hero in the Cultural Revolution Novel." *China Information: A Quarterly Journal on Contemporary China Studies* (Leiden) 12.4 (Spring 1998), pp. 68–95.

Lao She 老舍. *Luotuo Xiangzi* 駱駝祥子 (Camel Xiangzi). Hong Kong: Xuelin shudian, n.d. Translated by Jean James as *Rickshaw*. Honolulu: University of Hawaii Press, 1979.

Lau, Joseph S. M., C. T. Hsia, and Leo Ou-fan Lee, eds. *Modern Chinese Stories and Novellas, 1919–1949.* New York: Columbia University Press, 1981.

Lee Yee, ed. *The New Realism: Writings from China after the Cultural Revolution.* New York: Hippocrene, 1983.

Lei Yi 雷頤. *Qujingji* 取靜集 (Seeking quietude collection). Beijing: Xinhua chubanshe, 1998.

Leung, Laifong. *Morning Sun: Interviews with Chinese Writers of the Lost Generation.* Armonk, N.Y.: M.E. Sharpe, 1994.

Leyda, Jay. *Dianying: Electric Shadows*. Cambridge: MIT Press, 1972.

Li Boyuan 李伯元. *Guanchang xianxingji* 官場現形記 (Panorama of officialdom). Hong Kong: Guangzhi shuju, n.d.

Li Hong 里紅. "Xinglai ba, gege" 醒來吧, 哥哥 (Wake up, big brother). *Weilai* 3, 1979.2.21–24.

Li Hui 李輝. "Wentan beige" 文壇悲歌 (Mourning song on the literary scene). *Baihuazhou* 百花洲 (Land of the hundred flowers). N.p. 1988.4.4–193.

Li Jian 李劍. "'Gede' yu 'quede'" "歌德" 與 "缺德" ("Praise" and "shame"). *Hebei wenyi* 河北文藝 (Hebei literature and art) (Shijiazhuang) 1976.5–6.

Li Jiantong 李建彤. *Liu Zhidan* 劉志旦 (Liu Zhidan). Beijing: Wenhua yishu chubanshe, 1984.

Li Kewei 李克威. "Nüzei" 女賊 (Girl thief). *Dianying chuangzuo* 電影創作 (Beijing) 1979.11.30–55.

Li Oufan 李歐梵 (Leo Lee). "Liu Binyan yu 'Ren yao zhijian'" 劉賓雁與 "人妖之間" (Liu Binyan and "People or Monsters"). *Qishi niandai*, October 1980, pp. 79–82.

Li Qun 李羣. "Zhuanzhi kongmeibing" 專治恐美病 (Specializing in curing Americaphobia). *Wenhuibao*, 18 March 1951.

Li Shuoru 李碩儒 and Kuang Xiayu 鄺夏渝. "*Di'er ci woshou* chuban qianhou" "第二次握手" 出版前後 (The story of the publication of *The second handshake*). *Yangcheng wanbao* (Guangzhou), 2 June 1980.

Li Shusheng 李樹聲. "Zhongguo wenlian lilun yanjiushi zuotan 'shei shi qiangzhe?'" 中國文聯理論研究室座談 "誰是強者?" (The theoretical research section of the Chinese Federation of Literary and Art Workers discusses "Who is the stronger?"). *Juben* 1982.2.34.

Li Xinsheng 李新生. "Dui jixieyixi yinianji xuesheng youguan renshengguan wenti de diaocha jieguo" 對機械一系一年級學生有關人生觀問題的調查結果 (The results of a survey of the worldviews of freshmen in the no. 1 mechanics department). *Gaodeng jiaoyu yanjiu* 1985.1 (September 1985) pp. 51–54.

Li Yi (Lee Yee) 李怡. "Zhongguo xinxieshizhuyi wenyi de xingqi" 中國新寫實主義文藝的興起 ("The rise of neorealist Chinese literature"). *Qishiniandai* (Hong Kong) 1980.5.21–27.

Li Yingru 李英儒. *Yehuo chunfeng dou gucheng* 野火春風鬥古城 (Wildfire and spring wind in the old city). Beijing: Zuojia chubanshe, 1959. Abridged translation by Gladys Yang in *Chinese Literature* 1965.11.3–68; 1965.12.36–96.

Li Zhisui 李志綏. *Mao Zedong siren yisheng huiyilu* 毛澤東私人醫生回憶錄 (Memoires of the private doctor of Mao Zedong). Taibei: Shibao wenhua chuban qiye youxian gongsi, 1994.

———. *The Private Life of Chairman Mao*. Translated by Tai Hung-chao, edited by Anne Thurston. New York: Random House, 1994.

Liang Bin 梁斌. *Hongqipu* 紅旗譜 (Genealogy of the red flag). Beijing: Zhongguo qingnian chubanshe, 1957. Translated by Gladys Yang as *Keep the Red Flag Flying*. Beijing: Foreign Languages Press, 1961.

Liang Bingkun 梁秉堃. "Shei shi qiangzhe?" 誰是強者? (Who is the stronger?). *Juben* 1982, 1.10–49.

Liang Deming 梁德明. "Zhongshen dashi" 終身大事 (The great event in life). *Pugongying* 9 (1979), p. 2.

Liang Qichao 梁啓超. "Lun xiaoshuo yu qunzhi zhi guanxi" 論小說與群治之關係 (On the relation between fiction and popular sovereignty). *Xin xiaoshuo* 新小說 (New fiction) 1902.1. Reprinted in *Yinbingshi wenji* 飲冰室文集 (Collected works from the ice-drinker's studio). Vol. 10, pp. 6–9. Taibei: Taiwan zhonghua shuju, 1960. Translated by Gek Nai Cheng as "On the Relationship between Fiction and the Government of the People," in Denton, *Modern Chinese Literary Thought*, pp. 74–81.

Liang Xiaosheng 梁曉聲. '*93 duanxiang: shei shi choulou de Zhongguoren?* 九三斷想 — — 誰是醜陋的中國人? (Random thoughts in '93: who are the ugly Chinese?). Taiyuan: Shanxi gaoxiao lianhe chubanshe, 1994.

Lianhuan huabao bianjibu 連環畫報編輯部. "Guanyu lianhuanhua 'Feng' de zuotanhui fayan jilu" 關於連環畫 "楓" 的座談會發言紀錄 (Transcript of the conference on the cartoon strip "Maple"). Beijing, 11 August 1979.

Liao Bingxiong 廖冰兄. *Liao Bingxiong manhua* 廖冰兄漫畫 (The cartoons of Liao Bingxiong). Guangzhou: Lingnan meishu chubanshe, 1984.

Liaoning daxue Zhongwen xi 遼寧大學中文系. *Tiananmen shichao* 天安門詩抄 (Poems from Tiananmen). Beijing: Renmin wenxue chubanshe, 1979.

Lin Manshu 林曼叔 *et al. Zhongguo dangdai wenxueshi gao* 中國當代文學史稿 (A history of contemporary Chinese literature) Hong Kong: Centre de Publication Asie Orientale de l'Université Paris, 1978.

Lin, Yü-sheng. *The Crisis of Chinese Consciousness: Radical Anti-Traditionalism in the May Fourth Era*. Madison: University of Wisconsin Press, 1979.

Link, Perry. *Evening Chats in Beijing: Probing China's Predicament*. New York: W. W. Norton, 1992.

———. "Fiction and the Reading Public in Guangzhou and Other Chinese Cities," in Kinkley, *After Mao*, pp. 221–74.

———. "The Genie and the Lamp: Revolutionary *Xiangsheng*," in McDougall, *Popular Literature and Performing Arts*, pp. 83–111.

———. *Mandarin Ducks and Butterflies: Popular Fiction in Early Twentieth-Century Chinese Cities*. Berkeley and Los Angeles: University of California Press, 1981.

———, ed. *Roses and Thorns: The Second Blooming of the Hundred Flowers in Chinese Fiction, 1979–80*. Berkeley and Los Angeles: University of California Press, 1984.

———, ed. *Stubborn Weeds: Popular and Controversial Chinese Literature after the Cultural Revolution*. Bloomington: Indiana University Press, 1983.

———. "'Tu' yu 'yang': shi xi si pian dangdai Zhongguo xiaoshuoli de yige changjian de zhuti" "土" 與 "洋"——試析四篇當代中國小說裏的一個常見的主題 ("Earth" and "ocean": an analysis of a common theme as seen in four contemporary Chinese stories). *Wenyibao*, 22 November 1986, p. 2.

Link, Perry, Richard Madsen, and Paul G. Pickowicz, eds. *Unofficial China: Popular Culture and Thought in the People's Republic*. Boulder, Colo.: Westview, 1989.

Liu Binyan 劉賓雁. "Benbao neibu xiaoxi" 本報內部消息 (Our paper's inside news). *Renmin wenxue* 1956.6.6–21; 1956.10.48–59.

———. "China's Hidden Cannibalism." Translated by Perry Link, *New York Review of Books* 40.7 (8 April 1993), pp. 3–6.

———. "Diwuge chuan dayi de ren" 第五個穿大衣的人. *Beijing wenyi* no. 11, 1979. Reprinted in *Xiaoshuo yuebao* 小說月報 (Fiction Monthly) (Tianjin) 1980.2.12–18, 34. Translated by John Rohsenow as "The Fifth Man in the Overcoat" in Liu Binyan's *People or Monsters?*, pp. 79–97.

———. "Guanyu 'xie yin'anmian' he 'ganyu shenghuo'" 關於 "寫陰暗面" 和 "干預生活" (On "writing about the dark side" and "intervening in life"). *Shanghai wenxue* 1979.3.49–57.

———. "Jinggao" 警告. *Zuopin* 1980.1.1–12. Translated by Madeleine Ross as "Warning" in Liu Binyan, *People or Monsters?* pp. 69–78.

———. *Liu Binyan baogao wenxue jingxuan* 劉賓雁報告文學精選 (Selection of the finest of Liu Binyan's reportage). Taibei: Renjian chubanshe, 1987.

———. *People or Monsters? And Other Stories and Reportage from China after Mao*. Edited by Perry Link. Bloomington: Indiana University Press, 1983.

———. "Qingting renmin de shengyin" 傾聽人民的聲音 (Listen carefully to the voice of the people). Speech at the Fourth Congress of Chinese Literature and Art Workers, 9 November 1979, Beijing. Translated by Kyna Rubin and Perry Link in Liu Binyan, *People or Monsters?*, pp. 1–10.

———. "Ren yao zhijian" 人妖之間 (People or Monsters?), *Renmin wenxue* 1979.9.83–102. Translated by James Feinerman and Perry Link in Liu Binyan, *People or Monsters?*, pp. 12–68.

———. "Tan xin shiqi de wenxue chuangzuo wenti" 談新時期的文學創作問題 (On questions of literary work in the post-Mao years). *Dangdai wenxue yanjiu cankao ziliao* 當代文學研究參考資料 (Reference materials for research on contemporary literature) 1982.3.1–15.

———. "Zai Heilongjiang jianghua quanwen" 在黑龍江講話全文 (Complete text of speech at Heilongjiang). *Guangjiaojing* 廣角鏡 (Wide angle) (Hong Kong) 1980.3.10–23.

———. "Zai qiaoliang gongdishang" 在橋樑工地上 (On the bridge construction site). *Renmin wenxue* 1956.4.1–17.

Liu Fengzuo 劉風作. "Muqian daxuesheng baokan yuedu qingkuang de diaocha" 目前大學生報刊閱讀情況的調查 (An investigation into the current situation in the reading of newspapers and periodicals by university students). *Gaodeng jiaoyu yanjiu* (Liaoning University) 1985.1.96–97.

Liu, James J.Y. *The Chinese Knight-Errant*. Chicago: University of Chicago Press, 1967.

———. *Chinese Theories of Literature*. Chicago: University of Chicago Press, 1975.

Liu Ke 劉克. "Feitian" 飛天. *Shiyue* 1979.3.116–39.

Liu Liu 劉流. *Liehuo jin'gang* 烈火金鋼 (Diamond in the flames). Beijing: Zhongguo qingnian chubanshe, 1959.

Liu Qing 柳青. *Chuangyeshi* 創業史. 2 vols. Beijing: Zhongguo qingnian chubanshe, 1960, 1977. Translated by Sidney Shapiro as *The Builders*. Beijing: Foreign Languages Press, 1964.

Liu Qingbang 劉慶邦. "Kankan sheijia you fu" 看看誰家有福 (Look at whose family is blessed). *Benliu wenyi yuekan* 奔流文藝月刊 (Torrent literary monthly) (Zhengzhou) 1980.3.24–31. Translated by Donald Gibbs as "The Good Luck Bun" in Link, ed., *Roses and Thorns*, pp. 84–101.

Liu Qingren 劉慶仁 et al. "Guanyu zhongxuesheng sixiang zhuangkuang de diaocha" 關於中學生思想狀況的調查 (An investigation of the state of thinking among high school students) *Jiaoyu keyan tongxun* 教育科研通訊 (Scientific reports on education) (Heilongjiang) 1983.3.5–11, 39.

Liu Shijun 劉世俊. "Xiaoshile de qinsheng" 消逝了的琴聲. *Guangzhou wenyi* 1979.1.18–24.

Liu Xicheng 劉錫誠. "Tan dangqian duanpian xiaoshuo chuangzuo zhong de jige wenti" 談當前短篇小說創作中的幾個問題 (On some immediate problems in the creation of short stories). *Guangming ribao*, 30 March 1979.

———. "Wenxue yu dangdai shenghuo" 文學與當代生活 (Literature, art, and contemporary life). *Wenyibao* 1982.9.30–36.

Liu Xinwu 劉心武. "Aiqing de weizhi" 愛情的位置 (The place of love). *Shiyue* 1978.1.117–29.

———. "Ban zhuren" 班主任 (The homeroom teacher). *Renmin wenxue* 1977.11.16–29.

———. "Xinglai ba, didi" 醒來吧, 弟弟! (Wake up, little brother). *Zhongguo qingnian* 中國青年 (China's youth) (Beijing), 1978.2.

Liu Zaifu 劉再復. *Liu Zaifu ji* 劉再復集 (A collection of Liu Zaifu). (Haerbin: Heilongjiang jiaoyu chubanshe, 1988.

Liu Zhen 劉眞. "Heiqi" 黑旗 (Black flag). *Shanghai wenxue* 1979.3.4–17.

———. "Pengzong de gushi" 彭總的故事 (Stories of General Peng). *Beijing wenyi* 1979.5.46–49.

———. *Zai Pengzong shenbian* 在彭總身邊 (At the side of General Peng).

London, Miriam, and Ta-ling Lee. "Two Poems from the Chinese Underground." *American Spectator* 12.11 (November 1979), pp. 20–21.

London, Miriam, and Mu Yang-jen. "What Are They Reading in China?," *Saturday Review* 30 (September 1978), pp. 42–43.

Louie, Kam. "Between Paradise and Hell: Literary Double-Think in Post-Mao China." *Australian Journal of Chinese Affairs* 10 (July 1983), pp. 1–15.

Lu, Chao. "Popular Novels Leave Serious Stuff Standing." *China Daily*, 2 September 1986.

Lu Shuyuan 魯樞元. "Lun xin shiqi wenxue de 'xiang nei zhuan'" 論新時期文學的 "向內轉" (On the "inward turn" of literature in the new period). *Wenyibao*, 18 October 1986, p. 3.

Lu Wenfu 陸文夫. "Meishijia" 美食家. In *Lu Wenfu ji* 陸文夫集 (A collection of Lu Wenfu). (Fuzhou: Haixia wenyi chubanshe, 1986), pp. 1–85. Translated by Yu Fangyin as "The Gourmet" in Lu Wenfu, *A World of Dreams*, pp. 121–224.

———. *A World of Dreams*. Beijing: Panda Books, 1986.

Lu Xinhua 盧新華. *Mo* 魔 (Devil). Tianjin: Baihua chubanshe, 1985.

———. "Shanghen" 傷痕 (Scar) *Wenhuibao*, 11 August 1978. Translated by Bennett Lee as "The Wounded" in Lu Xinhua et al., *The Wounded*, pp. 9–24.

Lu Xinhua, et al. *The Wounded: New Stories of the Cultural Revolution, 77–78*. Hong Kong: Joint Publishing, 1979.

Lu Xun 魯迅. *The Complete Stories of Lu Xun*. Translated by Yang Xianyi and Gladys Yang. Bloomington: Indiana University Press, 1981.

———. "Li lun" 立論 (Establishing a viewpoint). In Lu Xun, *Yecao* 野草 (Wild grass). Beijing: Renmin wenxue chubanshe, 1973, pp. 45–46. Unattributed translation as "On Expressing an Opinion" in Lu Xun, *Wild Grass*. Beijing: Foreign Languages Press, 1974, pp. 50–51.

———. *Lu Xun yiwenji* 魯迅譯文集 (Collected translations of Lu Xun). 10 volumes. Beijing: Renmin wenxue chubanshe, 1959.

———. "Nahan zixu" 吶喊自序 (Preface to outcry). In Lu Xun, *Nahan* (Outcry). Hong Kong: Huitongshudian, 1972, pp. 1–6. Translated in Lu Xun, *Complete Stories*, pp. v–x.

———. "Shi zhong" 示衆 (A public example). In Lu Xun, *Panghuang* 彷徨 (Vacillation). Hong Kong: Xinyi chubanshe, 1972, pp. 91–98. Translated in *Complete Stories*, pp. 215–20.

Lu Yanzhou 魯彥周. "Huhuan" 呼喚 (Calling out). *Shouhuo* 1980.1.4–51.

———. "Tianyunshan chuanqi" 天雲山傳奇 (The fable of heavenly cloud mountain). *Qingming* 1979.1.95–139.

Lu Zhenkang 陸鎭康. "Yuanyuan qiyu ji" 元元奇遇記 (The strange experiences of Yuanyuan). *Guangdong wenyi* 廣東文藝 (Guangdong literature and art) 1977.6. 18–22.

Luo Guangbin 羅廣斌 and Yang Yiyan 楊益言. *Hongyan* 紅岩. Beijing: Zhongguo qingnian chubanshe, 1961). Translated as *Red Crag*. Beijing: Foreign Languages Press, 1978, without citation of translator.

Luo Guangbin, Liu Debin 劉德斌, and Yang Yiyan. *Zai liehuozhong yongsheng* 在烈火中永生 (Immortality in the raging flames). Beijing: Zhongguo qingnian chubanshe, 1978.

Luo Rujia 羅汝佳. "Jiujing shei 'chouhua' Zhonggong?" 究竟誰 "醜化" 中共? (Who is really "uglifying" the Chinese communists?). *Zhengming* 1981.5.56–57.

Ma Ji 馬季. "Duoceng fandian" 多層飯店. *Tianjin yanchang* 1979.5.3–7. Translated by Robert N. Tharp as "The Multi-level Hotel" in Link, ed., *Stubborn Weeds*, pp. 255–66.

Ma Ji and Tang Jiezhong 唐傑忠. *Baigujing xianxingji* 白骨精現形記 (White bone demon unmasked). Bai Li audiotapes (Hong Kong) BA–138. Audiocassette.

Ma, Yau-woon. "The Pao-kung Tradition in Chinese Popular Literature," Ph.D. dissertation, Yale University, 1971.

Ma Yixiang 馬憶湘. *Chaoyanghua* 朝陽花 (Sunflower). Beijing: Zhongguo qingnian chubanshe, 1961.

Mackerras, Colin. *The Chinese Theater in Modern Times*. Amherst: University of Massachusetts Press, 1975.

Mai Junru 麥均如. "'Wei wei,' 'e e' yu 'jingzi'" "唯唯," "鄂鄂," 與 "鏡子" ('Yes-men,' 'no-men,' and 'the mirror'). *Guangzhou ribao*, 28 February 1980, p. 3.

Mao Hanbin 毛漢斌, Lu Zhigao 盧志高, and Luo Hongyuan 羅宏元. "Bianhuazhong de qinggong sixiang guannian" 變化中的青工思想觀念 (The changing ideas and concepts of young workers). *Qingnian yanjiu* 1983.3.24–29.

Mao Zedong. *Selected Works*. New York: International Publishers, 1956.

———. *Selected Works*. Beijing: Foreign Languages Press, 1965.

May, Rachel, and Zhu Zhiyu. Translated by *A Chinese Winter's Tale* by Yu Luojin. Hong Kong: Chinese University of Hong Kong, Research Centre for Translations, 1986.

McDougall, Bonnie S. *Mao Zedong's "Talks at the Yan'an Conference on Literature and Art"*. Ann Arbor: University of Michigan, Center for Chinese Studies, 1980.

———. *Popular Literature and Performing Arts in the People's Republic of China, 1949–1979*. Berkeley and Los Angeles: University of California Press, 1984.

McDougall, Bonnie S., and Kam Louie. *The Literature of China in the Twentieth Century*. New York: Columbia University Press, 1997.

McLean, Hugh, and Walter N. Vickery, eds. *The Year of Protest, 1956: An Anthology of Soviet Literary Materials*. Westport, Conn.: Greenwood, 1956.

Meng Weizai 孟偉哉. "Guanyu 'linghun de gongchengshi' he 'shenghuo de jiaokeshu' de lijie" 關於 "靈魂的工程師" 和 "生活的教科書的理解 (An understanding of "engineer of the soul" and "textbooks for life"). *Guangming ribao*, 13 August 1980, p. 4.

Mingbao yuekan 明報月刊 (Ming bao monthly). Hong Kong.

Milosz, Czeslaw. *The Captive Mind*. Translated by Jane Zielonko. New York: Alfred A. Knopf, 1953.

Mo Yan 莫言. *Fengru feitun* 豐乳肥臀 (Full breasts and plump buttocks). Beijing: Zuojia chubanshe, 1995.

Mu Fu 牧夫 (pseud.). "Yichang daijia gaoang de biaoyan" 一場代價高昂的表演 (An extravagantly high–priced performance). *Qishiniandai* 145 (February 1982) pp. 12–14.

Mufson, Steven. "Let a Thousand Books Bloom." *Washington Post*, 20 August 1995, "Book World," pp. 1, 10.

Nanfang ribao 南方日報 (Southern daily). Guangzhou.

———. [Unsigned]. "Kuangfeng elang he suo ju? Yipian danxin wei renmin" 狂風惡浪何所懼? 一片丹心爲人民 (What is to be feared in wild winds and monstrous waves? The whole red heart is for the people), 23 September 1969, pp. 2–3.

———. [Unsigned]. "'Lao san pian' zhuzao de wuwei zhanshi" 老三篇鑄造的無畏戰士 (Fearless warriors forged by the three old articles), 24 September pp. 3–4.

Nathan, Andrew J. *Chinese Democracy*. New York: Alfred A. Knopf, 1985.

National Publishing Administration [of China], "Publishing in China Past and Present." N.p., n.d.

Ng, Mau-sang. *The Russian Hero in Modern Chinese Fiction*. Hong Kong: The Chinese University Press and Albany: State University of New York Press, 1988.

Nieh, Hualing, ed. and co-trans. *Literature of the Hundred Flowers*. 2 vols. New York: Columbia University Press, 1981.

Ōoka Shōhei 大岡昇平. *Nobi* 野火 (Prairie fire) in *Ōoka Shōhei shū* 大岡昇平集 (A collection of Ōoka Shōhei) (Tokyo: Iwanami Shoten, 1982–1984), vol. 3, pp.229–413. Translated by Ivan Morris as *Fires on the Plain*. New York: Alfred A. Knopf, 1957.

Ostrovskii, Nicholas. *Gangtie shi zenyang liancheng de* 鋼鐵是怎樣煉成的 (How steel is tempered). Beijing: Zhongguo qingnian chubanshe, 1958.

Ouyang Shan 歐陽山. *Kudou* 苦鬥 (Bitter struggle). Beijing: Zhongguo qingnian chubanshe, 1963.

———. *Sanjiaxiang* 三家巷 (Three-family lane). Guangzhou: Guangdong renmin chubanshe, 1959.

Pang Junlin 龐軍林 and Li Jie 李傑. "Dianying: xibu qingnian de kewang yu xuqiu" 電影: 西部青年的渴望與需求 (Film: the yearnings and demands of western young people). *Dangdai wenyi sichao* 1985.2.123–28.

Parks, Michael. "Gene Kelly Makes a Hit with 'Singin' in the Rain' in Peking." *Los Angeles Times*, 9 May 1981, part II, pp. 3, 5.

Pugongying 蒲公英 (Dandelions). Haidian qu wenhuazhan, Beijing.

Pusey, James R. *China and Charles Darwin*. Cambridge: Harvard University, Council on East Asian Studies, 1983.

Qian Gang 錢鋼. "Tangshan da dizhen: '7.28' jienan shi zhounian ji" 唐山大地震: "7.28" 劫難十週年記 (The great Tangshan earthquake: tenth anniversary memorial of the "July 28th" calamity). *Jiefangjun wenyi* 解放軍文藝 (Liberation army literature and art) (Beijing), March 1986, pp. 4–107.

Qian Yuxiang 錢玉祥. "Lishi a, shenpan wo ba!" 歷史啊, 審判我吧! (History, be my judge!). *Guangzhou wenyi* 1979.5.12–17.

Qin Mu 秦牧. "Bianzhengde tantao he chuli wenxue yishu wenti" 辯證地探討和處理文學藝術問題 (Explore and handle questions of literary art dialectically). *Guangdong wenyi* 廣東文藝 (Guangdong literature and art) (Guangzhou) 1977.3.8–12, 29.

Qingming 清明 (Qingming). Hefei.

Qingnian yanjiu 青年研究 (Research on youth). Beijing.

Qishiniandai 七十年代 (The seventies). Hong Kong.

Qu Bo 曲波. *Linhai xueyuan* 林海雪原. 2nd edition. Beijing: Renmin wenxue chubanshe, 1959. Translated by Sidney Shapiro as *Tracks in the Snowy Forest*. Beijing: Foreign Languages Press, 1962.

Quyi 曲藝 (Popular performing arts). Beijing.

Rawls, John. *A Theory of Justice*. Cambridge.: Harvard University Press, 1971). Translated by He Huaihong 何懷宏, He Baogang 何包鋼, and Liao Shenbai 廖申白 as *Zhengyilun* 正義論. Beijing: Zhongguo shehui kexue chubanshe, 1997.

Rawski, Evelyn S. *Education and Popular Literacy in Ch'ing China*. Ann Arbor: University of Michigan Press, 1979)

Renditions: A Chinese-English Translation Magazine. Chinese University of Hong Kong.

Renmin ribao 人民日報 (People's daily). Beijing.

———. [Unsigned]. "Jianchi Makesizhuyi de wenyi piping" 堅持馬克思主義的文藝批評 (Persist with Marxist criticism of literature and art), 14 January 1981, p. 5.

———. [Unsigned]. "Jiepi 'wenyi heixian zhuanzheng' lun, xunsu ba wenyi huoyue qilai" 揭批 "文藝黑線專政" 論迅速把文藝活躍起來 (Expose the concept of "black line dictatorship" and quickly revive literature and art) 24 December 1977, p. 2.

———. [Unsigned]. Pinglunyuan 評論員 (Commentator). "Renzhen taolun yixia wenyi chuangzuozhong biaoxian aiqing de wenti" 認眞討論一下文藝創作中表現愛情的問題 (Let us conscientiously discuss for a moment the question of depiction of love in literature and art), 4 November 1981.

———. [Unsigned]. "Rang renmin qunzhong dou neng kandao dianying he xi" 讓人民群眾都能看到電影和戲 (Let all the popular masses see films and plays), 25 December 1977, p. 3.

———. [Unsigned]. "Wenyi yao wei jianshe shehuizhuyi jingshen wenming zuochu gongxian" 文藝要爲建設社會主義精神文明作出貢獻 (Literature and art must make contributions to building socialist spiritual civilization), 4 February 1981, p. 5.

———. [Unsigned]. "Zaiqu renmin zai Mao zhuxi geming luxian zhidao xia fayang rendingshengtian de geming jingshen kangzhen jiuzai" 災區人民在毛主席革命路線指導下發揚人定勝天的革命精神抗震救災 (People in the disaster areas, under the revolutionary line of chairman Mao, press forward with the revolutionary spirit that man will certainly overcome nature to fight the earthquake and rescue [people from] disaster) 29 July 1976, p. 1.

Renmin wenxue 人民文學 (People's literature). Beijing.

Renmin zhi sheng bianjibu "人民之聲" 編輯部. "Guangzhou 'Renmin zhi sheng' bianjibu shengming" 廣州 "人民之聲" 編輯部聲明 (Declaration by the editors of Guangzhou's "Voice of the People"). *Guanchajia* 1980.5.15.

Roy, David. *The Plum in the Golden Vase, or Chin P'ing Mei*. Princeton: Princeton University Press, 1993– .

Ruan Yuanzhao 阮援昭. "Dianying de xin kunhuo" 電影的新困惑 (A new perplexity for film). *Zhongguo qingnian* 中國青年 (China's youth) (Beijing) 1987.1.38–39.

Said, Edward. *Orientalism*. New York: Vintage, 1979.

Schneider, Laurence A. *A Madman of Ch'u: The Chinese Myth of Loyalty and Dissent*. Berkeley and Los Angeles: University of California Press, 1980.

Schoenhals, Michael. *Doing Things with Words in Contemporary Chinese Culture: Five Studies*. University of California, Berkeley: Center for Chinese Studies, 1992.

Schwarcz, Vera. *Bridge across Broken Time: Chinese and Jewish Cultural Memory*. New Haven: Yale University Press, 1998.

———. *The Chinese Enlightenment: Intellectuals and the Legacy of the May Fourth Movement of 1919*. Berkeley and Los Angeles: University of California Press, 1986.

Schwartz, Alan U. "The State of Publishing, Censorship, and Copyright in the Soviet Union." *Publisher's Weekly*, 15 January 1973, pp. 32–35.

Seeberg, Vilma. *Literacy in China: the Effect of the National Development Context and Policy on Literary Levels, 1949–1979*. Bochum: Brockmeyer, 1990.

Sha Tian 沙田. "Liulanghan de qiyu" 流浪漢的奇遇 (Strange encounters of a wandering brave). *Guanchajia* 1978.2.82–85, 1978.3.81–85, 1978.4.83–85.

Sha Tong 沙童. "Renzhen kefu wenyi gongzuozhong de ziyouhua qingxiang" 認眞克服文藝工作中的自由化傾向 (Be serious about overcoming the trend toward liberalization in literature and art work"). *Hongqi* 1981.21 (1 November 1981), pp. 35–38. Translated in Foreign Broadcast Information Service, China Report, 3 December 1981, pp. K10–K15.

Sha Yexin 沙葉新, Yao Mingde 姚明德, and Li Shoucheng 李守成. "Jiaru wo shi zhende" 假如我是眞的 (What if I Really Were?) *Qishi niandai* (Hong Kong) 1980.1. 76–96.

Shamoyiluofu, L., and B. Sikeerbin 列·沙莫伊洛夫 and 鮑·斯柯爾賓 (hanyu pinyin transliterations). *Meizhou bao di shisan hao* 美洲豹第十三號 (The American leopard no. 13). Beijing: Shidai chubanshe, 1954.

Shanghai qingshaonian yanjiu 上海青少年研究 (Shanghai research on youth). Shanghai.

Shanghai wenxue 上海文學 (Shanghai literature). Shanghai.

Shehui 社會 (Society). Shanghai.

Shen Jiming 沈及明. "Guanzhong shenmei xinli de bianhua yu dianying de duice" 觀眾審美心理的變化與電影的對策 (Changes in aesthetic consciousness of audiences and how film can cope with them). *Dangdai dianying* 當代電影 (Contemporary film) (Beijing) 1985.2.16–26.

Shen Shuzhi 申述之. "Xi shi yan gei guanzhong kan de" 戲是演給觀眾看的 (Plays are performed for audiences). *Yangcheng wanbao*, 27 March 1980.

Shi Cheng 史乘. "Ping zhongpian xiaoshuo 'Diaodong'" 評中篇小說 "調動" (A review of the novella "Job Transfer") *Guangming ribao*, 9 April 1980, p. 4.

Shi Hua 施華. "Zhuozhou huiyi mijian beijing" 涿州會議密件背景 (Background to the secret documents of the Zhuozhou meeting). *Jiushiniandai* 九十年代 (The nineties) (Hong Kong) 1987.6.26–28.

Shi Tiesheng 史鐵生. "Wenge jikui" 文革記愧 (Remembering Cultural Revolution shame). *Dongfang jishi* 東方紀事 (Eastern chronicle) (Beijing) 1989.1.41–43.

Shidai de baogao zengkan 時代的報告增刊 (Supplement to report on the times). Beijing.

———. [Unsigned]. "'Kulian' de shifei, qing yu pingshuo" "苦戀" 的是非, 請與評說 (Please come forth with views on the "Unrequited Love" controversy), 23 April 1981, p. 1.

"Shijie wenxue" bianji bu "世界文學" 編輯部. *Xin bei* 心碑 (Monument in the heart). N.p., 1978.

Shikan 詩刊 (Poetry). Beijing.

Shiwubao 時務報 (China's progress). Shanghai.

Shiyue 十月 (October). Beijing.

Shouhuo 收穫 (Harvest). Shanghai.

Sima Yuchang 司馬玉常. "Manhua 'guanggao'" 漫話 "廣告" (Casual remarks on "advertising"). *Yangcheng wanbao*, 22 April 1980, p. 1.

Siu, Helen F., and Zelda Stern, eds. *Mao's Harvest: Voices from China's New Generation.* New York: Oxford University Press, 1983.

Solomon, Richard. *Mao's Revolution and the Chinese Political Culture.* Berkeley and Los Angeles: University of California Press, 1971.

Solzhenitsyn, Alexander. *Lecture.* Translated by Nicholas Bethell. London: Stenvalley Press, 1973.

Soong, Stephen C., and John Minford, eds. *Trees on the Mountain: An Anthology of New Chinese Writing*. Hong Kong: Chinese University Press, 1984.

Spechler, Dina. *Permitted Dissent in the USSR*. New York: Praeger, 1982.

Stavans, Ilan. *Antiheroes: Mexico and Its Detective Novel*. Translated by Jesse H. Lytle and Jennifer A. Mattson. Madison, N.J.: Fairleigh Dickinson University Press, 1997.

Su Manhua 蘇曼華. "Qing guanhuai yixia kexue wenyi" 請關懷一下科學文藝 (Please care a moment for science fiction). *Wenyibao*, 18 October 1986, p. 3.

Su Tong 蘇童. *Mi* 米. Taibei: Yuanliu chuban gongsi, 1991. Translated by Howard Goldblatt as *Rice*. New York: William Morrow, 1995.

―――. *Raise the Red Lantern: Three Novellas*. Translated by Michael Duke. New York: William Morrow, 1993.

―――. *Su Tong xiaoshuo jingpin xuan* 蘇童小說精品選 (A selection of the best fiction of Su Tong). Chongqing: Xi'nan shifan daxue chubanshe, 1993.

Su Xiaokang 蘇曉康 and Wang Luxiang 王魯湘. *Heshang* 河殤 (River elegy). Beijing: Xiandai chubanshe, 1988.

Su Xiaokang, Luo Shixu 羅時敘, and Chen Zheng 陳政, "*Wutuobang" ji: yi-jiu-wu-jiu nian Lushan zhi xia* (Memorial to utopia) 烏托邦祭: 一九五九年廬山之夏. Beijing: Zhongguo xinwen chubanshe, 1988.

Sun Li 孫犁. *Fengyun chuji* 風雲初記 (Stormy years). 3 vols. Beijing: Renmin wenxue chubanshe, 1951, Beijing: Zhongguo qingnian chubanshe, 1963 (vol. 3.

Sun Yuchun 孫玉春. "Jiu hou tu zhen yan" 酒後吐眞言 (The truth comes out with drink). *Anhui wenyi* 安徽文藝 (Anhui literature and art) (Hefei) 1979.4.16–18. Translated in *Chinese Literature* 1979.12.113–17 as "In Vino Veritas."

Swayze, Harold. *Political Control of Literature in the USSR, 1946–1959*. Cambridge: Harvard University Press, 1962.

Tai, Jeanne, ed. *Spring Bamboo: A Collection of Contemporary Chinese Short Stories*. New York: Random House, 1989.

Tam, King-fai. "The Detective Fiction of Ch'eng Hsiao-ch'ing." *Asia Major*, 3rd ser. 5.1 (1992), pp. 113–32.

Tang Xiaolou 唐曉樓. "Zhou Yang, Xia Yan, 'san bu'!" 周揚、夏衍、"三不"! (Zhou Yang, Xia Yan, and the "three noes"!). *Mingbao yuekan*, no. 172 (April 1980) pp. 26–27.

Tao Ye 陶冶, Sun Huimin 孫慧民, Zhang Youming 張酉鳴, and Hu Min 胡敏. "Shanghai chengshi jiating wenhua xiaofei xianzhuang ji fenxi" 上海城市家庭文化消費現狀及分析 (A survey and analysis of the cultural expenses of Shanghai households). *Shehui* 1985.6.13–15.

Thurston, Anne F. *Enemies of the People: The Ordeal of the Intellectuals in China's Great Cultural Revolution*. New York: Alfred A. Knopf, 1987.

―――. "Victims of China's Cultural Revolution: The Invisible Wounds," *Pacific Affairs*, part 1: 57.4.599–620 (Winter 1985); part 2: 58.1.5–27 (Spring 1985).

Tian Zhongquan 田中全. "'Maliezhuyi lao taitai': tan 'Ren dao zhongnian' li Qin Bo de xingxiang" 馬列主義老太太: 談 "人到中年" 裏秦波的形象 ("A Marxist-Leninist old lady": on the image of Qin Bo in "At middle age"). *Renmin ribao*, 16 July 1980, p. 5.

Tianjin yanchang 天津演唱 (Tianjin performance and song). Tianjin.

Today editorial board, ed. *Abandoned Wine: Chinese Writing Today*. London: Wellsweep Press, 1995.

Tong Enzheng 童恩正. "Shanhudaoshang de siguang" 珊瑚島上的死光 (Death rays from coral island). *Renmin wenxue* 1978.8.41–58.

Tong Enzheng et al. *Wuwan nian yiqian de keren* 五萬年以前的客人 (The visitor from fifty thousand years ago). Beijing: Ertong chubanshe, 1962.

Treat, John Whittier. *Writing Ground Zero: Japanese Literature and the Atomic Bomb.* Chicago: University of Chicago Press, 1995.

Tsai, Meishi. *Contemporary Chinese Novels and Short Stories, 1949–1974.* Cambridge: Harvard University, Council on East Asian Studies, 1979.

Tsau, Shu-ying. "Recent Developments in Spoken Drama." Paper for the 14th annual meeting of Chinese Oral and Performing Literature (CHINOPERL), 4 April 1982.

Tsuboi Sakae 壺井榮. *Nijūshi no hitomi* 二十四の瞳. Translated by Akira Miura as *Twenty-Four Eyes.* Tokyo: Kenkyusha, 1957.

Tsuboi Shigeji 壺井繁治. *Tsuboi Shigeji zenshishū* 壺井繁治全詩集 (Complete poems of Tsuboi Shigeji). Tokyo: Kokubunsha, 1970.

Van Crevel, Maghiel. *Language Shattered: Contemporary Chinese Poetry and Duoduo.* Leiden: Leiden University Research School CNWS, 1996)

Voinovich, Vladimir. *The Fur Hat.* Translated by Susan Brownsberger. San Diego: Harcourt Brace Jovanovich, 1989.

Wagner, Rudolf G. *Inside a Service Trade: Studies in Contemporary Chinese Prose.* Cambridge: Harvard University, Council on East Asian Studies, 1992.

Walder, Andrew G. *Communist Neo-Traditionalism: Work and Authority in Chinese Society.* Berkeley and Los Angeles: University of California Press, 1986.

———. "Organized Dependency and Cultures of Authority in Chinese Industry." *Journal of Asian Studies* 43.1 (November 1983), pp. 51–76.

Wang Anyi 王安憶. "Benci lieche zhongdianzhan" 本次列車終點站 (This train's final stop). *Shanghai wenxue* 1981.10.4–18. Translated by Yu Fanqin as "The Destination" in Wang Anyi, *Lapse of Time,* pp. 1–26.

———. *Changhen'ge: changpian xiaoshuo xuan* 長恨歌: 長篇小說選 (Songs of eternal sorrow: a selection of novels). Beijing: Zuojia chubanshe, 1996.

———. *Lapse of Time.* Beijing: Panda Books, 1988.

———. "Xiaoyuan suoji" 小院瑣記. *Xiaoshuo jikan* 小說季刊 (Fiction quarterly) (Beijing) 1980.3.68–75. Translated by Hu Zhihui as "Life in a Small Courtyard," *Chinese Literature* 1981.7.64–83.

———. "Yu, sha sha sha" 雨, 沙沙沙 (The rasping sound of rain). *Beijing wenyi* 1980.6.29–43. Translated by Michael Day as "And the Rain Patters On" in Wang Anyi, *Lapse of Time,* pp. 27–40.

Wang Binbin 王彬彬. "Mao Zedong zao yi shi baiwan fuweng" 毛澤東早已是百萬富翁 (Mao Zedong was a millionaire long ago) *Kaifang* 開放 (Open) (Hong Kong) 1998.12.72–73.

Wang, David Der-wei, ed. *Running Wild: New Chinese Writers.* New York: Columbia University Press, 1994.

Wang Dawen 王大聞. "Shouchaoben" 手抄本 (Hand-copied volumes). In Shi Xiaoyan 石效岩, *Beidahuang fengyunlu* 北大荒風雲錄 (Storms in the great north wastes). Beijing: China Youth Publishers, 1990, pp. 28–30.

Wang Jing 王靖 (pseud.). "Zai shehui de dang'anli" 在社會的檔案裏 (In society's archives). *Wotu* 沃土 (Fertile earth) (unofficial journal, Beijing) 1979.2.19–51). Reprinted in *Dianying chuangzuo* 電影創作 (Film creations) (Beijing) 1979.10.22–43.

Wang, Jing. *China's Avant-Garde.* Durham: Duke University Press, 1998.

Wang Jinmin 王晉民. "Jin sanshi nian Taiwan wenxue shuping" 近三十年臺灣文學述評 (A review of Taiwan literature over the last thirty years). 1980. Conference paper.

———. *Taiwan dangdai wenxue* 臺灣當代文學 (Contemporary Taiwan literature). Nanning: Guangxi renmin chubanshe, 1982.

———. *Taiwan yu haiwai huaren zuojia xiaozhuan* 臺灣與海外華人作家小傳 (Biographical sketches of Taiwanese and overseas Chinese writers). Fuzhou: Fujian renmin chubanshe, 1983.

Wang, Mason Y. H., ed. *Perspectives in Contemporary Chinese Literature*. University Center, Mich.: Green River Press, 1983.

Wang Meng 王蒙. "Buli" 布禮. *Dangdai*, March 1979, pp. 4–39 Translated by Wendy Larson as *Bolshevik Salute*. Seattle: University of Washington Press, 1989.

———. *Dongyu* 冬雨 (Winter rain). Beijing: Renmin wenxue chubanshe, 1980.

———. "Duobi chonggao" 躲避崇高 (Avoid the exalted). *Dushu* 1993.1.10–16.

———. "Guanyu gaige zhuanye zuojia tizhi de yixie tantao" 關於改革專業作家體制的一些探討 (Some thoughts on reforming the professional writing establishment). Reported in *Zhengming*, January 1983, p. 56.

———. "Hudie" 蝴蝶. *Shiyue* 1980.4.4–37. Translated by Gladys Yang as "Butterfly" in Wang Meng, *The Butterfly and Other Stories*, pp. 35–101. Beijing: Panda Books, 1983.

———. "Manhua wenyi xiaoguo" 漫畫文藝效果 ("A caricature of literary effects"). In Zhao Shilin 趙士林, ed. *Fang 'zuo' beiwanglu* 防 "左" 備忘錄 (Memoranda on guarding against the "left"). Taiyuan: Shuhai Chubanshe, 1992, pp. 409–12.

———. *Qingchun wansui* 青春萬歲 (Long live youth). Beijing: Renmin wenxue chubanshe, 1979.

———. "Ye de yan" 夜的眼 (Eye of the night). *Guangming ribao*, 2 October 1979.

———. "Zhongguo wenxue chuangzuo de huanjing yu qiantu" 中國文學創作的環境與前途 (The environment and the prospects for Chinese literary creation). *Xintu* 新土 (New earth) (New York) 1981.1.

———. "Zuzhibu xinlai de nianqingren" 組織部新來的年輕人. *Renmin wenxue* 1956.9.29–43. Translated as "A Newcomer Arrives in the Organization Department in Nieh, *Literature of the Hundred Flowers*, vol. 2, pp. 473–522.

Wang Ruowang 王若望. "Chuntianli de yigu leng feng" 春天裏的一股冷風 (A cold wind in springtime). *Guangming ribao*, 20 July 1979, p. 3.

———. "Ji'e sanbuqu" 飢餓三部曲. *Shouhuo* 1980.1.116–73. Translated by Kyna Rubin as *Hunger Trilogy*. Armonk, N.Y.: M. E. Sharpe, 1991.

———. "'Yuyong . . .' zhi lei" "御用 . . ." 之類 (" . . . Useful to the emperor" and their ilk). *Anhui wenxue* 1980.12.58–59.

Wang Shuo 王朔. "Wan de jiushi xin tiao" 玩得就是心跳. In Wang Shuo, *Qianwan bie ba wo dang ren* 千萬別把我當人 (Whatever you do, don't take me as human). Beijing: Renmin Zhongguo chubanshe, 1992, pp. 147–95. Translated by Howard Goldblatt as *Playing for Thrills*. New York: William Morrow, 1997.

Wang Weiling 王維玲. "Zai jiankuzhong molian, zai douzhengzhong chengzhang: ji 'Di'erci woshou' de xiezuo he zaoyu" 在艱苦中磨練, 在鬥爭中成長——記 "第二次握手" 的寫作和遭遇 (Tempered by hardships, raised in struggle: notes on the writing and the fate of *The second handshake*). *Wenyibao* 357 (September 1979), pp. 47–48.

Wang Yalin 王雅林 et al. "Qingnian zhigong yeyu wenhua shenghua kaocha" 青年職工業餘文化生活考察 (An examination of the after-hours cultural activity of young workers). *Xuexi yu tansuo* 學習與探索 (Study and exploration) (Harbin) 1983.1.37–43.

Wang Zhecheng 汪浙成 and Wen Xiaoyu 溫小鈺. "Cuowei de kouzi" 錯位的扣子 (A button in the wrong place). *Beifang wenxue* 北方文學 (Literature of the north)

(Harbin) 1980.8. Translated as "Out of Place" by Yu Fanqin in *Chinese Literature*, 1981.7.40–52.

———. "Jixu" 積蓄 (Savings). *Shouhuo* 1980.2.157–66. Translated by Donald Gibbs as "Nest Egg" in Link, ed., *Roses and Thorns*, pp. 57–82.

Wang Zhisheng 汪植生 and Li Zibiao 李子彪. "Guangzhoushi zhongxuesheng sixiang zhuangkuang de diaocha" 廣州市中學生思想狀況的調查 (An investigation into the thinking of middle school students in Guangzhou city). *Guangzhou yanjiu* 廣州研究 (Research on Guangzhou), pp. 43–44.

Wang Zisong. 汪子嵩. "Zhengzhixuejia de tianzhen" 政治學家的天眞 (The naiveté of political scientists). *Dushu*, 1994.6.15–22.

Watson, Burton, Translated by *The Complete Works of Chuang Tzu*. New York and London: Columbia University Press, 1968)

Wei Haibo 魏海波 et al. "Wuhui, daigou, disanzhe: Shanghai shimin daode yishi diaocha zhaji" 舞會、代溝、第三者——上海市民道德意識調查札記 (Dance parties, generation gaps, and third parties: notes on a survey of the moral consciousness of Shanghainese). *Minzhu yu fazhi* 民主與法制 (Democracy and Law) 1986.1.27–28.

Wei Haibo, Xu Honghai, Yu Bin 許宏海, 余斌, and Hu Yinkang 胡銀康. "Dianshi wenhua—panghuang zai fazhan de shizilukou" 電視文化彷徨在發展的十字路口 (Television culture: hesitating at the crossroads of development). *Shehui*, June 1985, pp. 8–15.

Wei Qiping 魏啓平. "Juzhangju" 局長局 (Bureau chief bureau) *Quyi* 1980.3.44–45.

Weilai 未來 (The future). Unofficial literary magazine, Guangzhou.

Weiminghu 未名湖 (Unnamed lake). Beijing University student literary magazine, Beijing.

Wen Lu 文路. "Zhongguo de changxiaoshu" 中國的暢銷書 (China's best-sellers). *Dongxiang* 1980.11.20.

Wen Yiduo 聞一多. *Wen Yiduo xuanji* 聞一多選集 (A Wen Yiduo selection). Hong Kong: Wenxue chubanshe, 1971.

Weng Dawei 翁達偉. "Chengshi qingnian shenghuo fangshi de quxiangxing" 城市青年生活方式的趨向性 (Trends in life style among urban youth). *Qingnian yanjiu* 1985.11.12–16.

Weng Mu 翁幕 "Shanghai daxuesheng dianying suzhi yipie" 上海大學生電影素質一瞥. (A glimpse of the sophistication in film of Shanghai university students). *Dianying xinzuo* 電影新作 (New works of film) (Shanghai) 1985.2.79–81.

Wenhuibao 文匯報 (Wenhui daily). Shanghai.

———. [Unsigned] Benbao pinglunyuan 本報評論員, "Wenyi yao wei sihua ouge" 文藝要爲四化謳歌 (Literature and art should sing the praises of the four modernizations), 23 February 1980.

———. [Unsigned] "Chuban tushu yao kaolü shehui xiaoguo" 出版圖書要考慮社會效果 (Social effects must be considered in book publishing), 22 April 1980.

———. [Unsigned] "'Gushihui' zai ge di nongcun da shou huanying" "故事會" 在各地農村大受歡迎 ("Story collections" gets a big welcome in peasant villages everywhere), 13 July 1980.

———. [Unsigned] "Jiaqiang dui zifa jutuan de zhengdun he guanli" 加強對自發劇團的整頓和管理 (Strengthen efforts to overhaul and regulate spontaneous drama troupes), 6 June 1980.

———. [Unsigned] "Nongmin yeyu yishu biaoyan zai Beijing bimu" 農民業餘藝術表演在北京閉幕 (Peasant-amateur artistic performances hold closing ceremony in Beijing), 12 June 1980.

———. [Unsigned] Pinglunyuan 評論員 (Commentator). "Manhuai xinxin, polang qianjin" 滿懷信心, 破浪前進 (Forge ahead full of confidence), 22 January 1980.

Wenyi qingkuang 文藝情況 (State of affairs in literature and art). N.p.

———. [Unsigned] "Qunian nongmin siren ban fangyingdui jin liuqiange" 去年農民 私人辦放映隊近六千個 (Peasant-run projection teams approached 6,000 last year) no. 5 (1984), p. 10.

Wenyibao 文藝報 (Literary gazette). Beijing.

Wiener, Philip P., ed. *Values in a Universe of Chance: Selected Writings of Charles S. Peirce*. Garden City, N.Y.: Doubleday Anchor, 1958.

Williams, Philip F. "'Remolding' and the Chinese Labor-Camp Novel" *Asia Major*. 3rd ser. 4.2 (1993), pp. 133–49.

———. Review of Liu Kang and Tang Xiaobin, *Politics, Ideology, and Literary Discourse in Modern China*. *Chinese Literature: Essays Articles and Reviews*, no. 17 (December 1995), pp. 173–82.

Womack, Brantly, ed. *Media and the Chinese Public: A Survey of the Beijing Media Audience*. Vol. 18.3–4 (Spring-Summer 1986) of *Chinese Sociology and Anthropology* (Armonk, N.Y.: M. E. Sharpe).

Wu Benxue 吳本雪. "Qingnian wenhua shenghuo yu jiazhi quxiang" 青年文化生活 與價值趨向 (Cultural life and value trends among youth). *Qingnian yanjiu* 1985.7.19– 23.

Wu Qiang 吳强. *Hongri* 紅日. Beijing: Zhongguo qingnian chubanshe, 1957. Translated by A. C. Barnes as *Red Sun*. Beijing: Foreign Languages Press, 1961.

Wu Woyao 吳沃堯 (also Jianren 趼人). *Ershinian mudu zhi guai xianzhuang* 二十年目 睹之怪現狀 (Strange events witnessed over twenty years). Hong Kong: Guangzhi shuju, n.d. Partially translated by Shih Shun Liu as *Vignettes from the Late Ch'ing: Bizarre Happenings Eyewitnessed over Two Decades*. Hong Kong: Chinese University of Hong Kong, 1975.

Wu, Yenna. *The Chinese Virago: A Literary Theme*. Cambridge: Harvard University, Council on East Asian Studies, 1995.

———. "Women as Sources of Redemption in Chang Hsien-liang's Labor-Camp Fiction," *Asia Major*, 3rd ser., 4.2 (1993), pp. 115–31.

Wu Yungang 吳運剛. "Ping 'ren yao zhi jian' de shishi" 評 "人妖之間" 的失實 (A criticism of the factual errors in "People or Monsters?"). *Beifang wenxue* 北方文學 (Literature of the north) (Harbin) 1982.2. Reprinted in *Heilongjiang ribao* 黑龍江 日報 18 February 1982.

Wu Zhengxin 吳政新. "Shishi qiu shi, qu xin yu min: cong yi ci guanzhong diaocha kan dianying pinglun de wenti" 實事求是, 取信於民: 從一次觀眾調查看電影 評論的問題 (Seek truth from facts, earn the trust of the people: viewing the question of film reviews from an audience survey) *Wenhuibao* 10 May 1986, p. 4.

Wu Zuxiang 吳組緗. "Guanguan de bupin" 官官的補品 (Guanguan's tonic). In *Wu Zuxiang xuanji* 吳組緗選集 (A collection of Wu Zuxiang). Hong Kong: Wenxue yanjiushe, n.d., pp. 16–32. Translated by Cyril Birch as "Young Master Gets His Tonic" in Lau et al., eds. *Modern Chinese Stories and Novellas*, pp. 372–81.

Wumingshi 無名氏. *Tali de nüren* 塔裏的女人 (Woman in the tower). Xi'an: Wuming shuwu, 1944). During the Cultural Revolution also a hand-copied volume.

Xi Xi 西西. "Xiang wo zheyang de yige nüzi" 像我這樣的一個女子 (A girl like me), in *Xi Xi juan* 西西卷 (Xi Xi volume). Hong Kong: Sanlian shudian, 1992, pp. 21–43. Translated by Rachel May and Zhu Zhiyu in Xi Xi, *A Girl Like Me and Other Stories*. Hong Kong: Chinese University of Hong Kong Press, 1986.

Xia Yan 夏衍. "Gei yige qingnian zuozhe de xin" 給一個青年作者的信 (A letter to a young writer). *Dianying xinzuo* 電影新作 (New works of film) 1979.5.2–5.

Xiangsheng chuangzuo zuotanhui bangongshi 相聲創作座談會辦公室, ed. "Xiangsheng chuangzuo zuotanhui jianbao" 相聲創作座談會簡報 (Bulletin on the conference on creating comedians' dialogues). N.p., 1980, no. 4.

Xiao Chen 曉晨. "Buyao gei shenghuo mengshang yiceng yinying: ping xiaoshuo 'Ren dao zhongnian'" 不要給生活蒙上一層陰影——評小說 "人到中年" (Let's not cover life with a layer of dark clouds: A critique of "At middle age"). *Wenhuibao*, 2 July 1980, p. 3.

Xiao Feng 小風. "Jiaru mingtian" 假如明天 (If tomorrow). *Weilai* 2, 1979.1.12–13.

Xiao Yi 小燚 (pseud.). "Mai jidan de xiao guniang" 賣雞蛋的小姑娘. *Zheyidai* pp. 28–33. Translated by Dale R. Johnson as "The Little Egg Girl" in Link, ed., *Stubborn Weeds*, pp. 162–170.

Xiao Yuying 蕭育瀛. "Ping yijiuwuba nian xin min'ge yundong" 評一九五八年新民歌運動 (On the new folksong movement of 1958). Yichun, 1980. Manuscript.

Xiaoshuo shibao 小說時報 (Fiction times). Shanghai.

Xiaoshuo yuebao 小說月報 (Fiction monthly). Tianjin.

Xin Shan 辛山. "Zhizhi 'qintun'" 制止 "侵吞" (Stop the "guzzling"). *Dushu* 1979.1.8–9.

Xin Xu 辛旭. "'Shiliunian' wu chabie ma?" "十六年" 無差別嗎? (Is there no distinction among "the sixteen years"?). *Wenyibao* 1982.6.37–41.

Xing Bensi 邢賁思. "Yihua wenti he jingshen wuran" 異化問題和精神污染 (The question of alienation and spiritual pollution). *Renmin ribao*, 5 November 1983, p. 5.

Xing Yixun 邢益勛. "Quan yu fa" 權與法 (Power and law) *Juben* 1979.10.2–33.

Xiong Zhaozheng 熊召政. "Qing juqi senlinban de shou, zhi zhi!" 請舉起森林般的手, 制止! (Raise your hands like the trees of a forest and stop it!) *Changjiang wenyi* 長江文藝 (Yangzi river literature and art) (Wuhan) 1980.1. 4–7.

Xu Haohua 徐浩華. "Jin ji nian biye de ligongke daxuesheng zai xiang shenme?" 近幾年畢業的理工科大學生在想甚麼? (What have graduates in science and engineering been thinking in recent years?). *Qingnian tansuo* 青年探索 (Youth's exploration) (Guangzhou) 1985.3.20–21, 8.

Xu Hui 徐慧. "Emeng: yige muqin de shouji" 噩夢——一個母親的手記) *Sichuan wenxue* 四川文學 (Sichuan literature) (Chengdu) 1979.4.46–50. Translated by William A. Lyell as "Nightmare: Notes from a Mother's Hand," in Link, ed., *Stubborn Weeds*, pp. 49–56.

Xu Liangying and Fan Dainian, *Science and Socialist Construction in China*. Armonk, N.Y.: M. E. Sharpe, 1982.

Xu Miaoting 許妙庭. "Shanghai shiqu qingnian dianying quwei qianxi" 上海市區青年電影趣味淺析 (A preliminary analysis of young people's preferences in film in the Shanghai area). *Qingnian yanjiu* 1983.1.39–46.

Xu Mingxu 徐明旭. "Diaodong" 調動 (Work transfer). *Qingming* 1979.2.58–95.

Xu Qing 許青. "Daxuesheng bangyang wenti diaocha" 大學生榜樣問題調查 (An investigation of the question of models among university students). *Qingnian yanjiu* 1984.2.48–57.

Xu Yihui 許宜輝. "Huangse luxiang dui qingshaonian de duhai" 黃色錄像對青少年的毒害 (The harm done to youth by pornographic videotapes). *Qingnian yanjiu* 1986.1.47–48.

Xuanchuan xuexi shouce 宣傳學習手冊 (Handbook for propaganda and study). Beijing.

Yan Jiayan 嚴家炎. "Lun sanshi niandai de xin ganjuepai xiaoshuo" 論三十年代的新感覺派小說 (On the new perceptionists of the 1930s). In Ma Liangchun 馬良

春, Zhang Daming 張大明, and Li Baoyan 李葆琰, *Zhongguo xiandai wenxue sichao liupai taolunji* 中國現代文學思潮流派討論集 (Collection of discussions on schools in modern Chinese literary thought). Beijing: Renmin wenxue chubanshe, 1984, pp. 246–88.

Yang, Daniel S. P. "Theater Activities in Post-Cultural Revolution China." In Constantine Tung and Colin MacKerras, eds. *Drama in the People's Republic of China*. (Albany: State University of New York Press, 1987, pp. 164–80.

Yang Ganhua 楊干花. "Jing zhe lei" 驚蟄雷 (A thunderclap to startle one from hibernation) *Huacheng* 1980.1.103–12.

Yang Jiang 楊絳. "Ganxiao liuji" 幹校六記 (Six chapters on cadre school). *Guangjiaojing* 廣角鏡 (Wide angle) (Hong Kong), no. 103 (April 1981). Translated by Howard Goldblatt as "Six Chapters from My Life 'Downunder'" in *Renditions*, no. 16 (Autumn 1981), pp. 6–61. Translated by Geremie Barmé and Bennet Lee as *A Cadre School Life: Six Chapters*. Hong Kong: Joint Publishing Company, 1982.

Yang, Ling. "The Last Three Years." *Beijing Review* 1979.52.7–15, 26.

Yang Mo 楊沫. *Qingchun zhi ge* 青春之歌. Beijing: Zuojia chubanshe, 1958. Translated by Nan Ying as *The Song of Youth*. Beijing: Foreign Languages Press, 1964.

Yang Qingyun 楊清雲. "Dalu xinshi minyi ceyan de jieguo" 大陸新詩民意測驗的結果 (The results of a survey of new poetry on the mainland). *Zhengming*, April 1980, p. 67.

Yang Yiyin 楊宜音. "Cong dushu jiegou kan daxuesheng de sixiang jiegou" 從讀書結構看大學生的思想結構 (Viewing the structure of university student thought from the structure of reading). *Qingnian yanjiu* 1983.3.33–39.

Yangcheng wanbao 羊城晚報 (Goat-city evening news). Guangzhou.

———. [Unsigned] "Guangzhoushi juchang buzu" 廣州市劇場不足 (There are not enough drama theaters in Guangzhou), 20 June 1980.

———. [Unsigned] "Zongzheng wenhuabu xiang quanjun tuijian sanshibu youxiu wenxue zuopin" 總政文化部向全軍推薦三十部優秀文學作品 (Cultural department of the general political department of the People's Liberation Army recommends 30 superior literary works to the entire army), 18 June 1980.

Yao Xueyin 姚雪垠. *Li Zicheng* 李自成. Beijing: Zhongguo qingnian chubanshe, 1976.

Ye Boquan 葉伯泉. "'Tamen shi zhenzheng de xin renwu': you Gaoerji de yige guandian suo xiangdao de" "他們是真正的新人物"——由高爾基的一個觀點所想到的 ("They are the true heroes": thoughts inspired by an opinion from Gorky) *Yalüjiang* 鴨綠江 (Yalü river) (Shenyang) 1980.1.65–67.

Ye Jun 葉俊. "Shanghai shifan daxue xuesheng sixiang guannian bianhua de qingkuang diaocha" 上海師範大學學生思想觀念變化的情況調查 (An investigation of the changes in ideas and concepts of students at Shanghai normal university). *Shanghai qingshaonian yanjiu* 1985.3.14–21.

Ye Zhaoyan 葉兆言. *Ye bo qinhuai* 夜泊秦淮 (Evening stop with the ladies of the night). Hangzhou: Zhejiang wenyi chubanshe, 1991.

You Kecun 尤可存 (pseud.), comp. "Daqiao fengyun" 大橋風雲 (The great bridge affair) *Guanchajia* 1977.11.81–85, 1977.12.80–85, 1978.1.82–85.

You Yicun 又一村. "'Neibu' jianwen" "內部" 見聞 (Seen and heard 'internally'). *Feng ye* 1979.7.1.

Yu Chen 雨辰. "Jiefang 'neibu shu'" 解放 '內部書' (Liberate "internal" books). *Dushu* 1979.1.8–9.

Yu Congzhe 余從哲. "Zhonggong de wenyi luxiang" 中共的文藝路向 (Trends in Chinese Communist literature and art). *Qishiniandai* (Hong Kong) 1979.12.15–19.

Yu Dong 雨東. "Yige zhide zhuyi de yuanze wenti" 一個值得注意的原則問題 (A noteworthy question of principle). *Wenyibao* 1982.5.50–51.

Yu Hua 余華. *Huozhe* 活著 (Living). Taibei: Maitian chuban, 1994.

———. "Xianshi yi zhong" 現實一種. *Beijing wenxue* 北京文學 (Beijing literature) 1988.1.4–25. Translated by Jeanne Tai as "One Kind of Reality" in David Wang, ed., *Running Wild*, pp. 21–68.

Yu Luojin 遇羅錦. "Chuntian de tonghua" 春天的童話 (A spring fairy tale). *Huacheng* 1982.1.141–221.

———. "Yige dongtian de tonghua" 一個冬天的的童話 (A winter fairy tale). *Dangdai* 1980.3.58–107. Unexpurgated English translation by Rachel May and Zhu Zhiyu, *A Chinese Winter's Tale*.

Yue Daiyun 樂黛雲. "Wo guan Zhongguo dangdai wenxue" 我觀中國當代文學 (My view of contemporary Chinese literature). Quoted in *Beijing wenxue* 北京文學 (Beijing literature) 1988.1.1.

Zha, Jianying. *China Pop: How Soap Operas, Tabloids, and Bestsellers are Transforming a Culture*. New York: New Press, 1995.

———. "China's Popular Culture in the 1990s." In William A. Joseph, ed. *China Briefing: The Contradictions of Change*. Armonk, N.Y.: M. E. Sharpe, 1997, pp. 109–50.

Zhang Aiping 張愛萍. "Daxue ya qingsong; qingsong ting qie zhi: du Chen Yi tongzhi shixuan yougan" 大雪壓青松, 青松挺且直——讀陳毅同志詩選有感 (The blizzard presses the evergreen; the evergreen stands ramrod straight: thoughts on reading the selected poems of Comrade Chen Yi). *Renmin ribao*, 2 September 1977, p. 3.

Zhang Aolie 張奧列. "'Shehui xiaoguo' xiaoyi" '社會效果' 小議 (Quibbles about "social effects"). *Yangcheng wanbao*, 16 June 1980.

Zhang Chengzhi 張承志. "Yi bi wei qi" 以筆爲旗 (With pen as banner). *Shiyue* 1993.3.52–53.

Zhang Jie 張潔. "Ai shi buneng wangji de" 愛是不能忘記的. *Beijing wenyi* 1979.11.19–26. Translated by William Crawford as "Love Must Not Be Forgotten" in Link., ed., *Roses and Thorns*, pp. 245–60.

———. *As Long as Nothing Happens, Nothing Will*. Translated by Gladys Yang et al. London: Virago, 1988

———. *Chenzhong de chibang* 沉重的翅膀 (Heavy wings). *Shiyue* 1981.4.4–107, and 1981.5.39-100. Also published by Beijing: Renmin wenxue chubanshe, 1994. Translated by Gladys Yang as *Leaden Wings*. London: Virago, 1987. Translated by Howard Goldblatt as *Heavy Wings*. New York: Grove Press, 1989.

———. "Pursuit." *China Reconstructs* 1981.12.44.

———. "Shei shenghuo de geng meihao?" 誰生活得更美好 (Who lives better?) In *Zhang Jie xiaoshuo juben xuan*. Beijing: Beijing chubanshe, 1980, pp. 54–70.

———. "Weiliao lu" 未了錄 (An unfinished record). *Shiyue* 1980.5.86–92.

Zhang Jinglu 張靜廬. *Zhongguo chuban shiliao bubian* 中國出版史料補編 (Supplement to historical materials on publishing in China). Beijing: Zhonghua shuju, 1957.

Zhang Xian 張弦. "Bei aiqing yiwang de jiaoluo" 被愛情遺忘的角落 (The corner forgotten by love). *Shanghai wenxue* 1980.1.4–14. Translated in Helen F. Siu and Zelda Stern, eds., *Mao's Harvest*, pp. 106–25.

———. "Zhengbuduan de hong si xian" 掙不斷的紅絲線 (The unbreakable red thread). *Shanghai wenxue* 1981.4.16–24, 49.

Zhang Xianliang 張賢亮. *Grass Soup*. Translated by Martha Avery. London: Secker & Warburg, 1994. An abridged translation of *Fannao jiushi zhihui* 煩惱就是智慧 (Vexation is wisdom). Beijing: Zuojia chubanshe, 1994.

———. "Ling yu rou" 靈與肉 (Spirit and flesh). *Shuofang* 朔方 (The north) (Yinchuan) 1980.9.3–16, 48. Translated by Philip Williams as "Body and Soul" in Chau, *Prize-winning Stories*, pp. 59–92.

———. "Lühuashu" 綠化樹. Translated by Gladys Yang as "Mimosa" in Zhang Xianliang, *Mimosa and Other Stories*.

———. *Mimosa and Other Stories*. Beijing: Panda Books, 1985.

———. *Nanren de yiban shi nüren* 男人的一半是女人. Chengdu: Sichuan wenyi chubanshe, 1986. Translated by Martha Avery as *Half of Man Is Woman*. New York: Ballantine Books, 1986.

———. *Wo de puti shu* 我的菩提樹. Beijing: Zuojia chubanshe, 1994. Translated by Martha Avery as *My Bodhi Tree*. London: Secker and Warburg, 1996.

———. "Xiaoerbulake" 蕭爾布拉克 (Xor Bulak). In Zhang Xianliang, *Xiaoerbulake*. Shanghai: Wenyi chubanshe, 1984, pp. 331–72.

———. *Xiguan siwang* 習慣死亡. Taibei: Yuanshen chubanshe, 1989. Translated by Martha Avery as *Getting Used to Dying*. New York: Harper Collins, 1991.

Zhang Xu 張戌 *et al* "Zhongxuesheng dui jitiwu de kanfa" 中學生對集體舞的看法 (The views of high school students on group dancing). *Tianjin qingnianbao* 天津青年報 (Tianjin youth news), 23 August 1985, p. 3.

Zhang Yang 張揚. *Di'erci woshou* 第二次握手 (The second handshake). Beijing: Zhongguo qingnian chubanshe, 1979.

Zhang Yigong 張一弓. "Fanren Li Tongzhong de gushi" 犯人李銅鐘的故事 (The story of the criminal Li Tongzhong). *Shouhuo* 1980.1.93–115, 193.

Zhang Yongzheng 張永正. "Zhongxuesheng lixiang wenti de diaocha" 中學生理想問題的調查 (A survey of ideals among high-school students). *Shanghai qingshaonian yanjiu* 1983.7.15–18, 31.

Zhao Dan 趙丹. "Guan de tai juti, wenyi mei xiwang" 管得太具體, 文藝沒希望 (Controlled too specifically, literature and art are hopeless). *Renmin ribao*, 8 October 1980, p. 5. Translated as "Rigid Control Ruins Art and Literature" in *Chinese Literature* 1981.1.108–11.

Zhao Guoqing 趙國慶. "Jiujiu ta!" 救救她! (Save her!). In Jiangxi daxue Zhongwenxi, ed. *Dangdai wenxue juben xuan*, pp. 151–226.

Zhao, Henry Y. H., ed. *The Lost Boat: Avant-Garde Fiction from China*. London: Wellsweep Press, 1993.

Zhao, Henry Y. H., and John Cayley, eds. *Abandoned Wine: Chinese Writing Today, II*. London: Wellsweep Press, 1996.

Zhao Zhenkai 趙振開. *Bodong* 波動 (Waves). *Jintian* 1979.4.31–71, 1979.5.1–13, 29–48, 1979.6.21–56 (June-October). Reprinted with minor revisions in *Changjiang wenxue congkan* 長江文學叢刊 (Yangzi river literary compendium) (Wuhan) 1981.1.21–76. Translated by Bonnie S. McDougall and Susette T. Cooke in Zhao Zhenkai, *Waves*. Hong Kong: Chinese University Press, 1985, pp. 1–146.

Zhao Zixiong 趙梓雄. "Weilai zai zhaohuan" 未來在召喚 (The future beckons). *Dangdai* 1979.1.8–40.

Zheiyidai 這一代 (This generation). Wuhan. Unofficial national student magazine, 1979.

Zheng Wen 鄭汶. "Chuangzuo de shuliang he zhiliang" 創作的數量和質量 (Quantity and quality in literary creation). *Guangming ribao*, 9 April 1980.

Zheng Wenguang 鄭文光. *Fei xiang Renmazuo* 飛向人馬座 (Flying toward Sagittarius). Beijing: People's Literature Publishing House, 1979.

Zheng Yi 鄭義. "Feng" 楓. *Wenhuibao*, 11 February 1979. Translated by Douglas Spelman as "Maple" in Link, ed. *Stubborn Weeds*, pp. 58–73.

———. *Hongse jinianbei* 紅色紀念碑 (Red memorial). Taibei: Huashi wenhua gongsi, 1993. Abridged and translated by T. P. Sym (pseud.) as *Scarlet Memorial*. Boulder, Colo.: Westview Press, 1996.

———. *Lishi de yibufen* 歷史的一部分 (A part of history). Taibei: Wanxiang tushu gongsi, 1993.

Zhengming 爭鳴 (Contending). Hong Kong.

Zhong Acheng 鍾阿城. "Qiwang" 棋王. *Shanghai wenxue* 1984.7.15–35. Translated by W. J. F. Jenner as "The Chess Master" in *Chinese Literature*, Summer 1985, pp. 84–131; and by Bonnie McDougall as "The King of Chess" in Ah Cheng, *Three Kings*. London: Collins Harvill, 1990, pp. 29–93.

Zhonggulou 鐘鼓樓 (Bell and drum tower). Dongcheng qu wenhuazhan, Beijing.

Zhongguo renmin daxue yi fenxiao "hunyin wenti diaocha zu" 中國人民大學一分校 "婚姻問題調查組" ("Research group on marriage questions" of the first campus of People's University of China). "Guowai 'xing ziyou' lilun dui bufen qingnian gongren de yingxiang" 國外 "性自由" 理論對部分青年工人的影響 (The influence of foreign theories of "sexual liberation" on certain young workers). *Qingnian yanjiu* 1982.17.17–26.

Zhongguo shehui kexueyuan wenxue yanjiusuo dangdai wenxue yanjiushi 中國社會科學院文學研究所當代文學研究室 (Contemporary literature section of the literature research institute of the Chinese Academy of Social Sciences). *Xin shiqi wenxue liu nian* 新時期文學六年 (Six years of the new period of literature). Beijing: Zhongguo shehuikexue chubanshe, 1985.

Zhongguo tongji nianjian 中國統計年鑑 (Yearbook of Chinese statistics). State Statistics Bureau, Beijing.

Zhongying gongsi 中影公司 (China film company). "Jing Jin Hu deng shiyige chengshi shangbannian dianying shichang qingkuang" 京津滬等十一個城市上半年電影市場情況 (The film market in the first half of the year in eleven cities including Beijing, Tianjin, and Shanghai). *Wenyijie tongxun* 文藝界通訊 (Bulletin of the world of literature and art) 1985.10.26–28.

Zhou Enlai 周恩來. "On Literature and Art." *Beijing Review*, 30 March 1979, pp. 9–16.

———. "You shenme fenbie?" 有甚麼分別? (What's the difference?). *Yuhua* 雨花 (Colored pebbles) (Nanjing) 1981.7.4–5.

———. "Zai wenyi gongzuo zuotanhui he gushipian chuangzuo huiyi shang de jianghua" 在文藝工作座談會和故事片創作會議上的講話 (Talk at the conference on literature and art work and on creation in film). *Wenyibao* 1979.2.2–13.

Zhou Erfu 周而復. *Shanghai de zaochen* 上海的早晨 (Morning in Shanghai). 2 vols. Shanghai: Zuojia chubanshe, 1958, 1962.

Zhou Libo 周立波. *Baofengzhouyu* 暴風驟雨 (Violent storm). Hong Kong: Xin minzhu chubanshe, 1949; Beijing: Renmin wenxue chubanshe, 1952. Translated by Xu Mengxiong as *The Hurricane*. Beijing: Foreign Languages Press, 1955.

Zhou Weibo 周惟波, Dong Yangsheng 董陽聲, and Ye Xiaonan 葉小楠, "Paobing siling de erzi" 炮兵司令的兒子 (Son of the artillery commander). *Wenhuibao*, 10 June 1979.

Zhou Yang 周揚. "Guanyu Makesizhuyi de jige lilun wenti de tantao" 關於馬克思主義的幾個理論問題的探討 (An enquiry into some theoretical questions in Marxism). *Renmin ribao*, 16 March 1983, pp. 4–5.

———. "Shehuizhuyi xianshizhuyi: Zhongguo wenxue qianjin de daolu" 社會主義 現實主義: 中國文學前進的道路 (Socialist realism: Chinese literature's path to progress). *Xinhua yuebao* 新華月報 (New China monthly) (Beijing) 1953. Reprinted in Beijing Shifan Daxue, ed. *Zhongguo xiandai wenxueshi cankao ziliao*, vol. 3, pp. 203–11.

———. "Xin min'ge kaituole shige de xin daolu" 新民歌開拓了詩歌的新道路. New poems have blazed the way to a new poetry). *Hongqi* 1958.1.33–38.

Zhou Yunfu 周雲夫. "Ye tan Mao de gaofei" 也談毛的稿費 (More on Mao's manuscript royalties). *Kaifang* 開放 (Open) (Hong Kong) 1999.1.99.

Zhou Zhiping 周質平 (C. P. Chou). "Hu Shi yu Lu Xun de jiaoyi" 胡適與魯迅的交 誼 (The friendship between Hu Shi and Lu Xun). *Mingbao yuekan*, no. 223 (July 1984), pp. 9–16.

Zhu Xiao 諸曉. "Yidai jiankuan zhong buhui" 衣帶漸寬終不悔 (In the end, no regrets for loosening the belt). *Wenhuibao*, 29 March 1980, p. 2.

Zhu Xueqin 朱學勤. "Chengtou bianhuan er wang qi" 城頭變幻二王旗 (The banners of two Wangs flashing above the city walls). *Ershiyi shiji* 二十一世紀 (Twenty-first century) (Hong Kong), no. 28 (April, 1995), pp. 119–22.

Zong Fuxian 宗福先. "Yu wusheng chu" 於無聲處 (From the silent zones). *Wenhuibao*, 28 October 1978, pp. 3–4; 29 October 1978, pp. 3–4; 30 October 1978, p. 4.

Zong Pu 宗璞. *See* Feng Zongpu.

Zuo Jianming 左建明. "Yinying" 陰影 (Shadow). *Shanghai wenxue* 1979.1.20–24.

Zuo Ni 左泥, ed. *Chongfang de xianhua* 重放的鮮花 (Fragrant flowers that bloom again). Shanghai: Wenyi chubanshe, 1979.

Zuopin 作品 (Literary works). Guangzhou. Called *Guangdong wenyi* before July 1978.

INDEX